AMERICAN VISIONS
AND REVISIONS
1607–1865

Also available from the Copley Series,
Sources of the American Tradition

CREATING THE CONSTITUTION

Edited by John P. Kaminski and Richard Leffler

THE UNION IN CRISIS, 1850–1877

Edited by Robert W. Johannsen

SOURCES OF THE AMERICAN TRADITION

AMERICAN VISIONS AND REVISIONS 1607–1865

EDITED BY DAVID GRIMSTED

Copley Publishing Group
Acton, Massachusetts 01720

ISBN 1-58390-000-4

Library of Congress Catalog Card Number: 98-073899

Cover: "He that Tilleth his Land Shall be Satisfied" (1850), artist unknown. Photographed by Graydon Wood. Reprinted by permission of the Philadelphia Museum of Art, The Edgar William and Bernice Chrysler Garbisch Collection.

Copley Publishing Group
138 Great Road
Acton, MA 01720
800.562.2147 • Fax: 978.263.9190
E-mail: publish@copleycustom.com

CONTENTS

Introduction   1

Chapter 1—New World Hopes—and Tragedies

Introduction   7

Native American Reactions   9

from A Description of New England   14
    John Smith

from A Model of Christian Charity   20
    John Winthrop

Chapter 2—A Troubled City on a Hill

Introduction   27

Selected Letters of John and Margaret Winthrop   29

from The Journal of John Winthrop   37

Selected Poems   65
    Anne Bradstreet

from A Key into the Language of America   68
    Roger Williams

from The Bloody Tenet of Persecution for the
Cause of Conscience   71
    Roger Williams

To the Town of Providence   75
    Roger Williams

from The Bloody Tenet Washed White in the
Blood of the Lamb   76
    John Cotton

Chapter 3—Quaker and Southern Visions

Introduction 79

Passenger Lists to Virginia and Massachusetts 81

from The General History of Virginia 85
    John Smith

from The History and Present State of Virginia 93
    Robert Beverley

from History of the Dividing Line 101
    William Byrd II

from The Secret Diary of William Byrd II 108

Upon a Fart 123
    William Byrd II

from The Journal of John Woolman 124

Chapter 4—This New Man

Introduction 137

The Way to Wealth 139
    Benjamin Franklin

from The Autobiography of Benjamin Franklin 143

Advice to a Friend 182
    Benjamin Franklin

The Speech of Miss Polly Baker 184
    Benjamin Franklin

from Letters from an American Farmer 187
    Michel-Guillaume-Jean de Crèvecoeur

Chapter 5—Revolutionary Ideas

Introduction 199

Declaration of Independence as Adopted by Congress 202

from The American Crisis 206
    Thomas Paine

On Slavery 211
    Patrick Henry

Family Correspondence 213
Abigail and John Adams

An Epitaph for John Jack 219
Daniel Bliss

Selected Writings 220
Phillis Wheatley

from Notes on the State of Virginia 225
Thomas Jefferson

from The Federalist Papers 233
James Madison

Chapter 6—Old Values in a New Democracy

Introduction 241

from Greenfield Hill 243
Timothy Dwight

from The Contrast 251
Royall Tyler

from Modern Chivalry 294
Hugh Henry Brackenridge

Chapter 7—Educating for Democracy

Introduction 309

from Notes on the State of Virginia 311
Thomas Jefferson

from Political Inquiries 315
Robert Coram

from Reports on Education 328
Horace Mann

from The Duty of American Women to Their Country 344
Catharine Beecher

Chapter 8—Democratic Faiths

Introduction   351

Importance of Religion to Society   353
  William Ellery Channing

from Unitarian Christianity   355
  William Ellery Channing

from Sinners Bound to Change Their Own Hearts   363
  Charles Grandison Finney

from Lectures on Revivals   370
  Charles Grandison Finney

from Catholicity Necessary to Sustain Popular Liberty   376
  Orestes Augustus Brownson

Shaker and Mormon Songs   382

Chapter 9—Keeping Democracy Wholesome

Introduction   397

from Democracy in America   399
  Alexis de Tocqueville

from Self-Reliance   428
  Ralph Waldo Emerson

from The Journals of Ralph Waldo Emerson   435

Chapter 10—The Democratic Self

Introduction   451

Selected Songs   453
  Samuel Woodworth

Selected Poems   466
  Henry Wadsworth Longfellow

from Song of Myself   479
  Walt Whitman

Selected Poems   487
  Emily Dickinson

Was He Henpecked?   494
  Phoebe Cary

Chapter 11—Keeping Capitalism Wholesome

Introduction	499
from A Short History of Paper Money and Banking in the United States *William M. Gouge*	501
from The Rights of Man to Property! *Thomas Skidmore*	512
from The Laboring Classes *Orestes Augustus Brownson*	521
from Sociology for the South *George Fitzhugh*	530

Chapter 12—Reforming Society

Introduction	537
Weld-Grimké Letters *Angelina Grimké, Sarah Grimké, and Theodore Weld*	540
Seneca Falls Declaration of Rights	563
from Fifth of July Speech *Frederick Douglass*	566
from Little Ferns for Fanny's Little Friends *Sara Payson Parton ("Fanny Fern")*	572
from Earth's Holocaust *Nathaniel Hawthorne*	578

Chapter 13—Which Minority's Rights?

Introduction	585
from The Perpetuation of Our Political Institutions *Abraham Lincoln*	587
from The Lincoln-Douglas Debates *Abraham Lincoln*	592
from Civil Disobedience *Henry David Thoreau*	601
from Slavery in Massachusetts *Henry David Thoreau*	606

from A Disquisition on Government 609
John C. Calhoun

from Twelve Years a Slave 614
Solomon Northup

Chapter 14—The Decision of War

Introduction 635

Debate on John P. Hale's Bill to Outlaw Rioting 637

from The Diary of George Templeton Strong 652

from The Diary of Mary Boykin Chesnut 666

from Army Life in a Black Regiment 692
Thomas Wentworth Higginson

Letter to Horace Greeley 709
Abraham Lincoln

Address Delivered at the Dedication of 711
the Cemetary at Gettysburg
Abraham Lincoln

Second Inaugural Address 712
Abraham Lincoln

INTRODUCTION

Dear Reader,

To study history by probing primary sources—documents written during the time one is trying to understand—is to accomplish much. Let me count, or recount, how much.

1. It is to meet people who lived earlier directly, sometimes intimately, not filtered through an intervening mind. It is to meet these folks, so to speak, on and in their own terms. You should like some, and dislike others of these new acquaintances, as well as find some boring. Whether you like them or dislike them, you should have emotive reactions to many of these people or their ideas.

2. It is to learn the basic skills responsible democratic citizens need: to understand what people say, to grasp the assumptions and implications of their argument, and to make judgements about what you see as true or false, promising or vicious in their positions. The story of the United States to 1865 involves the creation of history's first society dedicated to general equality of rights, opportunity and some influence for all, and then its near-dissolution because of long acceptance of slavery's gross mockery of such ideals. The nation and the ideal did last, however, and their continuing decencies depend on your integrity and good sense in influencing decisions and upholding standards.

3. To promote your capacities for citizenry, these sources should complicate and enrich your moral perceptions, and suggest how hard it is—perhaps socially impossible—to make decisions that don't have some dangers and disadvantages and potential viciousness. The broad story is of the world's first society to pronounce ideals of general human equality of worth, but the life of the nation announcing these ideals depended on the continuation of slavery that deprived millions not only of these rights but of almost all other social possibilities and protections. This institution was ended when both sides in the fight urged or ordered their young men to sacrifice life and liberty in try-

ing to kill each other, with some 620,000 of them dying. And there were the other contradictions less fully addressed: the building of American culture on the burying or transforming of Native American cultures; the development of vicious prejudices, especially racial ones; the deprivation of women of many rights and opportunities open to males; the existence of some people in poverty dire enough to mock equal dignity and opportunity.

To see how society struggled, never wholly successfully, with such issues is not to forgive them, but to condemn the failings more sadly, with some recognition of how hard it is for the best of humans to give fully satisfactory solutions, then or now. To read the arguments of Sarah and Angelina Grimké with Theodore Dwight Weld about whether women's rights should be yoked to the fight for slaves' rights is to sense how moral seriousness demands balancing ideals and practicalities in a world where one good often hurts another, and threatens to promote solutions that have horrors aplenty of their own.

4. It is to deepen ones' sense of how ongoing are the problems with which American society struggled, and how much they remain our problems. Choices always have to be made, and in fact are made as surely when we try to forget about problems as when we act. How does one keep democratic religion, schools, competition, cooperation, government activity and inactivity, capitalism, and power, contributing to rather than injuring the broadly decent balance in a good society between individual freedom, the common good, and the ideal of equal worth and opportunity for all? John Winthrop's "city on the hill" was never fully built by the Puritans, by his more secular American successors, or by us. No human society comes close to an immaculate conception, but ideals create, at best, some struggle to fend off or correct some of its worst failures, or most vicious realities. Then as now, a semblance of social decency depends on your—and others—caring, convictions, and choices, none of them easy nor perfect answers, but some of them better ones.

5. It demonstrates how all products of a society tell you important things. Not just formal or polemical or political arguments, but diaries, fictions, poems, personal letters, sermons, songs, writings for children, hymns—all documents of every kind in our society as well as in the past—are telling if one develops an eye to read the "signs" they give.

6. It is to sense the heart of history's interest: the deep differences and equally deep bonds between these earlier folks and us. They all have different voices, assumptions, and concerns than ours but share a common humanity and the struggle with the never fully answered questions that thread human life. They speak in accents made odd to our ears by time, but in words that we can comprehend, consider, care about.

7. It is not only to study history, but to learn to "write" it by doing precisely what all historians do: taking a small part of the past's documentary record and worrying it toward some interpretation. It sacrifices the passive absorption of others' facts or ideas for the harder active work of taking the facts of what some people said and working out some conclusions of your own about them and their society.

8. It is to gain some factual basis of your own for judging the historical stories that try to offer general patterns about past truth. How does the description you get in texts, lectures, or scholarly writings about Federalists and Jeffersonian Republicans accord with the social visions you find in the poem and play of Federalists Timothy Dwight and Royall Tyler and those writings of Republicans James Madison, Hugh Henry Brackeridge and Jefferson himself? How do descriptions of the South and slavery accord with the writings of William Byrd, George Fitzhugh, Mary Boykin Chesnut or of slaves Phillis Wheatley and Solomon Northup? What questions do the arguments of Abraham Lincoln and others about the coming of the Civil War raise about the interpretations you read and hear? Such questioning from evidence is the heart of beginning to be a good student of history. The process of moving from limited evidence to inclusive generalization should make clear how hard it is, how skeptical you should be about "final solutions" to historical riddles, and how easily new evidence can and should jar old answers.

Since this book, if well used, will do so much for you and your society, let me offer a few suggestions on how you can use it effectively. Though you may have as much trouble in arriving at intellectual-moral perfection as did Benjamin Franklin, here is a "plan" for improvement in accord with Franklin's practical good sense.

- Notice the dates of what you read because history is a journey through time. One can't travel without some map of dates and arrive anywhere. Sometimes they offer an important truth even aside from their necessity to the pattern, as when one notices that the death dates of Native Americans Miantonomo and Tecumseh come the year after their speeches urging united resistance to the European settlers/invaders.

- Read the brief introductions to the groups of writings. They will tell you a bit about the people involved and give you some idea concerning what to look for in their writings. They are far from a full map of what you will find in the readings but a nudge that will let you venture out with some sense of direction.

- Read over the "considerations" preceding the selections. There are more nudges here, and, if you have some fairly good answers to them when you're finished with the primary sources, you'll have learned a lot. Some of the questions here involve corollaries related to your thoughts about present society. Consider a bit your answers to these ahead of time, and ponder whether they've changed at all when you finish.

- Read the selections with an active mind and heart working to catch their tone of voice, their arguments and emotions, trying to figure out whether and why you like them or their ideas. Have the map of dates and data and considerations in the back of your mind, but keep your focus on the voices of these people who lived almost 400-150 years b.y. (before you) but which you can hear, like some very long distance call, almost perfectly if you try.

- Reread the considerations after you've read the primary sources and think through your answers to each of the questions. If you do that, you'll have answers to what I think most important in the documents

- Think of some things or issues that you noticed in the material that you weren't asked about. Doing that, you begin to be an intellectual Daniel Boone, able to discover the signs yourself not just read the signposts. And as you do that, you'll see that you should mistrust a bit even your genially intelligent guide on this book's intellectual trail. He deserves your mistrust.

- Write down in a notebook some basic ideas/impressions for each of the sources. This will 1) get them in mind much more completely than if you only think about them; 2) help you to think comparatively—as you should—about the people, times, and cultures in different sections of the book; and 3) provide easy mental refreshment should you let anyone test you about your intellectual journey.

- As you listen to lectures or read texts or scholarly arguments think about how well their conclusions or patternings jibe with the voices and concerns of the folks you've met firsthand. By this time you should have learned the basic lesson: everyone and every answer deserves an honest ear <u>and</u> some honest and informed skepticism. All instructors will doubtless show some doubts regarding your answers, and reciprocation is desirable.

If you follow these simple steps, you should learn a lot about earlier Americans, their times and choices—and about yourself and yours. You'll gain better sense of how Americans looked at and handled their world, and of the traditions, options, and dilemmas they passed on to you. You'll sharpen your historical and human understanding not by finding or defining any final solutions, but by a deepening sense of American aspirations, accomplishments, compromises and failures that are your, and to a degree the world's, heritage.

———————

So, dear Reader, isn't the American way of life great? Eight easy (well, "possible" anyway) steps to eight great goals, not to mention SUCCESS in this course of life. Happiness unfortunately is not insured, since our basic Declaration promises only that we can pursue—not attain—that. But I hope you find some moments of that, too, within these covers. There are a few good jokes as well as some very serious truths in here, none better than Franklin's project for arriving at moral perfection. He concluded, after some poor friend suggested he might well add humility to his list of virtues, that he despaired because he knew that if he ever became really humble he'd be proud of it. Don't worry; you have full permission to be proud of any virtues substantially improved by this course of study. I hope you, like Franklin, will find the exercise worthwhile even as you conclude with him that you won't keep grinding your intellectual-moral blade to perfect shining-ness but that you really "like a speckled axe best."

The Puritans and Franklin were right about themselves, you, me and any society: perfection is not to be expected. The saving grace is always some serious wish and work to make all a tad better, wiser, more caring. There's something to learn still from the "truths" with which the Puritans taught little children the alphabet:

> "Thy life to mend
> This book attend."

A NOTE ON THE DOCUMENTS

These writings are all taken from the sources unchanged, except for some modernization of spelling, punctuation, and capitalization in a few of the early sources, especially those of John Smith and John Winthrop. They are, of course, only a tiny part of the available documentation, and most of them only a tiny part of the writings of the few people used. Three dots appear where material is omitted <u>within</u> particular works or diary entries. I've tried to select documents of major human and intellectual interest to evoke what has come to be accepted as the "common culture" of these periods, while including a variety of less famous but equally telling sources.

These selections are from the most beautiful poems, the best diaries, the most pungent letters, the greatest debates, the richest folk music, the best play, the most famous political-religious documents of these times. And there are many less famous voices equally deep and important, suggesting how these selections could be increased ten-fold—yea, a hundredfold—with little diminution of intelligence, intensity and significance. For the decently curious and caring, they represent a good start to good ends, but only a beginning.

Most of the selections chosen have been condensed, some radically, but I believe there is no great distortion of anyone's argument or voice about the central issues they are brought forward to address.

CHAPTER 1

New World Hopes—and Tragedies

INTRODUCTION

NATIVE AMERICAN REACTIONS
Miantonomo, c. 1610–1643, Speech (1642)
Tenskwatawa, c. 1770–1837, Speech (1808)
Tecumseh, c. 1768–1813, Speeches (1810–11)
Pushmataha, c. 1785–1826, Speech (1811)
John Ross, 1790–1866, Letters (1834–36)

JOHN SMITH, 1580–1631
from A Description of New England (1616)

JOHN WINTHROP, 1588–1649
from A Model of Christian Charity (1630)

The rise of one vital culture often involves the vanquishing, or even vanishing, of others. This occurred as European immigrants built their new world communities by subduing varied Native American nations. Despite social, cultural, and agricultural sharing and the adaptive resilience of many Indian groups, European dominance steadily advanced, as the imperial conflicts of which Indians were sometimes able to take advantage declined and as Native Americans remained divided between and within tribal groupings.

The brief remarks by Narragansett warrior Miantonomo before one Puritan war, and by Shawnee leaders, Tenskwatawa, the Prophet, and Tecumseh before the War of 1812 suggest the difficulties faced by resistant Native Americans. The reply of Choctaw chief Pushmataha to Tecumseh underlines the problems of tribal and tactical divisions, though his siding with the Americans won his group no lasting benefits. Cherokee leader John Ross accurately described general American practices of breaking promises when they wanted more Indian lands, here in response to the 1832 uprooting of the flourishing Cherokee community in Georgia.

Representing European visions were the writings of adventurer Captain John Smith and Puritan leader John Winthrop. Smith was particularly active in the settlement of Virginia, but all his New World writings suggested the hope that England's hard-working poor would have the chance to become comfortable and productive in America— qualities denied them at home. While Smith's promise of "sufficient wealth" probably led on most immigrants, Winthrop's shipboard sermon as the first large group of Puritans sailed to Massachusetts reflected the religious-communal hopes of others. His vision was that his community might become God's "city on the hill" if people, through divine love, put the needs of others and society ahead of their own and firmly denied those other "gods, our pleasures and profits."

CONSIDERATIONS

- Did Europeans have any right to settle in the Americas or to dispossess Indians of their land? Could anything have been done to aid more peaceful accommodation or less violent confrontation?

- What were Smith's and Winthrop's visions of what might be, and how comparatively worthy do you judge them?

- Does today's United States have any ties to Winthrop's communal vision? Should it?

- Do you and your society subordinate pursuit of "pleasures and profits" to the needs of others or the community?

- Is this nation still Smith's land of immigrant opportunity? Should it be?

NATIVE AMERICAN REACTIONS

MIANTONOMO, 1642

Brothers, we must be as one as the English are or we shall all be destroyed. You know our fathers had plenty of deer and skins and our plains were full of game and turkeys, and our coves and rivers were full of fish.

But, brothers, since these Englishmen have seized our country, they have cut down the grass with scythes, and the trees with axes. Their cows and horses eat up the grass, and their hogs spoil our bed of clams; and finally we shall all starve to death; therefore, stand not in your own light, I ask you, but resolve to act like men. All the sachems both to the east and the west have joined with us, and we are resolved to fall upon them at a day appointed, and therefore I come secretly to you, because you can persuade your Indians to do what you will.

TENSKWATAWA TO
WILLIAM HENRY HARRISON, 1808

Father:—It is three years since I first began with that system of religion which I now practice. The white people and some of the Indians were against me; but I had no other intention but to introduce among the Indians, those good principles of religion which the white people profess. I was spoken badly of by the white people, who reproached me with misleading the Indians; but I defy them to say that I did anything amiss.

Father, I was told that you intended to hang me. When I heard this, I intended to remember it, and tell my father, when I went to see him, and relate to him the truth. . . .

The Great Spirit told me to tell the Indians that he had made them, and made the world—that he had placed them on it to do good, and not evil.

I told all the red skins, that the way they were in was not good, and that they ought to abandon it.

That we ought to consider ourselves as one man; but we ought to live agreeably to our several customs, the red people after their mode, and the white people after theirs; particularly, that they should not drink whiskey; that it was not made for them, but the white people, who alone knew how to use it; and that it is the cause of all the mischief which the Indians suffer; and that they must always follow the directions of the Great Spirit, and we must listen to him, as it was he that made us; determine to listen to nothing that is bad; do not take up the tomahawk, should it be offered by the British, or by the long knives; do not meddle with any thing that does not belong to you, but mind your own business, and cultivate the ground, that your women and your children may have enough to live on. . . .

You have promised to assist us; I now request you, in behalf of all the red people, to use your exertions to prevent the sale of liquor to us. . . .

Tecumseh to Harrison, 1810

You wish to prevent the Indians from doing as we wish them, to unite and let them consider their lands as the common property of the whole. You take the tribes aside and advise them not to come into this measure. . . . You want by your distinctions of Indian tribes, in allotting to each a particular, to make them war with each other. You never see an Indian endeavor to make the white people do this. You are continually driving the red people, when at last you will drive them onto the great lake, where they can neither stand nor walk.

Since my residence at Tippecanoe, we have endeavored to leave all distinctions, to destroy village chiefs, by whom all mischiefs are done. It is they who sell the land to the Americans. Brother, this land that was sold, and the goods that was given for it, was only done by a few. . . . In the future we are prepared to punish those who propose to sell land to the Americans. If you continue to purchase them, it will make war among the different tribes, and at last I do not know what will be the consequences among the white people. Brother, I wish you would take pity on the red people and do as I have requested. If you will not give up the land and do cross the boundary of our present settlement, it will be very hard, and produce great trouble between us.

The way, the only way to stop this evil is for the red men to unite in claiming a common and equal right in the land, as it was at first, and should be now—for it was never divided, but belongs to all. No tribe has the right to sell, even to each other, much less to strangers. . . . *Sell a country! Why not sell the air, the great sea, as well as the earth?* Did not the Great Spirit make them all for the use of his children?

How can we have confidence in the white people?

When Jesus Christ came upon the earth you killed Him and nailed Him to the cross. You thought He was dead and you were mistaken. . . .

TECUMSEH TO OTHER CHIEFS, 1811

Where today are the Pequot? Where are the Narragansett, the Mohican, the Pocanet, and other powerful tribes of our people? They have vanished before the avarice and oppression of the white man, as snow before the summer sun. . . . Will we let ourselves be destroyed in our turn, without making an effort worthy of our race? Shall we, without a struggle, give up our homes, our lands, bequeathed to us by the Great Spirit? The graves of our dead and everything that is dear and sacred to us? . . . I know you will say with me, Never! Never! . . .

Sleep not longer, O Choctaws and Chickasaws, in false security and delusive hopes. . . . Will not the bones of our dead be plowed up, and their graves turned into plowed fields?

PUSHMATAHA, 1811

The question before us now is not what wrongs they have inflicted upon our race, but what measures are best for us to adopt in regard to them; and though our race may have been unjustly treated and shamefully wronged by them, yet I shall not for that reason alone advise you to destroy them unless it was just and wise for you so to do; nor would I advise you to forgive them, though worthy of your commiseration, unless I believe it would be to the interest of our common good. . . .

My friends and fellow countrymen! You now have no just cause to declare war against the American people, or wreak your vengeance upon them as enemies, since they have ever manifested feelings of friendship towards you. It is . . . a disgrace to the memory of your fore-fathers, to wage war against the American people merely to gratify the malice of the English.

The war, which you are now contemplating against the Americans . . . forbodes nothing but destruction to our entire race. It is a war against a people whose territories are now far greater than our own, and who are far better provided with all the necessary implements of war, with men, guns, horses, wealth, far beyond that of all our race combined, and where is the necessity or wisdom to make war upon such a people?

JOHN ROSS, 1834

Ever since [the whites came] we have been made to drink of the bitter cup of humiliation; treated like dogs . . . our country and the graves of our Fathers torn from us . . . through a period of upwards of 200 years, rolled back, nation upon nation [until] we find ourselves fugitives, vagrants and strangers in our own country. . . .

The existence of the Indian Nations as distinct independent communities within the limits of the United States seems to be drawing to a close. . . . You are aware that our Brethren, the Choctaws, Chickasaws and Creeks of the South have severally disposed of their country to the United States and that a portion of our own Tribe have also emigrated West of the Mississippi—but that the largest portion of our Nation still remain firmly upon our ancient domain. . . . Our position there may be compared to a solitary tree in an open space, where all the forest trees around have been prostrated by a furious tornado.

JOHN ROSS, 1836

. . . [T]he United States solemnly guaranteed to said nation all their lands not ceded, and pledged the faith of the government, that "all white people who have intruded, or may hereafter intrude on the lands reserved for the Cherokees, shall be removed by the United States. . . ." The Cherokees were happy and prosperous under a scrupulous observance of treaty stipulations by the government of the United States, and from the fostering hand extended over them, they made rapid advances in civilization, morals, and in the arts and sciences. Little did they anticipate, that when taught to think and feel as the American citizen, and to have with him a common interest, they were to be *despoiled by their guardian,* to become strangers and wanderers in the land of their fathers, forced to return to the savage life, and to seek a new home in the wilds of the far west, and that without their consent. An instrument purporting to be a treaty with the Cherokee people, has recently been made public by the President of the United States, that will have such an operation if carried into effect. This instrument, the delegation aver before the civilized world, and in the presence of Almighty God, is fraudulent, false upon its face, made by unauthorized individuals, without the sanction, and against the wishes, of the great body of the Cherokee people. Upwards of fifteen thousand of those people have protested against it, solemnly declaring they will never acquiesce.

from A DESCRIPTION OF NEW ENGLAND

John Smith

Now because I have so oft asked such strange questions of the goodness and greatness of those spacious tracts of land, how they can be thus long unknown or not possessed by the Spaniards, and many such like demands, I entreat your pardons if I chance to be too plain or tedious in relating my knowledge for plain men's satisfaction.

• • •

And surely by reason of those sandy cliffs and cliffs of rocks, both which we saw so planted with gardens and corn fields, and so well inhabited with a goodly, strong, and well proportioned people, besides the greatness of the timber growing on them, the greatness of the fish, and the moderate temper of the air . . . who can but approve this a most excellent place, both for health and fertility? And of all the four parts of the world that I have yet seen not inhabited, could I have but means to transport a colony, I would rather live here than anywhere, and if it did not maintain itself, were we but once indifferently well fitted, let us starve.

The main staple, from hence to be extracted for the present to produce the rest, is fish, which however it may seem a mean and a base commodity, yet who[ever] will but truly take the pains and consider the sequel, I think will allow it well worth the labor. . . . Who doth not know that the poor Hollanders, chiefly by fishing at a great charge and labor in all weathers in the open sea, are made a people so hardy and industrious? . . . [The Hollanders] are made so mighty, strong, and rich as no state but Venice, of twice their magnitude, is so well furnished with so many fair cities, goodly towns, strong fortresses, and that abundance of shipping and all sorts of merchandise . . . What voyages and discoveries, east and west, north and south, yea about the world, make they? What an army by sea and land have they long maintained in despite of one of the greatest princes of the world? And never could the Spaniard with all his mines of gold and silver pay his debts, his friends, and army half so truly as the Hollanders still have done by this contemptible trade of fish.

•   •   •

. . . [W]hy should we more doubt than Holland, Portugal, Spaniards, French, or other, but to do much better than they, where there is victual to feed us; wood of all sorts to build boats, ships, or barks; the fish at our doors; pitch, tar, masts, yards, and most of other necessaries only for making? And here are no hard landlords to rack us with high rents or extorted fines to consume us, no tedious pleas in law to consume us with their many years' disputations for justice, no multitudes to occasion such impediments to good orders, as in popular states. So freely hath God and his Majesty bestowed those blessings on them that will attempt to obtain them, as here every man may be master and owner of his own labor and land, or the greatest part, in a small time. If he have nothing but his hands, he may set up this trade and by industry quickly grow rich, spending but half that time well which in England we abuse in idleness, worse or as ill.

•   •   •

The ground is so fertile that questionless it is capable of producing any grain, fruits, or seeds you will sow or plant . . .

All sorts of cattle may here be bred and fed in the isles or peninsulas, securely for nothing. In the interim, till they increase, if need be (observing the seasons) I dare undertake to have corn enough from the savages for 300 men, for a few trifles. And if they [the savages] should be untoward (as it is most certain they are), thirty or forty good men will be sufficient to bring them all in subjection. . . .

In March, April, May, and half June, here is cod in abundance; in May, June, July, and August, mullet and sturgeon, whose roes do make caviar and puttargo. Herring, if any desire them, I have taken many out of the bellies of cods, some in nets; but the savages compare their store in the sea to the hairs of their heads; and surely there are an incredible abundance upon this coast. . . .

Now young boys and girls, savages or any other, be they ever such idlers, may turn, carry, and return fish without either shame or any great pain; he is very idle that is past twelve years of age and cannot do so much, and she is very old that cannot spin a thread to make engines to catch them. . . .

Of beavers, otters, martens, black foxes, and furs of price may yearly be had six or seven thousand; and if the trade of the French were prevented, many more [could be had]. Twenty-five thousand [furs] this year were brought from those north parts into France, of which trade we may have as good part as the French, if we take good courses. . . .

Of woods, seeing there is such plenty of all sorts, if those that build ships and boats buy wood at so great a price as it is in England, Spain, France, Italy, and Holland and [buy] all other provisions for the nourishing of man's life live well by their trade when labor is all [that is] required to take those necessaries without any other tax, what hazard will be here but do much better?

* * *

The waters are most pure, proceeding from the entrails of rocky mountains.

The herbs and fruits are of many sorts and kinds: as alkermes, currants, or a fruit like currants, mulberries, vines, raspberries, gooseberries, plums, walnuts, chestnuts, small nuts, &c, pumpkins, gourds, strawberries, beans, peas, and maize, a kind or two of flax where with they make nets, lines, and ropes both small and great, very strong for their quantities.

Oak is the chief wood, of which there is great difference in regard [to the state] of the soil where it grows. [There are] fir, pine, walnut, chestnut, birch, ash, elm, cypress, cedar, mulberry, plum tree, hazel, sassafras, and many other sorts. . . .

All these and divers other good things do here, for want of use, still increase, and decrease with little diminution, whereby they grow to that abundance you shall scarce find any bay, shallow shore, or cove of sand where you may not take many clams, or lobsters, or both at your pleasure, and in many places load your boat if you please, nor [are there] isles where you find not fruits, birds, crabs, and mussels, or all of them for [the] taking, at a low water. And in the harbors we frequented, a little boy might take of cunners and pollocks and such delicate fish, at the ship's stern, more than six or ten can eat in a day; but with a casting net [we took] thousands when we pleased. . . .

Who can desire more content, that has small means or but only his merit to advance his fortune, than to tread and plant that ground he has purchased by the hazard of his life? If he have but the taste of virtue and magnanimity, what to such a mind can be more pleasant than planting and building a foundation for his posterity, got from the rude earth by God's blessing and his own industry, without prejudice to any? If he have any grain of faith or zeal in religion, what can he do less hurtful to any or more agreeable to God than to seek to convert those poor savages to know Christ and humanity, whose labors with discretion will triple requite thy charge and pains? What so truly suits with honor and honesty as the discovering things unknown, erecting towns, peopling countries, informing the ignorant, reforming things unjust, teaching virtue, and gain to our native mother-country a kingdom to attend her, find employment for those that are idle because they know not what to do? [This is] so far from wronging any as to cause posterity to remember thee and, remembering thee, ever honor that remembrance with praise.

•   •   •

I have not been so ill bred but I have tasted of plenty and pleasure as well as want and misery, nor does necessity yet, or occasion of discontent, force me to these endeavors, nor am I ignorant [of] what small thanks I shall have for my pains or that many would have the world imagine them to be of great judgement that can but blemish these my designs by their witty objections and detractions. Yet (I hope) my reasons with my deeds will so prevail with some that I shall not want employment in these affairs, to make the most blind see his own senselessness and incredulity, hoping that gain will make them effect that which religion, charity, and the common good cannot. It were but a poor device in me to deceive myself, much more the King, state, my friends, and country with these inducements which, seeing his Majesty has given permission, I wish all sorts of worthy, honest, industrious spirits would understand; and if they desire any further satisfaction I will do my best to give it; not to persuade them to go only, but go with them; not leave them there, but live with them there. . . .

I fear not want of company sufficient, were it but known what I know of those countries; and by the proof of that wealth I hope yearly to return, if God please to bless me from such accidents as are beyond my power . . . to prevent. For I am not so simple to think that ever any other motive than wealth will ever erect there a common wealth or draw company from their ease and humors at home to stay in New England to effect my purposes.

And lest any should think the toil might be insupportable, though these things may be had by labor and diligence, I assure myself there are [those] who delight extremely in vain pleasure, that take much more pains in England to enjoy it than I should do here to gain wealth sufficient; and yet I think they should not have half such sweet content, for our pleasure here is still gains; in England charges and loss. Here nature and liberty afford us that freely which in England we want, or it costs us dearly. What pleasure can be more than . . . in planting vines, fruits, or herbs, in contriving their own grounds, to the pleasure of their own minds, their fields, gardens, orchards, buildings, ships, and other works . . . to recreate themselves before their own doors, in their own boats upon the sea, where man, woman, and child, with a small hook and line, by angling may take divers sorts of excellent fish at their pleasures? And is it not pretty sport to pull up two pence, six pence, and twelve pence as fast as you can haul and veer a line? He is a very bad fisher [who] cannot kill in one day, with his hook and line, one, two, or three hundred cods, which dressed and dried, if they be sold there for ten shillings the hundred, though in England they will give more than twenty, may not both the servant, the master, and merchant be well content with this gain? If a man work but three days in seven he may get more than he can spend, unless he will be excessive. Now that carpenter, mason, gardener, tailor, smith, sailor . . . may they not make this a pretty recreation, though they fish but an hour in a day, to take more than they eat in a week? Or if they will not eat it, because there is so much better choice, yet [they can] sell it or change it with the fishermen or merchants for anything they want. And what sport does yield a more pleasing content and less hurt or charge than angling with a hook and crossing the sweet air from isle to isle, over the silent streams of a calm sea, wherein the most curious may find pleasure, profit, and content?

Thus, though all men be not fishers, yet all men, whatsoever, may in other matters do as well. . . .

For laborers, if those [in England] that sow hemp, rape, turnips, parsnips, carrots, cabbage, and such like, give twenty, thirty, forty, fifty shillings yearly for an acre of ground, and meat, drink, and wages to use it and yet grow rich, when better or at least as good ground may be had [in New England] and cost nothing but labor, it seems strange to me any such should there grow poor.

My purpose is not to persuade children from their parents, men from their wives, or servants from their masters, only such as with free consent may be spared. But that each parish or village, in city or country, that will but apparel their fatherless children of thirteen or fourteen years of age, or young married people that have small wealth to live on, here by their labor [they] may live exceeding well, provided always that first there be a sufficient power to command them, houses to receive them, means to defend them, and meet provisions for them; for any place may be overlain and it is most necessary to have a fortress (ere this grow to practice) and sufficient masters (as carpenters, masons, fishers, fowlers, gardeners, husbandmen, sawyers, smiths, spinners, tailors, weavers, and such like) to take ten, twelve, or twenty, or as there is occasion, for apprentices. The masters by this may quickly grow rich; these [apprentices] may learn their trades themselves to do the like, to a general and an incredible benefit for king and country, master and servant.

from A MODEL OF CHRISTIAN CHARITY

John Winthrop

God Almighty in His most holy and wise providence hath so disposed of the condition of mankind as in all times some must be rich, some poor, some high and eminent in power and dignity, others mean and in subjection.

THE REASON HEREOF:

First, to hold conformity with the rest of His works, being delighted to show forth the glory of His wisdom in the variety and difference of the creatures and the glory of His power, in ordering all these differences for the preservation and good of the whole, and the glory of His greatness; that as it is the glory of princes to have many officers, so this great King will have many stewards, counting Himself more honored in dispensing His gifts to man by man, than if He did it by His own immediate hand.

Secondly, that He might have the more occasion to manifest the work of His Spirit: first, upon the wicked in moderating and restraining them, so that the rich and mighty should not eat up the poor, nor the poor and despised rise up against their superiors and shake off their yoke; secondly, in the regenerate, in exercising His graces in them: as in the great ones, their love, mercy, gentleness, temperance, etc.; in the poor and inferior sort, their faith, patience, obedience, etc.

Thirdly, that every man might have need of other [men] and from hence they might be all knit more nearly together in the bond of brotherly affection. From hence it appears plainly that no man is made more honorable than another or more wealthy, etc., out of any particular and singular respect to himself but for the glory of his creator and the common good of the creature, man. Therefore God still reserves the property of these gifts to Himself, as Ezekial 16: 17; He there calls wealth His gold and His silver, etc. Proverbs 3: 9 He claims their service as His due, "Honor the Lord with thy riches," etc. . . . There are two rules whereby we are to walk, one towards another: justice and mercy. These are always distinguished in their act and in their object, yet may they both concur in the same subject in each respect: as sometimes there may be an occasion of showing mercy to a rich man in some sudden danger of distress, and also doing of mere justice to a poor man in regard of some particular contract. There is likewise a double law by which we are regulated in our conversation, one towards another, in both the former respects, the law of nature and the law of grace, or the moral law or the law of the Gospel, to omit the rule of justice as not properly belonging to this purpose, otherwise than it may fall into consideration in some particular cases. By the first of these laws, man, as he was enabled so withal, [is] commanded to love his neighbor as himself; upon this ground stand all the precepts of the moral law, which concerns our dealings with men. To apply this to the works of mercy, this law requires two things: first, that every man afford his help to another in every want or distress; secondly, that he perform this out of the same affection which makes him careful of his own good according to that of our savior, Matthew, 7: 12: "Whatsoever ye would that men should do to you.". . .

This law of the Gospel propounds likewise a difference of seasons and occasions. There is a time when a Christian must sell all and give to the poor as they did in the apostles' times. There is a time also when a Christian (though they give not all yet) must give beyond their ability, as they of Macedonia, II Corinthians 8, 9. Likewise, community of perils calls for extraordinary liberality and so doth community in some special service for the church. Lastly, when there is no other means whereby our Christian brother may be relieved in this distress, we must help him beyond our ability, rather than tempt God in putting Him upon help by miraculous or extraordinary means.

• • •

This duty of mercy is exercised in giving, lending, and forgiving.

QUEST. What rule shall a man observe in giving . . .?

ANS. If the time and occasion be ordinary he is to give out of his abundance—let him lay aside, as god hath blessed him. If the time and occasion be extraordinary, he must be ruled by them; a man cannot likely do too much, especially if he may leave himself and his family under probable means of comfortable subsistence.

OBJECTION. A man must lay up for posterity, and he is worse than an Infidel that provideth not for his own.

ANS. For the first, it is plain, it must be meant of the ordinary and usual course of fathers and cannot extend to times and occasions extraordinary; it is without question, that he is worse then an Infidel who through his own sloth and voluptuousness shall neglect to provide for his family.

OBJECTION. "The wise man's eyes are in his head" (saith Solomon) "and foreseeth the plague;" therefore we must forecast and lay up against evil times when he or his may stand in need of all he can gather.

ANS: This very argument Solomon uses to persuade to liberality. Eccle: [11. 1.] "Cast they bread upon the waters . . . ," "he that gives to the poor lends to the lord," and he will repay him even in this life a hundred fold to him or his. And I would know of those who plead so much for laying up for time to come, whether they hold to be Gospel Math: 16. 19. "Lay not up for yourselves treasures upon earth. They are subject to the moth, the rust, the thief." Secondly, they will steal away the heart, "where the treasure is there will the heart be also." He who hath this world's goods and sees his brother to need, and shuts up his compassion from him, how dwelleth the love of god in him . . .? If thy brother be in want and thou canst help him, thou needst not make doubt what thou shouldst do; if thou lovest god thou must help him.

QUEST: What rule must we observe in lending?

ANS: Thou must observe whether thy brother hath present or probable, or possible means of repaying thee; if there be none of these, thou must give him according to his necessity, rather than lend him as he requires; if he hath present means of repaying thee, thou art to look at him, not as an act of mercy, but by way of commerce, wherein thou art to walk by the rule of justice, but, if his means of repaying thee be only probable or possible then is he an object of thy mercy. Thou must lend him, though there be danger of losing it, Deut: 15. 7. "If any of thy brethren be poor etc. thou shalt lend him sufficient" that men might not shift off this duty by the apparent hazard. Math: 5. 42. "From him that would borrow of thee turn not away."

QUEST: What rule must we observe in forgiving?

ANS: Whether thou didst lend by way of commerce or mercy, if he have nothing to pay thee, thou must forgive him. . . . In all these and like cases Christ has a general rule, Math: 7. 22. "Whatsoever ye would that men should do to you, do ye the same to them also."

QUEST: What rule must we observe and walk by in case of community of peril?

ANS: The same as before, but with more enlargement towards others and less respect towards ourselves, and our own right. Hence it was that in the primitive church they all had all things in common, neither did any man say that that which he possessed with his own. Likewise in their return out of the captivity, because the work was great for the restoring of the church and the danger of enemies was common to all, Nehemiah exhorts the Jews to liberality and readiness in remitting their debts to their brethren, and disposes liberally of his own to such as wanted and stands not upon his own due, which he might have demanded of them. Thus did some of our forefathers in times of persecution here in England, and so did many of the faithful in other churches. The scripture gives no cause to restrain any from being over liberal this way; but all men to the liberal and cheerful practise hereof by the sweetest promises. To deal thy bread to the hungry and to bring the poor that wander into thy house, when thou seest the naked to cover them etc. then shall thy light break forth as the morning, and thy health shall grow speedily, thy righteousness shall go before thee, and the glory of the lord shall embrace thee. On the contrary most heavy curses are laid upon such as are straightened towards the Lord and his people: "He who shutteth his ears from hearing the cry of the poor, he shall cry and shall not be heard": Math: 25: 41 "Go ye cursed into everlasting fire etc. I was hungry and ye fed me not." Cor: 2. 9. 16. "He that soweth sparingly shall reap sparingly."

. . . The way to draw men to the works of mercy is not by force of argument from the goodness or necessity of the work, for though this course may enforce a rational mind to some present act of mercy as is frequent in experience, yet it cannot work such a habit in a soul as shall make it prompt upon all occasions to produce the same effect but by framing these affections of love in the heart which will as natively bring forth the other, as any cause doth produce the effect.

The definition which the Scripture gives us of love is this: Love is the bond of perfection. First, it is a bond, or ligament. 2ly, it makes the work perfect. There is no body but consists of parts and that which knits these parts together gives the body its perfection, because it makes each part so contiguous to the other as thereby they do mutually participate with each other, both in strength and infirmity, in pleasure and pain. In the most perfect of all bodies, Christ and his church make one body: the several parts of this body considered apart before they were united were as disproportionate and as much disordering as so many contrary qualities or elements, but when Christ comes and by his spirit and love knits all these parts to himself and each to the other, it is become the most perfect and best proportioned body in the world.

From the former considerations arise these conclusions.

1. First, this love among Christians is a real thing not imaginary.

2ly. This love is as absolutely necessary to the being of the body of Christ, as the sinews and other ligaments of a natural body are to the being of that body.

•   •   •

It rests now to make some application of this discourse by the present design which gave the occasion of writing it. Herein are four things to be propounded: first, the persons; secondly, the work; thirdly, the end; fourthly, the means.

1. For the persons, we are a company professing ourselves fellow members of Christ, in which respect only, though we were absent from each other many miles, and had our employments as far distant, yet we ought to account ourselves knit together by this bond of love, and live in the exercise of it, if we would have comfort in our being in Christ. . . .

2. For the work we have in hand, it is by mutual consent, through a special overruling providence and a more than an ordinary approbation of the churches of Christ, to seek out a place of cohabitation and consortship under a due form of government both civil and ecclesiastical. In such cases as this, the care of the public must oversway all private respects by which not only conscience but mere civil policy doth bind us; for it is a true rule that particular estates cannot subsist in the ruin of the public.

3. The end is to improve our lives to do more service to the Lord, the comfort and increase of the body of Christ whereof we are members, [so] that ourselves and posterity may be the better preserved from the common corruptions of this evil world, to serve the Lord and work out our salvation under the power and purity of His holy ordinances.

4. For the means whereby this must be effected, they are twofold: a conformity with the work and the end we aim at; these we see are extraordinary, therefore we must not content ourselves with usual ordinary means. Whatsoever we did or ought to have done when we lived in England, the same must we do, and more also where we go. That which the most in their churches maintain as a truth in profes-

sion only, we must bring into familiar and constant practice: as in this duty of love we must love brotherly without dissimulation; we must "love one another with a pure heart fervently;" we must "bear one another's burdens;" we must not look only on our own things but also on the things of our brethren. Neither must we think that the Lord will bear with such failings at our hands as He doth from those among whom we have lived.

• • •

Thus stands the cause between God and us: we are entered into covenant with Him for this work; we have taken out a commission; the Lord hath given us leave to draw our own articles. We have professed to enterprise these actions upon these and these ends; we have hereupon besought Him of favor and blessing. Now if the Lord shall please to hear us and bring us in peace to the place we desire, then hath He ratified this covenant and sealed our commission, [and He] will expect a strict performance of the articles contained in it. But if we shall neglect the observation of these articles which are the ends we have propounded and, dissembling with our God, shall fall to embrace this present world and prosecute our carnal intentions, seeking great things for ourselves and our posterity, the Lord will surely break out in wrath against us, be revenged of such a perjured people, and make us know the price of the breach of such a covenant.

Now the only way to avoid this shipwreck and to provide for our posterity is to follow the counsel of Micah: to do justly, to love mercy, to walk humbly with our God. For this end, we must be knit together in this work as one man. We must entertain each other in brotherly affection; we must be willing to abridge ourselves of our superfluities, for the supply of others' necessities; we must uphold a familiar commerce together in all meekness, gentleness, patience and liberality. We must delight in each other, make others' conditions our own, rejoice together, mourn together, labor and suffer together, always having before our eyes our commission and community in the work, our community as members of the same body. So shall we "keep the unity of the spirit in the bond of peace," the Lord will be our God and delight to dwell among us, as His own people, and [He] will command a blessing upon us in all our ways, so that we shall see much more of His wisdom, power, goodness, and truth than formerly we have been acquainted with. We shall find that the God of Israel is among us, when ten of us shall be able to resist a thousand of our enemies, when He shall make us a praise and glory [so] that men shall say of succeeding plantations, "The Lord make it like that of New England," for we must consider that we shall be as a city upon a hill, the eyes of all people are upon us. So that if we shall deal falsely with our God in this work we have undertaken, and so cause Him to withdraw His present help from us, we shall be made a story and a by-word through the world; we shall open the mouths of enemies to speak evil of the ways of God and all professors for God's sake; we shall shame the faces of many of God's worthy servants and cause their prayers to be turned into curses upon us, till we be consumed out of the good land whither we are going. And to shut up this discourse with that exhortation of Moses, that faithful servant of the Lord, in his last farewell to Israel, Deuteronomy 30: Beloved, there is now set before us "life and good, death and evil," in that we are commanded this day to love the Lord our God and to love one another, to walk in his ways and to keep His commandments, and His ordinance, and His laws, and the articles of our covenant with him [so] that we may live and be multiplied and [so] that the Lord our God may bless us in the land whither we go to possess it. But if our hearts shall turn away so that we will not obey, but shall be seduced and worship other gods, our pleasures and profits, and serve them, it is propounded unto us this day, we shall surely perish out of the good land whither we pass over this vast sea to possess it.

Therefore, let us choose life.
that we, and our seed,
may live; by obeying His
voice and cleaving to Him,
for He is our life and
our prosperity.

CHAPTER 2

A Troubled City on a Hill

INTRODUCTION

JOHN AND MARGARET WINTHROP, 1598–1644
Selected Letters (1629–1630)

JOHN WINTHROP
Journals (1631–1645)

ANNE BRADSTREET, 1612–1672
Selected Poems

ROGER WILLIAMS, 1603–1683
from A Key into the Language of America (1647, 1655),
from The Bloody Tenet of Persecution for
the Cause of Conscience (1643),
and To the Town of Providence (1655)

JOHN COTTON, 1584–1652
from The Bloody Tenet Washed White in
the Blood of the Lamb (1647)

Puritans, with good reason, never felt they achieved their hoped for "city on a hill," but their serious commitment to high ideals and their practical involvements in a secularizing world created a vital intellectual tradition. The most literate community in the world up to that time, Puritans did much to define the practices, aspirations, conflicts, and compromises of the American cultural tradition.

None of their writings gives better sense of the early community's conflicts, commitments, and everyday realities than the journals of John Winthrop, who served as governor of the colony for fourteen of its first twenty years. Winthrop chronicled conflicts with religious dissenters, with Indians, and with various sinners, and helped to define the political, economic and gender ideals and realities of the group. Some of

27

those gender relations are suggested also in the letters between John and Margaret Winthrop around the time of the 1630 removal to America, and in the poetry of Anne Bradstreet. Of a leading Puritan family, Bradstreet wrote her poems privately, but became the first colonist to publish a book of poetry upon the urging of relatives and clergy who took pride in her accomplishment. Winthrop wrote of the saddest case of banishment for dissent, that of Anne Hutchinson, and of another controversy that ended happier. Roger Williams was a well-loved Puritan minister driven from the colony because of his demands that Indians not the king be deemed the true owners of the land, that there be a sharper separation of church and state, and that the Puritans denounce all tie to the Church of England. Such things threatened the colony's charter; and, probably warned by Winthrop, Williams escaped to Rhode Island, where he developed one of the earliest arguments for toleration and wrote verse about the Indians, intended to emphasize the failings of white society. John Cotton, Boston's leading minister and long Anne Hutchinson's closest supporter, attacked Williams' doctrine of toleration on grounds common to that day.

CONSIDERATIONS

- How just and reasonable were the actions of the Puritan community against "dissenters" like Williams and Hutchinson?

- Has there been much change in the American definition of "liberty" versus "license" that Winthrop makes?

- What were the reasons that the Puritans and all Western nations (except Holland) rejected religious tolerance in the early 17th-century? How convincing are Williams' arguments for tolerance? What American circumstances aided the gradual acceptance of Williams' argument?

- What attitudes toward women do you find in Winthrop, and how important do you think them in explaining Hutchinson's banishment?

- What do Margaret Winthrop's letters and Bradstreet's poetry suggest about the position of women in the Puritan community? What do Winthrop and Williams suggest about the relations between whites and Native Americans?

Selected Letters of John and Margaret Winthrop

My most sweet Husband,

How dearly welcome thy kind letter was to me, I am not able to express. The sweetness of it did much refresh me. What can be more pleasing to a wife, than to hear of the welfare of her best beloved, and how he is pleased with her poor endeavours! I blush to hear myself commended, knowing my own wants. But it is your love that conceives the best, and makes all things seem better than they are. I wish that I may be always pleasing to thee, and that those comforts we have in each other may be daily increased, as far as they be pleasing to God. . . .

I have many reasons to make me love thee, whereof I will name two: First, because thou lovest God; and, secondly, because that thou lovest me. If these two were wanting, all the rest would be eclipsed. But I must leave this discourse, and go about my household affairs. I am a bad housewife to be so long from them; but I must needs borrow a little time to talk with thee, my sweet heart. The term is more than half done. I hope thy business draws to an end. It will be but two or three weeks before I see thee, though they be long ones. . . . And thus, with my mother's and my own best love to yourself and all the rest, I shall leave scribbling. The weather being cold, makes me make haste. Farewell, my good husband; the Lord keep thee.

Your obedient wife,
Margaret Winthrop

Groton, November 22, 1629

My dear Wife,

I have many things to thank thee for this week,—thy most kind letter, fowls, puddings, &c.; but I must first thank our heavenly Father, that I hear of thy health and the welfare of all our family; for I was in fear, because I left thee not well. But thus is the Lord pleased still to declare his goodness and mercy to his unworthy servants. Oh that we could learn to trust in him, and to love him as we ought!

. . . The Lord in mercy bring us well through all our troubles, as I trust he will. Thou must bear with my brevity. The Lord bless and keep thee, and all our children and company. So I kiss my sweet wife, and rest

Thy faithful husband,
Jo. Winthrop.

My brother and sister salute you all. Let the cow be killed against I come home; and let my son Henry provide such peas as will porridge well, or else none.

January 15, 1629

[To Margaret Winthrop]

The largeness and truth of my love to thee makes me always mindful of thy welfare, and set me on work to begin to write before I hear from thee. The very thought of thee affords me many a kind refreshing: What will then the enjoying of thy sweet society, which I prize above all worldly comforts?

Yet, such is the folly and misery of man, as he is easily brought to contemn the true good he enjoys, and to neglect the best things, which he holds only in hope, and both upon an ungrounded desire of some seeming good, which he promiseth to himself. And if it be thus with us, that are Christians, who have a sure word to direct us, and the holy faith to live by, what is the madness and bondage of those, who are out of Christ? . . . Let men talk what they will of riches, honours, pleasures, &c; let us have Christ crucified, and let them take all besides. For, indeed, he who hath Christ, hath all things with him; for he enjoyeth an all-sufficiency, which makes him abundantly rich in poverty, honourable in the lowest abasements, full of joy and consolation in the sharpest afflictions, living in death, and possessing eternity in this vale of misery. . . .

I am forced to patch up my letters, here a piece and there another. I have now received thine, the kindly fruits of thy most sweet affections. Blessed be the Lord for the welfare of thyself and all our family.

I received letters from my two sons with thee. Remember my love and blessing to them, and to my daughter Winthrop, for whose safety I give the Lord thanks. I have so many letters to write, as I cannot write to them now. Our friends here are in reasonable health, and desire to be kindly remembered to you all. Commend me to all my good friends, my loving neighbours, goodman Cole and his wife, to whom we are always much beholden. I will remember M_____ her gown and petticoat, and the children's girdles. So, with my most affectionate desires of thy welfare, and my blessing to all our children, I kiss my sweet wife, and commend thee and all ours to the gracious protection of our heavenly Father, and rest

Thy faithful husband, still present with thee in his most unkind absence,

Jo. Winthrop

May 8, 1629

Most loving and good Husband,

I have received your letters. The true tokens of your love and care of my good, now in your absence, as well as when you are present, make me think that saying false, Out of sight out of mind. I am sure my heart and thoughts are always near you, to do you good and not evil all the days of my life.

I hope, through God's blessing, your pains will not be altogether lost, which you bestow upon me in writing. Those serious thoughts of your own, which you sent me, did make a very good supply instead of a sermon. I shall often read them. . . . And I shall think long for your coming home. And thus, with my best love to you, I beseech the Lord to send us a comfortable meeting in his good time. I commit you to the Lord.

Your loving and obedient wife,
Margaret Winthrop

My sweet Husband,

I rejoice in the expectation of our happy meeting; for thy absence hath been very long in my conceit, and thy presence much desired. Thy welcome is always ready; make haste to entertain it.

I was yesterday at a meeting at goodman Cole's, upon the going of the young folk to Dedham, where thanks were given to God for the reformation of the young man, and amendment of his life. We had also a part in their prayers. My dear husband, I will now leave writing to thee, hoping to see thee shortly. The good Lord send us a comfortable meeting. . . . I received the things you sent, and thank you heartily for them. I will take order with my man to buy some trimming for my gown. And so I bid my good husband farewell, and commit him to the Lord.

Your loving and obedient wife,
Margaret Winthrop.

My dear Wife,

I praise the Lord that I hear of thy welfare, and of the rest of our family. I thank thee for thy most kind letter, and especially that sweet affection, from whence it flows. I am sorry I cannot come down to thee, as I hoped; but there is no remedy. The Lord so disposeth as I must stay yet (I doubt) a fortnight, but, assure thyself, not one day more than I must needs.

I pray thee have patience. God, in his due time, will bring us together in peace. . . . The Lord bless thee, my sweet wife, and all ours. Farewell.

Thy faithful husband,
Jo. Winthrop.

My most dear Husband,

I should not now omit any opportunity of writing to thee, considering I shall not long have thee to write unto. But, by reason of my unfitness at this time, I must entreat thee to accept of a few lines from me, and not to impute it to any want of love, or neglect of my duty to thee, to whom I owe more than I shall ever be able to express. My request now shall be to the Lord to prosper thee in thy voyage, and enable thee and fit thee for it, and give all graces and gifts for such employments as he shall call thee to. I trust God will once more bring us together before you go, that we may see each other with gladness, and take solemn leave, till we, through the goodness of our God, shall meet in New England, which will be a joyful day to us . . . And thus, with my best wishes to God for thy health and welfare, I take my leave, and rest

Thy faithful, obedient wife,
Margaret Winthrop.

My sweet Wife,

The opportunity of so fit a messenger, and my deep engagement of affection to thee, makes me write at this time, though I hope to follow soon after. The Lord our God hath oft brought us together with comfort, when we have been long absent; and, if it be good for us, he will do so still. . . . And is not he a God abroad as well as at home? Is not his power and providence the same in New England that it hath been in Old England? If our ways please him, he can command deliverance and safety in all places, and can make the stones of the field and the beasts, yea, the raging seas, and our very enemies, to be in league with us. But, if we sin against him, he can raise up evil against us out of our own bowels, houses, estates, &c. My good wife, trust in the Lord, whom thou hast found faithful. He will be better to thee than any husband, and will restore thee thy husband with advantage. But I must end, with all our salutations, with which I have laden this bearer, that he may be the more kindly welcome. So I kiss my sweet wife, and bless thee and all ours, and rest

Thine ever,
Jo. Winthrop.

February 14, 1629
Thou must be my valentine, for none hath challenged me.

London, March 2, 1629
Mine own dear Heart,

I must confess, thou hast overcome me with thy exceeding great love, and those abundant expressions of it in thy sweet letters, which savour of more than an ordinary spirit of love and piety. Blessed be the Lord our God, that gives strength and comfort to thee to undergo this great trial, which, I must confess, would be too heavy for thee, if the Lord did not put under his hand in so gracious a measure. Let this experience of his faithfulness to thee in this first trial, be a ground to establish thy heart to believe and expect his help in all that may follow. It grieveth me much, that I want time and freedom of mind to discourse with thee (my faithful yokefellow) in those things, which thy sweet letters offer me so plentiful occasion for. I beseech the Lord, I may have liberty to supply it, ere I depart; for I cannot thus leave thee. Our two boys and James Downing, John Samford and Mary M. and most of my servants, are gone this day towards South Hampton. The good Lord be with them and us all. Goodman Hawes was with me, and very kindly offers to bring his wife to Groton about the beginning of April, and so stay till thyself and my daughter be in bed; so as thou shalt not need take care for a midwife. Ah, my most kind and dear wife, how sweet is thy love to me! The Lord bless thee and thine with the blessings from above and from beneath, of the right hand and the left, with plenty of favour and peace here, and eternal glory hereafter. All here are in health, (I praise God,) and salute thee. Remember my love and blessing to our children, and my salutations to all as thou knowest. So I kiss and embrace thee, and rest

Thine ever,
Jo. Winthrop

My faithful and dear Wife,

It pleaseth God, that thou shouldest once again hear from me before our departure, and I hope this shall come safe to thy hands. I know it will be a great refreshing to thee. And blessed be his mercy, that I can write thee so good news, that we are all in very good health, and, having tried our ship's entertainment now more than a week, we find it agrees very well with us. Our boys are well and cheerful, and have no mind of home. They lie both with me, and sleep as soundly in a rug (for we use no sheets here) as ever they did at Groton; and so I do myself, (I praise God.) The wind hath been against us this week and more; but this day it is come fair to the north, so as we are preparing (by God's assistance) to set sail in the morning. . . . And now (my sweet soul) I must once again take my last farewell of thee in Old England. It goeth very near to my heart to leave thee; but I know to whom I have committed thee, even to him who loves thee much better than any husband can, who hath taken account of the hairs of thy head, and puts all thy tears in his bottle, who can, and (if it be for his glory) will bring us together again with peace and comfort. Oh, how it refresheth my heart, to think, that I shall yet again see thy sweet face in the land of the living!—that lovely countenance, that I have so much delighted in, and beheld with so great content! I have hitherto been so taken up with business, as I could seldom look back to my former happiness; but now, when I shall be at some leisure, I shall not avoid the remembrance of thee, nor the grief for thy absence. Thou hast thy share with me, but I hope the course we have agreed upon will be some ease to us both.

Mondays and Fridays, at five of the clock at night, we shall meet in spirit till we meet in person. Yet, if all these hopes should fail, blessed be our God, that we are assured we shall meet one day, if not as husband and wife, yet in a better condition. Let that stay and comfort thy heart. Neither can the sea drown thy husband, nor enemies destroy, nor any adversity deprive thee of thy husband or children. Therefore I will only take thee now and my sweet children in mine arms, and kiss and embrace you all, and so leave you with my God. . . .

Thine wheresoever,
Jo. Winthrop.

March 28, 1630

My Love, my Joy, my faithful One,

I suppose thou didst not expect to have any more letters from me till the return of our ships; but so is the good pleasure of God, that the winds should not serve yet to carry us hence. . . .

[T]his is the third letter I have written to thee, since I came to Hampton, in requital of those two I received from thee, which I do often read with much delight, apprehending so much love and sweet affection in them, as I am never satisfied with reading, nor can read them without tears; but whether they proceed from joy, sorrow or desire, or from that consent of affection, which I always hold with thee, I cannot conceive. Ah, my dear heart, I ever held thee in high esteem, as thy love and thy goodness hath well deserved; but (if it be possible) I shall yet prize thy virtue at a greater rate, and long more to enjoy thy sweet society than ever before. I am sure thou art not short of me in this desire. Let us pray hard, and pray in faith, and our God, in his good time, will accomplish our desire. Oh, how loath am I to bid thee farewell! but, since it must be, farewell, my sweet love, farewell. Farewell, my dear children and family. The Lord bless you all, and grant me to see your faces once again. Come, (my dear,) take him and let him rest in thine arms, who will ever remain,

Thy faithful husband,
Jo. Winthrop.

My dear Wife,

Blessed be the Lord, our good God and merciful Father, that hath preserved me in life and health to salute thee, and to comfort thy long longing heart with the joyful news of my welfare, and the welfare of thy beloved children.

We had a long and troublesome passage, but Lord made it safe and easy to us. . . .

I shall expect thee next summer, (if the Lord please,) and by that time I hope to be provided for thy comfortable entertainment. My most sweet wife, be not disheartened; trust in the Lord, and thou shalt see his faithfulness. . . . I kiss and embrace thee, my dear wife, and all my children, and leave thee in his arms, who is able to preserve you all, and to fulfil our joy in our happy meeting in his good time. Amen.

Thy faithful husband,
Jo. Winthrop.

from THE JOURNAL OF JOHN WINTHROP

APRIL 4, 1631

Wahginnacut, a sagamore upon the River Quonehtacut . . . came to the governour at Boston, with John Sagamore, and Jack Straw, (an Indian, who had lived in England and had served Sir Walter Earle and was now turned Indian again,) and divers of their sannops, and brought a letter to the governour from Mr. Endecott to this effect: That the said Wahginnacut was very desirous to have some Englishmen to come plant in his country, and offered to find them corn, and give them yearly eighty skins of beaver, and that the country was very fruitful, &c. and wished that there might be two men sent with him to see the country. The governour entertained them at dinner, but would send none with him. He discovered after, that the said sagamore is a very treacherous man and at war with the Pekoath . . . .

APRIL 12

At a court holden at Boston, (upon an information to the governour, that they of Salem had called Mr. Williams to the office of a teacher,) a letter was written from the court to Mr. Endecott to this effect: That whereas Mr. Williams had refused to join with the congregation at Boston, because they would not make a publick declaration of their repentance for having communion with the churches of England, while they lived there; and, besides, had declared his opinion, that the magistrate might not punish the breach of the Sabbath nor any other offence . . . therefore, they marvelled they would choose him without advising with the council. . . .

April 13, 1631

Chickatabot came to the governour, and desired to buy some English clothes for himself. The governour told him, that English sagamores did not use to truck; but he called his tailor and gave him order to make him a suit of clothes; whereupon he gave the governour two large skins of coat beaver, and, after he and his men had dined, they departed, and said he would come again three days after for his suit.

April 15

Chickatabot came to the governour again, and he put him into a very good new suit from head to foot, and after he set meat before them; but he would not eat till the governour had given thanks, and after meat he desired him to do the like, and so departed.

June 14

At a court, John Sagamore and Chickatabot being told at last court of some injuries that their men did to our cattle, and giving consent to make satisfaction, &c. now one of their men was complained of for shooting a pig, &c. for which Chickatabot was ordered to pay a small skin of beaver, which he presently paid.

At this court one Philip Ratcliff, a servant of Mr. Cradock, being convict, ore tenus, of most foul, scandalous invectives against our churches and government, was censured to be whipped, lose his ears, and be banished the plantation, which was executed.

July 13

Canonicus' son, the great sachem of Naraganset, came to the governour's house with John Sagamore. After they had dined, he gave the governour a skin, and the governour requited him with a fair pewter pot, which he took very thankfully, and stayed all night.

August 8

The Tarentines, to the number of one hundred, came in three canoes, and in the night assaulted the wigwam of the sagamore of

Agawam, by Merimack, and slew seven men, and wounded John Sagamore, and James, and some others.

MAY 8, 1632

The governour, among other things, used this speech to the people, after he had taken his oath: That he had received gratuities from divers towns, which he received with much comfort and content; he had also received many kindnesses from particular persons, which he would not refuse, lest he should be accounted uncourteous, &c.; but he professed that he received them with a trembling heart, in regard of God's rule, and the consciousness of his own infirmity; and therefore desired them, that hereafter they would not take it ill, if he did refuse presents from particular persons, except they were from the assistants, or from some special friends; to which no answer was made; but he was told after, that many good people were much grieved at it, for that he never had any allowance towards the charge of his place.

NOVEMBER 11, 1633

. . . At this meeting there arose some difference between the governour and Mr. Cottington, who charged the governour, that he took away the liberty of the rest, because (at the request of the rest) he had named some men to set out men's lands, &c. which grew to some heat of words; but the next Lord's day they both acknowledged openly their failing, and declared that they had been reconciled the next day.

DECEMBER 5

John Sagamore died of the small pox, and almost all his people; (above thirty buried by Mr. Maverick of Winesemett in one day.) The towns in the bay took away many of the children; but most of them died soon after.

James Sagamore of Sagus died also, and most of his folks. John Sagamore desired to be brought among the English, (so he was) and promised (if he recovered) to live with the English and serve their God. He left one son, which he disposed to Mr. Wilson, the pastor of Boston, to be brought up by him. He gave to the governour a good quantity of wampompeague, and to divers others of the English he gave gifts, and took order for the payment of his own debts and his men's. He died in a persuasion that he should go to the Englishmen's God. Divers of them, in their sickness, confessed that the Englishmen's God was a good God; and that, if they recovered, they would serve him.

It wrought much with them, that when their own people forsook them, yet the English came daily and ministered to them; and yet few, "only two families," took any [infection] by it. Among others, Mr. Maverick of Winesemett is worthy of a perpetual remembrance. Himself, his wife and servants, went daily to them, ministered to their necessities, and buried their dead, and took home many of their children. So did other of the neighbours.

This infectious disease spread to Pascataquack, where all the Indians (except one or two) died.

One Cowper of Pascataquack, going to an island, upon the Lord's day, to fetch some sack to be drank at the great house, he and a boy, coming back in a canoe, (being both drunk,) were driven to sea and never heard of after.

At the same plantation, a company having made a fire at a tree, one of them said, Here this tree will fall, and here will I lie; and accordingly it fell upon him and killed him.

It pleased the Lord to give special testimony of his presence in the church of Boston, after Mr. Cotton was called to office there. More were converted and added to that church, than to all the other churches in the bay . . . . Also, the Lord pleased greatly to bless the practice of discipline, wherein he gave the pastor, Mr. Wilson, a singular gift, to the great benefit of the church.

DECEMBER 27

The governour and assistants met at Boston, and took into consideration a treatise, which Mr. Williams (then of Salem) had sent to them, and which he had formerly written to the governour and council of Plimouth, wherein, among other things, he disputes their right to the lands they possessed here, and concluded that, claiming by the king's grant, they could have no title, nor otherwise, except they compounded with the natives. For this, taking advice with some of the most judicious ministers, (who much condemned Mr. Williams's errour and presumption,) they gave order, that he should be convented at the next court, to be censured, &c. . . . [P]assages chiefly whereat they were much offended: 1, for that he chargeth King James to have told a solemn publick lie, because in his patent he blessed God that he was the first Christian prince that had discovered this land; 2, for that he chargeth him and others with blasphemy for calling Europe Christendom, or the Christian world. . . .

. . . Mr. Williams also wrote to the governour, and also to him and the rest of the council, very submissively, professing his intent to have been only to have written for the private satisfaction of the [governor] &c. of Plimouth, without any purpose to have stirred any further in it, if the governour here had not required a copy of him; withal offering his book, or any part of it, to be burnt.

At the next court he appeared *penitently,* and gave satisfaction of his intention and loyalty. So it was left, and nothing done in it.

JANUARY 24, 1634

The governour and council met again at Boston, to consider of Mr. Williams's letter, &c. when, with the advice of Mr. Cotton and Mr. Wilson, and weighing his letter, and further considering of the aforesaid offensive passages in his book, (which, being written in very obscure and implicative phrases, might well admit of doubtful interpretation,) they found the matters not to be so evil as at first they seemed. Whereupon they agreed, that, upon his retractation, &c. or taking an oath of allegiance to the king, &c. it should be passed over.

NOVEMBER 24

One Scott and Eliot of Ipswich were lost in their way homewards, and wandered up and down six days and eat nothing. At length they were found by an Indian, being almost senseless for want of rest, &c.

About the same time one [blank] was twenty-one days upon Plumb Island, and found by chance frozen in the snow, yet alive, and did well. He had been missing twenty days, and himself said he had no food all that time.

NOVEMBER 27

. . . It was then informed us, how Mr. Eliot, the teacher of the church of Roxbury, had taken occasion, in a sermon, to speak of the peace made with the Pekods, and to lay some blame upon [the ministry] for proceeding therein, without consent of the people, and for other, failings (as he conceived.) We took order, that he should be dealt with by Mr. Cotton, Mr. Hooker, and Mr. Welde, to be brought to see his errour, and to heal it by some publick explanation of his meaning; for the people began to take occasion to murmur against us for it.

It was likewise informed, that Mr. Williams of Salem had broken his promise to us, in teaching publickly against the king's patent, and our great sin in claiming right thereby to this country, &c. and for usual terming the churches of England antichristian. We granted summons to him for his appearance at the next court.

The aforesaid three ministers, upon conference with the said Mr. Eliot, brought him to acknowledge his errour in that he had mistaken the ground of his doctrine . . .

JANUARY, 1635

The governour and assistants met at Boston to consider about Mr. Williams, for that they were credibly informed, that, notwithstanding the injunction laid upon him (upon the liberty granted him to stay till the spring) not to go about to draw others to his opinions, he did use to entertain company in his house, and to preach to them, even of such points as he had been censured for; and it was agreed to send him into England by a ship then ready to depart. The reason was, because he had drawn above twenty persons to his opinion, and they were intended to erect a plantation about the Naragansett Bay, from whence the infection would easily spread into these churches, (the people being, many of them, much taken with the apprehension of his godliness.) Whereupon a warrant was sent to him to come presently to Boston, to be shipped, &c. He returned answer, (and divers of Salem came with it), that he could not come without hazard of his life, &c. Whereupon a pinnace was sent with commission to Capt. Underhill, &c. to apprehend him, and carry him aboard the ship, (which then rode at Natascutt;) but, when they came at his house, they found he had been gone three days before; but whither they could not learn.

He had so far prevailed at Salem, as many there (especially of devout women) did embrace his opinions, and separated from the churches . . . .

Mr. Hugh Peter went from place to place labouring, both publick-ly and privately, to raise up men to a publick frame of spirit, and so prevailed, as he procured a good sum of money to be raised to set on foot the fishing business . . . and wrote into England to raise as much more. The intent was to set up a magazine of all provisions and other necessaries for fishing, that men might have things at hand, and for reasonable prices; whereas now the merchants and seamen took advantage to sell at most excessive rates . . . .

JULY 8, 1635

At the general court, Mr. Williams of Salem was summoned, and did appear. It was laid to his charge, that, being under question before the magistracy and churches for divers dangerous opinions, viz. 1, that the magistrate ought not to punish . . . otherwise than in such cases as did disturb the civil peace; 2, that he ought not to tender an oath to an unregenerate man; 3, that a man ought not to pray with such, though wife, child, &c.; 4, that a man ought not to give thanks after the sacrament nor after meat, &c.; and that the other churches were about to write to the church of Salem to admonish him of these errours; not-withstanding the church had since called him to the office of a teacher. Much debate was about these things. The said opinions were adjudged by all, magistrates and ministers, (who were desired to be present,) to be erroneous, and very dangerous, and the calling of him to office, at that time, was judged a great contempt of authority. So, in fine, time was given to him and the church of Salem to consider of these things till the next general court, and then either, to give satisfaction to the court, or else to expect the sentence. . . .

AUGUST 15

Mr. Williams, pastor of Salem, being sick and not able to speak, wrote to his church a protestation, that he could not communicate with the churches in the bay; neither would he communicate with them, except they would refuse communion with the rest; but the whole church was grieved herewith.

OCTOBER

At this general court Mr. Williams, the teacher of Salem, was again convented, and all the ministers in the bay being desired to be present, he was charged with the said two letters,—that to the churches, complaining of the magistrates for injustice, extreme oppression, &c. and the other to his own church, to persuade them to renounce communion with all the churches in the bay, as full of antichristian pollution, &c. He justified both these letters, and maintained all his opinions; and, being offered further conference or disputation, and a month's respite, he chose to dispute presently. So Mr. Hooker was appointed to dispute with him, but could not reduce him from any of his errours. So, the next morning, the court sentenced him to depart out of our jurisdiction within six weeks, all the ministers, save one, approving the sentence; and his own church had him under question also for the same cause; and he, at his return home, refused communion with his own church, who openly disclaimed his errours, and wrote an humble submission to the magistrates, acknowledging their fault in joining with Mr. Williams in that letter to the churches against them, &c.

JANUARY 18, 1636

... Mr. Winthrop answered, that his speeches and carriage had been part mistaken; but with all professed, that it was his judgment, that in the infancy of plantation, justice should be administered with more lenity than in a settled state, because people were then more apt to transgress, partly of ignorance of new laws and orders, partly through oppression of business and other straits; but, if it might be made clear to him, that it was an error, he would be ready to take up a stricter course. Then the ministers were desired to consider of the question by the next morning, and to set down a rule in the case. The next morning, they delivered their several reasons, which all sorted to this conclusion, that strict discipline, both in criminal offences and in martial affairs, was more needful in plantations than in a settled state, as tending to the honor and safety of the gospel. Whereupon Mr. Winthrop acknowledged that he was convinced, that he had failed in over much lenity and remissness, and would endeavor (by God's assistance) to take a more strict course hereafter. ...

OCTOBER 21, 1836

One Mrs. Hutchinson, a member of the church of Boston, a woman of a ready wit and bold spirit, brought over with her two dangerous errors: 1. That the person of the Holy Ghost dwells in a justified person. 2. That no sanctification can help to evidence to us our justification. . . .

There joined with her in these opinions a brother of hers, one Mr. Wheelwright, a silenced minister sometimes in England.

OCTOBER 21

Miantunnomoh, the sachem of Naragansett, (being sent for by the governour) came to Boston . . . about noon. The governour called together most of the magistrates and ministers, to give countenance to our proceedings, and to advise with them about the terms of peace. It was dinner time, and the sachems and their council dined by themselves in the same room where the governour dined, and their sanaps were sent to the inn. After dinner, Miantunnomoh declared what he had to say to us . . . . That they had always loved the English, and desired firm peace with us: That they would continue in war with the Pequods and their confederates, till they were subdued; and desired we should so do: They would deliver our enemies to us, or kill them: That if any of theirs should kill our cattle, that we would not kill them, but cause them to make satisfaction: That they would now make a firm peace, and two months hence they would send us a present. . . .

In the morning we met again, and concluded the peace upon the articles underwritten . . . . But because we could not well make them understand the articles perfectly, we agreed to send a copy of them to Mr. Williams, who could best interpret them to them. So, after dinner, they took leave, and were conveyed out of town by some musketeers, and dismissed with a volley of shot.

The Articles

1. A firm peace between us and our friends of other plantations, (if they consent,) and their confederates, (if they will observe the articles, &c.) and our posterities.

2. Neither party to make peace with the Pequods without the other's consent.

3. Not to harbour, &c. the Pequods, &c.

4. To put to death or deliver over murderers, &c.

5. To return our fugitive servants, &c.

6. We to give them notice when we go against the Pequods, and they to send us some guides.

7 . Free trade between us.

8. None of them to come near our plantations during the wars with the Pequods, without some Englishman or known Indian.

9. To continue to the posterity of both parties.

The governour of Plimouth wrote to the deputy, that we had occasioned a war, &c. by provoking the Pequods . . . . The deputy took it ill, (as there was reason,) and returned answer accordingly, and made it appear, 1. That there was as much done as could be expected, considering they fled from us, and we could not follow them in our armour, neither had any to guide us in their country. 2. We went not to make war upon them, but to do justice, &c.; and having killed thirteen of them for four or five, which they had murdered of [ours] and destroyed sixty wigwams, &c. we were not much behind with them. . . .

OCTOBER 25

The other ministers in the bay, hearing of these things, came to Boston at the time of a general court, and entered conference in private with them . . . to prevent (if it were possible) the dangers, which seemed hereby to hang over that and the rest of the churches. At this conference, Mr. Cotton was present, and gave satisfaction to them, so as he agreed with them all in the point of sanctification , and so did Mr. Wheelwright . . . .

DECEMBER 10

At this court the elders of the churches were called, to advise with them about discovering and pacifying the differences among, the churches in point of opinion. . . .

Mr. Wilson made a very sad speech of the condition of our churches, and the inevitable danger of separation, if these differences and alienations among brethren were not speedily remedied; and laid the blame upon these new opinions risen up amongst us, which all the magistrates, except the governor and two others, did confirm, and all the ministers but two. . . .

The speech of Mr. Wilson was taken very ill by Mr. Cotton and others of the same church, so as he and divers of them went to admonish him. But Mr. Wilson and some others could see no breach of rule, seeing he was called by the court about the same matter with the rest of the elders, and exhorted to deliver their minds freely and faithfully, both for discovering the danger, and the means to help; and the things he spake of were only in general, and such as were under a common fame. And being questioned about his intent, he professed he did not mean Boston church, nor the members thereof, more than others. But this would not satisfy, but they called him to answer publicly, [December] 31; and there the governor pressed it violently against him, and all the congregation, except the deputy and one or two more, and many of them with much bitterness and reproaches; but he answered them all with words of truth and soberness, and with marvellous wisdom. It was strange to see, how the common people were led, by example, to condemn him in that, which (it was very probable) divers of them did not understand, nor the rule which he was supposed to have broken; and that such as had known him so long, and what good he had done for that church, should fall upon him with such bitterness for justifying himself in a good cause; for he was a very holy, upright man, and for faith and love inferior to none in the country, and most dear to all men. . . . The next day Mr. Wilson preached, notwithstanding, and the Lord so assisted him and gave great satisfaction, and the governor himself gave public witness to him. . . .

JANUARY 20, 1637

The differences in the said points of religion increased more and more, and the ministers of both sides (there being only Mr. Cotton of one party) did publicly declare their judgments in some of them, so as all men's mouths were full of them. And there being, 12 mo. [February] 3, a ship ready to go for England, and many passengers in it, Mr. Cotton took occasion to speak to them about the differences, etc. . . . Thus every occasion increased the contention, and caused great alienation of minds; and the members of Boston (frequenting the lectures of other ministers) did make much disturbance by public questions, and objections to their doctrines, which did any way disagree from their opinions; and it began to be as common here to distinguish between men, by being under a covenant of grace or a covenant of works, as in other countries between Protestants and papists. . . .

MARCH 9, 1637

Mr. Wheelwright, one of the members of Boston, preaching at the last fast, inveighed against all that walked in a covenant of works . . . and called them antichrists, and stirred up the people against them with much bitterness and vehemency. For this he was called into the court, and his sermon being produced, he justified it, and confessed he did mean all that walk in such a way. Whereupon the elders of the rest of the churches were called, and asked whether they, in their ministry, did walk in such a way. They all acknowledged they did. So, after much debate, the court adjudged him guilty of sedition, and also of contempt, for that the court had appointed the fast as a means of reconciliation of the differences, etc., and he purposely set himself to kindle and increase them. . . .

MAY 17

Our court of elections was at Newtown. So soon as the court was set, being about one of the clock, a petition was preferred by those of Boston. The governor would have read it, but the deputy said it was out of order; it was a court for elections, and those must first be despatched, and then their petitions should be heard. Divers others also opposed that course, as an ill precedent, etc.; and the petition, being about pretence of liberty, etc., (though intended chiefly for revoking the sentence given against Mr. Wheelwright) would have spent all the day in debate, etc.; but . . . the people crying out for election, it was moved by the deputy, and people should divide themselves, and the greater number must carry it. And so it was done, and the greater number by many were for election. But the governor and that side kept their place still, and would not proceed. Whereupon the deputy told him, that, if he would not go to election, he and the rest of that side would proceed. Upon that, he came from his company, and they went to election; and Mr. Winthrop was chosen governor, Mr. Dudley deputy and Mr. Endecott of the standing council; and Mr. Israel Stoughton and Mr. Richard Saltonstall were called in to be assistants; and Mr.

Vane, Mr. Coddington, and Mr. Dummer, (being all of that faction,) were left quite out.

There was great danger of a tumult that day; for those of that side grew into fierce speeches, and some laid hands on others; but seeing themselves too weak, they grew quiet. . . .

MARCH 21, 1637

Miantunnomoh, etc., sent twenty-six, with forty fathom of wampom and a Pequod's hand. We gave four of the chief each a coat of fourteen shillings price, and deferred to return our present till after, according to their manner.

MAY 25

Our English from Connecticut, with their Indians, and many of the Naragansetts, marched in the night to a fort of the Pequods at Mistick, and, besetting the same about break of the day, after two hours' fight they took it, (by firing it,) and slew therein two chief sachems, and one hundred and fifty fighting men, and about one hundred and fifty old men, women and children, with the loss of two English, whereof but one was killed by the enemy. Divers of the Indian friends were hurt by the English because they had not some mark to distinguish them from the Pequods, as some of them had. . . .

JUNE 15

There was a day of thanksgiving kept in all the churches for the victory obtained against the Pequods, and for other mercies. . . .

NOVEMBER 1

There was great hope that the late general assembly would have had some good effect in pacifying the troubles and dissensions about matters of religion; but it fell out otherwise. For though Mr. Wheelwright and those of his party had been clearly confuted and confounded in the assembly, yet they persisted in their opinions, and were as busy in nourishing contentions . . . . Then the court sent for Mr. Wheelwright, and, he persisting to justify his sermon, and his whole practice and opinions, and refusing to leave either the place or his public exercisings, he was disfranchised and banished. . . .

The court also sent for Mrs. Hutchinson, and charged her with divers matters, as her keeping two public lectures every week in her house, whereto sixty or eighty persons did usually resort, and for reproaching most of the ministers (viz., all except Mr. Cotton) for not preaching a covenant of free grace, and that they had not the seal of the spirit, nor were able ministers of the New Testament; which were clearly proved against her, though she sought to shift it off. And, after many speeches to and fro, at last she was so full as she could not contain, but vented her revelations; amongst which this was one, that she had it revealed to her, that she should come into New England, and should here be persecuted, and that God would ruin us and our posterity, and the whole state, for the same. So the court proceeded and banished her; but, because it was winter, they committed her to a private house, where she was well provided, and her own friends and the elders permitted to go to her, but none else. . . .

JANUARY 16, 1638

. . . This year a plantation was begun at Tecticutt by a gentlewoman, an ancient maid, one Mrs. Poole. She went late thither, and endured much hardship, and lost much cattle. Called, after, Taunton.

MARCH 1

While Mrs. Hutchinson continued at Roxbury, divers of the elders and others resorted to her, and finding her to persist in maintaining those gross errors beforementioned, and many others, to the number of thirty or thereabout, some of them wrote to the church at Boston, offering to make proof of the same the church, etc., [March] 15; whereupon she was called, (the magistrates being desired to give her license to come,) and the lecture was appointed to begin at ten. . . . When she appeared, the errors were read to her. . . . These were also clearly confuted, but yet she held her own; so as the church (all but two of her sons) agreed she should be admonished, and because her sons would not agree to it, they were admonished also.

Mr. Cotton pronounced the sentence of admonition with great so-lemnity, and with much zeal and detestation of her errors and pride of spirit. The assembly continued till eight at night, and all did ac-knowledge the special presence of God's spirit therein; and she was appointed to appear again the next lecture day. . . .

MARCH 22, 1638

Mrs. Hutchinson appeared again (she, had been licensed by the court, in regard she had given hope of her repentance. . . . [S]he deliv-ered it in writing, wherein she made a retraction of near all, but, with such explanations and circumstances as gave no satisfaction to the church, so as she was required to speak further to them. Then she de-clared that it was just with God to leave her to herself, as he had done, for her slighting his ordinances both magistracy and ministry; and con-fessed that what she had spoken against the magistrates at the court (by way of revelation) was rash and ungrounded, and desired the church to pray for her. This gave the church good hope of her repen-tance; but when she was examined about some particulars, as that she had denied inherent righteousness, etc., she affirmed that it was nev-er her judgment; and though it was proved by many testimonies that she had been of that judgment, and so had persisted, and maintained it by argument against divers, yet she impudently persisted in her af-firmation, to the astonishment of all the assembly. So that, after much time and many arguments had been spent to bring her to see her sin, but all in vain, the church, with one consent, cast her out. . . .

After she was excommunicated, her spirits, which seemed before to be somewhat dejected, revived again, and she gloried in her suffer-ings, saying that it was the greatest happiness, next to Christ, that ever befell her. Indeed, it was a happy day to the churches of Christ here, and to many poor souls, who had been seduced by her, who, by what they heard and saw that day, were (through the grace of God) brought off quite from her errors, and settled again in the truth.

MARCH 27

. . . The wife of one William Dyer, a milliner in the New Exchange, a very proper and fair woman, and both of them notoriously infected with Mrs. Hutchinson's errours, and very censorious and troublesome, (she being of a very proud spirit, and much addicted to revelations,) had been delivered of a child some few months before, October 17, and the child buried, (being stillborn,) and viewed of none but Mrs. Hutchinson and the midwife, one Hawkins's wife, a rank familist also; and another woman had a glimpse of it, who, not being able to keep counsel, as the other two did, some rumour began to spread, that the child was a monster. One of the elders, hearing of it, asked Mrs. Hutchinson, when she was ready to depart; whereupon she told him how it was, and said she meant to have it chronicled, but excused her concealing of it till then, (by advice, as she said, of Mr. Cotton). . . . [I]t had a face, but no head, and the ears stood upon the shoulders and were like an ape's; it had no forehead, but over the eyes four horns, hard and sharp; two of them were above one inch long; the other two shorter; the eyes standing out, and the mouth also; . . . it had arms and legs as other children; but, instead of toes, it had on each foot three claws, like a young fowl, with sharp talons.

The governour speaking with Mr. Cotton about it, he told him the reason why he advised them to conceal it. . . . He considered, that, if it had been his own case, he should have desired to have had it concealed. . . . He had known other monstrous births, which had been concealed, and that he thought God might intend only the instruction of the parents, and such other to whom it was known, &c. The like apology he made for himself in publick, which was well accepted.

APRIL 2

The governour, with advice of some other of the magistrates and of the elders of Boston, caused the said monster to be taken up, and though it were much corrupted, yet most of those things were to be seen as the horns and claws, the scales, &c. . . .

Another thing observable was, the discovery of it, which was just when Mrs. Hutchinson was cast out of the church. For Mrs. Dyer going forth with her, a stranger asked, what young woman it was. The others answered, it was the woman which had the monster; which gave the first occasion to some that heard it to speak of it. The midwife, presently after this discovery, went out of the jurisdiction; and indeed it was time for her to be gone, for it was known, that she used to give young women oil of mandrakes and other stuff to cause conception; and she grew into great suspicion to be a witch, for it was credibly reported, that, when she gave any medicines, (for she practices physick,) she would ask the [party], if she did believe, she could help her, &c.

Another observable passage was, that the father of this monster, coming home at this very time, was, the next Lord's day, by an unexpected providence, questioned in the church for divers monstrous errours . . .

APRIL 21, 1638

Owsamekin, the sachem of Acooemeck, on this side Connecticut, came to the governour and brought a present of eighteen skins of beaver from himself and the sachems of Mohegan beyond Connecticut and Pakontuckett. The occasion was, (as he said,) it was reported, that we were angry with him, and intended to war upon them; so they came to seek peace. The governour received the present, and . . . answered them, that if they had done no wrong to the English, nor aided their enemies, we would be at peace with them. . . .

JUNE 5

Unkus, alias Okoco, the Monahegan sachem in the twist of Pequod River, came to Boston with thirty-seven men. He came from Connecticut with Mr. Haynes, and tendered the governour a present of twenty fathom of wampom. This was at the court, and it was thought fit by the council to refuse it, till he had given satisfaction about the Pequods he kept, etc. Upon this he was much dejected, and made account we would have killed him; but, two days after, having received good satisfaction of his innocency, etc., and he promising to submit to the order of the English touching the Pequods he had, and the differences between the Naragansetts and him, we accepted his present. And, about half an hour after, he came to the governour, and entertained him with these compliments: This heart (laying his hand upon his breast) is not mine, but yours; I have no men; they are all yours; command me any difficult thing, I will do it; I will not believe any Indians' words against the English; if any man shall kill an Englishman, I will put him to death, were he never so dear to me. So the governour gave him a fair, red coat, and defrayed his and his men's diet, and gave them corn to relieve them homeward, and a letter of protection to all men, etc., and he departed very joyful. . . .

September 25, 1638

. . . The court, taking into consideration the great disorder general through the country in costliness of apparel, and following new fashions, sent for the elders of the churches, and conferred with them about it, and laid it upon them, as belonging to them, to redress it, by urging it upon the consciences of their people, which they promised to do. But little was done about it; for divers of the elders' wives, &c. were in some measure partners in this general disorder.

December

At Providence, also, the devil was not idle. For whereas, at their first coming thither, Mr. Williams and the rest did make an order, that no man should be molested for his conscience, now men's wives, and children, and servants, claimed liberty hereby to go to all religious meetings, though never so often, or though private, upon the week days; and because one Verin refused to let his wife go to Mr. Williams so oft as she was called for, they required to have him censured. But there stood up one Arnold, a witty man of their own company, and withstood it, telling them that, when he consented to that order, he never intended it should extend to the breach of any ordinance of God, such as the subjection of wives to their husbands, etc., and gave divers solid reasons against it. . . .

March 16, 1639

. . . This is further to be observed in the delusions which this people were taken with: Mrs. Hutchinson and some of her adherents happened to be at prayer when the earthquake was at Aquiday, &c. and the house being shaken thereby, they were persuaded, (and boasted of it,) that the Holy Ghost did shake it in coming down upon them, as he did upon the apostles.

July

At Providence matters went after the old manner. Mr. Williams and many of his company, a few months since, were in all haste rebaptized, and denied communion with all others, and now he was come to question his second baptism, not being able to derive the authority of it from the apostles, otherwise than by the ministers of England, (whom he judged to be ill authority,) so as he conceived God would raise up some apostolick power. Therefore he bent himself that way, expecting (as was supposed) to become an apostle; and having, a little before, refused communion with all, save his own wife, now he would preach to and pray with all comers. Whereupon some of his followers left him and returned back from whence they went.

NOVEMBER 9, 1639

At a general court held at Boston, great complaint was made of the oppression used in the county in sale of foreign commodities; and Mr. Robert Keayne, who kept a shop in Boston, was notoriously above others observed and complained of; and, being convented, he was charged with many particulars; in some, for taking above six-pence in the shilling profit; in some above eight-pence; and, in some small things, above two for one; and being hereof convicted, (as appears by the records) he was fined £200. . . . After the court had censured him, the church of Boston called him also in question, where (as before he had done in the court) he did, with tears, acknowledge and bewail his covetous and corrupt heart, yet making some excuse for many of the particulars, which were charged upon him, as partly by pretence of ignorance of the true price of some wares and chiefly by being misled by some false principles. . . . These things gave occasion to Mr. Cotton, in his public exercise the next lecture day, to lay open the error of such false principles, and to give some rules of direction in the case.

Some false principles were these:

1. That a man might sell as dear as he can, and buy as cheap as he can.

2. If a man lose by casualty of sea, etc., in some of his commodities, he may raise the price of the rest.

3. That he may sell as he bought, though he paid too dear, etc., and though the commodity be fallen, etc.

4. That, as a man may take the advantage of his own skill or ability, so he may of another's ignorance or necessity. . . .

The rules for trading were these:

1. A man may not sell above the current price. i.e., such a price as is usual in the time and place, and as another (who knows the worth of

the commodity) would give for it, if he had occasion to use it; as that is called current money, which every man will take, etc.

2. When a man loseth in his commodity for want of skill, etc., he must look at it as his own fault or cross, and therefore not lay it upon another.

3. Where a man loseth by casualty of sea, or, etc., it is a loss cast upon himself by providence, and he may not ease himself of it by casting it upon another. . . .

The cause being debated by the church, some were earnest to have him excommunicated; but the most thought an admonition would be sufficient. . . . [I]n the end, the church consented to an admonition.

November, 1640

. . . Miantunnomoh, the sachem of Naragansett, came, and was met at Dorchester by Captain Gibbons and a guard of twelve musketeers, and well entertained at Roxbury by the governour; but when we came to parley, he refused to treat with us by our Pequod interpreter. . . . [D]eparting in a rude manner, without showing any respect or sign of thankfulness to the governour for his entertainment, whereof the governour informed the general court, and would show him no countenance, nor admit him to dine at our table, as formerly he had done, till he had acknowledged his failing, etc., which he readily did, so soon as he could be made to understand it, and did speak with our committees and us by a Pequod maid who could speak English perfectly. But it was conceived by some of the court that he kept back such things as he accounted secrets of state, and that he would carry home in his breast, as an injury, the strict terms he was put to. . . .

December

A wicked fellow, given up to bestiality, fearing to be taken by the hand of justice, fled to Long Island, and there was drowned. He had confessed to some that he was so given up to that abomination that he never saw any beast go before him but he lusted after it.

APRIL 13, 1641

A negro maid, servant to Mr. Stoughton of Dorchester, being well approved by divers years' experience, for sound knowledge and true godliness, was received into the church and baptized. . . .

A godly woman of the church of Boston, dwelling sometimes in London, brought with her a parcel of very fine linen of great value, which she set her heart too much upon, and had been at charge to have it all newly washed, and curiously folded and pressed, and so left it in press in her parlor over night. She had a negro maid went into the room very late, and let fall some snuff of the candle upon the linen, so as by the morning all the linen was burned to tinder, and the boards underneath, and some stools and a part of the wainscot burned, and never perceived by any in the house, though some lodged in the chamber over head, and no ceiling between. But it pleased God that the loss of this linen did her much good, both in taking off her heart from worldly comforts, and in preparing her for a far greater affliction by the untimely death of her husband, who was slain not long after at Isle of Providence.

SEPTEMBER 22, 1642

The sudden fall of land and cattle, and the scarcity of foreign commodities, and money, etc., with the thin access of people from England, put many into an unsettled frame of spirit, so as they concluded there would be no subsisting here, and accordingly they began to hasten away, some to the West Indies, others to the Dutch, at Long Island, etc., (for the governor there invited them by fair offers,) and others back for England. . . .

. . . . They fled for fear of want, and many of them fell into it, even to extremity, as if they had hastened into the misery which they feared and fled from, besides the depriving themselves of the ordinances and church fellowship, and those civil liberties which they enjoyed here; whereas, such as staid in their places, kept their peace and ease, and enjoyed still the blessing of the ordinances, and never tasted of those troubles and miseries, which they heard to have befallen those who departed. Much disputation there was about liberty of removing for outward advantages, and all ways were sought for an open door to get out at; but it is to be feared many crept out at a broken wall. For such as come together into a wilderness, where are nothing but wild beasts and beastlike men, and there confederate together in civil and church estate, whereby they do, implicitly at least, bind themselves to support each other, and all of them that society, whether civil or sacred, whereof they are members, how they can break from this without free consent, is hard to find, so as may satisfy a tender or good conscience in time of trial. . . . [T]hese all, being now thy brethren, as near to thee as the Isrealites were to Moses, it were much safer for thee, after his example, to choose rather to suffer affliction with thy brethren, than to enlarge thy ease and pleasure by furthering the occasion of their ruin. . . .

MARCH 21, 1644

One Dalkin and his wife dwelling near Meadford coming from Cambridge, where they had spent their Sabbath, and being to pass over the river at a ford, the tide not being fallen enough, the husband adventured over, and finding it too deep, persuaded his wife to stay a while, but it raining very sore, she would needs adventure over, and was carried away with the stream past her depth. Her husband not daring to go help her, cried out, and thereupon his dog, being at his house near by, came forth, and seeing something in the water, swam to her, and she caught hold on the dog's tail, so he drew her to the shore and saved her life.

MAY, 1643

Sacononoco and Pumham, two sachems near Providence, having under them between 2 and 300 men, finding themselves overborne by Miantunnomoh, the sachem of Naragansett, and Gorton and his company, who had so prevailed with Miantunnomoh, as he forced one of them to join with him in setting his hand or mark to a writing, whereby a part of his land was sold to Gorton and his company, for which Miantunnomoh received a price, but the other would not receive that which was for his part, alleging that he did not intend to sell his land, though through fear of Miantunnomoh he had put his mark to the writing. . . . We sent also to Miantunnomoh to signify the same to him. Whereupon, in the beginning of the court, Miantunnomoh came to Boston, and being demanded in open court, before divers of his own men and Cutshamekin and other Indians, whether he had any interest in the said two sachems as his subjects, he could prove none. Cutshamekin also in his presence affirmed, that he had no interest in them, but they were as free sachems as himself. . . .

AUGUST 6, 1643

Onkus, being provoked by Sequasson, a sachem of Connecticut, who would not be persuaded by the magistrates there to a reconciliation, made war upon him, and slew divers of his men and burnt his wigwams; whereupon Miantunnomoh, being his kinsman, took offence against Onkus, and went with near 1,000 men and set upon Onkus before he could be provided for defence, for he had not then with him above 3 or 400 men. But it pleased God to give Onkus the victory, after he had killed about 30 of the Narragansetts, and wounded many more, and among these two of Canonicus' sons and a brother of Miantunnomoh, who fled, but having on a coat of mail, he was easily overtaken, which two of his captains perceiving, they laid hold on him and carried him to Onkus, hoping thereby to procure their own pardon. . . . Onkus carries Miantunnomoh to Hartford to take advice of the magistrates there, and at Miantunnomoh's earnest entreaty he left him with them, yet as a prisoner. They kept him under guard, but used him very courteously, and so he continued till the commissioners of the United Colonies met at Boston, who taking into serious consideration what was safest and best to be done, were all of opinion that it would not be safe to set him at liberty, neither had we sufficient ground for us to put him to death. In this difficulty we called in five of the most judicious elders, (it being in the time of the general assembly of the elders,) and propounding the case to them, they all agreed that he ought to be put to death. Upon this concurrence we enjoined secrecy to ourselves and them, lest if it should come to the notice of the Narragansetts, they might set upon the commissioners, etc., in their return, to take some of them to redeem him, (as Miantunnomoh himself had told Mr. Haynes had been in consultation amongst them;) and agreed that, upon the return of the commissioners to Hartford, they should send for Onkus and tell him our determination, that Miantunnomoh should be delivered to him again, and he should put him to death so soon as he came within his own jurisdiction, and that two English should go along with him to see the execution, and that if any

Indians should invade him for it, we would send men to defend him: If Onkus should refuse to do it, then Miantunnomoh should be sent in a pinnace to Boston, there to be kept until further consideration.

The reasons of this proceeding with him were these. 1. It was now clearly discovered to us, that there was a general conspiracy among the Indians to cut off all the English, and that Miantunnomoh was the head and contriver of it. 2. He was of a turbulent and proud spirit, and would never be at rest. . . .

According to this agreement the commissioners, at their return to Connecticut, sent for Onkus, and acquainted him therewith, who readily undertook the execution, and taking Miantunnomoh along with him, in the way between Hartford and Windsor, (where Onkus hath some men dwell,) Onkus' brother, following after Miantunnomoh, clave his head with an hatchet, some English being present. And that the Indians might know that the English did approve of it, they sent 12 or 14 musketeers home with Onkus to abide a time with him for his defence, if need should be.

September, 1643

The Indians near the Dutch, having killed 15 men, as is before related, proceeded on and began to set upon the English who dwelt under the Dutch. They came to Mrs. Hutchinson's in way of friendly neighbourhood, as they had been accustomed, and taking their opportunity, killed her and Mr. Collins her son in law, (who had been kept prisoner in Boston, as is before related,) and all her family . . . in all sixteen, and put their cattle into their houses and there burnt them. By a good providence of God there was a boat came in there at the same instant, to which some women and children fled, and so were saved, but two of the boatmen going up to the houses were shot and killed.

These people had cast off ordinances and churches, and now at last their own people, and for larger accommodation had subjected themselves to the Dutch and dwelt scatteringly near a mile asunder: and some that escaped, who had removed only for want (as they said) of hay for their cattle which increased much, now coming back again to Aquiday, they wanted cattle for their grass. . . .

APRIL 13, 1645

Mr. Hopkins, the governor of Hartford upon Connecticut, came to Boston, and brought his wife with him, (a godly young woman, and of special parts,) who was fallen into a sad infirmity, the loss of her understanding and reason, which had been growing upon her divers years, by occasion of her giving herself wholly to reading and writing, and had written many books. Her husband, being very loving and tender of her, was loath to grieve her; but he saw his error, when it was too late. For if she had attended her household affairs, and such things as belong to women, and not gone out of her way and calling to meddle in such things as are proper for men, whose minds are stronger, etc., she had kept her wits, and might have improved them usefully and honorably in the place God had set her. . . .

MARCH 7, 1644

. . . At this court of assistants one James Britton, a man ill affected both to our church discipline and civil government, and one Mary Latham, a proper young woman about 18 years of age, whose father was a godly man and had brought her up well, were condemned to die for adultery, upon a law formerly made and published in print. It was thus occasioned and discovered. This woman, being rejected by a young man whom she had an affection unto, vowed she would marry the next that came to her, and accordingly, against her friends' minds, she matched with an ancient man who had neither honesty nor ability, and one whom she had no affection unto. Whereupon, soon after she was married, divers young men solicited her chastity, and drawing her into bad company, and giving her wine and other gifts, easily prevailed with her, and among others this Britton. But God smiting him with a deadly palsy and fearful horror of conscience withal, he could not keep secret, but discovered this, and other the like with other women, and was forced to acknowledge the justice of God in that having often called others fools, &c. for confessing against themselves, he was now forced to do the like. The woman dwelt now in Plimouth patent, and one of the magistrates there, hearing she was detected, &c. sent her to us. Upon her examination, she confessed he did attempt the fact, but did not commit it, and witness was produced that testified (which they both confessed) that in the evening of a day of humiliation through the country for England, &c. a company met at Britton's and there continued drinking sack, &c. till late in the night, and then Britton and the woman were seen upon the ground together, a little from the house. It was reported also that she did frequently abuse her husband, setting a knife to his breast and threatening to kill him, calling him old rogue and cuckold, and said she would make him wear horns as big as a bull. And yet some of the magistrates thought the evidence not sufficient against her, because there were not two direct witnesses; but the jury cast her, and then she confessed the fact, and accused twelve others, whereof two were married men. Five of these were apprehended and committed, (the rest were gone,) but denying it, and there being no other witness against them than the testimony of a condemned person, there could be no proceeding against them. The woman proved very penitent, and had deep apprehension of the foulness of her sin, and at length attained to hope of pardon by the blood of Christ, and was willing to die in satisfaction to justice. The man also was very much cast down for his sins, but was loth to die, and petitioned the general court for his life, but they would not grant it, though some of the magistrates spake much for it, and questioned the letter, whether adultery was death by God's law now. This Britton had been a professor in England, but coming hither he opposed our church government, &c. and grew dissolute, losing both power and profession of godliness.

March 21

They were both executed, they both died very penitently, especially the woman, who had some comfortable hope of pardon of her sin, and gave good exhortation to all young maids to be obedient to their parents, and to take heed of evil company, &c. . . .

July 3, 1645 [Speech to the General Court.]

I suppose something may be expected from me, upon this charge that is befallen me, which moves me to speak now to you; yet I intend not to intermeddle in the proceedings of the court, or with any of the persons concerned therein. Only I bless God, that I see an issue of this troublesome business. I also acknowledge the justice of the court, and, for mine own part, I am well satisfied, I was publicly charged, and I am publicly and legally acquitted, which is all I did expect or desire. And though this be sufficient for my justification before men, yet not so before the God, who hath seen so much amiss in my dispensations (and even in this affair) as calls me to be humble. For to be publicly and criminally charged in this court, is matter of humiliation, (and I desire to to make a right use of it) notwithstanding I be thus acquitted. . . . It may be of some good use, to inform and rectify the judgments of some of the people, and may prevent such distempers as have arisen amongst us. The great questions that have troubled the country are about the authority of the magistrates and the liberty of the people. It is yourselves who have called us to this office, and being called by you, we have our authority from God. . . . I entreat you to consider, that when you choose magistrates, you take them from among yourselves, men subject to like passions as you are. Therefore when you see infirmities in us, you should reflect upon your own, and that would make you bear the more with us, and not be severe censurers of the failings of your magistrates, when you have continual experience of the like infirmities in yourselves and others. We account him a good servant, who breaks not his covenant. The covenant between you and us is the oath you have taken of us, which is to this purpose, that we shall govern you and judge your causes by the rules of God's laws and our own, according to our best skill. When you agree with a workman to build you a ship or house, etc., he undertakes as well for his skill as for his faithfulness, for it is his profession, and you pay him for both. But when you call one to be a magistrate, he doth not profess nor undertake to have sufficient skill for that office, nor can you furnish him with gifts, etc., therefore you must run the hazard of his skill and ability. But if he fail in faithfulness, which by his oath he is bound unto, that he must answer for. . . . But if the case be doubtful, or the rule doubtful, to men of such understanding and parts as your magistrates are, if your magistrates should err here, yourselves must bear it.

For the other point concerning liberty, I observe a great mistake in the country about that. There is a twofold liberty, natural (I mean as our nature is now corrupt) and civil or federal. The first is common to man with beasts and other creatures. By this, man, as he stands in relation to man simply, hath liberty to do what he lists; it is a liberty to evil as well as to good. This liberty is incompatible and inconsistent with authority, and cannot endure the least restraint of the most just authority. The exercise and maintaining of this liberty makes men grow more evil, and in time to be worse than brute beasts. . . . This is that great enemy of truth and peace, that wild beast, which all the ordinances of God are bent against, to restrain and subdue it. The other kind of liberty I call civil or federal, it may also be termed moral, in reference to the covenant between God and man, in the moral law, and the politic covenants and constitutions, amongst men themselves. This liberty is the proper end and object of authority, and cannot subsist without it; and it is a liberty to that only which is good, just, and honest. This liberty you are to stand for, with the hazard (not only of your goods, but) of your lives, if need be. Whatsoever crosses this, is not authority, but a distemper thereof. This liberty is maintained and exercised in a way of subjection to authority; it is of the same kind of liberty wherewith Christ has made us free. The woman's own choice makes such a man her husband; yet being so chosen, he is her lord, and she is to be subject to him, yet in a way of liberty, not of bondage; and a true wife accounts her subjection her honor and freedom, and would not think her condition safe and free, but in her subjection to her husband's authority. Such is the liberty of the church under the authority of Christ, her king and husband; his yoke is so easy and sweet to her as a bride's ornaments; and if through forwardness or wantonness, etc., she shake it off, at any time, she is at no rest in her spirit, until she take it up again; and whether her lord smiles upon her and embraces her in his arms, or whether he frowns, or rebukes, or smites her, she apprehends the sweetness of his love in all, and is refreshed, supported, and instructed by every such dispensation of his authority over her. On the other side, ye know who they are that complain of this yoke and say, let us break their bands, etc., we will not have this man to rule over us. Even so, brethren, it will be between you and your magistrates. If you stand for your natural corrupt liberties, and will do what is good in your own eyes, you will not endure the least weight of authority, but will murmur, and oppose, and be always striving to shake off that yoke; but if you will be satisfied to enjoy such civil and lawful liberties, such as Christ allows you, then will you quietly and cheerfully submit unto that authority which is set over you, in all the administrations of it, for your good. Wherein, if we fail at any time, we hope we shall be willing (by God's assistance) to hearken to good advice from any of you, or in any other way of God; so shall your liberties be preserved, in upholding the honor and power of authority amongst you.

Selected Poems

Anne Bradstreet

The Author to Her Book

Thou ill-formed offspring of my feeble brain,
Who after birth didst by my side remain,
Till snatched from thence by friends, less wise than true,
Who thee abroad, exposed to public view,
Made thee in rags, halting to th' press to trudge,
Where errors were not lessened (all may judge).
At thy return my blushing was not small,
My rambling brat (in print) should mother call,
I cast thee by as one unfit for light,
Thy visage was so irksome in my sight;
Yet being mine own, at length affection would
Thy blemishes amend, if so I could:
I washed thy face, but more defects I saw,
And rubbing off a spot still made a flaw.
I stretched thy joints to make thee even feet,
Yet still thou run'st more hobbling than is meet;
In better dress to trim thee was my mind,
But nought save homespun cloth i' th' house I find.
In this array 'mongst vulgars may'st thou roam.
In critic's hands beware thou dost not come,
And take thy way where yet thou art not known;
If for thy father asked, say thou hadst none;
And for thy mother, she alas is poor,
Which caused her thus to send thee out of door.

BEFORE THE BIRTH OF ONE OF HER CHILDREN

All things within this fading world hath end,
Adversity doth still our joys attend;
No ties so strong, no friends so dear and sweet,
But with death's parting blow is sure to meet.
The sentence past is most irrevocable,
A common thing, yet oh, inevitable.
How soon, my Dear, death may my steps attend,
How soon't may be thy lot to lose thy friend,
We both are ignorant, yet love bids me
These farewell lines to recommend to thee,
That when that knot's untied that made us one,
I may seem thine, who in effect am none.
And if I see not half my days that's due,
What nature would, God grant to yours and you;
The many faults that well you know I have
Let be interred in my oblivious grave;
If any worth or virtue were in me,
Let that live freshly in thy memory
And when thou feel'st no grief, as I no harms,
Yet love thy dead, who long lay in thine arms.
And when thy loss shall be repaid with gains
Look to my little babes, my dear remains.
And if thou love thyself, or loved'st me,
These O protect from step-dame's injury.
And if chance to thine eyes shall bring this verse,
With some sad sighs honour my absent hearse;
And kiss this paper for thy love's dear sake,
Who with salt tears this last farewell did take.

To My Dear and Loving Husband

If ever two were one, then surely we.
If ever man were loved by wife, then thee;
If ever wife was happy in a man,
Compare with me, ye women, if you can.
I prize thy love more than whole mines of gold
Or all the riches that the East doth hold.
My love is such that rivers cannot quench,
Nor ought but love from thee, give recompense.
Thy love is such I can no way repay,
The heavens reward thee manifold, I pray.
Then while we live, in love let's so persevere
That when we live no more, we may live ever.

from A KEY INTO THE LANGUAGE OF AMERICA

Roger Williams

OF SALUTATION

There is a savor of civility and courtesy even amongst these wild
Americans, both among themselves and towards strangers.
More particular:

> The courteous pagan shall condemn
> Uncourteous Englishmen,
> Who live like foxes, bears, and wolves,
> Or lion in his den.
>
> •   •   •
>
> If nature's sons both wild and tame,
> Humane and courteous be,
> How ill becomes it sons of God
> To want humanity?
>
> •   •   •

OF SLEEP AND LODGING

Sweet rest is not confined to soft beds, for, not only God gives His
beloved sleep on hard lodgings, but also nature and custom give sound
sleep to these Americans on the earth, on a board or mat. Yet how is
Europe bound to God for better lodging, etc.
More particular:

> God gives them sleep on ground, on straw,
> On sedgie mats or board,
> When English softest beds of down,
> Sometimes no sleep afford.
>
> I have known them leave their house and mat,
> To lodge a friend or stranger,

When Jews and Christians oft have sent
    Christ Jesus to the manger.

  'Fore day they invoke their gods,
    Though many, false, and new;
O how should that God worshipped be,
    Who is but one and true?

         •   •   •

OF THEIR PERSONS AND PARTS OF BODY

Nature knows no difference between Europe and Americans in blood, birth, etc. God having of one blood made all mankind, Acts 17, and all by nature being children of wrath, Ephesians 2.

More particular:

  Boast not proud English, of thy birth and blood,
    Thy brother Indian is by birth as good.
Of one blood God made him, and thee, and all,
    As wise, as fair, as strong, as personal.

By nature wrath's his portion, thine no more,
    Till grace his soul and thine in Christ restore.
Make sure thy second birth, else thou shalt see,
    Heaven ope to Indians wild, but shut to thee.

         •   •   •

OF THEIR NAKEDNESS AND CLOTHING

How deep are the purposes and counsels of God? What should be the reason of this mighty difference of one man's children that all the sons of men on this side the way (in Europe, Asia, and Africa) should have such plenteous clothing for body, for soul! and the rest of Adam's sons and daughters on the other side, or America (some think as big as the other three), should neither have nor desire clothing for their naked souls or bodies.

More particular:

O what a tyrant's custom long,
    How do men make a tush
At what's in use, though ne'er so foul,
    Without once shame or blush?

Many thousand proper men and women,
    I have seen met in one place,
Almost all naked, yet not one,
    Thought want of clothes disgrace.

Israel was naked, wearing clothes!
    The best clad Englishman,
Not clothed with Christ, more naked is,
    Than naked Indian.

OF THEIR GOVERNMENT

The wildest of the sons of men have ever found a necessity (for preservation of themselves, their families, and properties) to cast themselves into some mold or form of government.

More particular:

Adulteries, murders, robberies, thefts,
    Wild Indians punish these!
And hold the scales of justice so,
    That no man farthing leese.

When Indians hear the horrid filths
    Of Irish, English men,
The horrid oaths and murders late,
    Thus say these Indians then,

"We wear no clothes, have many gods,
    And yet our sins are less.
You are barbarians, pagans wild,
    Your land's the wilderness."

from THE BLOODY TENET OF PERSECUTION FOR THE CAUSE OF CONSCIENCE

Roger Williams

TO EVERY COURTEOUS READER

While I plead the cause of truth and innocence against the bloody doctrine of persecution for cause of conscience, I judge it not unfit to give alarm to my self, and all men to prepare to be persecuted or hunted for cause of conscience. . . .

If you hunt any for cause of conscience, how can you say you followest the Lamb of God who so abhorred that practice? . . .

I confess I have little hope . . . that this discourse against the doctrine of persecution for cause of conscience should pass current (I say not amongst the wolves and lions, but even amongst the sheep of Christ themselves) . . .

However the proud . . . overlook the poor and cry out schismatics, heretics, shall blasphemers and seducers escape unpunished? Yet there is a sorer punishment in the Gospel for despising of Christ . . . "He that believeth not shall be damned," Mark 16.16.

Whatever worship, ministry, ministration, the best and purest, are practised without faith and true persuasion that they are the true institutions of God, they are sin. . . . And however in civil things we may be servants unto men, yet in divine and spiritual things the poorest peasant must disdain the service of the highest prince: "Be ye not the servants of men," I Cor. 14. . . .

In vain have English Parliaments permitted English Bibles in the poorest English houses, and the simplest man or woman to search the scriptures, if yet against their souls' persuasion from the scripture, they should be forced (as if they lived in Spain or Rome itself without the sight of a Bible) to believe as the Church believes. . . .

We must not let go for all the flea bitings of the present afflictions. Having bought truth dear, we must not sell it cheap, not the least grain of it for the whole world, for a little puff of credit and reputation from the changeable breath of uncertain sons of men. . . .

Peace. Dear *Truth,*
. . . [Y]our enemies, though they speak and rail against you, though they outrageously pursue, imprison, banish, kill your faithful witnesses, yet how is all colored over for "justice against the heretics"? Yea, if they kindle coals and blow the flames of devouring wars that leave neither spiritual nor civil state, but burn up branch and root, yet how do all pretend an holy war? He that kills, and he that is killed, they both cry out it is for God and for their conscience.

•   •   •

Truth. First, if the civil magistrates be Christians or members of the church . . . they are bound by this command of Christ to suffer opposition to their doctrine with meekness, and gentleness, and to be so far from striving to subdue their [religious] opposites with the civil sword that they are bound with patience and meekness to wait if God peradventure will please to grant repentance unto their [religious] opposites. . . .

Secondly, . . . True it is the sword may make . . . a whole nation of hypocrites. But to recover a soul from Satan by repentance, and to bring them from anti-Christian doctrine or worship to the doctrine or worship Christian . . . , that alone works the all-powerful God, by the sword of the spirit in the hand of His spiritual officers. . . .

. . . And I ask whether or not such as may hold forth other worships or religions (Jews, Turks, or anti-Christians), may not be peaceable and quiet subjects, loving and helpful neighbors, fair and just dealers, true and loyal to the civil government? It is clear they may from all reason and experience in many flourishing cities and kingdoms of the world, and so offend not against the civil state and peace; nor incur the punishment of the civil sword, notwithstanding that in spiritual and mystical account they are ravenous and greedy wolves.

•   •   •

Truth. . . . [T]he mischief of a blind Pharisee's blind guidance is greater than if he acted treasons, murders, etc.; and the loss of one soul by his seduction is a greater mischief than if he blew up parliaments and cut the throats of Kings or Emperors, so precious is that invaluable jewel of a soul, above all the present lives and bodies of all the men in the world! . . . [B]ut this sentence against him the Lord Jesus only pronounces in His Church, His spiritual judicature, and executes this sentence in part at present and hereafter to all eternity. Such a sentence no civil judge can pass, such a death no civil sword can inflict. . . .

So here, whatever be the soul infection breathed out from the lying lips of a plague-sick Pharisee, yet . . . not one elect or chosen of God shall perish. God's sheep are safe in His eternal hand and counsel, and He that knows His material, knows also His mystical stars, their numbers, and calls them every one by name; none falls into the ditch on the blind Pharisee's back, but such as were ordained to that condemnation, both guide and followers.

• • •

Peace. . . . [A] civil sword . . . is so far from bringing or helping forward an opposite in religion to repentance that magistrates sin grievously against the work of God and blood of souls by such proceedings [of persecution]. Because . . . (commonly) . . . the sufferings of false and anti-Christian teachers harden their followers, who, being blind by this means, are occasioned to tumble into the ditch of hell after their blind leaders with more inflamed zeal of lying confidence. So, secondly, violence and a sword of steel begets such an impression in the sufferers that, certainly, they conclude (as, indeed, that religion cannot be true which needs such instruments of violence to uphold it so) that persecutors are far from soft and gentle commiseration of the blindness of others. . . .

Truth. The souls of all men in the world are either naturally dead in sin or alive in Christ. If dead in sin, no man can kill them, no more than he can kill a dead man. Nor is it a false teacher or false religion that can so much prevent the means of spiritual life, as one of these two: Either the force of a material sword, imprisoning the souls of men in a state or national religion, ministry, or worship. Or secondly, civil wars and combustions for religion's sake, whereby men are immediately cut off without any longer means of repentance.

Now, again, for the souls that are alive in Christ, He has graciously appointed ordinances powerfully sufficient to maintain and cherish that life.

• • •

Truth. . . . Since all magistrates are God's ministers, essentially civil, bounded to a civil work, with civil weapons or instruments, and paid or rewarded with civil rewards. From all which, I say, . . . [it] cannot truly be alleged by any for the power of the civil magistrate to be exercised in spiritual and soul matters.

•   •   •

But . . . as it is most true that magistracy in general is of God for the preservation of mankind in civil order and peace (the world, otherwise, would be like the sea, wherein men, like fishes, would hunt and devour each other and the greater devour the lesser), so also it is true, that magistracy . . . is of man. Now what kind of magistrate soever the people shall agree to set up, whether he receive Christianity before he be set in office, or whether he receive Christianity after, he receives no more power of magistracy than a magistrate that has received no Christianity. For neither of them both can receive more than the commonweal, the body of people and civil state, as men, communicate unto them and betrust them with.

All lawful magistrates in the world . . . have, and can have no more power, than fundamentally lies in the bodies of fountains themselves, which power, might, or authority, is not religious, Christian, etc., but natural, human, and civil.

And hence, it is true, that a Christian captain, Christian merchant, physician, lawyer, pilot, father, master, and (so, consequently,) magistrate, etc., is no more a captain, merchant, physician, lawyer, pilot, father, master, magistrate, etc., than a captain, merchant, etc., of any other conscience or religion. . . .

A pagan or anti-Christian pilot may be as skillful to carry the ship to its desired port as any Christian mariner or pilot in the world, and may perform that work with as much safety and speed. . . .

To the Town of Providence

Roger Williams

That ever I should speak or write a tittle that tends to such an infinite liberty of conscience is a mistake, and which I have ever disclaimed and abhorred. To prevent such mistakes, I shall at present only propose this case: There goes many a ship to sea, with many hundred souls in one ship, whose weal and woe is common and is a true picture of a commonwealth, or a human combination or society. It hath fallen out sometimes, that both Papists and Protestants, Jews and Turks, may be embarked in one ship; upon which supposal I affirm, that all the liberty of conscience, that ever I pleaded for, turns upon these two hinges— that none of the Papists, Protestants, Jews, or Turks be forced to come to the ship's prayers or worship, nor compelled from their own particular prayers or worship, if they practice any. I further add, that I never denied, that notwithstanding this liberty, the commander of this ship ought to command the ship's course, yea, and also command that justice, peace, and sobriety be kept and practiced, both among the seamen and all the passengers. If any of the seamen refuse to perform their services, or passengers to pay their freight; if any refuse to help, in person or purse, towards the common charges or defense; if any refuse to obey the common laws and orders of the ship, concerning their common peace or preservation; if any shall mutiny and rise up against their commanders and officers; if any should preach or write that there ought to be no commanders or officers, because all are equal in Christ, therefore no masters nor officers, no laws nor orders, nor corrections nor punishments; I say, I never denied, but in such cases, whatever is pretended, the commander or commanders may judge, resist, compel, and punish such transgressors, according to their deserts and merits. This if seriously and honestly minded, may, if it so please the Father of lights, let in some light to such as willingly shut not their eyes.

I remain studious of your common peace and liberty.

Roger Williams
1655

from THE BLOODY TENET WASHED WHITE IN THE BLOOD OF THE LAMB

John Cotton

I expressly profess: 1. That no man is to be persecuted at all (much less for conscience sake), because all persecution is oppression for righteousness sake. 2. I profess further, that none is to be punished for his conscience sake, though erroneous, unless his errors be fundamental, or seditiously and turbulently promoted, and that after due conviction of conscience. That it may appear, he is not punished for his conscience, but for sinning against his conscience. . . .

In points of doctrine I said, . . . "some are fundamental, without right belief, whereof a man cannot be saved; others are circumstantial and less principal, wherein one man may differ from another in judgment without prejudice of salvation on either part. . . ."

I speak of . . . only . . . the foundation or fundamental points of Christian religion, which who so subverts and renounces, he renounces also his own salvation. . . .

That fundamentals are so clear, that a man cannot but be convinced in conscience of the truth of them after two or three admonitions; and that, therefore, such a person as still continues obstinate is condemned of himself. And if he then be punished, he is not punished for his conscience, but for sinning against his own conscience. . . .

For I thank God, God never left me to live in any such practices as to fall into any fundamental error, much less to persist therein after conviction and admonition, and least of all to seduce others thereinto. If God should leave me so far as to fall so fearfully into this three-fold degree of heretical wickedness, what am I better than other men? Better myself cut off by death or banishment, than the flock of Christ to be seduced and destroyed by my heretical wickedness. . . .

Nor is the righteous proceeding in civil states a disquieting of themselves, or any unmerciful disquieting of others. For it is no disquieting to a just man to do justice; and the disquieting of men in sin, it is no unmerciful dealing, but a compassionate healing, either of themselves or others. The false prophet reclaimed by stigmatizing with wounds in his hands will freely acknowledge: "Thus I was wounded in the house of my friends. Friends are not unmerciful disquieters. . . ."

But it was no part of my words or meaning to say that every heretic, though erring in some fundamental and weighty points, and for the same excommunicated [by the church], shall forthwith be punished by the civil magistrate; unless it does afterwards appear, that he break forth further either into blasphemy, or idolatry, or seducement of others to his heretical, pernicious ways. . . .

I would not say that every man that holds forth error in a boisterous and arrogant spirit to the disturbance of civil peace ought to be punished with death. This is too bloody a tenet, unless the boisterous arrogancy were such as did disturb the civil peace to the destruction of the lives and souls of men. . . .

. . . If it were true, that the magistrate has charge only of the bodies and goods of the subject, yet that might justly excite to watchfulness against such pollutions of religion as tend to apostasy. For if the church and people of God fall away from God, God will visit the city and country with public calamity, if not captivity, for the church's sake. . . .

. . . It is a carnal and worldly and, indeed, an ungodly imagination to confine the magistrate's charge to the bodies and goods of the subject, and to exclude them from the care of their souls. Did ever God commit the charge of the body to any governors to whom he did not commit (in His way) the care of souls also? Has God committed to parents the charge of the children's bodies, and not the care of their souls? To masters the charge of their servants' bodies, and not of their souls? To captains the charge of their soldiers' bodies, and not of their souls? Shall the captains suffer false worship, yea idolatry, publicly professed and practiced in the camp, and yet look to prosper in battle? . . . So civil governors, though to them be chiefly committed the bodies and goods of the people (as their adequate object), yet, in order to [accomplish] this, they may, and ought to, procure spiritual helps to their souls and to prevent such spiritual evils as that the prosperity of religion among them might advance the prosperity of the civil state. . . .

CHAPTER 3

Quaker and Southern Visions

INTRODUCTION

PASSENGER LISTS TO VIRGINIA AND
MASSACHUSETTS (1635)

CAPTAIN JOHN SMITH, 1580–1631
from The General History of Virginia (1624)

ROBERT BEVERLEY, 1673–1722
from The History and Present State of Virginia (1709)

WILLIAM BYRD II, 1674–1744
from History of the Dividing Line (1741)
from The Secret Diary (1709–1712), and
Upon a Fart (1704)

JOHN WOOLMAN, 1720–1772
Journal (1774)

The English mainland colonies absorbed many European stocks—
Dutch in New York, Swedes in Delaware, French Huguenots in
the Carolinas, Scots-Irish in the backcountry—each with its distinctive
culture and contributions. Probably those groups most influential on
later American developments, along with the Puritans, were the
planters of the Chesapeake and the Quakers.

The prominent colonial writings of Virginians capture some of the
themes and attitudes that were to remain central in the South: a sense
of pride in the possibilities and superior culture of the region combined
with a fear that such good qualities were tied to some falling behind
and failure to develop its potential. Smith's account centers on both
the drama of his Indian encounters, where personal heroics replaced
Puritan moralism, and on his struggles with his fellow planters who
he felt expected to find rather than sensibly develop wealth. Robert

Beverley and William Byrd II, the latter among the wealthiest and best educated Americans of his day, wrote in the early eighteenth century, as Virginia's slave society stabilized after decades of demographic (partly explained by the ships' lists) and social turmoil. Beverley's history (like Smith's) was partly recruiting tract, but his worry about Virginia society is as clear as his pride in it. Byrd was the colony's premier example of a self-defined aristocrat, writing gracefully humorous historical-literary works, as he expanded the fortune of his land speculator father. He kept check on his life in a secret coded diary demonstrating his amusedly superior indulgence—unless his authority was questioned. The entries for the week of October 27–November 2, 1709 are presented complete to suggest the formulaic way Byrd structured/chronicled his life.

Woolman was a successful Quaker businessman, one of several who, once wealth was gained, devoted energies to trying to make the world better accord with the Friends' belief in a benevolent God and humanity's capacity for good if one listened to one's inner voice.

CONSIDERATIONS

- What social vision divides Smith from his opponents among the first settlers?

- How does his relation with the Indians differ from those of the Puritans?

- What strengths and problems do Beverley and Byrd see in their Southern society? What is Byrd's view of his society and himself? How does this compare to Winthrop's? What might explain the differences between these sections?

- How do Smith, Beverley and Byrd use history? Do they have a vision of the common good?

- What differences are there in religion and social concern between the Puritans and the Quaker Woolman?

- What does Woolman see as the great dangers in American society? Is he right that, if some get too much, others will get too little?

Passenger Lists to Virginia and Massachusetts

(1635)

Passengers Bound for New England

1. Joseph Hull, of Somerset, a minister, aged 40 years
2. Agnes Hull, his wife, aged 25 years
3. Joan Hull, his daughter, aged 15 years
4. Joseph Hull, his son, aged 13 years
5. Tristram, his son, aged 11 years
6. Elizabeth Hull, his daughter, aged 7 years
7. Temperance, his daughter, aged 9 years
8. Grissell Hull, his daughter, aged 5 years
9. Dorothy Hull, his daughter, aged 3 years
10. Judith French, his servant, aged 20 years
11. John Wood, his servant, aged 20 years
12. Robert Dabyn, his servant, aged 28 years
13. Musachiell Bernard, of Batcombe, clotheir in the county of Somerset, 24 years
14. Mary Bernard, his wife, aged 28 years
15. John Bernard, his son, aged 3 years
16. Nathaniel, his son, aged 1 year
17. Rich. Persons, salter and his servant, 30 years
18. Francis Baber, chandler, aged 36 years
19. Jesope, joyner, aged 22 years
20. Walter Jesop, weaver, aged 21 years
21. Timothy Tabor, in Somerset of Batcombe, tailor, aged 35 years
22. Jane Tabor, his wife, aged 35 years
23. Jane Tabor, his daughter, aged 10 years
24. Anne Tabor, his daughter, aged 8 years
25. Sarah Tabor, his daughter, aged 5 years
26. William Fever, his servant, aged 20 years
27. John Whitmarke, aged 39 years
28. Alice Whitmarke, his wife, aged 35 years

29. James Whitmarke, his son, aged 11 years
30. Jane, his daughter, aged 7 years
31. Onseph Whitmarke, his son, aged 5 years
32. Rich. Whitmarke, his son, aged 2 years
33. William Read, of Batcombe, taylor in Somerset, aged 28 years
34. [Name not entered]
35. Susan Read, his wife, aged 29 years
36. Hannah Read, his daughter, aged 3 years
37. Susan Read, his daughter, aged 1 year
38. Rich. Adams, his servant, 29 years
39. Mary, his wife, aged 26 years
40. Mary Cheame, his daughter, aged 1 year

PASSENGERS BOUND FOR VIRGINIA

Edward Towers	26
Henry Woodman	22
Richard Seems	26
Vyncent Whatter	17
James Whithedd	14
Jonas Watts	21
Peter Loe	22
Geo. Brocker	17
Henry Ecles	26
Jo. Dennis	22
Tho. Swayne	23
Charles Rinsden	27
Jo. Exston	17
Wm. Luck	14
Jo. Thomas	19
Jo. Archer	21
Richard Williams	25
Francis Hutton	20
Savill Gascoyne	29
Rich. Bulfell	29
Rich. Jones	26
Tho. Wynes	30
Humphrey Williams	22

Edward Roberts	20
Martin Atkinson	32
Edward Atkinson	28
Wm. Edwards	30
Nathan Braddock	31
Jeffrey Gurrish	23
Henry Carrell	16
Tho. Ryle	24
Gamaliel White	24
Richard Marks	19
Tho. Clever	16
Jo. Kitchin	16
Edmond Edwards	20
Lewes Miles	19
Jo. Kennedy	20
Sam Jackson	24
Allin King	19
Rowland Sadler	19
Jo. Philllips	28
Daniel Endick	16
Jo. Chalk	25
Jo. Vynall	20
Edward Smith	20
Jo. Rowlidge	19
Wm. Westlie	40
Jo. Smith	18
Jo. Saunders	22
Tho. Bartcherd	16
Tho. Dodderidge	19
Richard Williams	18
Jo. Ballance	19
Wm. Baldin	21
Wm. Pen	26
Jo. Gerie	24
Henry Baylie	18
Rich. Anderson	50
Robert Kelum	51
Richard Fanshaw	22
Tho. Bradford	40

Wm. Spencer	15
Marmaduke Ella	22

Women

Ann Swayne	22
Eliz. Cote	22
Ann Rice	23
Kat. Wilson	23
Maudlin Lloyd	24
Mabell Busher	14
Annis Hopkins	24
Ann Mason	24
Bridget Crompe	18
Mary Hawkes	19
Ellin Hawkes	18

from THE GENERAL HISTORY OF VIRGINIA

John Smith

It might well be thought a country so fair (as Virginia is) and a people so tractable [as the Indians are] would long ere this have been quietly possessed, to the satisfaction of the adventurers' and the eternizing of the memory of those that effected it. But because all the world does see a defailment, this following treatise shall give satisfaction to all indifferent readers [by showing] how the business has been carried [out] whereby no doubt they will easily understand an answer to their question, how it came to pass there was no better speed and success in those proceedings.

•   •   •

Until the 13th of May they sought a place to plant in; then the Council was sworn [into office]; Master Wingfield was chosen President and an oration made why Captain Smith was not admitted to the Council as the rest.

Now falls every man to work, the Council contrive the fort, the rest cut down trees to make place to pitch their tents, some provide clapboard to reload the ships, some make gardens, some nets, &c. The savages often visited us kindly. The President's overweening jealousy would admit no exercise at arms or fortification but the boughs of trees cast together in the form of a half moon by the extraordinary pains and diligence of Captain Kendall.

Newport, Smith, and twenty others were sent to discover the head of the [James] river. By divers small habitations they passed; in six days they arrived at a town called Powhatan, consisting of some twelve houses pleasantly seated on a hill, before it three fertile isles, about it many of their cornfields; the place is very pleasant and strong by nature; of this place the Prince is called Powhatan and his people Powhatans. To this place the river is navigable; but higher, within a mile, by reason of the rocks and isles, there is not passage for a small boat; this they call the Falls. The people in all parts kindly entreated them. . . . [A]t the fort, where they arrived the next day, they found seventeen men hurt and a boy slain by the savages, and had it not chanced a cross-bar shot from the ships struck down a bough from a tree amongst them, that caused them to retire, our men had all been slain, being securely all at work and their arms in dry vats.

Hereupon the President was contented the fort should be palisaded, . . . for many were the assaults and ambuscades of the savages, and our men by their disorderly straggling were often hurt, when the savages by the nimbleness of their heels well escaped.

What toil we had, with so small a power to guard our workmen by day, watch all night, resist our enemies, and effect our business to re-load the ships, cut down trees, and prepare the ground to plant our corn. . . . Captain Smith, . . . all this time from their departure from the Canaries, was restrained as a prisoner upon the scandalous suggestions of some of the chief [colonists], (envying his repute) who feigned he intended to usurp the government, murder the Council, and make himself king. . . .

[H]e so much scorned their charity and publicly defied the uttermost of their cruelty he wisely prevented their policies, though he could not suppress their envies; yet so well he demeaned himself in this business as all the company did see his innocence and his adversaries' malice; and those suborned to accuse him, accused his accusers of subornation; many untruths were alleged against him, but being so apparently disproved, [the false charges] begot a general hatred in the hearts of the company against such unjust commanders, [and for] that the President was adjudged to give him £200 so that all he [President Wingfield] had was seized upon in part of satisfaction, which Smith presently returned to the store for the general use of the Colony.

Many were the mischiefs that daily sprung from their ignorant (yet ambitious) spirits, but the good doctrine and exhortation of our Preacher, Master Hunt, reconciled them and caused Captain Smith to be admitted to the Council. The next day all received the Communion; the day following, the savages voluntarily desired peace. . . .

Being thus left to our fortunes, it fortuned that within ten days, scarce ten amongst us could either go or well stand, such extreme weakness and sickness oppressed us. And thereat none need marvel if they consider the cause and reason which was this: While the ships stayed, our allowance was somewhat bettered by a daily proportion of biscuit, which the Sailors would pilfer to sell, give, or exchange with us for money, sassafras, furs, or love. But when they departed, there remained neither tavern, beer house, nor place of relief but the common kettle. Had we been as free from all sins as [from] gluttony and drunkenness, we might have been canonized for saints; but our President would never had been admitted [to sainthood]. . . . [O]ur drink was water, our lodgings castles in the air.

With this lodging and diet, our extreme toil in bearing and planting palisades so strained and bruised us, and our continual labor in the extremity of the heat had so weakened us, as were cause sufficient to have made us as miserable in our native country or any other place in the world. From May to September, those that escaped [death] lived upon sturgeon and sea crabs. Fifty in this time we buried; the rest seeing the President's projects to escape these miseries in our pinnace by flight (who all this time had neither felt want nor sickness) so moved our dead spirits as we deposed him . . . . But now was all our provision spent, the sturgeon gone, all helps abandoned, each hour expecting the fury of the savages, when God, the patron of all good endeavors, in that desperate extremity so changed the heart of the savages that they brought such plenty of their fruits and provision as no man wanted. . . .

The new President [Ratcliffe] and Martin, being little beloved, of weak judgment in dangers, and less industry in peace, committed the managing of all things abroad to Captain Smith, who, by his own example, good words, and fair promises, set some to mow, others to bind thatch, some to build houses, others to thatch them, himself always bearing the greatest task for his own share, so that in short time he provided most of them lodgings, neglecting any for himself. This done, seeing the savages superfluity begin to decrease, [Smith] (with some of his workmen) shipped himself in the shallop to search the country for trade. . . .

[A]t first they [the Indians] scorned him as a famished man and would in derision offer him a handful of corn, a piece of bread, for their swords and muskets, and such like proportions also for their apparel. But seeing by trade and courtesy there was nothing to be had, he made bold to try such conclusions as necessity enforced; though contrary to his commission, [he] let fly his muskets . . . whereat they all fled into the woods.

So marching towards their houses, they might see great heaps of corn; much ado he had to restrain his hungry soldiers from present taking of it, expecting as it happened that the savages would assault them, as not long after they did with most hideous noise. Sixty or seventy of them, some black, some red, some white, some parti-colored, came in a square order, singing and dancing out of the woods with their Okee (which was an idol made of skins, stuffed with moss, all painted and hung with chains and copper) borne before them; and in this manner, being well armed with clubs, targets, bows, and arrows, they charged the English that so kindly received them with their muskets loaded with pistol shot that down fell their god, and divers [Indians] lay sprawling on the ground; the rest fled again to the woods and ere long sent one of their Quiyoughcosucks to offer peace and redeem their Okee.

Smith told them if only six of them would come unarmed and load his boat, he would not only be their friend but restore them their Okee and give them beads, copper, and hatchets besides, which on both sides was to their contents performed, and then they brought him venison, turkeys, wild fowl, bread, and what they had, singing and dancing in sign of friendship till they departed.

• • •

. . . [Y]et what he carefully provided the rest carelessly spent.

• • •

The Spaniard never more greedily desired gold than he victual, nor his soldiers more to abandon the country than he to keep it. But . . . [he found] plenty of corn in the river of Chickahominy, where hundreds of savages in divers places stood with baskets expecting his coming. And now [with] the winter approaching, the rivers became so covered with swans, geese, ducks, and cranes that we daily feasted with good bread, Virginia peas, pumpkins, and persimmons, fish, fowl, and divers sorts of wild beasts as fat as we could eat them, so that none of our . . . humorists desired to go for England.

But our comedies never endured long without a tragedy; some idle exceptions being muttered against Captain Smith for not discovering the head of [the] Chickahominy river and [being] taxed by the Council to be too slow in so worthy an attempt, the next voyage he proceeded so far that with much labor by cutting of trees asunder he made his passage; but when his barge could pass no farther, he left her in a broad bay out of danger of shot, commanding none should go ashore till his return; himself with two English and two savages went up higher in a canoe, but he was not long absent but his men went ashore, whose want of government gave both occasion and opportunity to the savages to surprise one George Cassen, whom they slew. . . .

Smith little dreaming of that accident, being got to the marshes at the river's head twenty miles in the desert, had his two men slain (as is supposed) sleeping by the canoe, while himself by fowling sought them victual, who finding he was beset with 200 savages, two of them he slew, still defending himself with the aid of a savage his guide, whom he bound to his arm with his garter and used him as a buckler, yet he [Smith] was shot in his thigh a little, and had many arrows that stuck in his clothes but no great hurt, till at last they took him prisoner. . . .

He demanding for their captain, they showed him Opechancanough, King of Pamunkey, to whom he gave a round ivory double compass dial. Much they marveled at the playing of the fly and needle, which they could see so plainly and yet not touch it because of the glass that covered them. . . .

Notwithstanding, within an hour after, they tied him to a tree, and as many as could stand about him prepared to shoot him, but [seeing] the King holding up the compass in his hand, they all laid down their bows and arrows and in a triumphant manner led him to Orapaks, where he was after their manner kindly feasted and well used.

Their order in conducting him was thus: Drawing themselves all in file, the King in the midst had all their pieces and swords borne before him. Captain Smith was led after him by three great savages holding him fast by each arm. . . . A good time they continued this exercise and then cast themselves in a ring, dancing in such several postures and singing and yelling out such hellish notes and screeches; being strangely painted, every one [had] his quiver of arrows and at his back a club, on his arm a fox or an otter's skin or some such matter . . . their heads and shoulders were painted red with oil and pocones mingled together, which scarlet-like color made an exceeding handsome show; [each had] his bow in his hand and the skin of a bird with her wings abroad, dried, tied on his head, [with] a piece of copper, a white shell, a long feather with a small rattle growing at the tails of their snakes tied to it, or some such like toy. . . .

Smith they conducted to a long house where thirty or forty tall fellows did guard him, and ere long more bread and venison was brought him than would have served twenty men. I think his stomach at that time was not very good; what he left they put in baskets and tied over his head. About midnight they set the meat again before him . . . which made him think they would fat him to eat him. Yet in this desperate estate, to defend him from the cold, one Maocassater brought him his gown in requital of some beads and toys Smith had given him at his first arrival in Virginia. . . .

[They] made all the preparations they could to assault Jamestown, craving his advice, and for recompense he should have life, liberty, land, and women. . . . [H]e wrote his mind to them at the Fort, what was intended, how they should follow that direction to affright the messengers, and without fail send him such things as he wrote for, and an inventory with them. The difficult and danger he told the savages of . . . great guns, and other engines, exceedingly affrighted them, yet according to his request they went to Jamestown in as bitter weather as could be of frost and snow, and within three days returned with an answer.

But when they came to Jamestown, seeing men sally out as he had told them they would, they fled, yet in the night they came again to the same place where he had told them they should receive an answer and such things as he had promised them, which they found accordingly and with which they returned with no small expedition, to the wonder of them all that heard it, that he could either divine or the paper could speak. . . .

Not long after, early in a morning, a great fire was made in a long house and a mat spread on the one side as on the other; on the one they caused him to sit, and all the guard went out of the house, and presently came skipping in a great grim fellow all painted over with [char]coal mingled with oil, and many snakes' and weasels' skins stuffed with moss, and all their tails tied together so as they met on the crown of his head in a tassel, and round about the tassel was as a coronet of feathers, the skins hanging round about his head, back, and shoulders and in a manner covered his face, with a hellish voice, and a rattle in his hand. With most strange gestures and passions he began his invocation and environed the fire with a circle of meal; which done, three more such like devils came rushing in with the like antic tricks, painted half black, half red, but all their eyes were painted white and some red strokes like mustaches along their cheeks. Round about him those fiends danced a pretty while, and then came in three more as ugly as the rest, with red eyes and white strokes over their black faces; at last they all sat right opposite him, three of them on the one hand of the chief priest and three on the other. Then all with rattles began a song; which ended, the chief priest laid down five wheat corns; then, straining his arms and hands with such violence that he sweat and his veins swelled, he began a short oration; at the conclusion they all gave a short groan and then laid down three grains more. After that [they] began their song again and then another oration, ever laying down so many corns as before till they had twice encircled the fire; that done, they took a bunch of little sticks prepared for that purpose, continuing still their devotion, and at the end of every song and oration they laid down a stick betwixt the divisions of corn. Till night, neither he nor they did either eat or drink, and then they feasted merrily with the best provisions they could make.

Three days they used this ceremony; the meaning whereof, they told him, was to know if he intended them well or no. The circle of meal signified their country, the circles of corn the bounds of the sea, and the sticks his country. They imagined the world to be flat and round, like a trencher, and they in the midst. After this they brought him a bag of gunpowder, which they carefully preserved till the next spring, to plant as they did their corn, because they would be acquainted with the nature of that seed. . . .

At last they brought him to Werowocomoco, where was Powhatan, their Emperor. Here more than two hundred of those grim courtiers stood wondering at him, as [if] he had been a monster, till Powhatan and his train had put themselves in their greatest braveries. Before a fire, upon a seat like a bedstead, he sat covered with a great robe made of raccoon skins and all the tails hanging by. On either hand did sit a young wench of sixteen or eighteen years and along on each side [of] the house, two rows of men and behind them as many women, with all their heads and shoulders painted red, many of their heads bedecked with the white down of birds, but every one with something, and a great chain of white beads about their necks.

At his entrance before the King, all the people gave a great shout. The Queen of Appomattoc was appointed to bring him water to wash his hands, and another brought him a bunch of feathers, instead of a towel, to dry them. Having feasted him after their best barbarous manner they could, a long consultation was held, but the conclusion was, two great stones were brought before Powhatan; then as many as could laid hands on him, dragged him to them, and thereon laid his head, and being ready with their clubs to beat out his brains, Pocahontas, the King's dearest daughter, when no entreaty could prevail, got his head in her arms and laid her own upon his to save him from death, whereat the Emperor was contented he should live to make him hatchets, and her bells, beads, and copper, for they thought him as well [capable] of all occupations as themselves. For the King himself will make his own robes, shoes, bows, arrows, pots; plant; hunt; or do anything so well as the rest. . . .

Two days after, Powhatan, having disguised himself in the most fearfulest manner he could, caused Captain Smith to be brought forth to a great house in the woods and there upon a mat by the fire to be left alone. Not long after, from behind a mat that divided the house, was made the most dolefulest noise he ever heard; then Powhatan, more like a devil than a man, with some two hundred more as black as himself, came unto him and told him now they were friends, and presently he should go to Jamestown to send him two great guns and a grindstone for which he would give him the country of Capahowasic and forever esteem him as his son Nantaquond.

So to Jamestown with twelve guides Powhatan sent him. That night they quartered in the woods, he still expecting (as he had done all this long time of his imprisonment) every hour to be put to one death or other, for all their feasting. But almighty God (by His divine providence) had mollified the hearts of those stern barbarians with compassion. The next morning betimes they came to the fort, where Smith having used the savages with what kindness he could, he . . . gave them such toys and sent to Powhatan, his women, and children such presents as gave them in general full content.

from THE HISTORY AND PRESENT STATE OF VIRGINIA

Robert Beverley

PREFACE

'Tis agreed that travelers are of all men the most suspected of insincerity. . . .

I make no question, but the following account will come in for its share of this imputation. I shall be reputed as arrant a traveler as the rest, and my credit (like that of women) will be condemned for the sins of my company. . . .

If I might be so happy as to settle my credit with the reader, the next favor I would ask of him should be not to criticize too unmercifully upon my style. I am an Indian and don't pretend to be exact in my language. But I hope the plainness of my dress will give him the kinder impressions of my honesty, which is what I pretend to.

• • •

OF THE SERVANTS AND SLAVES IN VIRGINIA

Their servants they distinguish by the names of slaves for life and servants for a time.

Slaves are the Negroes and their posterity following the condition of the mother, according to the maxim *partus sequitur ventrem*. They are called slaves in respect of the time of their servitude because it is for life.

Servants are those which serve only for a few years, according to the time of their indenture or the custom of the country. The custom of the country takes place upon such as have no indentures. The law in this case is that if such servants be under nineteen years of age, they must be brought into court to have their age adjudged, and from the age they are judged to be of they must serve until they reach four and twenty. But if they be adjudged upwards of nineteen, they are then only to be servants for the term of five years.

The male servants and slaves of both sexes are employed together in tilling and manuring the ground, in sowing and planting tobacco,

93

corn, etc. Some distinction, indeed, is made between them in their clothes and food, but the work of both is no other than what the overseers, the freemen, and the planters themselves do.

Sufficient distinction is also made between the female servants and slaves, for a white woman is rarely or never put to work in the ground if she be good for anything else. And to discourage all planters from using any women so, their law imposes the heaviest taxes upon female servants working in the ground, while it suffers all other white women to be absolutely exempted. Whereas on the other hand, it is a common thing to work a woman slave out of doors; nor does the law make any distinction in her taxes, whether her work be abroad or at home.

Because I have heard how strangely cruel and severe the service of this country is represented in some parts of England, I can't forbear affirming that the work of their servants and slaves is no other than what every common freeman does. Neither is any servant required to do more in a day than his overseer. And I can assure you with a great deal of truth that generally their slaves are not worked near so hard nor so many hours in a day as the husbandmen and day laborers in England. An overseer is a man that having served his time has acquired the skill and character of an experienced planter and is therefore entrusted with the direction of the servants and slaves.

But to complete this account of servants I shall give you a short relation of the care their laws take that they be used as tenderly as possible.

By the Laws of Their Country

1. All servants whatsoever have their complaints heard without fee or reward, but if the master be found faulty the charge of the complaint is cast upon him, otherwise the business is done *ex officio.*

2. Any justice of peace may receive the complaint of a servant and order everything relating thereto till the next county court, where it will be finally determined.

3. All masters are under the correction and censure of the county courts to provide for their servants good and wholesome diet, clothing, and lodging.

4. They are always to appear upon the first notice given of the complaint of their servants, otherwise to forfeit the service of them until they do appear.

5. All servants' complaints are to be received at any time in court without process and shall not be delayed for want of form. But the merits of the complaint must be immediately inquired into by the justices, and if the master cause any delay therein the court may remove such servants if they see cause until the master will come to trial.

6. If a master shall at any time disobey an order of court made upon any complaint of a servant, the court is empowered to remove such servant forthwith to another master who will be kinder, giving to the former master the produce only (after fees deducted) of what such servants shall be sold for by public outcry.

7. If a master should be so cruel as to use his servant ill that is fallen sick or lame in his service and thereby rendered unfit for labor, he must be removed by the church wardens out of the way of such cruelty and boarded in some good planter's house till the time of his freedom, the charge of which must be laid before the next county court, which has power to levy the same from time to time upon the goods and chattels of the master. After which the charge of such boarding is to come upon the parish in general.

8. All hired servants are entitled to these privileges.

•   •   •

11. Each servant at his freedom receives of his master fifteen bushels of corn (which is sufficient for a whole year) and two new suits of clothes, both linen and woolen, and then becomes as free in all respects and as much entitled to the liberties and privileges of the country as any other of the inhabitants or natives are.

12. Each servant has then also a right to take up fifty acres of land, where he can find any unpatented; but that is no great privilege, for anyone may have as good a right for a piece of eight.

This is what the laws prescribe in favor of servants, by which you may find that the cruelties and severities imputed to that country are an unjust reflection. For no people more abhor the thoughts of such usage than the Virginians, nor take more precaution to prevent it.

OF THE OTHER PUBLIC CHARITABLE WORKS AND PARTICULARLY THEIR PROVISION FOR THE POOR

They live in so happy a climate and have so fertile a soil that nobody is poor enough to beg or want food, though they have abundance of people that are lazy enough to deserve it. I remember the time when five pound was left by a charitable testator to the poor of the parish he lived in, and it lay nine years before the executors could find one poor enough to be entitled to any part of this legacy; and at last it was all given to one old woman. So that this may in truth be termed the best poor man's country in the world. But as they have nobody that is poor to beggary, so they have few that are rich, because their goods are so heavily burdened with duties in England that they seldom can make any advantage of 'em.

When it happens that by accident or sickness any person is disabled from working and so is forced to depend upon the alms of the parish, he is then very well provided for, not at the common rate of some countries that give but sufficient to preserve the poor from perishing, but the unhappy creature is received into some charitable planter's house where he is at the public charge boarded very plentifully.

•   •   •

OF THE PEOPLE, INHABITANTS OF VIRGINIA

I can easily imagine that this as well as all the rest of the plantations was for the most part at first peopled by persons of low circumstances and by such as were willing to seek their fortunes in a foreign country. Nor was it hardly possible it should be otherwise, for 'tis not likely that any man of a plentiful estate should voluntarily abandon a happy certainty to roam after imaginary advantages in a New World. Besides which incertainty he must have proposed to himself to encounter the infinite difficulties and dangers that attend a new settlement. These discouragements were sufficient to terrify any man that could live easy in England from going to provoke his fortune in a strange land.

Those that went over to that country first were chiefly single men who had not the encumbrance of wives and children in England, and if they had they did not expose them to the fatigue and hazard of so long a voyage until they saw how it should fare with themselves. From hence it came to pass that when they were settled there in a comfortable way of subsisting a family they grew sensible of the misfortune of wanting wives, and such as had left wives in England sent for them. But the single men were put to their shifts. They excepted against the Indian women on account of their being pagans, and for fear they should conspire with those of their own nation to destroy their husbands. Under this difficulty they had no hopes but that the plenty in which they lived might invite modest women of small fortunes to go over thither from England. However, they would not receive any but such as could carry sufficient certificate of their modesty and good behavior. Those if they were but moderately qualified in all other respects might depend upon marrying very well in those days without any fortune. Nay, the first planters were so far from expecting money with a woman that 'twas a common thing for them to buy a deserving wife at the price of £100 and make themselves believe they had a hopeful bargain.

But this way of peopling the colony was only at first, for after the advantages of the climate and the fruitfulness of the soil were well known and all the dangers incident to infant settlements were over, people of better condition retired thither with their families, either to increase the estates they had before or else to avoid being persecuted for their principles of religion or government.

Thus in the time of the rebellion in England several good Cavalier families went thither with their effects to escape the tyranny of the usurper. . . . As for malefactors condemned to transportation, they have always received very few and for many years last past their laws have been severe against them.

• • •

OF THE RECREATIONS AND PASTIMES USED IN VIRGINIA

For their recreation the plantations, orchards, and gardens constantly afford 'em fragrant and delightful walks. In their woods and fields they have an unknown variety of vegetables and other rarities of nature to discover and observe. They have hunting, fishing, and fowling with which they entertain themselves a hundred ways. Here is the most good nature and hospitality practiced in the world, both towards friends and strangers. But the worst of it is this generosity is attended now and then with a little too much intemperance. . . .

. . . The admirable economy of the beavers deserves to be particularly remembered. They cohabit in one house, are incorporated in a regular form of government something like monarchy, and have over them a superintendent which the Indians call pericu. He leads them out to their several employments which consist in felling trees, biting off the branches, and cutting them into certain lengths suitable to the business they design them for, all which they perform with their teeth. When this is done, the governor orders several of his subjects to join together and take up one of those logs which they must carry to their house or dam, as occasion requires. He walks in state by them all the while and sees that everyone bears his equal share of the burden, while he bites with his teeth and lashes with his tail those that lag behind and do not lend all their strength. They commonly build their houses in swamps, and then to raise the water to a convenient height they make a dam with logs and a binding sort of clay so firm that though the water runs continually over, it cannot wash it away. Within these dams they enclose water enough to make a pool like a mill pond, and if a mill happen to be built upon the same stream below their dam, the miller in a dry season finds it worth his while to cut it to supply his mill with water. Upon which disaster the beavers are so expert at their work that in one or two nights' time they will repair the breach and make it perfectly whole again. . . .

The inhabitants are very courteous to travelers who need no other recommendation but the being human creatures. A stranger has no more to do but to inquire upon the road where any gentleman or good housekeeper lives, and there he may depend upon being received with hospitality. This good nature is so general among their people that the gentry when they go abroad order their principal servant to entertain all visitors with everything the plantation affords. And the poor planters who have but one bed will very often sit up or lie upon a form or couch all night to make room for a weary traveler to repose himself after his journey.

If there happen to be a churl that either out of covetousness or ill nature won't comply with this generous custom, he has a mark of infamy set upon him and is abhorred by all.

•   •   •

OF THE NATURAL PRODUCT OF VIRGINIA AND THE ADVANTAGES OF THEIR HUSBANDRY

. . . The fruit trees are wonderfully quick of growth, so that in six or seven years' time from the planting a man may bring an orchard to bear in great plenty, from which he may make store of good cider or distill great quantities of brandy, for the cider is very strong and yields abundance of spirit. Yet they have very few that take any care at all for an orchard. Nay, many that have good orchards are so negligent of them as to let them go to ruin and expose the trees to be torn and barked by the cattle.

Peaches, nectarines, and apricots as well as plums and cherries grow there upon standard trees. They commonly bear in three years from the stone and thrive so exceedingly that they seem to have no need of grafting or inoculating, if anybody would be so good a husband. And truly I never heard of any that did graft either plum, nectarine, peach, or apricot in that country. . . .

Grapevines of the English stock as well as those of their own production bear most abundantly . . .

When a single tree happens in clearing the ground to be left standing with a vine upon it open to the sun and air, that vine generally produces as much as four or five others that remain in the woods. I have seen in this case more grapes upon one single vine than would load a London cart. And for all this the people never remove any of them into their gardens but content themselves throughout the whole country with the grapes they find thus wild. Much less can they be expected to attempt the making of wine or brandy from the grape.

The almond, pomegranate, and fig ripen there very well, and yet there are not ten people in the country that have any of them in their gardens, much less endeavor to preserve any of them for future spending or to propagate to make a trade. . . .

It is thought too much for the same man to make the wheat and grind it, bolt it, and bake it himself; and it is too great a charge for every planter who is willing to sow barley to build a malt house and brewhouse too, or else to have no benefit of his barley; nor will it answer if he would be at the charge. These things can never be expected from a single family. But if they had cohabitations it might be thought worth attempting. Neither as they are now settled can they find any certain market for their other grain, which if they had towns would be quite otherwise. . . .

These and a thousand other advantages that country naturally affords which its inhabitants make no manner of use of . . . They receive no benefit nor refreshment from the sweets and precious things they have growing amongst them, but make use of the industry of England for all such things.

What advantages do they see the neighboring plantations make of their grain and provisions, while they who can produce them infinitely better not only neglect the making a trade thereof but even a necessary provision against an accidental scarcity—contenting themselves with a supply of food from hand to mouth, so that if it should please

God to send them an unseasonable year there would not be found in the country provision sufficient to support the people for three months extraordinary.

By reason of the unfortunate method of the settlement and want of cohabitation they cannot make a beneficial use of their flax, hemp, cotton, silk, silkgrass, and wool, which might otherwise supply their necessities, and leave the produce of tobacco to enrich them when a gainful market can be found for it.

Thus they depend altogether upon the liberality of nature without endeavoring to improve its gifts by art or industry. They sponge upon the blessings of a warm sun and a fruitful soil and almost grutch the pains of gathering in the bounties of the earth. I should be ashamed to publish this slothful indolence of my countrymen but that I hope it will rouse them out of their lethargy and excite them to make the most of all those happy advantages which nature has given them. And if it does this I am sure they will have the goodness to forgive me.

from HISTORY OF THE DIVIDING LINE

William Byrd II

As it happened some ages before to be the fashion to saunter to the Holy Land, and go upon other Quixote adventures so it was now grown the humor to take a trip to America. . . .

Happy was he, and still happier she, that could get themselves transported, fondly expecting their coarsest utensils, in that happy place, would be of massy silver.

This made it easy for the company to procure as many volunteers as they wanted for their new colony; but, like most other undertakers who have no assistance from the public, they starved the design by too much frugality; for, unwilling to launch out at first into too much expense, they shipped off but few people at a time, and those but scantily provided. The adventurers were, besides, idle and extravagant, and expected they might live without work in so plentiful a country.

These wretches were set ashore not far from Roanoke inlet, but by some fatal disagreement, or laziness, were either starved or cut to pieces by the Indians.

Several repeated misadventures of this kind did, for some time, allay the itch of sailing to this new world; but the distemper broke out again about the year 1606. . . .

This settlement stood its ground from that time forward in spite of all the blunders and disagreement of the first adventurers, and the many calamities that befell the colony afterwards. . . .

[T]hey extended themselves as far as James-town, where, like true Englishmen, they built a church that cost no more than fifty pounds, and a tavern that cost five hundred.

They had now made peace with the Indians, but there was one thing wanting to make that peace lasting. The natives could, by no means, persuade themselves that the English were heartily their friends, so long as they disdained to intermarry with them. And, in earnest, had the English consulted their own security and the good of the colony—

had they intended either to civilize or convert these gentiles, they would have brought their stomachs to embrace this prudent alliance.

The Indians are generally tall and well-proportioned, which may make full amends for the darkness of their complexions. Add to this, that they are healthy and strong, with constitutions untainted by lewdness, and not enfeebled by luxury. Besides, morals and all considered, I cannot think the Indians were much greater heathens than the first adventurers, who, had they been good Christians, would have had the charity to take this only method of converting the natives to Christianity. For, after all that can be said, a sprightly lover is the most prevailing missionary that can be sent amongst these, or any other infidels.

Besides, the poor Indians would have had less reason to complain that the English took away their land, if they had received it by way of portion with their daughters. Had such affinities been contracted in the beginning, how much bloodshed had been prevented, and how populous would the country have been, and, consequently, how considerable? Nor would the shade of the skin have been any reproach at this day; for if a Moor may be washed white in three generations, surely an Indian might have been blanched in two. . . .

About the same time New England was pared from Virginia by letters patent, bearing date April the 10th, 1608. Several gentlemen of the town and neighborhood of Plymouth obtained this grant. . . .

. . . [A]bout the year 1620, a large swarm of dissenters fled thither from the severities of their stepmother, the church. These saints conceiving the same aversion to the copper complexion of the natives, with that of the first adventurers to Virginia, would, on no terms, contract alliances with them, afraid perhaps, like the Jews of old, lest they might be drawn into idolatry by those strange women. . . .

. . . [T]he colony throve apace, and was thronged with large detachments of independents and presbyterians, who thought themselves persecuted at home.

Though these people may be ridiculed for some pharisaical particularities in their worship and behavior, yet they were very useful subjects, as being frugal and industrious, giving no scandal or bad example, at least by any open and public vices. By which excellent qualities they had much the advantage of the southern colony, who thought their being members of the established church sufficient to sanctify very loose and profligate morals. For this reason New England improved much faster than Virginia, and in seven or eight years New

Plymouth, like Switzerland, seemed too narrow a territory for its inhabitants. . . .

But what wounded Virginia deepest was the cutting off Maryland from it, by charter from king Charles I. to sir George Calvert, afterwards lord Baltimore, bearing date the 20th of June, 1632. The truth of it is, it begat much speculation in those days, how it came about that a good protestant king should bestow so bountiful a grant upon a zealous Roman catholic. But it is probable it was one fatal instance amongst many other of his majesty's complaisance to the queen.

However that happened, it is certain this province afterwards proved a commodious retreat for persons of that communion. The memory of the gunpowder treason-plot was still fresh in everybody's mind, and made England too hot for papists to live in, without danger of being burnt with the pope, every 5th of November; for which reason legions of them transplanted themselves to Maryland in order to be safe, as well from the insolence of the populace as the rigor of the government. . . .

The proprietors of New Jersey, finding more trouble than profit in their new dominions, made over their right to several other persons, who obtained a fresh grant from his royal highness, dated March the 14th, 1682.

Several of the grantees, being quakers and anabaptists, failed not to encourage many of their own persuasion to remove to this peaceful region. Amongst them were a swarm of Scots quakers, who were not tolerated to exercise the gifts of the spirit in their own country.

Besides the hopes of being safe from persecution in this retreat, the new proprietors inveigled many over by this tempting account of the country: that it was a place free from those three great scourges of mankind, priests, lawyers, and physicians. Nor did they tell them a word of a lie, for the people were yet too poor to maintain these learned gentlemen, who, everywhere, love to be well paid for what they do; and, like the Jews, cannot breathe in a climate where nothing is to be gotten.

The Jerseys continued under the government of these proprietors till the year 1702, when they made a formal surrender of the dominion to the queen, reserving however the property of the soil to themselves. So soon as the bounds of New Jersey came to be distinctly laid off, it appeared there was still a narrow slip of land, lying betwixt that colony and Maryland. Of this, William Penn, a man of much worldly wisdom, and some eminence among the quakers, got early notice, and, by the credit he had with the duke of York, obtained a patent for it, dated March the 4th, 1680.

It was a little surprising to some people how a quaker should be so much in the good graces of a popish prince; though, after all, it may be pretty well accounted for. This ingenious person had not been bred a quaker; but, in his earlier days, had been a man of pleasure about the town. He had a beautiful form and very taking address, which made him successful with the ladies, and particularly with a mistress of the duke of Monmouth. By this gentlewoman he had a daughter, who had beauty enough to raise her to be a dutchess, and continued to be a toast full 30 years. But this amour had like to have brought our fine gentleman in danger of a duel, had he not discreetly sheltered himself under this peaceable persuasion. Besides, his father having been a flag-officer in the navy, while the duke of York was lord high admiral, might recommend the son to his favor. This piece of secret history I thought proper to mention, to wipe off the suspicion of his having been popishly inclined.

This gentleman's first grant confined him within pretty narrow bounds, giving him only that portion of land which contains Buckingham, Philadelphia and Chester counties. But to get these bounds a little extended, he pushed his interest still further with his royal highness, and obtained a fresh grant of the three lower counties, called Newcastle, Kent and Sussex, which still remained within the New York patent, and had been luckily left out of the grant of New Jersey. The six counties being thus incorporated, the proprietor dignified the whole with the name of Pennsylvania.

The quakers flocked over to this country in shoals, being averse to go to heaven the same way with the bishops. Amongst them were not a few of good substance, who went vigorously upon every kind of improvement; and thus much I may truly say in their praise, that by diligence and frugality, for which this harmless sect is remarkable, and by having no vices but such as are private, they have in a few years made Pennsylvania a very fine country. The truth is, they have observed exact justice with all the natives that border upon them; they have purchased all their lands from the Indians; and though they paid but a trifle for them, it has procured them the credit of being more righteous than their neighbors. They have likewise had the prudence to treat them kindly upon all occasions, which has saved them from many wars and massacres wherein the other colonies have been indiscreetly involved. The truth of it is, a people whose principles forbid them to draw the carnal sword, were in the right to give no provocation.

• • •

[March] 10. The Sabbath happened very opportunely to give some ease to our jaded people, who rested religiously from every work but that of cooking the kettle. We observed very few cornfields in our walks and those very small, which seemed the stranger to us because we could see no other tokens of husbandry or improvement. But upon further inquiry we were given to understand people only made corn for themselves and not for their [live]stocks, which know very well how to get their own living. Both cattle and hogs ramble into the neighboring marshes and swamps, where they maintain themselves the whole winter long and are not fetched home till the spring. Thus these indolent wretches during one half of the year lose the advantage of the milk of their cattle, as well as their dung, and many of the poor creatures perish in the mire, into the bargain, by this ill management. Some who pique themselves more upon industry than their neighbors will now and then, in compliment to their cattle, cut down a tree whose limbs are loaded with the moss afore-mentioned. The trouble would be too great to climb the tree in order to gather this provender, but the shortest way (which in this country is always counted the best) is to fell it, just like the lazy Indians, who do the same by such trees as bear fruit and so make one harvest for all. By this bad husbandry milk is so scarce in the winter season that were a bigbellied woman to long for it she would tax her longing. And, in truth, I believe this is often the case, and at the same time a very good reason why so many people in this province are marked with a custard complexion.

The only business here is raising of hogs, which is managed with the least trouble and affords the diet they are most fond of. The truth of it is, the inhabitants of North Carolina devour so much swine's flesh that it fills them full of gross humors. . . . [A]nd . . . shows its spite to the poor nose, of which 'tis apt in a small time treacherously to undermine the foundation. This calamity is so common and familiar here that it ceases to be a scandal, and in the disputes that happen about beauty the noses have in some companies much ado to carry it. Nay, 'tis said that once, after three good pork years, a motion had like to have been made in the House of Burgesses that a man with a nose should be incapable of holding any place of profit in the province;

which extraordinary motion could never have been intended without some hopes of a majority. . . .

[March 11] We had encamped so early that we found time in the evening to walk near half a mile into the woods. There we came upon a family of mulattoes that called themselves free, though by the shyness of the master of the house, who took care to keep least in sight, their freedom seemed a little doubtful. It is certain many slaves shelter themselves in this obscure part of the world, nor will any of their righteous neighbors discover them. On the contrary, they find their account in settling such fugitives on some out-of-the-way corner of their land to raise stocks for a mean and inconsiderable share, well knowing their condition makes it necessary for them to submit to any terms. Nor were these worthy borderers content to shelter runaway slaves, but debtors and criminals have often met with the like indulgence. . . .

[March 15] . . . We saw no drones there, which are but too common, alas, in that part of the World. Though, in truth, the distemper of laziness seizes the men much oftener than the women. These last spin, weave, and knit, all with their own hands, while their husbands, depending on the bounty of the climate, are slothful in everythng but getting of children, and in that only instance make themselves useful members of an infant colony. . . .

[March 16] We passed by no less than two Quaker meetinghouses, one of which had an awkward ornament on the west end of it that seemed to ape a steeple. I must own I expected no such piece of foppery from a sect of so much outside simplicity. That persuasion prevails much in the lower end of Nansemond County, for want of ministers to pilot the people a decenter way to Heaven. . . . People uninstructed in any religion are ready to embrace the first that offers. 'Tis natural for helpless man to adore his Maker in some form or other, and were there any exception to this rule, I should suspect it to be among the Hottentots of the Cape of Good Hope and of North Carolina.

[March 17] . . . They account it among their greatest advantages that they are not priest-ridden, not remembering that the clergy is rarely guilty of bestriding such as have the misfortune to be poor. One thing may be said for the inhabitants of that province, that they are not troubled with any religious fumes and have the least superstition of any people living. They do not know Sunday from any other day, any more

than Robinson Crusoe did, which would give them a great advantage
were they given to be industrious. But they keep so many Sabbaths
every week that their disregard of the seventh day has no manner of
cruelty in it, either to servants or cattle. . . .

[March 25] Surely there is no place in the world where the inhabitants live with less labor than in North Carolina. It approaches nearer
to the description of Lubberland than any other, by the great felicity
of the climate, the easiness of raising provisions, and the slothfulness
of the people. Indian corn is of so great increase that a little pains will
subsist a very large family with bread, and then they may have meat
without any pains at all, by the help of the low grounds and the great
variety of mast that grows on the high land. The men, for their parts,
just like the Indians, impose all the work upon the poor women. They
make their wives rise out of their beds early in the morning, at the same
time that they lie and snore till the sun has risen one-third of his course,
and dispersed all the unwholesome damps. Then, after stretching and
yawning for half an hour, they light their pipes, and, under the protection of a cloud of smoke, venture out into the open air; though if it
happen to be never so cold they quickly return shivering into the chimney corner. When the weather is mild, they stand leaning with both
their arms upon the cornfield fence and gravely consider whether they
had best go and take a small heat at the hoe but generally find reasons
to put it off till another time. Thus they loiter away their lives, like
Solomon's sluggard, with their arms across, and at the winding up of
the year scarcely have bread to eat. To speak the truth, 'tis a thorough
aversion to labor that makes people file off to North Carolina, where
plenty and a warm sun confirm them in their disposition to laziness
for their whole lives. . . .

from THE SECRET DIARY
OF WILLIAM BYRD II

APRIL, 1709

3. . . . We prepared to go to church, but the parson did not come, notwithstanding good weather, so I read a sermon in Dr. Tillotson at home. . . .

5. . . . The Doctor had a fever and ague. We played at billiards. I read more Italian. In the evening we took a walk about the plantation. The brickmaker came this evening. I scolded with John about managing the tobacco. I read to the ladies Dr. Lister's *Journey to Paris*. I was ill treated by my wife, at whom I was out of humor. . . .

6. . . . My wife and I disagreed about employing a gardener. I ate milk for breakfast. John made an end of trimming the boat, which he performed very well. I settled my accounts and read Italian. I ate nothing but fish for dinner and a little asparagus. We played at billiards. . . .

7. . . . I reproached my wife with ordering the old beef to be kept and the fresh beef used first, contrary to good management, on which she was pleased to be very angry and this put me out of humor. I ate nothing but boiled beef for dinner. I went away presently after dinner to look after my people. When I returned I read more Italian and then my wife came and begged my pardon and we were friends again. I read in Dr. Lister again very late. I said my prayers. I had good health, good thoughts, and bad humor, unlike a philosopher. . . .

9. . . . My wife and I had another scold about mending my shoes but it was soon over by her submission. I settled my accounts and read Dutch. . . .

24. I rose at 6 o'clock and said my prayers very shortly. We breakfasted about 10 o'clock and I ate nothing but bread and butter and sack. We rode to Jamestown Church, where Mr. Commissary preached. When church was done I gave 10 shillings to the poor. Nothing could hinder me from sleeping at church, though I took a great deal of pains against it. . . .

25. I rose at 6 o'clock and said my prayers shortly. Mr. W-l-s and I fenced and I beat him. Then we played at cricket, Mr. W-l-s and John Custis against me and Mr. [H] but we were beaten. I ate nothing but milk for breakfast. . . .

MAY, 1709

1. . . . I endeavored to learn all I could from Major Burwell who is a sensible man skilled in matters relating to tobacco. In the evening we talked about religion and my wife and her sister had a fierce dispute about the infallibility of the Bible. . . .

2. . . . The women went to romping and I and my brother romped with them. . . .

JUNE, 1709

9. . . . My Eugene ran away this morning for no reason but because he had not done anything yesterday. I sent my people after him but in vain. The sloop came from Falling Creek with copper, timber, and planks. In the evening Captain Keeling came to see us to account with me for the quitrents of New Kent. . . .

10. . . . George B-th brought home my boy Eugene. . . . Captain and I had some discourse about the philosopher's stone which he is following with great diligence. . . . Eugene was whipped for running away and had the bit put on him. . . .

AUGUST, 1709

13. . . . Twelve Pamunkey Indians came over. We gave them some victuals and some rum and put them over the river. I danced my dance. I removed more books into the library. I read some geometry and walked to see the people at work. I ate fish for dinner. I was almost the whole afternoon in putting up my books. In the evening John Blackman came from the Falls and brought me word some of my people were sick and that my coaler was sick at the coal mine. I scolded with him about the little work he had done this summer. I took a walk about the plantation. . . .

19. . . . I rose at 6 o'clock and Mr. Randolph and I walked to the tannery, with which we were both pleased. Then we went and viewed all the work at the dam. Then we ate milk for breakfast and rode to the Falls where we found a good crop considering the great drought. . . .

OCTOBER, 1709

6. I rose at 6 o'clock and said my prayers and ate milk for breakfast. Then I proceeded to Williamsburg, where I found all well. I went to the capitol where I sent for the wench to clean my room and when I came I kissed her and felt her, for which God forgive me. . . .

19. . . . About ten o'clock we went to court where a man was tried for ravishing a very homely woman. There were abundance of women in the gallery. I recommended myself to God before I went into court. About one o'clock I went to my chambers for a little refreshment. The court rose about 4 o'clock and I dined with the Council. I ate boiled beef for dinner. I gave myself the liberty to talk very lewdly, for which God forgive me. . . .

27. I rose at 6 o'clock and read a chapter in Hebrew and some Greek in Lucian. I said my prayers and ate milk for breakfast. The President was so kind to offer to put off passing the accounts till my order came for increasing my salary. We went to court and sat till 4 o'clock. Then we went to dinner and I ate boiled beef for my dinner. In the evening we played at cards and I won £5. We drank some of Will Robinson's cider till we were very merry and then went to the coffeehouse and pulled poor Colonel Churchill out of bed. I went home about one o'clock in the morning. I neglected to say my prayers but had good health, good thoughts, and good humor, thanks be to God Almighty.

28. I rose at 6 o'clock but read nothing because Colonel Randolph came to see me in the morning. I neglected to say my prayers but I ate milk for breakfast. Colonel Harrison's vessel came in from Madeira and brought abundance of letters and among the rest I had ten from Mr. Perry with a sad account of tobacco. We went to court but much time was taken up in reading our letters and not much business was done. About 3 we rose and had a meeting of the College in which it was agreed to turn Mr. Blackamore out from being master of the school for being so great a sot. I ate boiled beef for dinner and in the evening went home after walking with Colonel Bassett. I said my prayers and had good health, good thoughts, and good humor, thanks be to God Almighty.

29. I rose at 6 o'clock and read nothing because the governors of the College were to meet again. However I said my prayers and ate milk for breakfast. When we met Mr. Blackamore presented a petition in which he set forth that if the governors of the College would for-

give him what was past, he would for the time to come mend his conduct. On which the governors at last agreed to keep him on, on trial, some time longer. Then we went to court where we sat till about 3 o'clock and then I learned that my sister Custis was at Mr. Bland's. I went to her and there was also Mrs. Chiswell. I went with them to Doctor B-r-t and ate beef for dinner. Here I stayed till 8 o'clock and then walked home. I said my prayers and had good health, good thoughts, and good humor, thanks be to God Almighty.

30. I rose at 6 o'clock but read nothing because by the time I was dressed Mr. Holloway, Mrs. Chiswell, and Mrs. Custis came to see me. However I said my prayers and ate milk for breakfast. I gave them a bottle of sack and as soon as they went away I waited on the President to church where Mr. Goodwin preached a good sermon. After church I went to Mr. Blair's to dinner with all the Council in attendance. I ate boiled beef for dinner. About 5 o'clock we returned home and then went to the coffeehouse where we sat an hour and then went home. I neglected to say my prayers, for which God forgive me. I had good health, good thoughts, and good humor, thanks be to God Almighty.

31. I rose at 6 o'clock and read two chapters in Hebrew and some Greek in Lucian. I said my prayers and ate milk for breakfast. About 10 o'clock we went to court. The committee met to receive proposals for the building the College and Mr. Tullitt undertook it for £2,000 provided he might wood off the College land and all assistants from England to come at the College's risk. We sat in court till about 4 o'clock and then I rode to Green Springs to meet my wife. I found her there and had the pleasure to learn that all was well at home, thanks be to God. There was likewise Mrs. Chiswell. I ate boiled beef for supper. Then we danced and were merry till about 10 o'clock. I neglected to say my prayers but had good health, good thoughts, and good humor, thanks be to God Almighty. This month I took above 400 of Colonel Quarry in money for bills at an allowance of 10 per cent.

NOVEMBER, 1709

1. I rose at 8 o'clock because I could not leave my wife sooner. Then I ate milk for breakfast. I neglected to say my [prayers] nor could I read anything. About 11 o'clock I went to Williamsburg and about 12 took my place in court. I sat there till about 4 and could not go out of town because I had accounts to settle with several people. About 5 o'clock we went to dinner and I ate boiled beef. Then the President took us

home to his house, where I played at cards and won 35 shillings. We were very merry and in that condition went to the coffeehouse and again disturbed Colonel Churchill. About 11 o'clock I went home and said a short prayer. I had good health, good thoughts, and good humor, thanks be to God Almighty.

2. I rose at 6 o'clock and read a chapter in Hebrew and some Greek in Lucian. I said my prayers and ate milk for breakfast, and settled some accounts, and then went to court where we made an end of the business. We went to dinner about 4 o'clock and I ate boiled beef again. In the evening I went to Dr. [Barret's] where my wife came this afternoon. Here I found Mrs. Chiswell, my sister Custis, and other ladies. We sat and talked till about 11 o'clock and then retired to our chambers. I played at [r-m] with Mrs. Chiswell and kissed her on the bed till she was angry and my wife also was uneasy about it, and cried as soon as the company was gone. I neglected to say my prayers, which I should not have done, because I ought to beg pardon for the lust I had for another man's wife. However I had good health, good thoughts, and good humor, thanks be to God Almighty. . . .

11. . . . [W]e returned in the dark to Arlington where we found some of the women sick and some out of humor and particularly my wife quarreled with Mr. Dunn and me for talking Latin and called it bad manners. This put me out of humor with her which set her to crying. I wholly made the reconciliation. The parson was more affronted than I, and went to bed. . . .

30. I rose at 3 o'clock and read two chapters in Hebrew and some Greek in Cassius. I went to bed again and lay till 7. I said my prayers, danced my dance, and ate milk for breakfast. Eugene was whipped for pissing in bed and Jenny for concealing it. I settled several accounts. I ate boiled beef for dinner. In the afternoon I played at billiards with my wife and then took a walk about the plantation to look over my affairs. I said my prayers. In the evening I read some Italian. About 8 o'clock we went to bed and I had good health, good thoughts, and good humor, thanks be to God Almighty.

DECEMBER, 1709

1. . . . Eugene was whipped again for pissing in bed and Jenny for concealing it. . . .

3. . . . Eugene pissed abed again for which I made him drink a pint of piss. I settled some accounts and read some news. . . .

JANUARY, 1710

13. . . . My daughter was not well and took a purge which did not work much. My wife was severe to her because she was fretful. In the afternoon I danced more dances, and then took a walk again about the plantation with my bow and arrow. . . .

23. . . . My daughter slept very well this night and was well this morning, thank God. . . .

24. I could not sleep all night for the disturbance my daughter gave me. . . . I had my father's grave opened to see him but he was so wasted there was not anything to be distinguished. . . . In the evening I read nothing by my wife's desire. I had good health, good thoughts, and good humor, thanks be to God Almighty. . . .

APRIL, 1710

21 . . . . About 8 o'clock I went to see the President and then went to court. I settled some accounts first. Two of the negroes were tried and convicted for treason. I wrote a letter to England and then went to court again. About 3 o'clock I returned to my chambers again and found above a girl who I persuaded to go with me into my chambers but she would not. I ate some cake and cheese and then went to Mr. Bland's where I ate some boiled beef. Then I went to the President's where we were merry till 11 o'clock. Then I stole away. I said a short prayer but notwithstanding committed uncleanness in bed. I had good health, bad thoughts, and good humor, thanks be to God Almighty. . . .

MAY, 1710

7. . . . I read a sermon of Dr. Tillotson's which affected me very much and made me shed some tears of repentance. The weather grew very hot. The sick boys were a little better. I ate [moderately], of roast beef for dinner. In the afternoon my wife and I took a long sleep which discomposed me. Then I read another sermon in Dr. Tillotson, after which we took a walk. . . .

JUNE, 1710

3. I rose at 6 o'clock and as soon as I came out news was brought that the child was very ill. We went out and found him just ready to die and he died about 8 o'clock in the morning. God gives and God takes away; blessed be the name of God. Mrs. Harrison and Mr. Ander-

son and his wife and some other company came to see us in our affliction. My wife was much afflicted but I submitted to His judgment better, notwithstanding I was very sensible of my loss, but God's will be done. Mr. Anderson and his wife with Mrs. B-k-r dined here. I ate roast mutton. In the afternoon I was griped in my belly very much but it grew better towards the night. In the afternoon it rained and was fair again in the evening. My poor wife and I walked in the garden. . . .

14. . . . My wife began to be comforted, thank God, and I lost my gripes. A poor woman brought her daughter over that was troubled with the vapors extremely. I let her know if her daughter would come and stay here for two months I would endeavor to cure her. I ate cold chicken for dinner. In the afternoon I read some Physics. . . .

July, 1710

9. . . . About 11 o'clock we went to church and had a good sermon. After church I invited nobody home because I design to break that custom that my people may go to church. I ate boiled pork for dinner. In the afternoon my wife and I had a terrible quarrel about the things she had come in but at length she submitted because she was in the wrong. . . .

14. . . . Billy Brayne and I had a quarrel because he would not learn his books and I whipped him extremely. In the evening we took a walk and I drank some milk warm from the cow. . . .

15. . . . My wife against my will caused little Jenny to be burned with a hot iron, for which I quarreled with her. It was so hot today that I did not intend to go to the launching of Colonel Hill's ship but about 9 o'clock the Colonel was so kind as to come and call us. My wife would not go at first but with much entreaty she at last consented. . . .

24. . . . I ate roast shoat for dinner. In the afternoon I settled my books again. In the evening I quarreled with my wife for not taking care of the sick woman, which she took very ill of me and was out of humor over it. . . .

25. . . . My wife was out of humor this evening for nothing, which I bore very well and was willing to be reconciled. . . .

26. . . . In the evening my wife and I took a walk about the plantation and were good friends. Mr. C-s went to Mrs. Harrison's. I said my prayers and had good health, good thoughts, and good humor, thanks be to God Almighty. I gave my wife a flourish. . . .

28. . . . In the afternoon my wife and I had a little quarrel because she moved my letters. Captain Burbydge came to see us and told me my great sloop was come round. I sent ten hogsheads more on board him. I walked with him some part of the way towards Mrs. Harrison's. When we came home my wife was pleased to be out of humor . . . .

30. . . . I read a sermon in Dr. Tillotson and then took a little [nap]. I ate fish for dinner. In the afternoon my wife and I had a little quarrel which I reconciled with a flourish. Then she read a sermon in Dr. Tillotson to me. It is to be observed that the flourish was performed on the billiard table. I read a little Latin. In the evening we took a walk about the plantation. I neglected to say my prayers but had good health, good thoughts, and good humor, thanks be to God. . . .

SEPTEMBER, 1710

22. I rose at 6 o'clock. . . . I neglected to say my prayers. About 10 o'clock we got on our horses and rode towards Henrico to see the militia. Colonel Randolph with a troop met us at Pleasant's mill and conducted us to his plantation, where all the men were drawn up in good order. The Governor was pleased with them and exercised them for two or three hours together. He presented me likewise to them to be their commander-in-chief [who] received me with an huzzah. About 3 o'clock we went to Colonel Randolph's house and had a dinner and several of the officers dined with us and my hogshead of punch entertained all the people and made them drunk and fighting all the evening, but without much mischief. . . .

OCTOBER, 1710

20. . . . Then I wrote a letter to my wife and after that went to dinner and ate roast beef for dinner. Then I went to the coffeehouse, where I played at hazard and lost £7 and returned home very peaceful. . . .

30. . . . Then Colonel Lewis and I walked to see the Governor's house and then went to the President's where we played at cards and I lost 35 shillings. I wrote a letter to Colonel Hunter which Mr. Hamilton undertook to carry to him. Then several of us went to the coffeehouse where we played at hazard and I won 23 shillings. I wrote a letter to my wife. I did not come home till 11 o'clock; however, I said my prayers and had good health, good thoughts, and good humor, thank God Almighty. . . .

NOVEMBER, 1710

4. . . . I was very weary and so went to bed about 8 o'clock. I neglected to say my prayers in form but had good health, good thoughts, and good humor, thank God Almighty. I gave my wife a flourish in which she had a great deal of pleasure. . . .

6. . . . I sent for the tailor to cut my coat shorter. At night my wife and I played at piquet and had a small quarrel about our count. . . .

DECEMBER, 1710

14. . . . I got home, where I arrived about 4 o'clock and found my wife better and the rest of the family pretty well only two people were sick without danger. I came just as my wife was at dinner with Mr. Dunn and his wife and ate some wild duck. In the evening I looked about me a little and found things in pretty good order. In the rest of the evening I read nothing because of the company that was here. I neglected to say my prayers but had good health, good thoughts, and good humor, thank God Almighty. I gave my wife a flourish, notwithstanding she was indisposed. . . .

16. I rose at 8 o'clock, having first rogered my wife. I read a chapter in Hebrew and some Greek in Lucian. I said my prayers and ate boiled milk for breakfast. I danced my dance and I set things in order in my library. Mrs. Dunn took physic and so did several of my people. The child continued out of order and Nurse was troubled with sore eyes. I ate boiled beef for dinner. In the afternoon my wife and I had a quarrel about learning to sing Psalms, in which she was wholly in the wrong, even in the opinion of Mrs. Dunn who was witness of it. . . .

17. . . . Mrs. Dunn read a sermon in Bishop Latimer which was written in a very comic style. Then we sat and talked till 8 o'clock when we went to bed because I intended to rise in the morning before day. My daughter lay with me. . . .

19. I rose about 7 o'clock and read nothing because I prepared to go to Falling Creek. I continued exceedingly out of humor, which was increased by the news of my dam being broken. About 10 o'clock I had a quarrel with my wife about lending my gun to John and about telling me I lied. However I was reconciled before I went away. . . .

JANUARY, 1711

9. . . . In the evening Joe Wilkinson's [wife] came to beg for her husband but I would not speak to her for fear of being persuaded by

her tears which women have always ready at command. At night I read some news and drank a bottle of cider. I said my prayers and had good health, good thoughts, and good humor, thank God Almighty. . . .

11. . . . I quarreled with my wife for being cruel to Suky Brayne, though she deserved it. . . .

22. . . . Redskin Peter pretended to be sick and I put a [branding-iron] on the place he complained of and put the [bit] upon him. The boy called the Doc was sent from Falling Creek with a swollen thigh. My sick people were better, thank God Almighty. . . .

23. . . . My sick people were better, thank God, and Redskin Peter was particularly well and worked as well as anybody. . . .

FEBRUARY, 1711

5. . . . My wife and I quarreled about her pulling her brows. She threatened she would not go to Williamsburg if she might not pull them; I refused, however, and got the better of her, and maintained my authority. . . .

MARCH, 1711

31. I rose about 6 o'clock and read two chapters in Hebrew and some Greek in Lucian. I said my prayers and ate boiled milk for breakfast. My wife told me of the misfortunes of Mrs. Dunn—that her husband had beat her, and that she had complained to Mr. Gee of it, who made Mr. Dunn swear that he would never beat her again; that he threatened to kill her and abused her extremely and told her he would go from her. I was sorry to hear it and told my wife if he did go from her she might come here. I read some news till dinner. I ate boiled beef for dinner. . . .

APRIL, 1711

20. . . . I wrote a letter to my wife in the morning and another in the afternoon. About 9 o'clock I went into court where we sat till past 5 dispensing justice. My case against Joe Wilkinson was called but not tried this day. I went to dine with the Governor and ate roast mutton for dinner. . . .

29. . . . I found a great deal of company with Colonel Ludwell who went away in the evening and we took a walk and romped with the girls at night. I ate some partridge and about 10 went to bed. I said a short prayer and had good health, good thoughts, and good humor,

thank God Almighty. I had wicked inclinations to Mistress Sarah Taylor.

30. . . . [G]ot home about 11 o'clock and found all well, only my wife was melancholy. We took a walk in the garden and pasture. We discovered that by the contrivance of Nurse and Anaka Prue got in at the cellar window and stole some strong beer and cider and wine. I turned Nurse away upon it and punished Anaka. I ate some fish for dinner. In the afternoon I caused Jack and John to be whipped for drinking . . . all last Sunday. In the evening I took a walk about the plantation and found things in good order. . . . The weather was very cold for the season. I gave my wife a powerful flourish and gave her great ecstasy and refreshment. . . .

MAY, 1711

26. . . . My wife continues very sick and peevish in her breeding and uses but little exercise. The wind was east and pretty cold. At night I read in the *Tatler*. . . .

JUNE, 1711

23. My wife was indisposed and was threatened with miscarriage. I again persuaded to bleed but she could not be persuaded to it. It rained again and I believe it was the rain that disposed my wife to that infirmity at this time. . . . I drank some syllabub and gave my daughter some with me. I said my prayers and had good health, good thoughts, and good humor, thank God Almighty. I had a small quarrel with my wife because she would not be bled but neither good words nor bad could prevail against her fear which is very uncontrollable.

24. . . . My wife was a little better, thank God, and gave me hope she would avoid miscarriage. . . .

25. . . . My wife grew worse and after much trial and persuasion was let blood when it was too late. . . . My wife grew very ill which made [me] weep for her. I ate roast mutton for dinner. In the afternoon my wife grew worse and voided a prodigious quantity of blood. I settled some accounts till the evening and then took a walk about the plantation. Before I returned my wife sent for me because she was very weak and soon after I came she was delivered of a false conception and then grew better. I sent for Mrs. Hamlin who came presently. I said my prayers and had good health, good thoughts, and good humor, thank God Almighty. . . .

OCTOBER, 1711

2. . . . About 11 we took horse and rode to Captain Jefferson's where the militia of that side of the river was drawn up. I viewed them a little and because they were not all come I went to Captain Jefferson's house where we drank some persico and then returned into the field where I caused the troops to be exercised by each captain and they performed but indifferently for which I reproved them. . . . [O]ne of the French was drunk and rude to his captain, for which I broke his head in two places. When all was over we went to dine with Captain Jefferson and I ate some roast beef. . . .

4. . . . I went to the militia court. . . . We fined all the Quakers and several others and the Captains agreed to send for trophies. Captain Royall neither came nor returned a list though he had two Quakers in his company I spoke gently to the Quakers which gave them a good opinion of me. . . . I told them they would certainly be fined five times in a year if they did not do as their fellow subjects did. . . .

21. I rose about 6 o'clock and we began to pack up our baggage in order to return. We drank chocolate with the Governor and about 10 o'clock we took leave of the Nottoway town and the Indian boys went away with us that were designed for the College. The Governor made three proposals to the Tuscaroras: that they would join with the English to cut off those Indians that had killed the people of Carolina, that they should have 40 shillings paid for every head they brought in of all those guilty Indians and be paid the price of a slave for all they brought in alive, and that they should send one of the chief men's sons out of every town to the College. . . . About 4 we dined and I ate some boiled beef. My man's horse was lame for which he was let blood. At night I asked a negro girl to kiss me, and when I went to bed I was very cold because I pulled off my clothes after lying in them so long. . . .

NOVEMBER, 1711

13. . . . Mr. Graeme and I went out with bows and arrows and shot at partridge and squirrel which gave us abundance of diversion but we lost some of our arrows. . . . We played at cards and drank some pressed wine and were merry till 10 o'clock. I neglected to say my prayers but rogered my wife, and had good health, good thoughts, and good humor, thank God Almighty. . . .

21. . . . About 2 o'clock we rose and went to dinner and I ate fish. Then Colonel Smith and I played at billiards and I won half a crown. Then we took a walk and afterwards went to the coffeehouse and played at whisk but lost 15 shillings. Then we played at dice and after losing £10 I recovered my money and won £8. . . .

22. . . . The House of Burgesses brought their address of thanks to which the Governor answered them that he would thank them when he saw them act with as little self interest as he had done. About 3 o'clock we went to dinner and I ate some roast goose. Then I took a walk to the Governor's new house with Frank W-l-s and then returned to the coffeehouse where I lost 12 pounds 10 shillings and about 10 o'clock returned home very much out of humor to think myself such a fool. . . .

23. . . . After dinner we went to Colonel Carter's room where we had bowl of punch of French brandy and oranges. We talked very lewdly and were almost drunk and in that condition we went to the coffeehouse and played at dice and I lost £12. We stayed at the coffeehouse till almost 4 o'clock in the morning talking with Major Harrison. Then I went to my lodging, where I committed uncleanness, for which I humbly beg God Almighty's pardon.

24. I rose about 8 o'clock and read a chapter in Hebrew and some Greek in Homer. I said my prayers and ate boiled milk for breakfast. Colonel Carter and several others came to my lodgings to laugh at me for my disorder last night. About 10 I went to the coffeehouse and drank some tea and then we went to the President's and read the law about probate and administration. Then I went to the capitol and danced my dance and wrote in my journal and read Italian. This day I make a solemn resolution never at once to lose more than 50 shillings and to spend less time in gaming, and I beg the God Almighty to give me grace to keep so good a resolution if it be His holy will. . . .

DECEMBER, 1711

30. . . . The weather was very clear and warm so that my wife walked out with Mrs. Dunn and forgot dinner, for which I had a little quarrel with her and another afterwards because I was not willing to let her have a book out of the library. . . .

31. . . . When I returned I was out of humor to find the negroes all at work in our chambers. . . . My wife and I had a terrible quarrel about whipping Eugene while Mr. Mumford was there but she had a mind

to show her authority before company but I would not suffer it, which she took very ill; however for peace sake I made the first advance towards a reconciliation which I obtained with some difficulty and after abundance of crying. However it spoiled the mirth of the evening, but I was not conscious that I was to blame in that quarrel. . . .

JANUARY, 1712

30. . . . I wrote a letter to my wife which I sent home by Tom again with my horse. . . . The Governor went to church but I did not because I heard of it too late but went to the coffeehouse where I played at piquet and won 50 shillings. Then I went to the capitol where I danced my dance and then read some Italian till 3 o'clock and then went to dinner and ate some roast turkey. . . .

FEBRUARY, 1712

5. I rose about 8 o'clock, my wife kept me so long in bed where I rogered her. I read nothing because I put my matters in order. I neglected to say my prayers but ate boiled milk for breakfast. My wife caused several of the people to be whipped for their laziness. . . .

MARCH, 1712

2. I rose about 7 o'clock and read a chapter in Hebrew but no Greek because Mr. Grills was here and I wished to talk with him. I ate boiled milk for breakfast and danced my dance. I reprimanded him for drawing so many notes on me. However I told him if he would let me know his debts I would pay them provided he would let a mulatto of mine that is his apprentice come to work at Falling Creek the last two years of his service, which he agreed. I had a terrible quarrel with my wife concerning Jenny that I took away from her when she was beating her with the tongs. She lifted up her hands to strike me but forbore to do it. She gave me abundance of bad words and endeavored to strangle herself, but I believe in jest only. However after acting a mad woman a long time she was passive again. . . .

APRIL, 1712

12. . . . I was a little out of humor this morning and beat Anaka a little unjustly for which I was sorry afterwards. . . .

17. . . . After dinner I went to Mrs. [Whaley's] where I saw my sister Custis and my brother who is just returned. Here we drank some

tea till the evening and then I took leave and went to the coffeehouse, where I played at cards and won 40 shillings but afterwards I played at dice and lost almost £10. This gave me a resolution to play no more at dice and so I went to my lodgings where I said a short prayer and had good health, good thoughts, and good humor, thank God Almighty. . . .

27. . . . About 3 o'clock we went to dinner and I ate some boiled beef. After dinner we took a walk in the orchard and then because my wife was tired she and I went to loll on the bed. There I rogered her. At night we drank some syllabub. . . .

MAY, 1712

9. . . . My people sheared the sheep today till noon. I ate some boiled mutton for dinner. In the afternoon it began to rain and grew very cold so that all my people went to plant the tobacco and planted 4,000 plants. . . .

10. . . . At night we ate some bread and butter and drank some Lisbon wine. . . .

22. . . . My wife caused Prue to be whipped violently notwithstanding I desired not, which provoked me to have Anaka whipped likewise who had deserved it much more, on which my wife flew into such a passion that she hoped she would be revenged of me. I was moved very much at this but only thanked her for the present lest I should say things foolish in my passion. I wrote more accounts to go to England. My wife was sorry for what she had said and came to ask my pardon and I forgave her in my heart but seemed to resent, that she might be the more sorry for her folly. She ate no dinner nor appeared the whole day. . . . I said my prayers and was reconciled to my wife and gave her a flourish in token of it. I had good health, good thoughts, but was a little out of humor, for which God forgive me.

23. . . . My wife and I were very good friends again. . . .

31. . . . I was out of humor with my wife for her foolish passions, of which she is often guilty, for which God forgive her and make her repent and amend.

Upon a Fart

(1704)

William Byrd II

Gentlest blast of ill concoction,
  Reverse of high-ascending belch:
Th' only stink abhorr'd by statesmen,
  Belov'd and practic'd by the Welch.

Softest notes of inward griping
  Your reverences' finest part,
So fine it needs no pains of wiping
  Except it prove a brewer's fart.

Swiftest ease of cholic pain,
  Vapour from a secret stench,
Is rattled out by th'unbred swain,
  But whisper'd by the bashful wench.

• • •

from THE JOURNAL OF JOHN WOOLMAN

I have often felt a motion of love to leave some hints in writing of my experience of the goodness of God, and now, in the thirty-sixth year of my age, I begin this work. I was born in Northampton, in Burlington County in West Jersey, AD 1720, and before I was seven years old I began to be acquainted with the operations of divine love. Through the care of my parents, I was taught to read near as soon as I was capable of it, and as I went from school one Seventh Day, I remember, while my companions went to play by the way, I went forward out of sight; and sitting down, I read the twenty-second chapter of the Revelations: "He showed me a river of water, clear as crystal, proceeding out of the throne of God and the Lamb, etc." And in reading it my mind was drawn to seek after that pure habitation which I then believed God had prepared for his servants. The place where I sat and the sweetness that attended my mind remain fresh in my memory.

This and the like gracious visitations had that effect upon me, that when boys used ill language it troubled me, and through the continued mercies of God I was preserved from it. The pious instructions of my parents were often fresh in my mind when I happened amongst wicked children, and was of use to me. . . .

I had a dream about the ninth year of my age as follows: I saw the moon rise near the west and run a regular course eastward, so swift that in about a quarter of an hour she reached our meridian, when there descended from her a small cloud on a direct line to the earth, which lighted on a pleasant green about twenty yards from the door of my father's house (in which I thought I stood) and was immediately turned into a beautiful green tree. The moon appeared to run on with equal swiftness and soon set in the east, at which time the sun arose at the place where it commonly does in the summer, and shining with full radiance in a serene air, it appeared as pleasant a morning as ever I saw.

All this time I stood still in the door in an awful frame of mind, and I observed that as heat increased by the rising sun, it wrought so powerfully on the little green tree that the leaves gradually withered; and before noon it appeared dry and dead. There then appeared a being, small of size, full of strength and resolution, moving swift from the north, southward, called a sun worm.

Another thing remarkable in my childhood was that once, going to a neighbor's house, I saw on the way a robin sitting on her nest; and as I came near she went off, but having young ones, flew about and with many cries expressed her concern for them. I stood and threw stones at her, till one striking her, she fell down dead. At first I was pleased with the exploit, but after a few minutes was seized with horror, as having in a sportive way killed an innocent creature while she was careful for her young. I beheld her lying dead and thought those young ones for which she was so careful must now perish for want of their dam to nourish them; and after some painful considerations on the subject, I climbed up the tree, took all the young birds and killed them, supposing that better than to leave them to pine away and die miserably, and believed in this case that Scripture proverb was fulfilled, "The tender mercies of the wicked are cruel." I then went on my errand, but for some hours could think of little else but the cruelties I had committed, and was much troubled.

Thus he whose tender mercies are over all his works hath placed a principle in the human mind which incites to exercise goodness toward every living creature; and this being singly attended to, people become tender-hearted and sympathizing, but being frequently and totally rejected, the mind shuts itself up in a contrary disposition.

• • •

I kept steady to meetings, spent First Days after noon chiefly in reading the Scriptures and other good books, and was early convinced in my mind that true religion consisted in all inward life, wherein the heart doth love and reverence God the Creator and learn to exercise true justice and goodness, not only toward all men but also toward the brute creatures; that as the mind was moved on an inward principle to love God as an invisible, incomprehensible being, on the same principle it was moved to love him in all his manifestations in the visible world; that as by his breath the flame of life was kindled in all animal and sensitive creatures, to say we love God as unseen and at the same time exercise cruelty toward the least creature moving by his life, or by life derived from him, was a contradiction in itself.

I found no narrowness respecting sects and opinions, but believed that sincere, upright-hearted people in every Society who truly loved God were accepted of him.

• • •

All this time I lived with my parents . . . having had schooling pretty well for a planter, I used to improve in winter evenings and other leisure times. And being now in the twenty-first year of my age, a man in much business shopkeeping and baking asked me if I would hire with him to tend shop and keep books. I acquainted my father with the proposal, and after some deliberation it was agreed for me to go.

At home I had lived retired, and now having a prospect of being much in the way of company, I felt frequent and fervent cries in my heart to God, the Father of Mercies, that he would preserve me from all taint and corruption, that in this more public employ I might serve him, my gracious Redeemer, in that humility and self-denial with which I had been in a small degree exercised in a very private life.

The man who employed me furnished a shop in Mount Holly, about five miles from my father's house and six from his own, and there I lived alone and tended his shop. Shortly after my settlement here I was visited by several young people, my former acquaintances, who knew not but vanities would be as agreeable to me now as ever; and at these times I cried to the Lord in secret for wisdom and strength, for I felt myself encompassed with difficulties and had fresh occasion to bewail the follies of time past in contracting a familiarity with a libertine people. And as I had now left my father's house outwardly, I found my Heavenly Father to be merciful to me beyond what I can express.

• • •

I went to meetings in an awful frame of mind and endeavored to be inwardly acquainted with the language of the True Shepherd. And one day being under a strong exercise of spirit, I stood up and said some words in a meeting, but not keeping close to the divine opening, I said more than was required of me; and being soon sensible of my error, I was afflicted in mind some weeks without any light or comfort, even to that degree that I could take satisfaction in nothing. I remembered God and was troubled, and in the depth of my distress he had pity upon me and sent the Comforter. I then felt forgiveness for my offense, and my mind became calm and quiet, being truly thankful to my gracious

Redeemer for his mercies. And after this, feeling the spring of divine love opened and a concern to speak, I said a few words in a meeting, in which I found peace. This . . . taught [me] to wait in silence sometimes many weeks together, until I felt that rise which prepares the creature to stand like a trumpet through which the Lord speaks to his flock.

About the time called Christmas I observed many people from the country and dwellers in town who, resorting to the public houses, spent their time in drinking and vain sports, tending to corrupt one another, on which account I was much troubled. At one house in particular there was much disorder, and I believed it was a duty laid on me to go and speak to the master of that house. I considered I was young and that several elderly Friends in town had opportunity to see these things, and though I would gladly have been excused, yet I could not feel my mind clear.

The exercise was heavy, and as I was reading what the Almighty said to Ezekiel respecting his duty as a watchman, the matter was set home more clearly; and then with prayer and tears I besought the Lord for his assistance, who in loving kindness gave me a resigned heart. Then at a suitable opportunity I went to the public house, and seeing the man amongst a company, I went to him and told him I wanted to speak with him; so we went aside, and there in the fear and dread of the Almighty I expressed to him what rested on my mind, which he took kindly, and afterward showed more regard to me than before. In a few years after, he died middle-aged, and I often thought that had I neglected my duty in that case it would have given me great trouble, and I was humbly thankful to my gracious Father, who had supported me herein.

My employer, having a Negro woman, sold her and directed me to write a bill of sale, the man being waiting who bought her. The thing was sudden, and though the thoughts of writing an instrument of slavery for one of my fellow creatures felt uneasy, yet I remembered I was hired by the year, that it was my master who directed me to do it, and that it was an elderly man, a member of our Society, who bought her; so through weakness I gave way and wrote it, but at the executing it, I was so afflicted in my mind that I said before my master and the Friend that I believed slavekeeping to be a practice inconsistent with the Christian religion. This in some degree abated my uneasiness, yet as often as I reflected seriously upon it I thought I should have been clearer if I had desired to be excused from it as a thing against my conscience, for such it was. And some time after this a young man of our Society spake to me to write an instrument of slavery, he having lately taken a Negro into his house. I told him I was not easy to write it, for though many kept slaves in our Society, as in others, I still believed the practice was not right, and desired to be excused from writing [it]. I spoke to him in good will, and he told me that keeping slaves was not altogether agreeable to his mind, but that the slave being a gift made to his wife, he had accepted of her.

• • •

[S]oon after this he left shopkeeping and we parted. I then wrought at my trade as a tailor, carefully attended meetings for worship and discipline, and found an enlargement of gospel love in my mind and therein a concern to visit Friends in some of the back settlements of Pennsylvania and Virginia.

• • •

Two things were remarkable to me in this journey. First, in regard to my entertainment: When I ate, drank, and lodged free-cost with people who lived in ease on the hard labor of their slaves, I felt uneasy; and as my mind was inward to the Lord, I found, from place to place, this uneasiness return upon me at times through the whole visit. Where the masters bore a good share of the burden and lived frugal, so that their servants were well provided for and their labor moderate, I felt more easy; but where they lived in a costly way and laid heavy burdens on their slaves, my exercise was often great, and I frequently had conversation with them in private concerning it. Secondly, this trade of importing them from their native country being much encouraged amongst them and the white people and their children so generally living without much labor was frequently the subject of my serious thoughts. And I saw in these southern provinces so many vices and corruptions increased by this trade and this way of life that it appeared to me as a dark gloominess hanging over the land; and though now many willingly run into it, yet in future the consequence will be grievous to posterity!

• • •

Scrupling to do writings relative to keeping slaves having been a means of sundry small trials to me, in which I have so evidently felt my own will set aside that I think it good to mention a few of them. Tradesmen and retailers of goods, who depend on their business for a living are naturally inclined to keep the good will of their customers; nor is it a pleasant thing for young men to be under a necessity to question the judgment or honesty of elderly men, and more especially of such who have a fair reputation. Deep-rooted customs, though wrong, are not easily altered, but it is the duty of everyone to be firm in that which they certainly know is right for them. A charitable, benevolent man, well acquainted with a Negro, may, I believe, under some certain circumstances keep him in his family as a servant on no other motives than the Negro's good; but man, as man, knows not what shall be after him, nor hath he any assurance that his children will attain to that perfection in wisdom and goodness necessary in every absolute governor. Hence it is clear to me that I ought not to be the scribe where wills are drawn in which some children are made absolute masters over others during life.

About this time an ancient man of good esteem in the neighborhood came to my house to get his will wrote. He had young Negroes, and I asking him privately how he purposed to dispose of them, he told me. I then said, "I cannot write thy will without breaking my own peace," and respectfully gave him my reasons for it. He signified that he had a choice that I should have wrote it, but as I could not consistent with my conscience, he did not desire it, and so he got it wrote by some other person. And a few years after, there being great alterations in his family, he came again to get me to write his will. His Negroes were yet young, and his son, to whom he intended to give them, was since he first spoke to me, from a libertine become a sober young man; and he supposed that I would have been free on that account to write it. We had much friendly talk on the subject and then deferred it, and a few days after, he came again and directed their freedom, and so I wrote his will.

•   •   •

Until the year 1756 I continued to retail goods, besides following my trade as a tailor, about which time I grew uneasy on account of my business growing too cumbersome. I began with selling trimmings for garments and from thence proceeded to sell clothes and linens, and at length having got a considerable shop of goods, my trade increased every year and the road to large business appeared open; but I felt a stop in my mind.

Through the mercies of the Almighty I had in a good degree learned to be content with a plain way of living. I had but a small family, that on serious consideration I believed Truth did not require me to engage in much cumbrous affairs. It had been my general practice to buy and sell things really useful. Things that served chiefly to please the vain mind in people I was not easy to trade in, seldom did it, and whenever I did I found it weaken me as a Christian.

The increase of business became my burden, for though my natural inclination was toward merchandise, yet I believed Truth required me to live more free from outward cumbers, and there was now a strife in my mind between the two; and in this exercise my prayers were put up to the Lord, who graciously heard me and gave me a heart resigned to his holy will. Then I lessened my outward business, and as I had opportunity, told my customers of my intentions that they might consider what shop to turn to, and so in a while wholly laid down merchandise, following my trade as a tailor, myself only, having no apprentice. I also had a nursery of apple trees, in which I employed some of my time hoeing, grafting, trimming, and inoculating.

* * *

The 13th day, 2nd month 1757. Being then in good health and abroad with Friends visiting families, I lodged at a Friend's house in Burlington, and going to bed about the time usual with me, I woke in the night and my meditations as I lay were on the goodness and mercy of the Lord, in a sense whereof my heart was contrite. After this I went to sleep again, and sleeping a short time I awoke. It was yet dark and no appearance of day nor moonshine, and as I opened my eyes I saw a light in my chamber at the apparent distance of five feet, about nine inches diameter, of a clear, easy brightness and near the center the most radiant. As I lay still without any surprise looking upon it, words were spoken to my inward ear which filled my whole inward man. They were not the effect of thought nor any conclusion in relation to the appearance, but as the language of the Holy One spoken in my mind. The words were, "Certain Evidence of Divine Truth," and were again repeated exactly in the same manner, whereupon the light disappeared.

* * *

[1757] We crossed the rivers Potomac and Rappahannock and lodged at Port Royal. And on the way, we happening in company with a colonel of the militia who appeared to be a thoughtful man, I took occasion to remark on the odds in general betwixt a people used to labor moderately for their living, training up their children in frugality and business, and those who live on the labor of slaves, the former in my view being the most happy life; with which he concurred and mentioned the trouble arising from the untoward, slothful disposition of the Negroes, adding that one of our laborers would do as much in a day as two of their slaves. I replied that free men whose minds were properly on their business found a satisfaction in improving, cultivating, and providing for their families, but Negroes, laboring to support others who claim them as their property and expecting nothing but slavery during life, had not the like inducement to be industrious.

After some further conversation I said that men having power too often misapplied it; that though we made slaves of the Negroes and the Turks made slaves of the Christians, I, however, believed that liberty was the natural right of all men equally, which he did not deny, but said the lives of the Negroes were so wretched in their own country that many of them lived better here than there. I only said, "There's great odds in regard to us on what principle we act." And so the conversation on that subject ended. And I may here add that another person some time afterward mentioned the wretchedness of the Negroes occasioned by their intestine wars as an argument in favor of our fetching them away for slaves, to which I then replied: "If compassion on the Africans in regard to their domestic troubles were the real motives of our purchasing them, that spirit of tenderness being attended to would incite us to use them kindly, among us; and as they are human creatures, whose souls are as precious as ours and who may receive the same help and comfort from the Holy Scriptures as we do, we could not omit suitable endeavors to instruct them therein. But while we manifest by our conduct that our views in purchasing them are to advance ourselves, and while our buying captives taken in war animates those parties to push on that war and increase desolations amongst them, to say they live unhappily in Africa is far from being an argument in our favour."

And I further said, "The present circumstances of these provinces to me appears difficult, that the slaves look like a burdensome stone to such who burden themselves with them, and that if the white people retain a resolution to prefer their outward prospects of gain to all other considerations and do not act conscientiously toward them as fellow creatures, I believe that burden will grow heavier and heavier till times change in a way disagreeable to us"—at which the person appeared very serious and owned that in considering their condition

and the manner of their treatment in these provinces, he had sometimes thought it might be just in the Almighty to so order it.

•   •   •

In my youth I was used to hard labour, and though I was middling
healthy, yet my nature was not fitted to endure so much as many others. Being often weary with it, I was prepared to sympathise with those
whose circumstances in life, as free men, required constant labour to
answer the demands of their creditors, as well as with others under
oppression in the uneasiness of body which I have many times felt by
too much labour, not as a forced but a voluntary oppression, I have
often been excited to think on the original cause of that oppression
which is imposed on many in the world. The latter part of the time
wherein I laboured on our plantation, my heart, through the fresh visitations of heavenly love, being often tender, and my leisure time being frequently spent in reading the life and doctrines of our blessed
Redeemer, the account of the sufferings of martyrs, and the history of
the first rise of our Society, a belief was gradually settled in my mind,
that if such as had great estates generally lived in that humility and
plainness which belong to a Christian life, and laid much easier rents
and interests on their lands and moneys, and thus led the way to a right
use of things, so great a number of people might be employed in things
useful, that labour both for men and other creatures would need to be
no more than an agreeable employ, and divers branches of business,
which serve chiefly to please the natural inclinations of our minds, and
which at present seem necessary to circulate that wealth which some
gather, might, in this way of pure wisdom, be discontinued. As I have
thus considered these things, a query at times hath arisen: Do I, in all
my proceedings, keep to that use of things which is agreeable to universal righteousness? And then there hath some degree of sadness at
times come over me, because I accustomed myself to some things
which have occasioned more labour than I believe Divine Wisdom
intended for us.

From my early acquaintance with truth I have often felt an inward
distress, occasioned by the striving of a spirit in me against the operation of the heavenly principle; and in this state I have been afflicted
with a sense of my own wretchedness, and in a mourning condition
have felt earnest longings for that Divine help which brings the soul
into true liberty. Sometimes on retiring into private places, the spirit
of supplication hath been given me, and under a heavenly covering I

have asked my gracious Father to give me a heart in all things resigned to the direction of His wisdom; in uttering language like this, the thought of my wearing hats and garments dyed with a dye injurious to them, has made lasting impression on me.

In visiting people of note in the Society who had slaves, and labouring with them in brotherly love on that account, I have seen, and the sight has affected me, that a conformity to some customs distinguishable from pure wisdom has entangled many, and that the desire of gain to support these customs has greatly opposed the work of truth. Sometimes when the prospect of the work before me has been such that in bowedness of spirit I have been drawn into retired places, and have besought the Lord with tears that He would take me wholly under His direction, and show me the way in which I ought to walk, it hath revived with strength of conviction that if I would be His faithful servant I must in all things attend to His wisdom, and be teachable; and so cease from all customs contrary thereto, however used amongst religious people.

As He is the perfection of power, of wisdom, and of goodness, so I believe He hath provided that so much labour shall be necessary for men's support in this world as would, being rightly divided, be a suitable employment of their time; and that we cannot go into superfluities, nor grasp after wealth in a way contrary to His wisdom, without having connection with some degree of oppression and with that spirit which leads to self-exaltation and strife, and which frequently brings calamities on countries by parties contending about their claims.

• • •

Having for many years felt love in my heart towards the natives of this land who dwell far back in the wilderness, whose ancestors were the owners and possessors of the country where we dwell, and who for a very small consideration assigned their inheritance to us, and being at Philadelphia in the eighth month 1761, on a visit to some Friends who had slaves, I fell in company with some of those natives who lived on the east branch of the river Susquehanna. . . . I believed some of them were measurably acquainted with that Divine power which subjects the rough and froward will of the creature. At times I felt inward drawings toward a visit to that place.

• • •

I was brought inwardly to commit myself to the Lord, to be disposed of as He saw good. So I took leave of my family and neighbours

in much bowedness of spirit. . . . [W]e met with an Indian-trader lately come from Wyoming. In conversation with him I perceived that
many white people do often sell rum to the Indians, which I believe is
a great evil. In the first place, they being thereby deprived of the use
of reason, and, their spirits violently agitated, quarrels often arise which
end in mischief, and the bitterness and resentments occasioned hereby are frequently of long continuance. Again, their skins and furs,
gotten through much fatigue and hard travels in hunting, with which
they intended to buy clothing, when they begin to be intoxicated they
often sell at a low rate for more rum; and afterwards when they suffer
for want of the necessaries of life are angry with those who for the sake
of gain, took advantage of their weakness. Their chiefs have often complained of this in their treaties with the English. Where cunning people pass counterfeits and impose on others that which is good for
nothing, it is considered as wickedness; but for the sake of gain to sell
that to people which we know does them harm and which often works
their ruin manifests a hardened and corrupt heart and is an evil which
demands the care of all true lovers of virtue in endeavouring to suppress. While my mind this evening was thus employed, I also remembered that the people on the frontier among whom this evil is too
common, are often poor people, who venture to the outside of a colony that they may live more independent of the wealthy, who often set
high rents on their land. I was renewedly confirmed in a belief, that if
all our inhabitants lived according to pure wisdom, labouring to promote universal love and righteousness, and ceased from every inordinate desire after wealth and from all customs which are tinctured with
luxury, the way would be easy for our inhabitants, though much more
numerous than at present, to live comfortable on honest employments,
without having that temptation they are often under of being drawn
into schemes to make settlements on lands which have not been honestly purchased of the Indians, or of applying to that wicked practice
of selling rum to them.

●　　●　　●

Near our tent, on the sides of large trees peeled for that purpose
were various representations of men going to and returning from the
wars, and of some being killed in battle. This was a path heretofore
used by warriors, and as I walked about viewing those Indian histo-
ries, which were painted mostly in red or black, and thinking on the
innumerable afflictions which the proud, fierce spirit produceth in the

world, thinking on the toils and fatigues of warriors in travelling over mountains and deserts; on their miseries and distresses when wounded far from home by their enemies; of their bruises and great weariness in chasing one another over the rocks and mountains; and of their restless, unquiet state of mind who live in this spirit, and of the hatred which mutually grows up in the minds of the children of those nations engaged in war with each other—the desire to cherish the spirit of love and peace amongst these people arose very fresh in me.

•   •   •

. . . [A]s I rode over the barren hills my meditations were on the alterations in the circumstances of the natives of this land since the coming of the English. The lands near the sea are conveniently situated for fishing; the lands near the rivers, where the tides flow, and some above, are in many places fertile, and not mountainous, while the running of the tides makes passing up and down easy with any kind of traffic. Those natives have in some places, for trifling considerations, sold their inheritance so favourably situated, and in other places been driven back by superior force; their way of clothing themselves is also altered from what it was, and they being far remote from us have to pass over mountains, swamps, and barren deserts, where travelling is very troublesome in bringing their furs and skins to trade with us. By the extending of English settlements, and partly by the increase of English hunters, the wild beasts which the natives chiefly depend on for subsistence are not so plentiful as they were, and people too often, for the sake of gain, induce them to waste their skins and furs in purchasing a liquor which tends to the ruin of them and their families.

My own will and desires were now very much broken, and my heart with much earnestness turned to the Lord, to whom alone I looked for help in the dangers before me. I had a prospect of the English along the coast for upward of nine hundred miles where I have travelled, and the favourable situation of the English and the difficulties attending the natives and the slaves amongst us in many places were open before me. A weighty and heavenly care came over my mind, and love filled my heart toward all mankind, in which I felt a strong engagement that we might be faithful to the Lord while His mercies are yet extended to us, and so attend to pure universal righteousness as to give no just cause of offense to the gentiles who do not profess Christianity, whether they be the blacks from Africa, or the native inhabitants of this continent. Here I was led into a close and laborious inquiry whether

I, as an individual, kept clear from all things which tended to stir up or were connected with wars, either in this land or in Africa; my heart was deeply concerned that in future I might in all things keep steadily to the pure truth, and live and walk in the plainness and simplicity of a sincere follower of Christ. In this lonely journey I did greatly bewail the spreading of a wrong spirit, believing that the prosperous, convenient situation of the English requires a constant attention to Divine love and wisdom, in order to guide and support us in a way answerable to the will of that good, gracious, and Almighty Being who hath an equal regard to all mankind. And here luxury and covetousness, with the numerous oppressions and other evils attending them, appeared very afflicting to me, and I felt in that which is immutable that the seeds of great calamity and desolation are sown and growing fast on this continent. Nor have I words sufficient to set forth the longing I then felt, that we who are placed along the coast, and have tasted the love and goodness of God, might arise in His strength and like faithful messengers labour to check the growth of these seeds, that they may not ripen to the ruin of our posterity.

CHAPTER 4

This New Man

INTRODUCTION

BENJAMIN FRANKLIN, 1706–1790
from The Way to Wealth (1758),
from The Autobiography of Benjamin Franklin (1791),
Advice to a Friend (1745), and The Speech of
Miss Polly Baker (1747)

HECTOR ST. JEAN DE CRÈVECOEUR, 1735–1813
from Letters of an American Farmer (1782)

Captain John Smith and others had argued that the American colonies could provide both work and a social chance for poor people who had none in Europe. But only in the eighteenth century did the idea develop that the broader opportunities might create a new sort of person. Benjamin Franklin, with his achievements in business, politics, diplomacy, science, invention, wit, literature and philanthropy, became the exemplar of this new American genius. As always, Franklin carefully and laughingly cultivated his image as the coonskin-capped product of a more natural and non-hierarchical society. Frenchman Hector St. Jean de Crèvecoeur, who became a New York citizen about ten years before the Revolution, wrote in France the book that first defined the idea of a new American social type, one vastly superior to his European peers, because he developed in a fostering rather than deforming socioeconomic climate.

Franklin owed much to his Puritan Boston background and to his Quaker Philadelphia home; like Woolman, he kept his shop until it kept him, and then he devoted himself to varied good works, intellectual and social. Yet his deism and humane scepticism led to rich satire on religious seriousness such as his project for achieving moral perfection, his worldly wise "moral" essays, his best selling secular "sermon" of Father Abraham, and his rechristening of sin as "errata." The *Auto-biography* was a success story, but one grounded in Franklin's enjoyment of the manipulative techniques useful in a society where people could become who they said, and who their neighbors agreed, they were. Crèvecoeur wrote his letters pretending to be a Pennsylvania farmer, living in what was judged "the best poor man's country." While first defining a glowing "American dream," he showed deep worry about the potential effects of war, of the frontier, of widescale slave-holding and of other tensions within it.

CONSIDERATIONS

- How similar are the two writers' pictures of the possibilities of American life? How do they relate to and differ from the pictures of earlier writers?

- What are the "democratic virtues" both men stress? Is "getting ahead" their primary value? How committed is Franklin to his welfare and to the common good?

- How does Franklin use humor in his account? What ties does he have to his Puritan origins?

- Are we taxed more by our vanities than by our taxes? Is Crèvecoeur right that more egalitarian socioeconomic circumstances produce a new kind of person?

- How important is possession of property to democratic institutions and human dignity?

from THE WAY TO WEALTH

(1758)

Benjamin Franklin

Courteous Reader,

I have heard that nothing gives an Author so great Pleasure, as to find his Words respectfully quoted by other learned Authors. This Pleasure I have seldom enjoyed; for tho' I have been, if I may say it without Vanity, an *eminent Author* of Almanacks annually now a full Quarter of a Century, my Brother Authors in the same Way, for what Reason I know not, have ever been very sparing in their Applauses; and no other Author has taken the least Notice of me, so that did not my Writings produce me some solid *Pudding*, the great Deficiency of *Praise* would have quite discouraged me.

I concluded at length, that the People were the best judges of my Merit; for they buy my Works; and besides, in my Rambles, where I am not personally known, I have frequently heard one or other of my Adages repeated, with, *as Poor Richard says*, at the End on't; this gave me some Satisfaction, as it showed not only that my Instructions were regarded, but discovered likewise some Respect for my Authority; and I own, that to encourage the Practice of remembering and repeating those wise Sentences, I have sometimes *quoted myself* with great Gravity.

Judge then how much I must have been gratified by an Incident I am going to relate to you. I stopt my Horse lately where a great Number of People were collected at a Vendue of Merchant Goods. The Hour of Sale not being come, they were conversing on the Badness of the Times, and one of the Company call'd to a plain clean old Man, with white Locks, *Pray, Father Abraham, what think you of the Times? Won't these heavy Taxes quite ruin the Country? How shall we be ever able to pay them? What would you advise us to?*—Father Abraham stood up, and reply'd, If you'd have my Advice, I'll give it you in short, for a *Word to the Wise is enough,* and *many Words won't fill a Bushel, as Poor Richard says.* They join'd in desiring him to speak his Mind, and gathering round him, he proceeded as follows;

"Friends, says he, and Neighbours, the Taxes are indeed very heavy, and if those laid on by the Government were the only Ones we had to pay, we might more easily discharge them; but we have many others, and much more grievous to some of us. We are taxed twice as much by our *Idleness*, three times as much by our *Pride*, and four times as much by our *Folly*, and from these Taxes the Commissioners cannot ease or deliver us by allowing an Abatement. However let us hearken to good Advice, and something may be done for us; *God helps them that help themselves*, as Poor Richard says, in his Almanack of 1733.

It would be thought a hard Government that should tax its People one tenth Part of their *Time*, to be employed in its Service. But *Idleness* taxes many of us much more, if we reckon all that is spent in absolute *Sloth*, or doing of nothing, with that which is spent in idle Employment or Amusements, that amount to nothing. *Sloth*, by bringing on Diseases, absolutely shortens Life. *Sloth, like Rust, consumes faster than Labour wears, while the used Key is always bright*, as Poor Richard says. But *dost thou love Life, then do not squander Time, for that's the Stuff Life is made of*, as Poor Richard says. How much more than is necessary do we spend in Sleep! forgetting that *The sleeping Fox catches no Poultry*, and that *there will be sleeping enough in the Grave*, as Poor Richard says. If Time be of all Things the most precious, *wasting Time* must be, as Poor Richard says, *the greatest Prodigality*, since, as he elsewhere tells us, *Lost Time is never found again*; and what we call *Time-enough, always proves little enough*: Let us then be up and be doing, and doing to the Purpose; so by Diligence shall we do more with less Perplexity. *Sloth makes all Things difficult, but Industry all easy*, as Poor Richard says; and *He that riseth late, must trot all Day, and shall scarce overtake his Business at Night*. While *Laziness travels so slowly, that Poverty soon overtakes him*, as we read in Poor Richard, who adds, *Drive thy Business, let not that drive thee*; and *Early to Bed, and early to rise, makes a Man healthy, wealthy and wise*.

So what signifies *wishing* and *hoping* for better Times. We may make these Times better if we bestir ourselves. *Industry need not wish*, as Poor Richard says, and *He that lives upon Hope will die fasting. There are no Gains, without Pains*.

• • •

And again, *Three Removes is as bad as a Fire;* and again, *Keep thy Shop, and thy Shop will keep thee*, and again, *If you would have your Business done, go; if not, send*. And again,

> *He that by the Plough would thrive,*
>
> *Himself must either hold or drive.*

And again, *The Eye of a Master will do more Work than both his Hands;* and again, *Want of Care does us more Damage than Want of Knowledge;* and again, *Not to oversee Workmen is to leave them your Purse open.* Trusting too much to others Care is the Ruin of many; for, as the Almanack says, *In the Affairs of this World, Men are saved, not by Faith, but by the Want of it.*

     •   •   •

> *Many Estates are spent in the Getting,*
>
> *Since Women for Tea forsook Spinning and Knitting,*
>
> *And Men for Punch forsook Hewing and Splitting.*

If you would be wealthy, says he, in another Almanack, *think of Saving as well as of Getting: The Indies have not made Spain rich, because her* Outgoes *are greater than her* Incomes. Away then with your expensive Follies, and you will not have so much Cause to complain of hard Times, heavy Taxes, and chargeable Families; for, as Poor Dick says,

> *Women and Wine, Game and Deceit,*
>
> *Make the Wealth small, and the Wants great.*

And farther, *What maintains one Vice, would bring up two Children.* You may think perhaps, That a *little* Tea, or a *little* Punch now and then, Diet a *little* more costly, Clothes a *little* finer, and a *little* Entertainment now and then, can be no *great* Matter; but remember what Poor Richard says, *Many a Little makes a Mickle;* and farther, *Beware of little Expences; a small Leak will sink a great Ship;* and again, *Who Dainties love, shall Beggars prove;* and moreover, *Fools make Feasts, and wise Men eat them.*

     •   •   •

And now to conclude, *Experience keeps a dear School, but Fools will learn in no other, and scarce in that;* for it is true, *we may give Advice, but we cannot give Conduct,* as Poor Richard says: However, remember this, *They that won't be counselled, can't be helped,* as Poor Richard says: And farther, *That if you will not hear Reason, she'll surely rap your Knuckles.*

Thus the old Gentleman ended his Harangue. The People heard it, and approved the Doctrine, and immediately practised the contrary, just as if it had been a common Sermon; for the Vendue opened, and they began to buy extravagantly, notwithstanding all his Cautions, and their own Fear of Taxes. I found the good Man had thoroughly studied my Almanacks, and digested all I had dropt on those Topicks during the Course of Five-and-twenty Years. The frequent Mention he made of me must have tired any one else, but my Vanity was wonderfully delighted with it, though I was conscious that not a tenth Part of the Wisdom was my own which he ascribed to me, but rather the *Gleanings* I had made of the Sense of all Ages and Nations. However, I resolved to be the better for the Echo of it; and though I had at first determined to buy Stuff for a new Coat, I went away resolved to wear my old One a little longer. *Reader*, if thou wilt do the same, thy Profit will be as great as mine.

from THE AUTOBIOGRAPHY
OF BENJAMIN FRANKLIN

PART ONE

Twyford, at the Bishop of St. Asaph's, 1771

Dear Son,

I have ever had a Pleasure in obtaining any little Anecdotes of my Ancestors. You may remember the Enquiries I made among the Remains of my Relations when you were with me in England; and the Journey I took for that purpose. Now imagining it may be equally agreeable to you to know the Circumstances of *my* Life, many of which you are yet unacquainted with; and expecting a Week's uninterrupted Leisure in my present Country Retirement, I sit down to write them for you. To which I have besides some other Inducements. Having emerg'd from the Poverty and Obscurity in which I was born and bred, to a State of Affluence and some Degree of Reputation in the World, and having gone so far thro' Life with a considerable Share of Felicity, the conducing Means I made use of, which, with the Blessing of God, so well succeeded, my Posterity may like to know, as they may find some of them suitable to their own Situations, and therefore fit to be imitated. That Felicity, when I reflected on it, has induc'd me sometimes to say, that were it offer'd to my Choice, I should have no Objection to a Repetition of the same Life from its Beginning, only asking the Advantage Authors have in a second Edition to correct some Faults of the first. So would I if I might, besides corr[ectin]g the Faults, change some sinister Accidents and Events of it for others more favourable, but tho' this were deny'd, I should still accept the Offer. However, since such a Repetition is not to be expected, the next Thing most like living one's Life over again, seems to be a *Recollection* of that Life; and to make that Recollection as durable as possible, the putting it down in Writing. Hereby, too, I shall indulge the Inclination so natural in old Men, to be talking of themselves and their own past Actions, and I shall indulge it, without being troublesome to others who thro' respect to Age might think themselves oblig'd to give me a Hearing, since this may be read or not as any one pleases. And lastly, (I may as well confess it, since my Denial of it will be believ'd by no body) perhaps I shall a good deal gratify my own *Vanity.* Indeed I scarce ever heard or saw the introductory Words, *Without Vanity I may say,* &c. but some vain thing immediately follow'd. Most People dislike Vanity in others whatever Share they have of it themselves, but I give it fair Quarter wherever I meet with it, being persuaded that it is often productive of Good to the Possessor and to others that are within his Sphere of Action: And therefore in many Cases it would not be quite absurd if a Man were to thank God for his Vanity among the other Comforts of Life.

And now I speak of thanking God, I desire with all Humility to acknowledge, that I owe the mention'd Happiness of my past Life to his kind Providence, which led me to the Means I us'd and gave them Success. My Belief of this, induces me to *hope,* tho' I must not *presume,* that the same Goodness will still be exercis'd towards me in continuing that Happiness, or in enabling me to bear a fatal Reverse, which I may experience as others have done, the Complexion of my future Fortune being known to him only: and in whose Power it is to bless to us even our Afflictions.

• • •

My elder Brothers were all put Apprentices to different Trades. I was put to the Grammar School at Eight Years of Age, my Father intending to devote me as the Tithe of his Sons to the Service of the Church. My early Readiness in learning to read (which must have been very early, as I do not remember when I could not read) and the Opinion of all his Friends that I should certainly make a good Scholar, encourag'd him in this Purpose of his. My Uncle Benjamin too approv'd of it, and propos'd to give me all his Shorthand Volumes of Sermons I suppose as a Stock to set up with, if I would learn his Character. I continu'd however at the Grammar School not quite one Year, tho' in that time I had risen gradually from the Middle of the Class of that Year to be the Head of it, and farther was remov'd into the next Class above it, in order to go with that into the third at the End of the Year. But my Father in the mean time, from a View of the Expence of a College Education which, having so large a Family, he could not well afford, and the mean Living many so educated were afterwards able to obtain, Reasons that he gave to his Friends in my Hearing, altered his first Intention, took me from the Grammar School, and set me to a School for Writing and Arithmetic kept by a then famous Man, Mr. Geo. Brownell, very successful in his Profession generally, and that by mild encouraging Methods. Under him I acquired fair Writing pretty soon, but I fail'd in the Arithmetic, and made no Progress in it.

At Ten Years old, I was taken home to assist my Father in his Business, which was that of a Tallow Chandler and Sope-Boiler. A Business he was not bred to, but had assumed on his Arrival in New England and on finding his Dying Trade would not maintain his Family, being in little Request. Accordingly I was employed in cutting Wick for the Candles, filling the Dipping Mold, and the Molds for cast Candles, attending the Shop, going of Errands, &c. I dislik'd the Trade and had a strong Inclination for the Sea; but my Father declar'd against it; however, living near the Water, I was much in and about it, learnt early to swim well, and to manage Boats, and when in a Boat or Canoe with other Boys I was commonly allow'd to govern, especially in any case of Difficulty; and upon other Occasions I was generally a Leader among the Boys, and sometimes led them into Scrapes, of which I will mention one Instance, as it shows an early projecting public Spirit, tho' not then justly conducted. There was a Salt Marsh that bounded part of the Mill Pond, on the Edge of which at Highwater, we us'd to stand to fish for Minews. By much Trampling, we had made it a mere Quagmire. My Proposal was to build a Wharf there fit for us to stand upon, and I show'd my Comrades a large Heap of Stones which were intended for a new House near the Marsh, and which would very well suit our Purpose. Accordingly in the Evening when the Workmen were gone, I assembled a Number of my Playfellows, and working with them diligently like so many Emmets, sometimes two or three to a Stone, we brought them all away and built our little Wharff. The next Morning the Workmen were surpriz'd at Missing the Stones; which were found in our Wharff; Enquiry was made after the Removers; we were discovered and complain'd of; several of us were corrected by our Fathers; and tho' I pleaded the Usefulness of the Work, mine convinc'd me that nothing was useful which was not honest.

I think you may like to know Something of his Person and Character. He had an excellent Constitution of Body, was of middle Stature, but well set and very strong. He was ingenious, could draw prettily, was skill'd a little in Music and had a clear pleasing Voice, so that when he play'd Psalm Tunes on his Violin and sung withal as he sometimes did in an Evening after the Business of the Day was over, it was extreamly agreable to hear. He had a mechanical Genius too, and on occasion was very handy in the Use of other Tradesmen's Tools. But his great Excellence lay in a sound Understanding, and solid Judgment in prudential Matters, both in private and publick Affairs. In the latter indeed he was never employed, the numerous Family he had to educate and the straitness of his Circumstances, keeping him close to his Trade, but I remember well his being frequently visited by leading People, who consulted him for his Opinion in Affairs of the Town or of the Church he belong'd to and show'd a good deal of Respect for his Judgment and Advice. He was also much consulted by private Persons about their Affairs when any Difficulty occur'd, and frequently chosen an Arbitrator between contending Parties. At his Table he lik'd to have as often as he could, some sensible Friend or Neighbour, to converse with, and always took care to start some ingenious or useful Topic for Discourse, which might tend to improve the Minds of his Children. By this means he turn'd our Attention to what was good, just, and prudent in the Conduct of Life; and little or no Notice was ever taken of what related to the Victuals on the Table, whether it was well or ill drest, in or out of season, of good or bad flavour, preferable or inferior to this or that other thing of the kind; so that I was bro't up in such a perfect Inattention to those Matters as to be quite Indifferent what kind of Food was set before me; and so unobservant of it, that to this Day, if I am ask'd I can scarce tell, a few Hours after Dinner, what I din'd upon. This has been a Convenience to me in travelling, where my Companions have been sometimes very unhappy for want of a suitable Gratification of their more delicate because better instructed Tastes and Appetites.

My Mother had likewise an excellent Constitution. She suckled all her 10 Children. I never knew either my Father or Mother to have any Sickness but that of which they dy'd, he at 89 and she at 85 Years of age. They lie buried together at Boston, where I some Years since plac'd a Marble stone over their Grave with this Inscription

Josiah Franklin

And Abiah his Wife

Lie here interred.

They lived lovingly together in Wedlock

Fifty-five Years.

Without an Estate or any gainful Employment,

By constant labour and Industry,
With God's Blessing,
They maintained a large Family
Comfortably;
And brought up thirteen Children,
And seven Grand Children
Reputably.
From this Instance, Reader,
Be encouraged to Diligence in thy Calling,
And distrust not Providence.
He was a pious & prudent Man,
She a discreet and virtuous Woman.
Their youngest Son,
In filial Regard to their Memory,
Places this Stone.
J.F. born 1655—Died 1744. Ætat—89
A.F. born 1667—died 1752—85

By my rambling Digressions I perceive my self to be grown old. I us'd to write more methodically. But one does not dress for private Company as for a publick Ball. 'Tis perhaps only Negligence.

To return, I continu'd thus employ'd in my Father's Business for two Years, that is till I was 12 Years old; and my Brother John who was bred to that Business having left my Father, married and set up for himself at Rhodeisland, there was all Appearance that I was destin'd to supply his Place and be a Tallow Chandler. But my Dislike to the Trade continuing, my Father was under Apprehensions that if he did not find one for me more agreable, I should break away and get to Sea, as his Son Josiah had done to his great Vexation. He therefore sometimes took me to walk with him, and see Joiners, Bricklayers, Turners, Braziers &c. at their Work, that he might observe my Inclination, and endeavour to fix it on some Trade or other on Land. It has ever since been a Pleasure to me to see good Workmen handle their Tools; and it has been useful to me, having learnt so much by it, as to be able to do little Jobs my self in my House, when a Workman could not readily be got; and to construct little Machines for my Experiments while the intention of making the Experiment was fresh and warm in my Mind. My Father at last fix'd upon the Cutler's Trade, and my Uncle Benjamin's Son Samuel who was bred to that Business in London being about that time establish'd in Boston, I was sent to be with him some time on liking. But his Expectations of a Fee with me displeasing my Father, I was taken home again.

From a Child I was fond of Reading, and all the little Money that came into my Hands was ever laid out in Books. Pleas'd with the Pilgrim's Progress, my first Collection was of John Bunyan's Works, in separate little Volumes. I afterwards sold them to enable me to buy R. Burton's Historical Collections; they were small Chapmen's books and cheap 40 or 50 in all. My Father's little Library consisted chiefly of Books in polemic Divinity, most of which I read, and have since often regretted, that at a time when I had such a Thirst for Knowledge, more proper Books had not fallen in my Way, since it was now resolv'd I should not be a Clergyman. Plutarch's Lives there was, in which I read abundantly, and I still think that time spent to great Advantage. There was also a Book of Defoe's, called an Essay on Projects, and another of Dr. Mather's, call'd Essays to do Good which perhaps gave me a Turn of Thinking that had an Influence on some of the principal future Events of my Life.

This Bookish Inclination at length determin'd my Father to make me a Printer, tho' he had already one Son, (James) of that Profession. In 1717 my Brother James return'd from England with a Press and Letters to set up his Business in Boston. I lik'd it much better than that of my Father, but still had a Hankering for the Sea. To prevent the apprehended Effect of such an Inclination, my Father was impatient to have me bound to my Brother. I stood out some time, but at last was persuaded and signed the Indentures, when I was yet but 12 Years old. I was to serve as an Apprentice till I was 21 Years of Age, only I was to be allow'd Journeyman's Wages during the last Year. In a little time I made great Proficiency in the Business, and became a useful Hand to my Brother. I now had Access to better Books. An Acquaintance with the Apprentices of Booksellers, enabled me sometimes to borrow a small one, which I was careful to return soon and clean. Often I sat up in my Room reading the greatest Part of the Night, when the Book was borrow'd in the Evening and to be return'd early in the Morning lest it should be miss'd or wanted. And after some time an ingenious Tradesman Mr. Matthew Adams who had a pretty Collection of Books, and who frequented our Printing House, took Notice of me, invited me to his Library, and very kindly lent me such Books as I chose to read. I now took a Fancy to Poetry, and made some little Pieces. My

Brother, thinking it might turn to account encourag'd me, and put me on composing two occasional Ballads. One was called the *Light House Tragedy,* and contain'd an Account of the drowning of Capt. Worthilake with his Two Daughters; the other was a Sailor Song on the Taking of *Teach* or Blackbeard the Pirate. They were wretched Stuff, in the Grubstreet Ballad Stile, and when they were printed he sent me about the Town to sell them. The first sold wonderfully, the Event being recent, having made a great Noise. This flatter'd my Vanity. But my Father discourag'd me, by ridiculing my Performances, and telling me Verse-makers were generally Beggars; so I escap'd being a Poet, most probably a very bad one. But as Prose Writing has been of great Use to me in the Course of my Life, and was a principal Means of my Advancement, I shall tell you how in such a Situation I acquir'd what little Ability I have in that Way.

There was another Bookish Lad in the Town, John Collins by Name, with whom I was intimately acquainted. We sometimes disputed, and very fond we were of Argument, and very desirous of confuting one another. Which disputacious Turn, by the way, is apt to become a very bad Habit, making People often extreamly disagreable in Company, by the Contradiction that is necessary to bring it into Practice, and thence, besides souring and spoiling the Conversation, is productive of Disgusts and perhaps Enmities where you may have occasion for Friendship. I had caught it by reading my Father's Books of Dispute about Religion. Persons of good Sense, I have since observ'd, seldom fall into it, except Lawyers, University Men, and Men of all Sorts that have been bred at Edinborough. A Question was once some how or other started between Collins and me, of the Propriety of educating the Female Sex in Learning, and their Abilities for Study. He was of Opinion that it was improper; and that they were naturally unequal to it. I took the contrary Side, perhaps a little for Dispute sake. He was naturally more eloquent, had a ready Plenty of Words, and sometimes as I thought bore me down more by his Fluency than by the Strength of his Reasons. As we parted without settling the Point, and were not to see one another again for some time, I sat down to put my Arguments in Writing, which I copied fair and sent to him. He answer'd and I reply'd. Three or four Letters of a Side had pass'd, when my Father happen'd to find my Papers, and read them. Without entering into the Discussion, he took occasion to talk to me about the Manner of my Writing, observ'd that tho' I had the Advantage of my Antagonist in correct Spelling and pointing (which I ow'd to the Printing House) I fell far short in elegance of Expression, in Method and in Perspicuity, of which he convinc'd me by several Instances. I saw the Justice of his Remarks, and thence grew more attentive to the *Manner* in Writing, and determin'd to endeavour at Improvement.

About this time I met with an odd Volume of the Spectator. It was the third. I had never before seen any of them. I bought it, read it over and over, and was much delighted with it. I thought the Writing excellent, and wish'd if possible to imitate it. With that View, I took some of the Papers, and making short Hints of the Sentiment in each Sentence, laid them by a few Days, and then without looking at the Book, try'd to compleat the Papers again, by expressing each hinted Sentiment at length and as fully as it had been express'd before, in any suitable Words, that should come to hand.

Then I compar'd my Spectator with the Original, discover'd some of my Faults and corrected them. But I found I wanted a Stock of Words or a Readiness in recollecting and using them, which I thought I should have acquir'd before that time, if I had gone on making Verses, since the continual Occasion for Words of the same Import but of different Length, to suit the Measure, or of different Sound for the Rhyme, would have laid me under a constant Necessity of searching for Variety, and also have tended to fix that Variety in my Mind, and make me Master of it. Therefore I took some of the Tales and turn'd them into Verse: And after a time, when I had pretty well forgotten the Prose, turn'd them back again. I also sometimes jumbled my Collections of Hints into Confusion, and after some Weeks, endeavour'd to reduce them into the best Order, before I began to form the full Sentences, and compleat the Paper. This was to teach me Method in the Arrangement of Thoughts. By comparing my work afterwards with the original, I discover'd many faults and amended them; but I sometimes had the Pleasure of Fancying that in certain Particulars of small Import, I had been lucky enough to improve the Method or the Language and this encourag'd me to think I might possibly in time come to be a tolerable English Writer, of which I was extreamly ambitious.

My Time for these Exercises and for Reading, was at Night, after Work or before Work began in the Morning; or on Sundays, when I contrived to be in the Printing house alone, evading as much as I could the common Attendance on publick Worship, which my Father used to exact of me when I was under his Care: And which indeed I still thought a Duty; tho' I could not, as it seemed to me, afford the Time to practise it.

When about 16 Years of Age, I happen'd to meet with a Book, written by one Tryon, recommending a Vegetable Diet. I determined to go into it. My Brother being yet unmarried, did not keep House, but boarded himself and his Apprentices in another Family. My refusing to eat Flesh occasioned an Inconveniency, and I was frequently chid for my singularity. I made my self acquainted with Tryon's Manner of preparing some of his Dishes, such as Boiling Potatoes or Rice, making Hasty Pudding and a few others, and then propos'd to my Brother, that if he would give me Weekly half the Money he paid for my Board I would board my self. He instantly agreed to it, and I presently found that I could save half what he paid me. This was an additional Fund for buying Books: But I had another Advantage in it. My Brother and the rest going from the Printing House to their Meals, I remain'd there alone, and dispatching presently my light Repast, (which often was no more than a Bisket or a Slice of Bread, a Handful of Raisins or a Tart from the Pastry Cook's, and a Glass of Water) had the rest of the Time till their Return, for Study, in which I made the greater Progress from that greater Clearness of Head and quicker Apprehension which usually attend Temperance in Eating and Drinking. And now it was that being on some Occasion made asham'd of my Ignorance in Figures, which I had twice failed in learning when at School, I took Cocker's Book of Arithmetick, and went thro' the whole by my self with great Ease. I also read Seller's and Sturmy's Books of Navigation, and became acquainted with the little Geometry they contain, but never proceeded far in that Science. And I read about this Time Locke on Human Understanding, and the Art of Thinking by Messrs. du Port Royal.

While I was intent on improving my Language, I met with an English Grammar (I think it was Greenwood's) at the End of which there were two little Sketches of the Arts of Rhetoric and Logic, the latter finishing with a Specimen of a Dispute in the Socratic Method. And soon after I procur'd Xenophon's Memorable Things of Socrates, wherein there are many Instances of the same Method. I was charm'd with it, adopted it, dropt my abrupt Contradiction, and positive Argumentation, and put on the humble Enquirer and Doubter. And being then, from reading Shaftsbury and Collins, become a real Doubter in many Points of our Religious Doctrine, I found this Method safest for my self and very embarassing to those against whom I used it, therefore I took a Delight in it, practis'd it continually and grew very artful and expert in drawing People even of superior Knowledge into concessions the Consequences of which they did not foresee, entangling them in Difficulties out of which they could not extricate themselves, and so obtaining Victories that neither my self nor my Cause always deserved.

I continu'd this Method some few Years, but gradually left it, retaining only the Habit of expressing my self in Terms of modest Diffidence, never using when I advance any thing that may possibly be disputed, the Words, *Certainly, undoubtedly,* or any others that give the Air of Positiveness to an Opinion; but rather say, I conceive, or I apprehend a Thing to be so or so, It appears to me, or I should think it so or so for such and such Reasons, or I imagine it to be so, or it is so if I am not mistaken. This Habit I believe has been of great Advantage to me, when I have had occasion to inculcate my Opinions and persuade Men into Measures that I have been from time to time engag'd in promoting. And as the chief Ends of Conversation are to *inform,* or to be *informed,* to *please* or to *persuade,* I wish wellmeaning sensible Men would not lessen their Power of doing Good by a Positive assuming Manner that seldom fails to disgust, tends to create Opposition, and to defeat every one of those Purposes for which Speech was given us, to wit, giving or receiving Information, or Pleasure: For if you would *inform,* a positive dogmatical Manner in advancing your Sentiments, may provoke Contradiction and prevent a candid Attention. If you wish Information and Improvement from the Knowledge of others and yet at the same time express your self as firmly fix'd in your present Opinions, modest sensible Men, who do not love Disputation, will probably leave you undisturb'd in the Possession of your Error . . .

• • •

My Brother had in 1720 or 21, begun to print a Newspaper. It was the second that appear'd in America, and was called *The New England Courant.* The only one before it, was *the Boston News Letter.* I remember his being dissuaded by some of his Friends from the Undertaking, as not likely to succeed, one newspaper being in their Judgment enough for America. At this time 1771 there are not less than five and twenty. He went on however with the Undertaking, and after having work'd in composing the Types and printing off the Sheets I was employ'd to carry the Papers thro' the Streets to the Customers. He had some ingenious Men among his Friends who amus'd themselves by writing little Pieces for this Paper, which gain'd it Credit, and made it more in Demand; and these Gentlemen often visited us. Hearing their Conversations, and their Accounts of the Approbation their Papers were receiv'd with, I was excited to try my Hand among them. But being still a Boy, and suspecting that my Brother would object to printing any Thing of mine in his Paper if he knew it to be mine, I contriv'd to disguise my Hand, and writing an anonymous Paper I put it in at Night under the Door of the Printing House. It was found in the Morning and communicated to his Writing Friends when they call'd in as usual. They read it, commented on it in my Hearing, and I had the exquisite Pleasure, of finding it met with their Approbation, and that in their different Guesses at the Author none were named but Men of some Character among us for Learning and Ingenuity.

I suppose now that I was rather lucky in my judges: And that perhaps they were not really so very good ones as I then esteem'd them. Encourag'd however by this, I wrote and convey'd in the same Way to the Press several more Papers, which were equally approv'd, and I kept my Secret till my small Fund of Sense for such Performances was pretty well exhausted, and then I discovered it; when I began to be considered a little more by my Brother's Acquaintance, and in a manner that did not quite please him, as he thought, probably with reason, that it tended to make me too vain. And perhaps this might be one Occasion of the Differences that we frequently had about this Time. Tho' a Brother, he considered himself as my Master, and me as his Apprentice; and accordingly expected the same Services from me as he would from another; while I thought he demean'd me too much in some he requir'd of me, who from a Brother expected more Indulgence. Our Disputes were often brought before our Father, and I fancy I was either generally in the right, or else a better Pleader, because the Judgment was generally in my favour: But my Brother was passionate and had often beaten me, which I took extreamly amiss; and thinking my Apprenticeship very tedious, I was continually wishing for some Opportunity of shortening it, which at length offered in a manner unexpected.

One of the Pieces in our News-Paper, on some political Point which I have now forgotten, gave Offence to the Assembly. He was taken up, censur'd and imprison'd for a Month by the Speaker's Warrant, I suppose because he would not discover his Author. I too was taken up and examin'd before the Council; but tho' I did not give them any Satisfaction, they contented themselves with admonishing me, and dismiss'd me; considering me perhaps as an Apprentice who was bound to keep his Master's Secrets. During my Brother's Confinement, which I resented a good deal, notwithstanding our private Differences, I had the Management of the Paper, and I made bold to give our Rulers some Rubs in it, which my Brother took very kindly, while others began to consider me in an unfavourable Light, as a young Genius that had a Turn for Libelling and Satyr. My Brother's Discharge was accompany'd with an Order of the House, (a very odd one) *that James Franklin should no longer print the Paper called the New England Courant.* There was a Consultation held in our Printing House among his Friends what he should do in this Case. Some propos'd to evade the Order by changing the Name of the paper; but my Brother seeing Inconveniences in that, it was finally concluded on as a better Way, to let it be printed for the future under the Name of *Benjamin Franklin.* And to avoid the Censure of the Assembly that might fall on him, as still printing it by his Apprentice, the Contrivance was, that my old Indenture should be return'd to me with a full Discharge on the Back of it, to be shown on Occasion; but to secure to him the Benefit of my Service I was to sign new Indentures for the Remainder of the Term, which were to be kept private. A very flimsy Scheme it was, but however it was immediately executed, and the Paper went on accordingly under my Name for several Months. At length a fresh Difference arising between my Brother and me, I took upon me to assert my Freedom, presuming that he would not venture to produce the new Indentures. It was not fair in me to take this Advantage, and this I therefore reckon one of the first Errata of my Life: But the Unfairness of it weigh'd little with me, when under the Impression of Resentment, for the Blows his Passion too often urg'd him to bestow upon me. Tho' he was otherwise not an ill-natur'd Man: Perhaps I was too saucy and provoking.

When he found I would leave him, he took care to prevent my getting Employment in any other Printing-House of the Town, by going round and speaking to every Master, who accordingly refus'd to give me Work. I then thought of going to New York as the nearest Place where there was a Printer: and I was the rather inclin'd to leave Boston, when I reflected that I had already made myself a little obnoxious to the governing Party; and from the arbitrary Proceedings of the Assembly in my Brother's Case it was likely I might if I stay'd soon bring myself into Scrapes; and farther that my indiscrete Disputations about

Religion began to make me pointed at with Horror by good People, as an Infidel or Atheist. I determin'd on the Point: but my Father now siding with my Brother, I was sensible that If I attempted to go openly, Means would be used to prevent me. My Friend Collins therefore undertook to manage a little for me. He agreed with the Captain of a New York Sloop for my Passage, under the Notion of my being a young Acquaintance of his that had got a naughty Girl with Child, whose Friends would compel me to marry her, and therefore I could not appear or come away publickly. So I sold some of my Books to raise a little Money, Was taken on board privately, and as we had a fair Wind in three Days I found my self in New York near 300 Miles from home, a Boy of but 17, without the least Recommendation to or Knowledge of any Person in the Place, and with very little Money in my Pocket.

• • •

I have been the more particular in this Description of my Journey, and shall be so of my first Entry into [Philadelphia], that you may in your Mind compare such unlikely Beginnings with the Figure I have since made there. I was in my Working Dress, my best Cloaths being to come round by Sea. I was dirty from my Journey; my Pockets were stuff'd out with Shirts and Stockings; I knew no Soul, nor where to look for Lodging. I was fatigu'd with Traveling, Rowing and Want of Rest. I was very hungry, and my whole Stock of Cash consisted of a Dutch Dollar and about a Shilling in Copper. The latter I gave the People of the Boat for my Passage, who at first refus'd it on Account of my Rowing; but I insisted on their taking it, a Man being sometimes more generous when he has but a little Money than when he has plenty, perhaps thro' Fear of being thought to have but little.

Then I walk'd up the Street, gazing about, till near the Market House I met a Boy with Bread. I had made many a Meal on Bread, and inquiring where he got it, I went immediately to the Baker's he directed me to in second Street; and ask'd for Bisket, intending such as we had in Boston, but they it seems were not made in Philadelphia, then I ask'd for a threepenny Loaf, and was told they had none such: so not considering or knowing the Difference of Money and the greater Cheapness nor the Names of his Bread, I bad him give me three penny worth of any sort. He gave me accordingly three great Puffy Rolls. I was surpriz'd at the Quantity, but took it, and having no room in my Pockets, walk'd off, with a Roll under each Arm, and eating the other. Thus I went up Market Street as far as fourth Street, passing by the Door of

Mr. Read, my future Wife's Father, when she standing at the Door saw me, and thought I made as I certainly did a most awkward ridiculous Appearance. Then I turn'd and went down Chestnut Street and part of Walnut Street, eating my Roll all the Way, and coming round found my self again at Market Street Wharff, near the Boat I came in, to which I went for a Draught of the River Water, and being fill'd with one of my Rolls, gave the other two to a Woman and her Child that came down the River in the Boat with us and were waiting to go farther. Thus refresh'd I walk'd again up the Street, which by this time had many clean dress'd People in it who were all walking the same Way; I join'd them, and thereby was led into the great Meeting house of the Quakers near the Market. I sat down among them, and after looking round a while and hearing nothing said, being very drowsy thro' Labour and want of Rest the preceding Night, I fell fast asleep, and continu'd so till the Meeting broke up, when one was kind enough to rouse me. This was therefore the first House I was in or slept in, in Philadelphia.

Walking again down towards the River, and looking in the Faces of People, I met a Young Quaker Man whose Countenance I lik'd, and accosting him requested he would tell me where a Stranger could get Lodging. We were then near the Sign of the Three Mariners. Here, says he, is one Place that entertains Strangers, but it is not a reputable House; if thee wilt walk with me, I'll show thee a better. He brought me to the Crooked Billet in Water-Street . Here I got a Dinner. And while I was eating it, several sly Questions were ask'd me, as it seem'd to be suspected from my youth and Appearance, that I might be some Runaway. After Dinner my Sleepiness return'd: and being shown to a Bed, I lay down without undressing, and slept till Six in the Evening; was call'd to Supper; went to Bed again very early and slept soundly till the next Morning. Then I made my self as tidy as I could, and went to Andrew Bradford the Printer's. I found in the Shop the old Man his Father, whom I had seen at New York, and who travelling on horse back had got to Philadelphia before me. He introduc'd me to his Son, who receiv'd me civilly, gave me a Breakfast, but told me he did not at present want a Hand, being lately supply'd with one. But there was another Printer in town lately set up, one Keimer, who perhaps might employ me; if not, I should be welcome to lodge at his House, and he would give me a little Work to do now and then till fuller Business should offer.

The old Gentleman said, he would go with me to the new Printer: And when we found him, Neighbour, says Bradford, I have brought to see you a young Man of your Business, perhaps you may want such a One. He ask'd me a few Questions, put a Composing Stick in my Hand to see how I work'd, and then said he would employ me soon, tho' he had just then nothing for me to do. And taking old Bradford whom he had never seen before, to be one of the Towns People that had a Good Will for him, enter'd into a Conversation on his present Undertaking and Prospects; while Bradford not discovering that he was the other Printer's Father, on Keimer's saying he expected soon to get the greatest Part of the Business into his own Hands, drew him on by artful Questions and starting little Doubts, to explain all his Views, what Interest he rely'd on, and in what manner he intended to proceed. I who stood by and heard all, saw immediately that one of them was a crafty old Sophister, and the other a mere Novice. Bradford left me with Keimer, who was greatly surpriz'd when I told him who the old Man was.

Keimer's Printing House I found, consisted of an old shatter'd Press, and one small worn-out Fount of English, which he was then using himself, composing in it an Elegy on Aquila Rose before-mentioned, an ingenious young Man of excellent Character much respected in the Town, Clerk of the Assembly, and a pretty Poet. Keimer made Verses, too, but very indifferently. He could not be said to write them, for his Manner was to compose them in the Types directly out of his Head; so there being no Copy, but one Pair of Cases, and the Elegy likely to require all the Letter, no one could help him. I endeavour'd to put his Press (which he had not yet us'd, and of which he understood nothing) into Order fit to be work'd with; and promising to come and print off his Elegy as soon as he should have got it ready, I return'd to Bradford's who gave me a little job to do for the present, and there I lodged and dieted. A few Days after Keimer sent for me to print off the Elegy. And now he had got another Pair of Cases, and a Pamphlet to reprint, on which he set me to work.

These two Printers I found poorly qualified for their Business. Bradford had not been bred to it, and was very illiterate; and Keimer tho' something of a Scholar, was a mere Compositor, knowing nothing of Presswork. He had been one of the French Prophets and could act their enthusiastic Agitations. At this time he did not profess any particular Religion, but something of all on occasion; was very ignorant of the

World, and had, as I afterwards found, a good deal of the Knave in his Composition. He did not like my Lodging at Bradford's while I work'd with him. He had a House indeed, but without Furniture, so he could not lodge me: But he got me a Lodging at Mr. Read's before-mentioned, who was the Owner of his House. And my Chest and Clothes being come by this time, I made rather a more respectable Appearance in the Eyes of Miss Read, than I had done when she first happen'd to see me eating my Roll in the Street.

•   •   •

I believe I have omitted mentioning that in my first Voyage from Boston, being becalm'd off Block Island, our People set about catching Cod and hawl'd up a great many. Hitherto I had stuck to my Resolution of not eating animal Food; and on this Occasion, I consider'd with my Master Tryon, the taking every Fish as a kind of unprovok'd Murder, since none of them had or ever could do us any Injury that might justify the Slaughter. All this seem'd very reasonable. But I had formerly been a great Lover of Fish, and when this came hot out of the Frying Pan, it smelt admirably well. I balanc'd some time between Principle and Inclination: till I recollected, that when the Fish were opened, I saw smaller Fish taken out of their Stomachs: Then thought I, if you eat one another, I don't see why we mayn't eat you. So I din'd upon Cod very heartily and continu'd to eat with other People, returning only now and then occasionally to a vegetable Diet. So convenient a thing it is to be a *reasonable Creature,* since it enables one to find or make a Reason for every thing one has a mind to do.

•   •   •

Mrs. Godfrey projected a Match for me with a Relation's Daughter, took Opportunities of bringing us often together, till a serious Courtship on my Part ensu'd, the Girl being in herself very deserving. The old Folks encourag'd me by continual Invitations to Supper, and by leaving us together, till at length it was time to explain. Mrs. Godfrey manag'd our little Treaty. I let her know that I expected as much Money with their Daughter as would pay off my Remaining Debt for the Printing-house, which I believe was not then above a Hundred Pounds. She brought me Word they had no such Sum to spare. I said they might mortgage their House in the Loan Office. The Answer to this after some Days was that they did not approve the Match . . . Mrs. Godfrey brought me afterwards some more favourable Accounts of their Disposition, and would have drawn me on again: but I declared absolutely my Resolution to have nothing more to do with that Family. . . .

But this Affair having turn'd my Thoughts to Marriage, I look'd round me, and made Overtures of Acquaintance in other Places; but soon found that the Business of a Printer being generally thought a poor one, I was not to expect Money with a Wife unless with such a one, as I should not otherwise think agreable. In the mean time, that hard-to-be-govern'd Passion of Youth, had hurried me frequently into Intrigues with low Women that fell in my Way, which were attended with some Expence and great Inconvenience, besides a continual Risque to my Health by a Distemper which of all Things I dreaded, tho' by great good Luck I escaped it.

A friendly Correspondence as Neighbours and old Acquaintances, had continued between me and Mrs. Read's Family, who all had a Regard for me from the time of my first Lodging in their House. I was often invited there and consulted in their Affairs, wherein I sometimes was of service. I pity'd poor Miss Read's unfortunate Situation, who was generally dejected, seldom chearful, and avoided Company. I consider'd my Giddiness and Inconstancy when in London as in a great degree the Cause of her Unhappiness; tho' the Mother was good enough to think the Fault more her own than mine, as she had prevented our Marrying before I went thither, and persuaded the other Match in my Absence. Our mutual Affection was revived, but there were now great Objections to our Union. That Match was indeed look'd upon as invalid, a preceding Wife being said to be living in England; but this could not easily be prov'd, because of the Distance. And tho' there was a Report of his Death, it was not certain. Then tho' it should be true, he had left many Debts which his Successor might be call'd on to pay. We ventured however, over all these Difficulties, and I [took] her to Wife Sept. 1, 1730. None of the Inconveniencies happened that we had apprehended, she prov'd a good and faithful Helpmate, assisted me much by attending the Shop, we throve together, and have ever mutually endeavour'd to make each other happy. Thus I corrected that great *Erratum* as well as I could.

• • •

Reading was the only Amusement I allow'd my self. I spent no time in Taverns, Games, or Frolicks of any kind. And my Industry in my Business continu'd as indefatigable as it was necessary. I was in debt for my Printing-house, I had a young Family coming on to be educated, and I had to contend with for Business two Printers who were establish'd in the Place before me. My Circumstances however grew daily easier: my original Habits of Frugality continuing. And my Father having among his Instructions to me when a Boy, frequently repeated a Proverb of Solomon, *"Seest thou a Man diligent in his Calling, he shall stand before Kings, he shall not stand before mean Men."* I from thence consider'd Industry as a Means of obtaining Wealth and Distinction, which encourag'd me, tho' I did not think that I should ever literally stand before Kings, which however has since happened.—for I have stood before five, and even had the honor of sitting down with one, the King of Denmark, to Dinner.

We have an English Proverb that says,

> He that would thrive
> Must ask his Wife;

it was lucky for me that I had one as much dispos'd to Industry and Frugality as my self. She assisted me chearfully in my Business, folding and stitching Pamphlets, tending Shop, purchasing old Linen Rags for the Paper-makers, &c. &c. We kept no idle Servants, our Table was plain and simple, our furniture of the cheapest. For instance my Breakfast was a long time Bread and Milk, (no Tea) and I ate it out of a twopenny earthen Porringer with a Pewter Spoon. But mark how Luxury will enter Families, and make a Progress, in Spite of Principle. Being call'd one Morning to Breakfast, I found it in a China Bowl with a Spoon of Silver. They had been bought for me without my Knowledge by my Wife, and had cost her the enormous Sum of three and twenty Shillings, for which she had no other Excuse or Apology to make, but that she thought *her* Husband deserv'd a Silver Spoon and China Bowl as well as any of his Neighbours. This was the first Appearance of Plate and China in our House, which afterwards in a Course of Years as our Wealth encreas'd augmented gradually to several Hundred Pounds in Value.

I had been religiously educated as a Presbyterian; and tho' some of the Dogmas of that Persuasion, such as the Eternal Decrees of God, Election, Reprobation, &c. appear'd to me unintelligible, others doubtful, I early absented myself from the Public Assemblies of the Sect, Sunday being my Studying-Day, I never was without some religious Principles; I never doubted, for instance, the Existance of the Deity, that he made the World, and govern'd it by his Providence; that the most acceptable Service of God was the doing Good to Man; that our Souls are immortal; and that all Crime will be punished and Virtue reward-ed either here or hereafter; these I esteem'd the Essentials of every Religion, and being to be found in all the Religions we had in our Coun-try I respected them all, tho' with different degrees of Respect as I found them more or less mix'd with other Articles which without any Ten-dency to inspire, promote or confirm Morality, serv'd principally to divide us and make us unfriendly to one another. This Respect to all, with an Opinion that the worst had some good Effects, induc'd me to avoid all Discourse that might tend to lessen the good Opinion anoth-er might have of his own Religion; and as our Province increas'd in People and new Places of worship were continually wanted, and gen-erally erected by voluntary Contribution, my Mite for such purpose, whatever might be the Sect, was never refused.

Tho' I seldom attended any Public Worship, I had still an Opinion of its Propriety, and of its Utility when rightly conducted, and I regu-larly paid my annual Subscription for the Support of the only Presby-terian Minister or Meeting we had in Philadelphia. He us'd to visit me sometimes as a Friend, and admonish me to attend his Administra-tions, and I was now and then prevail'd on to do so, once for five Sun-days successively. Had he been, *in my Opinion,* a good Preacher perhaps I might have continued, notwithstanding the occasion I had for the Sun-day's Leisure in my Course of Study: But his Discourses were chiefly either polemic Arguments, or Explications of the peculiar Doctrines of our Sect, and were all to me very dry, uninteresting and unedify-ing, since not a single moral Principle was inculcated or enforc'd their Aim seeming to be rather to make us Presbyterians than good Citizens. At length he took for his Text that Verse of the 4th Chapter of Philippi-ans, *Finally, Brethren, Whatsoever Things are true, honest, just, pure, love-ly, or of good report,* if *there be any virtue, or any praise, think on these Things;* and I imagin'd in a Sermon on such a Text, we could not miss of hav-ing some Morality: But he confin'd himself to five Points only as meant by the Apostle, viz. 1. Keeping holy the Sabbath Day. 2. Being diligent in Reading the Holy Scriptures. 3. Attending duly the Publick Worship. 4. Partaking of the Sacrament. 5. Paying a due Respect to God's Min-isters. These might be all good Things, but as they were not the kind of good Things that I expected from that Text, I despaired of ever meeting with them from any other, was disgusted, and attended his Preaching no more. I had some Years before compos'd a little Liturgy or Form of Prayer for my own private Use, viz, in 1728. entitled, *Arti-*

cles of Belief and Acts of Religion. I return'd to the Use of this, and went no more to the public Assemblies. My Conduct might be blameable, but I leave it without attempting farther to excuse it, my present purpose being to relate Facts, and not to make Apologies for them.

It was about this time that I conceiv'd the bold and arduous Project of arriving at moral Perfection. I wish'd to live without committing any Fault at any time; I would conquer all that either Natural Inclination, Custom, or Company might lead me into. As I knew, or thought I knew, what was right and wrong, I did not see why I might not *always* do the one and avoid the other. But I soon found I had undertaken a Task of more Difficulty than I had imagined. While my *Attention was taken up* in guarding against one Fault, I was often surpriz'd by another. Habit took the Advantage of Inattention. Inclination was sometimes too strong for Reason. I concluded at length, that the mere speculative Conviction that it was our Interest to be compleatly virtuous, was not sufficient to prevent our Slipping, and that the contrary Habits must be broken and good ones acquired and established, before we can have any Dependance on a steady uniform Rectitude of Conduct. For this purpose I therefore contriv'd the following Method.

In the various Enumerations of the moral Virtues I had met with in my Reading, I found the Catalogue more or less numerous, as different Writers included more or fewer Ideas under the same Name. Temperance, for Example, was by some confin'd to Eating and Drinking, while by others it was extended to mean the moderating every other Pleasure, Appetite, Inclination or Passion, bodily or mental, even to our Avarice and Ambition. I propos'd to myself, for the sake of Clearness, to use rather more Names with fewer Ideas annex'd to each, than a few Names with more Ideas; and I included under Thirteen Names of Virtues all that at that time occurr'd to me as necessary or desirable, and annex'd to each a short Precept, which fully express'd the Extent I gave to its Meaning.

These Names of Virtues with their Precepts were

1. Temperance.

Eat not to Dulness.
Drink not to Elevation.

2. Silence.

Speak not but what may benefit others or yourself. Avoid trifling Conversation.

3. Order.

Let all your Things have their Places. Let each Part of your Business have its Time.

4. Resolution.

Resolve to perform what you ought. Perform without fail what you resolve.

5. Frugality.

Make no Expence but to do good to others or yourself: i.e., Waste nothing.

6. Industry.

Lose no Time. Be always employ'd in something useful. Cut off all unnecessary Actions.

7. Sincerity.

Use no hurtful Deceit.
Think innocently and justly; and, if you speak, speak accordingly.

8. Justice.

Wrong none, by doing Injuries or omitting the Benefits that are your Duty.

9. Moderation.

Avoid Extreams. Forbear resenting Injuries so much as you think they deserve.

10. Cleanliness.

Tolerate no Uncleanness in Body, Cloaths or Habitation.

11. Tranquility.

Be not disturbed at Trifles, or at Accidents common or unavoidable.

12. Chastity.

Rarely use Venery but for Health or Offspring; Never to Dulness, Weakness, or the Injury of your own or another's Peace or Reputation.

13. Humility.

Imitate Jesus and Socrates.

My Intention being to acquire the *Habitude* of all these Virtues, I judg'd it would be well not to distract my Attention by attempting the whole at once, but to fix it on one of them at a time, and when I should be Master of that, then to proceed to another, and so on till I should have gone thro' the thirteen. And as the previous Acquisition of some might facilitate the Acquisition of certain others, I arrang'd them with that View as they stand above. *Temperance* first, as it tends to produce that Coolness and Clearness of Head, which is so necessary where constant Vigilance was to be kept up, and Guard maintained, against the unremitting Attraction of ancient Habits, and the Force of perpetual Temptations. This being acquir'd and establish'd, *Silence* would be more easy, and my Desire being to gain Knowledge at the same time that I improv'd in Virtue, and considering that in Conversation it was obtain'd rather by use of the Ears than of the Tongue, and therefore wishing to break a Habit I was getting into of Prattling, Punning and Joking, which only made me acceptable to trifling Company, I gave *Silence* the second Place. This, and the next, *Order*, I expected would allow me more Time for attending to my Project and my Studies; RESOLUTION, once become habitual, would keep me firm in my Endeavours to obtain all the subsequent Virtues; *Frugality* and *Industry*, by freeing me from my remaining Debt, and producing Affluence and Independance, would make more easy the Practice of *Sincerity* and *Justice*, &c. &c. Conceiving then that agreable to the Advice of Pythagoras in his Golden Verses daily Examination would be necessary, I contriv'd the following Method for conducting that Examination.

I made a little Book in which I allotted a Page for each of the Virtues. I rul'd each Page with red Ink, so as to have seven Columns, one for each Day of the Week, marking each Column with a Letter for the

Beginning of each Line with the first Letter of one of the Virtues, on which Line and in its proper Column I might mark by a little black Spot every Fault I found upon Examination to have been committed respecting that Virtue upon that Day.

I determined to give a Week's strict Attention to each of the Virtues successively. Thus in the first Week my great Guard was to avoid every the least Offence against Temperance, leaving the other Virtues to their ordinary Chance, only marking every Evening the Faults of the Day. Thus if in the first Week I could keep my first Line marked T clear of Spots, I suppos'd the Habit of that Virtue so much strengthen'd and its opposite weaken'd, that I might venture extending my Attention to include the next, and for the following Week keep both Lines clear of Spots. Proceeding thus to the last, I could go thro' a Course compleat in Thirteen Weeks, and four Courses in a year. And like him who having a Garden to weed, does not attempt to eradicate all the bad Herbs at once, which would exceed his Reach and his Strength, but works on one of the Beds at a time, and having accomplish'd the first proceeds to a Second; so I should have, (I hoped) the encouraging Pleasure of seeing on my Pages the Progress I made in Virtue, by clearing successively my Lines of their Spots, till in the End by a Number of Courses, I should be happy in viewing a clean Book after a thirteen Weeks daily Examination.

This my little Book had for its Motto these Lines from Addison's *Cato;*

Here will I hold: If there is a Pow'r above us,
(And that there is, all Nature cries aloud
Thro' all her Works) he must delight in Virtue,
And that which he delights in must be happy.

Another from Cicero.

O Vitoe, Philosophia Dux! O Virtutum indagatrix, expultrixque vitiorum! Unus dies bene, et ex preceptis tuis actus, peccanti immortalitati est anteponendus.

Another from the Proverbs of Solomon speaking of Wisdom or Virtue;

Length of Days is in her right hand, and in her Left Hand Riches and Honours; Her Ways are Ways of Pleasantness, and all her Paths are Peace. III, 16, 17.

And conceiving God to be the Fountain of Wisdom, I thought it right and necessary to solicit his Assistance for obtaining it; to this End I form'd the following little Prayer, which was prefix'd to my Tables of Examination; for daily Use.

O Powerful Goodness! bountiful Father! merciful Guide! Increase in me that Wisdom which discovers my truest Interests; Strengthen my Resolutions to perform what that Wisdom dictates. Accept my kind Offices to thy other Children, as the only Return in my Power for thy continual Favours to me.

I us'd also sometimes a little Prayer which I took from Thomson's Poems. viz

Father of Light and Life, thou Good supreme,
O teach me what is good, teach me thy self!
Save me from Folly, Vanity and Vice,
From every low Pursuit, and fill my Soul
With Knowledge, conscious Peace, and Virtue pure,
Sacred, substantial, neverfading Bliss!

• • •

I enter'd upon the Execution of this Plan for Self-Examination, and continu'd it with occasional Intermissions for some time. I was surpriz'd to find myself so much fuller of Faults than I had imagined, but I had the Satisfaction of seeing them diminish. To avoid the Trouble of renewing now and then my little Book, which by scraping out the Marks on the Paper of old Faults to make room for new Ones in a new Course, became full of Holes: I transferr'd my Tables and Precepts to the Ivory Leaves of a Memorandum Book, on which the Lines were drawn with red Ink that made a durable Stain, and on those Lines I mark'd my Faults with a black Lead Pencil, which Marks I could easily wipe out with a wet Sponge. After a while I went thro' one Course only in a Year, and afterwards only one in several years, till at length I omitted them entirely, being employ'd in Voyages and Business abroad with a Multiplicity of Affairs, that interfered, but I always carried my little Book with me.

My scheme of ORDER, gave me the most Trouble, and I found, that tho' it might be practicable where a Man's Business was such as to leave him the Disposition of his Time, that of a journey-man Printer for instance, it was not possible to be exactly observ'd by a Master, who must mix with the World, and often receive People of Business at their own Hours. *Order* too, with regard to Places for Things, Papers, &c. I found extreamly difficult to acquire. I had not been early accustomed to *Method*, and having an exceeding good Memory, I was not so sensible of the Inconvenience attending Want of Method. This Article therefore cost me so much painful Attention and my Faults in it vex'd me so much, and I made so little Progress in Amendment, and had such frequent Relapses, that I was almost ready to give up the Attempt, and content my self with a faulty Character in that respect. Like the Man who in buying an Ax of a Smith my neighbour, desired to have the whole of its Surface as bright as the Edge; The Smith consented to grind it bright for him if he would turn the Wheel. He turn'd while the Smith press'd the broad Face of the Ax hard and heavily on the Stone, which made the Turning of it very fatiguing. The Man came every now and then from the Wheel to see how the Work went on; and at length would take his Ax as it was without farther Grinding. No, says the Smith, Turn on, turn on; we shall have it bright by and by; as yet 'tis only speckled. Yes, says the Man; but—*I think I like a speckled Ax best.* And I believe this may have been the Case with many who having for want of some such Means as I employ'd found the Difficulty of obtaining good, and breaking bad Habits, in other Points of Vice and Virtue, have given up the Struggle, and concluded that *a speckled Ax was best.* For something that pretended to be Reason was every now and then suggesting to me, that such extream nicety as I exacted of my self might be a kind of Foppery in Morals, which if it were known would make me ridiculous; that a perfect Character might be attended with the Inconvenience of being envied and hated; and that a benevolent Man should allow a few Faults in himself, to keep his Friends in Countenance.

In Truth I found myself incorrigible with respect to *Order;* and now I am grown old, and my Memory bad, I feel very sensibly the want of it. But on the whole, tho' I never arrived at the Perfection I had been so ambitious of obtaining, but fell far short of it, yet I was by the Endeavour a better and a happier Man than I otherwise should have been, if I had not attempted it; As those who aim at perfect Writing by imitating the engraved Copies, tho' they never reach the wish'd for Excellence of those Copies, their Hand is mended by the Endeavour, and is tolerable while it continues fair and legible.

And it may be well my Posterity should be informed, that to this little Artifice, with the Blessing of God, their Ancestor ow'd the constant Felicity of his Life down to his 79th Year in which this is written. What Reserves may attend the Remainder is in the Hand of Providence. But if they arrive the Reflection on past Happiness enjoy'd ough help his Bearing them with more Resignation. To *Temperance* he asc his long-continu'd Health, and what is still left to him of a good stitution. To *Industry* and *Frugality* the early Easiness of his Circumstances, and Acquisition of his Fortune, with all that Knowledge which enabled him to be an useful Citizen, and obtain'd for him some Degree of Reputation among the Learned. To *Sincerity* and *Justice* the Confidence of his Country, and the honourable Employs it conferr'd upon him. And to the joint Influence of the whole Mass of the Virtues, even in the imperfect State he was able to acquire them, all that Evenness of Temper, and that Chearfulness in Conversation which makes his Company still sought for, and agreable even to his younger Acquaintance. I hope therefore that some of my Descendants may follow the Example and reap the Benefit.

It will be remark'd that, tho' my Scheme was not wholly without Religion there was in it no Mark of any of the distinguishing Tenets of any particular Sect. I had purposely avoided them; for being fully persuaded of the Utility and Excellency of my Method, and that it might be serviceable to People in all Religions, and intending some time or other to publish it, I would not have any thing in it that should prejudice any one of any Sect against it. I purposed writing a little Comment on each Virtue, in which I would have shown the Advantages of possessing it, and the Mischiefs attending its opposite Vice; and I should have called my Book the ART of *Virtue,* because it would have shown the *Means and Manner* of obtaining Virtue, which would have distinguish'd it from the mere Exhortation to be good, that does not instruct and indicate the Means; but is like the Apostle's Man of verbal Charity, who only, without showing to the Naked and the Hungry *how* or where they might get Cloaths or Victuals, exhorted them to be fed and clothed. *James* II, 15, 16.

But it so happened that my Intention of writing and publishing this ᵃment was never fulfilled. I did indeed, from time to time put down ᵗints of the Sentiments, Reasonings, &c. to be made use of in it; ᵛhich I have still by me: But the necessary close Attention to ⁿness in the earlier part of Life, and public Business since, ᵈ my postponing it. For it being connected in my Mind ˣtensive Project that required the whole Man to exe-ⁱnforeseen Succession of Employs prevented my ʰerto remain'd unfinish'd.

Design to explain and enforce this Doctrine, ᵗot hurtful because they are forbidden, but ᵗney are hurtful, the Nature of Man alone consider'd: That it was therefore every one's Interest to be virtuous, who wish'd to be happy even in this World. And I should from this Circumstance, there being always in the World a Number of rich Merchants, Nobility, States and Princes, who have need of honest Instruments for the Management of their Affairs, and such being so rare have endeavoured to convince young Persons, that no Qualities were so likely to make a poor Man's Fortune as those of Probity and Integrity.

My List of Virtues contain'd at first but twelve: But a Quaker Friend having kindly inform'd me that I was generally thought proud; that my Pride show'd itself frequently in Conversation; that I was not content with being in the right when discussing any Point, but was overbearing and rather insolent; of which he convinc'd me by mentioning several Instances; I determined endeavouring to cure myself if I could of this Vice or Folly among the rest, and I added *Humility* to my List, giving an extensive Meaning to the Word. I cannot boast of much Success in acquiring the *Reality* of this Virtue; but I had a good deal with regard to the *Appearance* of it. I made it a Rule to forbear all direct Contradiction to the Sentiments of others, and all positive Assertion of my own. I even forbid myself agreable to the old Laws of our Junto, the Use of every Word or Expression in the Language that imported a fix'd Opinion; such as *certainly, undoubtedly,* &c. and I adopted instead of them, I *conceive,* I *apprehend,* or I *imagine* a thing to be so or so, or it so appears to me at present. When another asserted something, that I thought an Error, I deny'd my self the Pleasure of contradicting him abruptly, and of showing immediately some Absurdity in his Proposition; and in answering I began by observing that in certain Cases or Circumstances his Opinion would be right, but that in the present case there *appear'd* or *seem'd* to me some Difference, &c. I soon found the Advantage of this Change in my Manners. The Conversations I engag'd in went on more pleasantly. The modest way in which I propos'd my Opinions, procur'd them a readier Reception and less Contradiction; I had less Mortification when I was found to be in the wrong, and I more easily prevail'd with others to give up their Mistakes and join with me when I happen'd to be in the right. And this Mode, which I at first put on, with some violence to natural Inclination, became at length so easy and so habitual to me, that perhaps for these Fifty Years past no one has ever heard a dogmatical Expression escape me. And to this Habit (after my Character of Integrity) I think it principally owing, that I had early so much Weight with my Fellow Citizens, when I proposed new Institutions, or Alterations in the old; and so much Influence in public Councils when I became a Member. For I was but a bad Speaker, never eloquent, subject to much Hesitation in my choice of Words, hardly correct in Language, and yet I generally carried my Points.

In reality there is perhaps no one of our natural Passions so hard to subdue as *Pride*. Disguise it, struggle with it, beat it down, stifle it, mortify it as much as one pleases, it is still alive, and will every now and then peep out and show itself. You will see it perhaps often in this History. For even if I could conceive that I had compleatly overcome it, I should probably by [be] proud of my Humility.

Thus far written at Passy 1784

PART THREE

I am now about to write at home, August 1788, but cannot have the help expected from my Papers, many of them being lost in the War: I have however found the following.

Having mentioned *a great and extensive Project* which I had conceiv'd, it seems proper that some Account should be here given of that Project and its Object. Its first Rise in my Mind appears in the following little Paper, accidentally preserved, viz

OBSERVATIONS on my Reading History in Library, May 9, 1731.

"That the great Affairs of the World, the Wars, Revolutions, &c. are carried on and effected by Parties.

"That the View of these Parties is their present general Interest, or what they take to be such.

"That the different Views of these different Parties, occasion all Confusion.

"That while a Party is carrying on a general Design, each Man has his particular private Interest in View.

"That as soon as a Party has gain'd its general Point, each Member becomes Intent upon his particular Interest, which thwarting others, breaks that Party into Divisions, and occasions more Confusion.

"That few in Public Affairs act from a meer View of the Good of their Country, whatever they may pretend; and tho' their Actings bring real Good to their Country, yet Men primarily consider'd that their own and their Country's Interest was united, and did not act from a Principle of Benevolence.

"That fewer still in public Affairs act with a View to the Good of Mankind.

"There seems to me at present to be great Occasion for raising an united Party for Virtue, by forming the Virtuous and good Men of all Nations into a regular body, to be govern'd by suitable good and wise Rules, which good and wise Men may probably be more unanimous in their Obedience to, than common People are to common Laws.

"I at present think, that whoever attempts this aright, and is well qualified, cannot fail of pleasing God, and of meeting with Success. B.F."

Revolving this Project in my Mind, as to be undertaken hereafter when my Circumstances should afford me the necessary Leisure, I put down from time to time on Pieces of Paper such Thoughts as occur'd to me respecting it. Most of these are lost; but I find one purporting to be the Substance of an intended Creed, containing as I thought the Essentials of every known Religion, and being free of every thing that might shock the Professors of any Religion. It is express'd in these Words. viz

"That there is one God who made all things.

"That he governs the World by his Providence.

"That he ought to be worshipped by Adoration, Prayer and Thanksgiving.

"But that the most acceptable Service of God is doing Good to Man.

"That the Soul is immortal.

"And that God will certainly reward Virtue and punish Vice either here or hereafter."

My Ideas at that time were, that the Sect should be begun and spread at first among young and single Men only; that each Person to be initiated should not only declare his Assent to such Creed, but should have exercis'd himself with the Thirteen Weeks Examination and Practice of the Virtues as in the before-mention'd Model; that the Existence of such a Society should be kept a Secret till it was become considerable, to prevent Solicitations for the Admission of improper Persons; but that the Members should each of them search among his Acquaintance for ingenuous well-disposed Youths, to whom with prudent Caution the Scheme should be gradually communicated: That the Members should engage to afford their Advice Assistance and Support to each other in promoting one another's Interest, Business and

Advancement in Life: That for Distinction, we should be call'd the Society of the *Free and Easy*; Free, as being by the general Practice and Habit of the Virtues, free from the Dominion of Vice, and particularly by the Practice of Industry and Frugality, free from Debt, which exposes a Man to Confinement and a Species of Slavery to his Creditors. This is as much as I can now recollect of the Project, except that I communicated it in part to two young Men, who adopted it with some Enthusiasm. But my then narrow Circumstances, and the Necessity I was under of sticking close to my Business, occasion'd my Postponing the farther Prosecution of it at that time, and my multifarious Occupations public and private induc'd me to continue postponing, so that it has been omitted till I have no longer Strength or Activity left sufficient for such an Enterprize: Tho' I am still of Opinion that it was a practicable Scheme, and might have been very useful, by forming a great Number of good Citizens: And I was not discourag'd by the seeming Magnitude of the Undertaking, as I have always thought that one Man of tolerable Abilities may work great Changes, and accomplish great Affairs among Mankind, if he first forms a good Plan, and, cutting off all Amusements or other Employments that would divert his Attention, makes the Execution of that same Plan his sole Study and Business.

In 1732 I first published my Almanack, under the Name of *Richard Saunders*; it was continu'd by me about 25 Years, commonly call'd *Poor Richard's* Almanack. I endeavour'd to make it both entertaining and useful, and it accordingly came to be in such Demand that I reap'd considerable Profit from it, vending annually near ten Thousand. And observing that it was generally read, scarce any Neighbourhood in the Province being without it, I consider'd it as a proper Vehicle for conveying Instruction among the common People, who bought scarce any other Books. I therefore filled all the little Spaces that occurr'd between the Remarkable Days in the Calendar, with Proverbial Sentences, chiefly such as inculcated Industry and Frugality, as the Means of procuring Wealth and thereby securing Virtue, it being more difficult for a Man in Want to act always honestly, as (to use here one of those Proverbs) *it is hard for an empty Sack to stand upright*. These Proverbs, which contained the Wisdom of many Ages and Nations, I assembled and form'd into a connected Discourse prefix'd to the Almanack of 1757, as the Harangue of a wise old Man to the People attending an Auction. The bringing all these scatter'd Counsels thus into a Focus, enabled them to make greater Impression. The Piece being universally approved was copied in all the Newspapers of the Continent, reprinted in Britain on a Broadside to be stuck up in Houses, two Translations were made of it in French, and great Numbers bought by the Clergy and Gentry to distribute gratis among their poor Parishioners and Tenants. In Pennsylvania, as it discouraged useless Expence in foreign Superfluities, some thought it had its share of Influence in producing that growing Plenty of Money which was observable for several Years after its Publication.

I consider'd my Newspaper also as another Means of Communicating Instruction, and in that View frequently reprinted in it Extracts from the Spectator and other moral Writers, and sometimes publish'd little Pieces of my own which had been first compos'd for Reading in our Junto. Of these are a Socratic Dialogue tending to prove, that, whatever might be his Parts and Abilities, a vicious Man could not properly be called a Man of Sense. And a Discourse on Self denial, showing that Virtue was not secure, till its Practice became a Habitude, and was free from the Opposition of contrary Inclinations. These may be found in the Papers about the beginning of 1735. In the Conduct of my Newspaper I carefully excluded all Libelling and Personal Abuse, which is of late Years become so disgraceful to our Country. Whenever I was solicited to insert any thing of that kind, and the Writers pleaded as they generally did, the Liberty of the Press, and that a Newspaper was like a Stage Coach in which any one who would pay had a Right to a Place, my Answer was, that I would print the Piece separately if desired, and the Author might have as many Copies as he pleased to distribute himself, but that I would not take upon me to spread his Detraction, and that having contracted with my Subscribers to furnish them with what might be either useful or entertaining, I could not fill their Papers with private Altercation in which they had no Concern without doing them manifest Injustice. Now many of our Printers make no scruple of gratifying the Malice of Individuals by false Accusations of the fairest Characters among ourselves, augmenting Animosity even to the producing of Duels, and are moreover so indiscreet as to print scurrilous Reflections on the Government of neighbouring States, and even on the Conduct of our best national Allies, which may be attended with the most pernicious Consequences. These Things I mention as a Caution to young Printers, and that they may be encouraged not to pollute their Presses and disgrace their Profession by such infamous

Practices, but refuse steadily; as they may see by my Example, that such a Course of Conduct will not on the whole be injurious to their Interests.

• • •

I began now to turn my Thoughts a little to public Affairs, beginning however with small Matters. The City Watch was one of the first Things that I conceiv'd to want Regulation. . . . [T]he Constable for a little Drink often got such Ragamuffins about him as a Watch, that reputable Housekeepers did not chuse to mix with. Walking the rounds too was often neglected, and most of the Night spent in Tippling. I thereupon wrote a Paper to be read in Junto, representing these Irregularities, but insisting more particularly on the Inequality of this Six Shilling Tax of the Constables, respecting the Circumstances of those who paid it, since a poor Widow Housekeeper, all whose Property to be guarded by the Watch did not perhaps exceed the Value of Fifty Pounds, paid as much as the wealthiest Merchant who had Thousands of Pounds-worth of Goods in his Stores. On the whole I proposed as a more effectual Watch, the Hiring of proper Men to serve constantly in that Business; and as a more equitable Way of supporting the Charge, the levying a Tax that should be proportion'd to Property. This Idea being approv'd by the Junto, was communicated to the other Clubs, but as arising in each of them. And tho' the Plan was not immediately carried into Execution, yet by preparing the Minds of People for the Change, it paved the Way for the Law obtain'd a few Years after, when the Members of our Clubs were grown into more Influence.

About this time I wrote a Paper, (first to be read in Junto but it was afterwards publish'd) on the different Accidents and Carelessnesses by which Houses were set on fire, with Cautions against them, and Means proposed of avoiding them. This was much spoken of as a useful Piece, and gave rise to a Project, which soon followed it, of forming a Company for the more ready Extinguishing of Fires, and mutual Assistance in Removing and Securing of Goods when in Danger. Associates in this Scheme were presently found amounting to Thirty. Our Articles of Agreement oblig'd every Member to keep always in good Order and fit for Use, a certain Number of Leather Buckets, with strong Bags and Baskets (for packing and transporting of Goods) which were to be brought to every Fire; and we agreed to meet once a Month and spend a social Evening together, in discoursing and communicating such Ideas as occur'd to us upon the Subject of Fires as might be useful in our Conduct on such Occasions.

The Utility of this Institution soon appear'd, and many more desiring to be admitted than we thought convenient for one Company, they were advised to form another, which was accordingly done. And this went on, one new Company being formed after another, till they became so numerous as to include most of the Inhabitants who were Men of Property; and now at the time of my Writing this, tho' upwards of Fifty Years since its Establishment, that which I first formed, called the Union Fire Company, still subsists and flourishes, tho' the first Members are all deceas'd but myself and one who is older by a Year than I am. The small Fines that have been paid by Members for Absence at the Monthly Meetings, have been apply'd to the Purchase of Fire Engines, Ladders, Firehooks, and other useful Implements for each Company, so that I question whether there is a City in the World better provided with the Means of putting a Stop to beginning Conflagrations; and in fact since those Institutions, the City has never lost by Fire more than one or two Houses at a time, and the Flames have often been extinguish'd before the House in which they began has been half consumed.

In 1739 arriv'd among us from England the Rev. Mr. Whitefield, who had made himself remarkable there as an intinerant Preacher. He was at first permitted to preach In some of our Churches; but the Clergy taking a Dislike to him, soon refus'd him their Pulpits and he was oblig'd to preach in the Fields. The Multitudes of all Sects and Denominations that attended his Sermons were enormous, and it was matter of Speculation to me who was one of the Number, to observe the extraordinary Influence of his Oratory on his Hearers, and how much they admir'd and respected him, notwithstanding his common Abuse of them, by assuring them they were naturally *half Beasts and half Devils.* It was wonderful to see the Change soon made in the Manners of our Inhabitants; from being thoughtless or indifferent about Religion, it seem'd as if all the World were growing Religious; so that one could not walk thro' the Town in an Evening without Hearing Psalms sung in different Families of every Street. And it being found inconvenient to assemble in the open Air, subject to its Inclemencies, the Building of a House to meet in was no sooner propos'd and Persons appointed to receive Contributions, but sufficient Sums were soon receiv'd to procure the Ground and erect the Building which was 100 feet long and 70 broad, about the Size of Westminster-hall; and the Work was carried on with such Spirit as to be finished in a much shorter time than could have been expected. Both House and Ground were vested in Trustees, expressly for the Use of any Preacher of any religious Persuasion who might desire to say something to the People of Philadelphia, the Design in building not being to accommodate any particular Sect, but the Inhabitants in general, so that even if the Mufti of Constantinople were to send a Missionary to preach Mahometanism to us, he would find a Pulpit at his Service. (The Contributions being made by People of different Sects promiscuously, Care was taken in the Nomination of Trustees to avoid giving a Predominancy to any Sect, so that one of each was appointed, viz. one Church of England-man, one Presbyterian, one Baptist, one Moravian, &c.).

Mr. Whitefield, in leaving us, went preaching all the Way thro' the Colonies to Georgia. The Settlement of that Province had lately been begun; but instead of being made with hardy industrious Husbandmen accustomed to Labour, the only People fit for such an Enterprise, it was with Families of broken Shopkeepers and other insolvent Debtors, many of indolent and idle habits, taken out of the Gaols, who being set down in the Woods, unqualified for clearing Land, and unable to endure the Hardships of a new Settlement, perished in Numbers, leaving many helpless Children unprovided for. The Sight of their miserable Situation inspired the benevolent Heart of Mr. Whitefield with the Idea of building an Orphan House there, in which they might be supported and educated. Returning northward he preach'd up this Charity, and made large Collections; for his Eloquence had a wonderful Power over the Hearts and Purses of his Hearers, of which I myself was an Instance. I did not disapprove of the Design, but as Georgia was then destitute of Materials and Workmen, and it was propos'd to send them from Philadelphia at a great Expence, I thought it would have been better to have built the House here and brought the Children to it. This I advis'd, but he was resolute in his first Project, and rejected my Counsel, and I thereupon refus'd to contribute. I happened soon after to attend one of his Sermons, in the Course of which I perceived he intended to finish with a Collection, and I silently resolved he should get nothing from me. I had in my Pocket a Handful of Copper Money, three or four silver Dollars, and five Pistoles in gold. As he proceeded I began to soften, and concluded to give the Coppers. Another Stroke of his Oratory made me asham'd of that, and determin'd me to give the Silver; and he finish'd so admirably, that I empty'd my Pocket wholly into the Collector's dish, Gold and all. At this Sermon there was also one of our Club, who being of my Sentiments respecting the Building in Georgia, and suspecting a Collection might be intended, had by Precaution emptied his Pockets before he came from home; towards the Conclusion of the Discourse however, he felt a strong Desire to give, and apply'd to a Neighbour who stood near him to borrow some Money for the Purpose. The Application was unfortunately to perhaps the only Man in the Company who had the firmness not to be affected by the Preacher. His Answer was, *At any other time, Friend Hopkinson, I would lend to thee freely; but not now; for thee seems to be out of thy right Senses.*

• • •

The Year following, a Treaty being to be held with the Indians at Carlisle, the Governor sent a Message to the House, proposing that they should nominate some of their Members to be join'd with some Members of Council as Commissioners for that purpose. The House nam'd the Speaker (Mr. Norris) and myself; and being commission'd we went to Carlisle, and met the Indians accordingly. As those People are extreamly apt to get drunk, and when so are very quarrelsome and disorderly, we strictly forbad the selling any Liquor to them; and when they complain'd of this Restriction, we told them that if they would continue sober during the Treaty, we would give them Plenty of Rum when Business was over. They promis'd this; and they kept their Promise—because they could get no Liquor—and the Treaty was conducted very orderly, and concluded to mutual Satisfaction. They then claim'd and receiv'd the Rum. This was in the Afternoon. They were near 100 Men, Women and Children, and were lodg'd in temporary Cabins built in the Form of a Square just without the Town. In the Evening, hearing a great Noise among them, the Commissioners walk'd out to see what was the Matter. We found they had made a great Bonfire in the Middle of the Square. They were all drunk Men and Women, quarrelling and fighting. Their dark-colour'd Bodies, half naked, seen only by the gloomy Light of the Bonfire, running after and beating one another with Firebrands, accompanied by their horrid Yellings, form'd a Scene the most resembling our Ideas of Hell that could well be imagin'd. There was no appeasing the Tumult, and we retired to our Lodging. At Midnight a Number of them came thundering at our Door, demanding more Rum; of which we took no Notice.

The next Day, sensible they had misbehav'd in giving us that Disturbance, they sent three of their old Counsellors to make their Apology. The Orator acknowledg'd the Fault, but laid it upon the Rum; and then endeavour'd to excuse the Rum, by saying, *"The great Spirit who made all things made every thing for some Use, and whatever Use he design'd any thing for, that Use it should always be put to; Now, when he made Rum, he said,* LET THIS BE FOR INDIANS TO GET DRUNK WITH. *And it must be so."* And indeed if it be the Design of Providence to extirpate these Savages in order to make room for Cultivators of the Earth, it seems not improbable that Rum may be the appointed Means. It has already annihilated all the Tribes who formerly inhabited the Sea-coast.

In 1751 Dr. Thomas Bond, a particular Friend of mine, conceiv'd the Idea of establishing a Hospital in Philadelphia, for the Reception and Cure of poor sick Persons, whether Inhabitants of the Province or Strangers. A very beneficent Design, which has been ascrib'd to me, but was originally his. He was zealous and active in endeavouring to procure subscriptions for it; but the Proposal in being a Novelty in America, and at first not well understood, he met with small Success. At length he came to me, with the Compliment that he found there was no such thing as carrying a public Spirited Project through, without my being concern'd in it; "for, says he, I am often ask'd by those to whom I propose Subscribing, Have you consulted Franklin upon this Business? and what does he think of it? And when I tell them that I have not, (supposing it rather out of your Line) they do not subscribe, but say they will consider of it." I enquir'd into the Nature, and probable Utility of his Scheme, and receiving from him a very satisfactory Explanation, I not only subscrib'd to it myself, but engag'd heartily in the Design of Procuring Subscriptions from others. Previous however to the Solicitation, I endeavoured to prepare the Minds of the People by writing on the Subject in the Newspapers, which was my usual Custom in such Cases, but which he had omitted.

The Subscriptions afterwards were more free and generous, but beginning to flag, I saw they would be insufficient without some Assistance from the Assembly, and therefore propos'd to petition for it, which was done. The Country Members did not at first relish the Project. They objected that it could only be serviceable to the City, and therefore the Citizens should alone be at the Expence of it; and they doubted whether the Citizens themselves generally approv'd of it: My Allegation on the contrary, that it met with such Approbation as to leave no doubt of our being able to raise £2000 by voluntary Donations, they considered as a most extravagant Supposition, and utterly impossible. On this I form'd my Plan; and asking Leave to bring in a Bill, for incorporating the Contributors according to the Prayer (of their) Petition, and granting them a blank Sum of Money, which Leave was obtain'd chiefly on the Consideration that the House could throw the Bill out if they did not like it, I drew it so as to make the important Clause a conditional One, viz. "And be it enacted by the Authority aforesaid That when the said Contributors shall have met and chosen their Managers and Treasurer, *and shall have raised by their Contributions a Capital Stock Of £2000 Value,* (the yearly Interest of which is to be applied to the Accommodating of the Sick Poor in the said Hospital, free of Charge for Diet, Attendance, Advice and Medicines) and *shall make the same appear to the Satisfaction of the Speaker of the Assembly* for the time being; that *then* it shall and may be lawful for the said Speaker, and he is hereby required to sign an Order on the Provincial Treasurer for the Payment of Two Thousand Pounds in two yearly Payments, to the Treasurer of the said Hospital, to be applied to the Founding, Building and Finishing of the same." This Condition carried the Bill through; for the Members who had oppos'd the Grant, and now conceiv'd they might have the Credit of being charitable without the Expence, agreed to its Passage; And then in soliciting Subscriptions among the People we urg'd the conditional Promise of the Law as an additional Motive to give, since every Man's Donation would be doubled. Thus the Clause work'd both ways. The Subscriptions accordingly soon exceeded the requisite sum, and we claim'd and receiv'd the Public Gift, which enabled us to carry the Design into Execution. A convenient and handsome Building was soon erected, the Institution has by constant Experience been found useful, and flourishes to this Day. And I do not remember any of my political Manoeuvres, the Success of which gave me at the time more Pleasure. Or that in afterthinking of it, I more easily excus'd my-self for having made some Use of Cunning. It was about this time that another Projector, the Revd. Gilbert Tennent, came to me, with a Request that I would assist him in procuring a Subscription for erecting a new Meeting-house. It was to be for the Use of a Congregation he had gathered among the Presbyterians who were originally Disciples of Mr. Whitefield. Unwilling to make myself disagreable to my fellow Citizens, by too frequently soliciting their Contributions, I absolutely refus'd. He then desir'd I would furnish them with a List of the Names of Persons I knew by Experience to be generous and public-spirited. I thought it would be unbecoming in me, after their kind Compliance with my Solicitations, to mark them out to be worried by other Beggars, and therefore refus'd also to give such a List. He then desir'd I would at least give him my Advice. That I will readily do, said I; and, in the first Place, I advise you to apply to all those whom you know will give something; next to those whom you are uncertain whether they will give any thing or not; and show them the List of those who have given: and lastly, do not neglect those who you are sure wil give nothing; for in some of them you may be mistaken. He laugh'd, thank'd me, and said he would take my Advice. He did so, for he ask'd of *every body*; and he obtain'd a much larger Sum than he expected, with which he erected the capacious and very elegant Meeting-house that stands in Arch Street.

Our City, tho' laid out with a beautiful Regularity, The Streets large, strait, and crossing each other at right Angles, had the Disgrace of suffering those Streets to remain long unpav'd, and in wet Weather the Wheel of heavy Carriages plough'd them into a Quagmire, so that it was difficult to cross them. And in dry Weather the Dust was offensive. I had liv'd near the Jersey Market, and saw with Pain the Inhabitants wading in Mud while purchasing their Provisions. A Strip of Ground down the middle of that Market was at length pav'd with Brick, so that being once in the Market they had firm Footing, but were often over Shoes in Dirt to get there. By talking and writing on the Subject, I was at length instrumental in getting the Street pav'd with Stone between the Market and the brick'd Foot-Pavement that was on each Side next the Houses. This for some time gave an easy Access to the Market, dry-shod. But the rest of the Street not being pav'd, whenever a Carriage came out of the Mud upon this Pavement, it shook off and left its Dirt upon it, and it was soon cover'd with Mire, which was not remov'd, the City as yet having no Scavengers. After some Enquiry I found a poor industrious Man, who was willing to undertake keeping the Pavement clean, by sweeping it twice a week and carrying off the Dirt from before all the Neighbours Doors, for the Sum of Sixpence per Month, to be paid by each House. I then wrote and printed a Paper, setting forth the Advantages to the Neighbourhood that might be obtain'd by this small Expence; the greater Ease in keeping our Houses clean, so much Dirt not being brought in by People's Feet; the Benefit to the Shops by more Custom, as Buyers could more easily get at them, and by not having in windy Weather the Dust blown in upon their Goods, &c. &c. I sent one of these Papers to each House, and in a Day or two went round to see who would subscribe an Agreement to pay these Sixpences. It was unanimously sign'd, and for a time well executed. All the Inhabitants of the City were delighted with the Cleanliness of the Pavement that surrounded the Market, it being a Convenience to all; and this rais'd a general Desire to have all the Streets paved; and made the People more willing to submit to a Tax for that purpose.

After some time I drew a Bill for Paving the City, and brought it into the Assembly. It was just before I went to England in 1757 and did not pass till I was gone, and then with an Alteration in the Mode of Assessment, which I thought not for the better, but with an additional Provision for lighting as well as Paving the Streets, which was a great Improvement. It was by a private Person, the late Mr. John Clifton, his giving a Sample of the Utility of Lamps by placing one at his Door, that the People were first impress'd with the Idea of enlightning all the City. The Honour of this public Benefit has also been ascrib'd to me, but it belongs truly to that Gentleman. I did but follow his Example; and have only some Merit to claim respecting the Form of our Lamps as differing from the Globe Lamps we at first were supply'd with from London. Those we found inconvenient in these respects; they admitted no Air below, the Smoke therefore did not readily go out above, but circulated in the Globe, lodg'd on its Inside, and soon obstructed the Light they were intended to afford; giving, besides, the daily Trouble of wiping them clean; and an accidental Stroke on one of them would demolish it, and render it totally useless. I therefore suggested the composing them of four flat Panes, with a long Funnel above to draw up the Smoke, and Crevices admitting Air below, to facilitate the Ascent of the Smoke. By this means they were kept clean, and did not grow dark in a few Hours as the London Lamps do, but continu'd bright till Morning; and an accidental Stroke would generally break but a single Pane, easily repair'd. . . .

ADVICE TO A FRIEND

Benjamin Franklin

My dear Friend, June 25, 1745

I know of no Medicine fit to diminish the violent natural Inclinations you mention; and if I did, I think I should not communicate it to you. Marriage is the proper Remedy. It is the most natural State of Man, and therefore the State in which you are most likely to find solid Happiness. Your Reasons against entring into it at present, appear to me not well-founded. The circumstantial Advantages you have in View by postponing it, are not only uncertain, but they are small in comparison with that of the Thing itself, the being *married and settled.* It is the Man and Woman united that make the compleat human Being. Separate, she wants his Force of Body and Strength of Reason; he, her Softness, Sensibility and acute Discernment. Together they are more likely to succeed in the World. A single Man has not nearly the Value he would have in that State of Union. He is an incomplete Animal. He resembles the odd Half of a Pair of Scissars. If you get a prudent healthy Wife, your Industry in your Profession, with her good Œconomy, will be a Fortune sufficient.

But if you will not take this Counsel, and persist in thinking a Commerce with the Sex inevitable, then I repeat my former Advice, that in all your Amours you should *prefer old Women to young ones.* You call this a Paradox, and demand my Reasons. They are these:

1. Because as they have more Knowledge of the World and their Minds are better stor'd with Observations, their Conversation is more improving and more lastingly agreable.

2. Because when Women cease to be handsome, they study to be good. To maintain their Influence over Men, they supply the Diminution of Beauty by an Augmentation of Utility. They learn to do a 1000 Services small and great, and are the most tender and useful of all Friends when you are sick. Thus they continue amiable. And hence there is hardly such a thing to be found as an old Woman who is not a good Woman.

3. Because there is no hazard of Children, which irregularly produc'd may be attended with much Inconvenience.

4. Because thro' more Experience, they are more prudent and discreet in conducting an Intrigue to prevent Suspicion. The Commerce with them is therefore safer with regard to your Reputation. And with regard to theirs, if the Affair should happen to be known, considerate People might be rather inclin'd to excuse an old Woman who would kindly take care of a young Man, form his Manners by her good Counsels, and prevent his ruining his Health and Fortune among mercenary Prostitutes.

5. Because in every Animal that walks upright, the Deficiency of the Fluids that fill the Muscles appears first in the highest Part: The Face first grows lank and wrinkled; then the Neck; then the Breast and Arms; the lower Parts continuing to the last as plump as ever: So that covering all above with a Basket, and regarding only what is below the Girdle, it is impossible of two Women to know an old from a young one. And as in the dark all Cats are grey, the Pleasure of corporal Enjoyment with an old Woman is at least equal, and frequently superior, every Knack being by Practice capable of Improvement.

6. Because the Sin is less. The debauching a Virgin may be her Ruin, and make her for Life unhappy.

7. Because the Compunction is less. The having made a young Girl *miserable* may give you frequent bitter Reflections; none of which can attend the making an old Woman *happy*.

8[thly and Lastly] They are *so grateful!!*

Thus much for my Paradox. But still I advise you to marry directly; being sincerely Your affectionate Friend.

THE SPEECH OF MISS POLLY BAKER

(1747)

Benjamin Franklin

The Speech of Miss Polly Baker, before a Court of Judicature, at Connecticut near Boston in New-England; where she was prosecuted the Fifth Time, for having a Bastard Child: Which influenced the Court to dispense with her Punishment, and induced one of her Judges to marry her the next Day.

May it please the Honourable Bench to indulge me in a few Words: I am a poor unhappy Woman, who have no Money to fee Lawyers to plead for me, being hard put to it to get a tolerable Living. I shall not trouble your Honours with long Speeches; for I have not the Presumption to expect, that you may, by any Means, be prevailed on to deviate in your Sentence from the Law, in my Favour. All I humbly hope is, That your Honours would charitably move the Governor's Goodness on my Behalf, that my Fine may be remitted. This is the Fifth Time, Gentlemen, that I have been dragg'd before your Court on the same Account; twice I have paid heavy Fines, and twice have been brought to Publick Punishment, for want of Money to pay those Fines. This may have been agreeable to the Laws, and I don't dispute it; but since Laws are sometimes unreasonable in themselves, and therefore repealed, and others bear too hard on the Subject in particular Circumstances; and therefore there is left a Power somewhat to dispense with the Execution of them; I take the Liberty to say, That I think this Law, by which I am punished, is both unreasonable in itself, and particularly severe with regard to me, who have always lived an inoffensive Life in the Neighbourhood where I was born, and defy my Enemies (if I have any) to say I ever wrong'd Man, Woman, or Child. Abstracted from the Law, I cannot conceive (may it please your Honours) what the Nature of my Offence is. I have brought Five fine Children into the World, at the Risque of my Life; I have maintain'd them well by my own Industry, without burthening the Township, and would have done it better, if it had not been for the heavy Charges and Fines I have paid. Can it be a Crime (in the Nature of Things I mean) to add to the Number of the King's Subjects, in a new Country that really wants People? I own it, I should think it a Praise-worthy, rather than a punishable Action. I have debauched no other Woman's Husband, nor enticed any Youth; these Things I never was charg'd with, nor has any one the least Cause of Complaint against me, unless, perhaps, the Minister, or Justice, because I have had Children without being married, by which they have missed a Wedding Fee. But, can ever this be a Fault of mine? I appeal to your Honours. You are pleased to allow I don't want Sense; but I must be stupified to the last Degree, not to prefer the Honourable State of Wedlock, to the Condition I have lived in. I always was, and still am willing to enter into it; and doubt not my behaving well in it, having all the Industry, Frugality, Fertility, and Skill in Oeconomy, appertaining to a good Wife's Character. I defy any Person to say, I ever refused an Offer of that Sort: On the contrary, I readily consented to the only Proposal o: Marriage that ever was made me, which was when I was a Virgin; but too easily confiding in the Person's Sincerity that made it, I unhappil‍y lost my own Honour, by trusting to his; for he got me with Child, and then forsook me: That very Person you all know; he is now become a Magistrate of this Country; and I had Hopes he would have appeared this Day on the Bench, and have endeavoured to moderate the Court in my Favour; then I should have scorn'd to have mention'd it; but I must now complain of it, as unjust and unequal, That my Betrayer and Undoer, the first Cause of all my Faults and Miscarriages (if they must be deemed such) should be advanc'd to Honour and Power in the Government, that punishes my Misfortunes with Stripes and Infamy. I should be told, 'tis like, That were there no Act of Assembly in the Case, the Precepts of Religion are violated by my Transgressions. If mine, then, is a religious Offence, leave it to religious Punishments. You have already excluded me from the Comforts of your Church-Communion. Is not that sufficient? You believe I have offended Heaven, and must suffer eternal Fire: Will not that be sufficient? What Need is there, then, of your additional Fines and Whipping? I own, I do not think as you do; for, if I thought what you call a Sin, was really such, I could not presumptuously commit it. But, how can it be believed, that Heaven is angry at my having Children, when to the little done by me towards it, God has been pleased to add his Divine Skill and admirable Workmanship in the Formation of their

Bodies, and crown'd it, by furnishing them with rational and immortal Souls. Forgive me, Gentlemen, if I talk a little extravagantly on these Matters; I am no Divine, but if you, Gentlemen, must be making Laws, do not turn natural and useful Actions into Crimes, by your Prohibitions. But take into your wise Consideration, the great and growing Number of Batchelors in the Country, many of whom from the mean Fear of the Expences of a Family, have never sincerely and honourably courted a Woman in their Lives; and by their Manner of Living, leave unproduced (which is little better than Murder) Hundreds of their Posterity to the Thousandth Generation. Is not this a greater Offence against the Publick Good, than mine? Compel them, then, by Law, either to Marriage, or to pay double the Fine of Fornication every Year. What must poor young Women do, whom Custom have forbid to solicit the Men, and who cannot force themselves upon Husbands, when the Laws take no Care to provide them any; and yet severely punish them if they do their Duty without them; the Duty of the first and great Command of Nature, and of Nature's God, *Encrease and Multiply.* A Duty, from the steady Performance of which, nothing has been able to deter me; but for its Sake, I have hazarded the loss of the Publick Esteem, and have frequently endured Publick Disgrace and Punishment; and therefore ought, in my humble Opinion, instead of a Whipping, to have a Statue erected to my Memory.

from LETTERS FROM AN AMERICAN FARMER

Michel-Guillaume-Jean de Crèvecoeur

LETTER III—WHAT IS AN AMERICAN?

I wish I could be acquainted with the feelings and thoughts which must agitate the heart and present themselves to the mind of an enlightened Englishman, when he first lands on this continent. He must greatly rejoice that he lived at a time to see this fair country discovered and settled; he must necessarily feel a share of national pride when he views the chain of settlements which embellishes these extended shores. When he says to himself, this is the work of my countrymen, who, when convulsed by factions, afflicted by a variety of miseries and wants, restless and impatient, took refuge here. . . .

[A] modern society offers itself to his contemplation, different from what he had hitherto seen. It is not composed, as in Europe, of great lords who possess everything, and of a herd of people who have nothing. Here are no aristocratical families, no courts, no kings, no bishops, no ecclesiastical dominion, no invisible power giving to a few a very visible one, no great manufacturers employing thousands, no great refinements of luxury. The rich and the poor are not so far removed from each other as they are in Europe. Some few towns excepted, we are all tillers of the earth, from Nova Scotia to West Florida. We are a people of cultivators, scattered over an immense territory, communicating with each other by means of good roads and navigable rivers, united by the silken bands of mild government, all respecting the laws without dreading their power, because they are equitable. We are all animated with the spirit of an industry which is unfettered and unrestrained because each person works for himself. If he travels through our rural districts he views not the hostile castle and the haughty mansion, contrasted with the clay-built hut and miserable cabin where cattle and men help to keep each other warm and dwell in meanness, smoke and indigence. A pleasing uniformity of decent competence appears throughout our habitations. The meanest of our loghouses is a dry and comfortable habitation. Lawyer or merchant are the fairest titles our towns afford; that of a farmer is the only appellation of the rural inhabitants of our country. It must take some time ere he can reconcile himself to our dictionary, which is but short in words of dignity and names of honor. There, on a Sunday, he sees a congregation of respectable farmers and their wives, all clad in neat homespun, well mounted, or riding in their own humble wagons. There is not among them an esquire, saving the unlettered magistrate. There he sees a parson as simple as his flock, a farmer who does not riot on the labor of others. We have no princes, for whom we toil, starve, and bleed; we are the most perfect society now existing in the world. Here man is free as he ought to be; nor is this pleasing equality so transitory as many others are. Many ages will not see the shores of our great lakes replenished with inland nations, nor the unknown bounds of North America entirely peopled. Who can tell how far it extends? Who can tell the millions of men whom it will feed and contain? for no European foot has yet travelled half the extent of this mighty continent!

•   •   •

In this great American asylum the poor of Europe have by some means met together and in consequence of various causes; to what purpose should they ask one another what countrymen they are? Alas, two thirds of them had no country. Can a wretch who wanders about, who works and starves, whose life is a continual scene of sore affliction or pinching penury, can that man call England or any other kingdom his country? A country that had no bread for him, whose fields procured him no harvest, who met with nothing but the frowns of the rich, the severity of the laws, with jails and punishments; who owned not a single foot of the extensive surface of this planet? No! urged by a variety of motives, here they came. Everything has tended to regenerate them: new laws, a new mode of living, a new social system; here they are become men; in Europe they were as so many useless plants, wanting vegetative mold and refreshing showers; they withered and were mowed down by want, hunger, and war; but now by the power of transplantation, like all other plants they have taken root and flourished! Formerly they were not numbered in any civil lists of their country, except in those of the poor; here they rank as citizens. By what invisible power has this surprising metamorphosis been performed? By that of the laws and that of their industry. The laws, the indulgent laws, protect them as they arrive, stamping on them the symbol of adoption; they receive ample rewards for their labors; these accumulated rewards procure them lands; those lands confer on them the title of freemen, and to that title every benefit is affixed which men can possibly require. This is the great operation daily performed by our laws. From whence proceed these laws? From our government. Whence the government? It is derived from the original genius and strong desire of the people ratified and confirmed by the crown. This is the great chain which links us all. . . .

What attachment can a poor European emigrant have for a country where he had nothing? The knowledge of the language, the love of a few kindred as poor as himself were the only cords that tied him; his country is now that which gives him land, bread, protection, and consequence; *Ubi panis ibi patria,* is the motto of all emigrants. What then is the American, this new man? He is either an European or the descendant of an European, hence that strange mixture of blood, which you will find in no other country. I could point out to you a family whose grandfather was an Englishman, whose wife was Dutch, whose son married a French woman, and whose present four sons have now four wives of different nations. *He* is an American who, leaving behind him all his ancient prejudices and manners, receives new ones from the new mode of life he has embraced, the new government he obeys, and the new rank he holds. He becomes an American by being received in the broad lap of our great *Alma Mater.* Here individuals of all nations are melted into a new race whose labors and posterity will one day cause great changes in the world. Americans are the western pilgrims who are carrying along with them that great mass of arts, sciences, vigor, and industry which began long since in the east; they will finish the great circle. The Americans were once scattered all over Europe; here they are incorporated into one of the finest systems of population which has ever appeared and which will hereafter become distinct by the power of the different climates they inhabit. The American ought therefore to love this country much better than that wherein either he or his forefathers were born. Here the rewards of his industry follow with equal steps the progress of his labor; his labor is founded on the basis of nature, *self-interest;* can it want a stronger allurement? Wives and children, who before in vain demanded of him a morsel of bread, now, fat and frolicsome, gladly help their father to clear those fields whence exuberant crops are to arise to feed and to clothe them all, without any part being claimed, either by a despotic prince, a rich abbot, or a mighty lord. Here religion demands but little of him, a small voluntary salary to the minister, and gratitude to God; can he refuse these? The American is a new man, who acts upon new principles; he must therefore entertain new ideas and form new opinions. From involuntary idleness, servile dependence, penury, and useless labor, he has passed to toils of a very different nature, rewarded by ample subsistence.—This is an American.

•   •   •

Men are like plants; the goodness and flavor of the fruit proceeds from the peculiar soil and exposition in which they grow. We are nothing but what we derive from the air we breathe, the climate we inhabit, the government we obey, the system of religion we profess, and the nature of our employment. . . .

Europe has no such class of men; the early knowledge they acquire, the early bargains they make, give them a great degree of sagacity. As freemen they will be litigious; pride and obstinacy are often the cause of law suits; the nature of our laws and governments may be another. As citizens it is easy to imagine that they will carefully read the newspapers, enter into every political disquisition, freely blame or censure governors and others. As farmers they will be careful and anxious to get as much as they can because what they get is their own. As northern men they will love the cheerful cup. As Christians, religion curbs them not in their opinions; the general indulgence leaves every one to think for themselves in spiritual matters; the laws inspect our actions, our thoughts are left to God. Industry, good living, selfishness, litigiousness, country politics, the pride of freemen, religious indifference, are their characteristics. If you recede still farther from the sea, you will come into more modern settlements; they exhibit the same strong lineaments in a ruder appearance. Religion seems to have still less influence, and their manners are less improved.

Now we arrive near the great woods, near the last inhabited districts; there men seem to be placed still farther beyond the reach of government, which in some measure leaves them to themselves. How can it pervade every corner; as they were driven there by misfortunes, necessity of beginnings, desire of acquiring large tracts of land, idleness, frequent want of economy, ancient debts, the reunion of such people does not afford a very pleasing spectacle. When discord, want of unity and friendship, when either drunkenness or idleness prevail in such remote districts, contention, inactivity, and wretchedness must ensue. There are not the same remedies to these evils as in a long established community. The few magistrates they have are in general little better than the rest; they are often in a perfect state of war; that of man against man, sometimes decided by blows, sometimes by means of the law; that of man against every wild inhabitant of these venerable woods, of which they are come to dispossess them. There men appear to be no better than carnivorous animals of a superior rank, living on the flesh of wild animals when they can catch them, and when they are not able, they subsist on grain. He who would wish to see America in its proper light, and have a true idea of its feeble beginnings and barbarous rudiments, must visit our extended line of frontiers where the last settlers dwell and where he may see the first labors of settlement, the mode of clearing the earth, in all their different appearances; where men are wholly left dependent on their native tempers and on the spur of uncertain industry, which often fails when not sanctified by the efficacy of a few moral rules. There, remote from the power of example and check of shame, many families exhibit the most hideous parts of our society. They are a kind of forlorn hope, preceding by ten or twelve years the most respectable army of veterans which come after them. In that space, prosperity will polish some, vice and the law will drive off the rest, who uniting again with others like themselves will recede still farther, making room for more industrious people who will finish their improvements, convert the loghouse into a convenient habitation, and, rejoicing that the first heavy labors are finished, will change in a few years that hitherto barbarous country into a fine, fertile, well regulated district. Such is our progress, such is the march of the Europeans toward the interior parts of this continent. . . .

As I have endeavored to show you how Europeans become Americans, it may not be disagreeable to show you likewise how the various Christian sects introduced, wear out, and how religious indifference becomes prevalent. When any considerable number of a particular sect happen to dwell contiguous to each other, they immediately erect a temple and there worship the Divinity agreeably to their own peculiar ideas. Nobody disturbs them. If any new sect springs up in Europe, it may happen that many of its professors will come and settle in America. As they bring their zeal with them, they are at liberty to make proselytes if they can, and to build a meeting and to follow the dictates of their consciences, for neither the government nor any other power interferes. If they are peaceable subjects and are industrious, what is it to their neighbors how and in what manner they think fit to address their prayers to the Supreme Being? But if the sectaries are not settled close together, if they are mixed with other denominations, their zeal will cool for want of fuel and will be extinguished in a little time. Then the Americans become as to religion, what they are as to country, allied to all. In them the name of Englishman, Frenchman, and European is lost, and in like manner, the strict modes of Christianity as practised in Europe are lost also. This effect will extend itself still farther hereafter, and though this may appear to you as a strange idea, yet it is a very true one. I shall be able perhaps hereafter to explain myself better; in the meanwhile, let the following example serve as my first justification.

Let us suppose you and I to be travelling; we observe that in this house, to the right, lives a Catholic who prays to God as he has been taught and believes in transubstantiation; he works and raises wheat, he has a large family of children, all hale and robust; his belief, his prayers, offend nobody. About one mile farther on the same road, his next neighbor may be a good honest plodding German Lutheran, who addresses himself to the same God, the God of all, agreeably to the modes he has been educated in, and believes in consubstantiation; by so doing he scandalizes nobody; he also works in his fields, embellishes the earth, clears swamps, &c. What has the world to do with his Lutheran principles? He persecutes nobody, and nobody persecutes him; he visits his neighbors, and his neighbors visit him. Next to him lives a seceder, the most enthusiastic of all sectaries; his zeal is hot and fiery, but separated as he is from others of the same complexion, he has no congregation of his own to resort to, where he might cabal and mingle religious pride with worldly obstinacy. He likewise raises good crops, his house is handsomely painted, his orchard is one of the fairest in the neighborhood. How does it concern the welfare of the country or of the province at large, what this man's religious sentiments are or really whether he has any at all? He is a good farmer, he is a sober, peaceable, good citizen; William Penn himself would not wish for more. This is the visible character, the invisible one is only guessed at, and is nobody's business.

· · ·

A European, when he first arrives, seems limited in his intentions as well as in his views, but he very suddenly alters his scale; two hundred miles formerly appeared a very great distance; it is now but a trifle; he no sooner breathes our air than he forms schemes and embarks in designs he never would have thought of in his own country. There the plentitude of society confines many useful ideas and often extinguishes the most laudable schemes which here ripen into maturity. Thus Europeans become Americans.

But how is this accomplished in that crowd of low, indigent people who flock here every year from all parts of Europe? I will tell you; they no sooner arrive than they immediately feel the good effects of that plenty of provisions we possess; they fare on our best food and are kindly entertained; their talents, character, and peculiar industry are immediately inquired into; they find countrymen everywhere disseminated, let them come from whatever part of Europe. Let me select one as an epitome of the rest; he is hired, he goes to work, and works moderately; instead of being employed by a haughty person, he finds himself with his equal, placed at the substantial table of the farmer or else at an inferior one as good; his wages are high, his bed is not like that bed of sorrow on which he used to lie; if he behaves with propriety and is faithful, he is caressed and becomes as it were a member of the family. He begins to feel the effects of a sort of resurrection; hitherto he had not lived but simply vegetated; he now feels himself a man because he is treated as such; the laws of his own country had overlooked him in his insignificancy; the laws of this cover him with their mantle. Judge what an alteration there must arise in the mind and thoughts of this man; he begins to forget his former servitude and dependence; his heart involuntarily swells and glows; this first swell inspires him with those new thoughts which constitute an American. What love can he entertain for a country where his existence was a burden to him; if he is a generous good man, the love of this new adoptive parent will sink deep into his heart. He looks around and sees many a prosperous person who but a few years before was as poor as himself. This encourages him much; he begins to form some little scheme, the first, alas, he ever formed in his life. If he is wise he thus spends two or three years, in which time he acquires knowledge, the use of tools, the modes of working the lands, felling trees, &c. This prepares the foundation of a good name, the most useful acquisition he can make. He is encouraged; he has gained friends; he is advised and directed; he feels bold; he purchases some land; he gives all the money he has brought over, as well as what he has earned, and trusts to the God of harvests for the discharge of the rest. His good name procures him credit. He is now possessed of the deed, conveying to him and his posterity the fee simple and absolute property of two hundred acres of land, situated on such a river. What an epoch in this man's life! He is become a freeholder, from perhaps a German boor—he is now an American, a Pennsylvanian, an English subject. He is naturalized, his name is enrolled with those of the other citizens of the province. Instead of being a vagrant, he has a place of residence; he is called the inhabitant of such a country or of such a district, and for the first time in his life counts for something; for hitherto he has been a cipher. I only repeat what I have heard many say, and no wonder their hearts should glow and be agitated with a multitude of feelings not easy to describe. From nothing to start into being; from a servant to the rank of a master; from being the slave of some despotic prince to become a free man invested with lands to which every municipal blessing is annexed! What a change indeed! It is in consequence of that change that he becomes an American. This great metamorphosis has a double effect; it extinguishes all his European prejudices, he forgets that mechanism of subordination, that servility of disposition which poverty had taught him; and sometimes he is apt to forget too much, often passing from one extreme to the other. If he is a good man, he forms schemes of future prosperity; he proposes to educate his children better than he has been educated himself; he thinks of future modes of conduct, feels an ardor to labor he never felt before. Pride steps in and leads him to everything that the laws do not forbid; he respects them; with a heartfelt gratitude he looks toward the east, toward that insular government from whose wisdom all his new felicity is derived and under whose wings and protection he now lives. These reflections constitute him the good man and the good subject. Ye poor Europeans, ye who sweat and work for the great—ye who are obliged to give so many sheaves to the church, so many to your lords, so many to your government, and have hardly any left for yourselves—ye who are held in less estimation than favorite hunters or useless lapdogs—ye who only breathe the air of nature, because it cannot be withheld from you; it is here that ye can conceive the possibility of those feelings I have been describing; it is here the laws of naturalization invite everyone to partake of our great labors and felicity, to till unrented, untaxed lands! Many, corrupted beyond the power of amendment, have brought with them all their vices and, disregarding the advantages held to them, have gone on in their former career of iniquity until they have been overtaken and punished by our laws. It is not every emigrant who succeeds; no, it is only the sober, the honest, and industrious; happy those to whom this transition has served as a powerful spur to labor, to prosperity, and to the good establishment of children, born in the days of their poverty, and who had no other portion to expect but the rags of their parents, had it not been for their happy emigration. . . .

After a foreigner from any part of Europe is arrived, and become a citizen, let him devoutly listen to the voice of our great parent which says to him, "Welcome to my shores, distressed European; bless the hour in which thou didst see my verdant fields, my fair navigable rivers, and my green mountains! If thou wilt work, I have bread for thee; if thou wilt be honest, sober, and industrious, I have greater rewards to confer on thee—ease and independence. I will give thee fields to feed and clothe thee, a comfortable fireside to sit by and tell thy children by what means thou hast prospered, and a decent bed to repose on. I shall endow thee beside with the immunities of a freeman. If thou wilt carefully educate thy children, teach them gratitude to God, and reverence to that government, that philanthropic government which has collected here so many men and made them happy, I will also provide for thy progeny; and to every good man this ought to be the most holy, the most powerful, the most earnest wish he can possibly form, as well as the most consolatory prospect when he dies. Go thou and work and till; thou shalt prosper, provided thou be just, grateful, and industrious."

LETTER IX—DESCRIPTION OF CHARLESTON; THOUGHTS ON SLAVERY; ON PHYSICAL EVIL; A MELANCHOLY SCENE

. . . While all is joy, festivity, and happiness in Charleston, would you imagine that scenes of misery overspread in the country? Their ears by habit are become deaf; their hearts are hardened; they neither see, hear, nor feel for the woes of their poor slaves from whose painful labors all their wealth proceeds. Here the horrors of slavery, the hardship of incessant toils, are unseen, and no one thinks with compassion of those showers of sweat and of tears which from the bodies of Africans daily drop and moisten the ground they till. The cracks of the whip urging these miserable beings to excessive labor are far too distant from the gay capital to be heard. The chosen race eat, drink, and live happy, while the unfortunate one grubs up the ground, raises indigo, or husks the rice, exposed to a sun full as scorching as their native one, without the support of good food, without the cordials of any cheering liquor. This great contrast has often afforded me subjects of the most afflicting meditation. On the one side, behold a people enjoying all that life affords most bewitching and pleasurable, without labor, without fatigue, hardly subjected to the trouble of wishing. With gold, dug from Peruvian mountains, they order vessels to the coasts of Guinea; by virtue of that gold, wars, murders, and devastations are committed in some harmless, peaceable African neighborhood where dwelt innocent people who even knew not but that all men were black. The daughter torn from her weeping mother, the child from the wretched parents, the wife from the loving husband, whole families swept away and brought through storms and tempests to this rich metropolis! There, arranged like horses at a fair, they are branded like cattle and then driven to toil, to starve, and to languish for a few years on the different plantations of these citizens. And for whom must they work? For persons they know not and who have no other power over them than that of violence, no other right than what this accursed metal has given them! Strange order of things! Oh, Nature, where are thou?—Are not these blacks thy children as well as we? On the other side, nothing is to be seen but the most diffusive misery and wretchedness, unrelieved even in thought or wish! Day after day they drudge on without any prospect of ever reaping for themselves; they are obliged to devote their lives, their limbs, their will, and every vital exertion to swell the wealth of masters who look not upon them with half the kindness and affection with which they consider their dogs and horses. Kindness and affection are not the portion of those who till the earth, who carry the burdens, who convert the logs into useful boards. This reward, simple and natural as one would conceive it, would border on humanity, and planters must have none of it! . . .

But is it really true, as I have heard it asserted here, that those blacks are incapable of feeling the spurs of emulation and the cheerful sound of encouragement? By no means; there are a thousand proofs existing of their gratitude and fidelity; those hearts in which such noble dispositions can grow are then like ours; they are susceptible of every generous sentiment, of every useful motive of action; they are capable of receiving lights, of imbibing ideas that would greatly alleviate the weight of their miseries. But what methods have in general been made use of to obtain so desirable an end? None; the day in which they arrive and are sold, is the first of their labors, labors which from that hour admit of no respite; for though indulged by law with relaxation on Sundays, they are obliged to employ that time which is intended for rest, to till their little plantations. What can be expected from wretches in such circumstances? Forced from their native country, cruelly treated when on board and not less so on the plantations to which they are driven; is there any thing in this treatment but what must kindle all the passions, sow the seeds of inveterate resentment, and nourish a wish of perpetual revenge? They are left to the irresistible effects of those strong and natural propensities; the blows they receive, are they conducive to extinguish them or to win their affections? They are neither soothed by the hopes that their slavery will ever terminate but with their lives nor yet encouraged by the goodness of their food or the mildness of their treatment. The very hopes held out to mankind by religion, that consolatory system so useful to the miserable, are never presented to them; neither moral nor physical means are made use of to soften their chains; they are left in their original and untutored state, that very state where in the natural propensities of revenge and warm passions are so soon kindled. Cheered by no one single motive that can impel the will, or excite their efforts, nothing but terrors and punishments are presented to them . . . .

The following scene will I hope account for these melancholy reflections and apologize for the gloomy thoughts with which I have filled this letter; my mind is, and always has been, oppressed since I became a witness to it. I was not long since invited to dine with a planter who lived three miles from——, where he then resided. In order to avoid the heat of the sun, I resolved to go on foot, sheltered in a small path leading through a pleasant wood. I was leisurely traveling along, attentively examining some peculiar plants which I had collected, when all at once I felt the air strongly agitated, though the day was perfectly calm and sultry. I immediately cast my eyes toward the cleared ground, from which I was but at a small distance, in order to see whether it was not occasioned by a sudden shower, when at that instant a sound resembling a deep rough voice, uttered, as I thought, a few inarticulate monosyllables. Alarmed and surprised, I precipitately looked all round, when I perceived at about six rods distance something resembling a cage, suspended to the limbs of a tree, all the branches of which appeared covered with large birds of prey fluttering about and anxiously endeavouring to perch on the cage. Actuated by an involuntary motion of my hands, more than by any design of my mind, I fired at them; they all flew to a short distance, with a most hideous noise, when, horrid to think and painful to repeat, I perceived a Negro, suspended in the cage and left there to expire! I shudder when I recollect that the birds had already picked out his eyes, his cheek bones were bare, his arms had been attacked in several places, and his body seemed covered with a multitude of wounds. From the edges of the hollow sockets and from the lacerations with which he was disfigured, the blood slowly dropped and tinged the ground beneath. No sooner were the birds flown, than swarms of insects covered the whole body of this unfortunate wretch, eager to feed on his mangled flesh and to drink his blood. I found myself suddenly arrested by the power of affright and terror; my nerves were convulsed; I trembled; I stood motionless, involuntarily contemplating the fate of this Negro, in all its dismal latitude. The living specter, though deprived of his eyes, could still distinctly hear, and in his uncouth dialect begged me to give him some water to allay his thirst. Humanity herself would have recoiled back with horror; she would have balanced whether to lessen such reliefless distress or mercifully with one blow to end this dreadful scene of agonizing torture! Had I had a ball in my gun, I certainly should have despatched him; but finding myself unable to perform so kind an office, I sought, though trembling, to relieve him as well as I could. A shell ready fixed to a pole, which had been used by some Negroes, presented itself to me; I filled it with water, and with trembling hands I guided it to the quivering lips of the wretched sufferer. Urged by the irresistible power of thirst, he endeavoured to meet it, as he instinctively guessed its approach by the noise it made in passing through the bars of the cage. "Tankè, you whitè man, tankè you, putè somè poison and givè me." How long have you been hanging there? I asked him. "Two days, and me no die; the birds, the birds; aaah me! " Oppressed with the reflections which this shocking spectacle afforded me, I mustered strength enough to walk away and soon reached the house at which I intended to dine. There I heard that the reason for this slave being thus punished, was on account of his having killed the overseer of the plantation. They told me that the laws of self-preservation rendered such executions necessary and supported the doctrine of slavery with the arguments generally made use of to justify the practice, with the repetition of which I shall not trouble you at present.

CHAPTER 5

Revolutionary Ideas

INTRODUCTION

THOMAS JEFFERSON, 1743–1826
Declaration of Independence as Adopted by Congress (1776)

THOMAS PAINE, 1737–1809
from The American Crisis (1776)

PATRICK HENRY, 1736–1799
On Slavery (1773)

ABIGAIL ADAMS, 1742–1822, AND
JOHN ADAMS, 1735–1826
Family Correspondence (1774–1776)

DANIEL BLISS, 1731–1786
An Epitaph for John Jack (1773)

PHILLIS WHEATLEY, 1754–1784
Selected Writings (1767–1774)

THOMAS JEFFERSON
from Notes on the State of Virginia (1785)

JAMES MADISON, 1751–1832
Federalist Papers No. 10 and 54 (1787–1788)

The American War for Independence was the first of "modern" revolutions where violence was justified by invocation of basic "human rights" that the old society violated and that the new would secure. Thomas Jefferson, with some help from Franklin and John Adams, wrote the basic statement of national principles, one that would later be used in support of causes that few endorsed at the time. In *Notes on the State of Virginia* Jefferson best revealed aspects of his American vision about economic development, slavery, and race. Thomas Paine, recently arrived from England and later to be both glorifier and sufferer of the French Revolution, was the only patriot who penned words that stirred broad popular support of the Revolution during its hard course.

Patrick Henry's letter was the most honest and uncalculated Southern reaction to the issue of slavery, remarkable for showing that as late as 1773 liberty's greatest orator had never thought about any tie between that principle and chattel slavery until a Quaker suggested some link. The letters of Abigail and John Adams, the era's richest family correspondence, suggest how sensitive Northerners were coming to see slavery as a brutal mockery of American ideals, and how their politicians knew that the nation might die if an effort was made to kill slavery generally. Abigail raised also, uniquely at the time, the status of another oppressed group whose political rights would not be much discussed for another three score years and ten. Daniel Bliss, who returned to England before the Revolution partly in disgust at colonies who talked liberty and practiced slavery, wrote an epitaph for an ex-slave he admired. Phillis Wheatley, an African-born Boston slave, became, with the strong support of her mistress and other evangelical women and ministers, the second American woman to publish a book of poems. Her Christianity and patriotism coated her plea for racial mutuality and respect, ideas put in clear prose in a much published letter she wrote to a Native American friend. Her poems became prime documents in the argument over black equality after Jefferson disparaged her and her race's intellectual capacities. James Madison was chief architect and justifier of the nation's Constitution. His Federalist Paper No. 10 was the classic argument that a large republic would protect stability and liberty better than a small, while No. 54 argued that the Constitution's three-fifths clause represented about the right amount of humanity left a slave. Perhaps Madison felt some unease with this last argument; only in this essay did he put his words into someone else's mouth.

CONSIDERATIONS

- What is Paine's justification for the American Revolution? Is it similar in tone and content to that of Jefferson's *Declaration*?

- Compare and contrast Jefferson's, Henry's, Wheatley's, and Bliss's reflections on slaves and slavery. How did the oppression of white men and of black slaves compare?

- What were the differences in gender roles in the Adams family? Were white women in a position similar to slaves? Do slave and gender realities lessen the justice of the American revolution? Would they have justified slave insurrection or a woman's war for equality and representation?

- How would you explain American revolutionaries insistence on their liberty and on black slavery?

- What theory does Madison use to justify the Constitution, and how valid is his argument? Is he in favor of strong or limited government? Do the Declaration, Paine and Madison agree about the role of government?

- Do you agree with his argument that three-fifths is about the proper amount of humanity left a slave?

DECLARATION OF INDEPENDENCE AS ADOPTED BY CONGRESS

In Congress, July 4, 1776

When in the Course of human events, it becomes necessary for one people to dissolve the political bands which have connected them with another, and to assume among the powers of the earth, the separate and equal station to which the Laws of Nature and of Nature's God entitle them, a decent respect to the opinions of mankind requires that they should declare the causes which impel them to the separation. We hold these truths to be self-evident, that all men are created equal, that they are endowed by their Creator with certain unalienable Rights, that among these are Life, Liberty, and the pursuit of Happiness. That to secure these rights, Governments are instituted among Men, deriving their just powers from the consent of the governed, That whenever any Form of Government becomes destructive of these ends, it is the Right of the People to alter or to abolish it, and to institute a new Government, laying its foundation on such principles and organizing its powers in such form, as to them shall seem most likely to effect their Safety and Happiness. Prudence, indeed, will dictate that Governments long established should not be changed for light and transient causes; and accordingly all experience hath shewn, that mankind are more disposed to suffer, while evils are sufferable, than to right themselves by abolishing the forms to which they are accustomed. But when a long train of abuses and usurpations, pursuing invariably the same Object evinces a design to reduce them under absolute Despotism, it is their right, it is their duty, to throw off such Government, and to provide New Guards for their future security. Such has been the patient sufferance of these Colonies; and such is now the necessity which constrains them to alter their former Systems of Government. The history of the present King of Great Britain is a history of repeated injuries and usurpations, all having in direct object the establishment of an absolute Tyranny over these States. To prove this, let facts be submitted to a candid world. He has refused his Assent to Laws, the most wholesome and necessary for the public good. He has forbidden his Governors to pass Laws of immediate and pressing importance, unless suspended in their operation till his Assent should be obtained; and when so suspended, he has utterly neglected to attend to them. He has refused to pass other Laws for the accommodation of large districts of people, unless those people would relinquish the right of Representation in the Legislature, a right inestimable o them and formidable to tyrants only. He has called together legislative bodies at places unusual, uncomfortable, and distant from the depository of their public Records, for the sole purpose of fatiguing them into compliance with his measures. He has dissolved Representative Houses repeatedly, for opposing with manly firmness, his invasions on the rights of the people. He has refused for a long time, after such dissolutions, to cause others to be elected; whereby the Legislative powers, incapable of Annihilation, have returned to the People at large for their exercise; the State remaining, in the mean time exposed to all the dangers of invasions from without, and convulsions within. He has endeavored to prevent the population of these States; for that purpose obstructing the Laws for Naturalization of Foreigners; refusing to pass others to encourage their migrations hither, and raising the conditions of new Appropriations of Lands. He has obstructed the Administration of Justice, by refusing his Assent to Laws for establishing Judiciary powers. He has made Judges dependent on his Will alone, for the tenure of their offices, and the amount and payment of their salaries. He has erected a multitude of New Offices, and sent hither swarms of Officers to harass our people, and eat out their substance. He has kept among us, in times of peace, standing Armies without the Consent of our legislatures. He has affected to render the Military independent of and superior to the Civil power. He has combined with others to subject us to a jurisdiction foreign to our constitution, and unacknowledged by our laws; giving his Assent to their Acts of pretended Legislation: For Quartering large bodies of armed troops among us: For protecting them, by a mock Trial, from punishment for any Murders which they should commit on the Inhabitants of these States: For cutting off our Trade with all parts of the world: For imposing Taxes on us without our Consent: For depriving us in many cases, of the benefits of Trial by Jury: For transporting us beyond Seas to be tried for pretended offences: For abolishing the free System of English Laws in a neighbouring Province, establishing therein an Arbitrary government, and enlarging its Boundaries so as to render it at once an example and fit instrument for introducing the same absolute rule into these Colonies: For taking away our Charters, abolishing our most valuable Laws, and altering fundamentally the Forms of our Governments: For suspending our own Legislatures, and declaring themselves invested with power to legislate for us in all cases whatsoever. He has abdicated Government here, by declaring us out of his Protection, and waging War against us. He has plundered our seas, ravaged our Coasts, burnt our towns, and destroyed the Lives of our people. He is at this time transporting large Armies of foreign Mercenaries to compleat the works of death, desolation, and tyranny, already begun with circumstances of Cruelty & perfidy scarcely paralleled in the most barbarous ages, and totally unworthy the Head of a civilized nation. He has constrained our fellow Citizens taken Captive on the high Seas to bear Arms against their Country, to become the executioners of their friends and Brethren, or to fall themselves by their Hands. He has excited domestic insurrections amongst us, and has endeavoured to bring on the inhabitants of our frontiers, the merciless Indian Savages, whose known rule of warfare, is an undistinguished destruction of all ages, sexes, and conditions. In every stage of these Oppressions We have Petitioned for Redress in the most humble terms: Our repeated Petitions have been answered only by repeated injury. A Prince, whose character is thus marked by every act which may define a Tyrant, is unfit to be the ruler of a free people. Nor have We been wanting in attentions to our British brethren. We have warned them from time to time of attempts by their legislature to extend an unwarrantable jurisdiction over us. We have reminded them of the circumstances of our emigration and settlement here. We have appealed to their native justice and magnanimity, and we have conjured them by the ties of our common kindred to disavow these usurpations, which, would inevitably interrupt our connections and correspondence. They too have been deaf to the voice of justice and of consanguinity. We must, therefore, acquiesce in the necessity, which denounces our Separation, and hold them, as we hold the rest of mankind, Enemies in War, in Peace Friends.

We, therefore, the Representatives of the united States of America, in General Congress, Assembled, appealing to the Supreme Judge of the world for the rectitude of our intentions, do, in the Name, and by Authority of the good People of these Colonies, solemnly publish and declare, That these United Colonies are, and of right ought to be Free and independent States; that they are absolved from all Allegiance to the British Crown, and that all political connection between them and the State of Great Britain, is and ought to be totally dissolved; and that as Free and Independent states, they have full Power to levy War, conclude Peace, contract Alliances, establish Commerce, and to do all other Acts and Things which Independent States may of right do. And for the support of this Declaration, with a firm reliance on the protection of divine Providence, we mutually pledge to each other our Lives, our Fortunes, and our sacred Honor.

from THE AMERICAN CRISIS

Thomas Paine

NUMBER 1

These are the times that try men's souls. The summer soldier and the sunshine patriot will, in this crisis, shrink from the service of their country; but he that stands it *now,* deserves the love and thanks of man and woman. Tyranny, like hell, is not easily conquered; yet we have this consolation with us, that the harder the conflict, the more glorious the triumph. What we obtain too cheap, we esteem too lightly: it is dearness only that gives every thing its value. Heaven knows how to put a proper price upon its goods; and it would be strange indeed if so celestial an article as FREEDOM should not be highly rated. Britain, with an army to enforce her tyranny, has declared that she has a right (*not only to* TAX) but "to BIND *us in* ALL CASES WHATSOEVER," and if being *bound in that manner,* is not slavery, then is there not such a thing as slavery upon earth. Even the expression is impious; for so unlimited a power can belong only to God.

Whether the independence of the continent was declared too soon, or delayed too long, I will not now enter into as an argument; my own simple opinion is, that had it been eight months earlier, it would have been much better. We did not make a proper use of last winter, neither could we, while we were in a dependent state. However, the fault, if it were one, was all our own; we have none to blame but ourselves. But no great deal is lost yet. All that Howe has been doing for this month past, is rather a ravage than a conquest, which the spirit of the Jerseys, a year ago, would have quickly repulsed, and which time and a little resolution will soon recover.

I have as little superstition in me as any man living, but my secret opinion has ever been, and still is, that God Almighty will not give up a people to military destruction, or leave them unsupportedly to perish, who have so earnestly and so repeatedly sought to avoid the calamities of war, by every decent method which wisdom could invent. Neither have I so much of the infidel in me, as to suppose that He has relinquished the government of the world, and given us up to the care of devils; and as I do not, I cannot see on what grounds the king of Britain can look up to heaven for help against us: a common murderer, a highwayman, or a house-breaker, has as good a pretense as he.

'Tis surprising to see how rapidly a panic will sometimes run through a country. All nations and ages have been subject to them: Britain has trembled like an ague at the report of a French fleet of flat bottomed boats; and in the fourteenth century the whole English army, after ravaging the kingdom of France, was driven back like men petrified with fear; and this brave exploit was performed by a few broken forces collected and headed by a woman, Joan of Arc. Would that heaven might inspire some Jersey maid to spirit up her countrymen, and save her fair fellow sufferers from ravage and ravishment! Yet panics, in some cases, have their uses; they produce as much good as hurt. Their duration is always short; the mind soon grows through them, and acquires a firmer habit than before. But their peculiar advantage is, that they are the touchstones of sincerity and hypocrisy, and bring things and men to light, which might otherwise have lain forever undiscovered. In fact, they have the same effect on secret traitors, which an imaginary apparition would have upon a private murderer. They sift out the hidden thoughts of man, and hold them up in public to the world. Many a disguised Tory has lately shown his head, that shall penitentially solemnize with curses the day on which Howe arrived upon the Delaware.

• • •

I shall conclude this paper with some miscellaneous remarks on the state of our affairs; and shall begin with asking the following question, Why is it that the enemy have left the New-England provinces, and made these middle ones the seat of war? The answer is easy: New-England is not infested with Tories, and we are. I have been tender in raising the cry against these men, and used numberless arguments to show them their danger, but it will not do to sacrifice a world either to their folly or their baseness. The period is now arrived, in which either they or we must change our sentiments, or one or both must fall. And what is a Tory? Good God! what is he? I should not be afraid to go with a hundred Whigs against a thousand Tories, were they to attempt to get into arms. Every Tory is a coward; for servile, slavish, self-interested fear is the foundation of Toryism; and a man under such influence, though he may be cruel, never can be brave.

But, before the line of irrecoverable separation be drawn between us, let us reason the matter together: Your conduct is an invitation to the enemy, yet not one in a thousand of you has heart enough to join him. Howe is as much deceived by you as the American cause is injured by you. He expects you will all take up arms, and flock to his standard, with muskets on your shoulders. Your opinions are of no use to him, unless you support him personally, for 'tis soldiers, and not Tories, that he wants.

I once felt all that kind of anger, which a man ought to feel, against the mean principles that are held by the Tories: a noted one, who kept a tavern at Amboy, was standing at his door, with as pretty a child in his hand, about eight or nine years old, as I ever saw, and after speaking his mind as freely as he thought was prudent, finished with this unfatherly expression, "*Well! give me peace in my day.*" Not a man lives on the continent but fully believes that a separation must some time or other finally take place, and a generous parent should have said, "*If there must be trouble, let it be in my day, that my child may have peace*"; and this single reflection, well applied, is sufficient to awaken every man to duty. Not a place upon earth might be so happy as America. Her situation is remote from all the wrangling world, and she has nothing to do but to trade with them. A man can distinguish himself between temper and principle, and I am as confident, as I am that God governs the world, that America will never be happy till she gets clear of foreign dominion. Wars, without ceasing, will break out till that period arrives, and the continent must in the end be conqueror; for though the flame of liberty may sometimes cease to shine, the coal can never expire.

•   •   •

I turn with the warm ardor of a friend to those who have nobly stood, and are yet determined to stand the matter out: I call not upon a few, but upon all: not on *this* state, but on *every* state: up and help us; lay your shoulders to the wheel; better have too much force than too little, when so great an object is at stake. Let it be told to the future world, that in the depth of winter, when nothing but hope and virtue could survive, that the city and the country, alarmed at one common danger, came forth to meet and to repulse it. Say not that thousands are gone, turn out your tens of thousands; throw not the burden of the day upon Providence, but "*show your faith by your works,*" that God may bless you. It matters not where you live, or what rank of life you hold, the evil or the blessing will reach you all. The far and the near, the home counties and the back, the rich and the poor, will suffer or rejoice alike. The heart that feels not now, is dead: the blood of his children will curse his cowardice, who shrinks back at a time when a little might have saved the whole, and made *them* happy. I love the man that can smile in trouble, that can gather strength from distress, and grow brave by reflection. 'Tis the business of little minds to shrink; but he whose heart is firm, and whose conscience approves his conduct, will pursue his principles unto death. My own line of reasoning is to myself as straight and clear as a ray of light. Not all the treasures of the world, so far as I believe, could have induced me to support an offensive war, for I think it murder; but if a thief breaks into my house, burns and destroys my property, and kills or threatens to kill me, or those that are in it, and to *"bind me in all cases whatsoever"* to his absolute will, am I to suffer it? What signifies it to me, whether he who does it is a king or a common man; my countryman or not my countryman; whether it be done by an individual villain, or an army of them? If we reason to the root of things we shall find no difference; neither can any just cause be assigned why we should punish in the one case and pardon in the other. Let them call me rebel, and welcome, I feel no concern from it; but I should suffer the misery of devils, were I to make a whore of my soul by swearing allegiance to one whose character is that of a sottish, stupid, stubborn, worthless, brutish man. I conceive likewise a horrid idea in receiving mercy from a being, who at the last day shall be shrieking to the rocks and mountains to cover him, and fleeing with terror from the orphan, the widow, and the slain of America.

There are cases which cannot be overdone by language, and this is one. There are persons, too, who see not the full extent of the evil which threatens them; they solace themselves with hopes that the enemy, if he succeed, will be merciful. It is the madness of folly, to expect mercy from those who have refused to do justice; and even mercy, where conquest is the object, is only a trick of war; the cunning of the fox is as murderous as the violence of the wolf, and we ought to guard equally against both. Howe's first object is, partly by threats and partly by promises, to terrify or seduce the people to deliver up their arms and receive mercy. The ministry recommended the same plan to Gage and this is what the Tories call making their peace, *"a peace which passeth all understanding"* indeed! A peace which would be the immediate forerunner of a worse ruin than any we have yet thought of. Ye men of Pennsylvania, do reason upon these things! Were the back counties to give up their arms, they would fall an easy prey to the Indians, who are all armed: this perhaps is what some Tories would not be sorry for. Were the home counties to deliver up their arms, they would be exposed to the resentment of the back counties, who would then have it in their power to chastise their defection at pleasure. And were any one state to give up its arms, *that* state must be garrisoned by all Howe's army of Britons and Hessians to preserve it from the anger of the rest. Mutual fear is the principal link in the chain of mutual love, and woe be to that state that breaks the compact. Howe is mercifully inviting you to barbarous destruction, and men must be either rogues or fools that will not see it. I dwell not upon the vapors of imagination; I bring reason to your ears, and, in language as plain as A, B, C, hold up truth to your eyes.

I thank God, that I fear not. I see no real cause for fear. I know our situation well, and can see the way out of it. While our army was collected, Howe dared not risk a battle; and it is no credit to him that he decamped from the White Plains, and waited a mean opportunity to ravage the defenceless Jerseys; but it is great credit to us, that, with a handful of men, we sustained an orderly retreat for near an hundred miles, brought off our ammunition, all our field pieces, the greatest part of our stores, and had four rivers to pass. None can say that our retreat was precipitate, for we were near three weeks in performing it, that the country might have time to come in. Twice we marched back to meet the enemy, and remained out till dark. The sign of fear was not seen in our camp, and had not some of the cowardly and disaffected inhabitants spread false alarms through the country, the Jerseys had never been ravaged. Once more we are again collected and collecting; our new army at both ends of the continent is recruiting fast, and we shall be able to open the next campaign with sixty thousand men, well armed and clothed. This is our situation, and who will may know it. By perseverance and fortitude we have the prospect of a glorious issue; by cowardice and submission, the sad choice of a variety of evils—a ravaged country—a depopulated city—habitations without safety, and slavery without hope —our homes turned into barracks and bawdyhouses for Hessians, and a future race to provide for, whose fathers we shall doubt of. Look on this picture and weep over it! and if there yet remains one thoughtless wretch who believes it not, let him suffer it unlamented.

On Slavery

Patrick Henry

Hanover, January 18, 1773

Dear Sir:

I take this opportunity to acknowledge the receipt of Anthony Benezet's book against the Slave Trade. I thank you for it.

It is not a little surprising that the professors of Christianity, whose chief excellence consists in softening the human heart, and in cherishing and improving its finer feelings, should encourage a practice [slavery] so totally repugnant to the first impressions of right and wrong.

What adds to the wonder is that this abominable practice has been introduced in the most enlightened ages. Times that seem to have pretensions to boast of high improvements in the arts and sciences and refined morality, have brought into general use, and guarded by many laws, a species of violence and tyranny which our more rude and barbarous, but more honest, ancestors detested.

Is it not amazing that at a time when the rights of humanity are defined and understood in a country, above all others, fond of liberty, that in such an age and country we find men professing a religion the most humane, mild, gentle, and generous, adopting a principle as repugnant to humanity as it is inconsistent with the Bible and destructive to liberty. Every thinking, honest man rejects it in speculation, how few in practice from conscientious motives!

Would anyone believe I am a master of slaves of my own purchase! I am drawn along by the general inconvenience of living here without them.

I will not, I cannot justify it. However culpable my conduct, I will so far pay my *devoir* to virtue as to own the excellence and rectitude of her precepts and lament my want of conformity to them.

I believe a time will come when an opportunity will be offered to abolish this lamentable evil. Everything we can do is to improve it, if it happens in our day. If not, let us transmit to our descendants, together with our slaves, a pity for their unhappy lot and an abhorrence of slavery.

211

If we cannot reduce this wished-for reformation to practice, let us treat the unhappy victims with lenity. It is the furthest advance we can make toward justice. It is a debt we owe to the purity of our religion, to show that it is at variance with that law which warrants slavery.

I know not when to stop. I could say many things on the subject, a serious view of which gives a gloomy perspective to future times.

FAMILY CORRESPONDENCE

Abigail and John Adams

JOHN ADAMS TO ABIGAIL ADAMS

My Dr.   Falmouth July 9, 1774

... I cannot with all my Philosophy and christian Resignation keep up my spirits. The dismal Prospect before me, my Family, and my country, are too much, for my Fortitude ...

At Table We were speaking about Captain Maccarty, which led to the Affrican Trade. J[udge] Trowbridge said that was a very humane and Christian Trade to be sure, that of making Slaves.—Ay, says I, It makes no great Odds, it is a Trade that almost all Mankind have been concerned in, all over the Globe, since Adam, more or less in one Way and another.—This occasioned a Laugh. . . .

ABIGAIL ADAMS TO JOHN ADAMS

October 22, 1774

... I wish most sincerely there was not a Slave in the province. It allways appeard a most iniquitious Scheme to me—fight ourselfs for what we are daily robbing and plundering from those who have as good a right to freedom as we have. You know my mind upon this Subject.

I left all our little ones well, and shall return to them to night. I hope to hear from you by the return of the bearer of this and by Revere. I long for the Day of your re turn, yet look upon you much safer where you are . . . .

Braintree March 31, 1776

... I am willing to allow the Colony great merrit for having produced a Washington but they have been shamefully duped by a Dunmore.

I have sometimes been ready to think that the passion for Liberty cannot be Eaquelly Strong in the Breasts of those who have been accustomed to deprive their fellow Creatures of theirs. Of this I am certain that it is not founded upon that generous and christian principal of doing to others as we would that others should do unto us.

Do not you want to see Boston; I am fearfull of the small pox, or I should have been in before this time. I got Mr. Crane to go to our House and see what state it was in. I find it has been occupied by one of the Doctors of a Regiment, very dirty, but no other damage has been done to it. . . .

I feel very differently at the approach of spring to what I did a month ago. We knew not then whether we could plant or sow with safety, whether when we had toiled we could reap the fruits of our own industery, whether we could rest in our own Cottages, or whether we should not be driven from the sea coasts to seek shelter in the wilderness, but now we feel as if we might sit under our own vine and eat the good of the land.

I feel a gaieti de Coar to which before I was a stranger. I think the Sun looks brighter, the Birds sing more melodiously, and Nature puts on a more chearfull countanance. We feel a temporary peace, and the poor fugitives are returning to their deserted habitations.

Tho we felicitate ourselves, we sympathize with those who are trembling least the ot of Boston should be theirs. But they cannot be in similar circumst nces unless pusilanimity and cowardise should take possession of them. They have time and warning given them to see the Evil and shun it.—I long to hear that you have declared an independancy—and by the way in the new Code of Laws which I suppose it will be necessary for you to make I desire you would Remember the Ladies, and be more generous and favourable to them than your ancestors. Do not put such unlimited power into the hands of the Husbands. Remember all Men would be tyrants if they could. If perticuliar care and attention is not paid to the Laidies we are determined to foment a Rebelion, and will not hold ourselves bound by any Laws in which we have no voice, or Representation.

That your Sex are Naturally Tyrannical is a Truth so thoroughly established as to admit of no dispute, but such of you as wish to be happy willingly give up the harsh title of Master for the more tender and endearing one of Friend. Why then, not put it out of the power of the vicious and the Lawless to use us with cruelty and indignity with impunity. Men of Sense in all Ages abhor those customs which treat us only as the vassals of your Sex. Regard us then as Beings placed by providence under your protection and in immitation of the Supreem Being make use of that power only for our happiness.

April 5

. . . I want to hear much oftener from you than I do. March 8 was the last date of any that I have yet had.—You inquire of whether I am making Salt peter. I have not yet attempted it, but after Soap making believe I shall make the experiment. I find as much as I can do to manufacture cloathing for my family which would else be Naked. . . .

JOHN ADAMS TO ABIGAIL ADAMS

Ap. 14, 1776

. . . But let Us take Warning and give it to our Children. Whenever Vanity, and Gaiety, a Love of Pomp and Dress, Furniture, Equipage, Buildings, great Company, expensive Diversions, and elegant Entertainments get the better of the Principles and Judgments of Men or Women there is no knowing where they will stop, nor into what Evils, natural, moral, or political, they will lead us.

Your Description of your own Gaiety de Coeur, charms me. Thanks be to God you have just Cause to rejoice—and may the bright Prospect be obscured by no Cloud.

As to Declarations of Independency, be patient. Read our Privateering Laws, and our Commercial Laws. What signifies a Word.

As to your extraordinary Code of Laws, I cannot but laugh. We have been told that our Struggle has loosened the bands of Governm ent every where. That Children and Apprentices were disobedient—that schools and Colledges were grown turbulent—that Indians slighted their Guardians and Negroes grew insolent to their Masters. But your Letter was the first Intimation that another Tribe more numerous and powerfull than all the rest were grown discontented.—This is rather too coarse a Compliment but you are so saucy, I wont blot it out.

Depend upon it, We know better than to repeal our Masculine systems. Altho they are in full Force, you know they are little more than Theory. We dare not exert our Power in its full Latitude. We are obliged to go fair, and softly, and in Practice you know We are the subjects. We have only the Name of Masters, and rather than give up this, which would compleatly subject Us to the Despotism of the Peticoat, I hope General Washington, and all our brave Heroes would fight. I am sure every good Politician would plot, as long as he would against Despotism, Empire, Monarchy, Aristocracy, Oligarchy, or Ochlocracy.—A fine Story indeed. I begin to think the Ministry as deep as they are wicked. After stirring up Tories, Landjobbers, Trimmers, Bigots, Canadians,

Indians, Negroes, Hanoverians, Hessians, Russians, Irish Roman Catholicks, Scotch Renegadoes, at last they have stimulated the [ladies] to demand new Priviledges and threaten to rebell. . . .

ABIGAIL ADAMS TO MERCY OTIS WARREN

Braintree April 27, 1776

. . . He is very sausy to me in return for a List of Female Grievances which I transmitted to him. I think I will get you to join me in a petition to Congress. I thought it was very probable our wise Statesmen would erect a New Goverment and form a new code of Laws. I ventured to speak a word in behalf of our Sex, who are rather hardly dealt with by the Laws of England which gives such unlimitted power to the Husband to use his wife Ill.

I requested that our Legislators would consider our case and as all Men of Delicacy and Sentiment are averse to Excercising the power they possess, yet as there is a natural propensity in Humane Nature to domination, I thought the most generous plan was to put it out of the power of the Arbitary and tyranick to injure us with impunity by Establisbing some Laws in our favour upon just and Liberal principals.

I believe I even threatned fomenting a Rebellion in case we were not considerd, and assured him we would not hold ourselves bound by any Laws in which we had neither a voice, nor representation.

In return he tells me he cannot but Laugh at My Extrodonary Code of Laws. That he had heard their Struggle had loosned the bands of Goverment, that children and apprentices were dissabedient, that Schools and Colledges were grown turbulant, that Indians slighted their Guardians, and Negroes grew insolent to their Masters. But my Letter was the first intimation that another Tribe more numerous and powerfull than all the rest were grown discontented. This is rather too coarse a complement, he adds, but that I am so sausy he wont blot it out.

So I have help'd the Sex abundantly, but I will tell him I have only been making trial of the Disintresstedness of his Virtue, and when weigh'd in the balance have found it wanting.

It would be bad policy to grant us greater power say they since under all the disadvantages we Labour we have the assendancy over their Hearts. . . .

ABIGAIL ADAMS TO JOHN ADAMS

B[raintre]e May 7, 1776

How many are the solitary hours I spend, ruminating upon the past, and anticipating the future, whilst you overwhelmd with the cares of State, have but few moments you can devote to any individual. All domestick pleasures and injoyments are absorbed in the great and important duty you owe your Country "for our Country is as it were a secondary God, and the First and greatest parent. It is to be preferred to Parents, Wives, Children, Friends and all things the Gods only excepted. For if our Country perishes it is as imposible to save an Individual, as to preserve one of the fingers of a Mortified Hand." Thus do I supress every wish, and silence every Murmer, acquiesceing in a painfull Seperation from the companion of my youth, and the Friend of my Heart. . . .

I can not say that I think you very generous to the Ladies, for whilst you are proclaiming peace and good will to Men, Emancipating all Nations, you insist upon retaining an absolute power over Wives. But you must remember that Arbitary power is like most other things which are very hard, very liable to be broken—and notwithstanding all your wise Laws and Maxims we have it in our power not only to free ourselves but to subdue our Masters, and without voilence throw both your natural and legal authority at our feet—

"Charm by accepting, by submitting sway
Yet have our Humour most when we obey,"

I thank you for several Letters which I have received since I wrote Last. They alleviate a tedious absence, and I long earnestly for a Saturday Evening, and experience a similar pleasure to that which I used to find in the return of my Friend upon that day after a weeks absence. The Idea of a year dissolves all my Phylosophy.

Our Little ones whom you so often recommend to my care and instruction shall not be deficient in virtue or probity if the precepts of a Mother have their desired Effect, but they would be doubly inforced could they be indulged with the example of a Father constantly before them; I often point them to their Sire. . . .

JOHN ADAMS TO ABIGAIL ADAMS

May 17, 1776

. . . Is it not a Saying of Moses, who am I, that I should go in and out before this great People? When I consider the great Events which are passed, and those greater which are rapidly advancing, and that I may have been instrumental of touching some Springs, and turning some small Wheels, which have had and will have such Effects, I feel an Awe upon my Mind, which is not easily described.

G[reat] B[ritain] has at last driven America, to the last Step, a compleat Seperation from her, a total absolute Independence, not only of her Parliament but of her Crown, for such is the Amount of the Resolve of the 15th. . . .

I have Reasons to believe that no Colony, which shall assume a Government under the People, will give it up. There is something very unnatural and odious in a Government 1000 Leagues off. An whole Government of our own Choice, managed by Persons whom We love, revere, and can confide in, has charms in it for which Men will fight. Two young Gentlemen from South Carolina, now in this City, who were in Charlestown when their new Constitution was promulgated, and when their new Governor and Council and Assembly walked out in Procession, attended by the Guards, Company of Cadetts, Light Horse &c., told me, that they were beheld by the People with Transports and Tears of Joy. The People gazed at them, with a Kind of Rapture. They both told me, that the Reflection that these were Gentlemen whom they all loved, esteemed and revered, Gentlemen of their own Choice, whom they could trust, and whom they could displace if any of them should behave amiss, affected them so that they could not help crying.

They say their People will never give up this Government. . . .

In one or two of your Letters you remind me to think of you as I ought. Be assured there is not an Hour in the Day, in which I do not think of you as I ought, that is with every Sentiment of Tenderness, Esteem, and Admiration.

AN EPITAPH FOR JOHN JACK

(1773)

Daniel Bliss

God
Wills us free
Man
Wills us slaves.
God's will be done.
Here lies the body of John Jack,
Native of Africa, who died March 1773
Aged about sixty years.
Tho' born in an land of slaves
He was born free.
Tho' he lived in a land of liberty
He lived a slave,
'Till by his honest tho' stolen labour
He acquired the source of slavery
Which gave him his freedom:
Tho' not long before
Death the grand tyrant
Gave him his final emancipation,
And put him on a footing with kings.
Tho' a slave to vice
He practiced those virtues
Without which kings are but slaves.

Selected Writings

Phillis Wheatley

To The University Of Cambridge, In New England

While an intrinsic ardor prompts to write,
The muses promise to assist my pen;
'Twas not long since I left my native shore
The land of errors, and *Egyptian* gloom:
Father of mercy, 'twas thy gracious hand
Brought me in safety from those dark abodes.

Students, to you 'tis giv'n to scan the heights
Above, to traverse the etheral space,
And mark the systems of revolving worlds.
Still more, ye sons of science, ye receive
The blissful news by messengers from heav'n
How *Jesus'* blood for your redemption flows.
See Him with hands outstretched upon the cross;
Immense compassion in His bosom glows;
He hears revilers, nor resents their scorn;
What matchless mercy in the Son of God!
When the whole human race by sin had fall'n,
He deign'd to die that they might rise again,
And share with Him in the sublimest skies,
Life without death, and glory without end.

Improve your privileges while they stay,
Ye pupils, and each hour redeem, that bears
Or good or bad report of you to heav'n.
Let sin, that baneful evil to the soul,
By you be shunned, nor once remit your guard;
Suppress the deadly serpent in its egg.
Ye blooming plants of human race divine,

An *Ethiop* tells you 'tis your greatest foe;
Its transient sweetness turns to endless pain,
And in immense perdition sinks the soul.

ON BEING BROUGHT FROM AFRICA
TO AMERICA

'Twas mercy brought me from my *Pagan* land,
Taught my benighted soul to understand
That there's a God, that there's a *Saviour* too:
Once I redemption neither sought nor knew.
Some view our sable race with scornful eye,
"Their colour is a diabolic dye."
Remember, *Christians*, *Negroes*, black as *Cain*,
May be refined, and join th' angelic train.

AN HYMN TO THE MORNING

Attend my lays, ye ever honour'd nine,
Assist my labours, and my strains refine;
In smoothest numbers pour the notes along,
For bright *Aurora* now demands my song.

Aurora hail, and all the thousand dyes,
Which deck thy progress through the vaulted skies:
The morn awakes, and wide extends her rays,
On ev'ry leaf the gentle zephyr plays;
Harmonious lays the feather'd race resume,
Dart the bright eye, and shake the painted plume.

Ye shady groves, your verdant gloom display
To shield your poet from the burning day:
Calliope awake the sacred lyre,
While thy fair sisters fan the pleasing fire:
The bow'rs, the gales, the variegated skies
In all their pleasures in my bosom rise.

See in the east th' illustrious king of day!
His rising radiance drives the shades away—
But Oh! I feel his fervid beams too strong,
And scarce begun, conclude th' abortive song.

AN HYMN TO THE EVENING

Soon as the sun forsook the eastern main
The pealing thunder shook the heav'nly plain;
Majestic grandeur! From the zephyr's wing,
Exhales the incense of the blooming spring.
Soft purl the streams, the birds renew their notes,
And through the air their mingled music floats.

Through all the heav'ns what beauteous dyes are
    spread!
But the west glories in the deepest red:
So may our breasts with ev'ry virtue glow,
The living temples of our God below!

Filled with the praise of him who gives the light;
And draws the sable curtains of the night,
Let placid slumbers soothe each weary mind,
At morn to wake more heav'nly, more refined;
So shall the labours of the day begin
More pure, more guarded from the snares of sin.

Night's leaden sceptre seals my drowsy eyes,
Then cease, my song, till fair *Aurora* rise.

TO THE RIGHT HONORABLE WILLIAM, EARL OF DARTMOUTH.

Hail, happy day! when, smiling like the morn,
Fair Freedom rose, New-England to adorn:
The northern clime, beneath her genial ray,
Dartmouth! congratulates thy blissful sway;
Elate with hope, her race no longer mourns,
Each soul expands, each grateful bosom burns,

While in thine hand with pleasure we behold
The silken reins, and Freedom's charms unfold.
Long lost to realms beneath the northern skies,
She shines Supreme, while hated faction dies:
Soon as appeared the Goddess long desired,
Sick at the view she languished and expired;
Thus from the splendors of the morning light
The owl in sadness seeks the caves of night.

No more, America, in mournful strain,
Of wrongs and grievance unredressed complain;
No longer shall thou dread the iron chain
Which wanton Tyranny, with lawless hand,
Has made, and with it meant t'enslave the land.

Should You, my lord, while you peruse my song,
Wonder from whence my love of Freedom sprung,
Whence flow these wishes for the common good,
By feeling hearts alone best understood,
I, young in life, by seeming cruel fate
Was snatched from Afric's fancied happy seat:
What pangs excruciating must molest,
What sorrows labor in my parent's breast!
Steeled was that soul, and by no misery moved,
That from a father seized his babe beloved:
Such, such my case. And can I then but pray
Others may never feel tyrannic sway?

For favors past, great Sir, our thanks are due,
And thee we ask thy favors to renew,
Since in thy power, as in thy will before,
To soothe the griefs which thou didst once deplore.
May heavenly grace the sacred sanction give
To all thy works, and thou forever live,
Not only on the wings of fleeting Fame,
Though praise immortal crowns the patriot's name,
But to conduct to heavens refulgent fane,
May fiery coursers sweep the etherial plain,
And bear thee upwards to that blest abode,
Where, like the prophet, thou shalt find thy God.

FROM A WHEATLEY LETTER OF 1774

The Israelites never accepted Egyptian rule, for in every human Breast, God has implanted a Principle, which we call Love of Freedom; it is impatient of Oppression, and pants for Deliverance; and by the Leave of our Modern Egyptians I will assert, that the Principle lives in us. God grant Deliverance in his own way and Time, and get him honor from all those whose Avarice impels them to countenance and help forward the Calamities of their Fellow Creatures. This I desire not for their Hurt, but to convince them of the strange Absurdity of their Conduct whose Words and Actions are so diametrically opposite. How well the Cry for Liberty, and the reverse Disposition for the Exercise of Oppressive Power over others agree,—I humbly think it does not require the Penetration of a Philosoper to determine.

from NOTES ON THE STATE OF VIRGINIA
(1787)

Thomas Jefferson

Slave children] should continue with their parents to a certain age, then be brought up, at the public expence, to tillage, arts or sciences, according to their geniusses, till the females should be eighteen, and the males twenty-one years of age, when they should be colonized to such place as the circumstances of the time should render most proper, sending them out with arms, implements of household and of the handicraft arts, seeds, pairs of the useful domestic animals, &c. to declare them a free and independant people, and extend to them our alliance and protection, till they have acquired strength; and to send vessels at the same time to other parts of the world for an equal number of white inhabitants; to induce whom to migrate hither, proper encouragements were to be proposed. It will probably be asked, Why not retain and incorporate the blacks into the state, and thus save the expence of supplying, by importation of white settlers, the vacancies they will leave? Deep rooted prejudices entertained by the whites; ten thousand recollections, by the blacks, of the injuries they have sustained; new provocations; the real distinctions which nature has made; and many other circumstances, will divide us into parties, and produce convulsions which will probably never end but in the extermination of the one or the other race.—To these objections, which are political, may be added others, which are physical and moral. The first difference which strikes us is that of colour. Whether the black of the negro resides in the reticular membrane between the skin and scarf-skin, or in the scarf-skin itself; whether it proceeds from the colour of the blood, the colour of the bile, or from that of some other secretion, the difference is fixed in nature, and is as real as if its seat and cause were better known to us. And is this difference of no importance? Is it not the foundation of a greater or less share of beauty in the two races? Are not the fine mixtures of red and white, the expressions of every passion by greater or less suffusions of colour in the one, preferable to that eternal monotony, which reigns in the countenances, that immoveable veil of black which covers all the emotions of the other race? Add to these, flowing hair, a more elegant symmetry of form, their own judgment in favour of the whites, declared by their preference of them, as uniformly as is the preference of the Oranootan for the black women over those of his own species. The circumstance of superior beauty, is thought worthy attention in the propagation of our horses, dogs, and other domestic animals; why not in that of man? Besides those of colour, figure, and hair, there are other physical distinctions proving a difference of race. They have less hair on the face and body. They secrete less by the kidnies, and more by the glands of the skin, which gives them a very strong and disagreeable odour. This greater degree of transpiration renders them more tolerant of heat, and less so of cold, than the whites. Perhaps too a difference of structure in the pulmonary apparatus, which a late ingenious experimentalist has discovered to be the principal regulator of animal heat, may have disabled them from extricating, in the act of inspiration, so much of that fluid from the outer air, or obliged them expiration, to part with more of it. They seem to require less sleep. A black, after hard labour through the day, will be induced by the slightest amusements to stir up till midnight, or later, though knowing he must be out with the first dawn of the morning. They are at least as brave, and more adventuresome. But this may perhaps proceed from a want of fore-thought, which prevents their seeing a danger till it be present. When present, they do not go through it with more coolness or steadiness than the whites. They are more ardent after their female: but love seems with them to be more an eager desire,.than a tender delicate mixture of sentiment and sensation. Their griefs are transient. Those numberless afflictions, which render it doubtful whether heaven has given life to us in mercy or in wrath, are less felt, and sooner forgotten with them. In general, their existence appears to participate more of sensation than reflection. To this be ascribed their disposition to sleep when abstracted from their diversions, and unemployed in labour. An animal whose body is at rest, and who does not reflect, must be disposed to sleep of course. Comparing them by their faculties of memory, reason, and imagination, it appears to me, that in memory they are equal to the whites; in reason much inferior, as I think one could scarcely be found capable of tracing and comprehending the investigations of Euclid; and that in imagination they are dull, tasteless, and anomalous. It would be unfair to follow them to

Africa for this investigation. We will consider them here, on the same stage with the whites, and where the facts are not apocryphal on which a judgment is to be formed. It will be right to make great allowances for the difference of condition, of education, of conversation, of the sphere in which they move. Many millions of them have been brought to, and born in America. Most of them indeed have been confined to tillage, to their own homes, and their own society: yet many have been so situated, that they might have availed themselves of the conversation of their masters; many have been brought up to the handicraft arts, from that circumstance have always been associated with the whites. Some have been liberally educated, and all have lived in countries where the arts and sciences are cultivated to a considerable degree, and have had before their eyes samples of the best works from abroad. The Indians, with no advantages of this kind, will often carve figures on their pipes not destitute of design and merit. They will crayon out an animal, a plant, or a country, so as to prove the existence of a germ in their minds which only wants cultivation. They astonish you with strokes of the most sublime oratory; such as prove their reason and sentiment strong, their imagination glowing and elevated. But never yet could I find that a black had uttered a thought above the level of plain narration; never see even an elementary trait of painting or sculpture. In music they are more generally gifted than the whites with accurate ears for tone and time, and they have been found capable of imagining a small catch.[1] Whether they will be equal to the composition of a more extensive run of melody, or of complicated harmony, is yet to be proved. Misery is often the parent of the most affecting touches in poetry.—Among the blacks is misery enough, God knows, but no poetry. Love is the peculiar œstrum of the poet. Their love is ardent, but it kindles the senses only, not the imagination. Religion indeed has produced a Phyllis Whately; but it could not produce a poet. The compositions published under her name are below the dignity of criticism. The heroes of the Dunciad are to her, as Hercules to the author of that poem. Ignatius Sancho has approached nearer to merit in composition, yet his letters do more honour to the heart than the head. They breathe the purest effusions of friendship and general philanthropy, and shew how great a degree of the latter may be compounded with strong religious zeal. He is often happy in the turn of his compliments, and his style is easy and familiar, except when he affects a Shandean fabrication of words. But his imagination is wild and extravagant, escapes incessantly from every restraint of reason and taste, and, in the course of its vagaries, leaves a tract of thought as incoherent and eccentric, as is the course of a meteor through the sky. His subjects should often have led him to a process of sober reasoning: yet we find him always substituting sentiment for demonstration. Upon the whole, though we admit him to the first place among those of his own colour who have presented themselves to the public judgment, yet when we compare him with the writers of the race among whom he lived, and particularly with the epistolary class, in which he has taken his own stand, we are compelled to enroll him at the bottom of the column. This criticism supposes the letters published under his name to be genuine, and to have received amendment from no other hand; points which would not be of easy investigation. The improvement of the blacks in body and mind, in the first instance of their mixture with the whites, has been observed by every one, and proves that their inferiority is not the effect merely of their condition of life. We know that among the Romans, about the Augustan age especially, the condition of their slaves was much more deplorable than that of the blacks on the continent of America. . . . Yet . . . their slaves were often their rarest artists. They excelled too in science, insomuch as to be usually employed as tutors to their master's children. Epictetus, Terence, and Phaedrus, were slaves. But they were of the race of whites. It is not their condition then, but nature, which has produced the distinction.—Whether further observation will or will not verify the conjecture, that nature has been less bountiful to them in the endowments of the head, I believe that in those of the heart she will be found to have done them justice. That disposition to theft with which they have been branded, must be ascribed to their situation, and not to any depravity of the moral sense. The man, in whose favour no laws of property exist, probably feels himself less bound to respect those made in favour of others. When arguing for ourselves, we lay it down as a fundamental, that laws, to be just, must give a reciprocation of right: that, without this, they are mere arbitrary rules of conduct, founded in force, and not in conscience: and it is a problem which I give to the master to solve, whether the religious precepts against the violation of property were not framed for him as well as his slave? And whether the slave may not as justifiably take a little from one, who has taken all from him, as he may slay one who would slay him? That a change in the relations in which a man is placed should change his ideas of moral right and wrong, is neither new, nor peculiar to the colour of the blacks. Homer tells us it was so 2600 years ago. . . .

> Jove fix'd it certain, that whatever day
> Makes man a slave, takes half his worth away.

But the slaves of which Homer speaks were whites. Notwithstanding these conditions which must weaken their respect for the laws of property, we find among them numerous instances of the most rigid integrity, and as many as among their better instructed masters, of benevolence, gratitude, and unshaken fidelity.—The opinion, that they are inferior in the faculties of reason and imagination, must be hazarded with great diffidence. To justify a general conclusion, requires many observations, even where the subject may be submitted to the anatomical knife, to optical glasses, to analysis by fire, or by solvents. How much more then where it is a faculty, not a substance, we are examining; where it eludes the research of all the senses; where the conditions of its existence are various and variously combined; where the effects of those which are present or absent bid defiance to calculation; let me add too, as a circumstance of great tenderness, where our conclusion would degrade a whole race of men from the rank in the scale of beings which their Creator may perhaps have given them. To our reproach it must be said, that though for a century and a half we have had under our eyes the races of black and of red men, they have never yet been viewed by us as subjects of natural history. I advance it therefore as a suspicion only, that the blacks, whether originally a distinct race, or made distinct by time and circumstances, are inferior to the whites in the endowments both of body and mind. It is not against experience to suppose, that different species of the same genus, or varieties of the same species, may possess different qualifications. Will not a lover of natural history then, one who views the gradations in all the races of animals with the eye of philosophy, excuse an effort to keep those in the department of man as distinct as nature has formed them? This unfortunate difference of colour, and perhaps of faculty, is a powerful obstacle to the emancipation of these people. Many of their advocates, while they wish to vindicate the liberty of human nature, are anxious also to preserve its dignity and beauty. Some of these, embarrassed by the question "What further is to be done with them?" join themselves in opposition with those who are actuated by sordid avarice only. Among the Romans emancipation required but one effort. The slave, when made free, might mix with, without staining the blood of his master. But with us a second is necessary, unknown to history. When freed, he is to be removed beyond the reach of mixture. . . .

MANNERS

. . . There must doubtless be an unhappy influence on the manners of our people produced by the existence of slavery among us. The whole commerce between master and slave is a perpetual exercise of the most boisterous passions, the most unremitting despotism on the one part, and degrading submissions on the other. Our children see this, and learn to imitate it; for man is an imitative animal. This quality is the germ of all education in him. From his cradle to his grave he is learning to do what he sees others do. If a parent could find no motive either in his philanthropy or his self-love, for restraining the intemperance of passion towards his slave, it should always be a sufficient one that his child is present. But generally it is not sufficient. The parent storms, child looks on, catches the lineaments of wrath, puts on the same airs in the circle of smaller slaves, gives a loose to his worst of passions, and thus nursed, educated, and daily exercised in tyranny, cannot but be stamped by it with odious peculiarities. The man must be a prodigy who can retain his manners and morals undepraved by such circumstances. And with what execration should the statesman be loaded, who permitting one half the citizens thus to trample on the rights of the other, transforms those into despots, and these into enemies, destroys the morals of the one part, and the amor patriæ of the other. For if a slave can have a country in this world, it must be any other in preference to that in which he is born to live and labour for another: in which he must lock up the faculties of his nature, contribute as far as depends on his individual endeavours to the evanishment of the human race, or entail his own miserable condition on the endless generations proceeding from him. With the morals of the people, their industry also is destroyed. For in a warm climate, no man will labour for himself who can make another labour for him. This is so true, that of the proprietors of slaves a very small proportion indeed are ever seen to labour. And can the liberties of a nation be thought secure when we have removed their only firm basis, a conviction in the minds of the people that these liberties are of the gift of God? That they are not to be violated but with his wrath? Indeed I tremble·for my country when I reflect that God is just: that his justice cannot sleep for ever: that considering numbers, nature and natural means only, a revolution of the wheel of fortune, an exchange of situation, is among possible events: that it may become probable by supernatural interference! The Almighty has no attribute which can take side with us in such a contest. . . .

MANUFACTURES

We never had an interior trade of any importance. Our exterior commerce has suffered very much from the beginning of the present contest. During this time we have manufactured within our families the most necessary articles of cloathing. Those of cotton will bear some comparison with the same kinds of manufacture in Europe; but those of wool, flax and hemp are very coarse, unsightly, and unpleasant: and such is our attachment to agriculture, and such our preference for foreign manufactures, that be it wise or unwise, our people will certainly return as soon as they can, to the raising [of] raw materials, and exchanging them for finer manufactures than they are able to execute themselves.

The political œconomists of Europe have established it as a principle that every state should endeavour to manufacture for itself: and this principle, like many others, we transfer to America, without calculating the difference of circumstance which should often produce a difference of result. In Europe the lands are either cultivated, or locked up against the cultivator. Manufacture must therefore be resorted to of necessity not of choice, to support the surplus of their people. But we have an immensity of land courting the industry of the husbandman. Is it best then that all our citizens should be employed in its improvement, or that one half should be called off from that to exercise manufactures and handicraft arts for the other? Those who labour in the earth are the chosen people of God, if ever he had a chosen people, whose breasts he has made his peculiar deposit for substantial and genuine virtue. It is the focus in which he keeps alive that sacred fire, which otherwise might escape from the face of the earth. Corruption of morals in the mass of cultivators is a phenomenon of which no age nor nation has furnished an example. It is the mark set on those, who not looking up to heaven, to their own soil and industry, as does the husbandman, for their subsistance, depend for it on the casualties and caprice of customers. Dependance begets subservience and venality, suffocates the germ of virtue, and prepares fit tools for the designs of ambition. This, the natural progress and consequence of the arts, has sometimes perhaps been retarded by accidental circumstances: but, generally speaking, the proportion which the aggregate of the other classes of citizens bears in any state to that of its husandmen, is the proportion of its unsound to its healthy parts, and is a good-enough barometer whereby to measure its degree of corruption. While we have land to labour then, let us never wish to see our citizens occupied at a work-bench, or twirling a distaff. Carpenters, masons, smiths, are wanting in husbandry: but, for the general operations of manufacture, let our workshops remain in Europe. It is better to carry provisions and materials to workmen there, than bring them to the provisions and materials, and with them their manners and principles. The loss by the transportation of commodities across the Atlantic will be made up in happiness and permanence of government. The mobs of great cities add just so much to the support of pure government, as sores do to the strength of the human body. It is the manners and spirit of a people which preserve a republic in vigor. A degeneracy in these is a canker which soon eats to the heart of its laws and constitution.

Note

1   The instrument proper to them is the Banjar, which they brought hither from Africa, and which is the original of the guitar, its chords being the four lower chords of the guitar.

from THE FEDERALIST PAPERS

James Madison

No. 10

To the People of the State of New York:

Among the numerous advantages promised by a well constructed union, none deserves to be more accurately developed than its tendency to break and control the violence of faction. The friend of popular governments, never finds himself so much alarmed for their character and fate, as when he contemplates their propensity to this dangerous vice. He will not fail therefore to set a due value on any plan which, without violating the principles to which he is attached, provides a proper cure for it. The instability, injustice and confusion introduced into the public councils, have in truth been the mortal diseases under which popular governments have everywhere perished, as they continue to be the favorite and fruitful topics from which the adversaries to liberty derive their most specious declamations. The valuable improvements made by the American Constitutions on the popular models, both ancient and modern, cannot certainly be too much admired; but it would be an unwarrantable partiality, to contend that they have as effectually obviated the danger on this side as was wished and expected. Complaints are every where heard from our most considerate and virtuous citizens, equally the friends of public and private faith, and of public and personal liberty; that our governments are too unstable; that the public good is disregarded in the conflicts of rival parties; and that measures are too often decided not according to the rules of justice and the rights of the minor party, but by the superior force of an interested and over-bearing majority. However anxiously we may wish that these complaints had no foundation, the evidence of known facts will not permit us to deny that they are in some degree true. It will be found indeed, on a candid review of our situation, that some of the distresses under which we labor, have been erroneously charged on the operation of our governments; but it will be found, at the same time, that other causes will not alone account for many of our heaviest misfortunes, and particularly for that prevailing and increasing distrust of public engagements, and alarm for private rights, which are echoed from one end of the continent to the other. These must be chiefly, if not wholly, effects of the unsteadiness and injustice with which a factious spirit has tainted our public administrations.

By a faction I understand a number of citizens, whether amounting to a majority or minority of the whole, who are united and actuated by some common impulse of passion, or of interest, adverse to the rights of other citizens or to the permanent and aggregate interests of the community. . . .

The latent causes of faction are thus sown in the nature of man; and we see them every where brought into different degrees of activity, according to the different circumstances of civil society. A zeal for different opinions concerning religion, concerning government and many other points, as well of speculation as of practice; an attachment to different leaders ambitiously contending for preeminence and power; or to persons of other descriptions whose fortunes have been interesting to the human passions, have in turn divided mankind into parties, inflamed them with mutual animosity, and rendered them much more disposed to vex and oppress each other, than to co-operate for their common good. So strong is this propensity of mankind to fall into mutual animosities, that where no substantial occasion presents itself, the most frivolous and fanciful distinctions have been sufficient to kindle their unfriendly passions and excite their most violent conflicts. But the most common and durable source of factions has been the various and unequal distribution of property. Those who hold and those who are without property have ever formed distinct interests in society. Those who are creditors and those who are debtors fall under a like discrimination. A landed interest, a manufacturing interest, a mercantile interest, a monied interest, with many lesser interests, grow up of necessity in civilized nations and divide them into different classes, actuated by different sentiments and views. The regulation of these various and interfering interests forms the principal task of modern legislation and involves the spirit of party and faction in the necessary and ordinary operations of government.

No man is allowed to be a judge in his own cause because his interest would certainly bias his judgment and, not improbably, corrupt his integrity. With equal, nay with greater reason, a body of men are unfit to be both judges and parties at the same time; yet, what are many of the most important acts of legislation but so many judicial determinations, not indeed concerning the right of single persons but concerning the rights of large bodies of citizens; and what are the different classes of legislators but advocates and parties to the causes which they determine? Is a law proposed concerning private debts? It is a question to which the creditors are parties on one side and the debtors on the other. Justice ought to hold the balance between them. Yet the parties are and must be themselves the judges; and the most numerous party, or, in other words, the most powerful faction must be expected to prevail. Shall domestic manufacturers be encouraged, and in what degree, by restrictions on foreign manufacturers? are questions which would be differently decided by the landed and the manufacturing classes, and probably by neither with a sole regard to justice and the public good. The apportionment of taxes on the various descriptions of property is an act which seems to require the most exact impartiality; yet, there is perhaps no legislative act in which greater opportunity and temptation are given to a predominant party, to trample on the rules of justice. Every shilling with which they over-burden the inferior number is a shilling saved to their own pockets.

It is in vain to say that enlightened statesmen will be able to adjust these clashing interests and render them all subservient to the public good. Enlightened statesmen will not always be at the helm; nor, in many cases, can such an adjustment be made at all, without taking into view indirect and remote considerations, which will rarely prevail over the immediate interest which one party may find in disregarding the rights of another, or the good of the whole.

The inference to which we are brought is that the *causes* of faction cannot be removed and that relief is only to be sought in the means of controlling its *effects*.

If a faction consists of less than a majority, relief is supplied by the republican principle, which enables the majority to defeat its sinister views by regular vote. It may clog the administration, it may convulse the society; but it will be unable to execute and mask its violence under the forms of the Constitution. When a majority is included in a faction, the form of popular government on the other hand enables it to sacrifice to its ruling passion or interest, both the public good and the rights of other citizens. To secure the public good, and private rights, against the danger of such a faction, and at the same time to preserve the spirit and the form of popular government, is then the great object to which our inquiries are directed. . . .

From this view of the subject, it may be concluded that a pure democracy, by which I mean a society consisting of a small number of citizens who assemble and administer the government in person, can admit of no cure for the mischiefs of faction. A common passion or interest will, in almost every case, be felt by a majority of the whole; a communication and concert results from the form of government itself; and there is nothing to check the inducements to sacrifice the weaker party or an obnoxious individual. Hence it is that such democracies have ever been spectacles of turbulence and contention, have ever been found incompatible with personal security or the rights of property, and have in general been as short in their lives as they have been violent in their deaths. Theoretic politicians, who have patronized this species of government have erroneously supposed that by reducing mankind to a perfect equality in their political rights, they would at the same time be perfectly equalized and assimilated in their possessions, their opinions, and their passions.

A republic, by which I mean a government in which the scheme of representation takes place, opens a different prospect and promises the cure for which we are seeking. Let us examine the points in which it varies from pure democracy, and we shall comprehend both the nature of the cure and the efficacy which it must derive from the union.

The two great points of difference between a democracy and a republic are first, the delegation of the government, in the latter, to a small number of citizens elected by the rest; secondly, the greater number of citizens and greater sphere of country over which the latter may be extended.

The effect of the first difference is, on the one hand, to refine and enlarge the public views by passing them through the medium of a chosen body of citizens whose wisdom may best discern the true interest of their country and whose patriotism and love of justice will be least likely to sacrifice it to temporary or partial considerations. Under such a regulation, it may well happen that the public voice pronounced by the representatives of the people will be more consonant to the public good than if pronounced by the people themselves convened for the purpose. . . .

. . . [H]owever small the republic may be, the representatives must be raised to a certain number in order to guard against the cabals of a few, and that however large it may be, they must be limited to a certain number in order to guard against the confusion of a multitude. Hence the number of representatives in the two cases, not being in proportion to that of the constituents, and being proportionally greatest in the small republic, it follows that if the proportion of fit characters be not less in the large than in the small republic, the former will present a greater option and consequently a greater probability of a fit choice. . . .

The other point of difference is, the greater number of citizens and extent of territory which may be brought within the compass of republican, than of democratic government; and it is this circumstance principally which renders factious combinations less to be dreaded in the former, than in the latter. The smaller the society, the fewer probably will be the distinct parties and interests composing it; the fewer the distinct parties and interests, the more frequently will a majority be found of the same party; and the smaller the number of individuals composing a majority, and the smaller the compass within which they are placed, the more easily will they concert and execute their plans of oppression. Extend the sphere, and you take in a greater variety of parties and interests; you make it less probable that a majority of the whole will have a common motive to invade the rights of other citizens; or if such a common motive exists, it will be more difficult for all who feel it to discover their own strength and to act in unison with each other. Besides other impediments, it may be remarked that where there is a consciousness of unjust or dishonorable purposes, communication is always checked by distrust, in proportion to the number whose concurrence is necessary.

Hence, it clearly appears that the same advantage which a republic has over a democracy, in controlling the effects of faction is enjoyed by a large over a small republic—is enjoyed by the union over the states composing it. Does this advantage consist in the substitution of representatives whose enlightened views and virtuous sentiments render them superior to local prejudices and to schemes of injustice? It will not be denied that the representation of the union will be most likely to possess these requisite endowments. Does it consist in the greater security afforded by a greater variety of parties, against the event of any one party being able to outnumber and oppress the rest? In an equal degree does the increased variety of parties, comprised within the union, increase this security. Does it, in fine, consist in the greater obstacles opposed to the concert and accomplishment of the secret wishes of an unjust and interested majority? Here, again, the extent of the union gives it the most palpable advantage.

The influence of factious leaders may kindle a flame within their particular states, but will be unable to spread a general conflagration through the other states; a religious sect, may degenerate into a political faction in a part of the confederacy; but the variety of sects dispersed over the entire face of it must secure the national councils against any danger from that source; a rage for paper money, for an abolition of debts, for an equal division of property, or for any other improper or wicked project, will be less apt to pervade the whole body of the union than a particular member of it; in the same proportion as such a malady is more likely to taint a particular county or district, than an entire state.

In the extent and proper structure of the union, therefore, we behold a republican remedy for the diseases most incident to republican government. And according to the degree of pleasure and pride, we feel in being republicans, ought to be our zeal in cherishing the spirit, and supporting the character of Federalists.

No. 54

The next view which I shall take of the House of Representatives relates to the apportionment of its members to the several States, which is to be determined by the same rule with that of direct taxes.

It is not contended that the number of people in each State ought not to be the standard for regulating the proportion of those who are to represent the people of each State. . . . [N]otwithstanding the imperfection of the rule as applied to the relative wealth and contributions of the States, it is evidently the least exceptionable among the practicable rules, and had too recently obtained the general sanction of America not to have found a ready preference with the convention.

All this is admitted, it will perhaps be said; but does it follow, from an admission of numbers for the measure of representation, or of slaves combined with free citizens as a ratio of taxation, that slaves ought to be included in the numerical rule of representation? Slaves are considered as property, not as persons. They ought therefore to be comprehended in estimates of taxation which are founded on property, and to be excluded from representation which is regulated by a census of persons. This is the objection, as I understand it, stated in its full force. I shall be equally candid in stating the reasoning which may be offered on the opposite side.

"We subscribe to the doctrine," might one of our Southern brethren observe, "that representation relates more immediately to persons, and taxation more immediately to property, and we join in the application of this distinction to the case of our slaves. But we must deny the fact that slaves are considered merely as property, and in no respect whatever as persons. The true state of the case is that they partake of both these qualities: being considered by our laws, in some respects, as persons, and in other respects as property. In being compelled to labor, not for himself, but for a master; in being vendible by one master to another master; and in being subject at all times to be restrained in his liberty and chastised in his body, by the capricious will of another—the slave may appear to be degraded from the human rank, and classed with those irrational animals which fall under the legal denomination of property. In being protected, on the other hand, in his life and in his limbs, against the violence of all others, even the master of his labor and his liberty; and in being punishable himself for all violence committed against others—the slave is no less evidently regarded by the law as a member of the society, not as a part of the irrational creation; as a moral person, not as a mere article of property. The federal Constitution, therefore, decides with great propriety on the case of our slaves, when it views them in the mixed character of persons and of property. This is in fact their true character. It is the character bestowed on them by the laws under which they live; and it will not be denied that these are the proper criterion; because it is only under the pretext that the laws have transformed the Negroes into subjects of property that a place is disputed them in the computation of numbers; and it is admitted that if the laws were to restore the rights which have been taken away, the Negroes could no longer be refused an equal share of representation with the other inhabitants.

"This question may be placed in another light. It is agreed on all sides that numbers are the best scale of wealth and taxation, as they are the only proper scale of representation. Would the convention have been impartial or consistent, if they had rejected the slaves from the list of inhabitants when the shares of representation were to be calculated, and inserted them on the lists when the tariff of contributions was to be adjusted? Could it be reasonably expected that the Southern States would concur in a system which considered their slaves in some degree as men when burdens were to be imposed, but refused to consider them in the same light when advantages were to be conferred? Might not some surprise also be expressed that those who reproach the Southern States with the barbarous policy of considering as property a part of their human brethren should themselves contend that the government to which all the States are to be parties ought to consider this unfortunate race more completely in the unnatural light of property than the very laws of which they complain?

"It may be replied, perhaps, that slaves are not included in the estimate of representatives in any of the States possessing them. They neither vote themselves nor increase the votes of their masters. Upon what principle, then, ought they to be taken into the federal estimate of representation? In rejecting them altogether, the Constitution would, in this respect, have followed the very laws which have been appealed to as the proper guide.

"This objection is repelled by a single observation. It is a fundamental principle of the proposed Constitution that as the aggregate number of representatives allotted to the several States is to be determined by a federal rule founded on the aggregate number of inhabitants, so the right of choosing this allotted number in each State is to be exercised by such part of the inhabitants as the State itself may designate. . . . Let the case of the slaves be considered, as it is in truth a peculiar one. Let the compromising expedient of the Constitution be mutually adopted which regards them as inhabitants, but as debased by servitude below the equal level of free inhabitants; which regards the *slave* as divested of two fifths of the *man*.

"After all, may not another ground be taken on which this article of the Constitution will admit of a still more ready defense? We have hitherto proceeded on the idea that representation related to persons only, and not at all to property. But is it a just idea? Government is instituted no less for protection of the property than of the persons of individuals. The one as well as the other, therefore, may be considered as represented by those who are charged with the government. Upon this principle it is that in several of the States, and particularly in the State of New York, one branch of the government is intended more especially to be the guardian of property and is accordingly elected by that part of the society which is most interested in this object of government. In the federal Constitution, this policy does not prevail. The rights of property are committed into the same hands with the personal rights. Some attention ought, therefore, to be paid to property in the choice of those hands. . . ."

Such is the reasoning which an advocate for the Southern interests might employ on this subject; and although it may appear to be a little strained in some points, yet on the whole, I must confess that it fully reconciles me to the scale of representation which the convention have established. . . .

CHAPTER 6

Old Values in a New Democracy

INTRODUCTION

TIMOTHY DWIGHT, 1752–1817
from Greenfield Hill (1794)

ROYALL TYLER, 1757–1826
from The Contrast (1787)

HUGH HENRY BRACKENRIDGE, 1748–1816
from Modern Chivalry (1793–1815)

The literature of the early republic shows authors' struggling to define and maintain traditional values in a time of substantial change. Timothy Dwight's *Greenfield Hill* glorified in the New England village the American socioeconomic moral economy where all might have a competence because no one took too much, in terms similar to those of Woolman and Crèvecoeur. He also shared their hatred of slavery, vicious in its gentlest New England guise, and vile in its worst form which Dwight, with patriotic tact, situated in the West Indies. Royall Tyler wrote the first successful American comedy in 1787 in New York City, where he spent a couple of weeks after a useless pursuit of the Shays' rebels routed by the Massachusetts militia. Putting a timely political essay in the mouth of his hero supporting a strong central government, Tyler concentrated on the contrast between Americans true to their own traditional values and those Americans who mindlessly aped new-fangled foreign fashions. This high moral argument was twined with the popular low comedy figures of Van Rough and especially Jonathan, both good souls if they followed their betters rather than their own instincts toward money-grubbing or uneducated decisions. Hugh Henry Brackenridge centered *Modern Chivalry* on a democratic Don Quoxiote who spends his life trying to save social decency and to keep an Irish servant by keeping him out of politics or the other "high" callings democratic citizens are ever anxious to bestow on his illiterate geniality. Brackenridge decided, good naturedly, that democrats wanted representatives no better than themselves and that the lowness of taste to which democratic liberty gave voice could be countered only by oppositional lowness.

Dwight and Tyler were New England Federalists, and Brackenridge a Pennsylvania Republican; the last two were influential judges and the first a prominent minister. Obviously literature at this point was not a paying profession, but a patriotic/pleasurable pastime.

CONSIDERATIONS

- What are the social ideals stressed in these early national works? What reservations or uneasiness about the new nation do they suggest?

- Who seems most hopeful and who most cynical about the process? Which authors would you connect with the Federalists and which to the Republicans?

- How important is the roughly equal "competence" that Dwight stresses to the advantages of American society?

- Why would Tyler stress old-fashioned virtues over fashionable ways? Does he see some danger to the common good in the economic graspingness of Van Rough and the political simplicity of Jonathan?

- Is Brackenridge right that democratic voters prefer someone incompetent to someone clearly better than they? Does American opportunity mean Teague O'Regan can become anything he wants?

- Do Brackenridge's dark truths deny Dwight's and Crèvecoeur's bright hopes?

from GREENFIELD HILL

Timothy Dwight

PART II THE FLOURISHING VILLAGE

Fair Verna! loveliest village of the west;
Of every joy, and every charm, possess'd;
How pleas'd amid thy varied walks I rove,
Sweet, cheerful walks of innocence, and love,
And o'er thy smiling prospects cast my eyes,
And see the seats of peace, and pleasure, rise,
And hear the voice of Industry resound,
And mark the smile of Competence, around!
Hail, happy village! O'er thy cheerful lawns,
With earliest beauty, spring delighted dawns;
The northward sun begins his vernal smile;
The spring-bird carols o'er the cressy rill:
The shower, that patters in the ruffled stream,
The ploughboy's voice, that chides the lingering team,
The bee, industrious, with his busy song,
The woodman's axe, the distant groves among,
The waggon, rattling down the rugged steep,
The light wind, lulling every care to sleep,
All these, with mingled music, from below,
Deceive intruding sorrow, as I go.

How pleas'd, fond Recollection, with a smile,
Surveys the varied round of wintery toil!
How pleas'd amid the flowers, that scent the plain,
Recalls the vanish'd frost, and sleeted rain;
The chilling damp, the ice-endangering street,
And treacherous earth that slump'd beneath the feet.

Yet even stern winter's glooms could joy inspire:
Then social circles grac'd the nutwood fire;
The axe resounded, at the sunny door;

The swain, industrious, trimm'd his flaxen store;
Or thresh'd, with vigorous flail, the bounding wheat,
His poultry round him pilfering for their meat;
Or slid his firewood on the creaking snow,
Or bore his produce to the main below;
Or o'er his rich returns exulting laugh'd;
Or pledg'd the healthful orchard's sparkling draught:
While, on his board, for friends and neighbours spread,
The turkey smoak'd, his busy housewife fed;
And Hospitality look'd smiling round,
And Leisure told his tale, with gleeful sound.

Then too, the rough road hid beneath the sleigh,
The distant friend despis'd a length of way,
And join'd the warm embrace, and mingling smile,
And told of all his bliss, and all his toil;
And, many a month elaps'd, was pleas'd to view
How well the household far'd, the children grew;
While tales of sympathy deceiv'd the hour,
And Sleep, amus'd, resign'd his wonted power.

Yes! let the proud despise, the rich deride,
These humble joys, to Competence allied:
To me, they bloom, all fragrant to my heart,
Nor ask the pomp of wealth, nor gloss of art.
And as a bird, in prison long confin'd,
Springs from his open'd cage, and mounts the wind,
Thro' fields of flowers, and fragrance, gaily flies,
Or re-assumes his birth-right, in the skies:
Unprison'd thus from artificial joys,
Where pomp fatigues, and fussful fashion cloys,
The soul, reviving, loves to wander free
Thro' native scenes of sweet simplicity;
Thro' Peace' low vale, where Pleasure lingers long,
And every songster tunes his sweetest song,
And Zephyr hastes, to breathe his first perfume,
And Autumn stays, to drop his latest bloom:
'Till grown mature, and gathering strength to roam,
She lifts her lengthen'd wings, and seeks her home.

But now the wintery glooms are vanish'd all;
The lingering drift behind the shady wall;
The dark-brown spots, that patch'd the snowy field;
The surly frost, that every bud conceal'd;
The russet veil, the way with slime o'erspread,
And all the saddening scenes of March are fled.

Sweet-smiling village! loveliest of the hills!
How green thy groves! How pure thy glassy rills!
With what new joy, I walk thy verdant streets!
How often pause, to breathe thy gale of sweets;
To mark thy well-built walls! thy budding fields!
And every charm, that rural nature yields;
And every joy, to Competence allied,
And every good, that Virtue gains from Pride!

No griping landlord here alarms the door,
To halve, for rent, the poor man's little store.
No haughty owner drives the humble swain
To some far refuge from his dread domain;
Nor wastes, upon his robe of useless pride,
The wealth, which shivering thousands want beside;
Nor in one palace sinks a hundred cots;
Nor in one manor drowns a thousand lots;
Nor, on one table, spread for death and pain,
Devours what would a village well sustain.
O Competence, thou bless'd by Heaven's decree,
How well exchang'd is empty pride for thee!
Oft to thy cot my feet delighted turn,
To meet thy chearful smile, at peep of morn;
To join thy toils, that bid the earth look gay;
To mark thy sports, that hail the eve of May;
To see thy ruddy children, at thy board,
And share thy temperate meal, and frugal hoard;
And every joy, by winning prattlers giv'n,
And every earnest of a future Heaven.

There the poor wanderer finds a table spread,
The fireside welcome, and the peaceful bed.
The needy neighbour, oft by wealth denied,

There finds the little aids of life supplied;
The horse, that bears to mill the hard-earn'd grain;
The day's work given, to reap the ripen'd plain;
The useful team, to house the precious food,
And all the offices of real good.

There too, divine Religion is a guest,
And all the Virtues join the daily feast.
Kind Hospitality attends the door,
To welcome in the stranger and the poor;
Sweet Chastity, still blushing as she goes;
And Patience smiling at her train of woes;
And meek-eyed Innocence, and Truth refin'd,
And Fortitude, of bold, but gentle mind.

Thou pay'st the tax, the rich man will not pay;
Thou feed'st the poor, the rich man drives away.
Thy sons, for freedom, hazard limbs, and life,
While pride applauds, but shuns the manly strife:
Thou prop'st religion's cause, the world around,
And shew'st thy faith in works, and not in sound.

Say, child of passion! while, with idiot stare,
Thou seest proud grandeur wheel her sunny car;
While kings, and nobles, roll bespangled by,
And the tall palace lessens in the sky;
Say, while with pomp thy giddy brain runs round,
What joys, like these, in splendour can be found?
Ah, yonder turn thy wealth-inchanted eyes,
Where that poor, friendless wretch expiring lies!
Hear his sad partner shriek, beside his bed,
And call down curses on her landlord's head,
Who drove, from yon small cot, her household sweet,
To pine with want, and perish in the street.
See the pale tradesman toil, the live-long day,
To deck imperious lords, who never pay!
Who waste, at dice, their boundless breadth of soil,
But grudge the scanty meed of honest toil.
See hounds and horses riot on the store,
By HEAVEN created for the hapless poor!

See half a realm one tyrant scarce sustain,
While meagre thousands round him glean the plain!
See, for his mistress' robe, a village sold,
Whose matrons shrink from nakedness and cold!
See too the Farmer prowl around the shed,
To rob the starving household of their bread;
And seize, with cruel fangs, the helpless swain,
While wives, and daughters, plead, and weep, in vain;
Or yield to infamy themselves, to save
Their sire from prison, famine, and the grave.

There too foul luxury taints the putrid mind,
And slavery there imbrutes the reasoning kind:
There humble worth, in damps of deep despair,
Is bound by poverty's eternal bar:
No motives bright the etherial aim impart,
Nor one fair ray of hope allures the heart.

But, O sweet Competence! how chang'd the scene,
Where thy soft footsteps lightly print the green!
Where Freedom walks erect, with manly port,
And all the blessings to his side resort,
In every hamlet, Learning builds her schools,
And beggars' children gain her arts, and rules;
And mild Simplicity o'er manners reigns
And blameless morals Purity sustains.

From thee the rich enjoyments round me spring,
Where every farmer reigns a little king;
Where all to comfort, none to danger, rise;
Where pride finds few, but nature all supplies;
Where peace and sweet civility are seen,
And meek good-neighbourhood endears the green.
Here every class (if classes those we call,
Where one extended class embraces all,
All mingling, as the rainbow's beauty blends,
Unknown where every hue begins or ends)
Each following each, with uninvidious strife,
Wears every feature of improving life.
Each gains from other comeliness of dress,

And learns, with gentle mien to win and bless,
With welcome mild the stranger to receive,
And with plain, pleasing decency to live;
Refinement hence even humblest life improves;
Not the loose fair, that form and frippery loves;
But she, whose mansion is the gentle mind,
Is thought, and action, virtuously refin'd.
Hence, wives and husbands act a lovelier part,
More just the conduct, and more kind the heart;
Hence brother, sister, parent, child, and friend,
The harmony of life more sweetly blend;
Hence labour brightens every rural scene;
Hence cheerful plenty lives along the green;
Still Prudence eves her hoard, with watchful care,
And robes of thrift and neatness, all things wear.

But hark! what voice so gaily fills the wind ?
Of care oblivious, whose that laughing mind?
'Tis yon poor black, who ceases now his song,
And whistling, drives the cumbrous wain along.
He never, dragg'd, with groans, the galling chain;
Nor hung, suspended, on th' infernal crane;
No dim, white spots deform his face, or hand,
Memorials hellish of the marking brand!
No seams of pincers, fears of scalding oil;
No waste of famine, and no wear of toil.
But kindly fed, and clad, and treated, he
Slides on, thro' life, with more than common glee.
For here mild manners good to all impart,
And stamp with infamy th' unfeeling heart;
Here law, from vengeful rage, the slave defends,
And here the gospel peace on earth extends.

He toils, 'tis true; but shares his master's toil;
With him, he feeds the herd, and trims the soil;
Helps to sustain the house, with clothes, and food,
And takes his portion of the common good:
Lost liberty his sole, peculiar ill,
And fix'd submission to another's will.
Ill, ah, how great! without that cheering sun,

The world is chang'd to one wide, frigid zone;
The mind, a chill'd exotic, cannot grow,
Nor leaf with vigour, nor with promise blow;
Pale, sickly, shrunk, it strives in vain to rise,
Scarce lives, while living, and untimely dies.

See fresh to life the Afric infant spring,
And plume its powers, and spread its little wing!
Firm is its frame, and vigorous is its mind,
Too young to think, and yet to misery blind.
But soon he sees himself to slavery born;
Soon meets the voice of power, the eye of scorn;
Sighs for the blessings of his peers, in vain;
Condition'd as a brute, tho' form'd a man.
Around he casts his fond, instinctive eyes,
And sees no good, to fill his wishes, rise:
(No motive warms, with animating beam,
Nor praise, nor property nor kind esteem,
Bless'd independence, on his native ground,
Nor sweet equality with those around;)
Himself, and his, another's shrinks to find,
Levell'd below the lot of human kind.
Thus, shut from honour's paths, he turns to shame,
And filches the small good, he cannot claim.
To sour, and stupid, sinks his active mind;
Finds joys in drink, he cannot elsewhere find;
Rule disobeys; of half his labour cheats;
In some safe cot, the pilfer'd turkey eats;
Rides hard, by night, the steed, his art purloins;
Serene from conscience' bar himself essoins;
Sees from himself his sole redress must flow,
And makes revenge the balsam of his woe.

Thus slavery's blast bids sense and virtue die;
Thus lower'd to dust the sons of Afric lie.
Hence sages grave, to lunar systems given,
Shall ask, why two-legg'd brutes were made by HEAVEN?

•   •   •

O thou chief curse, since curses here began;
First guilt, first woe, first infamy of man;
Thou spot of hell, deep smirch'd on human kind,
The uncur'd gangrene of the reasoning mind;
Alike in church, in state, and household all,
Supreme memorial of the world's dread fall;
O slavery ! laurel of the Infernal mind,
Proud Satan's triumph over lost mankind!

from THE CONTRAST

A Comedy in Five Acts

Royall Tyler

EXULT, each patriot heart!—this night is shown
A piece, which we may fairly call our own;
Where the proud titles of "My Lord! Your Grace!"
To humble *Mr.* and plain *Sir* give place.
Our Author pictures not from foreign climes
The fashions or the follies of the times;
But has confin'd the subject of his work
To the gay scenes—the circles of New-York.
On native themes his Muse displays her pow'rs;
If ours the faults, the virtues too are ours.
Why should our thoughts to distant countries roam,
When each refinement may be found at home?
Who travels now to ape the rich or great,
To deck an equipage and roll in state;
To court the graces, or to dance with ease,
Or by hypocrisy to strive to please?
Our free-born ancestors such arts despis'd;
Genuine sincerity alone they priz'd;
Their minds, with honest emulation fir'd;
To solid good—not ornament—aspir'd;
Or, if ambition rous'd a bolder flame,
Stern virtue throve, where indolence was shame.

But modern youths, with imitative sense,
Deem taste in dress the proof of excellence;
And spurn the meanness of your homespun arts,
Since homespun habits would obscure their parts;
Whilst all, which aims at splendour and parade,
Must come from Europe, *and be ready made.*
Strange! we should thus our native worth disclaim,
And check the progress of our rising fame.

Yet *one*, whilst imitation bears the sway,
Aspires to nobler heights, and points the way.
Be rous'd, my friends ! his bold example view;
Let your own Bards be proud to copy *you!*
Should rigid critics reprobate our play,
At least the patriotic heart will say,
"Glorious our fall, since in a noble cause,
The bold *attempt alone* demands applause."
Still may the wisdom of the Comic Muse
Exalt your merits, or your faults accuse.
But think not, 't is her aim to be severe;—
We all are mortals, and as mortals err.
If candor pleases, we are truly blest;
Vice trembles, when compell'd to stand confess'd.
Let not light Censure on your faults offend,
Which aims not to expose them, but amend.
Thus does our Author to your candor trust;
Conscious, the *free* are generous, as just.

ACT I

LETITIA. And so, Charlotte, you really think the pocket-hoop unbecoming.

CHARLOTTE. No, I don't say so. It may be very becoming to saunter round the house of a rainy day; to visit my grand-mamma, or to go to Quakers' meeting: but to swim in a minuet, with the eyes of fifty well-dressed beaux upon me, to trip it in the Mall, or walk on the battery, give me the luxurious, jaunty, flowing, bell-hoop. It would have delighted you to have seen me the last evening, my charming girl! I was dangling o'er the battery with Billy Dimple; a knot of young fellows were upon the platform; as I passed them I faltered with one of the most bewitching false steps you ever saw, and then recovered myself with such a pretty confusion, flirting my hoop to discover a jet black shoe and brilliant buckle. Gad! how my little heart thrilled to hear the confused raptures of—"*Demme, Jack, what a delicate foot!*" "*Ha! General, what a well-turned—*"

LETITIA. Fie! fie! Charlotte [*stopping her mouth*], I protest you are quite a libertine.

CHARLOTTE. Why, my dear little prude, are we not all such libertines? Do you think, when I sat tortured two hours under the hands of my friseur, and an hour more at my toilet, that I had any thoughts of my Aunt Susan, or my cousin Betsey? though they are both allowed to be critical judges of dress.

LETITIA. Why, who should we dress to please, but those who are judges of its merit?

CHARLOTTE. Why, a creature who does not know *Buffon* from *Soufflé*—Man!—my Letitia—Man! for whom we dress, walk, dance, talk, lisp, languish, and smile. Does not the grave Spectator assure us that even our much bepraised diffidence, modesty, and blushes are all directed to make ourselves good wives and mothers as fast as we can? Why, I'll undertake with one flirt of this hoop to bring more beaux to my feet in one week than the grave Maria, and her sentimental circle, can do, by sighing sentiment till their hairs are grey.

LETITIA. Well, I won't argue with you; you always out-talk me; let us change the subject. I hear that Mr. Dimple and Maria are soon to be married.

CHARLOTTE. You hear true. I was consulted in the choice of the wedding clothes. She is to be married in a delicate white satin, and has a monstrous pretty brocaded lutestring for the second day. It would have done you good to have seen with what an affected indifference the dear sentimentalist turned over a thousand pretty things, just as if her heart did not palpitate with her approaching happiness, and at last made her choice and arranged her dress with such apathy as if she did not know that plain white satin and a simple blond lace would show her clear skin and dark hair to the greatest advantage.

LETITIA. But they say her indifference to dress, and even to the gentleman himself, is not entirely affected.

CHARLOTTE. How?

LETITIA. It is whispered that if Maria gives her hand to Mr. Dimple, it will be without her heart.

CHARLOTTE. Though the giving the heart is one of the last of all laughable considerations in the marriage of a girl of spirit, yet I should like to hear what antiquated notions the dear little piece of old-fashioned prudery has got in her head.

LETITIA. Why, you know that old Mr. John-Richard-Robert-Jacob-Isaac-Abraham-Cornelius Van Dumpling, Billy Dimple's father (for he has thought fit to soften his name, as well as manners, during his English tour), was the most intimate friend of Maria's father. The old folks, about a year before Mr. Van Dumpling's death, proposed this match;

the young folks were accordingly introduced, and told they must love one another. Billy was then a good-natured, decent-dressing young fellow, with a little dash of the coxcomb, such as our young fellows of fortune usually have. At this time, I really believe she thought she loved him; and had they then been married, I doubt not they might have jogged on, to the end of the chapter, a good kind of a sing-song lack-a-daysaical life, as other honest married folks do.

CHARLOTTE. Why did they not then marry?

LETITIA. Upon the death of his father, Billy went to England to see the world and rub off a little of the patroon rust. During his absence, Maria, like a good girl, to keep herself constant to her *own true-love,* avoided company, and betook herself, for her amusement, to her books, and her dear Billy's letters. But, alas! how many ways has the mischievous demon of inconstancy of stealing into a woman's heart! Her love was destroyed by the very means she took to support it.

CHARLOTTE. How?—Oh! I have it—some likely young beau found the way to her study.

LETITIA. Be patient, Charlotte; your head so runs upon beaux. Why, she read *Sir Charles Grandison, Clarissa Harlowe,* Shenstone, and the *Sentimental Journey;* and between whiles, as I said, Billy's letters. But, as her taste improved, her love declined. The contrast was so striking betwixt the good sense of her books and the flimsiness of her love-letters, that she discovered she had unthinkingly engaged her hand without her heart; and then the whole transaction, managed by the old folks, now appeared so unsentimental, and looked so like bargaining for a bale of goods, that she found she ought to have rejected, according to every rule of romance, even the man of her choice, if imposed upon her in that manner. Clary Harlowe would have scorned such a match.

CHARLOTTE. Well, how was it on Mr. Dimple's return? Did he meet a more favourable reception than his letters?

LETITIA. Much the same. She spoke of him with respect abroad, and with contempt in her closet. She watched his conduct and conversation, and found that he had by travelling acquired the wickedness of Lovelace without his wit, and the politeness of Sir Charles Grandison without his generosity. The ruddy youth, who washed his face at the cistern every morning, and swore and looked eternal love and constancy, was now metamorphosed into a flippant, palid, polite beau, who devotes the morning to his toilet, reads a few pages of Chesterfield's letters, and then minces out, to put the infamous principles in practice upon every woman he meets.

CHARLOTTE. But, if she is so apt at conjuring up these sentimental bugbears, why does she not discard him at once?

LETITIA. Why, she thinks her word too sacred to be trifled with. Besides, her father, who has a great respect for the memory of his deceased friend, is ever telling her how he shall renew his years in their union, and repeating the dying injunctions of old Van Dumpling.

CHARLOTTE. A mighty pretty story! And so you would make me believe that the sensible Maria would give up Dumpling manor, and the all-accomplished Dimple as a husband, for the absurd, ridiculous reason, forsooth, because she despises and abhors him. Just as if a lady could not be privileged to spend a man's fortune, ride in his carriage, be called after his name, and call him her *own dear love* when she wants money, without loving and respecting the great he-creature. Oh! my dear girl, you are a monstrous prude.

LETITIA. I don't say what I would do; I only intimate how I suppose she wishes to act.

CHARLOTTE. No, no, no! A fig for sentiment! If she breaks, or wishes to break, with Mr. Dimple, depend upon it, she has some other man in her eye. A woman rarely discards one lover until she is sure of another. Letitia little thinks what a clue I have to Dimple's conduct. The generous man submits to render himself disgusting to Maria, in order that she may leave him at liberty to address me. I must change the subject.

[*Aside, and rings a bell.*

Enter SERVANT

Frank, order the horses to.—Talking of marriage, did you hear that Sally Bloomsbury is going to be married next week to Mr. Indigo, the rich Carolinian?

LETITIA. Sally Bloomsbury married!—why, she is not yet in her teens.

CHARLOTTE. I do not know how this is, but you may depend upon it, 'tis a done affair. I have it from the best authority. There is my aunt Wyerly's Hannah. You know Hannah; though a black, she is a wench that was never caught in a lie in her life. Now, Hannah has a brother who courts Sarah, Mrs. Catgut the milliner's girl, and she told Hannah's brother, and Hannah, who, as I said before, is a girl of undoubted veracity, told it directly to me, that Mrs. Catgut was making a new cap for Miss Bloomsbury, which, as it was very dressy, it is very probable is designed for a wedding cap. Now, as she is to be married, who can it be but to Mr. Indigo? Why, there is no other gentleman that visits at her papa's.

LETITIA. Say not a word more, Charlotte. Your intelligence is so direct and well grounded, it is almost a pity that it is not a piece of scandal.

CHARLOTTE. Oh! I am the pink of prudence. Though I cannot charge myself with ever having discredited a tea-party by my silence, yet I take care never to report anything of my acquaintance, especially if it is to their credit—*discredit,* I mean—until I have searched to the bottom of it. It is true, there is infinite pleasure in this charitable pursuit. Oh! how delicious to go and condole with the friends of some backsliding sister, or to retire with some old dowager or maiden aunt of the family, who love scandal so well that they cannot forbear gratifying their appetite at the expense of the reputation of their nearest relations! And then to return full fraught with a rich collection of circumstances, to retail to the next circle of our acquaintance under the strongest injunctions of secrecy—ha, ha, ha!—interlarding the melancholy tale with so many doleful shakes of the head, and more doleful "Ah! who would have thought it! so amiable, so prudent a young lady, as we all thought her, what a monstrous pity! well, I have nothing to charge myself with; I acted the part of a friend, I warned her of the principles of that rake, I told her what would be the consequence; I told her so, I told her so."—Ha, ha, ha!

LETITIA. Ha, ha, ha! Well, but, Charlotte, you don't tell me what you think of Miss Bloomsbury's match.

CHARLOTTE. Think! why I think it is probable she cried for a plaything, and they have given her a husband. Well, well, well, the puling chit shall not be deprived of her plaything: 'tis only exchanging London dolls for American babies.—Apropos, of babies, have you heard what Mrs. Affable's high-flying notions of delicacy have come to?

LETITIA. Who, she that was Miss Lovely?

CHARLOTTE. The same; she married Bob Affable of Schenectady. Don't you remember?

Enter SERVANT

SERVANT. Madam, the carriage is ready.

LETITIA. Shall we go to the stores first, or visiting?

CHARLOTTE. I should think it rather too early to visit, especially Mrs. Prim; you know she is so particular.

LETITIA. Well, but what of Mrs. Affable?

CHARLOTTE. Oh, I'll tell you as we go; come, come, let us hasten. I hear Mrs. Catgut has some of the prettiest caps arrived you ever saw. I shall die if I have not the first sight of them.[*Exeunt.*

SCENE II

A Room in VAN ROUGH'S *House*
MARIA sitting disconsolate at a Table,
with Books, & c.

• • •

Who is it that considers the helpless situation of our sex, that does not see that we each moment stand in need of a protector, and that a brave one too? Formed of the more delicate materials of nature, endowed only with the softer passions, incapable from our ignorance of the world, to guard against the wiles of mankind, our security for happiness often depends upon their generosity and courage. Alas! how little of the former do we find! How inconsistent! that man should be leagued to destroy that honour upon which solely rests his respect and esteem. Ten thousand temptations allure us, ten thousand passions betray us; yet the smallest deviation from the path of rectitude is followed by the contempt and insult of man, and the more remorseless pity of woman; years of penitence and tears cannot wash away the stain, nor a life of virtue obliterate its remembrance. Reputation is the life of woman; yet courage to protect it is masculine and disgusting; and the only safe asylum a woman of delicacy can find is in the arms of a man of honour. How naturally, then, should we love the brave and the generous; how gratefully should we bless the arm raised for our protection, when nerv'd by virtue and directed by honour! Heaven grant that the man with whom I may be connected—may be connected! Whither has my imagination transported me—whither does it now lead me? Am I not indissolubly engaged, by every obligation of honour which my own consent and my father's approbation can give, to a man who can never share my affections, and whom a few days hence it will be criminal for me to disapprove—to disapprove! would to heaven that were all—to despise. For, can the most frivolous manners, actuated by the most depraved heart, meet, or merit, anything but contempt from every woman of delicacy and sentiment?

[VAN ROUGH *without*. Mary!]

Ha! my father's voice—Sir!—

Enter VAN ROUGH

VAN ROUGH. What, Mary, always singing doleful ditties, and moping over these plaguy books.

MARIA. I hope, Sir, that it is not criminal to improve my mind with books, or to divert my melancholy with singing, at my leisure hours.

VAN ROUGH. Why, I don't know that, child; I don't know that. They us'd to say, when I was a young man, that if a woman knew how to make a pudding, and to keep herself out of fire and water, she knew enough for a wife. Now, what good have these books done you? have they not made you melancholy? as you call it. Pray, what right has a girl of your age to be in the dumps? haven't you everything your heart can wish; an't you going to be married to a young man of great fortune; an't you going to have the quit-rent of twenty miles square?

MARIA. One-hundredth part of the land, and a lease for life of the heart of a man I could love, would satisfy me.

VAN ROUGH. Pho, pho, pho! child; nonsense, downright nonsense, child. This comes of your reading your story-books; your Charles Grandisons, your Sentimental Journals, and your Robinson Crusoes, and such other trumpery. No, no, no! child, it is money makes the mare go; keep your eye upon the main chance, Mary.

MARIA. Marriage, Sir, is, indeed, a very serious affair.

VAN ROUGH. You are right, child; you are right. I am sure I found it so, to my cost.

MARIA. I mean, Sir, that as marriage is a portion for life, and so intimately involves our happiness, we cannot be too considerate in the choice of our companion.

VAN ROUGH. Right, child; very right. A young woman should be very sober when she is making her choice, but when she has once made it, as you have done, I don't see why she should not be as merry as a grig; I am sure she has reason enough to be so. Solomon says that "there is a time to laugh, and a time to weep." Now, a time for a young woman to laugh is when she has made sure of a good rich husband. Now, a time to cry, according to you, Mary, is when she is making choice of him; but I should think that a young woman's time to cry was when she despaired of *getting* one. Why, there was your mother, now: to be sure, when I popp'd the question to her she did look a little silly; but when she had once looked down on her apron-strings, as all modest young women us'd to do, and drawled out ye-s, she was as brisk and as merry as a bee.

MARIA. My honoured mother, Sir, had no motive to melancholy; she married the man of her choice.

VAN ROUGH. The man of her choice! And pray, Mary, an't you going to marry the man of your choice—what trumpery notion is this? It is these vile books [*throwing them away*]. I'd have you to know, Mary, if you won't make young Van Dumpling the man of *your* choice, you shall marry him as the man of *my* choice.

MARIA. You terrify me, Sir. Indeed, Sir, I am all submission. My will is yours.

VAN ROUGH. Why, that is the way your mother us'd to talk. "My will is yours, my dear Mr. Van Rough, my will is yours"; but she took special care to have her own way, though, for all that.

MARIA. Do not reflect upon my mother's memory, Sir—

VAN ROUGH. Why not, Mary, why not? She kept me from speaking my mind all her *life*, and do you think she shall henpeck me now she is *dead* too? Come, come; don't go to sniveling; be a good girl, and mind the main chance. I'll see you well settled in the world.

MARIA. I do not doubt your love, Sir, and it is my duty to obey you. I will endeavour to make my duty and inclination go hand in hand.

VAN ROUGH. Well, well, Mary; do you be a good girl, mind the main chance, and never mind inclination. Why, do you know that I have been down in the cellar this very morning to examine a pipe of Madeira which I purchased the week you were born, and mean to tap on your wedding day?—That pipe cost me fifty pounds sterling. It was well worth sixty pounds; but I overreach'd Ben Bulkhead, the super-cargo. I'll tell you the whole story. You must know that—

Enter SERVANT

SERVANT. Sir, Mr. Transfer, the broker, is below.   [*Exit.*

VAN ROUGH. Well, Mary, I must go. Remember, and be a good girl, and mind the main chance.

[*Exit.*

MARIA [*alone*]. How deplorable is my situation! How distressing for a daughter to find her heart militating with her filial duty! I know my father loves me tenderly; why then do I reluctantly obey him? Heaven knows! with what reluctance I should oppose the will of a parent, or set an example of filial disobedience; at a parent's command, I could wed awkwardness and deformity. Were the heart of my husband good, I would so magnify his good qualities with the eye of conjugal affection, that the defects of his person and manners should be lost in the emanation of his virtues. At a father's command, I could embrace poverty. Were the poor man my husband, I would learn resignation to my lot; I would enliven our frugal meal with good humour, and chase away misfortune from our cottage with a smile. At a father's command, I could almost submit to what every female heart knows to be the most mortifying, to marry a weak man, and blush at my husband's folly in every company I visited. But to marry a depraved wretch, whose only virtue is a polished exterior; who is actuated by the unmanly ambition of conquering the defenceless; whose heart, insensible to the emotions of patriotism, dilates at the plaudits of every unthinking girl; whose laurels are the sighs and tears of the miserable victims of his specious behaviour—can he, who has no regard for the peace and happiness of other families, ever have a due regard for the peace and happiness of his own? Would to heaven that my father were not so hasty in his temper! Surely, if I were to state my reasons for declining this match, he would not compel me to marry a man, whom, though my lips may solemnly promise to honour, I find my heart must ever despise.

[*Exit.*

END OF THE FIRST ACT

ACT II. SCENE I

Enter CHARLOTTE *and* LETITIA

CHARLOTTE [*at entering*]. Betty, take those things out of the carriage and carry them to my chamber; see that you don't tumble them. My dear, I protest, I think it was the homeliest of the whole. I declare I was almost tempted to return and change it.

LETITIA. Why would you take it?

CHARLOTTE. Didn't Mrs. Catgut say it was the most fashionable?

LETITIA. But, my dear, it will never fit becomingly on you.

CHARLOTTE. I know that; but did not you hear Mrs. Catgut say it was fashionable?

LETITIA. Did you see that sweet airy cap with the white sprig?

CHARLOTTE. Yes, and I longed to take it; but, my dear, what could I do? Did not Mrs. Catgut say it was the most fashionable; and if I had not taken it, was not that awkward gawky, Sally Slender, ready to purchase it immediately?

LETITIA. Did you observe how she tumbled over the things at the next shop, and then went off without purchasing anything, nor even thanking the poor man for his trouble? But, of all the awkward creatures, did you see Miss Blouze endeavouring to thrust her unmerciful arm into those small kid gloves?

CHARLOTTE. Ha, ha, ha, ha!

LETITIA. Then did you take notice with what an affected warmth of friendship she and Miss Wasp met? when all their acquaintance know how much pleasure they take in abusing each other in every company.

CHARLOTTE. Lud! I Letitia, is that so extraordinary? Why, my dear, I hope you are not going to turn sentimentalist. Scandal, you know, is but amusing ourselves with the faults, foibles, follies, and reputations of our friends; indeed, I don't know why we should have friends, if we are not at liberty to make use of them. But no person is so ignorant of the world as to suppose, because I amuse myself with a lady's faults, that I am obliged to quarrel with her person every time we meet; believe me, my dear, we should have very few acquaintances at that rate.

SERVANT *enters and delivers a letter to* CHARLOTTE, *and—*

[*Exit.*

CHARLOTTE. You'll excuse me, my dear.

[*Opens and reads to herself*

LETITIA. Oh, quite excusable.

CHARLOTTE. As I hope to be married, my brother Henry is in the city.

LETITIA. What, your brother, Colonel Manly?

CHARLOTTE. Yes, my dear; the only brother I have in the world.

LETITIA. Was he never in this city?

CHARLOTTE. Never nearer than Harlem Heights, where he lay with his regiment.

LETITIA. What sort of a being is this brother of yours? If he is as chatty, as pretty, as sprightly as you, half the belles in the city will be pulling caps for him.

CHARLOTTE. My brother is the very counterpart and reverse of me: I am gay, he is grave; I am airy, he is solid; I am ever selecting the most pleasing objects for my laughter, he has a tear for every pitiful one. And thus, whilst he is plucking the briars and thorns from the path of the unfortunate, I am strewing my own path with roses.

LETITIA. My sweet friend, not quite so poetical, and a little more particular.

CHARLOTTE. Hands off, Letitia. I feel the rage of simile upon me; I can't talk to you in any other way. My brother has a heart replete with the noblest sentiments, but then, it is like—it is like—Oh! you provoking girl, you have deranged all my ideas—it is like—Oh! I have it—his heart is like an old maiden lady's bandbox; it contains many costly things, arranged with the most scrupulous nicety, yet the misfortune is that they are too delicate, costly, and antiquated for common use.

LETITIA. By what I can pick out of your flowery description, your brother is no beau.

CHARLOTTE. No, indeed, he makes no pretension to the character. He'd ride, or rather fly, an hundred miles to relieve a distressed object, or to do a gallant act in the service of his country; but should you drop your fan or bouquet in his presence, it is ten to one that some beau at the farther end of the room would have the honour of presenting it to you before he had observed that it fell. I'll tell you one of his antiquated, anti-gallant notions. He said once in my presence, in a room full of company—would you believe it?—in a large circle of ladies, that the best evidence a gentleman could give a young lady of his respect and affection was to endeavour in a friendly manner to rectify her foibles. I protest I was crimson to the eyes, upon reflecting that I was known as his sister.

LETITIA. Insupportable creature! tell a lady of her faults! if he is so grave, I fear I have no chance of captivating him.

CHARLOTTE. His conversation is like a rich, old-fashioned brocade—it will stand alone; every sentence is a sentiment. Now you may judge what a time I had with him, in my twelve months' visit to my father. He read me such lectures, out of pure brotherly affection, against the extremes of fashion, dress, flirting, and coquetry, and all the other dear things which he knows I dote upon, that I protest his conversation made me as melancholy as if I had been at church; and heaven knows, though I never prayed to go there but on one occasion, yet I would have exchanged his conversation for a psalm and a sermon. Church is rather melancholy, to be sure; but then I can ogle the beaux, and be regaled with "here endeth the first lesson," but his brotherly *here,* you would think had no end. You captivate him! Why, my dear, he would as soon fall in love with a box of Italian flowers. There is Maria, now, if she were not engaged, she might do something. Oh! how I should like to see that pair of penserosos together, looking as grave as two sailors' wives of a stormy night, with a flow of sentiment meandering through their conversation like purling streams in modern poetry.

LETITIA. Oh! my dear fanciful—

CHARLOTTE. Hush! I hear some person coming through the entry.

Enter SERVANT

SERVANT. Madam, there's a gentleman below who calls himself Colonel Manly; do you choose to be at home?

CHARLOTTE. Show him in. [*Exit* SERVANT.] Now for a sober face.

Enter COLONEL MANLY

MANLY. My dear Charlotte, I am happy that I once more enfold you within the arms of fraternal affection. I know you are going to ask (amiable impatience!) how our parents do—the venerable pair transmit you their blessing by me. They totter on the verge of a well-spent life, and wish only to see their children settled in the world, to depart in peace.

CHARLOTTE. I am very happy to hear that they are well. [*Coolly.*] Brother, will you give me leave to introduce you to our uncle's ward, one of my most intimate friends?

MANLY [*saluting* LETITIA]. I ought to regard your friends as my own.

CHARLOTTE. Come, Letitia, do give us a little dash of your vivacity; my brother is so sentimental and so grave, that I protest he'll give us the vapours.

MANLY. Though sentiment and gravity, I know, are banished the polite world, yet I hoped they might find some countenance in the meeting of such near connections as brother and sister.

CHARLOTTE. Positively, brother, if you go one step further in this strain, you will set me crying, and that, you know, would spoil my eyes; and then I should never get the husband which our good papa and mamma have so kindly wished me—never be established in the world.

MANLY. Forgive me, my sister—I am no enemy to mirth; I love your sprightliness; and I hope it will one day enliven the hours of some worthy man; but when I mention the respectable authors of my existence—the cherishers and protectors of my helpless infancy, whose hearts glow with such fondness and attachment that they would willingly lay down their lives for my welfare—you will excuse me if I am so unfashionable as to speak of them with some degree of respect and reverence.

CHARLOTTE. Well, well, brother; if you won't be gay, we'll not differ; I will be as grave as you wish. [*Affects gravity.*] And so, brother, you have come to the city to exchange some of your commutation notes for a little pleasure?

MANLY. Indeed you are mistaken; my errand is not of amusement, but business; and as I neither drink nor game, my expenses will be so trivial, I shall have no occasion to sell my notes.

CHARLOTTE. Then you won't have occasion to do a very good thing. Why, here was the Vermont General—he came down some time since, sold all his musty notes at one stroke, and then laid the cash out in trinkets for his dear Fanny. I want a dozen pretty things myself; have you got the notes with you?

MANLY. I shall be ever willing to contribute, as far as it is in my power, to adorn or in any way to please my sister; yet I hope I shall never be obliged for this to sell my notes. I may be romantic, but I preserve them as a sacred deposit. Their full amount is justly due to me, but as embarrassments, the natural consequences of a long war, disable my country from supporting its credit, I shall wait with patience until it is rich enough to discharge them. If that is not in my day, they shall be transmitted as an honourable certificate to posterity, that I have humbly imitated our illustrious WASHINGTON, in having exposed my health and life in the service of my country, without reaping any other reward than the glory of conquering in so arduous a contest.

CHARLOTTE. Well said heroics. Why, my dear Henry, you have such a lofty way of saying things, that I protest I almost tremble at the thought of introducing you to the polite circles in the city. The belles would think you were a player run mad, with your head filled with old scraps of tragedy; and as to the beaux, they might admire, because they would not understand you. But, however, I must, I believe, introduce you to two or three ladies of my acquaintance.

LETITIA. And that will make him acquainted with thirty or forty beaux.

CHARLOTTE. Oh! brother, you don't know what a fund of happiness you have in store.

MANLY. I fear, sister, I have not refinement sufficient to enjoy it.

CHARLOTTE. Oh! you cannot fail being pleased.

LETITIA. Our ladies are so delicate and dressy.

CHARLOTTE. And our beaux so dressy and delicate.

LETITIA. Our ladies chat and flirt so agreeably.

CHARLOTTE. And our beaux simper and bow so gracefully.

LETITIA. With their hair so trim and neat.

CHARLOTTE. And their faces so soft and sleek.

LETITIA. Their buckles so tonish and bright.

CHARLOTTE. And their hands so slender and white.

LETITIA. I vow, Charlotte, we are quite poetical.

CHARLOTTE. And then, brother, the faces of the beaux are of such a lily-white hue! None of that horrid robustness of constitution, that vulgar cornfed glow of health, which can only serve to alarm an unmarried lady with apprehension, and prove a melancholy memento to a married one, that she can never hope for the happiness of being a widow. I will say this to the credit of our city beaux, that such is the delicacy of their complexion, dress, and address, that, even had I no reliance upon the honour of the dear Adonises, I would trust myself in any possible situation with them, without the least apprehensions of rudeness.

MANLY. Sister Charlotte!

CHARLOTTE. Now, now, now, brother [*interrupting him*], now don't go to spoil my mirth with a dash of your gravity; I am so glad to see you, I am in tip-top spirits. Oh! that you could be with us at a little snug party. There is Billy Simper, Jack Chaffé, and Colonel Van Titter, Miss Promonade, and the two Miss Tambours, sometimes make a party, with some other ladies, in a side-box at the play. Everything is conducted with such decorum. First we bow round to the company in general, then to each one in particular, then we have so many inquiries after each other's health, and we are so happy to meet each other, and it is so many ages since we last had that pleasure, and if a married lady is in company, we have such a sweet dissertation upon her son Bobby's chin-cough; then the curtain rises, then our sensibility is all awake, and then, by the mere force of apprehension, we torture some harmless expression into a double meaning, which the poor author never dreamt of, and then we have recourse to our fans, and then we blush, and then the gentlemen jog one another, peep under the fan, and make the prettiest remarks; and then we giggle and they simper, and they giggle and we simper, and then the curtain drops, and then for nuts and oranges, and then we bow, and it's pray, Ma'am, take it, and pray, Sir, keep it, and oh! not for the world, Sir; and then the curtain rises again, and then we blush and giggle and simper and bow all over again. Oh! the sentimental charms of a side-box conversation! [*All laugh.*]

MANLY. Well, sister, I join heartily with you in the laugh; for, in my opinion, it is as justifiable to laugh at folly as it is reprehensible to ridicule misfortune.

CHARLOTTE. Well, but, brother, positively I can't introduce you in these clothes: why, your coat looks as if it were calculated for the vulgar purpose of keeping yourself comfortable.

MANLY. This coat was my regimental coat in the late war. The public tumults of our state have induced me to buckle on the sword in support of that government which I once fought to establish. I can only say, sister, that there was a time when this coat was respectable, and some people even thought that those men who had endured so many winter campaigns in the service of their country, without bread, clothing, or pay, at least deserved that the poverty of their appearance should not be ridiculed.

CHARLOTTE. We agree in opinion entirely, brother, though it would not have done for me to have said it: it is the coat makes the man respectable. In the time of the war, when we were almost frightened to death, why, your coat was respectable, that is, fashionable; now another kind of coat is fashionable, that is, respectable. And pray direct the tailor to make yours the height of the fashion.

MANLY. Though it is of little consequence to me of what shape my coat is, yet, as to the height of the fashion, there you will please to excuse me, sister. You know my sentiments on that subject. I have often lamented the advantage which the French have over us in that particular. In Paris, the fashions have their dawnings, their routine, and declensions, and depend as much upon the caprice of the day as in other countries; but there every lady assumes a right to deviate from the general *ton* as far as will be of advantage to her own appearance. In America, the cry is, what is the fashion? and we follow it indiscriminately, because it is so.

CHARLOTTE. Therefore it is, that when large hoops are in fashion, we often see many a plump girl lost in the immensity of a hoop-petticoat, whose want of height and *en-bon-point* would never have been remarked in any other dress. When the high head-dress is the mode, how then do we see a lofty cushion, with a profusion of gauze, feathers, and ribbon, supported by a face no bigger than an apple! whilst a broad full-faced lady, who really would have appeared tolerably handsome in a large head-dress, looks with her smart chapeau as masculine as a soldier.

MANLY. But remember, my dear sister, and I wish all my fair country-women would recollect, that the only excuse a young lady can have for going extravagantly into a fashion is because it makes her look extravagantly handsome.—Ladies, I must wish you a good morning.

CHARLOTTE. But, brother, you are going to make home with us.

MANLY. Indeed I cannot. I have seen my uncle and explained that matter.

CHARLOTTE. Come and dine with us, then. We have a family dinner about half-past four o'clock.

MANLY. I am engaged to dine with the Spanish ambassador. I was introduced to him by an old brother officer; and instead of freezing me with a cold card of compliment to dine with him ten days hence, he, with the true old Castilian frankness, in a friendly manner, asked me to dine with him to-day—an honour I could not refuse. Sister, adieu—Madam, your most obedient—   [*Exit.*

CHARLOTTE. I will wait upon you to the door, brother; I have something particular to say to you.   [*Exit.*

LETITIA [*alone*]. What a pair!—She the pink of flirtation, he the essence of everything that is *outré* and gloomy.—I think I have completely deceived Charlotte by my manner of speaking of Mr. Dimple; she's too much the friend of Maria to be confided in. He is certainly rendering himself disagreeable to Maria, in order to break with her and proffer his hand to me. This is what the delicate fellow hinted in our last conversation.   [*Exit.*

SCENE II. *THE MALL*

Enter JESSAMY

JESSAMY. Positively this Mall is a very pretty place. I hope the cits won't ruin it by repairs. To be sure, it won't do to speak of in the same day with Ranelagh or Vauxhall; however, it's a fine place for a young fellow to display his person to advantage. Indeed, nothing is lost here; the girls have taste, and I am very happy to find they have adopted the elegant London fashion of looking back, after a genteel fellow like me has passed them.—Ah! who comes here? This, by his awkwardness, must be the Yankee colonel's servant. I'll accost him.

Enter JONATHAN

Votre très-humble, serviteur, Monsieur. I understand Colonel Manly, the Yankee officer, has the honour of your services.

JONATHAN. Sir!—

JESSAMY. I say, Sir, I understand that Colonel Manly has the honour of having you for a servant.

JONATHAN. Servant! Sir, do you take me for a neger—I am Colonel Manly's waiter.

JESSAMY. A true Yankee distinction, egad, without a difference. Why, Sir, do you not perform all the offices of a servant? do you not even blacken his boots?

JONATHAN. Yes; I do grease them a bit sometimes; but I am a true blue son of liberty, for all that. Father said I should come as Colonel Manly's waiter, to see the world, and all that; but no man shall master me. My father has as good a farm as the colonel.

JESSAMY. Well, Sir, we will not quarrel about terms upon the eve of an acquaintance from which I promise myself so much satisfaction—therefore, sans ceremonie—

JONATHAN. What?—

JESSAMY. I say I am extremely happy to see Colonel Manly's waiter.

JONATHAN. Well, and I vow, too, I am pretty considerably glad to see you; but what the dogs need of all this outlandish lingo? Who may you be, Sir, if I may be so bold?

JESSAMY. I have the honour to be Mr. Dimple's servant, or, if you please, waiter. We lodge under the same roof, and should be glad of the honour of your acquaintance.

JONATHAN. You a waiter! by the living jingo, you look so topping, I took you for one of the agents to Congress.

JESSAMY. The brute has discernment, notwithstanding his appearance.—Give me leave to say I wonder then at your familiarity.

JONATHAN. Why, as to the matter of that, Mr.—; pray, what's your name?

JESSAMY. Jessamy, at your service.

JONATHAN. Why, I swear we don't make any great matter of distinction in our state between quality and other folks.

JESSAMY. This is, indeed, a levelling principle.—I hope, Mr. Jonathan, you have not taken part with the insurgents.

JONATHAN. Why, since General Shays has sneaked off and given us the bag to hold, I don't care to give my opinion; but you'll promise not to tell—put your ear this way—you won't tell?—I vow I did think the sturgeons were right.

JESSAMY. I thought, Mr. Jonathan, you Massachusetts men always argued with a gun in your hand. Why didn't you join them?

JONATHAN. Why, the colonel is one of those folks called the Shin—Shin—dang it all, I can't speak them lignum vitæ words—you know who I mean—there is a company of them—they wear a china goose at their button-hole—a kind of gilt thing.—Now the colonel told father and brother—you must know there are, let me see—there is Elnathan, Silas, and Barnabas, Tabitha—no, no, she's a she—tarnation, now I have it—there's Elnathan, Silas, Barnabas, Jonathan, that's I—seven of us, six went into the wars, and I stayed at home to take care of mother. Colonel said that it was a burning shame for the true blue Bunker Hill sons of liberty, who had fought Governor Hutchinson, Lord North, and the Devil, to have any hand in kicking up a cursed dust against a government which we had, every mother's son of us, a hand in making.

JESSAMY. Bravo!—Well, have you been abroad in the city since your arrival? What have you seen that is curious and entertaining?

JONATHAN. Oh! I have seen a power of fine sights. I went to see two marblestone men and a leaden horse that stands out in doors in all weathers; and when I came where they was, one had got no head, and t'other weren't there. They said as how the leaden man was a damn'd tory, and that he took wit in his anger and rode off in the time of the troubles.

JESSAMY. But this was not the end of your excursion?

JONATHAN. Oh, no; I went to a place they call Holy Ground. Now I counted this was a place where folks go to meeting; so I put my hymn-book in my pocket, and walked softly and grave as a minister; and when I came there, the dogs a bit of a meeting-house could I see. At last I spied a young gentlewoman standing by one of the seats which they have here at the doors. I took her to be the deacon's daughter, and she looked so kind, and so obliging, that I thought I would go and ask her the way to lecture, and—would you think it?—she called me dear, and sweeting, and honey, just as if we were married: by the living jingo, I had a month's mind to buss her.

JESSAMY. Well, but how did it end?

JONATHAN. Why, as I was standing talking with her, a parcel of sailor men and boys got round me, the snarl- headed curs fell a-kicking and cursing of me at such a tarnal rate, that I vow I was glad to take to my heels and split home, right off, tail on end, like a stream of chalk.

JESSAMY. Why, my dear friend, you are not acquainted with the city; that girl you saw was a—   [*Whispers.*

JONATHAN. Mercy on my soul! was that young woman a harlot!— Well! if this is New-York Holy Ground, what must the Holy-day Ground be!

JESSAMY. Well, you should not judge of the city too rashly. We have a number of elegant, fine girls here that make a man's leisure hours pass very agreeably. I would esteem it an honour to announce you to some of them.— Gad! that announce is a select word; I wonder where I picked it up.

JONATHAN. I don't want to know them.

JESSAMY. Come, come, my dear friend, I see that I must assume the honour of being the director of your amusements. Nature has given us passions, and youth and opportunity stimulate to gratify them. It is no shame, my dear Blueskin, for a man to amuse himself with a little gallantry.

JONATHAN. Girl huntry! I don't altogether understand. I never played at that game. I know how to play hunt the squirrel, but I can't play anything with the girls; I am as good as married.

JESSAMY. Vulgar, horrid brute! Married, and above a hundred miles from his wife, and thinks that an objection to his making love to every woman he meets! He never can have read, no, he never can have been in a room with a volume of the divine Chesterfield.—So you are married?

JONATHAN. No, I don't say so; I said I was as good as married, a kind of promise.

JESSAMY. As good as married!—

JONATHAN. Why, yes; there's Tabitha Wymen, the deacon's daughter, at home; she and I have been courting a great while, and folks say as how we are to be married; and so I broke a piece of money with her when we parted, and she promised not to spark it with Solomon Dyer while I am gone. You wouldn't have me false to my true-love, would you?

JESSAMY. May be you have another reason for constancy; possibly the young lady has a fortune? Ha! Mr. Jonathan, the solid charms; the chains of love are never so binding as when the links are made of gold.

JONATHAN. Why, as to fortune, I must needs say her father is pretty dumb rich; he went representative for our town last year. He will give her—let me see-four times seven is—seven times four—nought and carry one—he will give her twenty acres of land—somewhat rocky though—a Bible, and a cow.

JESSAMY. Twenty acres of rock, a Bible, and a cow! Why, my dear Mr. Jonathan, we have servant-maids, or, as you would more elegantly express it, waitresses, in this city, who collect more in one year from their mistresses' cast clothes.

JONATHAN. You don't say so!—

JESSAMY. Yes, and I'll introduce you to one of them. There is a little lump of flesh and delicacy that lives at next door, waitress to Miss Maria; we often see her on the stoop.

JONATHAN. But are you sure she would be courted by me?

JESSAMY. Never doubt it; remember a faint heart never—blisters on my tongue—I was going to be guilty of a vile proverb; flat against the authority of Chesterfield. I say there can be no doubt that the brilliancy of your merit will secure you a favourable reception.

JONATHAN. Well, but what must I say to her?

JESSAMY. Say to her! why, my dear friend, though I admire your profound knowledge on every other subject, yet, you will pardon my saying that your want of opportunity has made the female heart escape the poignancy of your penetration. Say to her! Why, when a man goes a-courting, and hopes for success, he must begin with doing, and not saying.

JONATHAN. Well, what must I do?

JESSAMY. Why, when you are introduced, you must make five or six elegant bows.

JONATHAN. Six elegant bows! I understand that; six, you say? Well—

JESSAMY. Then you must press and kiss her hand; then press a kiss, and so on to her lips and cheeks; then talk as much as you can about hearts, darts, flames, nectar and ambrosia—the more incoherent the better.

JONATHAN. Well, but suppose she should be angry with I?

JESSAMY. Why, if she should pretend—please to observe, Mr. Jonathan—if she should pretend to be offended, you must—But I'll tell you how my master acted in such a case: He was seated by a young lady of eighteen upon a sofa, plucking with a wanton hand the blooming sweets of youth and beauty. When the lady thought it necessary to check his ardour, she called up a frown upon her lovely face, so irresistibly alluring, that it would have warmed the frozen bosom of age; remember, said she, putting her delicate arm upon his, remember your character and my honour. My master instantly dropped upon his knees, with eyes swimming with love, cheeks glowing with desire, and in the gentlest modulation of voice he said: My dear Caroline, in a few months our hands will be indissolubly united at the altar; our hearts I feel are already so; the favours you now grant as evidence of your affection are favours indeed; yet, when the ceremony is once past, what will now be received with rapture will then be attributed to duty.

JONATHAN. Well, and what was the consequence?

JESSAMY. The consequence!—Ah! forgive me, my dear friend, but you New England gentlemen have such a laudable curiosity of seeing the bottom of everything—why, to be honest, I confess I saw the blooming cherub of a consequence smiling in its angelic mother's arms, about ten months afterwards.

JONATHAN. Well, if I follow all your plans, make them six bows, and all that, shall I have such little cherubim consequences?

JESSAMY. Undoubtedly.—What are you musing upon?

JONATHAN. You say you'll certainly make me acquainted?—Why, I was thinking then how I should contrive to pass this broken piece of silver—won't it buy a sugar-dram?

JESSAMY. What is that, the love-token from the deacon's daughter?—You come on bravely. But I must hasten to my master. Adieu, my dear friend.

JONATHAN. Stay, Mr. Jessamy—must I buss her when I am introduced to her?

JESSAMY. I told you, you must kiss her.

JONATHAN. Well, but must I buss her?

JESSAMY. Why kiss and buss, and buss and kiss, is all one.

JONATHAN. Oh! my dear friend, though you have a profound knowledge of all, a pugnency of tribulation, you don't know everything. [*Exit.*

JESSAMY [*alone.*]. Well, certainly I improve; my master could not have insinuated himself with more address into the heart of a man he despised. Now will this blundering dog sicken Jenny with his nauseous pawings, until she flies into my arms for very ease. How sweet will the contrast be between the blundering Jonathan and the courtly and accomplished Jessamy!

END OF THE SECOND ACT

ACT III. SCENE I

•   •   •

DIMPLE. Now, did not my lord expressly say that it was unbecoming a well-bred man to be in a passion, I confess I should be ruffled. [*Reads.*] "There is no accident so unfortunate, which a wise man may not turn to his advantage; nor any accident so fortunate, which a fool will not turn to his disadvantage." True, my lord; but how advantage can be derived from this I can't see. Chesterfield himself, who made, however, the worst practice of the most excellent precepts, was never in so embarrassing a situation. I love the person of Charlotte, and it is necessary I should command the fortune of Letitia. As to Maria!—I doubt not by my *sang-froid* behaviour I shall compel her to decline the match; but the blame must not fall upon me. A prudent man, as my lord says, should take all the credit of a good action to himself, and throw the discredit of a bad one upon others. I must break with Maria, marry Letitia, and as for Charlotte—why, Charlotte must be a companion to my wife.—Here, Jessamy!

Enter JESSAMY

DIMPLE *folds and seals two letters*
DIMPLE. Here, Jessamy, take this letter to my love.
[*Gives one.*

JESSAMY. To which of your honour's loves?—Oh! [*reading*] to Miss
Letitia, your honour's rich love.

DIMPLE. And this [*delivers another*] to Miss Charlotte Manly. See that
you deliver them privately.

JESSAMY. Yes, your honour.   [*Going.*

DIMPLE. Jessamy, who are these strange lodgers that came to the
house last night?

JESSAMY. Why, the master is a Yankee colonel; I have not seen much
of him; but the man is the most unpolished animal your honour ever
disgraced your eyes by looking upon. I have had one of the most *outré*
conversations with him! He really h is a most prodigious effect upon
my risibility.

DIMPLE. I ought, according to every rule of Chesterfield, to wait on
him and insinuate myself into his good graces.—Jessamy, wait on the
colonel with my compliments, and if he is disengaged I will do myself
the honour of paying him my respects.—Some ignorant, unpolished
boor—

JESSAMY *goes off and returns*

JESSAMY. Sir, the colonel is gone out, and Jonathan his servant says
that he is gone to stretch his legs upon the Mall.—Stretch his legs! what
an indelicacy of diction!

DIMPLE. Very well. Reach me my hat and sword. I'll accost him there,
in my way to Letitia's, as by accident; pretend to be struck by his person and address, and endeavour to steal into his confidence. Jessamy,
I have no business for you at present.   [*Exit.*

JESSAMY [*taking up the book*]. My master and I obtain our knowledge
from the same source—though, gad! I think myself much the prettier
fellow of the two. . . . [*Laughing without.*] Ha! that's Jenny's titter. I protest I despair of ever teaching that girl to laugh; she has something so
execrably natural in her laugh, that I declare it absolutely discompos-
es my nerves. How came she into our house! [*Calls.*] Jenny!

Enter JENNY

Prythee, Jenny, don't spoil your fine face with laughing.

JENNY. Why, mustn't I laugh, Mr. Jessamy?

JESSAMY. You may smile, but, as my lord says, nothing can authorise a laugh.

JENNY. Well, but I can't help laughing.—Have you see him, Mr. Jessamy? ha, ha, ha!

JESSAMY. Seen whom?

JENNY. Why, Jonathan, the New England colonel's servant. Do you know he was at the play last night, and the stupid creature don't know where he has been. He would not go to a play for the world; he thinks it was a show, as he calls it.

JESSAMY. As ignorant and unpolished as he is, do you know, Miss Jenny, that I propose to introduce him to the honour of your acquaintance?

JENNY. Introduce him to me! for what?

JESSAMY. Why, my lovely girl, that you may take him under your protection, as Madame Rambouillet did young Stanhope; that you may, by your plastic hand, mould this uncouth cub into a gentleman. He is to make love to you.

JENNY. Make love to me!—

JESSAMY. Yes, Mistress Jenny, make love to you; and, I doubt not, when he shall become *domesticated* in your kitchen, that this boor, under your auspices, will soon become *un amiable petit Jonathan.*

JENNY. I must say, Mr. Jessamy, if he copies after me, he will be vastly, monstrously polite.

JESSAMY. Stay here one moment, and I will call him.—Jonathan!—Mr. Jonathan!—   [*Calls.*

JONATHAN [*within*]. Holla! there.—[*Enters.*] You promise to stand by me—six bows you say.   [*Bows.*

JESSAMY. Mrs. Jenny, I have the honour of presenting Mr. Jonathan, Colonel Manly's waiter, to you. I am extremely happy that I have it in my power to make two worthy people acquainted with each other's merits

JENNY, So, Mr. Jonathan, I hear you were at the play last night.

JONATHAN. At the play! why, did you think I went to the devil's drawing-room?

JENNY. The devil's drawing-room!

JONATHAN. Yes; why an't cards and dice the devil's device, and the play-house the shop where the devil hangs out the vanities of the world upon the tenterhooks of temptation? I believe you have not heard how they were acting the old boy one night, and the wicked one came among them sure enough, and went right off in a storm, and carried one quarter of the play-house with him. Oh! no, no, no! you won't catch me at a play-house, I warrant you.

JENNY. Well, Mr. Jonathan, though I don't scruple your veracity, I have some reasons for believing you were there: pray, where were you about six o'clock?

JONATHAN. Why, I went to see one Mr. Morrison, the *hocus pocus* man; they said as how he could eat a case knife.

JENNY. Well, and how did you find the place?

JONATHAN. As I was going about here and there, to and again, to find it, I saw a great crowd of folks going into a long entry that had lanterns over the door; so I asked a man whether that was not the place where they played *hocus pocus?* He was a very civil, kind man, though he did speak like the Hessians; he lifted up his eyes and said, "They play *hocus pocus* tricks enough there, Got knows, mine friend."

JENNY. Well—

JONATHAN. So I went right in, and they showed me away, clean up to the garret, just like meeting-house gallery. And so I saw a power of topping folks, all sitting round in little cabins, "just like father's corn-cribs"; and then there was such a squeaking with the fiddles, and such a tarnal blaze with the lights, my head was near turned. At last the people that sat near me set up such a hissing—hiss—like so many mad cats; and then they went thump, thump, thump, just like our Peleg threshing wheat, and stamped away, just like the nation; and called out for one Mr. Langolee—I suppose he helps act the tricks.

JENNY. Well, and what did you do all this time?

JONATHAN. Gor, I—I liked the fun, and so I thumped away, and hiss'd as lustily as the best of 'em. One sailor-looking man that sat by me, seeing me stamp, and knowing I was a cute fellow, because I could make a roaring noise, clapped me on the shoulder and said, "You are a d——d hearty cock, smite my timbers!" I told him so I was, but I thought he need not swear so, and make use of such naughty words.

JESSAMY. The savage!—Well, and did you see the man with his tricks?

JONATHAN. Why, I vow, as I was looking out for him, they lifted up a great green cloth and let us look right into the next neighbour's house. Have you a good many houses in New-York made so in that 'ere way?

JENNY. Not many; but did you see the family?

JONATHAN. Yes, swamp it; I see'd the family.

JENNY. Well, and how did you like them?

JONATHAN. Why, I vow they were pretty much like other families—there was a poor, good-natured, curse of a husband, and a sad rantipole of a wife.

JENNY. But did you see no other folks?

JONATHAN. Yes. There was one youngster; they called him Mr. Joseph; he talked as sober and as pious as a minister; but, like some ministers that I know, he was a sly tike in his heart for all that. He was going to ask a young woman to spark it with him, and—the Lord have mercy on my soul!—she was another man's wife.

•   •   •

JENNY. Well, Mr. Jonathan, you were certainly at the play-house.

JONATHAN. I at the play-house!—Why didn't I see the play then?

JENNY. Why, the people you saw were players.

JONATHAN. Mercy on my soul! did I see the wicked players?—Mayhap that 'ere Darby that I liked so was the old serpent himself, and had his cloven foot in his pocket. Why, I vow, now I come to think on't, the candles seemed to burn blue, and I am sure where I sat it smelt tarnally of brimstone.

JESSAMY. Well, Mr. Jonathan, from your account, which I confess is very accurate, you must have been at the play-house.

JONATHAN. Why, I vow, I began to smell a rat. When I came away, I went to the man for my money again; you want your money? says he; yes, says I; for what? says he; why, says I, no man shall jockey me out of my money; I paid my money to see sights, and the dogs a bit of a sight have I seen, unles you call listening to people's private business a sight. Why, says he, it is the School for Scandalization.—The School for Scandalization!—Oh! ho! no wonder you New-York folks are so cute at it, when you go to school to learn it; and so I jogged off.

JESSAMY. My dear Jenny, my master's business drags me from you; would to heaven I knew no other servitude than to your charms.

JONATHAN. Well, but don't go; you won't leave me so—

JESSAMY. Excuse me.—Remember the cash.

[Aside to him, and—Exit.

JENNY. Mr. Jonathan, won't you please to sit down? Mr. Jessamy tells me you wanted to have some conversation with me.

[Having brought forward two chairs, they sit.

JONATHAN. Ma'am!—

JENNY. Sir!

JONATHAN. Ma'am!—

JENNY. Pray, how do you like the city, Sir?

JONATHAN. Ma'am!—

JENNY. I say, Sir, how do you like New-York?

JONATHAN. Ma'am!—

JENNY. The stupid creature! but I must pass some little time with him, if it is only to endeavour to learn whether it was his master that made such an abrupt entrance into our house, and my young mistress's heart, this morning. [*Aside.*] As you don't seem to like to talk, Mr. Jonathan—do you sing?

• • •

JONATHAN. . . . I can sing . . . some other time, when you and I are better acquainted, I'll sing the whole of it—no, no-that's a fib—I can't sing but a hundred and ninety verses; our Tabitha at home can sing it all.— [*Sings.*

Marblehead's rocky place,
And Cape-Cod is sandy;
Charleston is burnt down,
Boston is the dandy.
Yankee doddle, doodle do, etc.

I vow, my own town song has put me into such topping spirits that I believe I'll begin to do a little, as Jessamy says we must when we go a-courting—[*Runs and kisses her.*] Burning rivers! cooling flames! red-hot roses! pig-nuts! hasty-pudding and ambrosia!

JENNY. What means this freedom? you insulting wretch.
[*Strikes him.*

JONATHAN. Are you affronted?

JENNY. Affronted! with what looks shall I express my anger?

JONATHAN. Looks! why as to the matter of looks, you look as cross as a witch.

JENNY. Have you no feeling for the delicacy of my sex?

JONATHAN. Feeling! Gor, I—I feel the delicacy of your sex pretty smartly [*rubbing his cheek*], though, I vow, I thought when you city ladies courted and married, and all that, you put feeling out of the question. But I want to know whether you are really affronted, or only pretend to be so? 'Cause, if you are certainly right down affronted, I am at the end of my tether; Jessamy didn't tell me what to say to you.

JENNY. Pretend to be affronted!

JONATHAN. Aye aye, if you only pretend, you shall hear how I'll go to work to make cherubim consequences.   [*Runs up to her.*

JENNY. Begone, you brute!

JONATHAN. That looks like mad; but I won't lose my speech. My dearest Jenny—your name is Jenny, I think?—My dearest Jenny, though I have the highest esteem for the sweet favours you have just now granted me—Gor, that's a fib, though; but Jessamy says it is not wicked to tell lies to the women. [*Aside.*] I say, though I have the highest esteem for the favours you have just now granted me, yet you will consider that, as soon as the dissolvable knot is tied, they will no longer be favours, but only matters of duty and matters of course.

JENNY. Marry you! you audacious monster! get out of my sight, or, rather, let me fly from you.   [*Exit hastily.*

JONATHAN. Gor! she's gone off in a swinging passion, before I had time to think of consequences. If this is the way with your city ladies, give me the twenty acres of rock, the Bible, the cow, and Tabitha, and a little peaceable bundling.

SCENE II. THE MALL

Enter MANLY

MANLY. It must be so, Montague! and it is not all the tribe of Mandevilles that shall convince me that a nation, to become great, must first become dissipated. Luxury is surely the bane of a nation: Luxury! which enervates both soul and body, by opening a thousand new sources of enjoyment, opens, also, a thousand new sources of contention and want: Luxury! which renders a people weak at home, and accessible to bribery, corruption, and force from abroad. When the Grecian states knew no other tools than the axe and the saw, the Grecians were a great, a free and a happy people. The kings of Greece devoted their lives to the service of their country, and her senators knew no other superiority over their fellow-citizens than a glorious pre-eminence in danger and virtue. They exhibited to the world a noble spectacle—a number of independent states united by a similarity of language, sentiment, manners, common interest, and common consent in one grand mutual league of protection. And, thus united, long might they have continued the cherishers of arts and sciences, the protectors of the oppressed, the scourge of tyrants, and the safe asylum of liberty. But when foreign gold, and still more pernicious foreign luxury, had crept among them, they sapped the vitals of their virtue. The virtues of their ancestors were only found in their writings. Envy and suspicion, the vices of little minds, possessed them. The various states engendered jealousies of each other; and, more unfortunately, growing jealous of their great federal council, the Amphictyons, they forgot that their common safety had existed, and would exist, in giving them an honourable extensive prerogative. The common good was lost in the pursuit of private interest; and that people who, by uniting, might have stood against the world in arms, by dividing, crumbled into ruin—their name is now only known in the page of the historian, and what they once were is all we have left to admire. Oh! that America! Oh! that my country, would, in this her day, learn the things which belong to her peace!

Enter DIMPLE

DIMPLE. You are Colonel Manly, I presume?

MANLY. At your service, Sir.

DIMPLE. My name is Dimple, Sir. I have the honour to be a lodger in the same house with you, and, hearing you were in the Mall, came hither to take the liberty of joining you.

MANLY. You are very obliging, Sir.

DIMPLE. As I understand you are a stranger here, Sir, I have taken the liberty to introduce myself to your acquaintance, as possibly I may have it in my power to point out some things in this city worthy your notice.

MANLY. An attention to strangers is worthy a liberal mind, and must ever be gratefully received. But to a soldier, who has no fixed abode, such attentions are particularly pleasing.

DIMPLE. Sir, there is no character so respectable as that of a soldier. And, indeed, when we reflect how much we owe to those brave men who have suffered so much in the service of their country, and secured to us those inestimable blessings that we now enjoy, our liberty and independence, they demand every attention which gratitude can pay. For my own part, I never meet an officer, but I embrace him as my friend, nor a private in distress, but I insensibly extend my charity to him.—I have hit the Bumkin off very tolerably.[*Aside.*

MANLY. Give me your hand, Sir! I do not proffer this hand to everybody; but you steal into my heart. I hope I am as insensible to flattery as most men; but I declare (it may be my weak side) that I never hear the name of soldier mentioned with respect, but I experience a thrill of pleasure which I never feel on any other occasion.

DIMPLE. Will you give me leave, my dear Colonel, to confer an obligation on myself, by showing you some civilities during your stay here, and giving a similar opportunity to some of my friends?

MANLY. Sir, I thank you; but I believe my stay in this city will be very short.

DIMPLE. I can introduce you to some men of excellent sense, in whose company you will esteem yourself happy; and, by way of amusement, to some fine girls, who will listen to your soft things with pleasure.

MANLY. Sir, I should be proud of the honour of being acquainted with those gentlemen—but, as for the ladies, I don't understand you.

DIMPLE. Why, Sir, I need not tell you, that when a young gentleman is alone with a young lady he must say some soft things to her fair cheek—indeed, the lady will expect it. To be sure, there is not much pleasure when a man of the world and a finished coquette meet, who perfectly know each other; but how delicious is it to excite the emotions of joy, hope, expectation, and delight in the bosom of a lovely girl who believes every tittle of what you say to be serious!

MANLY. Serious, Sir! In my opinion, the man who, under pretensions of marriage, can plant thorns in the bosom of an innocent, unsuspecting girl is more detestable than a common robber, in the same proportion as private violence is more despicable than open force, and money of less value than happiness.

DIMPLE. How he awes me by the superiority of his sentiments. [*Aside.*] As you say, Sir, a gentleman should be cautious how he mentions marriage.

MANLY. Cautious, Sir! No person more approves of an intercourse between the sexes than I do. Female conversation softens our manners, whilst our discourse, from the superiority of our literary advantages, improves their minds. But, in our young country, where there is no such thing as gallantry, when a gentleman speaks of love to a lady, whether he mentions marriage or not, she ought to conclude either that he meant to insult her or that his intentions are the most serious and honourable. How mean, how cruel, is it, by a thousand tender assiduities, to win the affections of an amiable girl, and, though you leave her virtue unspotted, to betray her into the appearance of so many tender partialities, that every man of delicacy would suppress his inclination towards her, by supposing her heart engaged! Can any man, for the trivial gratification of his leisure hours, affect the happiness of a whole life! His not having spoken of marriage may add to his perfidy, but can be no excuse for his conduct.

DIMPLE. Sir, I admire your sentiments—they are mine. The light observations that fell from me were only a principle of the tongue; they came not from the heart; my practice has ever disapproved these principles.

MANLY. I believe you, sir. I should with reluctance suppose that those pernicious sentiments could find admittance into the heart of a gentleman.

• • •

ACT IV. SCENE I

CHARLOTTE's *Apartment*

• • •

CHARLOTTE. . . . . But, my dear friend, your happiness depends on yourself Why don't you discard him? Though the match has been of long standing, I would not be forced to make myself miserable: no parent in the world should oblige me to marry the man I did not like.

MARIA. Oh! my dear, you never lived with your parents, and do not know what influence a father's frowns have upon a daughter's heart. Besides, what have I to alledge against Mr. Dimple, to justify myself to the world? He carries himself so smoothly, that every one would impute the blame to me, and call me capricious.

CHARLOTTE. And call her capricious! Did ever such an objection start into the heart of woman? For my part, I wish I had fifty lovers to discard, for no other reason than because I did not fancy them. My dear Maria, you will forgive me; I know your candour and confidence in me; but I have at times, I confess, been led to suppose that some other gentleman was the cause of your aversion to Mr. Dimple.

MARIA. No, my sweet friend, you may be assured, that though I have seen many gentlemen I could prefer to Mr. Dimple, yet I never saw one that I thought I could give my hand to, until this morning.

CHARLOTTE. This morning!

MARIA. Yes; one of the strangest accidents in the world. The odious Dimple, after disgusting me with his conversation, had just left me, when a gentleman, who, it seems, boards in the same house with him, saw him coming out of our door, and, the houses looking very much alike, he came into our house instead of his lodgings; nor did he discover his mistake until he got into the parlour, where I was; he then bowed so gracefully, made such a genteel apology, and looked so manly and noble!—

CHARLOTTE. I see some folks, though it is so great an impropriety, can praise a gentleman, when he happens to be the man of their fancy. [*Aside.*

MARIA. I don't know how it was—I hope he did not think me indelicate—but I asked him, I believe, to sit down, or pointed to a chair. He sat down, and, instead of having recourse to observations upon the weather, or hackneyed criticisms upon the theatre, he entered readily into a conversation worthy a man of sense to speak, and a lady of delicacy and sentiment to hear. He was not strictly handsome, but he spoke the language of sentiment, and his eyes looked tenderness and honour.

CHARLOTTE. Oh! [*eagerly*] you sentimental, grave girls, when your hearts are once touched, beat us rattles a bar's length. And so you are quite in love with this he-angel?

MARIA. In love with him! How can you rattle so, Charlotte? am I not going to be miserable? [*Sighs.*] In love with a gentleman I never saw but one hour in my life, and don't know his name! No; I only wished that the man I shall marry may look, and talk, and act, just like him. Besides, my dear, he is a married man.

CHARLOTTE. Why, that was good-natured—he told you so, I suppose, in mere charity, to prevent you falling in love with him?

MARIA. He didn't tell me so; [*peevishly*] he looked as if he was married.

CHARLOTTE. How, my dear; did he look sheepish?

MARIA. I am sure he has a susceptible heart, and the ladies of his acquaintance must be very stupid not to—

CHARLOTTE. Hush! I hear some person coming.

• • •

Enter DIMPLE *and* MANLY

DIMPLE. Ladies, your most obedient.

CHARLOTTE. Miss Van Rough, shall I present my brother Henry to you? Colonel Manly, Maria—Miss Van Rough, brother.

MARIA. Her brother! [*Turns and sees* MANLY.] Oh! my heart! the very gentleman I have been praising.

MANLY. The same amiable girl I saw this morning!

CHARLOTTE. Why, you look as if you were acquainted.

MANLY. I unintentionally intruded into this lady's presence this morning, for which she was so good as to promise me her forgiveness.

CHARLOTTE. Oh! ho! is that the case! Have these two penserosos been together? Were they Henry's eyes that looked so tenderly? [*Aside.*] And so you promised to pardon him? and could you be so good-natured? have you really forgiven him? I beg you would do it for my sake [*whispering loud to* MARIA]. But, my dear, as you are in such haste, it would be cruel to detain you; I can show you the way through the other room.

MARIA. Spare me, my sprightly friend.

MANLY. The lady does not, I hope, intend to deprive us of the pleasure of her company so soon.

CHARLOTTE. She has only a mantua-maker who waits for her at home. But, as I am to give my opinion of the dress, I think she cannot go yet. We were talking of the fashions when you came in, but I suppose the subject must be changed to something of more importance now. Mr. Dimple, will you favour us with an account of the public entertainments?

DIMPLE. Why, really, Miss Manly, you could not have asked me a question more *mal-apropos*. For my part, I must confess that, to a man who has travelled, there is nothing that is worthy the name of amusement to be found in this city.

CHARLOTTE. Except visiting the ladies.

DIMPLE. Pardon me, Madam; that is the avocation of a man of taste. But for amusement, I positively know of nothing that can be called so, unless you dignify with that title the hopping once a fortnight to the sound of two or three squeaking fiddles, and the clattering of the old tavern windows, or sitting to see the miserable mummers, whom you call actors, murder comedy and make a farce of tragedy.

MANLY. Do you never attend the theatre, Sir?

DIMPLE. I was tortured there once.

CHARLOTTE. Pray, Mr. Dimple, was it a tragedy or a comedy?

DIMPLE. Faith, Madam, I cannot tell; for I sat with my back to the stage all the time, admiring a much better actress than any there—a lady who played the fine woman to perfection; though, by the laugh of the horrid creatures round me, I suppose it was comedy. Yet, on second thoughts, it might be some hero in a tragedy, dying so comically as to set the whole house in an uproar. Colonel, I presume you have been in Europe?

MANLY. Indeed, Sir, I was never ten leagues from the continent.

DIMPLE. Believe me, Colonel, you have an immense pleasure to come; and when you shall have seen the brilliant exhibitions of Europe, you will learn to despise the amusements of this country as much as I do.

MANLY. Therefore I do not wish to see them; for I can never esteem that knowledge valuable which tends to give me a distaste for my native country.

DIMPLE. Well, Colonel, though you have not travelled, you have read.

MANLY. I have, a little; and by it have discovered that there is a laudable partiality which ignorant, untravelled men entertain for everything that belongs to their native country. I call it laudable; it injures no one; adds to their own happiness; and, when extended, becomes the noble principle of patriotism. Travelled gentlemen rise superior, in their own opinion, to this; but if the contempt which they contract for their country is the most valuable acquisition of their travels, I am far from thinking that their time and money are well spent.

MARIA. What noble sentiments!

CHARLOTTE. Let my brother set out where he will in the fields of conversation, he is sure to end his tour in the temple of gravity.

MANLY. Forgive me, my sister. I love my country; it has its foibles undoubtedly—some foreigners will with pleasure remark them—but such remarks fall very ungracefully from the lips of her citizens.

DIMPLE. You are perfectly in the right, Colonel—America has her faults.

MANLY. Yes, Sir; and we, her children, should blush for them in private, and endeavour, as individuals, to reform them. But, if our country has its errors in common with other countries, I am proud to say America—I mean the United States—has displayed virtues and achievements which modern nations may admire, but of which they have seldom set us the example.

CHARLOTTE. But, brother, we must introduce you to some of our gay folks, and let you see the city, such as it is. Mr. Dimple is known to almost every family in town; he will doubtless take a pleasure in introducing you?

DIMPLE. I shall esteem every service I can render your brother an honour.

MANLY. I fear the business I am upon will take up all my time, and my family will be anxious to hear from me.

MARIA. His family! but what is it to me that he is married! [*Aside.*]. Pray, how did you leave your lady, Sir?

CHARLOTTE. My brother is not married [*observing her anxiety*]; it is only an odd way he has of expressing himself. Pray, brother, is this business, which you make your continual excuse, a secret?

MANLY. No, sister; I came hither to solicit the honourable Congress, that a number of my brave old soldiers may be put upon the pension-list, who were, at first, not judged to be so materially wounded as to need the public assistance. My sister says true [*to* MARIA]; I call my late soldiers my family. Those who were not in the field in the late glorious contest, and those who were, have their respective merits; but, I confess, my older brother-soldiers are dearer to me than the former description. Friendships made in adversity are lasting; our countrymen may forget us, but that is no reason why we should forget one another. But I must leave you; my time of engagement approaches.

CHARLOTTE. Well, but, brother, if you will go, will you please to conduct my fair friend home? You live in the same street—I was to have gone with her myself—[*Aside.*] A lucky thought.

MARIA. I am obliged to your sister, Sir, and was just intending to go.
[*Going.*

MANLY. I shall attend her with pleasure.
[*Exit with* MARIA, *followed by* DIMPLE *and* CHARLOTTE.

MARIA. Now, pray, don't betray me to your brother.

CHARLOTTE. [*Just as she sees him make a motion to take his leave.*] One word with you, brother, if you please.   [*Follows them out.*
[*Manent* DIMPLE *and* LETITIA.

DIMPLE. You received the billet I sent you, I presume?

LETITIA. Hush!—Yes.

DIMPLE. When shall I pay my respects to you?

LETITIA. At eight I shall be unengaged.

Reënter CHARLOTTE

DIMPLE. Did my lovely angel receive my billet? [*To* CHARLOTTE.]

CHARLOTTE. Yes.

DIMPLE. What hour shall I expect with impatience?

CHARLOTTE. At eight I shall be at home unengaged.

DIMPLE. Unfortunate! I have a horrid engagement of business at that hour. Can't you finish your visit earlier and let six be the happy hour?

CHARLOTTE. You know your influence over me.
[*Exeunt severally.*

SCENE II

VAN ROUGH'S *House*

VAN ROUGH [*alone*]. It cannot possibly be true! The son of my old friend can't have acted so unadvisedly. Seventeen thousand pounds! in bills! Mr. Transfer must have been mistaken. He always appeared so prudent, and talked so well upon money matters, and even assured me that he intended to change his dress for a suit of clothes which would not cost so much, and look more substantial, as soon as he married. No, no, no! it can't be; it cannot be. But, however, I must look out sharp. I did not care what his principles or his actions were, so long as he minded the main chance. Seventeen thousand pounds! If he had lost it in trade, why the best men may have ill-luck; but to game it away, as Transfer says—why, at this rate, his whole estate may go in one night, and, what is ten times worse, mine into the bargain. No, no; Mary is right. Leave women to look out in these matters; for all they look as if they didn't know a journal from a ledger, when their interest is concerned they know what's what; they mind the main chance as well as the best of us. I wonder Mary did not tell me she knew of his spending his money so foolishly. Seventeen thousand pounds! Why, if my daughter was standing up to be married, I would forbid the banns, if I found it was to a man who did not mind the main chance.—Hush! I hear somebody coming. 'Tis Mary's voice; a man with her too! I shouldn't be surprised if this should be the other string to her bow. Aye, aye, let them alone; women understand the main chance.— Though, i' faith, I'll listen a little.   [*Retires into a closet.*

MANLY *leading in* MARIA

MANLY. I hope you will excuse my speaking upon so important a subject so abruptly; but, the moment I entered your room, you struck me as the lady whom I had long loved in imagination, and never hoped to see.

MARIA. Indeed, Sir, I have been led to hear more upon this subject than I ought.

MANLY. Do you, then, disapprove my suit, Madam, or the abruptness of my introducing it? If the latter, my peculiar situation, being obliged to leave the city in a few days, will, I hope, be my excuse; if the former, I will retire, for I am sure I would not give a moment's inquietude to her whom I could devote my life to please. I am not so indelicate as to seek your immediate approbation; permit me only to be near you, and by a thousand tender assiduities to endeavour to excite a grateful return.

MARIA. I have a father, whom I would die to make happy; he will disapprove—

MANLY. Do you think me so ungenerous as to seek a place in your esteem without his consent? You must—you ever ought to consider that man as unworthy of you who seeks an interest in your heart contrary to a father's approbation. A young lady should reflect that the loss of a lover may be supplied, but nothing can compensate for the loss of a parent's affection. Yet, why do you suppose your father would disapprove? In our country, the affections are not sacrificed to riches or family aggrandizement; should you approve, my family is decent, and my rank honourable.

MARIA. You distress me, Sir.

MANLY. Then I will sincerely beg your excuse for obtruding so disagreeable a subject, and retire.   [*Going.*

MARIA. Stay, Sir! your generosity and good opinion of me deserve a return; but why must I declare what, for these few hours, I have scarce suffered myself to think?—I am—

MANLY. What?

MARIA. Engaged, Sir; and, in a few days to be married to the gentleman you saw at your sister's.

MANLY. Engaged to be married! And I have been basely invading the rights of another? Why have you permitted this? Is this the return for the partiality I declared for you?

MARIA. You distress me, Sir. What would you have me say? you are too generous to wish the truth. Ought I to say that I dared not suffer myself to think of my engagement, and that I am going to give my hand without my heart? Would you have me confess a partiality for you? If so, your triumph is complete, and can be only more so when days of misery with the man I cannot love will make me think of him whom I could prefer.

MANLY [*after a pause*]. We are both unhappy; but it is your duty to obey your parent—mine to obey my honour. Let us, therefore, both follow the path of rectitude; and of this we may be assured, that if we are not happy, we shall, at least, deserve to be so. Adieu! I dare not trust myself longer with you.   [*Exeunt severally.*

END OF THE FOURTH ACT

•   •   •

ACT V. SCENE II

•   •   •

Enter DIMPLE *leading* LETITIA

LETITIA. And will you pretend to say now, Mr. Dimple, that you propose to break with Maria? Are not the banns published? Are not the clothes purchased? Are not the friends invited? In short, is it not a done affair?

DIMPLE. Believe me, my dear Letitia, I would not marry her.

LETITIA. Why have you not broke with her before this, as you all along deluded me by saying you would?

DIMPLE. Because I was in hopes she would, ere this, have broke with me.

LETITIA. You could not expect it.

DIMPLE. Nay, but be calm a moment; 'twas from my regard to you that I did not discard her.

LETITIA. Regard to me!

DIMPLE. Yes; I have done everything in my power to break with her, but the foolish girl is so fond of me that nothing can accomplish it. Besides, how can I offer her my hand when my heart is indissolubly engaged to you?

LETITIA. There may be reason in this; but why so attentive to Miss Manly?

DIMPLE. Attentive to Miss Manly! For heaven's sake, if you have no better opinion of my constancy, pay not so ill a compliment to my taste.

LETITIA. Did I not see you whisper her to-day?

DIMPLE. Possibly I might—but something of so very trifling a nature that I have already forgot what it was.

LETITIA. I believe she has not forgot it.

DIMPLE. My dear creature, how can you for a moment suppose I should have any serious thoughts of that trifling, gay, flighty coquette, that disagreeable—

Enter CHARLOTTE

My dear Miss Manly, I rejoice to see you; there is a charm in your conversation that always marks your entrance into company as fortunate.

LETITIA. Where have you been, my dear?

CHARLOTTE. Why, I have been about to twenty shops, turning over pretty things, and so have left twenty visits unpaid. I wish you would step into the carriage and whisk round, make my apology, and leave my cards where our friends are not at home; that, you know, will serve as a visit. Come, do go.

LETITIA. So anxious to get me out! but I'll watch you. [*Aside.*] Oh! yes, I'll go; I want a little exercise. Positively [DIMPLE *offering to accompany her*], Mr. Dimple, you shall not go; why, half my visits are cake and caudle visits; it won't do, you know, for you to go.

[*Exit, but returns to the door in the back scene and listens.*

DIMPLE. This attachment of your brother to Maria is fortunate.

CHARLOTTE. How did you come to the knowledge of it?

DIMPLE. I read it in their eyes.

CHARLOTTE. And I had it from her mouth. It would have amused you to have seen her! She, that thought it so great an impropriety to praise a gentleman that she could not bring out one word in your favour, found a redundancy to praise him.

DIMPLE. I have done everything in my power to assist his passion there: your delicacy, my dearest girl, would be shocked at half the instances of neglect and misbehaviour.

CHARLOTTE. I don't know how I should bear neglect; but Mr. Dimple must misbehave himself indeed, to forfeit my good opinion.

DIMPLE. Your good opinion, my angel, is the pride and pleasure of my heart; and if the most respectful tenderness for you, and an utter indifference for all your sex besides, can make me worthy of your esteem, I shall richly merit it.

CHARLOTTE. All my sex besides, Mr. Dimple!—you forgot your tête-à-tête with Letitia.

DIMPLE. How can you, my lovely angel, cast a thought on that insipid, wry-mouthed, ugly creature!

CHARLOTTE. But her fortune may have charms.

DIMPLE. Not to a heart like mine. The man, who has been blessed with the good opinion of my Charlotte, must despise the allurements of fortune.

CHARLOTTE. I am satisfied.

DIMPLE. Let us think no more on the odious subject, but devote the present hour to happiness.

CHARLOTTE. Can I be happy, when I see the man I prefer going to be married to another?

DIMPLE. Have I not already satisfied my charming angel, that I can never think of marrying the puling Maria? But, even if it were so, could that be any bar to our happiness? for, as the poet sings,

"Love, free as air, at sight of human ties,
Spreads his light wings, and in a moment flies."

Come, then, my charming angel! why delay our bliss? The present moment is ours; the next is in the hand of fate. [*Kissing her.*

CHARLOTTE. Begone, Sir! By your delusions you had almost lulled my honour asleep.

DIMPLE. Let me lull the demon to sleep again with kisses.

[*He struggles with her; she screams.*

Enter MANLY

MANLY. Turn, villain! and defend yourself—   [*Draws.*

VAN ROUGH enters and beats down their swords

VAN ROUGH. Is the devil in you? are you going to murder one another?   [*Holding* DIMPLE.

DIMPLE. Hold him, hold him—I can command my passion.

Enter JONATHAN

JONATHAN. What the rattle ails you? Is the old one in you? Let the
colonel alone, can't you? I feel chock-full of fight—do you want to kill
the colonel?

MANLY. Be still, Jonathan; the gentleman does not want to hurt me.

JONATHAN. Gor! I—I wish he did; I'd show him Yankee boys play,
pretty quick.—Don't you see you have frightened the young woman
into the *hystrikes?*

VAN ROUGH. Pray, some of you explain this; what has been the occasion of all this racket?

MANLY. That gentleman can explain it to you; it will be a very di-
verting story for an intended father-in-law to hear.

VAN ROUGH. How was this matter, Mr. Van Dumpling?

DIMPLE. Sir—upon my honour—all I know is, that I was talking to
this young lady, and this gentleman broke in on us in a very extraordinary manner.

VAN ROUGH. Why, all this is nothing to the purpose; can you explain
it, Miss?   [*To* CHARLOTTE.

Enter LETITIA *through the back scene*

LETITIA. I can explain it to that gentleman's confusion. Though long
betrothed to your daughter [*to* VAN ROUGH], yet, allured by my fortune,
it seems (with shame do I speak it) he has privately paid his address
to me. I was drawn in to listen to him by his assuring me that the match
was made by his father without his consent, and that he proposed to
break with Maria, whether he married me or not. But, whatever were
his intentions respecting your daughter, Sir, even to me he was false;
for he has repeated the same story, with some cruel reflections upon
my person, to Miss Manly.

JONATHAN. What a tarnal curse!

LETITIA. Nor is this all, Miss Manly. When he was with me this very
morning, he made the same ungenerous reflections upon the weakness
of your mind as he has so recently done upon the defects of my person.

JONATHAN. What a tarnal curse and damn, too.

DIMPLE. Ha! since I have lost Letitia, I believe I had as good make it up with Maria. Mr. Van Rough, at present I cannot enter into particulars; but, I believe, I can explain everything to your satisfaction in private.

VAN ROUGH. There is another matter, Mr. Van Dumpling, which I would have you explain. Pray, Sir, have Messrs. Van Cash & Co. presented you those bills for acceptance?

DIMPLE. The deuce! Has he heard of those bills! Nay, then, all's up with Maria, too; but an affair of this sort can never prejudice me among the ladies; they will rather long to know what the dear creature possesses to make him so agreeable. [*Aside.*] Sir, you'll hear from me. [*To* MANLY.

MANLY. And you from me, Sir—

DIMPLE. Sir, you wear a sword—

MANLY. Yes, Sir. This sword was presented to me by that brave Gallic hero, the Marquis De la Fayette. I have drawn it in the service of my country, and in private life, on the only occasion where a man is justified in drawing his sword, in defence of a lady's honour. I have fought too many battles in the service of my country to dread the imputation of cowardice. Death from a man of honour would be a glory you do not merit; you shall live to bear the insult of man and the contempt of that sex whose general smiles afforded you all your happiness.

DIMPLE. You won't meet me, Sir? Then I'll post you for a coward.

MANLY. I'll venture that, Sir. The reputation of my life does not depend upon the breath of a Mr. Dimple. I would have you to know, however, Sir, that I have a cane to chastise the insolence of a scoundrel, and a sword and the good laws of my country to protect me from the attempts of an assassin—

DIMPLE. Mighty well! Very fine, indeed! Ladies and gentlemen, I take my leave; and you will please to observe in the case of my deportment the contrast between a gentleman who has read Chesterfield and received the polish of Europe and an unpolished, untravelled American.   [*Exit.*

Enter MARIA

MARIA. Is he indeed gone?

LETITIA. I hope, never to return.

VAN ROUGH. I am glad I heard of those bills; though it's plaguy unlucky; I hoped to see Mary married before I died.

MANLY. Will you permit a gentleman, Sir, to offer himself as a suitor to your daughter? Though a stranger to you, he is not altogether so to her, or unknown in this city. You may find a son-in-law of more fortune, but you can never meet with one who is richer in love for her, or respect for you.

VAN ROUGH. Why, Mary, you have not let this gentleman make love to you without my leave?

MANLY. I did not say, Sir—

MARIA. Say, Sir!—I—the gentleman, to be sure, met me accidentally.

VAN ROUGH. Ha, ha, ha! Mark me, Mary; young folks think old folks to be fools; but old folks know young folks to be fools. Why, I knew all about this affair. This was only a cunning way I had to bring it about. Hark ye! I was in the closet when you and he were at our house. [*Turns to the company.*] I heard that little baggage say she loved her old father, and would die to make him happy! Oh! how I loved the little baggage! And you talked very prudently, young man. I have inquired into your character, and find you to be a man of punctuality and mind the main chance. And so, as you love Mary and Mary loves you, you shall have my consent immediately to be married. I'll settle my fortune on you, and go and live with you the remainder of my life.

MANLY. Sir, I hope—

VAN ROUGH. Come, come, no fine speeches; mind the main chance, young man, and you and I shall always agree.

LETITIA. I sincerely wish you joy [*advancing to* MARIA]; and hope your pardon for my conduct.

MARIA. I thank you for your congratulations, and hope we shall at once forget the wretch who has given us so much disquiet, and the trouble that he has occasioned.

CHARLOTTE. And I, my dear Maria—how shall I look up to you for forgiveness? I; who, in the practice of the meanest arts, have violated the most sacred rights of friendship? I never can forgive myself, or hope charity from the world; but, I confess, I have much to hope from such a brother; and I am happy that I may soon say, such a sister.

MARIA. My dear, you distress me; you have all my love.

MANLY. And mine.

CHARLOTTE. If repentance can entitle me to forgiveness, I have already much merit; for I despise the littleness of my past conduct. I now find that the heart of any worthy man cannot be gained by invidious attacks upon the rights and characters of others—by countenancing the address of a thousand—or that the finest assemblage of features, the greatest taste in dress, the genteelest address, or the most brilliant wit, cannot eventually secure a coquette from contempt and ridicule.

MANLY. And I have learned that probity, virtue, honour, though they should not have received the polish of Europe, will secure to an honest American the good graces of his fair countrywomen, and I hope, the applause of THE PUBLIC.

THE END

from MODERN CHIVALRY

Hugh Henry Brackenridge

VOLUME I, BOOK I

Chapter I

John Farrago was a man of about fifty-three years of age, of good natural sense, and considerable reading; but in some things whimsical, owing perhaps to his greater knowledge of books than of the world; but, in some degree, also, to his having never married, being what they call an old bachelor, a characteristic of which is, usually, singularity and whim. He had the advantage of having had in early life, an academic education; but having never applied himself to any of the learned professions, he had lived the greater part of his life on a small farm, which he cultivated with servants or hired hands, as he could conveniently supply himself with either. The servant he had at this time, was an Irishman, whose name was Teague O'Regan. I shall say nothing of the character of this man, because the very name imports what he was.

A strange idea came into the head of Captain Farrago about this time; for, by the bye, I had forgot to mention that having been chosen captain of a company of militia in the neighbourhood, he had gone by the name of Captain ever since; for the rule is, once a captain, and always a captain; but, as I was observing, the idea had come in to his head, to saddle an old horse that he had, and ride about the world a little, with his man Teague at his heels, to see how things were going on here and there, and to observe human nature. For it is a mistake to suppose, that a man cannot learn man by reading him in a corner, as well as on the widest space of transaction. At any rate, it may yield amusement. . . .

Chapter III

The Captain rising early next morning, and setting out on his way, had now arrived at a place where a number of people were convened, for the purpose of electing persons to represent them in the legislature of the state. There was a weaver who was a candidate for this appointment, and seemed to have a good deal of interest among the people. But another, who was a man of education, was his competitor. Relying on some talent of speaking which he thought he possessed, he addressed the multitude.

Said he, "Fellow citizens, I pretend not to any great abilities; but am conscious to myself that I have the best good will to serve you. But it is very astonishing to me, that this weaver should conceive himself qualified for the trust. For though my acquirements are not great, yet his are still less. The mechanical business which he pursues, must necessarily take up so much of his time, that he cannot apply himself to political studies, I should therefore think it would be more answerable to your dignity, and conducive to your interest, to be represented by a man at least of some letters, than by an illiterate handicraftsman like this. It will be more honourable for himself, to remain at his loom and knot threads, than to come forward in a legislative capacity: because, in the one case, he is in the sphere where God and nature has placed him; in the other, he is like a fish out of water, and must struggle for breath in a new element.

"Is it possible he can understand the affairs of government, whose mind has been concentered to the small object of weaving webs; to the price by the yard, the grist of the thread, and such like matters as concern a manufacturer of cloths? The feet of him who weaves, are more occupied than the head, or at least as much; and therefore the whole man must be, at least, but in half accustomed to exercise his mental powers. For these reasons, all other things set aside, the chance is in my favour, with respect to information. However, you will decide, and give your suffrages to him or to me, as you shall judge expedient."

The Captain hearing these observations, and looking at the weaver, could not help advancing, and undertaking to subjoin something in support of what had been just said. Said he, "I have no prejudice against a weaver more than another man. Nor do I know any harm in the trade; save that from the sedentary life in a damp place, there is usually a paleness of the countenance: but this is a physical, not a moral evil. Such usually occupy subterranean apartments; not for the purpose, like Demosthenes, of shaving their heads, and writing over eight times the history of Thucydides, and perfecting a style of oratory; but rather to keep the thread moist; or because this is considered but as an inglorious sort of trade, and is frequently thrust away into cellars, and damp outhouses, which are not occupied for a better use.

"But to rise from the cellar to the senate house, would be an unnatural hoist. To come from counting threads, and adjusting them to the splits of a reed, to regulate the finances of a government, would be preposterous; there being no congruity in the case. There is no analogy between knotting threads and framing laws. It would be a reversion of the order of things. Not that a manufacturer of linen or woolen, or other stuff, is an inferior character, but a different one, from that which ought to be employed in affairs of state. It is unnecessary to enlarge on this subject; for you must all be convinced of the truth and propriety of what I say. But if you will give me leave to take the manufacturer aside a little, I think I can explain to him my ideas on the subject; and very probably prevail with him to withdraw his pretensions." The people seeming to acquiesce, and beckoning to the weaver, they drew aside, and the Captain addressed him in the following words:

"Mr. Traddle," said he, for that was the name of the manufacturer, "I have not the smallest idea of wounding your sensibility; but it would seem to me, it would be more your interest to pursue your occupation, than to launch out into that of which you have no knowledge. When you go to the senate house, the application to you will not be to warp a web; but to make laws for the commonwealth. Now, suppose that the making these laws, requires a knowledge of commerce, or of the interests of agriculture, or those principles upon which the different manufacturers depend, what service could you render? It is possible you might think justly enough; but could you speak? You are not in the habit of public speaking. You are not furnished with those common place ideas, with which even very ignorant men can pass for knowing something. There is nothing makes a man so ridiculous as to attempt what is above his sphere. You are no tumbler for instance; yet should you give out that you could vault upon a man's back; or turn head over heels, like the wheels of a cart; the stiffness of your joints would encumber you; and you would fall upon your backside to the ground. Such a squash as that would do you damage. The getting up to ride on the state is an unsafe thing to those who are not accustomed to such horsemanship. It is a disagreeable thing for a man to be laughed at, and there is no way of keeping one's self from it but by avoiding all affectation."

While they were thus discoursing, a bustle had taken place among the crowd. Teague hearing so much about elections, and serving the government, took it into his head, that he could be a legislator himself. The thing was not displeasing to the people, who seemed to favour his pretensions; owing, in some degree, to there being several of his countrymen among the crowd; but more especially to the fluctuation of the popular mind, and a disposition to what is new and ignoble. For though the weaver was not the most elevated object of choice, yet he was still preferable to this tatter-demalion, who was but a menial servant, and had so much of what is called the brogue on his tongue, as to fall far short of an elegant speaker.

The Captain coming up, and finding what was on the carpet, was greatly chagrined at not having been able to give the multitude a better idea of the importance of a legislative trust; alarmed also, from an apprehension of the loss of his servant. Under these impressions he resumed his address to the multitude. Said he, "This is making the matter still worse, gentlemen; this servant of mine is but a bog-trotter; who can scarcely speak the dialect in which your laws ought to be written; but certainly has never read a single treatise on any political subject; for the truth is, he cannot read at all. The young people of the lower class, in Ireland, have seldom the advantage of a good education; especially the descendants of the ancient Irish, who have most of them a great assurance of countenance, but little information, or literature. This young man, whose family name is O'Regan, has been my servant for several years. And, except a too great fondness for women, which now and then brings him into scrapes, he has demeaned himself in a manner tolerable enough. But he is totally ignorant of the great principles of legislation; and more especially, the particular interests of the government. A free government is a noble possession to a people: and this freedom consists in an equal right to make laws, and to have the benefit of the laws when made. Though doubtless, in such a government, the lowest citizen may become chief magistrate; yet it is sufficient to possess the right; not absolutely necessary to exercise it. Or even if you should think proper, now and then, to show your privilege, and exert, in a signal manner, the democratic prerogative, yet is it not descending too low to filch away from me a hireling, which I cannot well spare, to serve your purpose? You are surely carrying the matter too far, in thinking to make a senator of this hostler; to take him away from an employment to which he has been bred, and put him to another, to which he has served no apprenticeship: to set those hands which have been lately employed in currying my horse, to the draughting of bills, and preparing of business for the house."

The people were tenacious of their choice, and insisted on giving Teague their suffrages; and by the frown upon their brows, seemed to indicate resentment at what had been said; as indirectly charging them with want of judgment; or calling in question their privilege to do what they thought proper. "It is a very strange thing," said one of them, who was a speaker for the rest, "that after having conquered Burgoyne and Cornwallis, and got a government of our own, we cannot put in it whom we please. This young man may be your servant, or another man's servant; but if we choose to make him a delegate, what is that to you? He may not be yet skilled in the matter, but there is a good day a-coming. We will impower him; and it is better to trust a plain man like him, than one of your high flyers, that will make laws to suit their own purpose."

Said the Captain, "I had much rather you would send the weaver, though I thought that improper, than to invade my household, and thus detract from me the very person that I have about me to brush my boots, and clean my spurs." The prolocutor of the people gave him to understand that his surmises were useless, for the people had determined on the choice, and Teague they would have, for a representative.

Finding it answered no end to expostulate with the multitude, he requested to speak a word with Teague by himself. Stepping aside, he said to him, composing his voice, and addressing him in a soft manner; "Teague, you are quite wrong in this matter they have put into your head. Do you know what it is to be a member of a deliberate body? What qualifications are necessary? Do you understand anything of geography? If a question should be, to make a law to dig a canal in some part of the state, can you describe the bearing of the mountains, and the course of the rivers? Or if commerce is to be pushed to some new quarter, by the force of regulations, are you competent to decide in such a case? There will be questions of law, and astronomy on the carpet. How you must gape and stare like a fool, when you come to be asked your opinion on these subjects. Are you acquainted with the abstract principles of finance; with the funding public securities; the ways and means of raising the revenue; providing for the discharge of the public debts, and all other things which respect the economy of the government? Even if you had knowledge, have you a facility of speaking? I would suppose you would have too much pride to go to the house just to say, 'Ay,' or 'No.' This is not the fault of your nature, but of your education; having been accustomed to dig turf in your early years, rather than instructing yourself in the classics, or common school books.

"When a man becomes a member of a public body, he is like a racoon, or other beast that climbs up the fork of a tree; the boys pushing at him with pitchforks, or throwing stones, or shooting at him with an arrow, the dogs barking in the meantime. One will find fault with your not speaking; another with your speaking, if you speak at all. They will have you in the newspapers, and ridicule you as a perfect beast. There is what they call the caricatura; that is, representing you with a dog's head, or a cat's claw. As you have a red head, they will very probably make a fox of you, or a sorrel horse, or a brindled cow. It is the devil in hell to be exposed to the squibs and crackers of the gazette wits and publications. You know no more about these matters than a goose; and yet you would undertake rashly, without advice, to enter on the office; nay, contrary to advice. For I would not for a thousand guineas, though I have not the half of it to spare, that the breed of the O'Regans should come to this; bringing on them a worse stain than stealing sheep; to which they are addicted. You have nothing but your character, Teague, in a new country to depend upon. Let it never be said, that you quitted an honest livelihood, the taking care of my horse, to follow the new fangled whims of the times, and to be a statesman."

Teague was moved chiefly with the last part of the address, and consented to give up the object.

The Captain, glad of this, took him back to the people, and announced his disposition to decline the honour which they had intended him.

Teague acknowledged that he had changed his mind, and was willing to remain in a private station.

The people did not seem well pleased with the Captain, but as nothing more could be said about the matter, they turned their attention to the weaver, and gave him their suffrages. . . .

VOLUME II, BOOK IV

Chapter I

The insuing day, the Captain arrived in a certain city, and put up at the sign of the Indian Queen. Taking a day or two to refresh himself, and get a new pair of breeches made and his coat mended, which was a little worn at the elbows, he went to look about the city. The fourth day, when he had proposed to set out to prerambulate this modern Babylon, and called for Teague to bring him his boots, there was no Teague there. The hostler being called, with whom he used to sleep, informed, that he had disappeared the day before. The Captain was alarmed: and, from the recollection of former incidents, began to enquire if there were any elections going on at that time. As it so happened, there was one that very day. Thinking it probable the bog-trotter, having still a hankering after an appointment, might offer himself on that occasion, he set out to the place where the people were convened, to see if he could discover Teague amongst the candidates. He could see nothing of him; and though he made enquiry, he could hear no account. But the circumstance of the election drawing his attention for some time, he forgot Teague.

The candidates were all remarkably pot-bellied; and waddled in their gait. The Captain enquiring what were the pretensions of these men to be elected; he was told, that they had all stock in the funds, and lived in large brick buildings; and some of them entertained fifty people at a time, and eat and drank abundantly; and, living an easy life, and pampering their appetites, they had swollen to this size.

It is a strange thing, said the Captain, that in the country, in my route, they would elect no one but a weaver, or a whiskey distiller; and here none but fat swabs, that guzzle wine, and smoke segars. It was not so in Greece, where Phocion came with his plain coat, from his humble dwelling, and directed the counsels of the poeple; or in Rome, where Cincinnatus was made dictator from the plough. Something must be wrong, where the inflate, and the pompous are the objects of choice. Though there is one good arising from it, that there is no danger of my Teague here. He could not afford to give a dinner; and as to funds, he has not a single shilling in them. They will make him neither mayor nor legislator in this city.

Na faith, said Mr. M'Donald, the Scotch gentleman who had been present at the embarrassment of the Captain, on the occasion of the former election; and having, a few days before, come to the city, and observing the Captain in the crowd, had come up to accost him, just as he was uttering these last words to himself: Na faith, said he, there is na danger of Teague here, unless he had his scores o' shares in the bank; and was in league with the brokers, and had a brick house at his hurdies, or a ship or twa on the stocks. A great deal used to be done, by employing advocates with the tradesmen, to listen to the news, and tell them fair stories; but all is now lost in substantial interest, and the funds command every thing. Besides, this city is swarming with Teagues, and O'Regans, and O'Brians, and O'Murphys, and O'Farrels; I see, that they cannot be at a loss without your bog-trotter.

The Captain having his fears eased, in this particular, returned home, greatly troubled, nevertheless, that he could not come up with the Irishman. . . .

BOOK V

Chapter V

The next day, revolving everything in his mind, it occurred to the Captain, that the Irishman might have gone out of town, hearing of an election at a district, and have been elected to Congress. As that body was then sitting, he thought it could be no great trouble to go to the house, and cast an eye from the gallery, and see if the ragamuffin had got there. There was one that had a little of the brogue of Teague upon his tongue, but nothing of his physiognomy; others had a good deal of his manner, but there was none that came absolutely up to the physic of his person.

However, being here, the Captain tho't it not amiss to listen a while to the debates upon the carpet. A certain bill was depending, and made, it seems, the order of the day. Mr. Cogan being on the floor, spoke:— Sir, said he, addressing himself to the chair, the bill in contemplation, is, in my opinion, of a dangerous tendency. I will venture to foretel, that, if it goes into a law, the cows will have fewer calves, and the sheep less wool; hens will lay fewer eggs, and cocks forget to crow daylight. The horses will be worse shod, and stumble more; our watches go too slow; corns grow upon our toes; young women have the stomach ach; old men the gout; and middle aged persons fainting fits. The larks will fall dead in the field; the frogs croak till they burst their bags; and the leaves of the trees fall before the autumn. Snow will be found in the heat of harvest, and dog days in winter. The rivers will revert; and the shadows fall to the east in the morning. The moon will be eclipsed; and the equinoxes happen at a wrong season of the year. Was it not such a bill as this, that changed the old stile; that made the eclipse in the time of Julius Cesar; that produced an earthquake at Jamaica, and sunk Port Royal? All history, both ancient and modern, is full of the mischiefs of such a bill. I shall, therefore, vote against it.

Mr. Bogan was now on the floor, and advocated the good effects of the bill.

Sir, said he, addressing himself to the chair, I appear in support of the bill. I say, it will have a good effect on the physical world especially. The ducks will be fatter, the geese heavier, the swans whiter, the red-birds sing better, and partridges come more easily into traps. It will kill rats, muzzle calves, and cut colts; and multiply the breed of oysters, and pickle cod-fish. It will moderate the sun's heat, and the winter's cold; prevent fogs, and cure the ague. It will help the natural brain; brace the nerves, cure sore eyes, and the cholic, and remove rheumatisms. Consult experience, and it will be found, that provisions of the nature proposed by this bill have all astonishing influence in this respect, where they have been tried. I must take the liberty to say, the gentleman's allegations are totally *unfounded;* and he has *committed* himself in the matter of his history; the earthquake in Jamaica, not happening in the time of Julius Cesar; and therefore could have nothing do with the eclipse of the sun. I shall, therfore, vote in favour of the bill.

Mr. Cogan rose to explain; and said, that he did not say, that the earthquake at Jamaica was at the same time with the eclipse of the sun, which happened at the birth of Julius Cesar.

Mr. Bogan rose to correct the gentleman: It was not at the birth of Julius Cesar, but at his death, that the earthquake happened.

Mr. Hogan was on the floor: Said, he thought he could reconcile the gentlemen on that head. It was well known Julius Cesar lived about the time of the rebellion in Scotland, a little after Nebuchadnezzar, king of the Jews. As to the earthquake, he did not remember what year it happened; and therefore could say nothing about it.

At this period, the question being called, it was put, and carried by a majority of 25.

The Captain, satisfied with this sample of Congressional debates, retired, and came to his lodging. . . .

PART II (1804)

Chapter I

We shall go no farther back upon the steps of the Captain, with the bog-trotter at his heels, than where we find them within a mile, or less of the village where his home was, and where he had resided some years, before he had set out on his peregrinations. Passing through a wood just as he approached the town, he saw at some distance before him the semblance of men suspended on the limbs of trees, or at least the exuviae of men, coats, waist-coats, breeches, and hats. What can this be, said the Captain? It is probable that hearing of your return, Teague, the wags of the village have been making what are called Padies, and have set them up on these trees, knowing that this way we should come along. By St. Patrick, said Teague, but I will Pady dem wid dis shalelah. I will tache dem to make Padies, and hang dem up for sign posts in de wood here. Dis is not St. Patrick's day in de morning neider: Bad luck to dem, it may be some poor fellows dat dey have hanged up in reality, for shape-stealing as dey do in Ireland.

I see nothing said the Captain, drawing nearer, but the emptyings of ward-robes, jibbeted on these trees, through the grove: stretched on limbs, or suspended from them, a phenomenon, which I am unable to comprehend, or explain; For I see no corn growing underneath, or near about, from which, a priapus, or scarecrow might affright the birds; nor can they be the vestments of people at work, near hand, or stripped to bathe, as I see no water pond, or river, but a dry grove.

The fact is, these habiliments were of the people of the town, who had hung them up to take the dew, in order to take off the musk of a pole-cat which had affected them from the perfusions of one of these animals. The story is as follows.

Not long before this, a typographist had set up a paper in the village and having reference to the sharpness of his writing, the editor had chosen to assume the symbol, or hieroglyphic of the Porcupine, and in allusion to his quills called himself Peter Porcupine . . . The truth is he had been bred in the barracks, and had at his finger ends, the familiar phrases of the common soldiery, with that peculiar species of wit, which is common with that occupation of men, and in that grade.

. . . I have been turning in my mind what word in our English language, best expresses it, and I have found it to be that which has been given it by Thomas Paine, *black-guardism*. The editor of the Porcupine had scored the village not a little. I do not say rubbed. For that is a translation of the phrase of Horace; *urbem defricuit;* and conveys the idea of tickling, and causing a sensation in part pleasant, yet hurting a little. That was not the case here. For what man without indignation and bitter resentment, can bear the touch of the slanderer, more especially if that slander is of a private, and domestic nature and alludes to what cannot be explained or defended. Not that it is true, but a man in the just pride of standing in society, would scorn to appeal to the public or bring it before a court!

There was in the village a man of understanding, and sensibility who had been the subject of caricature by Peter, and not chusing for reasons that weighed with himself, to take it in good part, thought of retaliation. But what could he do? The same language was unbecoming a gentleman. The like strictures of foibles or of faults on the part of an adversary, could only become the character of a subordinate. Nor was it so much his object to repress the licentiousness of this buffoon as to correct the taste and judgment of the public who did not all at once distinguish the impropriety of countenancing such ribaldry. This they continued to do by receiving his papers.

With a view to this having taken a pole-cat on the mountains, he had put it in a cage and hiring an office contiguous to that of Porcupine, he kept it, suffering the boys of the village to provoke it, and the dogs to bark at it through the bars. The consequence was, that Peter himself, and not unfrequently the female part of his family passing and repassing, were besprinkled with the effluvia and offended with the odour of the animal. The effusions were excited by the irritations of others; but friend and foe were indiscriminately the object of the vapour when they came in the way of its ascension. It was in vain to complain; the owner called himself Paul Pole-cat, and when Peter expostulated and justified his gall on the *freedom of the Press,* Paul fortified himself on the liberty of the *Express.*

But it was not Peter alone, nor his unoffending wife and family that had reason to complain of this nuisance. The children running home to their parents, and the dogs with them, brought the perfume to the houses of the village. The wearing apparel of almost every one was affected with the musk; the women buried their dresses; the men in some instances did so, and in others, hung them up to the action of the air; and the dews of the adjoining wood.

The vestiges of these were the phenomena, which the Captain saw, in his approach to the town. . . .

The Captain advancing to the populace was recognized by them, and his appearance contributed not a little to a longer suspension of hostilities.

Countrymen and fellow-citizens, said he, is this the satisfaction that I have, in returning amongst you after an absence of several years, to see man armed against man, and war waged not only in the very bosom of the republic, but in the village which I have instructed by many precepts? What can be the madness that possesses you? are not the evils of life sufficient? but you must increase them by the positive acts of your own violence. You cannot wholly preserve yourselves at all times free from the maladies of the body, or the distresses of the mind. But it is in your power greatly to assuage these, by the virtues of temperance and moderation. What fury can prompt you, to this degree of apparent resentment, and approaching tumult? Is it local or general politics? Is it any disagreement with regard to your corporate interests, or is religion the cause? Has any flagrant instance of moral turpitude, or exceeding knavery in an individual, roused you to this excess of violence, and exclamation? . . .

I advise therefore, and so far as my weak judgment deserves to be regarded would recommend, that each man lay down his shalelah, baton, or walking-stick, and retire for the evening; and convene tomorrow in a regular town meeting, where the adversaries and advocates on both sides may have an opportunity of being heard. . . .

Chapter II

Containing Proceedings of the Town Meeting

The day following, a meeting being held, and the Chief Burgess in the chair, an advocate of Porcupine took the ground and spoke.

Gentlemen, said he, the press is the palladium of liberty. "The image that fell down from Jupiter." The freedom of the press is essential to liberty. Shackle the press, and you restrain freedom. The constitutions of the states have provided that the press shall be free. If you muzzle this, you may as well muzzle the mouth of man.

It is not the freedom of the press, said one interrupting him, it is the abuse of it that is in question.

The chief burgess called to order, and the speaker went on.

That is the point, said he, to which I meant to come. What shall be said to be the abuse of the press? In order to determine this, we must consider its use. This is,

1. The amusement of the editor. For as some men amuse themselves, shooting, fishing, or chacing with the hound, wild beasts, so men of literary taste, find their recreation in penning paragraphs for a paper, sometimes containing information, or observations on the state of empires, and the characters of great men; at other times by descending, or not rising at all, but confining themselves to the subordinate, affairs of individuals, and private persons.

2. The profit of the editor: and this depends on the number of subscribers. It is not every one that has a taste for refined writing. An editor must be "all things to all men, that he may gain some." Guts and garbage delight bears; and swine swill the trough in preference to the running stream. Black-guardism is the gout of many. Nay it is the more prevailing taste;

The world is naturally averse
To all the truth it sees or hears;
But swallows nonsense and a lie,
With greediness and gluttony.

In Britain, or some other countries, delicacy may succeed. But the coarse stomachs of the Americans crave rather indelicacy and indecency, at least a portion of it. Rough like their own woods, and wild beasts, they digest scurrility.

Well done Porcupine, said the pole-cat man, taking the ground in his turn: well said. But this furnishes a ground to justify the introduction of the pole-cat. You talk of the freedom of the press. Here is the freedom of the express. Nay the word *expression* which is common to both institutions, the artificial one of the types, and the natural one of the cat, shews the original to be similar, and the comparison to *run on all-fours*. If the ink cast into black letter, and carrying with it pain and pungency from the ideas communicated, is tolerated; much more the volatile alkali of the animal that is now set up is to be born, as not more offensive to body or mind. Shall the bark of trees made into powder, and this powder into a liquid, impregnated with thought, and put upon paper, and carried to the press, be accounted harmless, notwithstanding like violence of the decoction, yet the wild cats that inhabit those trees, and are denizens of the forest, be prohibited the haunts of men, because of a bag under their tails which contains all unsavory distillation, and may occasionally be spurted upon men?

• • •

There is hardship both ways, said an elderly inhabitant. In a community different interests will exist. Family interests; family attachments; party conceptions; and party interests. The passions of the heart will create differences. To have a printer all of one side, even though he be a dunce, is an inequality. What if we prevail upon the owner, or as he would call himself the publisher of the pole-cat, to give up or sell out his establishment, dismiss the wild beast, or return it to the mountains, and institute in its place, a counter press of types and blackball that may be a match for Porcupine. O Jehu! Said a man laughing, where will you get a match for Porcupine? A man neither of conscience or shame, taught and educated as he is, with typography that is adequate? Who will be willing to be the ostensible vehicle of language becoming a scavenger? Can any one be found who will have front from insensibility of heart, or the forehead of brass, to bear the imputation? If we could get some Teague O'Regan now, that did not know what we were doing with him: that would think it an honour to be employed; that would not take amiss the proposition of making him the conduit of reproach, and dishonourable inuendo; in short, from whom it could be concealed on what account he was chosen; the project might be plausible.

The Captain, at this rising hastily; a thing unusual with him; for he was naturally grave and sedate; but suddenly feeling the impulse of the congruity, he started from his seat, and seconded the proposition of another press; for said he, the very Teague O'Regan that you want is at hand; a waiter of mine. A bog-trotter, taken, not on the Balagate, but, on the Irish mountains: an aboriginal of the island; not your Scotch-Irish, so called, a colony planted in Ulster, by king James the first of England, when he subdued the natives; but a real Paddy, with the brogue on his tongue, and none on his feet; brought up to sheep-stealing from his youth; for his ancestors inhabiting the hills, were a kind of freebooters, time immemorial, coming down to the low grounds, and plundering the more industrious inhabitants. Captured by traps set upon the hills, or surrounded in the bogs, attempting his escape, he had been tamed and employed, many years, digging Turf, before he came to my hands, I bought him from an Irish vessel, just as a curiosity, not that I expected much service from him; but to see what could be made of a rude man by care and patience. The rogue has a low humour, and a sharp tongue; unbounded impudence. And what may be a restraint upon the licentiousness of his press, should he set up one, he is a most abominable coward; the idea of cudgeling will keep him in bounds; should he over-match Porcupine, and turn upon his employers. He has all the low phrases, cant expressions, illiberal reflections, that could be collected from the company he has kept since he has had the care of my horse, and run after my heels in town and country for several years past. What is more, he has been in France, and has a spice of the language, and a tang of Jacobinism in his principles, and conversation, that will match the contrary learning carried to an exorbitant excess in Peter Porcupine. I do not know that you can do better than contribute to a paper of his setting up. He may call it the Mully-Grub, or give it some such title as will bespeak the nature, of the matter it will usually contain.

• • •

I never had intended, continued the other, more than to reach the sensations of the multitude, and bring them to their senses.

It is only by an appeal to feeling that mind sometimes can be awakened. The public have now some idea of what I mean, that the licentiousness of the press, is not more a nuisance in the moral, than offensive smells are in the physical world. I agree that the cat be removed, and as a substitute, that we may taper off gradually, shall subscribe to the Mully-Grub.

The speech was applauded, and the vote taken.

CHAPTER 7

Educating for Democracy

INTRODUCTION

THOMAS JEFFERSON
from Notes on the State of Virginia (1785)

ROBERT CORAM, 1761–96
from Political Inquiries (1792)

HORACE MANN, 1796–1859
from Reports on Education (1839–48)

CATHARINE BEECHER, 1800–1878
from The Duty of American Women to Their Country (1845)

In the new nation talk of the ties of education to both individual opportunity and the common good quickly developed. But not until the 1830s did Northern states begin instituting a general system of public schools. Among early devisors of education plans, Thomas Jefferson was the best known. However, when Virginia later considered instituting public schools, the ex-president and his supporters chose to spend the money on a second state university instead. The least famous advocate of an early plan was a young editor of a Republican newspaper in Delaware, Robert Coram. His ideas drew from that days' leading public school promoter, Noah Webster, but were grounded in a much broader class analysis that suggested (like Woolman and Dwight) that a decent democratic society depended on reasonably equitable wealth and opportunity. Webster's plan provided six years of general education for all girls and boys at public expense.

Horace Mann of Massachusetts perhaps did most to establish in the 1830s what became the American system of public schools—state mandated, locally organized and financed, and free and compulsory for six years for all children. His stress on trained professional teachers and student learning through active involvement with ideas rather than by rote memorization or corporal punishment were tied to his faith that free schools were necessary for personal opportunity and responsibility as well as society's political and financial welfare, the latter now tied to expectations of an expanding economic pie. Catharine Beecher's educational concerns grew from a desire to curb democratic excess, triggered partly by the riots of the mid-1830s. She also saw schools as providing career opportunities for women. Accepting conventional gender definitions, she argued that a woman's "nurturing" nature, on which the moral world depended, peculiarly suited women to teach the young.

CONSIDERATIONS

- Is basic education necessary for a democratic society and citizenry? Does it promote society's political and financial well-being? Is it necessary to the individual's equality of opportunity and political participation?

- Should basic public education be paid for by taxes, be compulsory, be equal, or empahsize morality?

- How democratic, and how different, are the plans of Jefferson, Coram, and Mann? How attuned are they to good educational practice?

- Why were Mann's ideas about education accepted so readily? Are women especially suited to teaching? Have the American educational system and goals changed much from Mann's time?

- Can or does education cure any social problems? Does the lack of it create problems?

from NOTES ON THE STATE OF VIRGINIA

Thomas Jefferson

Another object of the revisal is, to diffuse knowledge more generally through the mass of the people. This bill proposes to lay off every county into small districts of five or six miles square, called hundreds, and in each of them to establish a school for teaching reading, writing, and arithmetic. The tutor to be supported by the hundred, and every person in it entitled to send their children three years gratis, and as much longer as they please, paying for it. These schools to be under a visitor, who is annually to chuse the boy, of best genius in the school, of those whose parents are too poor to give them further education, and to send him forward to one of the grammar schools, of which twenty are proposed to be erected in different parts of the country, for teaching Greek, Latin, geography, and the higher branches of numerical arithmetic. Of the boys thus sent in any one year, trial is to be made at the grammar schools one or two years, and the best genius of the whole selected, and continued six years, and the residue dismissed. By this means twenty of the best geniusses will be raked from the rubbish annually, and be instructed, at the public expence, so far as the grammar schools go. At the end of six years instruction, one half are to be discontinued (from among whom the grammar schools will probably be supplied with future masters); and the other half, who are to be chosen for the superiority of their parts and disposition, are to be sent and continued three years in the study of such sciences as they shall chuse, at William and Mary college, the plan of which is proposed to be enlarged, as will be hereafter explained, and extended to all the useful sciences. The ultimate result of the whole scheme of education would be the teaching all the children of the state reading, writing, and common arithmetic: turning out ten annually of superior genius, well taught in Greek, Latin, geography, and the higher branches of arithmetic: turning out ten others annually, of still superior parts, who, to those branches of learning, shall have added such of the sciences as their genius shall have led them to: the furnishing to the wealthier part of the people convenient schools, at which their children may be educated, at their own expence.—The general objects of this law are to provide an education adapted to the years, to the capacity, and the condition of every one, and directed to their freedom and happiness. Specific details were not proper for the law. These must be the business of the visitors entrusted with its execution. The first stage of this education being the schools of the hundreds, wherein the great mass of the people will receive their instruction, the principal foundations of future order will be laid here. Instead therefore of putting the Bible and Testament into the hands of the children, at an age when their judgments are not sufficiently matured for religious inquiries, their memories may here be stored with the most useful facts from Grecian, Roman, European and American history. The first elements of morality too may be instilled into their minds; such as, when further developed as their judgments advance in strength, may teach them how to work out their own greatest happiness, by shewing them that it does not depend on the condition of life in which chance has placed them, but is always the result of a good conscience, good health, occupation, and freedom in all just pursuits.—Those whom either the wealth of their parents or the adoption of the state shall destine to higher degrees of learning, will go on to the grammar schools, which constitute the next stage, there to be instructed in the languages. The learning Greek and Latin, I am told, is going into disuse in Europe. I know not what their manners and occupations may call for: but it would be very ill-judged in us to follow their example in this instance. There is a certain period of life, say from eight to fifteen or sixteen years of age, when the mind, like the body, is not yet firm enough for laborious and close operations. If applied to such, it falls an early victim to premature exertion; exhibiting indeed at first, in these young and tender subjects, the flattering appearance of their being men while they are yet children, but ending in reducing them to be children when they should be men. The memory is then most susceptible and tenacious of impressions; and the learning of languages being chiefly a work of memory, it seems precisely fitted to the powers of this period, which is long enough too for acquiring the most useful languages ancient and modern. I do not pretend that language is science. It is only an instrument for the attainment of science. But that time is not lost which is employed in providing tools for future operation: more especially as in this case the books put into the hands of the youth for this purpose may be such as will at the same time impress their minds with useful facts and good principles. If this period be suffered to pass in idleness, the mind becomes lethargic and impotent, as would the body it inhabits if unexercised during the same time. The sympathy between body and mind during their rise, progress and decline, is too strict and obvious to endanger our being misled while we reason from the one to the other.—As soon as they are of sufficient age, it is supposed they will be sent on from the grammar schools to the university, which constitutes our third and last stage, there to study those sciences which may be adapted to their views.—By that part of our plan which prescribes the selection of the youths of genius from among the classes of the poor, we hope to avail the state of those talents which nature has sown as liberally among the poor as the rich, but which perish without use, if not sought for and cultivated.—But of all the views of this law none is more important, none more legitimate, than that of rendering the people the safe, as they are the ultimate, guardians of their own liberty. For this purpose the reading in the first stage, where *they* will receive their whole education, is proposed, as has been said, to be chiefly historical. History by apprising them of the past will enable them to judge of the future; it will avail them of the experience of other times and other nations; it will qualify them as judges of the actions and designs of men; it will enable them to know ambition under every disguise it may assume; and knowing it, to defeat its views. In every government on earth is some trace of human weakness, some germ of corruption and degeneracy, which cunning will discover, and wickedness insensibly open, cultivate, and improve. Every government degenerates when trusted to the rulers of the people alone. The people themselves therefore are its only safe depositories. And to render even them safe their minds must be improved to a certain degree. This indeed is not all that is necessary, though it be essentially necessary. An amendment of our constitution must here come in aid of the public education. The influence over government must be shared among all the people. If every individual which composes their mass participates of the ultimate authority, the government will be safe; because the corrupting the whole mass will exceed any private resources of wealth: and public ones cannot be provided but by levies on the people. In this case every man would have to pay his own price. The government of Great-Britain has been corrupted, because but one man in ten has a right to vote for members of parliament. The sellers of the government there-

fore get nine-tenths of their price clear. It has been thought that corruption is restrained by confining the right of suffrage to a few of the
wealthier of the people: but it would be more effectually restrained by
an extension of that right to such numbers as would bid defiance to
the means of corruption.

from POLITICAL INQUIRIES

To Which Is Added a Plan for the Establishment of Schools Throughout the United States

Robert Coram

Above all, watch carefully over the education of your children. It is from public schools, be assured, that come the wise magistrates—the well trained and courageous soldiers—the good fathers—the good husbands—the good brothers—the good friends—the good man.—
RAYNAL.

INTRODUCTION

It is serious truth, whatever may have been advanced by European writers to the contrary, that the aborigines of the American continent have fewer vices, are less subject to diseases, and are a happier people than the subjects of any government in the Eastern world....

Europeans have been taught to believe that mankind have something of the Devil ingrafted in their nature, that they are naturally ferocious, vicious, revengeful, and as void of reason as brutes, etc., etc. Hence their sanguinary laws, which string a man to a gibbet for the value of twenty pence. They first frame an hypothesis, by which they prove men to be wolves, and then treat them as if they really were such.

But notwithstanding the Europeans have proved men to be naturally wolves, yet they will assert that "men owe everything to education. The minds of children are like blank paper, upon which you may write any characters you please." Thus will they every day refute the fundamental principles upon which their laws are built, and yet not grow a jot the wiser.

Whoever surveys the history of nations with a philosophic eye will find that the civilized man in every stage of his civilization and under almost every form of government has always been a very miserable being. When we consider the very splendid advantages which the citizen seems to possess, the grand scheme of Christianity, the knowledge of sciences and of arts, the experience of all ages and nations recorded in his libraries for a guide, how mortifying must it be to him to reflect that with all his boasted science and philosophy he had made but a retrograde advance to happiness and that the savage, by superior instinct or natural reason, has attained what he, the citizen, by all his powers of refined and artificial intellect could never reach.

There must be some fundamental error, therefore, common to all civilized nations, and this error appears to me to be in education. In savage state education is perfect. In the civilized state education is the most imperfect part of the whole scheme of government or civilization; or, rather, it is not immediately connected with either, for I know of no modern governments, except perhaps the New England states, in which education is incorporated with the government or regulated by it.

In the savage state, as I said before, the system of education is perfect. To explain this, it will be necessary to define the word *education*, or at least what I mean by it. Education, then, means the instruction of youth in certain rules of conduct by which they will be enabled to support themselves when they come to age and to know the obligations they are under to that society of which they constitute a part. Nature, then, in the savage state is the unerring instructor of their youth in the first or principal part of education, for, when their bodily powers are complete, that part of education which relates to their support is complete also. When they can subdue the wild animals, they can procure subsistence. The second, or less essential part, is taught by their parents: their laws, or rather *customs*, being few and simple, are easily remembered and understood.

But the unfortunate civilized man, to obtain a livelihood, must be acquainted with some art or science, in which he is neither instructed by nature, by government, by his parents, or oftentimes by any means at all. He is then absolutely unable to procure himself subsistence without violating some law, and as to the obligations he is under to society, he knows indeed but very little if anything about them. In this state of the case, the situation of the civilized man is infinitely worse than that of the savage, nay, worse than that of the brute creation, for the birds have nests, the foxes have holes, and all animals in their wild state have permanent means of subsistence, but the civilized man has nowhere to lay his head: he has neither habitation nor food, but forlorn and outcast, he perishes for want and starves in the midst of universal plenty. . . .

CHAPTER I

Inquiry into the Origin of Government . . .

No question has puzzled philosophers of all ages more than the origin of government. The wants and vices of mankind have been generally held out to be the causes of all the good and bad governments with which mankind have alternately been blessed or cursed from the earliest ages to the present day. But there is no satisfactory reason to believe that government originated from either of those causes. We can never believe it originated from his wants, considering the very small proportion of cultivated land in proportion to the uncultivated at this day in every part of the globe, some small islands excepted; nor will his vices afford a better solution of the question, since the savages of North America are infinitely more virtuous than the inhabitants of the most polished nations of Europe. . . .

Since, then, we are unable to discover the origin of government from the impenetrable obscurity in which it is involved, let us consider its end as equally applicable to our purpose. The end of government, we are told, is public good, by which is to be understood the happiness of the community. The great body of the people in Europe are unhappy, not to say miserable: there needs no other argument to prove that all the European governments have been founded upon wrong principles, since the means used have not produced the end intended.

• • •

In the comparative view of the civilized man and the savage, the most striking contrast is the division of property. To the one, it is the source of all his happiness: to the other, the fountain of all his misery. By holy writ we are informed that God gave to man dominion over the earth, the living creatures, and the herbs; human laws have, however, limited this jurisdiction to certain orders or classes of men; the rest are to feed upon air if they can or fly to another world for subsistence. This parceling out to individuals what was intended for the general stock of society leads me to inquire farther into the nature and origin of property. I am not quite so visionary as to expect that the members of any civilized community will listen to an equal division of lands: had that been the object of this work, the author had infallibly lost his labor. But a substitute, and perhaps the only one, is highly practicable, as will hereafter appear.

CHAPTER II

Inquiry into the Origin of Property . . .

. . . The right to exclusive property is a question of great importance, and, of all others, perhaps, deserves the most candid and equitable solution. Such a solution will afford a foundation for laws which will totally eradicate from the civilized man a very large portion of those vices which such legislators as Dr. Blackstone pretend to be natural to the human race. One deplorable inquiry, at least, which has filled the earth with tears and the hearts of all good men with deep regret—I mean the slave trade—could never have existed among any people who had distinct ideas of property. . . .

Any person possessed of common sense and some erudition who was not previously bent upon establishing a favorite system at the expense of truth might give us a rational account in what manner property should be regulated under the law of nature. Such a person would probably say all things subject to the dominion of man may be included in two classes, land and movables; the rational foundation of the tenure of each is labor. Thus fruit growing on a tree was common, but when collected it became the exclusive property of the collector; land uncultivated was common but when cultivated, it became the exclusive possession of the cultivator. Men, then, according to the laws of nature, had an exclusive property in movables and an exclusive possession in lands, both of which were founded on labor and bounded by it. For as labor employed in the collection of fruit could give an exclusive right only to the fruit so collected, so labor in the soil could give exclusive possession only to the spot so labored.

•   •   •

[W]hen, with the sword of violence and the pen of sophistry, a few had plundered or cheated the bulk of their rights, the few became ennobled and the many were reduced from mere animals of prey to beasts of burden. But why not mention a few more concomitants of civil society, such as poverty, vices innumerable, and diseases unknown in the state of nature. Look around your cities, ye who boast of having established the civilization and happiness of man, see at every corner of your streets some wretched object with tattered garments, squalid look, and hopeless eye, publishing your lies, in folio to the world. Hedged in the narrow strait, between your sanguinary laws and the pressing calls of hunger, he has no retreat, but like an abortive being, created to no manner of purpose, his only wish is death. For of what use can life be but to augment his sufferings by a comparison of his desperate lot with yours?

• • •

Reduced to light, air, and water for an inheritance, one would have thought their situation could not be easily made worse, but it is not difficult to be mistaken. The bulk of mankind were not only cheated out of their right to the soil but were held ineligible to offices in the government because they were not freeholders. First cruelly to wrest from them the paternal inheritance of their universal Father, and then to make this outrageous act an excuse for denying them the rights of citizenship. This is the history of civil society in which our duty and happiness are so admirably interwoven together. We will, however, never believe that men originally entered into a compact by which they excluded themselves from all right to the bounties of Providence; and if they did, the contract could not be binding on their posterity, for although a man may give away his own right, he cannot give away the right of another. . . .

. . . [I]f the European governments were erected to supply the wants and lessen the fears of individuals, we may venture to assert that the first projectors of them were errant blockheads. The wants of man, instead of having been lessened, have been multiplied, and that in proportion to his boasted civilization; and the fear of poverty alone is more than sufficient to counterbalance all the fears to which he was subject in the rudest stage of natural liberty.

From this source arise almost all the disorders in the body politic. The fear of poverty has given a double spring to avarice, the deadliest passion in the human breast; it has erected a golden image to which all mankind, with reverence, bend the knee regardless of their idolatry. Merit is but an abortive useless gift to the possessor, unless accompanied with wealth; he might choose which tree whereon to hang himself, did not his virtuous mind tell him to "dig, beg, rot, and perish well content, so he but wrap himself in honest rags at his last gasp and die in peace." . . .

. . . [I]n the age in which Dr. Blackstone lived, he should have known better, he should have known that the unequal distribution of property was the parent of almost all the disorders of government; nay, he did know it, for he had read Beccaria, who treating upon the crime of robbery, says, "But this crime, alas!, is commonly the effect of misery and despair, the crime of that unhappy part of mankind to whom the right of exclusive property (a terrible and perhaps unnecessary right) has left but a bare subsistence." There is no necessity for concealing this important truth, but much benefit may be expected from its promulgation—It offers a foundation whereon to erect a system, which like the sun in the universe, will transmit light, life, and harmony to all under its influence—I mean—A SYSTEM OF EQUAL EDUCATION.

CHAPTER III

Consequences Drawn from the Preceding Chapters by Which It Is Proved that All Governments Are Bound To Secure to Their Subjects the Means of Acquiring Knowledge in Sciences and in Arts.

• • •

We will now inquire the best mode of alleviating his miseries, without disturbing the established rules of property. In the savage state, as there is no learning, so there is no need of it. Meum & tuum, which principally receives existence with civil society, is but little known in the rude stages of natural liberty; and where all property is unknown, or rather, where all property is in common, there is no necessity of learning to acquire or defend it. If in adverting from a state of nature to a state of civil society, men gave up their natural liberty and their common right to property, it is but just that they should be protected in their civil liberty and furnished with means of gaining exclusive property, in lieu of that natural liberty and common right of property which they had given up in exchange for the supposed advantages of civil society; otherwise the change is for the worse, and the general happiness is sacrificed for the benefit of a few. . . .

Education should not be left to the caprice or negligence of parents, to chance, or confined to the children of wealthy citizens; it is a shame, a scandal to civilized society, that part only of the citizens should be sent to colleges and universities to learn to cheat the rest of their liberties. Are ye aware, legislators, that in making knowledge necessary to the subsistence of your subjects, ye are in duty bound to secure to them the means of acquiring it? Else what is the bond of society but a rope of sand, incapable of supporting its own weight? A heterogenous jumble of contradiction and absurdity, from which the subject knows not how to extricate himself, but often falls a victim to his natural wants or to cruel and inexorable laws—starves or is hanged. . . .

We despise thieves, not caring to reflect that human nature is always the same: that when it is a man's interest to be a thief he becomes one, but when it is his interest to support a good character he becomes an honest man; that even thieves are honest among each other, because it is their interest to be so. We seldom hear of a man in independent circumstances being indicted for petit felony: the man would be an idiot indeed who would stake a fair character for a few shillings which he did not need, but the greatest part of those indicted for petit felonies are men who have no characters to lose, that is—no substance, which the world always takes for good character.

If a man has no fortune and through poverty or neglect of his parents he has had no education and learned no trade, in such a forlorn situation, which demands our charity and our tears, the equitable and humane laws of England spurn him from their protection, under the harsh term of a vagrant or a vagabond, and he is cruelly ordered to be whipped out of the county. . . .

How can those English vagrant acts be reconciled to that law which pretends to protect every man in his just rights? Or have poor men no rights? How will they square with the doctrines of the Christian religion which preach poverty, charity, meekness, and disinterestedness, after the example of their humble founder. . . .

But how comes this injustice in the arrangements of policy? Is it not evident that it is all the work of men's hands? Thus it is that the sins of the fathers are visited upon the children unto the third and fourth generation. A tyrant, a madman, or a fool forms a society; to aggrandize his own family and his dependants, he creates absurd and unnatural distinctions; to make one part of the people fools, he makes the other part slaves. . . .

We are told by Sir William Blackstone that it is a settled rule at common law that no prisoner shall be allowed counsel upon his trial upon the general issue in any capital crime unless some point of law shall arise proper to be debated. This is without doubt a barbarous law, and it is a little surprising that while every other art and science is daily improving, such inconsistencies should have been suffered to continue to this time of day in a science on which our lives depend. . . . Those governments, therefore, which think the instruction of youth worthy [of] their attention, would do well to cause an abridgement of their statute law to be read in their schools at stated times, as often as convenient. . . .

Mr. Noah Webster is the only American author, indeed the only author of any nation, . . . who has taken up the subject of education upon that liberal and equitable scale which it justly deserves. . . .

I think it a debt due to Mr. Webster to introduce part of his sentiments on this subject—"A good system of education," says this author, "should be the first article in the code of political regulations, for it is much easier to introduce and establish an effectual system for preserving morals than to correct by penal statutes the ill effects of a bad system. . . .

"Two regulations are essential to the continuance of republican governments: 1. Such a distribution of lands and such principles of descent and alienation as shall give every citizen a power of acquiring what his industry merits. 2. Such a system of education as gives every citizen an opportunity of acquiring knowledge and fitting himself for places of trust. These are fundamental articles, the *sine qua non* of the existence of the American republics.". . .

Suffer me then, Americans, to arrest, to command your attention to this important subject. To make mankind better is a duty which every man owes to his posterity, to his country, and to his God; and remember, my friends, there is but one way to effect this important purpose—which is—by incorporating education with government.—*This is the rock on which you must build your political salvation!*

CHAPTER IV

The System of Education Should Be Equal . . .

That the system of education should be equal is evident, since the rights given up in the state of nature and for which education is the substitute were equal. But as I know it will be objected by some that the natural inequality of the human intellect will obviate any attempt to diffuse knowledge equally, it seems necessary to make some inquiry concerning the natural equality of men.

That all men are by nature equal was once the fashionable phrase of the times, and men gloried in this equality and really believed it, or else they acted their parts to the life! Latterly, however, this notion is laughed out of countenance, and some very grave personages have not scrupled to assert that as we have copied the English in our form of federal government, we ought to imitate them in the establishment of a nobility also. . . .

But to return to our inquiry—If an elegant silver vase and some ore of the same metal were shown to a person ignorant of metals, it would not require much argument to convince him that the vase could never be produced from the ore. Such is the mode of reasoning upon the inequality of the human species. Effects purely artificial have been ascribed to nature, and the man of letters who from his cradle to his grave has trod the paths of art is compared with the untutored Indian and the wretched African in whom slavery has deadened all the springs of the soul.

And the result of this impartial and charitable investigation is that there is an evident gradation in the intellectual faculties of the human species. There are various grades in the human mind is the fashionable phrase of the times. Scarce a superficial blockhead is to be met with but stuns you with a string of trite commonplace observations upon gradation, and no doubt thinks himself *in primo gradu* or at the top of the ladder. . . .

The minds of children are like blank paper, upon which you may write any characters you please. But what tends most to establish this idea of natural equality [is that] we find it always uniform in the savage state.

Now if there was a natural inequality in the human mind, would it not be as conspicuous in the savage as in the civilized state? The contrary of which is evident to every observer acquainted with the American Indians. Among those people all the gifts of Providence are in common. We do not see, as in civilized nations, part of the citizens sent to colleges to learn to cheat the rest of their liberties who are condemned to be hewers of wood and drawers of water. The mode of acquiring information, which is common to one, is common to all; hence we find a striking equality in form, size, and intellectual faculties nowhere to be found in civilized nations.

It is only in civilized nations where extremes are to be found in the human species—it is here where wealthy and dignified mortals roll along the streets in all the parade and trappings of royalty, while the lower class are not half so well fed as the horses of the former. It is this cruel inequality which has given rise to the epithets of nobility, vulgar, mob, canaille, etc. and the degrading, but common observation— Man differs more from man, than man from beast—The difference is purely artificial. Thus do men create an artificial inequality among themselves and then cry out it is all natural.

If we would give ourselves time to consider, we would find an idea of natural intellectual equality everywhere predominant but more particularly in free countries. The trial by jury is a strong proof of this idea in that nation; otherwise would they have suffered the unlettered peasant to decide against lawyers and judges? Is it not here taken for granted that the generality of men, although they are ignorant of the phrases and technical terms of the law, have notwithstanding sufficient mother wit to distinguish between right and wrong, which is all the lawyer with his long string of cases and reports is able to do? From whence also arises our notion of common sense? Is it not from an idea that the bulk of mankind possess what is called common understanding?

•   •   •

It is generally observed that most of the American legislatures are composed of lawyers and merchants. What is the reason? Because the farmer has no opportunity of getting his son instructed without sending him to a college, the expense of which is more than the profits of his farm. An equal representation is absolutely necessary to the preservation of liberty. But there can never be an equal representation until there is an equal mode of education for all citizens. For although a rich farmer may, by the credit of his possessions, help himself into the legislature, yet if through a deficiency in his education he is unable to speak with propriety, he may see the dearest interest of his country basely bartered away and be unable to make any effort except his single vote against it. Education, therefore, to be generally useful should be brought home to every man's door.

CHAPTER V

Wretched State of the Country Schools throughout the United States, and the Absolute Necessity of a Reformation.

The country schools through most of the United States, whether we consider the buildings, the teachers, or the regulations, are in every respect completely despicable, wretched, and contemptible. The buildings are in general sorry hovels, neither windtight nor watertight, a few stools serving in the double capacity of bench and desk and the old leaves of copy books making a miserable substitute for glass windows.

The teachers are generally foreigners, shamefully deficient in every qualification necessary to convey instruction to youth . . . and the children who are advanced are beat and cuffed to forget the former mode they have been taught, which irritates their minds and retards their progress. The quarter being finished, the children lie idle until another master offers, few remaining in one place more than a quarter. . . . All these blockheads are equally absolute in their own notions and will by no means suffer the children to pronounce the letter as they were first taught, but every three months the school goes through a reform—error succeeds error—and dunce the second reigns like dunce the first. . . .

The necessity of a reformation in the country schools is too obvious to be insisted on, and the first step to such reformation will be by turning private schools into public ones. The schools should be public, for several reasons—1st. Because, as has been before said, every citizen has an equal right to subsistence and ought to have an equal opportunity of acquiring knowledge. 2d. Because public schools are easiest maintained, as the burden falls upon all the citizens.

The man who is too squeamish or lazy to get married contributes to the support of public schools as well as the man who is burdened with a large family. But private schools are supported only by heads of families, and by those only while they are interested, for as soon as the children are grown up their support is withdrawn, which makes the employment so precarious that men of ability and merit will not submit to the trifling salaries allowed in most country schools and which, by their partial support, cannot afford a better.

Let public schools then be established in every county of the United States, at least as many as are necessary for the present population;

and let those schools be supported by a general tax. Let the objects of those schools be to teach the rudiments of the English language, writing, bookkeeping, mathematics, natural history, mechanics, and husbandry—and let every scholar be admitted gratis and kept in a state of subordination without respect to persons.

The other branch of education, I mean, instruction in arts, ought also to be secured to every individual by laws enacted for that purpose, by which parents and others having authority over youth should be compelled to bind them out at certain ages and for a limited time to persons professing mechanical or other branches, and the treatment of apprentices during their apprenticeship should be regulated by laws expressly provided. . . .

It would be superfluous to insist on the necessity of trades—their use is obvious. I shall only remark that, considering the transitory nature of all human advantages, how soon a man may be dispossessed of a very considerable property—how many avenues there are to misfortunes; a good trade seems to be the only sheet anchor on which we may firmly rely for safety in the general storms of human adversity. How much then is it to be lamented that ever the tyranny of fashion or pride of birth gave an idea of disgrace to those virtuous and useful occupations.

To demonstrate the practicability of establishing public schools throughout the United States, let us suppose the states to be divided into districts according to the population, and let every district support one school by a tax on the acre on all lands within the district. . . .

Now when we consider that such a trifling tax, by being applied to this best of purposes, may be productive of consequences amazingly glorious, can any man make a serious objection against public schools? "It is unjust," says one, "that I should pay for the schooling of other people's children." But, my good sir, it is more unjust that your posterity should go without any education at all. And public schools is the only method I know of to secure an education to your posterity forever. . . .

Perhaps no plan of private education can ever be so cheap as public. In the instances of public schools a considerable part of the master's salary would be spent in the district. The farmer might supply him with provisions, and the receipts might be tendered as a part of his tax to the collector. Thus the farmer would scarcely feel the tax.

No modes of faith, systems of manners, or foreign or dead languages should be taught in those schools. As none of them are necessary to obtain a knowledge of the obligations of society, the government is not bound to instruct the citizens in any thing of the kind—No medals or premiums of any kind should be given under the mistaken notion of exciting emulation. Like titles of nobility, they are not productive of a single good effect but of many very bad ones: my objections are founded on reason and experience. In republican governments the praises of good men, and not medals, should be esteemed the proper reward of merit, but by substituting a bauble instead of such rational applause, do we not teach youth to make a false estimate of things and to value them for their glitter, parade, and finery? This single objection ought to banish medals from schools forever.

• • •

To conclude, to make men happy, the first step is to make them independent. For if they are dependent, they can neither manage their private concerns properly, retain their own dignity, or vote impartially for their country: they can be but tools at best. And to make them independent, to repeat Mr. Webster's words, two regulations are essentially necessary. First, such a distribution of lands and principles of descent and alienation as shall give every citizen a power of acquiring what his industry merits. Secondly, such a system of education as gives every citizen an opportunity of acquiring knowledge and fitting himself for places of trust. It is said that men of property are the fittest persons to represent their country because they have least reason to betray it. If the observation is just, every man should have property, that none be left to betray their country.

• • •

Let us keep nature in view and form our policy rather by the fitness of things than by a blind adherence to contemptible precedents from arbitrary and corrupt governments. Let us begin by perfecting the system of education as the proper foundation whereon to erect a temple to liberty and to establish a wise, equitable, and durable policy, that our country may become *indeed* an asylum to the distresses of every clime—the abode of liberty, peace, virtue, and happiness—a land on which the Deity may deign to look down with approbation—and whose government may last till time shall be no more!

from REPORTS ON EDUCATION

Horace Mann

CHALLENGES TO A NEW AGE (1845)

... The great doctrine which it is desirable to maintain, and carry out ... is, *equality of school-privileges for all the children of the town, whether they belong to a poor district or a rich one, a small district or a large one.* ...

... The great, the all-important, the only important question still remains: By what spirit are our schools animated? Do they cultivate the higher faculties in the nature of childhood,—its conscience, its benevolence, a reverence for whatever is true and sacred? or are they only developing, upon a grander scale, the lower instincts and selfish tendencies of the race,—the desires which prompt men to seek, and the powers which enable them to secure, sensual ends,—wealth, luxury, preferment,—irrespective of the well-being of others? Knowing, as we do, that the foundations of national greatness can be laid only in the industry, the integrity, and the spiritual elevation of the people, are we equally sure that our schools are forming the character of the rising generation upon the everlasting principles of duty and humanity? or, on the other hand, are they only stimulating the powers which lead to a base pride of intellect, which prompt to the ostentation instead of the reality of virtue, and which give augury that life is to be spent only in selfish competitions between those who should be brethren? Above all others, must the children of a republic be fitted for society as well as for themselves. As each citizen is to participate in the power of governing others, it is an essential preliminary that he should be imbued with a feeling for the wants, and a sense of the rights, of those whom he is to govern; because the power of governing others, if guided by no higher motive than our own gratification, is the distinctive attribute of oppression; an attribute whose nature and whose wickedness are the same, whether exercised by one who calls himself a republican, or by one born an irresponsible despot. In a government like ours, each individual must think of the welfare of the State, as well as of the welfare of his own family, and, therefore, of the children of others as well as his own. It becomes, then, a momentous question, whether the children in our schools are educated in reference to themselves and their private interests only, or with a regard to the great social duties and prerogatives that await them in after-life. Are they so educated, that, when they grow up, they will make better philanthropists and Christians, or only grander savages? For, however loftily the intellect of man may have been gifted, however skillfully it may have been trained, if it be not guided by a sense of justice, a love of mankind, and a devotion to duty, its possessor is only a more splendid, as he is a more dangerous barbarian.

We have had admirable essays and lectures on the subject of morality in our schools. . . . [W]hile specific directions and practical aids in regard to the training of children in those every-day domestic and social duties on which their own welfare and the happiness of society depend are comparatively unknown. How shall this great disideratum be supplied? How shall the rising generation be brought under purer moral influences, by way of guaranty and suretyship, that, when they become men, they will surpass their predecessors, both in the soundness of their speculations and in the rectitude of their practice? Were children born with perfect natures, we might expect that they would gradually purify themselves from the vices and corruptions which are now almost enforced upon them by the examples of the world. But the same nature by which the parents sunk into error and sin pre-adapts the children to follow in the course of ancestral degeneracy. . . . But man has not yet applied his highest wisdom and care to the young of his own species. They have been comparatively neglected until their passions had taken deep root, and their ductile feelings had hardened into the iron inflexibility of habit; and then how often have the mightiest agencies of human power and terror been expanded upon them in vain! Governments do not see the future criminal or pauper in the neglected child, and therefore they sit calmly by, until roused from their stupor by the cry of hunger or the spectacle of crime. Then they erect the almshouse, the prison, and the gibbet, to arrest or mitigate the evils which timely caution might have prevented. The courts and the ministers of justice sit by until the petty delinquencies of youth glare out in the enormities of adult crime; and then they doom to prison or the gallows those enemies to society, who, under wise and well-applied influences, might have been supports and ornaments of the social fabric. . . . Who will deny, that, if one tithe of the talent and culture which have been expended in legislative halls, in defining offences, and in devising and denouncing punishments for them; or of the study and knowledge which have been spent in judicial courts, in trying and in sentencing criminals; or of the eloquence and the piety which have preached repentance and remission of sins to adult men and women,—had been consecrated to the instruction and training of the young, the civilization of mankind would have been adorned by virtues and charities and Christian graces to which it is now a stranger?

What an appalling fact it is to every contemplative mind, that even wars and famines and pestilences—terrible calamities as they are acknowledged to be—have been welcomed as blessings and mercies, because they swept away, by thousands and tens of thousands, the pests which ignorance and guilt had accumulated! But the efficiency or sufficiency of these comprehensive remedies is daily diminishing. A large class of men seem to have lost that moral sense by which the liberty and life of innocent men are regarded as of more value than the liberty and life of criminals. There is not a government in Christendom which is not growing weaker every day, so far as its strength lies in an appeal to physical force. The criminal code of most nations is daily shorn of some of its terrors. Where, as with us, the concurrence of so many minds is a prerequisite, the conviction of the guilty is often a matter of difficulty; and every guilty man who escapes is a missionary, going through society, and preaching the immunity of guilt wherever he goes. War will never again be waged to disburden the crowded prisons, or to relieve the weary executioner. The arts of civilization have so multiplied the harvests of the earth, that a general famine will not again lend its aid to free the community of its surplus members. Society at large has emerged from that barbarian and semi-barbarian state where pestilence formerly had its birth, and committed its ravages. These great outlets and sluice-ways, which, in former times, relieved nations of the dregs and refuse of their population, being now closed, whatever want or crime we engender, or suffer to exist, we must live with. If improvidence begets hunger, that hunger will break into our garners. . . .

In the history of the world, that period which opened with the war of the American Revolution, and with the adoption of the Constitution of the United States, forms a new era. Those events, it is true, did not change human nature; but they placed that nature in circumstances so different from any it had ever before occupied, that we must expect a new series of developments in human character and conduct. Theoretically, and, to a great extent, practically, the nation passed at once, from being governed by others, to self-government. Hereditary misrule was abolished; but power and opportunity for personal misrule were given in its stead. In the hour of exultation at the achievement of liberty, it was not considered that the evils of license may be more formidable than the evils of oppression, because a man may sink himself to a profounder depth of degradation than it is in the power of any other mortal to sink him, and because the slave of the vilest tyrant is less debased than the thrall of his own passions. Restraints of physical force were cast off; but no adequate measures were taken to supply their place with the restraints of moral force. In the absence of the latter, the former, degrading as they are, are still desirable,—as a strait-jacket for the maniac is better than the liberty by which he would inflict wounds or death upon himself. The question now arises,—and it is a question on whose decision the worth or worthlessness of our free institutions are suspended,—whether some more powerful agency cannot be put in requisition to impart a higher moral tone to the public mind; to enthrone the great ideas of justice, truth, benevolence, and reverence, in the breasts of the people, and give them a more authoritative sway over conduct than they have ever yet possessed.

●　　●　　●

In Prussia and a few of the smaller States of Continental Europe, the action of the intellect, for reasons too obvious to be mentioned, has taken more of a speculative turn. In Great Britain, it has been turned towards practical or utilitarian objects; and, in the United States, it has been pre-eminently so turned. The immense natural resources of our country would have stimulated to activity a less enterprising and a less energetic race than the Anglo-Saxon. But such glittering prizes, placed within the reach of such fervid natures and such capacious desires, turned every man into a competitor and an aspirant. The exuberance that overspread the almost interminable valleys of the West drew forth hosts of colonists to gather their varied harvests. The tide of emigration rolled on, and it still continues to roll, with a volume and a celerity never before known in any part of the world, or in any period of history. Unlike all other nations, we have had no fixed, but a rapidly growing frontier. . . . But scarcely had the immigrant and the adventurer surveyed the richness of vegetation which covered the surface of the earth, before they discovered an equal vastness of mineral wealth beneath it,—wealth which had been laid up, of old, in subterranean chambers, no man yet knows how capacious. Thus every man, however poor his parentage, became the heir-apparent of a rich inheritance. And while millions were thus appropriating fortunes to themselves out of the great treasure-house of the West, other millions on the Atlantic seaboard, with equal enterprise and equal avidity, were amassing the means of refinement and luxury. In one section, where Nature had adapted the soil to the production of new and valuable staples, the planter seized the opportunity,—literally a golden one,—and soon filled the markets of the world with some of the cheapest and most indispensable necessaries of life. In another section, foreign commerce invited attention; and the hardy and fearless inhabitants went forth to the uttermost parts of the earth in quest of gain. . . . Meantime, science and invention applied themselves to the mechanic arts. They found that Nature, in all her recesses, had hidden stores of power, surpassing the accumulated strength of the whole human race, though all its vigor could be concentrated in a single arm. They found that whoever would rightly apply to Nature, by a performance of the true scientific and mechanical conditions, for the privilege of using her agencies, should forthwith be invested with a power such as no Babylonian or Egyptian king, with all his myriads of slaves, could ever command. . . .

. . . [I]ndividual opulence has increased; and the sum total or valuation of the nation's capital has doubled and redoubled with a rapidity to which the history of every other nation that has ever existed must acknowledge itself to be a stranger. This easy accumulation of wealth has inflamed the laudable desire of competence into a culpable ambition for superfluous riches. To convert natural resources into the means of voluptuous enjoyments, to turn mineral wealth into metallic currency, to invent more productive machinery, to open new channels of intercommunication between the States, and to lengthen the prodigious inventory of capital invested in commerce, has spurred the energies and quickened the talent of a people, every one of whom is at liberty to choose his own employment, and to change it, when chosen, for any other that promises to be more lucrative.

Nor is this the only side on which hope has been stimulated and ambition aroused. Others of the most craving instincts of human nature have been called into fervid activity. Political ambition, the love of power,—whether it consists in the base passion of exercising authority over the will of others, or in the more expansive and generous desire of occupying a conspicuous place among our fellows by their consent,—these motives have acted upon a strong natural instinct in the hearts of all. . . .

Now, it is too obvious to need remark, that the main tendency of institutions and of a state of society like those here depicted is to cultivate the intellect and to inflame the passions, rather than to teach humility and lowliness to the heart. Our civil and social condition holds out splendid rewards for the competitions of talent, rather than motives for the practice of virtue. It sharpens the perceptive faculties in comparing different objects of desire, it exercises the judgment in arranging means for the production of ends, it gives a grasp of thought and a power of combination which nothing else could so effectively impart; but, on the other hand, it tends not merely to the neglect of the moral nature, but to an invasion of its rights, to a disregard of its laws, and, in cases of conflict, to the silencing of its remonstrances and the denial of its sovereignty.

And has not experience proved what reason might have predicted? Within the last half-century, has not speculation, to a fearful extent, taken the place of honest industry? Has not the glare of wealth so dazzled the public eye as often to blind it to the fraudulent means by which the wealth itself had been procured? Have not men been honored for the offices of dignity and patronage they have held, rather than for the ever-enduring qualities of probity, fidelity, and intelligence, which alone are meritorious considerations for places of honor and power? . . .

And who will say, even of the most favored portions of our country, that their advancement in moral excellence, in probity, in purity, and in the practical exemplification of the virtues of a Christian life, has kept pace with their progress in outward conveniences and embellishments? Can virtue recount as many triumphs in the moral world as intellect has won in the material? Can our advances towards perfection in the cultivation of private and domestic virtues, and in the feeling of brotherhood and kindness towards all the members of our households, bear comparison with the improvements in our dwellings, our furniture, or our equipages? Have our charities for the poor, the debased, the ignorant, been multiplied in proportion to our revenues? Have we subdued low vices, low indulgences, and selfish feelings? and have we fertilized the waste places in the human heart as extensively as we have converted the wilderness into plenteous harvest-fields, or enlisted the running waters in our service? . . .

END POVERTY THROUGH EDUCATION (1848)

Another cardinal object which the government of Massachusetts, and all the influential men in the State, should propose to themselves, is the physical well-being of all the people,—the sufficiency, comfort, competence, of every individual in regard to food, raiment, and shelter. And these necessaries and conveniences of life should be obtained by each individual for himself, or by each family for themselves, rather than accepted from the hand of charity or extorted by poor-laws. It is not averred that this most desirable result can, in all instances, be obtained; but it is, nevertheless, the end to be aimed at. True statesmanship and true political economy, not less than true philanthropy, present this perfect theory as the goal, to be more and more closely approximated by our imperfect practice. The desire to achieve such a result cannot be regarded as an unreasonable ambition; for, though all mankind were well fed, well clothed, and well housed, they might still be but half civilized.

Poverty is a public as well as a private evil. There is no physical law necessitating its existence. The earth contains abundant resources for ten times—doubtless for twenty times—its present inhabitants. Cold, hunger, and nakedness are not, like death, an inevitable lot. There are many single States in this Union which could supply an abundance of edible products for the inhabitants of the thirty States that compose it. There are single States capable of raising a sufficient quantity of cotton to clothe the whole nation; and there are other States having sufficient factories and machinery to manufacture it. The coal-fields of Pennsylvania are sufficiently abundant to keep every house in the land at the temperature of sixty-five degrees for centuries to come. Were there to be a competition, on the one hand, to supply wool for every conceivable fabric, and, on the other, to wear out these fabrics as fast as possible, the single State of New York would beat the whole country. There is, indeed, no assignable limit to the capacities of the earth for producing whatever is necessary for the sustenance, comfort, and improvement of the race. Indigence, therefore, and the miseries and degradations incident to indigence, seem to be no part of the eternal ordinances of Heaven. The bounty of God is not brought into question or suspicion by its existence; for man who suffers it might have avoided it. Even the wealth which the world now has on hand is more than sufficient to supply all the rational wants of every individual in it. Privations and sufferings exist, not from the smallness of its sum, but from the inequality of its distribution. Poverty is set over against profusion. In some, all healthy appetite is cloyed and sickened by repletion; while in others, the stomach seems to be a supernumerary organ in the system, or, like the human eye or human lungs before birth, is waiting to be transferred to some other region, where its functions may come into use. One gorgeous palace absorbs all the labor and expense that might have made a thousand hovels comfortable. That one man may ride in carriages of Oriental luxury, hundreds of other men are turned into beasts of burden. To supply a superfluous wardrobe for the gratification of one man's pride, a thousand women and children shiver with cold; and, for every flash of the diamonds that royalty wears, there is a tear of distress in the poor man's dwelling. . . . Millions are perishing in the midst of superfluities.

According to the European theory, men are divided into classes, some toil to earn, others seize and enjoy. According to the Massachusetts theory, all are to have an equal chance for earning, and equal security in the enjoyment of what they earn. The latter tends to equality of condition; the former, to the grossest inequalities. Tried by any Christian standard of morals, or even by any of the better sort of heathen standards, can any one hesitate, for a moment, in declaring which of the two will produce the greater amount of human welfare, and which, therefore, is the more comfortable to the divine will? . . . The present condition of Ireland cancels all the glories of the British crown. . . . Where standards like these exist, and are upheld by council and by court, by fashion and by law, *Christianity is yet to be discovered;* at least, it is yet to be applied in practice to the social condition of men.

Our ambition as a State should trace itself to a different origin, and propose to itself a different object. Its flame should be lighted at the skies. Its radiance and its warmth should reach the darkest and the coldest abodes of men. It should seek the solution of such problems as these: To what extent can competence displace pauperism? How nearly can we free ourselves from the low-minded and the vicious, not by their expatriation, but by their elevation? To what extent can the resources and powers of Nature be converted into human welfare, the peaceful arts of life be advanced, and the vast treasures of human talent and genius be developed? How much of suffering, in all its forms, can be relieved? or, what is better than relief, how much can be prevented? Cannot the classes of crimes be lessened, and the number of criminals in each class be diminished? Our exemplars, both for public and for private imitation, should be the parables of the lost sheep and of the lost piece of silver. When we have spread competence through all the abodes of poverty, when we have substituted knowledge for ignorance in the minds of the whole people, when we have reformed the vicious and reclaimed the criminal, then may we invite all neighboring nations to behold the spectacle, and say to them, in the conscious elation of virtue, "Rejoice with me," for I have found that which is lost. Until that day shall arrive, our duties will not be wholly fulfilled, and our ambition will have new honors to win.

But is it not true that Massachusetts, in some respects, instead of adhering more and more closely to her own theory, is becoming emulous of the baneful examples of Europe? The distance between the two extremes of society is lengthening, instead of being abridged. With every generation, fortunes increase on the one hand, and some new privation is added to poverty on the other. We are verging towards those extremes of opulence and of penury, each of which unhumanizes the human mind. A perpetual struggle for the bare necessaries of life, without the ability to obtain them, makes men wolfish. Avarice, on the other hand, sees, in all the victims of misery around it, not objects for pity and succor, but only crude materials to be worked up into more money.

I suppose it to be the universal sentiment of all those who mingle any ingredient of benevolence with their notions on political economy, that vast and overshadowing private fortunes are among the greatest dangers to which the happiness of the people in a republic can be subjected. Such fortunes would create a feudalism of a new kind, but one more oppressive and unrelenting than that of the middle ages. The feudal lords in England and on the Continent never held their retainers in a more abject condition of servitude than the great majority of foreign manufacturers and capitalists hold their operatives and laborers at the present day. The means employed are different; but the similarity in results is striking. What force did then, money does now. The villein of the middle ages had no spot of earth on which he could live, unless one were granted to him by his lord. The operative or laborer of the present day has no employment, and therefore no bread, unless the capitalist will accept his services. The vassal had no shelter but such as his master provided for him. Not one in five thousand of English operatives or farm-laborers is able to build or own even a hovel; and therefore they must accept such shelter as capital offers them. The baron prescribed his own terms to his retainers: those terms were peremptory, and the serf must submit or perish. The British manufacturer or farmer prescribes the rate of wages he will give to his work-people; he reduces these wages under whatever pretext he pleases; and they, too, have no alternative but submission or starvation. In some respects, indeed, the condition of the modern dependant is more forlorn than that of the corresponding serf class in former times. Some attributes of the patriarchal relation did spring up between the lord and his lieges to soften the harsh relations subsisting between them. . . .

Now, two or three things will doubtless be admitted to be true, beyond all controversy, in regard to Massachusetts. By its industrial condition, and its business operations, it is exposed, far beyond any other State in the Union, to the fatal extremes of overgrown wealth and desperate poverty. Its population is far more dense than that of any other state. . . . [F]rom the last of June, 1848, to the first of August, 1848, the amount of money invested by the citizens of Massachusetts "in manufacturing cities, railroads, and other improvements," is "fifty-seven millions of dollars, of which more than fifty has been paid in and expended." The dividends to be received by citizens of Massachusetts from June, 1848, to April, 1849, are estimated by the same writer at ten millions, and the annual increase of capital a "little short of twenty-two millions." If this be so, are we not in danger of neutralizing and domesticating among ourselves those hideous evils which are always engendered between capital and labor, when all the capital is in the hands of one class, and all the labor is thrown upon another?

Now, surely nothing but universal education can counterwork this tendency to the domination of capital and the servility of labor. If one class possesses all the wealth and the education, while the residue of society is ignorant and poor, it matters not by what name the relation between them may be called: the latter, in fact and in truth, will be the servile dependants and subjects of the former. But, if education be equably diffused, it will draw property after it by the strongest of all attractions; for such a thing never did happen, and never can happen, as that an intelligent and practical body of men should be permanently poor. Property and labor in different classes are essentially antagonistic; but property and labor in the same class are essentially fraternal.

The people of Massachusetts have, in some degree, appreciated the truth, that the unexampled prosperity of the State—its comfort, its competence, its general intelligence and virtue—is attributable to the education, more or less perfect, which all its people have received: but are they sensible of a fact equally important; namely, that it is to this same education that two-thirds of the people are indebted for not being to-day the vassals of as severe a tyranny, in the form of capital, as the lower classes of Europe are bound to in the form of brute force?

Education, then, beyond all other devices of human origin, is the great equalizer of the conditions of men,—the balance-wheel of the social machinery. I do not here mean that it so elevates the moral nature as to make men disdain and abhor the oppression of their fellow-men. This idea pertains to another of its attributes. But I mean that it gives each man the independence and the means by which he can resist the selfishness of other men. It does better than to disarm the poor of their hostility towards the rich: it prevents being poor. . . . [A] fellow-feeling for one's class or caste is the common instinct of hearts not wholly sunk in selfish regards for person or for family. The spread of education, by enlarging the cultivated class or caste, will open a wider area over which the social feelings will expand; and, if this education should be universal and complete, it would do more than all things else to obliterate distinctions in society.

The main idea set forth in the creeds of some political reformers, or revolutionizers, is, that some people are poor *because* others are rich. This idea supposes a fixed amount of property in the community, which by fraud or force, or arbitrary law, is unequally divided among men; and the problem presented for solution is, how to transfer a portion of this property from those who are supposed to have too much to those who feel and know that they have too little. At this point, both their theory and their expectation of reform stop. But the beneficent power of education would not be exhausted, even though it should peaceably abolish all the miseries that spring from the co-existence, side by side, of enormous wealth and squalid want. It has a higher function. Beyond the power of diffusing old wealth, it has the prerogative of creating new. It is a thousand times more lucrative than fraud, and adds a thousand-fold more to a nation's resources than the most successful conquests. Knaves and robbers can obtain only what was before possessed by others. But education creates or develops new treasures,—treasures not before possessed or dreamed of by any one.

•   •   •

Now, these powers of Nature, by being enlisted in the service of man ADD to the wealth of the world,—unlike robbery or slavery or agrarianism, which aim only at the appropriation, by one man or one class, of the wealth belonging to another man or class. One man, with a Foudrinier, will make more paper in a twelvemonth than all Egypt could have made in a hundred years during the reign of the Ptolemies. One man, with a power-press, will print books faster than a million of scribes could copy them before the invention of printing. One man, with an iron-foundry, will make more utensils or machinery than Tubal-Cain could have made had he worked diligently till this time. And so in all the departments of mechanical labor, in the whole circle of useful arts. These powers of Nature are able to give to all the inhabitants of the earth, not merely shelter, covering, and food, but all the means of refinement, embellishment, and mental improvement. In the most strict and literal sense, they are bounties which God gives for proficiency in knowledge. . . .

. . . [T]he question has often forced itself upon reflecting minds, why there was this preposterousness, this inversion of what would appear to be the natural order of progress. Why was it, for instance, that men should have learned the courses of the stars, and the revolutions of the planets, before they found out how to make a good wagon-wheel? Why was it that they built the Parthenon and the Colosseum before they knew how to construct a comfortable, healthful dwelling-house? Why did they construct the Roman aqueducts before they constructed a sawmill? Or why did they achieve the noblest models in eloquence, in poetry, and in the drama, before they invented movable types? I think we have now arrived at a point where we can unriddle this enigma. *The labor of the world has been performed by ignorant men,* by classes doomed to ignorance from sire to son, by the bondmen and bondwomen of the Jews, by the helots of Sparta, by the captives who passed under the Roman yoke, and by the villeins and serfs and slaves of more modern times. The masters—the aristocratic or patrician orders—not only disdained labor for themselves and their children, which was one fatal mistake, but they supposed that knowledge was of no use to a laborer, which was a mistake still more fatal. Hence, ignorance, for almost six thousand years, has gone on plying its animal muscles, and dropping its bloody sweat, and never discovered any way, nor dreamed that there was any way, by which it might accomplish many times more work with many times less labor. And yet nothing is more true than that an ignorant man will toil all his life long, moving to and fro within an inch of some great discovery, and will never see it. All the elements of a great discovery may fall into his hands, or be thrust into his face; but his eyes will be too blind to behold it. If he is a slave, what motive has he to behold it? Its greater profitableness will not redound to his benefit; for another stands ready to seize all the gain. Its abridgment of labor will not conduce to his ease; for other toils await him. . . .

If a savage will learn how to swim, he can fasten a dozen pounds' weight to his back, and transport it across a narrow river or other body of water of moderate width. If he will invent an axe, or other instrument, by which to cut down a tree, he can use the tree for a float, and one of its limbs for a paddle, and can thus transport many times the former weight many times the former distance. Hollowing out this log, he will increase what may be called its tonnage, or rather its *poundage;* and, by sharpening its ends, it will cleave the water both more easily and more swiftly. Fastening several trees together, he makes a raft, and thus increases the buoyant power of his embryo water-craft. Turning up the ends of small poles, or using knees of timber instead of straight pieces, and grooving them together, or filling up the interstices between them in some other way, so as to make them water-tight, he brings his rude raft literally into *ship-shape.* Improving upon hull below and rigging above, he makes a proud merchantman, to be wafted by the winds from continent to continent. But even this does not content the adventurous naval architect. He frames iron arms for his ship; and, for oars, affixes iron wheels, capable of swift revolution, and stronger than the strong sea. Into iron-walled cavities in her bosom he puts iron organs of massive structure and strength, and of cohesion insoluble by fire. Within these he kindles a small volcano; and then, like a sentient and rational existence, this wonderful creation of his hands cleaves oceans, breasts tides, defies tempests, and bears its living and jubilant freight around the globe. Now, take away intelligence from the ship-builder, and the steamship—that miracle of human art—falls back into a floating log; the log itself is lost; and the savage swimmer, bearing his dozen pounds on his back, alone remains.

And so it is, not in one department only, but in the whole circle of human labors. The annihilation of the sun would no more certainly be followed by darkness than the extinction of human intelligence would plunge the race at once into the weakness and helplessness of barbarism. To have created such beings as we are, and to have placed them in this world without the light of the sun, would be no more cruel than for a government to suffer its laboring classes to grow up without knowledge.

In this fact, then, we find a solution of the problem that so long embarrassed inquirers. The reason why the mechanical and useful arts,—those arts which have done so much to civilize mankind, and which have given comforts and luxuries to the common laborer of the present day, such as kings and queens could not command three centuries ago,—the reason why these arts made no progress, and until recently, indeed, can hardly be said to have had any thing more than a beginning, is, that the labor of the world was performed by ignorant men. As soon as some degree of intelligence dawned upon the workman, then a corresponding degree of improvement in his work followed. . . .

For the creation of wealth, then,—for the existence of a wealthy people and a wealthy nation,—intelligence is the grand condition. The number of improvers will increase as the intellectual constituency, if I may so call it, increases. In former times, and in most parts of the world even at the present day, not one man in a million has ever had such a development of mind as made it possible for him to become a contributor to art or science. Let this development precede, and contributions, numberless, and of inestimable value, will be sure to follow. That political economy, therefore, which busies itself about capital and labor, supply and demand, interest and rents, favorable balances of trade, but leaves out of account the element of a widespread mental development, is nought but stupendous folly. The greatest of all the arts in political economy is to change a consumer into a producer; and the next greatest is to increase the producer's producing power,—an end to be directly attained by increasing his intelligence. For mere delving, an ignorant man is but little better than a swine, whom he so much resembles in his appetites, and surpasses in his powers of mischief.

"WORDS, WORDS, WORDS" (1839)

. . . In Scotland, the Spelling Book is called the *Spell Book,* and we ought to adopt that appellation here, for, as it is often used with us, it does cast a spell over the faculties of children, which, generally, they do not break for years;—and oftentimes, we believe, never. If any two things on earth should be put together and kept together, one would suppose that it should be the idea of a thing and the name of that thing.

The spelling book, however, is a most artful and elaborate contrivance, by which words are separated from their meanings, so that the words can be transferred into the mind of the pupil, without permitting any glimmer of the meaning to accompany them. A spelling book is a collection of signs without the things signified;—of words without sense;—a dictionary without definitions. It is a place where words are shut up and impounded so that their significations cannot get at them. The very notion of language is that it is a vehicle of thought and feeling, from mind to mind. Without the thought and feeling the vehicle goes empty. Pretending to carry freight, it carries no freight. To become familiar with things and their properties, without any knowledge of the names by which they are called, would be the part of beings, who had intelligence, but no faculty of speech; but to learn names, without the things or properties signified is surely the part of beings, who have speech, but no intelligence. . . .

In the school of Pestalozzi, a series of engravings was prepared, representing a variety of objects, whose names, structure and use, the children were to learn. One day the master having presented to his class the engraving of a ladder, a lively little boy exclaimed, "But there is a real ladder in the court-yard; why not talk about that rather than the picture?" "The engraving is here," said the master, "and it is more convenient to talk about what is before your eyes, than to go into the yard to talk about the other." The boy's remark, thus eluded, was for that time disregarded. Soon after, the engraving of a window formed the subject of examination. "But why," exclaimed the same little objector, "why talk of this picture of a window, when there is a real window in the room, and there is no need to go into the court-yard for it?" In the evening both circumstances were mentioned to Pestalozzi. "The boy is right," said he, "the reality is better than the counterfeit;—put away the engravings and let the class be instructed in real objects." This was the origin of a better mode of instruction, suggested by the wants and the pleasures of an active mind. . . .

If one wished to prepare a boy to work upon a farm, or to be a salesman in a store, would he shut him up in a closet, giving him a list of names of all the farming utensils and seeds and products; or a list of all the commodities in a trader's invoice, and when he had learned these, send him to his place of destination as one acquainted with the objects, the materials, with which he is to be occupied? . . .   .

Again, the things, the relations, of art, of science, of business, are to the mind of a child, what the nutriment of food is to his body; and the mind will be enervated, if fed on the names of things, as much as the body would be emaciated, if fed upon the names of food. Yet, formerly, it was the almost universal practice,—and we fear it is now nearly so,—to keep children two or three years in the spelling book, where the mind's eye is averted from the objects, qualities, and relations of existing things, and fastened upon a few marks, of themselves wholly uninteresting.

Who has ever looked at a child, above the age of nine months, without witnessing his eager curiosity to gaze at and handle the objects within his reach. He loves to play with a bright shovel and tongs, to pull the dishes from the table by the corner of the cloth, to disperse the contents of a work-basket, because these are something. There is substance, color, motion, in them. What an imagination it is, which turns a stick into a horse; and makes a little girl dress and undress a doll to prepare it for going to visit or to bed. But what is there in the alphabet or in monosyllables, to stimulate this curiosity or to gratify it? The senseless combinations of letters into *ba, be, bi, bo, bu,* deaden this curiosity. And after it has been pretty effectually extinguished, so that, by the further aid of the spelling book, the child can perform the feat of speaking without thinking,—as circus horses are taught to trot without advancing,—then let him be carried into reading lessons, where there are but few words he has ever seen or heard before, and where the subject is wholly beyond the reach of his previous attainments, and if by this process, the very faculty of thought be not subjugated, it must be because the child is incorrigibly strong-minded. These are the most efficient means of stultification. . . .

from THE DUTY OF AMERICAN WOMEN TO THEIR COUNTRY

Catharine Beecher

Do you say that such cruelty and bloodthirsty rage can never appear among us; that our countrymen can never be so deluded by falsehood and blinded by passion? . . .

Look, again, at the Southwest, and see gamblers swinging uncondemned from a gallows, and among them a harmless man, whom the fury of the mob hung up without time for judge or jury to detect his innocence.

See, on the banks of the Mississippi, fires blazing, and American citizens *roasted alive* by their fellow-citizens! See, even in New-England, the boasted land of law and steady habits, a raging mob besets a house filled with women and young children. They set fire to it, and the helpless inmates are driven forth by the flames to the sole protection of darkness and the pitiless ruffians. See, in Cincinnati, the poor blacks driven from their homes, insulted, beaten, pillaged, seeking refuge in prisons and private houses, and for days kept in constant terror and peril.

See, in Philadelphia, one class of citizens arrayed in arms against another, both excited to the highest pitch of rage, both thirsting for each other's blood, while the civil authority can prevent universal pillage, misrule, and murder, only by volleys that shoot down neighbours, brothers, and friends.

See, too, how the rage of political strife has threatened the whole nation with a civil war. South Carolina declares that she will not submit to certain laws, which she claims are unconstitutional. Her own citizens are divided into fierce parties, so exasperated that each is preparing to shoot down the other. . . .

And all these materials of combustion are now slumbering in our bosom, pent up for a while, but ready to burst forth, like imprisoned lava, and deluge the land. How easy it would be to bring the nation into fierce contest on the subject of slavery, that internal cancer which inflames the whole body politic! How easy to array native citizens against foreign immigrants, who at once oppose the prejudices and diminish the wages of those around them! . . . How easy to make one class of humbler means, believe that bank, or monopoly, is destroying the fruit of their toil, to increase the overgrown wealth of a class above them!

• • •

What, then, has saved our country from those wide-sweeping horrors that desolated France? Why is it that, in the excitements of embargoes, and banks, and slavery, and abolition, and foreign immigration, the besom of destruction has not swept over the land? It is because there has been such a large body of *educated* citizens, who have had intelligence enough to understand how to administer the affairs of state, and a proper sense of the necessity of sustaining law and order; who have had moral principle enough to subdue their own passions, and to use their influence to control the excited minds of others. Change our large body of moral, intelligent, and religious people to the ignorant, impulsive, excitable population of France, and in one month the horrors of the Reign of Terror would be before our eyes. Nothing can preserve this nation from such scenes but perpetuating this preponderance of intelligence and virtue. This is our only safeguard.

• • •

My countrywomen, what is before us? What awful forebodings arise! Intelligence and virtue our only safeguards, and yet all this mass of ignorance among us, and hundreds of thousands of ignorant foreigners being yearly added to augment our danger! . . .

The grand reason is, the *selfish apathy* of the educated classes, and the *stupid apathy* of those who are too ignorant to appreciate an education for their children. In those states where no school system is established by law, the intelligent and wealthy content themselves with securing a good education for their own children, and care nothing for the rest. When any project, therefore, is presented for obtaining a good school system, the rich and intelligent do not wish to be taxed for the children of others, and the rest do not care whether their children are educated or not, or else are too poor to pay the expense.

In those states where a school system is established, parents of intelligence and moral worth, seeing the neglected state of the common school, withdraw their children to private schools. And feeling no interest in schools which they do not patronise, they pass them with utter neglect. And thus, neither rich nor poor care enough to be willing to be taxed for their elevation and improvement.

•   •   •

Look, then, at the work to be done. Two millions of destitute children to be supplied with schools! To meet this demand, *sixty thousand* teachers and *fifty thousand* schoolhouses are required. . . . Where are we to raise such an army of teachers? Not from the sex which finds it so much more honourable, easy, and lucrative to enter the many roads to wealth and honour open in this land. But a few will turn from these, to the humble, unhonoured toils of the schoolroom and its penurious reward.

It is *woman* who is to come in at this emergency, and meet the demand; woman, whom experience and testimony has shown to be the best, as well as the cheapest guardian and teacher of childhood, in the school as well as the nursery. Already, in those parts of our country where education is most prosperous, the larger part of the teachers of common schools are women. In Massachusetts, three out of five of all the teachers are women. In the State of New-York and in Philadelphia similar results are seen.

Women, then, are to be educated for teachers, and sent to the destitute children of this nation by hundreds and by thousands. This is the way in which *a profession* is to be created for woman—a profession as honourable and as lucrative for her as the legal, medical, and theological are for men. This is the way in which thousands of intelligent and respectable women, who toil for a pittance scarcely sufficient to sustain life, are to be relieved and elevated. This is the way, and *the only way*, in which our nation can be saved from impending perils. Though we are now in such a condition that many have given over our case in despair, as too far gone for remedy—though the peril is immense, and the work to be done enormous, yet *it is in the power of American women to save their country*. There is benevolence enough, there are means enough at their command. All that is needed is a knowledge of the danger, and a faithful use of the means within their reach.

And who else, in such an emergency as this, can so appropriately be invoked to aid? It is woman who is the natural and appropriate guardian of childhood. It is woman who has those tender sympathies which can most readily feel for the wants and sufferings of the young. It is woman, who is especially interested in all efforts which tend to elevate and dignify her own sex. It is woman, too, who has that conscientiousness and religious devotion, which, in any worthy cause, are the surest pledges of success.

And it is the pride and honour of our country, that woman holds a commanding influence in the domestic and social circle, which is accorded to the sex in no other nation, and such as will make her wishes and efforts, if united for a benevolent and patriotic object, almost omnipotent.

• • •

. . . [I]f the tastes and principles are not formed aright, the probability is, that blank ignorance would be better than the poisonous food, which a mind, thus sent forth to seek its own supplies, would inevitably select. But in those sections of our country that are most deficient in schools, there are neither books, nor the desire, or the taste for reading them. And among those who are taught to read, thousands go from the portals of knowledge to daily toil, or to vicious indulgences, leaving the mind as empty and stupid as if no such ability were gained. And how many there are, who have sharpened their faculties only as edged tools for greater mischief! No; the American people are to be educated *for their high duties.* The children who, ere long, are to decide whether we shall have tariff or no tariff, bank or no bank, slavery or no slavery, naturalization laws or no such laws, must be trained so that they cannot be duped and excited by demagogues, and thus led on to the ruin that overwhelmed the people of France. They must be trained to read, and think, and decide *intelligently* on all matters where they are to act as legislators, judges, jury, and executive. The children who, ere long, are to be thrown into the heats and passion of political strife and sectional jealousy, must be trained to rule their passions, and to control themselves by reason, religion, and law. The young daughters of this nation, too, must be trained to become the educators of all the future statesmen, legislators, judges, juries, and magistrates of this land.

• • •

While it is universally conceded by all intelligent persons, that there is no nation on earth, whose prosperity, and even existence, so much depends on the *moral training* of the mass of the people, there is no nation, *where schools are established by law*, in which so little of it is done. It is mournful to reflect, that by far the larger part of our schools banish religious and moral training altogether, and confine their efforts entirely to the training of *the intellect*, and a great part of them merely to that of *the memory.* . . .

Many persons justify the neglect of moral training in our schools, by claiming that religion must be banished from schools, on account of the great diversity of sects, who cannot agree in this matter. Such are little aware on how many important points all sects are agreed. . . .

In the first place, all children in schools, can be taught, that *the Bible* contains the rules of duty given by God, which all men are bound to obey. This is what all denominations allow, and if there is any dispute about *which translation* is the proper one, each child can be allowed to use the Bible his parents think to be right.

When this is duly taught, the children can be required, for several successive mornings, each to repeat a passage from the Bible, which teaches the *character* of God.

When this subject is exhausted, then the teacher can compose a form of prayer consisting exclusively of passages from the Bible, to be used as the first act of school duty.

• • •

A PLAN PROPOSED

It is the object of what follows, to enable every woman, who wishes to do something for the cause of education and her country, *to act immediately*, before the interest awakened is absorbed by other pursuits. The thing to be aimed at is, the *employment of female talent and benevolence in educating ignorant and neglected American children.*

In order to give an idea of what *needs* to be done, and of what *can* be done, some facts will be stated of which the writer of this volume has personal knowledge. There are, in all parts of this country, women of education and benevolence, and some of them possessing wealth, who are longing for something to do, which is more worthy of their cultivated energies than the ordinary pursuits of women of leisure. There is a still greater multitude of women of good sense and benevolence, who, if educated, would make admirable teachers, but who now have no resource but the needle and the manufactory.

• • •

In the Catholic Church, a wisdom is shown on this subject, which Protestants as yet have not exhibited. In that Church, if a lady of wealth and family is led to devote herself to benevolent enterprises, a post is immediately found for her as Lady Abbess, or Lady Patroness, or Lady Superior, where she secures the power, consideration, and rank, which even ambition might covet. There is now a Catholic institution in one of our principal western cities, known to the writer, which is superintended by a lady of rank and family from Belgium, and which is only a branch of a still larger institution in Belgium, over which another titled lady presides. And there are several other ladies of family and fortune from Europe, who are spending their time and wealth in gathering American children into the Catholic Church. Meantime, all women of humbler station have places provided, as *Nuns* or *Sisters of Charity*, where they can spend their benevolent energies in honoured activity. . . .

But among Protestants there is no system of organization instituted, thus to secure and employ the benevolent energies of the female sex in the cause of education. . . . [W]omen in humbler circumstances find almost as insurmountable obstacles; they know of no place where they can go, it is the business of no one to aid them, they know of no one to whom to apply for assistance, and thus it is that hundreds and hundreds of women, abundantly competent to act as missionary teachers, are pining in secret over wasted energies, which they are longing to spend in the most appropriate duty of women, the training of young minds for usefulness and for Heaven. . . .

By the census, it appears that the excess of female population in New-England over that of the other sex is more than 14,000. From extensive inquiries and consultation, the writer believes that *one fourth* of these women would gladly engage as teachers; that a large part are already qualified, and that the others could be fitted for these duties at an *average* expense of two hundred dollars each. . . .

There is no just foundation for the remark not unfrequently made, that the Catholic Church contains more *self-denying* benevolence than other communions, while *sisters of charity* and *nuns* are pointed out as illustrations. There are hundreds and thousands of women in this Protestant land, who, without the mistaken principles, possess all the self-denying benevolence which, in Catholic communities, leads to cloistered vows.

CHAPTER 8

Democratic Faiths

INTRODUCTION

WILLIAM ELLERY CHANNING, 1780–1842
Importance of Religion to Society (1832) and
from On Unitarian Christianity (1817)

CHARLES GRANDISON FINNEY, 1792–1875
from Sinners Bound to Change Their Own Hearts (1836)
and *from* Lectures on Revivals (1845)

ORESTES AUGUSTUS BROWNSON, 1803–1876
from Catholicity Necessary to Sustain Popular Liberty (1845)

SHAKER AND MORMON SONGS (1804–1865)

Many Americans saw religion, like public education, as a needed moral anchor in a free society, where self-restraint for most would replace legal controls. Religion in the United States was strengthened by being separated from the state and its support; church membership and attendance steadily climbed from its low point in the late eighteenth century. Churches' dependence on private enthusiasm and funding assured great efforts to meet people's needs and interests so that both theology and practice were brought into close accord with democratic sensibilities.

William Ellery Channing founded the Unitarian faith—a union of Christianity and enlightened rationalism—that flourished in New England from 1815 to 1825. Former lawyer Charles Grandison Finney led the second Great Awakening that swept the nation after 1825. Finney put his religious ideas in democratic/legal political metaphors, while his theology emphasized human choice and God as law-guided ruler rather than the Puritans' absolute sovereign. Finney's "techniques" for revivals suggested how churches pragmatically competed for popular support.

Orestes Brownson became the nation's leading spokesman for Roman Catholicism after a conversion that climaxed a long intellectual journey from evangelicalism, to Jacksonian politics, to a brief proto-Marxian radicalism. He (like Channing) argued that religion was a necessary rudder for democratic freedom, but insisted that only Catholicism was solid enough for the job.

Two of the many "new" faiths of the era, both based on additional revelations to Christianity, were popularly known as the Shakers and the Mormons. The Shakers lived in celibate and egalitarian communities with great economic and aesthetic success, where they expressed their cooperative spirituality in song and ecstatic dance. Mormons, with their New World religious history and revelation, grew rapidly despite deadly riots that drove them from Missouri and then Illinois, where founder Joseph Smith was mob-murdered. Brigham Young led the Mormon exodus to "Deseret" or Utah in 1845, in which isolated setting the faith flourished.

CONSIDERATIONS

- What ideas are shared in these of faiths? How do they differ from the Puritan beliefs? How would you explain the change? What are the major disagreements?

- Is religion essential or important to American society? Is any form of religion more helpful than others? Does the American system of no direct support or sanction of any faith help or hurt religion?

- How do the new "sects" of the age—Shakers and Mormons—differ from the other faiths? Why did they and similar groups flower in these years?

- Should government support religion through the tax breaks given churches or through subsidies to their schools and social programs? Do or should churches influence social policy?

- Are the nation's varied religions a source of national division or strength? Is the U.S. a religious nation? Is it a Christian one?

Importance of Religion to Society

William Ellery Channing

Few men suspect, perhaps no man comprehends, the extent of the support given by religion to the virtues of ordinary life. No man, perhaps, is aware how much our moral and social sentiments are fed from this fountain; how powerless conscience would become without the belief of a God; how palsied would be human benevolence, were there not the sense of a higher benevolence to quicken and sustain it; how suddenly the whole social fabric would quake, and with what a fearful crash it would sink into hopeless ruins, were the ideas of a Supreme Being, of accountableness, and of a future life, to be utterly erased from every mind. Once let men thoroughly believe that they are the work and sport of chance; that no superior intelligence concerns itself with human affairs; that all their improvements perish for ever at death; that the weak have no guardian and the injured no avenger; that there is no recompense for sacrifices to uprightness and the public good; that an oath is unheard in heaven; that secret crimes have no witness but the perpetrator; that human existence has no purpose, and human virtue no unfailing friend; that this brief life is every thing to us, and death is total, everlasting extinction;—once let men thoroughly abandon religion, and who can conceive or describe the extent of the desolation which would follow? We hope, perhaps, that human laws and natural sympathy would hold society together. As reasonably might we believe that, were the sun quenched in the heavens, our torches could illuminate and our fires quicken and fertilize the earth. What is there in human nature to awaken respect and tenderness, if man is the unprotected insect of a day? and what is he more, if atheism be true? Erase all thought and fear of God from a community, and selfishness and sensuality would absorb the whole man. Appetite knowing no restraint, and poverty and suffering having no solace or hope, would trample in scorn on the restraints of human laws. Virtue, duty, principle, would be mocked and spurned as unmeaning sounds. A sordid self-interest would supplant every other feeling, and man would become in fact, what the theory of atheism declares him to be, a companion for brutes.

It particularly deserves attention in this discussion, that the Christian religion is singularly important to free communities. In truth, we may doubt whether civil freedom can subsist without it. This at least we know, that equal rights and an impartial administration of justice have never been enjoyed where this religion has not been understood. It favors free institutions, first, because its spirit is the very spirit of liberty; that is, a spirit of respect for the interests and rights of others. Christianity recognizes the essential equality of mankind; beats down with its whole might those aspiring and rapacious principles of our nature which have subjected the many to the few; and, by its refining influence, as well as by direct precept, turns to God, and to him only, that supreme homage which has been so impiously lavished on crowned and titled fellow-creatures. Thus its whole tendency is free. It lays deeply the only foundations of liberty, which are the principles of benevolence, justice, and respect for human nature. The spirit of liberty is not merely, as multitudes imagine, a jealousy of our own particular rights, an unwillingness to be oppressed ourselves, but a respect for the rights of others, and an unwillingness that any man, whether high or low, should be wronged and trampled under foot. Now this is the spirit of Christianity; and liberty has no security, any farther than this uprightness and benevolence of sentiment actuates a community.

In another method religion befriends liberty. It diminishes the necessity of public restraints, and supersedes in a great degree the use of force in administering the laws; and this it does by making men a law to themselves, and by repressing the disposition to disturb and injure society. Take away the purifying and restraining influence of religion, and selfishness, rapacity, and injustice will break out in new excesses. . . . Diminish principle, and you increase the need of force in a community. In this country government needs not the array of power which you meet in other nations. . . . This is the perfection of freedom; and to what do we owe this condition? I answer, to the power of those laws which religion writes on our hearts, which unite and concentrate public opinion against injustice and oppression, which spread a spirit of equity and good-will through the community. Thus religion is the soul of freedom, and no nation under heaven has such an interest in it as ourselves.

from UNITARIAN CHRISTIANITY

William Ellery Channing

We regard the Scriptures as the records of God's successive revelations to mankind, and particularly of the last and most perfect revelation of his will by Jesus Christ. Whatever doctrines seem to us to be clearly taught in the Scriptures, we receive without reserve or exception. We do not, however, attach equal importance to all the books in this collection. Our religion, we believe, lies chiefly in the New Testament. The dispensation of Moses compared with that of Jesus, we consider as adapted to the childhood of the human race, a preparation for a nobler system, and chiefly useful now as serving to confirm and illustrate the Christian Scriptures. Jesus Christ is the only Master of Christians, and whatever he taught, either during his personal ministry or by his inspired Apostles, we regard as of divine authority, and profess to make the rule of our lives. . . .

Our leading principle in interpreting Scripture is this, that the Bible is a book written for men, in the language of men, and that its meaning is to be sought in the same manner as that of other books. We believe that God, when He speaks to the human race, conforms, if we may so say, to the established rules of speaking and writing. How else would the Scriptures avail us more than if communicated in an unknown tongue?

Now all books and all conversation require in the reader or hearer the constant exercise of reason; or their true import is only to be obtained by continual comparison and inference. Human language, you well know, admits various interpretations; and every word and every sentence must be modified and explained according to the subject which is discussed, according to the purposes, feelings, circumstances, and principles of the writer, and according to the genius and idioms of the language which he uses. These are acknowledged principles in the interpretation of human writings; and a man whose words we should explain without reference to these principles would reproach us justly with a criminal want of candour, and an intention of obscuring or distorting his meaning. . . .

We profess not to know a book which demands a more frequent exercise of reason than the Bible. In addition to the remarks now made on its infinite connections, we may observe, that its style nowhere affects the precision of science or the accuracy of definition. Its language is singularly glowing, bold, and figurative, demanding more frequent departures from the literal sense than that of our own age and country, and consequently demanding more continual exercise of judgment. We find, too, that the different portions of this book, instead of being confined to general truths, refer perpetually to the times when they were written, to states of society, to modes of thinking, to controversies in the church, to feelings and usages which have passed away, and without the knowledge of which we are constantly in danger of extending to all times and places what was of temporary and local application.—We find, too, that some of these books are strongly marked by the genius and character of their respective writers, that the Holy Spirit did not so guide the Apostles as to suspend the peculiarities of their minds, and that a knowledge of their feelings, and of the influences under which they were placed, is one of the preparations for understanding their writings. With these views of the Bible, we feel it our bounden duty to exercise our reason upon it perpetually, to compare, to infer, to look beyond the letter to the spirit, to seek in the nature of the subject and the aim of the writer his true meaning; and, in general, to make use of what is known for explaining what is difficult, and for discovering new truths.

Need I descend to particulars to prove that the Scriptures demand the exercise of reason? Take, for example, the style in which they generally speak of God, and observe how habitually they apply to Him human passions and organs. Recollect the declarations of Christ, that he came not to send peace, but a sword; that unless we eat his flesh and drink his blood we have no life in us; that we must hate father and mother, and pluck out the right eye; and a vest number of passages equally bold and unlimited. Recollect the unqualified manner in which it is said of Christians that they possess all things, know all things, and can do all things. Recollect the verbal contradiction between Paul and James, and the apparent clashing of some parts of Paul's writings with the general doctrines and end of Christianity. I might extend the enumeration indefinitely; and who does not see that we must limit all these passages by the known attributes of God, of Jesus Christ, and of human nature, and by the circumstances under which they were written, so as to give the language a quite different import from what it would require had it been applied to different beings, or used in different connections?

Enough has been said to show in what sense we make use of reason in interpreting Scripture. From a variety of possible interpretations we select that which accords with the nature of the subject and the state of the writer, with the connection of the passage, with the general strain of Scripture, with the known character and will of God, and with the obvious and acknowledged laws of nature. In other words, we believe that God never contradicts in one part of Scripture what He teaches in another; and never contradicts in revelation what He teaches in his works and providence. And we therefore distrust every interpretation which, after deliberate attention, seems repugnant to any established truth. We reason about the Bible precisely as civilians do about the constitution under which we live; who, you know, are accustomed to limit one provision of that venerable instrument by others, and to fix the precise import of its parts by inquiring into its general spirit, into the intentions of its authors, and into the prevalent feelings, impressions, and circumstances of the time when it was framed. Without these principles of interpretation, we frankly acknowledge that we cannot defend the divine authority of the Scriptures. Deny us this latitude, and we must abandon this book to its enemies. . . .

We grant that the passions continually, and sometimes fatally, disturb the rational faculty in its inquiries into revelation. The ambitious contrive to find doctrines in the Bible which favour their love of dominion. The timid and dejected discover there a gloomy system, and the mystical and fanatical a visionary theology. The vicious can find examples or assertions on which to build the hope of a late repentance, or of acceptance on easy terms. The falsely refined contrive to light on doctrines which have not been soiled by vulgar handling. But the passions do not distract the reason in religious any more than in other inquiries which excite strong and general interest; and this faculty, of consequence, is not to be renounced in religion, unless we are prepared to discard it universally. The true inference from the almost endless errors which have darkened theology is, not that we are to neglect and disparage our powers, but to exert them more patiently, circumspectly, uprightly; the worst errors, after all, having sprung up in that church which proscribes reason, and demands from its members implicit faith. The most pernicious doctrines have been the growth of the darkest times, when the general credulity encouraged bad men and enthusiasts to broach their dreams and inventions, and to stifle the faint remonstrances of reason by the menaces of everlasting perdition. Say what we may, God has given us a rational nature, and will call us to account for it. We may let it sleep, but we do so at our peril. Revelation is addressed to us as rational beings. . . .

To the views now given an objection is commonly urged from the character of God. We are told that God being infinitely wiser than men, his discoveries will surpass human reason. In a revelation from such a teacher we ought to expect propositions which we cannot reconcile with one another, and which may seem to contradict established truths; and it becomes us not to question or explain them away, but to believe, and adore, and to submit our weak and carnal reason to the Divine Word. To this objection we have two short answers. We say, first, that it is impossible that a teacher of infinite wisdom should expose those whom he would teach to infinite error. But if once we admit that propositions which in their literal sense appear plainly repugnant to one another, or to any known truth, are still to be literally understood and received, what possible limit can we set to the belief of contradictions? . . .

[I]f God be infinitely wise, He cannot sport with the understandings of his creatures. A wise teacher discovers his wisdom in adapting himself to the capacities of his pupils, not in perplexing them with what is unintelligible, not in distressing them with apparent contradictions, not in filling them with a sceptical distrust of their own powers. An infinitely wise teacher, who knows the precise extent of our minds and the best method of enlightening them, will surpass all other instructors in bringing down truth to our apprehension, and in showing its loveliness and harmony. . . . A revelation is a gift of light. It cannot thicken our darkness and multiply our perplexities.

Having thus stated the principles according to which we interpret Scripture, I now proceed to the second great head of this discourse, which is, to state some of the views which we derive from that sacred book, particularly those which distinguish us from other Christians.

(I.) In the first place, we believe in the doctrine of Gods' unity, or that there is one God, and one only. To this truth we give infinite importance, and we feel ourselves bound to take heed lest any man spoil us of it by vain philosophy. The proposition that there is one God seems to us exceedingly plain. We understand by it that there is one being, one mind, one person, one intelligent agent, and one only, to whom underived and infinite perfection and dominion belong. . . .

We find the Father continually distinguished from Jesus by this title. 'God sent his Son.' 'God anointed Jesus.' Now, how singular and inexplicable is this phraseology, which fills the New Testament, if this title belong equally to Jesus, and if a principal object of this book is to reveal him as God, as partaking equally with the Father in supreme divinity! We challenge our opponents to adduce one passage in the New Testament where the word God means three persons, where it is not limited to one person, and where, unless turned from its usual sense by the connection, it does not mean the Father. Can stronger proof be given, that the doctrine of three persons in the Godhead is not a fundamental doctrine of Christianity? . . .

We believe in *the moral perfection of God*. We consider no part of theology so important as that which treats of God's moral character; and we value our views of Christianity chiefly as they assert his amiable and venerable attributes.

It may be said that in regard to this subject all Christians agree, that all ascribe to the Supreme Being infinite justice, goodness, and holiness. We reply, that it is very possible to speak of God magnificently, and to think of Him meanly; to apply to his person high-sounding epithets, and to his government principles which make Him odious. The Heathens called Jupiter the greatest and the best; but his history was black with cruelty and lust. We cannot judge of men's real ideas of God by their general language, for in all ages they have hoped to soothe the Deity by adulation. We must inquire into their particular views of his purposes, of the principles of his administration, and of his disposition towards his creatures.

We conceive that Christians have generally leaned towards a very injurious view of the Supreme Being. They have too often felt as if he were raised, by his greatness and sovereignty, above the principles of morality, above those eternal laws of equity and rectitude to which all other beings are subjected. We believe that in no being is the sense of right so strong, so omnipotent, as in God. We believe that his almighty power is entirely submitted to his perceptions of rectitude; and this is the ground of our piety. It is not because He is our Creator merely, but because He created us for good and holy purposes; it is not because his will is irresistible, but because his will is the perfection of virtue, that we pay him allegiance. We cannot bow before a being, however great and powerful, who governs tyrannically. We respect nothing but excellence, whether on earth or in heaven. We venerate not the loftiness of God's throne, but the equity and goodness in which it is established.

We believe that God is infinitely good, kind, benevolent, in the proper sense of these words; good in disposition as well as in act; good not to a few, but to all; good to every individual, as well as to the general system.

We believe, too, that God is just: but we never forget that this justice is the justice of a good being, dwelling in the same mind, and acting in harmony, with perfect benevolence. By this attribute we understand God's infinite regard to virtue or moral worth expressed in a moral government; that is, in giving excellent and equitable laws, and in conferring such rewards, and inflicting such punishments, as are best fitted to secure their observance. . . .

To give our views of God in one word, we believe in his parental character. We ascribe to him not only the name, but the dispositions and principles of a father. We believe that he has a father's concern for his creatures, a father's desire for their improvement, a father's equity in proportioning his commands to their powers, a father's joy in their progress, a father's readiness to receive the penitent, and a father's justice for the incorrigible. We look upon this world as a place of education, in which He is training men by prosperity and adversity, by aids and obstructions, by conflicts of reason and passion, by motives to duty and temptations to sin, by a various discipline suited to free and moral beings, for union with Himself, and for a sublime and ever-growing virtue in heaven.

Now, we object to the systems of religion which prevail among us, that they are adverse, in a greater or less degree, to these purifying, comforting, and honourable views of God; that they take from us our Father in heaven, and substitute for Him a being whom we cannot love if we would, and whom we ought not to love if we could. . . .

This system also teaches that God selects from this corrupt mass a number to be saved, and plucks them, by a special influence, from the common ruin; that the rest of mankind, though left without that special grace which their conversion requires, are commanded to repent, under penalty of aggravated woe; and that forgiveness is promised to them on terms which their very constitution infallibly disposes them to reject, and in rejecting which they awfully enhance the punishments of hell. These proffers of forgiveness and exhortations of amendment, to beings born under a blighting curse, fill our minds with a horror which we want words to express. . . .

The false and dishonourable views of God which have now been stated, we feel ourselves bound to resist unceasingly. . . .We cling to the Divine perfections. We meet them everywhere in creation, we read them in the Scriptures, we see a lovely image of them in Jesus Christ; and gratitude, love, and veneration call on us to assert them. . . .

We believe that all virtue has its foundation in the moral nature of man, that is, in conscience, or his sense of duty, and in the power of forming his temper and life according to conscience. We believe that these moral faculties are the grounds of responsibility, and the highest distinctions of human nature, and that no act is praiseworthy any further than it springs from their exertion. . . .

Among the virtues we give the first place to the love of God. We believe that this principle is the true end and happiness of our being, that we are made for union with our Creator, that his infinite perfection is the only sufficient object and true resting-place for the insatiable desires and unlimited capacities of the human mind, and that without Him our noblest sentiments, admiration, veneration, hope, and love would wither and decay. We believe, too, that the love of God is not only essential to happiness, but to the strength and perfection of all the virtues; that conscience, without the sanction of God's authority and retributive justice, would be a weak director; that benevolence, unless nourished by communion with his goodness and encouraged by his smile, could not thrive amidst the selfishness and thanklessness of the world; and that self-government, without a sense of the divine inspection, would hardly extend beyond an outward and partial purity. God, as he is essentially goodness, holiness, Justice, and virtue, so He is the life, motive, and sustainer of virtue in the human soul.

But whilst, we earnestly inculcate the love of God, we believe that great care is necessary to distinguish it from counterfeits. . . . If religion be the shipwreck of understanding, we cannot keep too far from it. On this subject we always speak plainly. We cannot sacrifice our reason to the reputation of zeal. We owe it to truth and religion to maintain that fanaticism, partial insanity, sudden impressions, and ungovernable transports are anything rather than piety.

We conceive that the true love of God is a moral sentiment, founded on a clear perception, and consisting in a high esteem and veneration of his moral perfections. Thus, it perfectly coincides, and is in fact the same thing, with the love of virtue, rectitude, and goodness. You will easily judge, then, what we esteem the surest and only decisive signs of piety. We lay no stress on strong excitements. We esteem him, and him only, a pious man, who practically conforms to God's moral perfections and government; who shows his delight in God's benevolence by loving and serving his neighbour; his delight in God's justice by being resolutely upright; his sense of God's purity by regulating his thoughts, imagination, and desires; and whose conversation, business and domestic life are swayed by a regard to God's presence and authority. . . .

We would not, by these remarks, be understood as wishing to exclude from religion warmth, and even transport. We honour and highly value true religious sensibility. We believe that Christianity is intended to act powerfully on our whole nature, on the heart as well as the understanding and the conscience. We conceive of heaven as a state where the love of God will be exalted into an unbounded fervour and joy; and we desire, in our pilgrimage here, to drink into the spirit of that better world. But we think that religious warmth is only to be valued when it springs naturally from an improved character, when it comes unforced, when it is the recompense of obedience, when it is the warmth of a mind which understands God by being like Him, and when, instead of disordering, it exalts the understanding, invigorates conscience, gives a pleasure to common duties, and is seen to exist in connection with cheerfulness, judiciousness, and a reasonable frame of mind. When we observe a fervor called religious in men whose general character expresses little refinement and elevation, and whose piety seems at war with reason, we pay it little respect. We honor religion too much to give its sacred name to a feverish, forced, fluctuating zeal, which has little power over the life. . . .

from SINNERS BOUND TO CHANGE THEIR OWN HEARTS

Charles Grandison Finney

Make you a new heart and a new spirit, for why will ye die?
—Ezek. xviii, 31

The command here addressed to the Israelites is binding upon every impenitent sinner to whom the gospel shall be addressed. He is required to perform the same duty, upon the same penalty. It becomes, therefore, a matter of infinite importance that we should well understand, and fully and immediately obey, the requirement. The questions that would naturally arise to a reflecting mind on reading this text, are the following:

1. What are we to understand by the requirement to make a new heart and a new spirit?

2. Is it reasonable to require the performance of this duty on pain of eternal death?

3. How is this requirement, that we should make to us a new heart and a new spirit, consistent with the often repeated declarations of the Bible, that a new heart is the gift and work of God? . . .

It should here be observed, that although the Bible was not given to teach us mental philosophy, yet we may rest assured that all its declarations are in accordance with the true philosophy of mind. . . .

A change of heart, then, consists in changing the controlling preference of the mind in regard to the *end* of pursuit. The selfish heart is a preference of self-interest to the glory of God and the interests of his kingdom. A new heart consists in a preference of the glory of God and the interests of his kingdom to one's own happiness. In other words, it is a change from selfishness to benevolence, from having a supreme regard to one's own interest to an absorbing and controlling choice of the happiness and glory of God and his kingdom.

It is a change in the choice of a *Supreme Ruler*. The conduct of impenitent sinners demonstrates that they prefer Satan as the ruler of the world, they obey his laws, electioneer for him, and are zealous for his interests, even to martyrdom. They carry their attachment to him and his government so far as to sacrifice both body and soul to promote his interest and establish his dominion. A new heart is the choice of JEHOVAH as the supreme ruler; a deep-seated and abiding preference of his laws, and government, and character, and person, as the supreme Legislator and Governor of the universe.

Thus the world is divided into two great political parties; the difference between them is, that one party choose Satan as the god of this world, yield obedience to his laws, and are devoted to his interest. Selfishness is the law of Satan's empire, and all impenitent sinners yield it a willing obedience. The other party choose Jehovah for their governor, and consecrate themselves, with all their interests, to his service and glory. Nor does this change imply a constitutional alteration of the powers of body or mind, any more than a change of mind in regard to the form or administration of a human government. . . .

Suppose a human sovereign should establish a government, and propose as the great end of pursuit, to produce the greatest amount of happiness possible within his kingdom. He enacts wise and benevolent laws, calculated to promote this object to which he conforms all his own conduct; in the administration of which, he employs all his wisdom and energies, and requires all his subjects to sympathize with him; to aim at the same object; to be governed by the same principles; to aim supremely and constantly at the same end; the promotion of the highest interests of the community. Suppose these laws to be so framed, that universal obedience would necessarily result in universal happiness. Now suppose that one individual, after a season of obedience and devotion to the interest of the government and the glory of his sovereign, should be induced to withdraw his influence and energies from promoting the public good, and set up for himself; suppose him to say, I will no longer be governed by the principles of good will to the community, and find my own happiness in promoting the public interest; but will aim at promoting my own happiness and glory, in my own way, and let the sovereign and the subjects take care for themselves. "Charity begins at home." Now suppose him thus to set up for himself; to propose his own happiness and aggrandizement as the supreme object of his pursuit, and should not hesitate to trample upon the laws and encroach upon the rights, both of his sovereign and the subjects, wherever those laws or rights lay in the way of the accomplishment of his designs. It is easy to see, that he has become a rebel; has changed his *heart*, and consequently his conduct; has set up in interest not only separate from, but opposed to the interest of his rightful sovereign. He has changed his heart from good to bad; from being an obedient subject he has become a rebel; from obeying his sovereign, he has set up an independent sovereignty; from trying to influence all men to obey the government, from seeking supremely the prosperity and the glory of his sovereign, he becomes himself a little sovereign. . . .

Now this is the case with the sinner; God has established a government, and proposed by the exhibition of his own character, to produce the greatest practicable amount of happiness in the universe. He has enacted laws wisely calculated to promote this object, to which he conforms all his own conduct, and to which he requires all his subjects perfectly and undeviatingly to conform theirs. After a season of obedience, Adam changed his heart, and set up for himself. So with every sinner, although he *does not first obey, as Adam did;* yet his wicked heart consists in setting up his own interest in opposition to the interest and government of God. In aiming to promote his own private happiness, in a way that is opposed to the general good. Self-gratification becomes the law to which he conforms his conduct. It is that minding of the flesh, which is enmity against God. A change of heart, therefore, is to prefer a different *end.* To prefer supremely the glory of God and the public good, to the promotion of his own interest; and whenever this preference is changed, we see of course a corresponding change of conduct. If a man change sides in politics, you will see him meeting with those that entertain the same views and feelings with himself; devising plans and using his influence to elect the candidate which he has now chosen. He has new political friends on the one side, and new political enemies on the other. So with a sinner; if his heart is changed, you will see that Christians become his friends—Christ his candidate. He aims at honoring him and promoting his interest in all his ways. Before, the language of his conduct was, "Let Satan govern the world." Now, the language of his heart and of his life is, "Let Christ rule King of nations, as he is King of saints." Before, his conduct said, "O Satan, let thy kingdom come, and let thy will be done." Now, his heart, his life, his lips cry out, "O Jesus, let thy kingdom come, let thy will be done on earth as it is in heaven.". . .

To maintain that we are under obligation to do what we have no power to do, is absurd. If we are under no obligation to do a thing, and do it not, we sin. For the blame-worthiness of sin consists in its being the violation of an obligation. But if we are under an obligation to do what we have no power to do, then sin is unavoidable; we are forced to sin by a natural necessity. But this is contrary to right reason, to make sin to consist in any thing that is forced upon us by the necessity of nature. Besides, if it is sin, we are bound to repent of it, heartily to blame ourselves, and justify the requirement of God; but it is plainly impossible for us to blame ourselves for not doing what we are conscious we never had any power to do. Suppose God should command a man to fly; would the command impose upon him any obligation, until he was furnished with wings? Certainly not. But suppose, on his failing to obey, God should require him to repent of his disobedience, and threaten to send him to hell if he did not heartily blame himself, and justify the requirement of God. He must cease to be a reasonable being before he can do this. He knows that God never gave him power to fly, and therefore he had no right to require it of him. His natural sense of justice, and of the foundation of obligation, is outraged, and he indignantly and conscientiously throws back the requirement into his Maker's face. Repentance, in this case, is a natural impossibility; while he is a reasonable being, he knows that he is not to blame for not flying without wings; and however much he may regret his not being able to obey the requirement, and however great may be his fear of the wrath of God, still to blame himself and justify God is a natural impossibility. As, therefore, God requires men to make to themselves a new heart, on pain of eternal death, it is the strongest possible evidence that they are able to do it. To say that he has commanded them to do it, without telling them they are able, is consummate trifling. Their ability is implied as strongly as it can be, in the command itself. . . .

The very terms used by our Savior in the promise of the Spirit to reprove the world of sin, of righteousness, and of a judgment to come, strongly imply the mode of his agency. The term rendered *Comforter* in our translation of the Bible, is Parakletos; it is the same term which, in one of the epistles of John, is rendered *Advocate*. The term is there applied to Jesus Christ. It is there said, "If any man sin, we have a *Parakletos*, or an Advocate with the Father, even Jesus Christ the righteous." In this passage Jesus Christ is spoken of as the Advocate of men with God. The Parakletos, or Comforter, promised by our Savior, is represented as God's Advocate, to plead His cause with men. The term rendered *reprove* or *convince* in our translation is a law term, and signifies the summing up of an argument, and establishing or demonstrating the sinner's guilt. Thus the strivings of the Spirit of God with men, is not a physical scuffling, but a debate; a strife not of body with body, but of mind with mind; and that in the action and reaction of vehement argumentation. From these remarks, it is easy to answer the question sometimes put by individuals who seem to be entirely in the dark upon this subject, whether in converting the soul the Spirit acts directly on the mind, or on the truth. This is the same nonsense as if you should ask, whether an earthly advocate who had gained his cause, did it by acting directly and physically on the jury, or on his argument. . . .

You see from this subject that a sinner, under the influence of the Spirit of God, is just as free as a jury under the arguments of an advocate.

Here also you may see the importance of right views on this point. Suppose a lawyer, in addressing a jury, should not expect to change their minds by any thing he could say, but should wait for an invisible, and physical agency, to be exerted by the Holy Ghost upon them. And suppose, on the other hand, that the jury thought that in making up their verdict, they must be passive, and wait for a direct physical agency to be exerted upon them. In vain might the lawyer plead, and in vain might the jury hear, for until he pressed his arguments as if he was determined to bow their hearts, and until they make up their minds, and decide the question, and thus act like rational beings, both his pleading, and their hearing is in vain. So if a minister goes into a desk to preach to sinners, believing that they have no power to obey the truth, and under the impression that a direct physical influence must be exerted upon them before they *can* believe, and if his audience be of the same opinion, in vain does he preach, and in vain do they hear, "for they are yet in their sins;" they sit and quietly wait for some invisible hand to be stretched down from heaven, and perform some surgical operation, infuse some new principle, or implant some constitutional taste; *after* which they suppose they shall be *able* to obey God. Ministers should labor with sinners, as a lawyer does with a jury, and upon the same principles of mental philosophy; and the sinner should weigh his arguments, and make up his mind as upon oath and for his life, and give a verdict upon the spot, according to law and evidence. . . .

But here perhaps another objection may arise—*If the sinner is able to convert himself, why does he need the Spirit of God?*

Suppose a man owed you one hundred dollars, was abundantly able, but wholly unwilling to pay you; you obtain a writ, and prepare, by instituting a suit against him, to ply him with a motive that will constrain him to be honest and pay his debts. Now suppose that he should say, I am perfectly able to pay this hundred dollars, of what use then is this writ, and a sheriff, and a lawsuit? The answer is, It is to make him willing—to be sure, he is able, but he is unwilling. Just so with the sinner—he is able to do his duty, but is unwilling, therefore the Spirit of God plies him with motives to make him willing. . . .

Sinner! your obligation to love God is equal to the excellence of his character, and your guilt in not obeying him is of course equal to your obligation. You cannot therefore for an hour or a moment defer obedience to the commandment in the text, without deserving eternal damnation. . . .

If men would act as wisely and as philosophically in attempting to make men Christians, as they do in attempting to sway mind upon other subjects; if they would suit their subject to the state of mind, conform "the action to the word and the word to the action," and press their subject with as much address, and warmth, and perseverance, as lawyers and statesmen do their addresses; the result would be the conversion of hundreds of thousands, and converts would be added to the Lord "like drops of the morning dew." Were the whole church and the whole ministry right upon this subject; had they right views, were they imbued with a right spirit, and would they "go forth with tears, bearing precious seed, they would soon reap the harvest of the whole earth, and return bearing their sheaves with them." . . .

And now sinner. . . [l]et the truth take hold upon your conscience— throw down your rebellious weapons—give up your refuges of lies— fix your mind steadfastly upon the world of considerations that should instantly decide you to close in with the offer of reconciliation while it now lies before you. Another moment's delay, and it may be too late forever. The Spirit of God may depart from you—the offer of life may be made no more, and this one more slighted offer of mercy may close up your account, and seal you over to all the horrors of eternal death. Hear, then, O sinner, I beseech you, and obey the word of the Lord— "Make you a new heart and a new spirit, for why will ye die?". . .

Sinners . . . have been perplexed and confounded by abstract doctrines, metaphysical subtleties, absurd exhibitions of the sovereignty of God, inability, physical regeneration, and constitutional depravity, until the agonized mind, discouraged and mad with contradiction from the pulpit, and absurdity in conversation, dismissed the subject as altogether incomprehensible, and postponed the performance of duty as impossible.

FROM A FINNEY SERMON

"A thing is not right or good because God commands it. The principles of right are as eternal as God, and He is good because His being is in accordance with them. God cannot make anything right any more than He can make the three angles of a triangle equal to two right angles."

FROM A FINNEY PRAYER

"O Lord, I have been walking down Broadway today, and I have seen a good many of my friends and Thy friends, and I wondered, O Lord! if they seemed as poor, and vapid, and empty, and worldly to Thee as they did to me."

from LECTURES ON REVIVALS

Charles Grandison Finney

R*eligion is the work of man*. It is something for man to do. It consists in obeying God. It is man's duty. It is true, God induces him to do it. He influences him by his Spirit, because of his great wickedness and reluctance to obey. If it were not necessary for God to influence men—if men were disposed to obey God, there would be no occasion to pray, "O Lord, revive thy work." The ground of necessity for such a prayer is, that men are wholly indisposed to obey; and unless God interpose the influence of his Spirit, not a man on earth will ever obey the commands of God.

A "Revival of Religion" presupposes a declension. Almost all the religion in the world has been produced by revivals. God has found it necessary to take advantage of the excitability there is in mankind, to produce powerful excitements among them, before he can lead them to obey. Men are so sluggish, there are so many things to lead their minds off from religion, and to oppose the influence of the gospel, that it is necessary to raise an excitement among them, till the tide rises so high as to sweep away the opposing obstacles. They must be so excited that they will break over these counteracting influences, before they will obey God.

Look back at the history of the Jews, and you will see that God used to maintain religion among *them* by special occasions, when there would be a great excitement, and people would turn to the Lord. And after they had been thus revived, it would be but a short time before there would be so many counteracting influences brought to bear upon them, that religion would decline, and keep on declining, till God could have time— so to speak—to shape the course of events so as to produce another excitement, and then pour out his Spirit again to convert sinners. . . .

The state of this world is still such, and probably will be till the millennium is fully come, that religion must be mainly promoted by these excitements. How long and how often has the experiment been tried, to bring the church to act steadily for God, without these periodical excitements! Many good men have supposed, and still suppose, that the best way to promote religion, is to go along *uniformly*, and gather in the ungodly gradually, and without excitement. But however such reasoning may appear in the abstract, *facts* demonstrate its futility. If the church were far enough advanced in knowledge, and had stability of principle enough to *keep awake*, such a course would do; but the church is so little enlightened, and there are so many counteracting causes, that the church will not go steadily to work without a special excitement. As the millennium advances, it is probable that these periodical excitements will be unknown. Then the church will be enlightened, and the counteracting causes removed, and the entire church will be in a state of habitual and steady obedience to God. . . .

Then . . . Christians will not sleep the greater part of the time, and once in a while wake up, and rub their eyes, and bluster about, and vociferate, a little while, and then go to sleep again. Then there will be no need that ministers should wear themselves out, and kill themselves, by their efforts to roll back the flood of worldly influence that sets in upon the church. But as yet the state of the Christian world is such, that to expect to promote religion without excitements is unphilosophical and absurd. The great political, and other worldly excitements that agitate Christendom, are all unfriendly to religion, and divert the mind from the interests of the soul. Now these excitements can only be counteracted by *religious* excitements. And until there is religious principle in the world to put down irreligious excitements, it is in vain to try to promote religion, except by counteracting excitements. This is true in philosophy, and it is a historical fact. . . .

Ordinarily, there are three agents employed in the work of conversion, and one instrument. The agents are God,—some person who brings the truth to bear on the mind,—and the sinner himself. The instrument is the truth. There are *always two* agents, God and the sinner, employed and active in every case of genuine conversion.

1. The agency of God is two-fold; by his Providence and by his spirit.

(1.) By his providential government, he so arranges events as to bring the sinner's mind and the truth in contact. He brings the sinner where the truth reaches his ears or his eyes. It is often interesting to trace the manner in which God arranges events so as to bring this about, and how he sometimes makes every thing seem to favor a revival. The state of the weather, and of the public health, and other circumstances concur to make every thing just right to favor the application of truth with the greatest possible efficacy. How he sometimes sends a minister along, just at the time he is wanted! How he brings out a particular truth, just at the particular time when the individual it is fitted to reach is in the way to hear! . . . If men were *disposed* to obey God, the truth is given with sufficient clearness in the Bible; and from preaching they could learn all that is necessary for them to know. But because they are wholly *disinclined* to obey it, God clears it up before their minds, and pours in a blaze of convincing light upon their souls, which they cannot withstand, and they yield to it, and obey God, and are saved.

2. The agency of men is commonly employed. Men are not mere *instruments* in the hands of God. Truth is the instrument. The preacher is a moral agent in the work; he acts; he is not a mere passive instrument; he is voluntary in promoting the conversion of sinners.

3. The agency of the sinner himself. The conversion of a sinner consists in his obeying the truth. It is therefore impossible it should take place without his agency, for it consists in *his* acting right. He is influenced to this by the agency of God, and by the agency of men. Men act on their fellow-men, not only by language, but by their looks, their tears, their daily deportment. See that impenitent man there, who has a pious wife. Her very looks, her tenderness, her solemn, compassionate dignity, softened and molded into the image of Christ, are a sermon to him all the time. He has to turn his mind away, because it is such a reproach to him. He feels a sermon ringing in his ears all day long. . . .

REMARKS

1. Revivals were formerly regarded as miracles. And it has been so by some even in our day. And others have ideas on the subject so loose and unsatisfactory, that if they would only *think*, they would see their absurdity. For a long time, it was supposed by the church, that a revival was a miracle, an interposition of Divine power which they had nothing to do with, and which they had no more agency in producing, than they had in producing thunder, or a storm of hail, or an earthquake. It is only within a few years that ministers generally have supposed revivals were to be *promoted* by the use of means designed and adapted specifically to that object. . . .

2. Mistaken notions concerning the sovereignty of God, have greatly hindered revivals.

Many people have supposed God's sovereignty to be something very different from what it is. They have supposed it to be such an arbitrary disposal of events, and particularly of the gift of his Spirit, as precluded a rational employment of means for promoting a revival of religion. But there is no evidence from the Bible, that God exercises any such sovereignty as that. There are no facts to prove it. But every thing goes to show, that God has connected means with the end through all the departments of his government—in nature and in grace. There is no *natural* event in which his own agency is not concerned. He has not built the creation like a vast machine, that will go on alone without his further care. He has not retired from the universe, to let it work for itself. This is mere atheism. He exercises a universal superintendence and control. And yet every event in nature has been brought about by means. He neither administers providence nor grace with that sort of sovereignty, that dispenses with the use of means. . . .

[M]en cannot do the devil's work more effectually, than by preaching up the sovereignty of God, as a reason why we should not put forth efforts to produce a revival.

3. You see the error of those who are beginning to think that religion can be better promoted in the world without revivals, and who are disposed to give up all efforts to produce religious excitements. Because there are evils arising in some instances out of great excitements on the subject of religion, they are of opinion that it is best to dispense with them altogether. This cannot, and must not be. True, there is danger of abuses. In cases of great *religious* as well as all other excitements, more or less incidental evils may be expected of course. But this is no reason why they should be given up. The best things are always liable to abuses. Great and manifold evils have originated in the providential and moral governments of God. But these *foreseen* perversions and evils were not considered a sufficient reason for giving them up. For the establishment of these governments was on the whole the best that could be done for the production of the greatest amount of happiness. So in revivals of religion, it is found by experience, that in the present state of the world, religion cannot be promoted to any considerable extent without them. The evils which are sometimes complained of, when they are real, are incidental, and of small importance when compared with the amount of good produced by revivals.

• • •

There are three things in particular, which have chiefly attracted remark, and therefore I shall speak of them. They are *Anxious Meetings, Protracted Meetings*, and the *Anxious Seat*. These are all opposed, and are called new measures.

(1.) *Anxious Meetings*. The first that I ever heard of under that name, was in New England, where they were appointed for the purpose of holding personal conversation with anxious sinners, and to adapt instruction to the cases of individuals, so as to lead them immediately to Christ. The design of them is evidently philosophical, but they have been opposed because they were new. . . .

(2.) *Protracted Meetings*. These are not new, but have always been practised, in some form or other, ever since there was a church on earth. The Jewish festivals were nothing else but protracted meetings. In regard to the *manner*, they were conducted differently from what they are now. But the *design* was the same, to devote a series of days to religious services, in order to make a more powerful impression of divine things upon the minds of the people. . . . I will suggest a few things that ought to be considered in regard to them.

(*a.*) In appointing them, regard should be had *to the circumstances of the people;* whether the church are able to give their attention and devote their time to carry on the meaning. . . . Now there are particular seasons of the year, in which God in his providence calls upon men to attend to business, because worldly business at the time is particularly urgent, and must be done at that season, if done at all; seed time and harvest for the farmer, and the business seasons for the merchant. And we have no right to say, in those particular seasons, that we will quit *our business* and have a protracted meeting. . . .

(*b.*) Ordinarily a protracted meeting should be conducted through, and the labor chiefly performed, by *the same minister*, if possible. . . . Suppose a person who was sick should call in a different physician every day. He would not know what the symptoms had been, nor what was the course of the disease or of the treatment, nor what remedies had been tried, nor what the patient could bear. Why, he would certainly kill the patient. Just so in a protracted meeting, carried on by a succession of ministers. None of them get into the spirit of it, and generally they do more hurt than good. . . .

(*f.*) *All sectarianism* should be carefully avoided. If a sectarian spirit breaks out, either in the preaching, or praying, or conversation, it will counteract all the good of the meeting.

(*g.*) Be watchful against *placing dependence* on a protracted meting, *as if that of itself would produce a revival.* This is a point of great danger, and has always been so. This is the great reason why the church in successive generations has always had to give up her measures—because Christians had come to rely on them for success. . . .

(*h.*) Avoid adopting the idea that a revival cannot be enjoyed *without a Protracted Meeting.* Some churches have got into a morbid state of feeling on this subject. Their zeal has become all spasmodic, and feverish, so that they never think of doing anything to promote a revival, *only in that way.* When a protracted meeting is held, they will seem to be wonderfully zealous, and then sink down to a torpid state till another protracted meeting produces another spasm. . . .

(3.) *The Anxious Seat.*

By this I mean the appointment of some particular seat in the place of the meeting, where the anxious may come and be addressed particularly, and be made subjects of prayer, and sometimes conversed with individually. Of late this measure has met with more opposition than any of the others. What is the great objection? I cannot see it. The *design* of the anxious seat is undoubtedly philosophical, and according to the laws of mind. It has two bearings:

1. When a person is seriously troubled in mind, every body knows that there is a powerful tendency to try to keep it private that he is so, and it is a great thing to get the individual willing to have the fact known to others. And as soon as you can get him willing to make known his feelings, you have accomplished a great deal. . . .

2. Another bearing of the anxious seat, is to detect deception and delusion. . . . If you say to him. "There is the anxious seat, come out and avow your determination to be on the Lord's side," and if he is not willing to do so small a thing as that, then he is not willing to do *any thing,* and there he is, brought out before his own conscience. It uncovers the delusion of the human heart, and prevents a great many spurious conversations, by showing those who might otherwise imagine themselves willing to do any thing for Christ, that in fact they are willing to do *nothing.*

from CATHOLICITY NECESSARY TO SUSTAIN POPULAR LIBERTY

Orestes Augustus Brownson

By popular liberty, we mean democracy; by democracy, we mean the democratic form of government; by the democratic form of government, we mean that form of government which vests the sovereignty in the people as population, and which is administered by the people, either in person or by their delegates. By sustaining popular liberty, we mean, not the introduction or institution of democracy, but preserving it when and where it is already introduced, and securing its free, orderly, and wholesome action. By Catholicity, we mean the Roman Catholic Church, faith, morals, and worship. The thesis we propose to maintain is, therefore, that without the Roman Catholic religion it is impossible to preserve a democratic government, and secure its free, orderly, and wholesome action. Infidelity, Protestantism, heathenism may institute a democracy, but only Catholicity can sustain it.

Our own government, in its origin and constitutional form, is not a democracy, but, if we may use the expression, a limited *elective* aristocracy. In its theory, the representative, within the limits prescribed by the Constitution, when once elected, and during the time for which he is elected, is, in his official action, independent of his constituents, and not responsible to them for his acts. . . . Since 1828, it has been becoming in practice, and is now, substantially, a pure democracy, with no effective constitution but the will of the majority for the time being. Whether the change has been for the better or the worse, we need not stop to inquire. The change was inevitable, because men are more willing to advance themselves by flattering the people and perverting the Constitution, than they are by self-denial to serve their country. The change has been effected, and there is no return to the original theory of the government. . . . Your Calhouns must give way for your Polks and Van Burens, your Websters for your Harrisons and Tylers. No man, who is not prepared to play the demagogue, to stoop to flatter the people, and, in one direction or another, to exaggerate the democratic tendency, can receive the nomination for an important office, or have influence in public affairs. The reign of great men, of distinguished statesmen and firm patriots, is over, and that of the demagogues has begun. . . .

The theory of democracy is, . . . the people are assumed to be what Almighty God is to the universe, the first cause, the medial cause, the final cause. . . .

It is a beautiful theory, and would work admirably, if it were not for one little difficulty, namely,—*the people are fallible, both individually and collectively, and governed by their passions and interests, which not unfrequently lead them far astray, and produce much mischief.* The government must necessarily follow their will; and whenever that will happens to be blinded by passion, or misled by ignorance or interest, the government must inevitably go wrong; and government can never go wrong without doing injustice. . . .

Do not answer by referring us to the virtue and intelligence of the people. We are writing seriously, and have no leisure to enjoy a joke, even if it be a good one. . . . [W]e think we hazard nothing in saying, our free institutions cannot be sustained without an augmentation of popular virtue and intelligence. . . .

The press makes readers, but does little to make virtuous and intelligent readers. . . . Your popular literature caters to popular taste, passions, prejudices, ignorance, and errors; it is by no means above the average degree of virtue and intelligence which already obtains, and can do nothing to create a higher standard of virtue or tone of thought. On what, then, are we to rely?

"On Education," answer Frances Wright, Abner Kneeland, the Hon. Secretary of the Massachusetts Board of Education, and the Educationists generally. But we must remember that we must have virtue *and* intelligence. . . . Education, moreover, demands educators, and educators of the right sort. Where are these to be obtained? Who is to select them, judge of their qualifications, sustain or dismiss them? The people? Then you place education in the same category with democracy. You make the people through their representatives the educators. The people will select and sustain only such educators as represent their own virtues, vices, intelligence, prejudices, and errors. . . .

We know of but one solution of the difficulty, and that is in RELIGION. There is no foundation for virtue but in religion, and it is only religion that can command the degree of popular virtue and intelligence requisite to insure to popular government the right direction and a wise and just administration. A people without religion, however successful they may be in throwing off old institutions, or in introducing new ones, have no power to secure the free, orderly, and wholesome working of any institutions. . . .

But what religion? It must be a religion which is above the people and controls them, or it will not answer the purpose. If it depends on the people, if the people are to take care of it, to say what it shall be, what it shall teach, what it shall command, what worship or discipline it shall insist on being observed, we are back in our old difficulty. The people take care of religion; but who or what is to take care of the people? We repeat then, what religion? It cannot be Protestantism, in all or any of its forms; for Protestantism assumes as its point of departure that Almighty God has indeed given us a religion, but *has given it to us not to take care of us, but to be taken care of by us.* It makes religion the ward of the people; assumes it to be sent on earth a lone and helpless orphan, to be taken in by the people, who are to serve as its nurse. . . .

The first stage of Protestantism was to place religion under the charge of the civil government. The Church was condemned, among other reasons, for the control it exercised over princes and nobles, that is, over the temporal power; and the first effect of Protestantism was to emancipate the government from this control, or, in other words, to free the government from the restraints of religion, and to bring religion in subjection to the temporal authority. . . . But, if the government control the religion, it can exercise no control over the sovereign people, for they control the government. Through the government the people take care of religion, but who or what takes care of the people? This would leave the people ultimate, and we have no security unless we have something more ultimate than they, something which they cannot control, but which they must obey.

The second stage in Protestantism is to reject, in matters of religion, the authority of the temporal government, and to subject religion to the control of the faithful. This is the full recognition in matters of religion of the democratic principle. The people determine their faith and worship, select, sustain, or dismiss their own religious teachers. They who are to be taught judge him who is to teach, and say whether he teaches them truth or falsehood, wholesome doctrine or unwholesome. . . .

The third and last stage of Protestantism is Individualism. This leaves religion entirely to the control of the individual, who selects his own creed, or makes a creed to suit himself, devises his own worship and discipline, and submits to no restraints but such as are self-imposed. This makes a man's religion the effect of his virtue and intelligence, and denies it all power to augment or to direct them. So this will not answer. . . .

The faith and discipline of a sect take any and every direction the public opinion of that sect demands. All is loose, floating,—is here to-day, is there to-morrow, and, next day, may be nowhere. The holding of slaves is compatible with Christian character south of a geographical line, and incompatible north; and Christian morals change according to the prejudices, interests, or habits of the people,—as evinced by the recent divisions in our own country among the Baptists and Methodists. The Unitarians of Savannah refuse to hear a preacher accredited by Unitarians of Boston.

The great danger in our country is from the predominance of material interests. Democracy has a direct tendency to favor inequality and injustice. . . . What our people demand of government is, that it adopt and sustain such measures as tend most directly to facilitate the acquisition of wealth. It must, then, follow the passion for wealth, and labor especially to promote worldly interests. . . .

Now, what is wanted is some power to prevent this, to moderate the passion for wealth, and to inspire the people with such a true and firm sense of justice, as will prevent any one interest from struggling to advance itself at the expense of another. Without this the stronger material interests proedominate, make the government the means of securing their predominance, and of extending it by the burdens which, through the government, they are able to impose on the weaker interests of the country. . . .

Protestantism is insufficient to restrain these, for it does not do it, and is itself carried away by them. The Protestant sect governs its religion, instead of being governed by it. . . . If the minister attempts to do his duty, reproves a practice by which his parishioners "get gain," or insists on their practising some real self-denial not compensated by some self-indulgence, a few leading members will tell him very gravely, that they hired him to preach and pray for them, not to interfere with their business concerns and relations; and if he does not mind his own business, they will no longer need his services. . . .

If Protestantism will not answer the purpose, what religion will? The Roman Catholic, or none. The Roman Catholic religion assumes, as its point of departure, that it is instituted not to be taken care of by the people, but to take care of the people; not to be governed by them, but to govern them. The word is harsh in democratic ears, we admit; but it is not the office of religion to say soft or pleasing words. It must speak the truth even in unwilling ears, and it has few truths that are not harsh and grating to the worldly mind or the depraved heart. The people need governing, and must be governed, or nothing but anarchy and destruction await them. They must have a master. The word must be spoken. . . . The first lesson to the child is, *obey;* the first and last lesson to the people, individually or collectively, is, OBEY;—and there is no obedience where there is no authority to enjoin it.

The Roman Catholic religion, then, is necessary to sustain popular liberty, because popular liberty can be sustained only by a religion free from popular control, above the people, speaking from above and able to command them,—and such a religion is the Roman Catholic. It acknowledges no master but God, and depends only on the divine will in respect to what it shall teach, what it shall ordain, what it shall insist upon as truth, piety, moral and social virtue. It was made not by the people, but for them; is administered not by the people, but for them; is accountable not to the people, but to God. . . .

The only influence on the political or governmental action of the people which we ask from Catholicity, is that which it exerts on the mind, the heart, and the conscience;—an influence which it exerts by enlightening the mind to see the true end of man, the relative value of all worldly pursuits, by moderating the passions, by weaning the affections from the world, inflaming the heart with true charity, and by making each act in all things seriously, honestly, conscientiously. The people will thus come to see and to will what is equitable and right, and will give to the government a wise and just direction, and never use it to effect any unwise or unjust measures. . . .

[W]hen God speaks, man has nothing to do but to listen and obey. So, having decided that Catholicity is from God, save in condescension to the weakness of our Protestant brethren, we must refuse to consider it in its political bearings. It speaks from God, and its speech overrides every other speech, its authority every other authority. It is the sovereign of sovereigns. He who could question this, admitting it to be from God, has yet to obtain his first religious conception, and to take his first lesson in religious liberty; for we are to hear God, rather than hearken unto men. But we have met the Protestants on their own ground, because, though in doing so we surrendered the vantage-ground we might occupy, we know the strength of Catholicity and the weakness of Protestantism. We know what Protestantism has done for liberty, and what it can do. It can take off restraints, and introduce license, but it can do nothing to sustain true liberty. Catholicity depends on no form of government; it leaves the people to adopt such forms of government as they please, because under any or all forms of government it can fulfil its mission of training up souls for heaven; and the eternal salvation of one single soul is worth more than, is a good far outweighing, the most perfect civil liberty, nay, all the wordly prosperity and enjoyment ever obtained or to be obtained by the whole human race. . . .

The universal restlessness of Protestant nations, the universal disposition to change, the constant movements of the populations, so much admired by shortsighted philosophers, are a sad spectacle to the soberminded Christian, who would, as far as possible, find in all things a type of that eternal fixedness and repose he looks forward to as the blessed reward of his trials and labors here. Catholicity comes here to our relief. All else may change, but it changes not.

SHAKER AND MORMON SONGS

SHAKER SONGS

RIGHTS OF CONSCIENCE

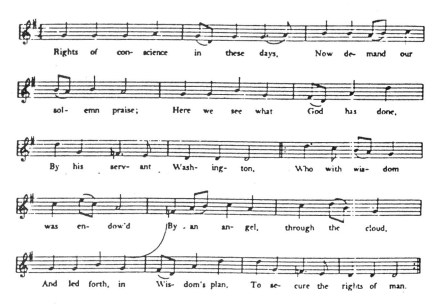

Rights of con- science in these days, Now de- mand our sol- emn praise; Here we see what God has done, By his serv- ant Wash- ing- ton, Who with wis- dom was en- dow'd By an an- gel, through the cloud, And led forth, in Wis- dom's plan, To se- cure the rights of man.

2 "Arm yourselves, unsheath the sword!
  (Cries this servant of the Lord,)
  Rights of freedom we'll maintain,
  And our independence gain."
  Fleets and armies he withstood,
  In the strength of Jehu's God;
  Proud Cornwallis and Burgoyne,
  With their armies soon resign.

3 Thus the valiant conqu'ror stood
  To defend his country's good,
  Till a treaty he confirms,

Settling peace on his own terms.
Having clos'd these warlike scenes,
Chosen men he then convenes;
These a constitution plan'd,
To protect this ransom'd land.

4   Prince of all the host he stands,
Keeps the helm in his own hands,
Till a law stands to declare,
Bind the conscience if you dare!
Then he spreads the eagle's wings
(Signs of freedom) on all things,
Form'd an order to his mind,
Blest the earth and then resign'd.

5   When by precept he had shown
What kind heaven had made known,
By example aids the cause,
Forms his own domestic laws,
Breaks the yoke at his own door,
Clothes the naked, feeds the poor,
Bondage from his house he hurl'd,
Freed his slaves and left the world.

•   •   •

10   Mighty Christians, stout and bold!
Full of lust as you can hold,
Fighting for religious rights!
God has notic'd all such fights;
Still your souls are not releas'd,
Bound by sin and wicked priests:
Tho' your country has been sav'd,
You in bondage are enslav'd.

11   With all this you're not content;
Still on bondage you are bent,
Binding the poor negro too,
He must be a slave to you!
Yet of Washington you boast,
Spread his fame thro' every coast,

Bury him with great ado,
Precepts and examples, too!

12 Did you think in seventy five,
When the states were all alive,
When they did for freedom sue,
God was deaf and blind like you?
You were fighting on one side,
To build up your lust and pride;
God was bringing in a plan.
To defeat the pride of man.

•   •   •

15 See the woman's seed advance,
Glor'ous in Emmanuel's dance!
At this arrange victor'ous play,
Earth and heavens flee away:
Swift as light'ning see them move,
Labouring in unfeigned love:
God, thro' Mother we adore,
Hate the flesh and sin no more.

SPIRITUAL WINE

I have found the true vine, and have tast- ed its wine Which has
made me to stag- ger and reel; And to such it be- longs to break
forth in- to songs, To ex- press how de- light- ful they feel; By a
boun- ti- ful use of this heav- en- ly juice, I forget all my sor- rows and woes; Give me plen- ty of this, I want
no oth- er bliss, And I care not much how the world goes goes
goes, And I care not much how the world goes.

• • •

4   Since my sins I confess'd, some are greatly distress'd,
    And lament how deluded I be;
    But at every fresh draught, I have heartily laugh'd,
    At their crocodile weeping for me.
    In my free happy choice, I can daily rejoice
    In this blest holy way that I've chose;
    If they will not pursue, I shall bid them adieu,
    And I care not much how the world goes—

5   All the pleasures they boast are but bubbles at most,
    And by heaven were never design'd,
    In their bondage to hold an enlightened soul,
    Or an honest believer to bind.
    As the mighty and rich have to fall in the ditch,
    Then let me have my victuals and clothes,
    And I ask not a cent, but shall still be content,
    And I care not much how the world goes—

6   Of their honors, I own, I desire to have none,
    For their titles are only a lie;
    When the bishop and squire are brought into the fire,
    They'll not be a whit greater than I:
    I should then be a fool if I wanted to rule,
    In a kingdom so near to a close;
    From such honor I fly, and myself I deny,
    And I care not much how the world goes—

A WORK SONG

I work thirteen hours, in each twenty-four
Or more if necessity call;
In point of distinction, I want nothing more
Than just to be servant of all:
I peaceably work at whatever I'm set,
From no other motive but love,
To honor the gospel and keep out of debt,
And lay up a treasure above.

I eat for refreshment, my strength to repair,—
Not merely to gratify taste;
Whatever's provided, I thankfully share,
And nothing that's good do I waste;
I still realize that my Elders are nigh,
Their modest example I view,
By which I am furnish'd with power from on high
The beastly old man to subdue.

At half after seven, from work I retire,
And noise and confusion I shun.
And just before meeting I settle the fire,
To see that no mischief be done:
I go into meeting to find some increase,
And never withdraw till it close,
And when we're dimiss'd I retire in peace,
Prepar'd for a pleasant repose.

I sleep seven hours, with little recess,
And O how refreshing they seem:
At four in the morning I get up and dress,
Regardless of vision or dream.
When meeting is over I chuse to give way,
And be at my work very soon,
And more than one half that's laid out for the day,
Must always be done before noon.

I keep in the circle assigned to me,
With which I am fully content,
And nothing beyond it I'm anxious to see,
Unless in a gift I am sent.
In all kinds of company, I am among,
My words I do carefully weigh,
And rather than speak with an unbridled tongue,
I chuse to have nothing to say.

By temperance, prudence, industry and care,
My faith is to lay up in store
A good gospel treasure, enough and to spare,
To give to the needy and poor.
That this is the gospel I have not a doubt,
Nor am I a tittle afraid,
But in true obedience my strength will hold out
Until the foundation is laid.

MOTHER ANN'S PLUMB CAKE

GREAT I LITTLE I

PINCH'D UP, NIP'D UP

Pentatonic, mode 3 (I II III — V VI —)   [♩=128–168]
SM198, p. 93

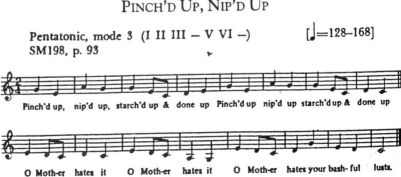

SIMPLE GIFTS

'Tis the gift to be sim- ple, 'tis the gift to be free; 'Tis the gift to come down where we ought to be; And when we find our- selves in the place just right, 'Twill be in the val- ley of love and de- light. When true sim- plic- i- ty is gaind, To bow and to bend we shan't be a- sham'd To turn, turn will be our de- light, 'Till by turn- ing, turn- ing we come round right.

CIVIL WAR SUPPLICATION

Dark is the cloud that rests o- ver the na- tion

Wild is the war cry that pier- ces the air

God's heav- y judg- ments spread wide de- so- la- tion

Strong hearts are bowed in the depths of dis- pair.

2   Lord, may the bands of the captive be broken,
     O! may this struggle bring true liberty,
     Teach man that love is a heaven born token
     And that the truth can alone make him free.

•   •   •

JUBILEE

The gos-pel is ad-vanc-ing And free-dom is com-menc-ing With leap-ing and with danc-ing We'll hail the ju-bi-lee The fire is in-creas-ing The flame is nev-er ceas-ing I feel I am re-leas-ing, And now I will be free.

3   With freedom I'm delighted
     I will not feel affrighted
     Come let us be united
     And sound the jubilee.
     The bands of sin are breaking
     The devel's kingdom shaking
     And his foundation quaking
     Because we will be free.

4   And now each true believer
     Will bind the old deceiver
     And keep him bound forever
     Throughout the jubilee.

This work of tribulation
Is free from condemnation
And brings complete salvation
To all who will be free.

5   The gospell fire is blazing
The world with wonder gazing
They say it is amazing
Is this your jubilee.
But we will shout like thunder
And fill the world with wonder
We'll break our bands asunder
And then we will be free.

MORMON HYMNS

THE SEER, JOSEPH, THE SEER

Words by John Taylor
Tune by Sigismond Neukomm—
Arr. by Ebenezer Beesley

The Seer, the Seer, Joseph the Seer!
I'll sing of the Prophet ever dear;
His equal now cannot be found,
By searching the wide world around.
With Gods he soared in the realms of day,
And men he taught the heavenly way,
The earthly Seer! the heavenly Seer!
I love to dwell on his memory dear;
The chosen of God and the friend of man,
He brought the Priesthood back again;
He gazed on the past and the future too,
And opened the heavenly world to view.

•   •   •

The Saints, the Saints, his only pride!
For them he lived, for them he died;
Their joys were his, their sorrows too,

He loved the Saints, he loved Nauvoo,
Unchanged in death, with a Savior's love,
He pleads their case in the courts above.
The Seer, the Seer! Joseph the Seer!
O, how I love his memory dear!
The just and wise, the pure and free,
A father he was, and is to be.
Let fiends now rage in their dark hour—
No matter, no matter, he is beyond their power.

He's free! he's free! the Prophet's free!
He is where he will ever be,
Beyond the reach of mobs and strife,
He rests unharmed in endless life.
His home's in the sky, he dwells with the Gods,
Far from the furious rage of mobs,
He died, he died for those he loved.
He reigns, he reigns in the realms above,
He waits with the just who have gone before,
To welcome the Saints to Zion's shore.
Shout, shout, ye Saints, this boon is given;
We'll meet our martyred Seer in Heaven.

We Thank Thee, O God, for a Prophet

Words by William Fowler
Music by Caroline Elizabeth Sarah Norton

We thank Thee, O God, for a Prophet,
To guide us in these latter days;
We thank Thee for sending the Gospel
To lighten our minds with its rays;
We thank Thee for every blessing
Bestowed by Thy bounteous hand;
We feel it a pleasure to serve Thee,
And love to obey Thy command.

• • •

We doubt not the Lord, nor His goodness,
We've proved Him in days that are past;
The wicked who fight against Zion
Will surely be smitten at last.

● ● ●

Thus on to eternal perfection
The honest and faithful will go,
While they who reject this glad message
Shall never such happiness know.

PRAISE TO THE MAN

Hymn by William W. Phelps

Praise to the Man who communed with Jehovah!
Jesus anointed "that Prophet and Seer"
Blessed to open the last dispensation;
Kings shall extol him, and nations revere.

Chorus
Hail to the Prophet, ascended to heaven!
Traitors and tryants now fight him in vain;
Mingling with Gods, he can plan for his brethren;
Death cannot conquer the Hero again.
Praise to his mem'ry, he died as a martyr,
Honored and blest be his ever great name!
Long shall his blood, which was shed by assassins,
Plead unto heav'n while the earth lauds his fame.

● ● ●

Sacrifice brings forth the blessings of heaven;
Earth must stone for the blood of that man;
Wake up the world for the conflict of justice;
Millions shall know "Brother Joseph" again.

O MY FATHER

Hymn by Eliza R. Snow
Tune by James McGranahan

O my Father, Thou that dwellest
In the high and glorious place!
When shall I regain Thy presence,
And again behold Thy face?
In Thy holy habitation,
Did my spirit once reside;
In my first primeval childhood
Was I nurtured near Thy side?

For a wise and glorious purpose
Thou hast placed me here on earth,
And withheld the recollection
Of my former friends and birth;
Yet ofttimes a secret something
Whispered, "You're a stranger here;"
And I felt that I had wandered
From a more exalted sphere.

I had learned to call Thee Father,
Through Thy spirit from on high;
But until the Key of Knowledge
Was restored, I knew not why.
In the heavens are parents single?
No; the thought makes reason stare!
Truth is reason, Truth eternal
Tells me I've a Mother there.

When I leave this frail existence,
When I lay this mortal by,
Father, Mother, may I meet you
In your royal courts on high?
Then, at length, when I've completed
All you sent me forth to do,
With your mutual approbation
Let me come and dwell with you.

THOUGH DEEP'NING TRIALS THRONG YOUR WAY

Words by Eliza R. Snow
Music by George Careless

Though deep'ning trials throng your way,
Press on, press on, ye Saints of God!
Ere long the resurrection day
Will spread its life and truth abroad.

•　•　•

What though our rights have been assailed?
What though by foes we've been despoiled?
Jehovah's promise has not failed,
Jehovah's purpose is not foiled.

His work is moving on apace,
And great events are rolling forth;
The Kingdom of the latter days—
The "little stone"—must fill the earth.

NOW LET US REJOICE IN THE DAY OF SALVATION

Words by William W. Phelps

Hymn

Now let us rejoice in the day of salvation,
No longer as strangers on earth need we roam,
Good tidings are sounding to us and each nation,
And shortly the hour of redemption will come.
When all that was Promised the Saints will be given,
And none will molest them from morn until ev'n,
And earth will appear as the garden of Eden,
And Jesus will say to all Israel, Come Home.

We'll love one another, and never dissemble,
But cease to do evil, and ever be one;
And when the ungodly are fearing and tremble,
We'll watch for the day when the Savior will come.

• • •

HIGH ON THE MOUNTAIN TOP

Words by Joel H. Johnson
Music by Ebenezer Beesley

High on the mountain top
A banner is unfurled;
Ye nations, now look up;
It waves to all the world;
In Deseret's sweet, peaceful land—
On Zion's mount behold it stand!

For there we shall be taught
The law that will go forth,
With truth and wisdom fraught,
To govern all the earth;
Forever there His ways we'll tread,
And save ourselves with all our dead.

• • •

Then hail to Deseret!
A refuge for the good,
And safety for the great,
It they but understood
That God with plagues will shake the world
'Till all its thrones shall down be hurled.

CHAPTER 9

Keeping Democracy Wholesome

INTRODUCTION

ALEXIS DE TOCQUEVILLE, 1805–1859
from Democracy in America (1835,1840)

RALPH WALDO EMERSON, 1803–1882
from Self Reliance (1841) and
from The Journals of Ralph Waldo Emerson (1820–1864)

Both Europeans and Americans by the 1830s saw the United States as pointing in the direction the world was likely to go, and worried about what kind of people and society would develop. None worried more thoughtfully than American Transcendentalist Ralph Waldo Emerson and French visitor Alexis de Tocqueville.

Tocqueville came to the United States technically to look at its reformed prison system, but actually to understand "democracy" so that it might be structured to accentuate its good features and guard against its bad when it came to his native France and other countries. He saw the broad process as inevitable, but, unlike Karl Marx (who developed his alternative version of "modern" society at the same time) he believed its quality was not decreed but depended on how people chose to structure and live within it.

Ralph Waldo Emerson headed the United States' first literary movement—the Transcendentalists centered in Concord, Massachusetts—and became, through his essays and lectures, the nation's best known intellectual. Emerson's fear of conformity, of the voluntary sacrifice of personal vision, in democratic society paralleled that of Tocqueville about tyranny of the majority, but his solution was to stress individualism rather than communal involvement. His private journals, the best intellectual diary of the era, are a good introduction to his breadth of interest and insight.

CONSIDERATIONS

- For Tocqueville, what are the main traits of democratic society? What does he find its greatest strengths and dangers? Why is he so concerned about it? Is he right to fear majority tyranny in democracy?

- What are the differences between Tocqueville's view of individualism and that of Emerson? What criticisms of American society are suggested by Emerson?

- How similar are the two men's views of slavery and sectional discord?

- Is self-reliance and truth to one's personal vision a better social answer than conformity to accepted standards or commitments to communal responsibility? Are "self-interest rightly understood" and "self-reliance" the same thing as "looking out for number one"?

- What are democracy's dangers today, and the best guards aginst them?

from DEMOCRACY IN AMERICA

Alexis de Tocqueville

AUTHOR'S INTRODUCTION

Amongst the novel objects that attracted my attention during my stay in the United States, nothing struck me more forcibly than the general equality of condition among the people. I readily discovered the prodigious influence which this primary fact exercises on the whole course of society; it gives a peculiar direction to public opinion, and a peculiar tenor to the laws; it imparts new maxims to the governing authorities, and peculiar habits to the governed.

I soon perceived that the influence of this fact extends far beyond the political character and the laws of the country, and that it has no less empire over civil society than over the government; it creates opinions, gives birth to new sentiments, founds novel customs, and modifies whatever it does not produce. The more I advanced in the study of American society, the more I perceived that this equality of condition is the fundamental fact from which all others seem to be derived, and the central point at which all my observations constantly terminated.

I then turned my thoughts to our own hemisphere, and thought that I discerned there something analogous to the spectacle which the New World presented to me. I observed that equality of condition, though it has not there reached the extreme limit which it seems to have attained in the United States, is constantly approaching it; and that the democracy which governs the American communities appears to be rapidly rising into power in Europe. Hence I conceived the idea of the book which is now before the reader. . . .

I look back for a moment on the situation of France seven hundred years ago, when the territory was divided amongst a small number of families, who were the owners of the soil and the rulers of the inhabitants; the right of governing descended with the family inheritance from generation to generation; force was the only means by which man

could act on man; and landed property was the sole source of power.
. . .

Whilst the kings were ruining themselves by their great enterprises, and the nobles exhausting their resources by private wars, the lower orders were enriching themselves by commerce. The influence of money began to be perceptible in state affairs. The transactions of business opened a new road to power, and the financier rose to a station of political influence in which he was at once flattered and despised.

Gradually the diffusion of intelligence, and the increasing taste for literature and art, caused learning and talent to become a means of government; mental ability led to social power, and the man of letters took a part in the affairs of the state. The value attached to high birth declined just as fast as new avenues to power were discovered. . . .

As soon as land began to be held on any other than a feudal tenure, and personal property in its turn became able to confer influence and power, every discovery in the arts, every improvement in commerce or manufactures, created so many new elements of equality among men. Henceforward every new invention, every new want which it occasioned, and every new desire which craved satisfaction, was a step towards a general levelling. The taste for luxury, the love of war, the empire of fashion, and the most superficial as well as the deepest passions of the human heart, seemed to co-operate to enrich the poor and to impoverish the rich.

From the time when the exercise of the intellect became a source of strength and of wealth, we see that every addition to science, every fresh truth, and every new idea became a germ of power placed within the reach of the people. . . .

In running over the pages of our history for seven hundred years, we shall scarcely find a single great event which has not promoted equality of condition. The Crusades and the English wars decimated the nobles and divided their possessions: the municipal corporations introduced democratic liberty into the bosom of feudal monarchy; the invention of fire-arms equalized the vassal and the noble on the field of battle; the art of printing opened the same resources to the minds of all classes; the post-office brought knowledge alike to the door of the cottage and to the gate of the palace; and Protestantism proclaimed that all men are alike able to find the road to heaven. The discovery of America opened a thousand new paths to fortune, and led obscure adventurers to wealth and power. . . .

Whithersoever we turn our eyes, we perceive the same revolution going on throughout the Christian world. The various occurrences of national existence have everywhere turned to the advantage of democracy: all men have aided it by their exertions, both those who have intentionally labored in its cause, and those who have served it unwittingly; those who have fought for it, and those who have declared themselves its opponents, have all been driven along in the same track, have all labored to one end; some ignorantly and some unwillingly, all have been blind instruments in the hands of God.

The gradual development of the principle of equality is, therefore, a Providential fact. It has all the chief characteristics of such a fact: it is universal, it is durable, it constantly eludes all human interference, and all events as well as all men contribute to its progress.

Would it, then, be wise to imagine that a social movement, the causes of which lie so far back, can be checked by the efforts of one generation? Can it be believed that the democracy which has overthrown the feudal system, and vanquished kings, will retreat before tradesmen and capitalists? Will it stop now that it has grown so strong, and its adversaries so weak? Whither, then, are we tending? . . .

The whole book which is here offered to the public has been written under the impression of a kind of religious terror produced in the author's mind by the view of that irresistible revolution which has advanced for centuries in spite of every obstacle, and which is still advancing in the midst of the ruins it has caused. It is not necessary that God himself should speak in order that we may discover the unquestionable signs of his will. It is enough to ascertain what is the habitual course of nature and the constant tendency of events. I know, without a special revelation, that the planets move in the orbits traced by the Creator's hand.

If the men of our time should be convinced, by attentive observation and sincere reflection, that the gradual and progressive development of social equality is at once the past and the future of their history, this discovery alone would confer the sacred character of a Divine decree upon the change. To attempt to check democracy would be in that case to resist the will of God; and the nations would then be constrained to make the best of the social lot awarded to them by Providence.

The Christian nations of our day seem to me to present a most alarming spectacle; the movement which impels them is already so strong that it cannot be stopped, but it is not yet so rapid that it cannot be guided. Their fate is still in their own hands; yet a little while, and it may be so no longer.

The first of the duties which are at this time imposed upon those who direct our affairs, is to educate the democracy; to renovate, if possible, its religious belief; to purify its morals; to regulate its movements; to substitute by degrees a knowledge of business for its inexperience, and an acquaintance with its true interests for its blind instincts; to adapt its government to time and place, and to make it conform to the occurrences and the men of the times. A new science of politics is needed for a new world. . . .

In no country in Europe has the great social revolution which I have just described made such rapid progress as in France; but it has always advanced without guidance. The heads of the state have made no preparation for it, and it has advanced without their consent or without their knowledge. The most powerful, the most intelligent, and the most moral classes of the nation have never attempted to take hold of it in order to guide it. . . .

Thus we have a democracy without anything to lessen its vices and bring out its natural advantages; and although we perceive the evils it brings, we are ignorant of the benefits it may confer. . . .

Gradually the distinctions of rank are done away; the barriers which once severed mankind are falling down; property is divided, power is shared by many, the light of intelligence spreads, and the capacities of all classes are equally cultivated. The State becomes democratic, and the empire of democracy is slowly and peaceably introduced into the institutions and the manners of the nation.

I can conceive of a society in which all men would feel an equal love and respect for the laws of which they consider themselves as the authors; in which the authority of the government would be respected as necessary, though not as divine; and in which the loyalty of the subject to the chief magistrate would not be a passion, but a quiet and rational persuasion. Every individual being in the possession of rights which he is sure to retain, a kind of manly confidence and reciprocal courtesy would arise between all classes, alike removed from pride and servility. The people, well acquainted with their own true interests, would understand that, in order to profit by the advantages of society, it is necessary to satisfy its requisitions. The voluntary association of the citizens might then take the place of the individual exertions of the nobles, and the community would be alike protected from anarchy and from oppression. . . .

The nation, taken as a whole, will be less brilliant, less glorious, and perhaps less strong; but the majority of the citizens will enjoy a greater degree of prosperity, and the people will remain quiet, not because they despair of a change for the better, but because they are conscious that they are well off already. . . .

If society is tranquil, it is not because it is conscious of its strength and its well-being, but because it fears its weakness and its infirmities; a single effort may cost it its life. Everybody feels the evil, but no one has courage or energy enough to seek the cure. The desires, the repinings, the sorrows, and the joys of the present time lead to no visible or permanent result, like the passions of old men, which terminate in impotence.

We have, then, abandoned whatever advantages the old state of things afforded, without receiving any compensation from our present condition; we have destroyed an aristocracy, and we seem inclined to survey its ruins with complacency, and to fix our abode in the midst of them. . . .

Where are we, then?

The religionists are the enemies of liberty, and the friends of liberty attack religion; the high-minded and the noble advocate bondage, and the meanest and most servile preach independence; honest and enlightened citizens are opposed to all progress, whilst men without patriotism and without principle put themselves forward as the apostles of civilization and intelligence. Has such been the fate of the centuries which have preceded our own? and has man always inhabited a world like the present, where all things are out of their natural connections, where virtue is without genius, and genius without honor; where the love of order is confounded with a taste for oppression, and the holy rites of freedom with a contempt of law; where the light thrown by conscience on human actions is dim, and where nothing seems to be any longer forbidden or allowed, honorable or shameful, false or true?

I cannot believe that the Creator made man to leave him in an endless struggle with the intellectual miseries which surround us. God destines a calmer and a more certain future to the communities of Europe. I am ignorant of his designs, but I shall not cease to believe in them because I cannot fathom them, and I had rather mistrust my own capacity than his justice.

There is a country in the world where the great social revolution which I am speaking of seems to have nearly reached its natural limits. It has been effected with ease and quietness; say rather that this country is reaping the fruits of the democratic revolution which we are undergoing, without having had the revolution itself.

The emigrants who colonized the shores of America in the beginning of the seventeenth century somehow separated the democratic principle from all the principles which it had to contend with in the old communities of Europe, and transplanted it alone to the New World. It has there been able to spread in perfect freedom, and peaceably to determine the character of the laws by influencing the manners of the country. . . .

It is not, then, merely to satisfy a legitimate curiosity that I have examined America; my wish has been to find there instruction by which we may ourselves profit. . . .

ADVANTAGES OF DEMOCRACY IN THE UNITED STATES

. . . The defects and weaknesses of a democratic government may readily be discovered; they are demonstrated by flagrant instances, whilst its salutary influence is insensible, and, so to speak, occult. A glance suffices to detect its faults, but its good qualities can be discerned only by long observation. The laws of the American democracy are frequently defective or incomplete; they sometimes attack vested rights, or sanction others which are dangerous to the community; and even if they were good, their frequency would still be a great evil. How comes it, then, that the American republics prosper and continue?. . .

Democratic laws generally tend to promote the welfare of the greatest possible number; for they emanate from the majority of the citizens, who are subject to error, but who cannot have an interest opposed to their own advantage. The laws of an aristocracy tend, on the contrary, to concentrate wealth and power in the hands of the minority; because an aristocracy, by its very nature, constitutes a minority. It may therefore be asserted, as a general proposition, that the purpose of a democracy in its legislation is more useful to humanity than that of an aristocracy. This is, however, the sum total of its advantages.

Aristocracies are infinitely more expert in the science of legislation than democracies ever can be. They are possessed of a self-control which protects them from the errors of temporary excitement; and they form far-reaching designs, which they know how to mature till a favorable opportunity arrives. Aristocratic government proceeds with the dexterity of art; it understands how to make the collective force of all its laws converge at the same time to a given point. Such is not the case with democracies, whose laws are almost always ineffective or inopportune. The means of democracy are therefore more imperfect than those of aristocracy, and the measures which it unwittingly adopts are frequently opposed to its own cause; but the object it has in view is more useful. . . .

In the United States, . . . all parties are willing to recognize the rights of the majority, because they all hope at some time to be able to exercise them to their own advantage. The majority, therefore, in that country, exercise a prodigious actual authority, and a power of opinion which is nearly as great; no obstacles exist which can impede or even retard its progress, so as to make it heed the complaints of those whom it crushes upon its path. This state of things is harmful in itself, and dangerous for the future. . . .

Tyranny of the Majority

I hold it to be an impious and detestable maxim, that, politically speaking, the people have a right to do anything; and yet I have asserted that all authority originates in the will of the majority. Am I, then, in contradiction with myself?

A general law, which bears the name of justice, has been made and sanctioned, not only by a majority of this or that people, but by a majority of mankind. The rights of every people are therefore confined within the limits of what is just. A nation may be considered as a jury which is empowered to represent society at large, and to apply justice, which is its law. . . .

Some have not feared to assert that a people can never outstep the boundaries of justice and reason in those affairs which are peculiarly its own; and that consequently full power may be given to the majority by which they are represented. But this is the language of a slave.

A majority taken collectively is only an individual, whose opinions, and frequently whose interests, are opposed to those of another individual, who is styled a minority. If it be admitted that a man possessing absolute power may misuse that power by wronging his adversaries, why should not a majority be liable to the same reproach? . . .

The form of government which is usually termed *mixed* has always appeared to me a mere chimera. Accurately speaking, there is no such thing as a *mixed government*, in the sense usually given to that word, because, in all communities, some one principle of action may be discovered which preponderates over the others. . . .

I am therefore of opinion, that social power superior to all others must always be placed somewhere; but I think that liberty is endangered when this power finds no obstacle which can retard its course, and give it time to moderate its own vehemence.

Unlimited power is in itself a bad and dangerous thing. Human beings are not competent to exercise it with discretion. God alone can be omnipotent, because his wisdom and his justice are always equal to his power. . . .

In my opinion, the main evil of the present democratic institutions of the United States does not arise, as is often asserted in Europe, from their weakness, but from their irresistible strength. I am not so much alarmed at the excessive liberty which reigns in that country, as at the inadequate securities which one finds there against tyranny.

When an individual or a party is wronged in the United States, to whom can he apply for redress? If to public opinion, public opinion constitutes the majority; if to the legislature, it represents the majority, and implicitly obeys it; if to the executive power, it is appointed by the majority, and serves as a passive tool in the hands. The public force consists of the majority under arms; the jury is the majority invested with the right of hearing judicial cases; and in certain States, even the judges are elected by the majority. However iniquitous or absurd the measure of which you complain, you must submit to it as well as you can. . . .

I do not say that there is a frequent use of tyranny in America, at the present day; but I maintain that there is no sure barrier against it, and that the causes which mitigate the government there are to be found in the circumstances and the manners of the country, more than in its laws. . . .

It is in the examination of the exercise of thought in the United States, that we clearly perceive how far the power of the majority surpasses all the powers with which we are acquainted in Europe. Thought is an invisible and subtile power, that mocks all the efforts of tyranny. At the present time, the most absolute monarchs in Europe cannot prevent certain opinions hostile to their authority from circulating in secret through their dominions, and even in their courts. It is not so in America; as long as the majority is still undecided, discussion is carried on; but as soon as its decision is irrevocably pronounced, every one is silent, and the friends as well as the opponents of the measure unite in assenting to its propriety. The reason of this is perfectly clear: no monarch is so absolute as to combine all the powers of society in his own hands, and to conquer all opposition, as a majority is able to do, which has the right both of making and of executing the laws.

The authority of a king is physical, and controls the actions of men without subduing their will. But the majority possesses a power which is physical and moral at the same time, which acts upon the will as much as upon the actions, and represses not only all contest, but all controversy.

I know of no country in which there is so little independence of mind and real freedom of discussion as in America. In any constitutional state in Europe, every sort of religious and political theory may be freely preached and disseminated. . . . [I]n a nation where democratic institutions exist, organized like those of the United States, there is but one authority, one element of strength and success, with nothing beyond it.

In America, the majority raises formidable barriers around the liberty of opinion: within these barriers, an author may write what he pleases; but woe to him if he goes beyond them. Not that he is in danger of an *auto-da-fé*, but he is exposed to continued obloquy and persecution. His political career is closed forever, since he has offended the only authority which is able to open it. Every sort of compensation, even that of celebrity, is refused to him. Before publishing his opinions, he imagined that he held them in common with others; but no sooner has he declared them, than he is loudly censured by his opponents, whilst those who think like him, without having the courage to speak out, abandon him in silence. He yields at length, overcome by the daily effort which he has to make, and subsides into silence, as if he felt remorse for having spoken the truth.

Fetters and headsmen were the coarse instruments which tyranny formerly employed; but the civilization of our age has perfected despotism itself, though it seemed to have nothing to learn. Monarchs had, so to speak, materialized oppression: the democratic republics of the present day have rendered it as entirely an affair of the mind, as the will which it is intended to coerce. Under the absolute sway of one man, the body was attacked in order to subdue the soul; but the soul escaped the blows which were directed against it, and rose proudly superior. Such is not the course adopted by tyranny in democratic republics; there the body is left free, and the soul is enslaved. The master no longer says, "You shall think as I do, or you shall die"; but he says, "You are free to think differently from me, and to retain your life, your property, and all that you possess; but you are henceforth a stranger among your people. You may retain your civil rights, but they will be useless to you, for you will never be chosen by your fellow-citizens, if you solicit their votes; and they will affect to scorn you, if you ask for their esteem. You will remain among men, but you will be deprived of the rights of mankind. Your fellow-creatures will shun you like an impure being; and even those who believe in your innocence will abandon you, lest they should be shunned in their turn. Go in peace! I have given you your life, but it is an existence worse than death."

Absolute monarchies had dishonored despotism; let us beware lest democratic republics should reinstate it, and render it less odious and degrading in the eyes of the many, by making it still more onerous to the few. . . .

[T]he ruling power in the United States is not to be made game of. The smallest reproach irritates its sensibility, and the slightest joke which has any foundation in truth renders it indignant; from the forms of its language up to the solid virtues of its character, everything must be made the subject of encomium. No writer, whatever be his eminence, can escape paying this tribute of adulation to his fellow-citizens. The majority lives in the perpetual utterance of self-applause; and there are certain truths which the Americans can only learn from strangers or from experience.

If America has not as yet had any great writers, the reason is given in these facts; there can be no literary genius without freedom of opinion, and freedom of opinion does not exist in America. The Inquisition has never been able to prevent a vast number of anti-religious books from circulating in Spain. The empire of the majority succeeds much better in the United States, since it actually removes any wish to publish them. . . .

This irresistible authority is a constant fact, and its judicious exercise is only an accident.

Effects of the Tyranny of the Majority upon the National Character of the Americans

The tendencies which I have just mentioned are as yet but slightly perceptible in political society; but they already exercise an unfavorable influence upon the national character of the Americans. I attribute the small number of distinguished men in political life to the ever-increasing despotism of the majority in the United States.

When the American Revolution broke out, they arose in great numbers; for public opinion then served, not to tyrannize over, but to direct the exertions of individuals. . . .

Democratic republics extend the practice of currying favor with the many, and introduce it into all classes at once: this is the most serious reproach that can be addressed to them. This is especially true in democratic states organized like the American republics, where the power of the majority is so absolute and irresistible that one must give up his rights as a citizen, and almost abjure his qualities as a man, if he intends to stray from the track which it prescribes. . . .

CAUSES WHICH TEND TO MAINTAIN DEMOCRACY

. . . A thousand circumstances, independent of the will of man, facilitate the maintenance of a democratic republic in the United States. . . .

The Americans have no neighbors, and consequently they have no great wars, or financial crises, or inroads, or conquest, to dread; they require neither great taxes, nor large armies, nor great generals; and they have nothing to fear from a scourge which is more formidable to republics than all these evils combined, namely, military glory. It is impossible to deny the inconceivable influence which military glory exercises upon the spirit of a nation. . . .

The Americans had the chances of birth in their favor; and their forefathers imported that equality of condition and of intellect into the country whence the democratic republic has very naturally taken its rise. Nor was this all; for besides this republican condition of society, the early settlers bequeathed to their descendants the customs, manners, and opinions which contribute most to the success of a republic. When I reflect upon the consequences of this primary fact, methinks I see the destiny of America embodied in the first Puritan who landed on those shores, just as the whole human race was represented by the first man.

The chief circumstance which has favored the establishment and the maintenance of a democratic republic in the United States, is the nature of the territory which the Americans inhabit. Their ancestors gave them the love of equality and of freedom; but God himself gave them the means of remaining equal and free, by placing them upon a boundless continent. General prosperity is favorable to the stability of all governments, but more particularly of a democratic one, which depends upon the will of the majority, and especially upon the will of that portion of the community which is most exposed to want. When the people rule, they must be rendered happy. . . .

THE THREE RACES IN THE UNITED STATES

. . . [T]he first in enlightenment, power, and happiness, is the white man, the European, man par excellence; below him come the Negro and the Indian.

These two unlucky races have neither birth, physique, language, nor mores in common; only their misfortunes are alike. Both occupy an equally inferior position in the land where they dwell; both suffer the effects of tyranny, and, though their afflictions are different, they have the same people to blame for them.

Seeing what happens in the world, might one not say that the European is to men of other races what man is to the animals? He makes them serve his convenience, and when he cannot bend them to his will he destroys them. . . .

The Negro has reached the ultimate limits of slavery, whereas the Indian lives on the extreme edge of freedom. The effect of slavery on the former is not more fatal than that of independence on the latter.

The Negro has lost even the ownership of his own body and cannot dispose of his own person without committing a sort of larceny.

But the savage is his own master as soon as he is capable of action. . . . Having nothing but the resources of the wilderness with which to oppose our well-developed arts, undisciplined courage against our tactics, and the spontaneous instincts of his nature against our profound designs, he fails in the unequal contest.

The Negro would like to mingle with the European and cannot. The Indian might to some extent succeed in that, but he scorns to attempt it. The servility of the former delivers him over into slavery; the pride of the latter leads him to death. . . .

When they have abolished slavery, the moderns still have to eradicate three much more intangible and tenacious prejudices: the prejudice of the master, the prejudice of race, and the prejudice of the white.

•   •   •

Turning my attention to the United States of our own day, I plainly
see that in some parts of the country the legal barrier between the two
races is tending to come down, but not that of mores: I see that slavery
is in retreat, but the prejudice from which it arose is immovable.

In that part of the Union where the Negroes are no longer slaves,
have they come closer to the whites? Everyone who has lived in the
United States will have noticed just the opposite.

Race prejudice seems stronger in those states that have abolished
slavery than in those where it still exists, and nowhere is it more intol-
erant than in those states where slavery was never known.

It is true that in the North of the Union the law allows legal mar-
riages between Negroes and whites, but public opinion would regard
a white man married to a Negro woman as disgraced, and it would be
very difficult to quote an example of such an event.

In almost all the states where slavery has been abolished, the Negroes have been given electoral rights, but they would come forward
to vote at the risk of their lives. When oppressed, they can bring an
action at law, but they will find only white men among their judges. It
is true that the laws make them eligible as jurors, but prejudice wards
them off. The Negro's son is excluded from the school to which the
European's child goes. In the theaters he cannot for good money buy
the right to sit by his former master's side; in the hospitals he lies apart.
He is allowed to worship the same God as the white man but must not
pray at the same altars. He has his own clergy and churches. . . .

Perhaps the northern American might have allowed some Negro
woman to be the passing companion of his pleasures, had the legislators declared that she could not hope to share his nuptial bed; but she
can become his wife, and he recoils in horror from her.

Thus it is that in the United States the prejudice rejecting the Negroes seems to increase in proportion to their emancipation, and inequality cuts deep into mores as it is effaced from the laws.

But if the relative position of the two races inhibiting the United
States is as I have described it, why is it that the Americans have abol-

ished slavery in the North of the Union, and why have they kept it in the South and aggravated its rigors?

The answer is easy. In the United States people abolish slavery for the sake not of the Negroes but of the white men. . . . [S]lavery, so cruel to the slave, was fatal to the master.

But the banks of the Ohio provided the final demonstration of this truth.

The stream that the Indians had named the Ohio, or Beautiful River par excellence, waters one of the most magnificent valleys in which man has ever lived. On both banks of the Ohio stretched undulating ground with soil continually offering the cultivator inexhaustible treasures; on both banks the air is equally healthy and the climate temperate. . . . There is only one difference between the two states: Kentucky allows slaves, but Ohio refuses to have them.

So the traveler who lets the current carry him down the Ohio till it joins the Mississippi sails, so to say, between freedom and slavery; and he has only to glance around him to see instantly which is best for mankind.

On the left bank of the river the population is sparse; from time to time one sees a troop of slaves loitering through half-deserted fields; the primeval forest is constantly reappearing; one might say that society had gone to sleep; it is nature that seems active and alive, whereas man is idle.

But on the right bank a confused hum proclaims from afar that men are busily at work; fine crops cover the fields; elegant dwellings testify to the taste and industry of the workers; on all sides there is evidence of comfort; man appears rich and contented; he works. . . .

The influence of slavery extends even further, penetrating the master's soul and giving a particular turn to his ideas and tastes.

On both banks of the Ohio live people with characters by nature enterprising and energetic, but these common characteristics are turned to different use on one side and the other.

The white man on the right bank, forced to live by his own endeavors, has made material well-being the main object of his existence; as he lives in a country offering inexhaustible resources to his industry and continual inducements to activity, his eagerness to possess things goes beyond the ordinary limits of human cupidity; tormented by a longing for wealth, he boldly follows every path to fortune that is open to him; he is equally prepared to turn into a sailor, pioneer, artisan, or cultivator, facing the labors or dangers of these various ways of life with even constancy; there is something wonderful in his resourcefulness and a sort of heroism in his greed for gain.

The American on the left bank scorns not only work itself but also enterprises in which work is necessary to success; living in idle ease, he has the tastes of idle men; money has lost some of its value in his eyes; he is less interested in wealth than in excitement and pleasure and expends in that direction the energy which his neighbor puts to other use; he is passionately fond of hunting and war; he enjoys all the most strenuous forms of bodily exercise; he is accustomed to the use of weapons and from childhood has been ready to risk his life in single combat . . . he is passionately fond of hunting and war.

• • •

We have seen that slavery, which is abolished in the North, still exists in the South, and I have traced its fatal influence on the well-being of the master himself.

Trade and industry are bound to flourish more in the North than in the South. It is natural that both population and wealth should pile up there more quickly. . . .

It is difficult to conceive of a lasting relation between two peoples, one of whom is poor and weak, the other rich and strong, even if it is proved that the strength and wealth of the one are in no way the cause of the weakness and poverty of the other. The Union is even harder to maintain at a time when the one is gaining the strength which the other is losing. . . .

The weak seldom have confidence in the justice and reasonableness of the strong. States which are growing comparatively slowly therefore look with jealous distrust on fortune's favorites. That is the reason for the deep uneasiness and vague restlessness which one notices in one part of the Union, in contrast to the well-being and confidence prevailing in the other. I think there are no other reasons for the hostile attitude of the South.

Of all Americans the southerners are those who ought to be most attached to the Union, for it is they who would suffer most if left to themselves; nevertheless, they alone threaten to break the federal bond. Why is that so? The answer is easy: the South, which provided the Union with four Presidents, which now knows that federal power is slipping from it, which yearly sees its number of representatives in Congress falling and that of the North and West rising—the South, whose men are ardent and irascible, is getting angry and restless. It turns its melancholy gaze inward and back to the past, perpetually fancying that it may be suffering oppression. . . .

Hence the greatest danger threatening the United States springs from its very prosperity, for in some of the confederate states it brings that intoxication which goes with sudden access of fortune, and in others it brings the envy, distrust, and regrets which most often follow where it is lost. . . .

RESTLESSNESS IN THE MIDST OF PROSPERITY

. . . In America I have seen the freest and best educated of men in circumstances the happiest to be found in the world; yet it seemed to me that a cloud habitually hung on their brow, and they seemed serious and almost sad even in their pleasures. . . . [T]he latter never stop thinking of the good things they have not got.

It is odd to watch with what feverish ardor the Americans pursue prosperity and how they are ever tormented by the shadowy suspicion that they may not have chosen the shortest route to get it.

Americans cleave to the things of this world as if assured that they will never die, and yet are in such a rush to snatch any that come within their reach, as if expecting to stop living before they have relished them. They clutch everything but hold nothing fast, and so lose grip as they hurry after some new delight.

An American will build a house in which to pass his old age and sell it before the roof is on; he will plant a garden and rent it just as the trees are coming into bearing; he will clear a field and leave others to reap the harvest; he will take up a profession and leave it, settle in one place and soon go off elsewhere with his changing desires. If his private business allows him a moment's relaxation, he will plunge at once into the whirlpool of politics. . . .

Add to this taste for prosperity a social state in which neither law nor custom holds anyone in one place, and that is a great further stimulus to this restlessness of temper. One will then find people continually changing path for fear of missing the shortest cut leading to happiness. . . .

When all prerogatives of birth and fortune are abolished, when all professions are open to all and a man's own energies may bring him to the top of any of them, an ambitious man may think it easy to launch on a great career and feel that he is called to no common destiny. But that is a delusion which experience quickly corrects. The same equality which allows each man to entertain vast hopes makes each man by himself weak. His power is limited on every side, though his longings may wander where they will. . . .

One can imagine men who have found a degree of liberty completely satisfactory to them. In that case they will enjoy their independence without anxiety or excitement. But men will never establish an equality which will content them. . . .

RELIGION IN DEMOCRACY

. . . [T]his great utility of religions is still more obvious amongst nations where equality of conditions prevails, than amongst others. It must be acknowledged that equality, which brings great benefits into the world, nevertheless suggests to men . . . some very dangerous propensities. It tends to isolate them from each other, to concentrate every man's attention upon himself; and it lays open the soul to an inordinate love of material gratification. The greatest advantage of religion is to inspire diametrically contrary principles. There is no religion which does not place the object of man's desires above and beyond the treasures of earth, and which does not naturally raise his soul to regions far above those of the senses. Nor is there any which does not impose on man some duties toward his kind, and thus draw him at times from the contemplation of himself. This occurs in religions the most false and dangerous.

Religious nations are therefore naturally strong on the very point on which democratic nations are weak, which shows of what importance it is for men to preserve their religion as their conditions become more equal. . . .

. . . [R]eligions ought . . . to confine themselves within their own precincts; for in seeking to extend their power beyond religious matters, they incur a risk of not being believed at all. The circle within which they seek to restrict the human intellect ought therefore to be carefully traced, and, beyond its verge, the mind should be left entirely free to its own guidance. . . .

. . . [T]he principle opinions which constitute a creed, and which theologians call articles of faith, must be very carefully distinguished from the accessories connected with them. Religions are obliged to hold fast to the former, whatever be the peculiar spirit of the age; but they should take good care not to bind themselves in the same manner to the latter, at a time when everything is in transition, and when the mind, accustomed to the moving pageant of human affairs, reluctantly allows itself to be fixed on any point. The fixity of eternal and secondary things can afford a chance of duration only when civil society is itself fixed; under any other circumstances, I hold it to be perilous.

We shall see that, of all the passions which originate in or are fostered by equality, there is one which it renders peculiarly intense, and which it also infuses into the heart of every man,—I mean the love of well-being. The taste for well-being is the prominent and indelible feature of democratic times.

It may be believed that a religion which should undertake to destroy so deep-seated a passion, would in the end be destroyed by it; and if it attempted to wean men entirely from the contemplation of the good things of this world, in order to devote their faculties exclusively to the thought of another, it may be foreseen that the minds of men would at length escape its grasp, to plunge into the exclusive enjoyment of present and material pleasures. The chief concern of religion is to purify, to regulate, and to restrain the excessive and exclusive taste for well-being which men feel at periods of equality; but it would be an error to attempt to overcome it completely, or to eradicate it. Men cannot be cured of the love of riches; but they may be persuaded to enrich themselves by none but honest means.

This brings me to a final consideration, which comprises, as it were, all the others. The more the conditions of men are equalized and assimilated to each other, the more important is it for religion; whilst it carefully abstains from the daily turmoil of secular affairs, not needlessly to run counter to the ideas which generally prevail, or to the permanent interests which exist in the mass of the people. . . .

I showed in my former volume how the American clergy stand aloof from secular affairs. . . . [H]e leaves men to themselves, and surrenders them to the independence and instability which belong to their nature and their age. I have seen no country in which Christianity is clothed with fewer forms, figures, and observances than in the United States; or where it presents more distinct, simple, and general notions to the mind. Although the Christians of America are divided into a multitude of sects, they all look upon their religion in the same light. This applies to Roman Catholicism as well as to the other forms of belief. There are no Romish priests who show less taste for the minute individual observances, for extraordinary or peculiar means of salvation, or who cling more to the spirit, and less to the letter, of the law, than the Roman Catholic priests of the United States. Nowhere is that doctrine of the Church which prohibits the worship reserved to God alone from being offered to the saints, more clearly inculcated or more generally followed. Yet the Roman Catholics of America are very submissive and very sincere.

Another remark is applicable to the clergy of every communion. The American ministers of the Gospel do not attempt to draw or to fix all the thoughts of man upon the life to come; they are willing to surrender a portion of his heart to the cares of the present; seeming to consider the goods of this world as important, though secondary, objects. If they take no part themselves in productive labor, they are at least interested in its progress, and they applaud its results; and whilst they never cease to point to the other world as the great object of the hopes and fears of the believer, they do not forbid him honestly to court prosperity in this. Far from attempting to show that these things are distinct and contrary to one another, they study rather to find out on what point they are most nearly and closely connected.

All the American clergy know and respect the intellectual supremacy exercised by the majority: they never sustain any but necessary conflicts with it. . . .

America is the most democratic country in the world, and it is at the same time (according to reports worthy of belief) the country in which the Roman Catholic religion makes most progress. . . .

Nor is this difficult of explanation. The men of our days are naturally little disposed to believe; but, as soon as they have any religion, they immediately find in themselves a latent instinct which urges them unconsciously towards Catholicism. Many of the doctrines and practices of the Romish Church astonish them; but they feel a secret admiration for its discipline, and its great unity attracts them. If Catholicism could at length withdraw itself from the political animosities to which it has given rise, I have hardly any doubt but that the same spirit of the age which appears to be so opposed to it would become so favorable as to admit of its great and sudden advancement. . . .

EQUALITY SUGGESTS TO THE AMERICANS THE IDEA OF THE INDEFINITE PERFECTIBILITY OF MAN.

. . . In proportion as castes disappear and the classes of society approximate,—as manners, customs, and laws vary, from the tumultuous intercourse of men,—as new facts arise,—as new truths are brought to light,—as ancient opinions are dissipated, and others take their place,—the image of an ideal but always fugitive perfection presents itself to the human mind. Continual changes are then every instant occurring under the observation of every man: the position of some is rendered worse; and he learns but too well that no people and no individual, how enlightened soever they may be, can lay claim to infallibility: the condition of others is improved; whence he infers that man is endowed with an indefinite faculty of improvement. His reverses teach him that none have discovered absolute good,—his success stimulates him to the never-ending pursuit of it. Thus, forever seeking, forever falling to rise again,—often disappointed, but not discouraged,—he tends unceasingly towards that unmeasured greatness so indistinctly visible at the end of the long track which humanity has yet to tread. . . .

I accost an American sailor, and inquire why the ships of his country are built so as to last but for a short time; he answers without hesitation, that the art of navigation is every day making such rapid progress, that the finest vessel would become almost useless if it lasted beyond a few years. In these words, which fell accidentally, and on a particular subject, from an uninstructed man, I recognize the general and systematic idea upon which a great people direct all their concerns.

Aristocratic nations are naturally too apt to narrow the scope of human perfectibility; democratic nations, to expand it beyond reason. . . .

HISTORY IN DEMOCRACY

. . . In aristocratic ages, as the attention of historians is constantly drawn to individuals, the connection of events escapes them; or, rather, they do not believe in any such connection. To them, the clew of history seems every instant crossed and broken by the step of man. In democratic ages, on the contrary, as the historian sees much more of actions than of actors, he may easily establish some kind of sequence and methodical order amongst the former. . . .

Historians who live in democratic ages, then, not only deny that the few have any power of acting upon the destiny of a people, but they deprive the people themselves of the power of modifying their own condition, and they subject them either to an inflexible Providence or to some blind necessity. According to them, each nation is indissolubly bound by its position, its origin, its antecedents, and its character, to a certain lot which no efforts can ever change. . . .

In perusing the historical volumes which our age has produced, it would seem that man is utterly powerless over himself and over all around him. The historians of antiquity taught how to command: those of our time teach only how to obey; in their writings the author often appears great, but humanity is always diminutive. . . .

Our contemporaries are but too prone to doubt of human free-will, because each of them feels himself confined on every side by his own weakness; but they are still willing to acknowledge the strength and independence of men united in society. Let not this principle be lost sight of; for the great object in our time is to raise the faculties of men, not to complete their prostration. . . .

OF INDIVIDIALISM IN DEMOCRATIC COUNTRIES

I have shown how it is that, in ages of equality, every man seeks for his opinions within himself: I am now to show how it is that, in the same ages, all his feelings are turned towards himself alone. *Individualism* is a novel expression, to which a novel idea has given birth. Our fathers were only acquainted with *égoïsme* (selfishness). Selfishness is a passionate and exaggerated love of self, which leads a man to connect everything with himself, and to prefer himself to everything in the world. Individualism is a mature and calm feeling, which disposes each member of the community to sever himself from the mass of his fellows, and to draw apart with his family and his friends; so that, after he has thus formed a little circle of his own, he willingly leaves society at large to itself. Selfishness originates in blind instinct: individualism proceeds from erroneous judgment more than from depraved feelings; it originates as much in deficiencies of mind as in perversity of heart.

Selfishness blights the germ of all virtue: individualism, at first, only saps the virtues of public life; but, in the long run, it attacks and destroys all others, and is at length absorbed in downright selfishness. Selfishness is a vice as old as the world, which does not belong to one form of society more than to another: individualism is of democratic origin, and it threatens to spread in the same ratio as the equality of condition.

Amongst aristocratic nations, as families remain for centuries in the same condition, often on the same spot, all generations become, as it were, contemporaneous. A man almost always knows his forefathers, and respects them: he thinks he already sees his remote descendants, and he loves them. . . . Aristocratic institutions have, moreover, the effect of closely binding every man to several of his fellow-citizens. As the classes of an aristocratic people are strongly marked and permanent, each of them is regarded by its own members as a sort of lesser country, more tangible and more cherished than the country at large. As, in aristocratic communities, all the citizens occupy fixed positions, one above the other, the result is, that each of them always sees a man above himself whose patronage is necessary to him, and, below himself, another man whose co-operation he may claim. . . .

Amongst democratic nations, new families are constantly springing up, others are constantly falling away, and all that remain change their condition; the woof of time is every instant broken, and the track of generations effaced. Those who went before are soon forgotten; of those who will come after, no one has any idea: the interest of man is confined to those in close propinquity to himself. As each class approximates to other classes, and intermingles with them, its members become indifferent, and as strangers to one another. Aristocracy had made a chain of all the members of the community, from the peasant to the king: democracy breaks that chain, and severs every link of it.

As social conditions become more equal, the number of persons increases who, although they are neither rich nor powerful enough to exercise any great influence over their fellows, have nevertheless acquired or retained sufficient education and fortune to satisfy their own wants. They owe nothing to any man, they expect nothing from any man; they acquire the habit of always considering themselves as standing alone, and they are apt to imagine that their whole destiny is in their own hands.

Thus, not only does democracy make every man forget his ancestors, but it hides his descendants and separates his contemporaries from him; it throws him back forever upon himself alone, and threatens in the end to confine him entirely within the solitude of his own heart.

THAT THE AMERICANS COMBAT THE EFFECTS OF INDIVIDUALISM BY FREE INSTITUTIONS

. . . Equality places men side by side, unconnected by any common tie; despotism raises barriers to keep them asunder: the former predisposes them not to consider their fellow-creatures, the latter makes general indifference a sort of public virtue.

Despotism, then, which is at all times dangerous, is more particularly to be feared in democratic ages. It is easy to see that in those same ages men stand most in need of freedom. When the members of a community are forced to attend to public affairs, they are necessarily drawn from the circle of their own interests, and snatched at times from self-observation. As soon as a man begins to treat of public affairs in public, he begins to perceive that he is not so independent of his fellow-men as he had at first imagined, and that, in order to obtain their support, he must often lend them his co-operation.

When the public govern, there is no man who does not feel the value of public good-will, or who does not endeavor to court it by drawing to himself the esteem and affection of those amongst whom he is to live. Many of the passions which congeal and keep asunder human hearts, are then obliged to retire and hide below the surface. Pride must be dissembled; disdain dares not break out; selfishness fears its own self. . . .

It is difficult to draw a man out of his own circle to interest him in the destiny of the state, because he does not clearly understand what influence the destiny of the state can have upon his own lot. But if it be proposed to make a road cross the end of his estate, he will see at a glance that there is a connection between this small public affair and his greatest private affairs; and he will discover, without its being shown to him, the close tie which unites private to general interest. Thus, far more may be done by intrusting to the citizens the administration of minor affairs by then surrendering to them the control of important ones, towards interesting them in the public welfare, and convincing them that they constantly stand in need one of another in order to provide for it. A brilliant achievement may win for you the favor of a people at one stroke; but to earn the love and respect of the population which surrounds you, a long succession of little services rendered and of obscure good deeds,— a constant habit of kindness, and an established reputation for disinterestedness,—will be required. Local freedom, then, which leads a great number of citizens to value the affection of their neighbors and of their kindred, perpetually brings men together, and forces them to help one another, in spite of the propensities which sever them.

In the United States, the more opulent citizens take great care not to stand aloof from the people; on the contrary, they constantly keep on easy terms with the lower classes: they listen to them, they speak to them every day. They know that the rich in democracies always stand in need of the poor; and that, in democratic times, you attach a poor man to you more by your manner than by benefits conferred....

The best-informed inhabitants of each district constantly use their information to discover new truths which may augment the general prosperity; and, if they have made any such discoveries, they eagerly surrender them to the mass of the people.

When the vices and weaknesses frequently exhibited by those who govern in America are closely examined, the prosperity of the people occasions, but improperly occasions, surprise. Elected magistrates do not make the American democracy flourish; it flourishes because the magistrates are elective.

It would be unjust to suppose that the patriotism and the zeal which every American displays for the welfare of his fellow-citizens are wholly insincere. Although private interest directs the greater part of human actions in the United States, as well as elsewhere, it does not regulate them all. I must say that I have often seen Americans make great and real sacrifices to the public welfare; and I have remarked a hundred instances in which they hardly ever failed to lend faithful support to each other. The free institutions which the inhabitants of the United States possess, and the political rights of which they make so much use, remind every citizen, and in a thousand ways, that he lives in society. They every instant impress upon his mind the notion that it is the duty, as well as the interest, of men to make themselves useful to their fellow-creatures; and as he sees no particular ground of animosity to them, since he is never either their master or their slave, his heart readily leans to the side of kindness. Men attend to the interests of the public, first by necessity, afterwards by choice: what was intentional becomes an instinct; and by dint of working for the good of one's fellow-citizens, the habit and the taste for serving them is at length acquired....

OF THE USE WHICH AMERICANS MAKE OF PUBLIC ASSOCIATIONS IN CIVIL LIFE

. . . [A]ssociations only which are formed in civil life, without reference to political objects, are here adverted to. The political associations which exist in the United States are only a single feature in the midst of the immense assemblage of associations in that country. Americans of all ages, all conditions, and all dispositions, constantly form associations. They have not only commercial and manufacturing companies, in which all take part, but associations of a thousand other kinds,—religious, moral, serious, futile, general or restricted, enormous or diminutive. The Americans make associations to give entertainments, to found seminaries, to build inns, to construct churches, to diffuse books, to send missionaries to the antipodes; they found in this manner hospitals, prisons, and schools. If it be proposed to inculcate some truth, or to foster some feeling by the encouragement of a great example, they form a society. Wherever, at the head of some new undertaking, you see the government in France, or a man of rank in England, in the United States you will be sure to find an association. . . .

Thus, the most democratic country on the face of the earth is that in which men have, in our time, carried to the highest perfection the art of pursuing in common the object of their common desires, and have applied this new science to the greatest number of purposes. Is this the result of accident? or is there in reality any necessary connection between the principle of association and that of equality? . . .

Amongst democratic nations, . . . all the citizens are independent and feeble; they can do hardly anything by themselves, and none of them can oblige his fellow-men to lend him their assistance. They all, therefore, become powerless, if they do not learn voluntarily to help each other. If men living in democratic countries had no right and no inclination to associate for political purposes, their independence would be in great jeopardy but they might long preserve their wealth and their cultivation: whereas, if they never acquired the habit of forming associations in ordinary life, civilization itself would be endangered. A people amongst whom individuals should lose the power of achieving great things single-handed, without acquiring the means of producing them by united exertions, would soon relapse into barbarism. . . .

As soon as several of the inhabitants of the United States have taken up an opinion or a feeling which they wish to promote in the world, they look out for mutual assistance; and as soon as they have found each other out, they combine. From that moment they are no longer isolated men, but a power seen from afar, whose actions serve for an example, and whose language is listened to. The first time I heard in the United States that a hundred thousand men had bound themselves publicly to abstain from spirituous liquors, it appeared to me more like a joke than a serious engagement; and I did not at once perceive why these temperate citizens could not content themselves with drinking water by their own firesides. I at last understood that these hundred thousand Americans, alarmed by the progress of drunkenness around them, had made up their minds to patronize temperance. . . .

In democratic countries, the science of association is the mother of science; the progress of all the rest depends upon the progress it has made. . . . [A] stranger is constantly amazed by the immense public works executed by a nation which contains, so to speak, no rich men. The Americans arrived but as yesterday on the territory which they inhabit, and they have already changed the whole order of nature for their own advantage. They have joined the Hudson to the Mississippi, and made the Atlantic Ocean communicate with the Gulf of Mexico, across a continent of more than five hundred leagues in extent which separates the two seas. The longest railroads which have been constructed, up to the present time, are in America.

But what most astonishes me in the United States is not so much the marvellous grandeur of some undertakings, as the innumerable multitude of small ones. Almost all the farmers of the United States combine some trade with agriculture; most of them make agriculture itself a trade. It seldom happens that an American farmer settles for good upon the land which he occupies: especially in the districts of the Far West, he brings land into tillage in order to sell it again, and not to farm it: he builds a farm-house on the speculation, that, as the state of the country will soon be changed by the increase of population, a good price may be obtained for it. . . .

As they are all more or less engaged in productive industry, at the least shock given to business, all private fortunes are put in jeopardy at the same time, and the state is shaken. I believe that the return of these commercial panics is an endemic disease of the democratic nations of our age. It may be rendered less dangerous, but it cannot be cured; because it does not originate in accidental circumstances, but in the temperament of these nations.

HOW AN ARISTOCRACY MAY BE CREATED BY MANUFACTURES

I have shown how democracy favors the growth of manufactures, and increases without limit the numbers of the manufacturing classes: we shall now see by what side-road manufacturers may possibly, in their turn, bring men back to aristocracy.

It is acknowledged, that, when a workman is engaged every day upon the same details, the whole commodity is produced with greater ease, promptitude, and economy. It is likewise acknowledged, that the cost of production of manufactured goods is diminished by the extent of the establishment in which they are made, and by the amount of capital employed or of credit. These truths had long been imperfectly discerned, but in our time they have been demonstrated. They have been already applied to many very important kinds of manufactures, and the humblest will gradually be governed by them. I know of nothing in politics which deserves to fix the attention of the legislator more closely than these two new axioms of the science of manufactures.

When a workman is unceasingly and exclusively engaged in the fabrication of one thing, he ultimately does his work with singular dexterity; but, at the same time, he loses the general faculty of applying his mind to the direction of the work. He every day becomes more adroit and less industrious; so that it may be said of him, that, in proportion as the workman improves, the man is degraded. What can be expected of a man who has spent twenty years of his life in making heads for pins? and to what can that mighty human intelligence, which has so often stirred the world, be applied in him, except it be to investigate the best method of making pins' heads? When a workman has spent a considerable portion of his existence in this manner, his thoughts are forever set upon the object of his daily toil; his body has contracted certain fixed habits, which it can never shake off: in a word, he no longer belongs to himself, but to the calling which he has chosen. It is in vain that laws and manners have been at pains to level all the barriers round such a man, and to open to him on every side a thousand different paths to fortune; a theory of manufactures more powerful than manners and laws binds him to a craft, and frequently to a spot, which he cannot leave: it assigns him to a certain place in society, beyond which he cannot go: in the midst of universal movement, it has rendered him stationary. . . .

Thus, at the very time at which the science of manufactures lowers the class of workmen, it raises the class of masters. . . . The master and the workman have then here no similarity, and their differences increase every day. They are only connected as the two rings at the extremities of a long chain. Each of them fills the station which is made for him, and which he does not leave: the one is continually, closely, and necessarily dependent upon the other, and seems as much born to obey, as that other is to command. What is this but aristocracy?

As the conditions of men constituting the nation become more and more equal, the demand for manufactured commodities becomes more general and extensive; and the cheapness which places these objects within the reach of slender fortunes becomes a great element of success. Hence, there are every day more men of great opulence and education who devote their wealth and knowledge to manufactures; and who seek, by opening large establishments, and by a strict division of labor, to meet the fresh demands which are made on all sides. Thus, in proportion as the mass of the nation turns to democracy, that particular class which is engaged in manufactures becomes more aristocratic. Men grow more alike in the one, more different in the other; and inequality increases in the less numerous class, in the same ratio in which it decreases in the community. Hence it would appear, on searching to the bottom, that aristocracy should naturally spring out of the bosom of democracy.

But this kind of aristocracy by no means resembles those kinds which preceded it. . . . To say the truth, though there are rich men, the class of rich men does not exist; for these rich individuals have no feelings or purposes in common, no mutual traditions or mutual hopes; there are individuals, therefore, but no definite class.

Not only are the rich not compactly united amongst themselves, but there is no real bond between them and the poor. Their relative position is not a permanent one; they are constantly drawn together or separated by their interests. The workman is generally dependent on the master, but not on any particular master: these two men meet in the factory, but know not each other elsewhere; and whilst they come into contact on one point, they stand very wide apart on all others. The manufacturer asks nothing of the workman but his labor; the workman expects nothing from him but his wages. The one contracts no obligation to protect, nor the other to defend; and they are not permanently connected either by habit or duty. . . .

. . . [T]he manufacturing aristocracy of our age first impoverishes and debases the men who serve it, and then abandons them to be supported by the charity of the public. This is a natural consequence of what has been said before. Between the workman and the master there are frequent relations, but no real association.

I am of opinion, upon the whole, that the manufacturing aristocracy which is growing up under our eyes is one of the harshest which ever existed in the world; but, at the same time, it is one of the most confined and least dangerous. Nevertheless, the friends of democracy should keep their eyes anxiously fixed in this direction; for if ever a permanent inequality of conditions and aristocracy again penetrate into the world, it may be predicted that this is the gate by which they will enter.

from SELF-RELIANCE

Ralph Waldo Emerson

There is a time in every man's education when he arrives at the conviction that envy is ignorance; that imitation is suicide; that he must take himself for better, for worse, as his portion; that though the wide universe is full of good, no kernel of nourishing corn can come to him but through his toil bestowed on that plot of ground which is given to him to till. . . .

Trust thyself: every heart vibrates to that iron string. Accept the place the divine providence has found for you, the society of your contemporaries, the connection of events. Great men have always done so, and confided themselves childlike to the genius of their age, betraying their perception that the absolutely trustworthy was seated at their heart, working through their hands, predominating in all their being. And we are now men, and must accept in the highest mind the same transcendent destiny; and not minors and invalids in a protected corner, not cowards fleeing before a revolution, but guides, redeemers, and benefactors, obeying the Almighty effort, and advancing on Chaos and the Dark.

What pretty oracles nature yields us on this text, in the face and behavior of children, babes, and even brutes! That divided and rebel mind, that distrust of a sentiment because our arithmetic has computed the strength and means opposed to our purpose, these have not. Their mind being whole, their eye is as yet unconquered, and when we look in their faces we are disconcerted. Infancy conforms to nobody: all conform to it, so that one babe commonly makes four or five out of the adults who prattle and play to it. So God has armed youth and puberty and manhood no less with its own piquancy and charm, and made it enviable and gracious and its claims not to be put by, if it will stand by itself. Do not think the youth has no force, because he cannot speak to you and me. Hark! in the next room his voice is sufficiently clear and emphatic. It seems he knows how to speak to his contemporaries.

Bashful or bold, then, he will know how to make us seniors very unnecessary.

The nonchalance of boys who are sure of a dinner, and would disdain as much as a lord to do or say aught to conciliate one, is the healthy attitude of human nature. A boy is in the parlor what the pit is in the playhouse; independent, irresponsible, looking out from his corner on such people and facts as pass by, he tries and sentences them on their merits, in the swift, summary way of boys, as good, bad, interesting, silly, eloquent, troublesome. He cumbers himself never about consequences, about interests: he gives an independent, genuine verdict. You must court him: he does not court you. But the man is, as it were, clapped into jail by his consciousness. . . .

Society everywhere is in conspiracy against the manhood of every one of its members. Society is a joint-stock company, in which the members agree, for the better securing of his bread to each shareholder, to surrender the liberty and culture of the eater. The virtue in most request is conformity. Self-reliance is its aversion. It loves not realities and creators, but names and customs.

Whoso would be a man must be a nonconformist. He who would gather immortal palms must not be hindered by the name of goodness, but must explore if it be goodness. Nothing is at last sacred but the integrity of your own mind. Absolve you to yourself, and you shall have the suffrage of the world. I remember an answer which when quite young I was prompted to make a valued adviser, who was wont to importune me with the dear old doctrines of the church. On my saying, What have I to do with the sacredness of traditions, if I live wholly from within? my friend suggested: "But these impulses may be from below, not from above." I replied: "They do not seem to me to be such; but if I am the Devil's child, I will live then from the Devil." No law can be sacred to me but that of my nature. Good and bad are but names very readily transferable to that or this; the only right is what is after my constitution, the only wrong what is against it. . . . If an angry bigot assumes this bountiful cause of Abolition, and comes to me with his last news from Barbadoes, why should I not say to him: "Go love thy infant; love thy woodchopper: be good-natured and modest: have that grace; and never varnish your hard, uncharitable ambition with this incredible tenderness for black folk a thousand miles off. Thy love afar is spite at home." Rough and graceless would be such greeting, but truth is handsomer than the affectation of love. Your goodness must have some edge to it,—else it is none. The doctrine of hatred must be preached as the counteraction of the doctrine of love when that pules and whines. I shun father and mother and wife and brother, when my genius calls me. I would write on the lintels of the door-post, *Whim*. I hope it is somewhat better than whim at last, but we cannot spend the day in explanation. Expect me not to show cause why I seek or why I exclude company. Then, again, do not tell me, as a good man did to-day, of my obligation to put all poor men in good situations. Are they *my* poor? I tell thee, thou foolish philanthropist, that I grudge the dollar, the dime, the cent, I give to such men as do not belong to me and to whom I do not belong. There is a class of persons to whom by all spiritual affinity I am bought and sold; for them I will go to prison, if need be; but your miscellaneous popular charities; the education at college of fools; the building of meeting-houses to the vain end to which many now stand; alms to sots; and the thousandfold Belief Societies;—though I confess with shame I sometimes succumb and give the dollar, it is a wicked dollar which by and by I shall have the manhood to withhold.

• • •

What I must do is all that concerns me, not what the people think. This rule, equally arduous in actual and in intellectual life, may serve for the whole distinction between greatness and meanness. It is the harder, because you will always find those who think they know what is your duty better than you know it. It is easy in the world to live after the world's opinion; it is easy in solitude to live after our own; but the great man is he who in the midst of the crowd keeps with perfect sweetness the independence of solitude. . . .

For non-conformity the world whips you with its displeasure. And therefore a man must know how to estimate a sour face. The bystanders look askance on him in the public street or in the friend's parlor. If this aversation had its origin in contempt and resistance like his own, he might well go home with a sad countenance; but the sour faces of the multitude, like their sweet faces, have no deep cause, but are put on and off as the wind blows and a newspaper directs. Yet is the discontent of the multitude more formidable than that of the senate and the college? It is easy enough for a firm man who knows the world to brook the rage of the cultivated classes. Their rage is decorous and prudent, for they are timid as being very vulnerable themselves. But when to their feminine rage the indignation of the people is added, when the ignorant and the poor are aroused, when the unintelligent brute force that lies at the bottom of society is made to growl and mow, it needs the habit of magnanimity and religion to treat it godlike as a trifle of no concernment.

The other terror that scares us from self-trust is our consistency; a reverence for our past act or word, because the eyes of others have no other data for computing our orbit than our past acts, and we are loath to disappoint them.

But why should you keep your head over your shoulder? Why drag about this corpse of your memory, lest you contradict somewhat you have stated in this or that public place? . . .

A foolish consistency is the hobgoblin of little minds, adored by little statesmen and philosophers and divines. With consistency a great soul has simply nothing to do. He may as well concern himself with his shadow on the wall. Speak what you think now in hard words and to-morrow speak what to-morrow thinks in hard words again, though it contradict everything you said to-day.—"Ah, so you shall be sure to be misunderstood?"—Is it so bad, then, to be misunderstood? Pythagoras was misunderstood, and Socrates, and Jesus, and Luther, and Copernicus, and Galileo, and Newton, and every pure and wise spirit that ever took flesh. To be great is to be misunderstood.

I suppose no man can violate his nature. All the sallies of his will are rounded in by the law of his being, as the inequalities of Andes and Himmaleh are insignificant in the curve of the sphere. Nor does it matter how you gauge and try him. A character is like an acrostic or Alexandrian stanza;—read it forward, backward, or across, it still spells the same thing. In this pleasing, contrite wood-life which God allows me, let me record day by day my honest thought without prospect or retrospect, and, I cannot doubt, it will be found symmetrical, though I mean it not and see it not. My book should smell of pines and resound with the hum of insects. The swallow over my window should interweave that thread or straw he carries in his bill into my web also. We pass for what we are. Character teaches above our wills. Men imagine that they communicate their virtue or vice only by overt actions, and do not see that virtue or vice emit a breath every moment.

There will be an agreement in whatever variety of actions, so they be each honest and natural in their hour. . . .

Is the acorn better than the oak which is its fulness and completion? Is the parent better than the child into whom he has cast his ripened being? Whence, then, this worship of the past? The centuries are conspirators against the sanity and authority of the soul. Time and space are but physiological colors which the eye makes, but the soul is light; where it is, is day; where it was, is night; and history is an impertinence and an injury, if it be anything more than a cheerful apologue or parable of my being and becoming.

Man is timid and apologetic; he is no longer upright; he dares not say "I think," "I am," but quotes some saint or sage. He is ashamed before the blade of grass or the blowing rose. These roses under my window make no reference to former roses or to better ones; they are for what they are; they exist with God to-day. There is no time to them. There is simply the rose; it is perfect in every moment of its existence. Before a leaf-bud has burst, its whole life acts; in the full-blown flower there is no more; in the leafless root there is no less. Its nature is satisfied, and it satisfies nature, in all moments alike. But man postpones or remembers; he does not live in the present, but with reverted eye laments the past, or, heedless of the riches that surround him, stands on tiptoe to foresee the future. He cannot be happy and strong until he too lives with nature in the present, above time.

. . . If we live truly, we shall see truly. It is as easy for the strong man to be strong, as it is for the weak to be weak. When we have new perception, we shall gladly disburden the memory of its hoarded treasures as old rubbish. When a man lives with God, his voice shall be as sweet as the murmur of the brook and the rustle of the corn. . . .

If we cannot at once rise to the sanctities of obedience and faith, let us at least resist our temptations; let us enter into the state of war, and wake Thor and Woden, courage and constancy in our Saxon breasts. This is to be done in our smooth times by speaking the truth. Check this lying hospitality and lying affection. Live no longer to the expectation of these deceived and deceiving people with whom we converse. Say to them, "O father, O mother, O wife, O brother, O friend, I have lived with you after appearances hitherto. Henceforward I am the truth's. Be it known unto you that henceforward I obey no law less than the eternal law. I will have no convenants but proximities. I shall endeavor to nourish my parents, to support my family, to be the chaste husband of one wife,—but these relations I must fill after a new and unprecedented way. I appeal from your customs. I must be myself. I cannot break myself any longer for you, or you. If you can love me for what I am, we shall be the happier. If you cannot, I will still seek to deserve that you should. I will not hide my tastes or aversions. I will so trust that what is deep is holy, that I will do strongly before the sun and moon whatever inly rejoices me, and the heart appoints. If you are noble, I will love you; if you are not, I will not hurt you and myself by hypocritical attentions. If you are true, but not in the same truth with me, cleave to your companions; I will seek my own. I do this not selfishly, but humbly and truly. It is alike your interest, and mine, and all men's, however long we have dwelt in lies, to live in truth. Does this sound harsh to-day? You will soon love what is dictated by your nature as well as mine, and, if we follow the truth, it will bring us out safe at last." But so you may give these friends pain. Yes, but I cannot sell my liberty and my power, to save their sensibility. Besides, all persons have their moments of reason, when they look out into the region of absolute truth; then will they justify me, and do the same thing.

The populace think that your rejection of popular standards is a rejection of all standard, and mere antinomianism; and the bold sensualist will use the name of philosophy to gild his crimes. But the law of consciousness abides. There are two confessionals, in one or the other of which we must be shriven. You may fulfil your round of duties by clearing yourself in the *direct*, or in the *reflex* way. Consider whether you have satisfied your relations to father, mother, cousin, neighbor, town, cat, and dog; whether any of these can upbraid you. But I may also neglect this reflex standard, and absolve me to myself. I have my own stern claims and perfect circle. It denies the name of duty to many offices that are called duties. But if I can discharge its debts, it enables me to dispense with the popular code. If any one imagines that this law is lax, let him keep its commandment one day.

And truly it demands something godlike in him who has cast off the common motives of humanity, and has ventured to trust himself for a taskmaster. High be his heart, faithful his will, clear his sight, that he may in good earnest be doctrine, society, law, to himself, that a simple purpose may be to him as strong as iron necessity is to others! . . .

Society is a wave. The wave moves onward, but the water of which it is composed does not. The same particle does not rise from the valley to the ridge. Its unity is only phenomenal. The persons who make up a nation to-day, next year die, and their experience with them.

And so the reliance on property, including the reliance on governments which protect it, is the want of self-reliance. Men have looked away from themselves and at things so long, that they have come to esteem the religious, learned, and civil institutions as guards of property, and they deprecate assaults on these, because they feel them to be assaults on property. They measure their esteem of each other by what each has, and not by what each is. But a cultivated man becomes ashamed of his property, out of new respect for his nature. Especially he hates what he has, if he see that it is accidental,—came to him by inheritance, or gift, or crime; then he feels that it is not having; it does not belong to him, has no root in him, and merely lies there, because no revolution or no robber takes it away. . . . Our dependence on these foreign goods leads to our slavish respect for numbers. The political parties meet in numerous conventions; the greater the concourse, and with each new uproar of announcement, The delegation from Essex! The Democrats from New Hampshire! The Whigs of Maine! the young patriot feels himself stronger than before by a new thousand of eyes and arms. In like manner the reformers summon conventions, and vote and resolve in multitude. Not so, O friends, will the God deign to enter and inhabit you, but by a method precisely the reverse. It is only as a man puts off all foreign support, and stands alone, that I see him to be strong and to prevail. He is weaker by every recruit to his banner. Is not a man better than a town? Ask nothing of men, and in the endless mutation, thou only firm column must presently appear the upholder of all that surrounds thee. He who knows that power is inborn, that he is weak because be has looked for good out of him and elsewhere, and so perceiving, throws himself unhesitatingly on his thought, instantly rights himself, stands in the erect position, commands his limbs, works miracles; just as a man who stands on his feet is stronger than a man who stands on his head. . . .

from THE JOURNALS OF
RALPH WALDO EMERSON

OCTOBER 25, 1820

I find myself often idle, vagrant, stupid and hollow. This is somewhat appalling and, if I do not discipline myself with diligent care, I shall suffer severely from remorse and the sense of inferiority hereafter. All around me are industrious and will be great, I am indolent and shall be insignificant. Avert it, heaven! avert it, virtue! I need excitement.

[JANUARY, 1822]

. . . This fact, that the seeds of corruption are buried in the causes of improvement strikes us everywhere in the political, moral, and national history of the world. It seems to indicate the intentions of Providence to limit human perfectibility and to bind together good and evil, like life and death, by indissoluble connection. . . .

MAY 12, 1822

I have a nasty appetite which I will not gratify.

MAY 13, 1822

In twelve days I shall be nineteen years old; which I count a miserable thing. Has any other educated person lived so many years and lost so many days? . . .

Look next from the history of my intellect to the history of my heart. A blank, my lord. I have not the kind affections of a pigeon. Ungenerous and selfish, cautious and cold, I yet wish to be romantic; have not sufficient feeling to speak a natural, hearty welcome to a friend or stranger. . . .

[April 8, 1823]

Good men desire, and the great cause of human nature demands that this abundant and overflowing richness wherewith God has blessed this country be not misapplied and made a curse of; that this new storehouse of nations shall never pour out upon the world an accursed tribe of barbarous robbers. . . . And on the contrary, if the senates that shall meet hereafter in those wilds shall be made to speak a voice of wisdom and virtue, the reformation of the world would be to be expected from America. . . .

December 21, 1823

Who is he that shall controul me? Why may not I act & speak & write & think with entire freedom? What am I to the Universe, or, the Universe, what is it to me? Who hath forged the chains of Wrong & Right, of Opinion & Custom? And must I wear them? Is Society my anointed King? Or is there any mightier community or any man or more than man, whose slave I am? I am solitary in the vast society of beings; I consort with no species; I indulge no sympathies. I see the world, human, brute & inanimate nature; I am in the midst of them, but not *of* them; I hear the song of the storm—the Winds & warring Elements sweep by me—but they mix not with my being. I see cities & nations & witness passions—the roar of their laughter—but I partake it not;—the yell of their grief—it touches no chord in me; their fellowships & fashions, lusts & virtues, the words & deeds they call glory & shame—I disclaim them all. I say to the Universe, Mighty one! thou art not my mother; Return to chaos, if thou wilt, I shall still exist. I live. If I owe my being, it is to a destiny greater than thine. Star by Star, world by world, system by system shall be crushed—but I shall live.

[January, 1827]

Peculiarities of the Present Age

1. Instead of systematic pursuit of science, men cultivate the knowledge of anecdotes.

2. It is said to be the age of the first person singular.

3. The reform of the Reformation.

4. Transcendentalism. Metaphysics and Ethics look inwards.

• • •

6. The paper currency. Joint stock companies.

7. The disposition among men of associating themselves to promote any purpose. (Millions of societies.)

FEBRUARY 16, 1827

. . . The only dispensers of fame are the middle class of mankind, and they will not value the far-sought abstraction, no matter how inaccessible or sublime, more than the fowl on the dunghill regards the pearl. . . . But those writings which indicate valuable genius treat of common things. Those minds which God has formed for any powerful influence over men, have never effeminately shrunk from intercourse with unnurtured minds. They scorned to be tender and squeamish. Human destiny is not nice. . . .

FEBRUARY 27, 1827 [ST. AUGUSTINE, FLA.]

A fortnight since I attended a meeting of the Bible Society. The Treasurer of this institution is Marshal of the district & by a somewhat unfortunate arrangement has appointed a special meeting of the Society & a Slave Auction at the same time & place, one being in the Government house & the other in the adjoining yard. One ear therefore heard the glad tidings of great joy whilst the other was regaled with "Going gentlemen, Going!" And almost without changing our position we might aid in sending the scriptures into Africa or bid for "four children without the mother who had been kidnapped therefrom. . . ."

JUNE 25, 1828

What is the matter with the world that it is so out of joint? Simply that men do not rule themselves but let circumstances rule them. . . .

NOVEMBER, 1830

. . . God finds his perfection in himself; so must man. . . .

JULY 15, [1831]

. . . God in us worships God. . . .

The things taught in colleges and schools are not an education, but the means of education. . . .

JULY 29, 1831

Suicidal is this distrust of reason; this fear to think; this doctrine that 't is pious to believe on other's words, impious to trust entirely to yourself. . . .

JANUARY 20, [1832]

Don't trust children with edge tools. Don't trust man, great God, with more power than he has, until he has learned to use that little better. What a hell should we make of the world if we could do what we would! Put a button on the foil till the young fencers have learned not to put each other's eyes out. . . .

FEBRUARY 18, 1832

What can we see, read, acquire, but ourselves. Cousin is a thousand books to a thousand persons. Take the book, my friend, and read your eyes out, you will never find there what I find. . . .

JUNE 2, 1832

I have sometimes thought that, in order to be a good minister, it was necessary to leave the ministry. The profession is antiquated. In an altered age, we worship in the dead forms of our forefathers. Were not a Socratic paganism better than an effete, superannuated Christianity? . . .

NOVEMBER 23, [1834]

The root and seed of democracy is the doctrine, Judge for yourself. Reverence thyself. It is the inevitable effect of that doctrine, where it has any effect (which is rare), to insulate the partisan, to make each man a state. . . .

DECEMBER 21, [1834]

. . . Blessed is the day when the youth discovers that Within and Above are synonyms. . . .

[DECEMBER 22, 1834]

. . . If I were more in love with life and as afraid of dying . . . , I would go to a Jackson Caucus or to the Julien Hall, and I doubt not the unmixed malignity, the withering selfishness, the impudent vulgarity, that mark those meetings would speedily cure me of my appetite for longevity. In the hush of these woods I find no Jackson placards affixed to the trees. . . .

[DECEMBER 29? 1834]

Extremes meet. Misfortunes even may be so accumulated as to be ludicrous. To be shipwrecked is bad; to be shipwrecked on an iceberg is horrible; to be shipwrecked on an iceberg in a snowstorm, confounds us; to be shipwrecked on an iceberg in a storm and to find a bear on the snow bank to dispute the sailor's landing which is not driven away till he has bitten off a sailor's arm, is rueful to laughter.

Some people smile spite of themselves in communicating the worst news. . . .

[JULY 30, 1835]

. . . You affirm that the moral development contains all the intellectual, and that Jesus was the perfect man. I bow in reverence unfeigned before that benign man. I know more, hope more, am more, because he has lived. But, if you tell me that in your opinion he has fulfilled all the conditions of man's existence, carried out to the utmost, at least by implication, all man's powers, I suspend my assent. I do not see in him cheerfulness: I do not see in him the love of natural science: I see in him no kindness for art; I see in him nothing of Socrates, of Laplace, of Shakspear. The perfect man should remind us of all great men. Do you ask me if I would rather resemble Jesus than any other man? If I should say Yes, I should suspect myself of superstition. . . .

[OCTOBER 6, 1836]

. . . Transcendentalism means, says our accomplished Mrs. B., with a wave of her hand, *a little beyond.* . . .

NOVEMBER 3–4, 1836

. . . This age will be characterized as the era of Trade, for every thing is made subservient to that agency. The very savage on the shores of the N.W. America, holds up his shell & cries 'a dollar!' Government at home is conducted on such principles. Superstition gives way; Patriotism; Martial Ardor; Romance in the people; but avarice does not.

Meantime, it is also a social era; the age of associations, the powers of Combination are discovered. & hence of course the age of Constitutions, of Universal suffrage, of schools, of revision of laws, abolition of imprisonment, of railroads. . . .

NOVEMBER 19, 1836

. . . [T]he great man should occupy the whole space between God and the mob. . . . Thus did Jesus, dwelling in mind with pure God, and dwelling in social position and hearty love with fishers and women. Thus did Shakspear, the great Englishman, drawing direct from the soul at one end, and piercing into the play-going populace at the other. . . .

[SEPTEMBER 19, 1837]

. . . I received a letter from the Salem Lyceum, signed I. F. Worcester, requesting me to lecture before the institution next winter, and adding, "The subject is, of course, discretionary with yourself, provided no allusions are made to religious controversy, or other exciting topics upon which the public mind is honestly divided!" I replied, on the same day, to Mr. W. by quoting these words, and adding, "I am really sorry that any person in Salem should think me capable of accepting an invitation so incumbered." . . .

OCTOBER 6, [1837]

A great man must not grumble at his contemporaries. . . . If you don't like the world, make it to suit you. All true men have done so before you. . . .

OCTOBER 8, [1837]

. . . The young Southerner comes here a spoiled child, with graceful manners, excellent self-command, very good to be spoiled more, but good for nothing else,—a mere parader. He has conversed so much with rifles, horses and dogs that he has become himself a rifle, a horse and a dog, and in civil, educated company, where anything human is going forward, he is dumb and unhappy, like an Indian in a church. Treat them with great deference, as we often do, and they accept it all as their due without misgiving. Give them an inch, and they take a mile. They are mere bladders of conceit. Each snipper-snapper of them all undertakes to speak for the entire Southern States. "At the South, the reputation of Cambridge," etc., etc., which being interpreted, is, In my negro village of Tuscaloosa, or Cheraw, or St. Mark's, I supposed so and so. "We, at the South," forsooth. They are more civilized than the Seminoles, however, in my opinion; a little more. Their question respecting any man is like a Seminole's,—How can he fight? In this country, we ask, What can he do? His pugnacity is all they prize in man, dog, or turkey. The proper way of treating them is not deference, but to say as Mr. Ripley does, "Fiddle faddle," in answer to each solemn remark about "The South." "It must be confessed," said the young man, "that in Alabama, we are dead to everything, as respects politics." "Very true," replied Mr. Ripley, "leaving out the last clause.". . .

FEBRUARY 15, 1839

In the morning a man walks with his whole body; in the evening, only with his legs; the trunk is carried along almost motionless.

"A lovely child! I promise you he will be a great scholar." A dear little child with soft hair. Tomorrow he will defy you.

August 27, 1839

. . . On Sunday we heard sulphurous Calvinism. The preacher railed at Lord Byron. I thought Lord Byron's vice better than Rev. Mr M's Virtue. . . .

September 14, 1839

. . . [W]e all are involved in the condemnation of words, an Age of words. We are shut up in schools & college recitation rooms for ten or fifteen years & come out at last with a bellyfull of words & do not know a thing. We cannot use our hands or our legs or our eyes or our arms. We do not know an edible root in the woods. We cannot tell our course by the stars nor the hour of the day by the sun. It is well if we can swim & skate. We are afraid of a horse, of a cow, of a dog, of a cat, of a spider. Far better was the Roman rule to teach a boy nothing that he could not learn standing. . . .

September 14–17, 1839

. . . The mob are always interesting. We hate editors, preachers, & all manner of scholars, and fashionists. A blacksmith, a truckman, a farmer we follow into the barroom & watch with eagerness what they shall say, for such as they, do not speak because they are expected to, but because they have somewhat to say. . . .

[June 24, 1840]

The language of the street is always strong. What can describe the folly and emptiness of scolding like the word *jawing?* I feel too the force of the double negative, though clean contrary to our grammar rules. And I confess to some pleasure from the stinging rhetoric of a rattling oath in the mouth of truckmen and teamsters. How laconic and brisk it is by the side of a page of the *North American Review*. Cut these words and they would bleed; they are vascular and alive; they walk and run. Moreover they who speak them have this elegancy, that they do not trip in their speech. It is a shower of bullets, whilst Cambridge men and Yale men correct themselves and begin again at every half sentence. . . .

[JUNE 29, 1840]

. . . The simplest things are always better than curiosities. The most imposing part of this Harrison celebration of the Fourth of July in Concord, as in Baltimore, was this ball, twelve or thirteen feet in diameter, which, as it mounts the little heights and descends the little slopes of the road, draws all eyes with a certain sublime movement, especially as the imagination is incessantly addressed with its political significancy. So the Log Cabin is a lively watchword. . . .

JULY 6, [1840]

. . . We see the river glide below us, but we see not the river that glides over us and envelopes us in its floods. A month ago, I met myself, as I was speeding away from some trifle to chase a new one, and knew that I had eaten lotus and been a stranger from my home all this time. . . .

APRIL 20, 1841

. . . We are a puny and fickle folk. Hesitation and following are our diseases. The rapid wealth which hundreds in the community acquire in trade or by the incessant expansions of our population and arts, enchants the eyes of all the rest, the luck of one is the hope of thousands, and the whole generation is discontented with the tardy rate of growth which contents every European community. America is . . . the country of small adventures, of short plans, of daring risks, not of patience, not of great combinations, not of long, persistent, close-woven schemes, demanding the utmost fortitude, temper, faith, and poverty. Our books are tents; not pyramids: our reformers are slight and wearisome talkers. . . .

[OCTOBER, 1841]

"What are you doing, Zeke?" said Judge Webster to his eldest boy.
"Nothing."
"What are you doing, Daniel?"
"Helping Zeke."
A tolerably correct account of most of our activity to-day. . . .

The sum of life ought to be valuable when the fractions & particles are so sweet. A man cannot resist the sweet excitements of opium or brandy. Well then, the universe must be worth somewhat.

The *Daguerrotype* is good for its authenticity. No man quarrels with his shadow, nor will he with his miniature when the sun was the painter. Here is no interference and the distortions are not the blunders of an artist, but only those of motion, imperfect light, & the like.

The view taken of Transcendentalism in State Street is that it threatens to invalidate contracts. . . .

I told Garrison that I thought he must be a very young man or his time hang very heavy on his hands who can afford to think much & talk much about the foibles of his neighbors, or *'denounce'* and play 'the son of thunder' as he called it. I am one who believe all times to be pretty much alike and yet I sympathize so keenly with this. We want to be expressed, yet you take from us War, that great opportunity which allowed the accumulations of electricity to stream off from both poles, the positive & the negative. Well, now you take from us our cup of alcohol as before you took our cup of wrath. We had become canting moths of peace, our helm was a skillet, & now we must become temperance watersops. You take away, but what do you give me? . . .

DECEMBER 31, [1843]

. . . We rail at trade, but the historian of the world will see that it was the principle of liberty; that it settled America, and destroyed feudalism, and made peace and keeps peace; that it will abolish slavery. . . .

The two parties in life are the believers and unbelievers, variously named. The believer is poet, saint, democrat, theocrat, free-trade, no church, no capital punishment, idealist.

The unbeliever supports the church, education, the fine arts, etc., as *amusements*.

But the unbelief is very profound: Who can escape it? I am nominally a believer: yet I hold on to property: I eat my bread with unbelief. . . .

[JANUARY 30, 1844]

. . . "And fools rush in where angels fear to tread." So say I of Brook Farm. Let it live. Its merit is that it is a new life. Why should we have only two or three ways of life, and not thousands and millions? This is a new one so fresh and expensive that they are all homesick when they go away. . . .

[MARCH, 1844]

Somebody said of me after the lecture at Amory Hall . . . "The secret of his popularity is, that he has a *damn* for everybody.". . .

[APRIL, 1844]

The Shaker told me they . . . read the Bible and their own publications. They write their own poetry. "All their hymns and songs of every description are manufactured in the Society.". . .

[JUNE 15, 1844]

. . . My fellow men could hardly appear to less advantage before me than in this senseless jumping. The music seemed to me dragged down nearly to the same bottom. . . . Yet the women were well dressed and appeared with dignity as honored persons. And I judge the whole society to be cleanly and industrious, but stupid people. . . .

[JULY, 1844]

Does he not do more to abolish Slavery who works all day steadily in his garden than he who goes to the Abolition meeting and makes a speech? The Anti-slavery agency, like so many of our employments, is a suicidal business. . . . The planter does not want slaves; give him money; give him a machine that will provide him with as much money as the slaves yield, and he will thankfully let them go; he does not love whips, or usurping overseers, or sulky, swarthy giants creeping round his house and barns by night with lucifer matches in their hands and knives in their pockets. No; only he wants his luxury, and he will pay even this price for it. . . .

. . . Intense selfishness which we all share. Planter will not hesitate to eat his negro, because he can. We eat him in milder fashion by pelting the negro's friend. We cannot lash him with a whip, because we dare not. We lash him with our tongues. I like the Southerner the best;

he deals roundly and does not cant. . . . I do not wonder at feeble men being strong advocates for slavery. . . . I do not wonder that such would fain raise a mob, for fear is very cruel. . . .

A gentleman may have many innocent propensities, but if he chances to have the habit of slipping arsenic into the soup of whatever person sits next him at table, he must expect some inconvenience. He may call it his "peculiar institution," a mere way of his; he never puts it in his own soup, only in the soup of his neighbor. . . .

The conscience of the white and the improvement of the black coöperated, and the emancipation became inevitable. It is a great deed with a great sequel, and cannot now be put back . . . the conscience is more tender, and the black more respectable. . . . [T]he haters of Garrison have lived to rejoice in that grand world-movement which, every age or two, casts out so masterly an agent of good. I cannot speak of that gentleman without respect.

• • •

The Superstitions of our Age:
The fear of Catholicism;
The fear of pauperism;
The fear of immigration;
The fear of manufacturing interests;
The fear of radicalism or democracy,
And faith in the steam engine.

Nemesis takes care of all these things, balances fear with fear, eradicates nobles by upstarts, supplants one set of nobodies by new nobodies.

• • •

[April–May, 1851]

Bad Times. . . .

[T]he infamy that has fallen on Massachusetts, that clouds the daylight and takes away the comfort out of every hour. We shall never feel well again until that detestable law is nullified in Massachusetts and until the Government is assured that once for all it cannot and shall not be executed here. . . .

I opened a paper to-day in which he pounds on the old strings in a letter to the Washington Birthday feasters at New York. "Liberty! liberty!" Pho! Let Mr. Webster, for decency's sake, shut his lips once and forever on this word. The word *liberty* in the mouth of Mr. Webster sounds like the word *love* in the mouth of a courtezan. . . .

Wolf, however long his nails have been pared, however neatly he has been shaved and tailored and taught and tuned to say "virtue" and "religion," cannot be relied on when it comes to a pinch; he will forget his morality, and say morality means sucking blood. . . .

[N]othing seems to me more bitterly futile than this bluster about the Union. A year ago we were all lovers and prizers of it. . . . But in the new attitude in which we find ourselves, the degradation and personal dishonour which now rest like miasma on every house in Massachusetts, the sentiment is entirely changed. No man can look his neighbor in the face. We sneak about with the infamy of crime in the streets and cowardice in ourselves. . . .

Another year, and a standing army, officered by Southern gentlemen to protect the Commissioners and to hunt the fugitives, will be illustrating the new sweets of Union in Boston, Worcester, and Springfield. . . .

The fame of Webster ends in this nasty law. . . .

It will be his distinction to have changed in one day, by the most detestable law that was ever enacted by a civilized state, the fairest and most triumphant national escutcheon the sun ever shone upon, the free, the expanding, the hospitable, the irresistible America, home of the homeless, and pregnant with the blessing of the world, into a jail or barracoon for the slaves of a few thousand Southern planters, and all the citizens of this hemisphere into kidnappers and drivers for the same. . . .

This Slavery shall not be, it poisons and depraves everything it touches. . . .

[FEBRUARY, 1855]

"Fortune and Hope! I 've made my port,
Farewell, ye twin deceivers;
Ah! many a time I've been your sport,
Go, cozen new believers."

• • •

[FALL?] 1859

The resistance to slavery—it is the old mistake of the slaveholder to impute the resistance to Clarkson or Pitt, to Channing or Garrison, or to some John Brown whom he has just captured, & to make a personal affair of it; & he believes, whilst he chains & chops him, that he is getting rid of his tormentors; and does not see that the air which this man breathed is liberty, & is breathed by thousands & millions; that men of the same complexion as he, will look at slaveholders as felons who have disentitled themselves to the protection of law, as the burglar has, whom I see breaking into my neighbor's house; and therefore no matter how many Browns he can catch & kill, he does not make the number less, for the air breeds them, every school, every church, every domestic circle, every home of courtesy, genius, & conscience is educating haters of him & his misdeeds.

APRIL–MAY, 1860

. . . *Advantages of old age.* I reached the other day the end of my fifty seventh year, and am easier in my mind than hitherto. I could never give much reality to evil & pain. But now when my wife says, perhaps this tumor on your shoulder is a cancer, I say, what if it is? It would not make the gentleman on his way in a cart to the gallows very unhappy, to tell him that the pain in his knee threatened a white swelling. . . .

[FEBRUARY 27, 1861]

. . . In the South, slavery and hunting, sportsmanship and the climate and politics give the men self-reliance; and the South is well officered, and, with some right, they despise the peaceful North people, leaning on the law and on each other. In proportion to the number of self-reliant persons will the power and attitude of the State be. . . .

OCTOBER 9, 1864

Right-minded men would very easily bring order out of our American chaos, if working with courage, & without by-ends. These Tennessee slaveholders in the land of Midian are far in advance of our New-England politicians. They see & front the real questions. The two points would seem to be absolute Emancipation—establishing the fact that the United States henceforward knows no color, no race, in its law, but legislates for all alike—one law for all men: *that* first; and, secondly, make the confiscation of rebel property final, as you did with the tories in the Revolution.

Thereby you at once open the whole South to the enterprise & genius of new men of all nations, & extend New England from Canada to the Gulf, & to the Pacific. You redeem your wicked Indian policy, & leave no murderous complications to sow the sure seed of future wars.

[SUMMER,] 1865

. . . We see the dawn of a new era, worth to mankind all the treasure & all the lives it has cost, yes, worth to the world the lives of all this generation of American men, if they had been demanded.

. . . The present war, on a prodigiously enlarged scale, has cost us how many valuable lives; but it has made many lives valuable that were not so before, through the start & expansion it has given. It has fired selfish old men to an incredible liberality, & young men to the last devotion. The journals say, it has demoralized many rebel regiments, but also it has *moralized* many of our regiments, & not only so, but *moralized* cities & states. It added to every house & heart a vast enlargement. In every house & shop, an American map has been unrolled, & daily studied,—& now that peace has come, every citizen finds himself a skilled student of the condition, means, & future, of this continent. . . .

The War has made the Divine Providence credible to a good many people. They did not believe that Heaven was quite honest. I think it a singular & marked result, that it has established a conviction in so many minds that the right will get done; has established a chronic hope for a chronic despair.

CHAPTER 10

The Democratic Self

INTRODUCTION

SAMUEL WOODWORTH, 1785–1842
Selected Songs (1812–1828)

HENRY WADSWORTH LONGFELLOW, 1807–1882
Selected Poems (1838–1863)

WALT WHITMAN, 1819–1892
from Song of Myself (1855)

EMILY DICKINSON, 1830–1886
Selected Poems

PHOEBE CARY, 1823–1869
Was He Henpecked? (1859)

Some of Tocqueville's and Emerson's differences relate to varying ideas about the proper space between the responsible individual and society. As Franklin and Brackenridge suggested, people in a democratic society are self-defined—with considerable help from their neighbors. Hence they struggle with the relation of their personal vision to the masses, with being both a part of, and apart from, the general will. Antebellum poets offer one example of the democratic Everyman's effort to establish a socially and individually responsible vision.

Longfellow, Whitman, and Dickinson suggest the citizen's range of options. Harvard professor Longfellow was the best of the "household poets" who became the center of the nation's common culture by writing gracefully conventional poetry attuned to offering comfort, faith, and a sense of connectedness to his fellow citizens. Longfellow understood both the value and limitations of his poetic role, and predicted that some American would develop a democratic poetry as vibrant as the great works of more heroic ages.

Whitman attempted that, collapsing all conventional rhyme and meter into a rhapsodically inclusive river of rhythm. His "myself and "I" asserted the individual's union with all other things and people, a transcendent spiritual and sensual bond that joined all to self.

Dickinson, unpublished in her lifetime, chose instead a reclusive and intensely personal life and poetry that argued that honesty of vision was the price and the prize of those who remained social "nobodies"—her individual version of the Shakers' communal "small i." Her off-rhythms and near-rhymes within a conventional structure italicized her wariness of social and aesthetic expectations.

Samuel Woodworth wrote probably the most popular songs, as well as the most successful musical comedy, in the nationalistic wake of the War of 1812. His songs of moral sentiment and patriotism showed high seriousness, while his comic ones admitted the more aggressive, aggrandizing, and conning American interest in money and sex.

Cincinnati-born Phoebe Cary wrote popular verse, none better than her comic woman's eye view of the joke of patriarchal pretension.

CONSIDERATIONS

- How do the poets balance their need for a personal vision with the pressures of—or their commitments to—the common good of mass democratic society?

- Does Emily Dickinson's poetry represent primarily a woman's social vision? Is Cary's more "feminist"?

- What do Woodworth's songs tell you about American national feelings and social values at the time? Are there differences between the values of his serious and comic songs?

- Does the work of society's artists have much to do with the "history" of most people in the era? What are the advantages and problems of trying to speak to or for society or of deciding to turn one's back on it?

- Do your religion, ethnicity, background, values, and/or interests set you apart from American society? Are you a part of it?

SELECTED SONGS

Samuel Woodworth

COLUMBIA, THE PRIDE OF THE WORLD

Oh, there is a region, a realm in the West,
    To Tyranny's shackles unknown,
A country with union and liberty blest,
    That fairest of lands is our own.
Where commerce has opened her richest of marts,
    Where freedom's bright flag is unfurled,
The garden of science, the seat of the arts,
    Columbia, the pride of the world.
Her clime is a refuge for all the oppressed,
    Whom tyranny urges to roam;
And every exile we greet as a guest,
    Soon feels like a brother at home.
Then hail to our country, the land of our birth,
    Where freedom's bright flag is unfurled;
The rays of whose glory have lighted the earth,
    Columbia, the pride of the world.

OUR NATIVE LAND

In this vast rising empire of the west,
With freedom, science, fame, and plenty blest,
Where earthly comforts in profusion flow,
Each virtuous bosom must with rapture glow;
For here, where Liberty her fane has built,
No grief is found, but in the path of guilt;
No pains, nor fears, the good man's heart annoy,
No tears are shed but those of sympathy or joy.

THE HUNTERS OF KENTUCKY

Air—"Miss Bailey"

Ye gentlemen and ladies fair,
      Who grace this famous city,
Just listen, if ye've time to spare,
      While I rehearse a ditty;
And for the opportunity,
      Conceive yourselves quite lucky,
For 'tis not often that you see,
      A hunter from Kentucky.
Oh! Kentucky, the hunters of Kentucky,
      The hunters of Kentucky.

We are a hardy free-born race,
      Each man to fear a stranger,
Whate'er the game, we join in chase,
      Despising toil and danger;
And if a daring foe annoys,
      Whate'er his strength and forces,
We'll show him that Kentucky boys
      Are "alligator horses."
Oh! Kentucky, the hunters of Kentucky,
      The hunters of Kentucky.

I s'pose you've read it in the prints,
      How Packenham attempted
To make Old Hickory JACKSON wince,
      But soon his scheme repented;
For we with rifles ready cock'd,
      Thought such occasion lucky,
And soon around the General flock'd
      The hunters of Kentucky.
           Oh! Kentucky, &c.

You've heard, I spose, how New-Orleans
      Is famed for wealth and beauty—
There's girls of every hue, it seems,
      From snowy white to sooty;
So Packenham he made his brags,
      If he in fight was lucky,

He'd have their girls and cotton bags,
    In spite of Old Kentucky.
            Oh! Kentucky, &c.

But JACKSON, he was wide awake,
    And wasn't scared at trifles;
For well he knew what aim we take,
    With our Kentucky rifles;
So he led us down to Cypress swamp,
    The ground was low and mucky;
There stood John Bull, in martial pomp,
    And here was Old Kentucky.
            Oh! Kentucky, &c.

A bank was raised to hide our breast,
    Not that we thought of dying,
But then we always like to rest,
    Unless the game is flying;
Behind it stood our little force—
    None wished it to be greater,
For every man was half a horse,
    And half an alligator.
            Oh! Kentucky, &c.

They did not let our patience tire,
    Before they showed their faces—
We did not choose to waste our fire,
    So snugly kept our places;
But when so near we saw them wink,
    We thought it time to stop them;
And 'twould have done you good, I think,
    To see Kentucky pop them.
            Oh! Kentucky, &c.

They found at last 'twas vain to fight
    Where lead was all their booty,
And so they wisely took to flight,
    And left us all the beauty.
And now, if danger e'er annoys,
    Remember what our trade is,

Just send for us Kentucky boys,
    And we'll protect you, Ladies.
        Oh! Kentucky, &c.

THE GRAND CANAL

While millions awaken to Freedom the chorus,
    In wreathing for valor the blood-sprinkled bay,
The new brilliant era which opens before us,
    Demands the rich tribute of gratitude's lay;
For ours is a boast unexampled in story,
    Unequaled in splendor, unrivaled in grace,
A conquest that gains us a permanent glory,
    The triumph of science o'er matter and space!
For realms that were dreary, are now smiling cheery,
Since Hudson and Erie like sisters embrace.

From heroes whose wisdom and chivalrous bearing
    Secured us the rights which no power can repeal,
Have spirits descended as brilliantly daring,
    To fix on the charter Eternity's seal.
Behold them consummate the giant conception,
    Unwearied in honor's beneficent race,
While nature submits to the daring surreption,
    And envy and ignorance shrink in disgrace.
For realms that were dreary, are now smiling cheery,
Since Hudson and Erie like sisters embrace.

The nymphs of our rivers, our lakes, and our fountains,
    Are now by the monarch of ocean caressed;
While spurning the barriers of forests and mountains,
    Bold Commerce enriches the wilds of the West.
Then hail to the sages, whose wisdom and labors
    Conceived and perfected the brilliant design;
Converting the remotest strangers to neighbors,
    By weaving a ligament nought can disjoin;
For regions once dreary, are now smiling cheery,
Since Hudson and Erie like their waters combine.

THE BUCKET

Air—"The Flower of Dumblane"

How dear to this heart are the scenes of my childhood,
　　When fond recollection presents them to view!
The orchard, the meadow, the deep-tangled wild-wood,
　　And every loved spot which my infancy knew!
The wide-spreading pond and the mill that stood by it,
　　The bridge, and the rock where the cataract fell,
The cot of my father, the dairy-house nigh it,
　　And e'en the rude bucket that hung in the well—
The old oaken bucket, the iron-bound bucket,
The moss-covered bucket which hung in the well.

That moss-covered vessel I hail'd as a treasure,
　　For often at noon, when return'd from the field,
I found it the source of an exquisite pleasure,
　　The purest and sweetest that nature can yield.
How ardent I seized it, with hands that were glowing,
　　And quick to the white-pebbled bottom it fell;
Then soon, with the emblem of truth overflowing,
　　And dripping with coolness, it rose from the well—
The old oaken bucket, the iron-bound bucket,
The moss-covered bucket, arose from the well.

How sweet from the green mossy brim to receive it,
　　As poised on the curb it inclined to my lips!
Not a full blushing goblet could tempt me to leave it,
　　The brightest that beauty or revelry sips.
And now, far removed from the loved habitation,
　　The tear of regret will intrusively swell,
As fancy reverts to my father's plantation,
　　And sighs for the bucket that hangs in the well—
The old oaken bucket, the iron-bound bucket,
The moss-covered bucket that hangs in the well!

BANKRUPTCY OF THE HEART

Air—"Erin go Bragh"

Let infamy cover the dastard, that meanly
  Can sport with the peace of an innocent maid,
For there is no pang which the heart feels so keenly
  As finding its confidence basely betray'd.
No power can retrieve such a wide desolation,
As spreads o'er the face of the mental creation,
When once a sincere trusting heart's adoration
  Has been with a cold-blooded treason repaid.

For woman, dear woman, ne'er traffics by measure,
  But risks her whole heart, without counting the cost;
And if the dear youth whom she trusts with the treasure
  Be shipwreck'd, or faithless, her capital's lost.
For all she was worth, was her stock of affection,
And bankruptcy follows, with sad retrospection,
And nothing can ever remove the dejection
  That preys on a bosom whose prospects are cross'd.

VARIETY

The noblest talent love can claim,
Is never to appear the same;
For 'tis variety alone,
That props the urchin-tyrant's throne.
So do the seasons, as they range,
Afford new pleasure when they change:
The sweetest flower would cease to cheer,
Should fragrant spring bloom all the year.

THE NEEDLE

The gay belles of fashion may boast of excelling
  In waltz or cotillion—at whist or quadrille;
And seek admiration by vauntingly telling,
  Of drawing, and painting, and musical skill;

But give me the fair one, in country or city,
 Whose home and its duties are dear to her heart,
Who cheerfully warbles some rustical ditty,
 While plying the needle with exquisite art.
The bright little needle—the swift-flying needle,
 The needle directed by beauty and art.

If Love have a potent, a magical token,
 A talisman, ever resistless and true—
A charm that is never evaded or broken,
 A witchery certain the heart to subdue—
'Tis this—and his armory never has furnished
 So keen and unerring, or polished a dart;
Let Beauty direct it, so pointed and burnished,
 And oh! it is certain of touching the heart.

Be wise then, ye maidens, nor seek admiration
 By dressing for conquest, and flirting with all;
You never, whate'er be your fortune or station,
 Appear half so lovely at rout or at ball,
As gayly convened at a work-covered table
 Each cheerfully active and playing her part,
Beguiling the task with a song or a fable,
 And plying the needle with exquisite art.

OH, WOMEN ARE ANGELS

Oh, women are angels, in limbs,
 In person, and manners, and features,
But what shall we say of the whims,
 That govern these comical creatures?
By turns they will fondle and tease—
 With what would you have me compare them?
Though buzzing and stinging like bees,
 For the sake of the honey we bear them.

  Yet, women are angels, you see,
   There's something so charming about them,
  Whatever their oddities be,
   Oh, we never could manage without them.

There are some that resemble ice-cream,
 Which coldly forbids you to sip, sir;
But however frosty it seem,
 It will melt with the warmth of your lip, sir.
While others, like counterfeit grapes,
 The best imitations are hollow,
With beautiful colors and shapes,
 But oh, they're the devil to swallow.
   Yet women are angels, &c.

What strange contradictions they show,
 In matters of conjugal bliss, sir,
While frowning and crying "no, no!"
 They wish you to take it for "yes, sir."
Pursue, and how swift they will fly,
 All panting with fears and alarms, sir,
Retreat—and I'll bet you my eye,
 They'll pant, by-and-by, in your arms, sir.
   Yet women are angels, &c.

Jonathan's Courting

JONATHAN:

I cannot tell the reason, but I really want a wife,
And every body tells me 'tis the sweetest thing in life;
But as for cheeks like roses, with pouting lips, and such,
I know no more about them, than Ponto does of Dutch.
   Tol de rol lol, &c.

HARRIET [*Imitating*]:

If you expect to please me and win me for your bride,
You'll have to lie and flatter, and swear, my lad, beside—
So now begin to practice, and if you'd have me wed,
Declare you even love, sir, the ground on which I tread.
   Tol de rol lol, &c.

JONATHAN:

I'll tell you that sincerely, nor think it any harm,
I love the ground you walk on, for 'tis your father's farm,

Could that be mine without you, I'd be a happy man,
But since you go together, I will love you if I can.

> Tol de rol lol, &c.

HARRIET:

If I consent to have you, we must reside in town,
And sport a coach and horses, to travel up and down—
With footmen all in livery, to make a splendid show,
And when you don't attend me, I will get another beau.

> Tol de rol lol, &c.

JONATHAN:

If that's your calculation, we never can agree,
For such a mode of living will never do for me—
And as for beaux and lovers, though you may like the fun,
I guess the deacon's Sally will be content with one.

> Tol de rol lol, &c.

KATE ROMPWELL

Kate Rompwell is a funny lass, with lips as sweet as treacle,
And for a partner in a jig, I never know'd her equal,
She'll run, and jump, and wrestle, too, although she's fat and
    weighty,
And many a time upon the green I've tripped the heels of Katy.
    O, my Katy! my pretty bouncing Katy.

Her eyes are blue as indigo, or high-bush huckle-berry,
Her cheek and lips are red as beets, or like a full ripe cherry;
Her teeth are white, her hair is brown as a rusty-coat petate,
And like two dumplins are the breasts of pretty buxom Katy.
    O, my Katy! my pretty buxom Katy.

One 'lection night, the candle out, perhaps a little tipsy,
I caught a female in my arms, and thought it was the gipsy.
But zounds, it prov'd her maiden aunt, a little short of eighty,
That I'd mistaken in the dark for pretty buxom Katy.
    O, my Katy, my pretty buxom Katy.

COTTAGE NEAR THE WOOD

The fortune I crave, and I sigh for no more,
    Is health and contentment, apparel and food,
The smile of affection from one I adore,
    And a neat little cottage that stands near a wood.

While the slaves of ambition sell comfort for fame,
    Be mine the applause of the wise and the good,
A conscience that daily acquits me of blame,
    And a neat little cottage that stands near a wood.

Let others for grandeur and opulence toil,
    I'd share not their turbulent joys if I could,
The treasure I seek is affection's sweet smile,
    And a neat little cottage that stands near a wood.

from AMERICAN FARMERS

MILLER:

And now relieved from day's turmoil,
    Let festive pleasures fill each breast,
And no intruding sorrows spoil,
    The song or mirthful jest.
For lords of the soil, and fed by our toil,
American farmers are blest, my boys,
    American farmers are blest.

CHORUS:

    For lords of the soil, &c.

LYDIA:

Ye fair, who seek a splendid lot,
    Behold content, a richer prize,
Within the humblest ploughman's cot,
    That rank and pride despise.
And palace or cot, whatever your lot,
The farmer your table supplies, my dear,
    The farmer your table supplies.

CHORUS:

>   For lords of the soil, &c.

• • •

JONATHAN:

By girls we may be thus cajoled,
>   But not by any dandy blade,
A Yankee's honour can't be sold,
>   Whatever price be paid.
But tempters are told, as we pocket the gold,
>   'Tis all in the way of trade, my boys,
>   'Tis all in the way of trade.

CHORUS:

>   For the lords of the soil, &c.

BELLAMY:

Would you a maiden's heart assail,
>   Be careful or you'll miss the mark,
For Hymen's torch with some prevail,
>   While others choose a spark;
But modest or frail, peep under her veil,
>   Before you make love in the dark, my boy,
>   Before you make love in the dark.

CHORUS:

>   For the lords of the soil, &c.

from DOCTOR STRAMONIUM

Air—"Nothing at All"

• • •

2

I next taught the gamut, the sharps, and the flats,
To a nasal-twang'd bass, and a treble of cats;
Till my *private* duet with a miss, got abroad,

Which chang'd the *key note,* and produced a *discord.*

Spoken

A little love affair, that ran *counter* to my wishes, and induced some slanderous tongues to pronounce the whole *tenor* of my conduct to be thorough *bass.* . . .
Fa, sol, la; fa, sol, la; fa, sol, la, me;
Hop a twig, such a rig ought not to be.

3

A travelling merchant I quickly became,
With a new stock in trade, a new dress, and new name;
And I bartered my goods with such exquisite grace,
That I left a fair mourner in every place.

Spoken

"O Tabitha, what will become of me! The dear sweet Mr. Rover, (for that was my travelling name) my dear sweet Mr. Rover, the pedlar, is gone, and perhaps I shall never see him again. O dear!" "*Your* dear sweet Mr. Rover, indeed! I'd have you to know, cousin Keziah, th ɪt he is *my* dear sweet Mr. Rover, and he has left me something to remember him by."—"O the base, wicked deceiver! He has left me something too." Thus would they sympathize with each other, or tear caps for poor Rover, while I was unconsciously preparing a similar mine to spring in the next village, or jogging quietly along the road, inviting every one to buy my
Dutch ovens, cullenders, dippers and pans,
Broaches and buckles, with ear-rings and fans.

4

A schoolmaster, next, with a visage severe,
Board, lodging and washing, and twelve pounds a year,
For teaching the rustics to spell, and to read
The New-England Primer, the Psalter and Creed.

• • •

5

I then became preacher without any call,
When a sweet village lass came to hear brother Paul;
And told her experience o'er with such grace,
That I gave the dear creature an ardent embrace.

• • •

6

And now a physician, with cock'd hat and wig,
I can feel ladies' pulses, look wise, and talk big;
With a fine ruffled shirt, and good coat to my back,
I pluck the poor *geese*, while the ducks exclaim *quack*!

Spoken

. . . "Let me see your tongue, Miss."—"My tongue! Law
souls, Doctor, what in the world has the tongue to do with the
heart?" "In general, Miss, not much; but your case is an exception." "An exception! O goody gracious! now, you don't
say so; is an exception a dangerous disorder, Doctor?" "Not
at all dangerous, Miss. An application of stramonium exter-
nally, and copious draughts of catnip tea internally, will soon
restore you."—The lady's heart becomes composed, I pocket
my fee, and make my exit, singing—
Feel the pulse, smell the cane, look at the tongue,
Touch the gold, praise the old, flatter the young.

SELECTED POEMS

Henry Wadsworth Longfellow

A PSALM OF LIFE, 1838

Tell me not, in mournful numbers,
    Life is but an empty dream!—
For the soul is dead that slumbers,
    And things are not what they seem.

Life is real! Life is earnest!
    And the grave is not its goal;
Dust thou art, to dust returnest,
    Was not spoken of the soul.

Not enjoyment, and not sorrow,
    Is our destined end or way;
But to act, that each to-morrow
    Find us farther than to-day.

Art is long, and Time is fleeting,
    And our hearts, though stout and brave,
Still, like muffled drums, are beating
    Funeral marches to the grave.

In the world's broad field of battle,
    In the bivouac of Life,
Be not like dumb, driven cattle!
    Be a hero in the strife!

Trust no Future, howe'er pleasant!
    Let the dead Past bury its dead!
Act,—act in the living Present!
    Heart within, and God o'erhead!

Lives of great men all remind us
    We can make our lives sublime,

And, departing, leave behind us
    Footprints on the sands of time;

Footprints, that perhaps another,
    Sailing o'er life's solemn main,
A forlorn and shipwrecked brother,
    Seeing, shall take heart again.

Let us, then, be up and doing,
    With a heart for any fate;
Still achieving, still pursuing,
    Learn to labor and to wait.

HYMN TO THE NIGHT, 1839

I heard the trailing garments of the Night
    Sweep through her marble halls!
I saw her sable skirts all fringed with light
    From the celestial walls!

I felt her presence, by its spell of might,
    Stoop o'er me from above;
The calm, majestic presence of the Night,
    As of the one I love.

I heard the sounds of sorrow and delight,
    The manifold, soft chimes,
That fill the haunted chambers of the Night,
    Like some old poet's rhymes.

From the cool cisterns of the midnight air
    My spirit drank repose;
The fountain of perpetual peace flows there,—
    From those deep cisterns flows.

O holy Night! from thee I learn to bear
    What man has borne before!
Thou layest thy finger on the lips of Care,
    And they complain no more.

Peace! Peace! Orestes-like I breathe this prayer
    Descend with broad-winged flight,

The welcome, the thrice-prayed for, the most fair,
 The best-beloved Night!

THE DAY IS DONE, 1844

The day is done, and the darkness
 Falls from the wings of Night,
As a feather is wafted downward
 From an eagle in his flight.

I see the lights of the village
 Gleam through the rain and the mist,
And a feeling of sadness comes o'er me
 That my soul cannot resist:

A feeling of sadness and longing,
 That is not akin to pain,
And resembles sorrow only
 As the mist resembles the rain.

Come, read to me some poem,
 Some simple and heartfelt lay,
That shall soothe this restless feeling,
 And banish the thoughts of day.

Not from the grand old masters,
 Not from the bards sublime,
Whose distant footsteps echo
 Through the corridors of Time.

For, like strains of martial music,
 Their mighty thoughts suggest
Life's endless toil and endeavor;
 And tonight I long for rest.

Read from some humbler poet,
 Whose songs gushed from his heart,
As showers from the clouds of summer,
 Or tears from the eyelids start;

Who, through long days of labor,
 And nights devoid of ease,

Still heard in his soul the music
    Of wonderful melodies.

Such songs have power to quiet
    The restless pulse of care,
And come like the benediction
    That follows after prayer.

Then read from the treasured volume
    The poem of thy choice,
And lend to the rhyme of the poet
    The beauty of thy voice.

And the night shall be filled with music,
    And the cares, that infest the day,
Shall fold their tents, like the Arabs,
    And as silently steal away.

THE JEWISH CEMETERY AT NEWPORT, 1854

How strange it seems! These Hebrews in their graves,
    Close by the street of their fair seaport town,
Silent beside the never-silent waves,
    At rest in all this moving up and down!

The trees are white with dust, that o'er their sleep
    Wave their broad curtains in the south wind's breath,
While underneath these leafy tents they keep
    The long, mysterious Exodus of Death.

And these sepulchral stones, so old and brown,
    That pave with level flags their burial place,
Seem like the tablets of the Law, thrown down
    And broken by Moses at the mountain's base.

The very names recorded here are strange,
    Of foreign accent, and of different climes;
Alvares and Rivera interchange
    With Abraham and Jacob of old times.

"Blessed be God, for he created death!"
    The mourners said, "and death is rest and peace";

Then added, in the certainty of faith,
    "And giveth life that nevermore shall cease."

Closed are the portals of their synagogue,
    No Psalms of David now the silence break,
No Rabbi reads the ancient Decalogue
    In the grand dialect the prophets spake.

Gone are the living, but the dead remain,
    And not neglected; for a hand unseen,
Scattering its bounty, like a summer rain,
    Still keeps their graves and their remembrance green.

How came they here? What burst of Christian hate,
    What persecution, merciless and blind,
Drove o'er the sea—that desert desolate—
    These Ishmaels and Hagars of mankind?

They lived in narrow streets and lanes obscure,
    Ghetto and Judenstrass, in murk and mire;
Taught in the school of patience to endure
    The life of anguish and the death of fire.

All their lives long, with the unleavened bread
    And bitter herbs of exile and its fears,
The wasting famine of the heart they fed,
    And slaked its thirst with Marah of their tears.

Anathema maranatha! was the cry
    That rang from town to town, from street to street:
At every gate the accursed Mordecai
    Was mocked and jeered, and spurned by Christian feet.

Pride and humiliation hand in hand
    Walked with them through the world where'er they went;
Trampled and beaten were they as the sand,
    And yet unshaken as the continent.

For in the background figures vague and vast
    Of patriarchs and of prophets rose sublime,
And all the great traditions of the past
    They saw reflected in the coming time.

And thus forever with reverted look
　　The mystic volume of the world they read,
Spelling it backward, like a Hebrew book,
　　Till life became a legend of the dead.

But ah! what once has been shall be no more!
　　The groaning earth in travail and in pain
Brings forth its races, but does not restore,
　　And the dead nations never rise again.

from MY LOST YOUTH, 1855

Often I think of the beautiful town
　　That is seated by the sea;
Often in thought go up and down
　　The pleasant streets of that dear old town,
　　And my youth comes back to me.
　　　　And a verse of a Lapland song
　　　　Is haunting my memory still:
　　　　"A boy's will is the wind's will,
And the thoughts of youth are long, long thoughts."

I can see the shadowy lines of its trees,
　　And catch, in sudden gleams,
The sheen of the far-surrounding seas,
And islands that were the Hesperides
　　Of all my boyish dreams.
　　　　And the burden of that old song,
　　　　It murmurs and whispers still:
　　　　"A boy's will is the wind's will,
And the thoughts of youth are long, long thoughts."

•　　•　　•

from THE VILLAGE BLACKSMITH, 1841

　　Under a spreading chestnut-tree
　　　　The village smithy stands;
　　The smith, a mighty man is he,

With large and sinewy hands;
And the muscles of his brawny arms
  Are strong as iron bands.

His hair is crisp, and black, and long,
  His face is like the tan;
His brow is wet with honest sweat,
  He earns whate'er he can,
And looks the whole world in the face,
  For he owes not any man.

* * *

He goes on Sunday to the church,
  And sits among his boys;
He hears the parson pray and preach,
  He hears his daughter's voice,
Singing in the village choir,
  And it makes his heart rejoice.
It sounds to him like her mother's voice,
  Singing in Paradise!
He needs must think of her once more,
  How in the grave she lies;
And with his hard, rough hand he wipes
  A tear out of his eyes.

Toiling,—rejoicing,—sorrowing,
  Onward through life he goes;
Each morning sees some task begin,
  Each evening sees it close;
Something attempted, something done,
  Has earned a night's repose.

Thanks, thanks to thee, my worthy friend,
  For the lesson thou hast taught!
Thus at the flaming forge of life
  Our fortunes must be wrought;
Thus on its sounding anvil shaped
  Each burning deed and thought.

from THE BIRDS OF KILLINGWORTH, 1863

• • •

The robin and the bluebird, piping loud,
      Filled all the blossoming orchards with their glee;
The sparrows chirped as if they still were proud
      Their race in Holy Writ should mentioned be;
And hungry crows, assembled in a crowd,
      Clamored their piteous prayer incessantly,
Knowing who hears the ravens cry, and said:
"Give us, O Lord, this day, our daily bread!"

• • •

Thus came the jocund Spring in Killingworth,
      In fabulous days, some hundred years ago;
And thrifty farmers, as they tilled the earth,
      Heard with alarm the cawing of the crow,
That mingled with the universal mirth,
      Cassandra-like, prognosticating woe;
They shook their heads, and doomed with dreadful words
To swift destruction the whole race of birds.

And a town-meeting was convened straightway
      To set a price upon the guilty heads
Of these marauders, who, in lieu of pay,
      Levied black-mail upon the garden beds
And cornfields, and beheld without dismay
      The awful scarecrow, with his fluttering shreds;
The skeleton that waited at their feast,
Whereby their sinful pleasure was increased.

Then from his house, a temple painted white,
      With fluted columns, and a roof of red,
The Squire came forth, august and splendid sight
      Slowly descending, with majestic tread,
Three flights of steps, nor looking left nor right,
      Down the long street he walked, as one who said,
"A town that boasts inhabitants like me
Can have no lack of good society!"

The Parson, too, appeared, a man austere,
    The instinct of whose nature was to kill;
The wrath of God he preached from year to year,
    And read, with fervor, Edwards on the Will;
His favorite pastime was to slay the deer
    In Summer on some Adirondac hill;
E'en now, while walking down the rural lane,
He lopped the wayside lilies with his cane.

From the Academy, whose belfry crowned
    The hill of Science with its vane of brass,
Came the Preceptor, gazing idly round,
    Now at the clouds, and now at the green grass,
And all absorbed in reveries profound
    Of fair Almira in the upper class,
Who was, as in a sonnet he had said,
As pure as water, and as good as bread.

And next the Deacon issued from his door,
    In his voluminous neck-cloth, white as snow;
A suit of sable bombazine he wore;
    His form was ponderous, and his step was slow;
There never was so wise a man before;
    He seemed the incarnate "Well, I told you so!"
And to perpetuate his great renown
There was a street named after him in town.

These came together in the new town-hall,
    With sundry farmers from the region round.
The Squire presided, dignified and tall,
    His air impressive and his reasoning sound;
Ill fared it with the birds, both great and small;
    Hardly a friend in all that crowd they found,
But enemies enough, who every one
Charged them with all the crimes beneath the sun.

When they had ended, from his place apart
    Rose the Preceptor, to redress the wrong,
And, trembling like a steed before the start,
    Looked round bewildered on the expectant throng ;
Then thought of fair Almira, and took heart

To speak out what was in him, clear and strong,
Alike regardless of their smile or frown,
And quite determined not to be laughed down.

"Plato, anticipating the Reviewers,
   From his Republic banished without pity
The Poets; in this little town of yours,
   You put to death, by means of a Committee,
The ballad-singers and the Troubadours,
   The street-musicians of the heavenly city,
The birds, who make sweet music for us all
In our dark hours, as David did for Saul.

● ● ●

"You slay them all! and wherefore? for the gain
   Of a scant handful more or less of wheat,
Or rye, or barley, or some other grain,
   Scratched up at random by industrious feet,
Searching for worm or weevil after rain!
   Or a few cherries, that are not so sweet
As are the songs these uninvited guests
Sing at their feast with comfortable breasts.

● ● ●

"What! would you rather see the incessant stir
   Of insects in the windrows of the hay,
And hear the locust and the grasshopper
   Their melancholy hurdy-gurdies play?
Is this more pleasant to you than the whir
   Of meadow-lark, and her sweet roundelay,
Or twitter of little field-fares, as you take
Your nooning in the shade of bush and brake?

"You call them thieves and pillagers; but know,
   They are the winged wardens of your farms,
Who from the cornfields drive the insidious foe,
   And from your harvests keep a hundred harms;
Even the blackest of them all, the crow,
   Renders good service as your man-at-arms,
Crushing the beetle in his coat of mail,

And crying havoc on the slug and snail.

"How can I teach your children gentleness,
      And mercy to the weak, and reverence
For Life, which, in its weakness or excess,
      Is still a gleam of God's omnipotence,
Or Death, which, seeming darkness, is no less
      The selfsame light, although averted hence,
When by your laws, your actions, and your speech,
You contradict the very things I teach?"

With this he closed; and through the audience went
      A murmur, like the rustle of dead leaves;
The farmers laughed and nodded, and some bent
      Their yellow heads together like their sheaves;
Men have no faith in fine-spun sentiment
      Who put their trust in bullocks and in beeves.
The birds were doomed; and, as the record shows,
A bounty offered for the heads of crows.

There was another audience out of reach,
      Who had no voice nor vote in making laws,
But in the papers read his little speech,
      And crowned his modest temples with applause;
They made him conscious, each one more than each,
      He still was victor, vanquished in their cause.
Sweetest of all the applause he won from thee,
O fair Almira at the Academy!

And so the dreadful massacre began;
      O'er fields and orchards, and o'er woodland crests,
The ceaseless fusillade of terror ran.
      Dead fell the birds, with blood-stains on their breasts,
Or wounded crept away from sight of man,
      While the young died of famine in their nests;
A slaughter to be told in groans, not words,
The very St. Bartholomew of Birds!

The Summer came, and all the birds were dead;
      The days were like hot coals; the very ground

Was burned to ashes; in the orchards fed
  Myriads of caterpillars, and around
The cultivated fields and garden beds
  Hosts of devouring insects crawled, and found
No foe to check their march, till they had made
The land a desert without leaf or shade.

Devoured by worms, like Herod, was the town,
  Because, like Herod, it had ruthlessly
Slaughtered the Innocents. From the trees spun down
  The canker-worms upon the passers-by,
Upon each woman's bonnet, shawl, and gown,
  Who shook them off with just a little cry;
They were the terror of each favorite walk,
The endless theme of all the village talk.

The farmers grew impatient, but a few
  Confessed their error, and would not complain,
For after all, the best thing one can do
  When it is raining, is to let it rain.
Then they repealed the law, although they knew
  It would not call the dead to life again;
As school-boys, finding their mistake too late,
Draw a wet sponge across the accusing slate.

•   •   •

But the next Spring a stranger sight was seen,
  A sight that never yet by bard was sung,
As great a wonder as it would have been
  If some dumb animal had found a tongue!
A wagon, overarched with evergreen,
  Upon whose boughs were wicker cages hung,
All full of singing birds, came down the street,
Filling the air with music wild and sweet.

From all the country round these birds were brought,
  By order of the town, with anxious quest,
And, loosened from their wicker prisons, sought
  In woods and fields the places they loved best,
Singing loud canticles, which many thought

Were satires to the authorities addressed,
While others, listening in green lanes, averred
Such lovely music never had been heard!

But blither still and louder carolled they
    Upon the morrow, for they seemed to know
It was the fair Almira's wedding-day,
    And everywhere, around, above, below,
When the Preceptor bore his bride away,
    Their songs burst forth in joyous overflow,
And a new heaven bent over a new earth
Amid the sunny farms of Killingworth.

POSSIBILITIES, 1854

Where are the poets, unto whom belong
    The Olympian heights; whose singing shafts were sent
    Straight to the mark, and not from bows half bent,
    But with the utmost tension of the thong?
Where are the stately argosies of song,
    Whose rushing keels made music as they went
    Sailing in search of some new continent,
    With all sail set, and steady winds and strong?
Perhaps there lives some dreamy boy, untaught
    In schools, some graduate of the field or street,
    Who shall become a master of the art,
An admiral sailing the high seas of thought,
    Fearless and first, and steering with his fleet
    For lands not yet laid down in any chart.

from SONG OF MYSELF

Walt Whitman

1

I celebrate myself, and sing myself,
And what I assume you shall assume,
For every atom belonging to me as good belongs to you.
I loaf and invite my soul,
I lean and loaf at my case observing a spear of summer grass.
My tongue, every atom of my blood, formed from this soil, this air,
Born here of parents born here from parents the same, and their par-
    ents the same,
I, now thirty-seven years old in perfect health begin,
Hoping to cease not till death.
Creeds and schools in abeyance,
Retiring back awhile sufficed at what they are, but never forgotten,
I harbor for good or bad, I permit to speak at every hazard,
Nature without check with original energy.

2

•   •   •

I will go to the bank by the wood and become undisguised and naked,
I am mad for it to be in contact with me.

The smoke of my own breath,
Echoes, ripples, buzzed whispers, love root, silk thread, crotch and
    vine,
My respiration and inspiration, the beating of my heart, the passing
    of blood and air through my lungs.
The sniff of green leaves and dry leaves, and of the shore and dark-
    colored sea rocks, and of hay in the barn,
The sound of the belched words of my voice loosed to the eddies of
    the wind,

A few light kisses, a few embraces, a reaching around of arms,
The play of shine and shade on the trees as the supple boughs wag,
The delight alone or in the rush of the streets, or along the fields and
    hillsides,
The feeling of health, the full-noon trill, the song of me rising from bed
    and meeting the sun.

Have you reckoned a thousand acres much? have you reckoned the
    earth much?
Have you practiced so long to learn to read?
Have you felt so proud to get at the meaning of poems?

Stop this day and night with me and you shall possess the origin of all
    poems,
You shall possess the good of the earth and sun (there are millions of
    suns left),
You shall no longer take things at second or third hand, nor look
    through the eyes of the dead, nor feed on the specters in books,
You shall not look through my eyes either, nor take things from me,
You shall listen to all sides and filter them from yourself.

3

I have heard what the talkers were talking, the talk of the beginning
    and the end,
But I do not talk of the beginning or the end.

There was never any more inception than there is now,
Nor any more youth or age than there is now,
And will never be any more perfection than there is now,
Nor any more heaven or hell than there is now.

Urge and urge and urge,
Always the procreant urge of the world.
Out of the dimness opposite equals advance, always substance and
    increase, always sex,
Always a knit of identity, always distinction, always a breed of life.
To elaborate is no avail, learned and unlearned feel that it is so.

Sure as the most certain sure, plumb in the uprights, well entretied,
    braced in the beams,
Stout as a horse, affectionate, haughty, electrical,

I and this mystery here we stand.

Clear and sweet is my soul, and clear and sweet is all that is not my
    soul.

Lack one lacks both, and the unseen is proved by the seen,
Till that becomes unseen and receives proof in its turn.

Showing the best and dividing it from the worst age vexes age,
Knowing the perfect fitness and equanimity of things, while they dis-
    cuss I am silent, and go bathe and admire myself.

Welcome is every organ and attribute of me, and of any man hearty
    and clean,
Not an inch nor a particle of an inch is vile, and none shall be less fa-
    miliar than the rest.

I am satisfied—I see, dance, laugh, sing;
As the hugging and loving bedfellow sleeps at my side through the
    night, and withdraws at the peep of the day with stealthy tread,
Leaving me baskets covered with white towels swelling the house with
    their plenty,
Shall I postpone my acceptation and realization and scream at my eyes,
That they turn from gazing after and down the road,
And forthwith cipher and show me to a cent,
Exactly the value of one and exactly the value of two, and which is
    ahead?

4

Trippers and askers surround me,
People I meet, the effect upon me of my early life or the ward and city
    I live in, or the nation,
The latest dates, discoveries, inventions, societies, authors old and new,
My dinner, dress, associates, looks, compliments, dues,
The real or fancied indifference of some man or woman I love,
The sickness of one of my folks or of myself, or ill-doing or loss or lack
    of money, or depressions or exaltations,
Battles, the horrors of fratricidal war, the fever of doubtful news, the
    fitful events;
These come to me days and nights and go from me again,

But they are not the Me myself.
Apart from the pulling and hauling stands what I am,
Stands amused, complacent, compassionating, idle, unitary,
Looks down, is erect, or bends an arm on an impalpable certain rest,
Looking with side-curved head curious what will come next,
Both in and out of the game and watching and wondering at it.
Backward I see in my own days where I sweated through fog with lin-
    guists and contenders,
I have no mockings or arguments, I witness and wait.

5

I believe in you my soul, the other I am must not abase itself to you,
And you must not be abased to the other.
Loaf with me on the grass, loose the stop from your throat,
Not words, not music or rhyme I want, not custom or lecture, not even
    the best,
Only the lull I like, the hum of your valvèd voice.
I mind how once we lay such a transparent summer morning,
How you settled your head athwart my hips, and gently turned over
    upon me,
And parted the shirt from my bosom bone, and plunged your tongue
    to my bare-stripped heart,
And reached till you felt my beard, and reached till you held my feet.
Swiftly arose and spread around me the peace and knowledge that pass
    all the argument of the earth,
And I know that the hand of God is the promise of my own,
And I know that the spirit of God is the brother of my own,
And that all the men ever born are also my brothers, and the women
    my sisters and lovers,
And that a kelson of the creation is love,
And limitless are leaves stiff or drooping in the fields,
And brown ants in the little wells beneath them,
And mossy scabs of the worm fence, heaped stones, elder, mullein and
    pokeweed.

6

A child said *What is the grass?* fetching it to me with full hands,
How could I answer the child? I do not know what it is any more than he.

I guess it must be the flag of my disposition, out of hopeful green stuff
    woven.
Or I guess it is the handkerchief of the Lord,
A scented gift and remembrancer designedly dropped,
Bearing the owner's name someway in the corners, that we may see
    and remark, and say *Whose?*

Or I guess the grass is itself a child, the produced babe of the vegetation.

Or I guess it is a uniform hieroglyphic,
And it means, Sprouting alike in broad zones and narrow zones,
Growing among black folks as among white,
Canuck, Tuckahoe, Congressman, Cuff, I give them the same, I receive
    them the same.

And now it seems to me the beautiful uncut hair of graves.
Tenderly will I use you curling grass,
It may be you transpire from the breasts of young men,
It may be if I had known them I would have loved them,
It may be you are from old people, or from offspring taken soon out of
    their mothers' laps,
And here you are the mothers' laps.
This grass is very dark to be from the white heads of old mothers,
Darker than the colorless beards of old men,
Dark to come from under the faint red roof of mouths.
O I perceive after all so many uttering tongues,
And I perceive they do not come from the roofs of mouths for nothing.
I wish I could translate the hints about the dead young men and women,
And the hints about old men and mothers, and the offspring taken soon
    out of their laps.
What do you think has become of the young and old men?
And what do you think has become of the women and children?
They are alive and well somewhere,
The smallest sprout shows there is really no death,
And if ever there was it led forward life, and does not wait at the end
    to arrest it,
And ceased the moment life appeared.
All goes onward and outward, nothing collapses,
And to die is different from what anyone supposed, and luckier.

•　•　•

8

The little one sleeps in its cradle.

I lift the gauze and look a long time, and silently brush away flies with my hand.

The youngster and the red-faced girl turn aside up the bushy hill,

I peeringly view them from the top.

The suicide sprawls on the bloody floor of the bedroom,

I witness the corpse with its dabbled hair, I note where the pistol has fallen.

The blab of the pave, tires of carts, sluff of boot soles, talk of the promenaders,

The heavy omnibus, the driver with his interrogating thumb, the clank of the shod horses on the granite floor,

The snow sleighs, clinking, shouted jokes, pelts of snowballs,

The hurrahs for popular favorites, the fury of roused mobs,

The flap of the curtained litter, a sick man inside borne to the hospital.

The meeting of enemies, the sudden oath, the blows and fall,

The excited crowd, the policeman with his star quickly working his passage to the center of the crowd,

The impassive stones that receive and return so many echoes,

What groans of overfed or half-starved who fall sunstruck or in fits,

What exclamations of women taken suddenly who hurry home and give birth to babes,

What living and buried speech is always vibrating here, what howls restrained by decorum,

Arrests of criminals, slights, adulterous offers made, acceptances, rejections with convex lips,

I mind them or the show or resonance of them—I come and I depart.

•　•　•

10

•　•　•

The runaway slave came to my house and stopped outside,

I heard his motions crackling the twigs of the woodpile,

Through the swung half-door of the kitchen I saw him limpsy and
    weak,
And went where he sat on a log and led him in and assured him,
And brought water and filled a tub for his sweated body and bruised
    feet,
And gave him a room that entered from my own, and gave him some
    coarse clean clothes,
And remember perfectly well his revolving eyes and his awkwardness,
And remember putting plasters on the galls of his neck and ankles;
He stayed with me a week before he was recuperated and passed north,
I had him sit next me at table, my firelock leaned in the corner.

11

Twenty-eight young men bathe by the shore,
Twenty-eight young men and all so friendly;
Twenty-eight years of womanly life and all so lonesome.
She owns the fine house by the rise of the bank,
She hides handsome and richly dressed aft the blinds of the window.
Which of the young men does she like the best?
Ah, the homeliest of them is beautiful to her.

Where are you off to, lady? for I see you,
You splash in the water there, yet stay stock still in your room.
Dancing and laughing along the beach came the twenty-ninth bather,
The rest did not see her, but she saw them and loved them.
The beards of the young men glistened with wet, it ran from their long
    hair,
Little streams passed all over their bodies.
An unseen hand also passed over their bodies,
It descended tremblingly from their temples and ribs.

The young men float on their backs, their white bellies bulge to the
    sun, they do not ask who seizes fast to them,
They do not know who puffs and declines with pendant and bending
    arch,
They do not think whom they souse with spray.

12

The butcher boy puts off his killing clothes, or sharpens his knife at the stall in the market,
I loiter enjoying his repartee and his shuffle and breakdown.
Blacksmiths with grimed and hairy chests environ the anvil,
Each has his main sledge, they are all out, there is a great heat in the fire.
From the cinder-strewed threshold I follow their movements,
The lithe sheer of their waists plays even with their massive arms,
Overhand the hammers swing, overhand so slow, overhand so sure,
They do not hasten, each man hits in his place.

13

The Negro holds firmly the reins of his four horses, the block swags underneath on its tied-over chain.
The Negro that drives the long dray of the stoneyard, steady and tall he stands poised on one leg on the stringpiece,
His blue shirt exposes his ample neck and breast and loosens over his hip band,
His glance is calm and commanding, he tosses the slouch of his hat away from his forehead,
The sun falls on his crispy hair and mustache, falls on the black of his polished and perfect limbs.
I behold the picturesque giant and love him, and I do not stop there,
I go with the team also.

In me the caresser of life wherever moving, backward as well as forward sluing,
To niches aside and junior bending, not a person or object missing,
Absorbing all to myself and for this song.

Selected Poems

Emily Dickinson

I'm Nobody. Who Are You?

I'm nobody. Who are you?
Are you nobody too?
Then there's a pair of us.
Don't tell—they'd banish us, you know.

How dreary to be somebody,
How public—like a frog—
To tell your name the livelong June
To an admiring bog.

The Soul Selects Her Own Society

The soul selects her own society,
Then shuts the door.
To her divine majority
Present no more.

Unmoved she notes the chariots pausing
At her low gate;
Unmoved, an emperor be kneeling
Upon her mat.

I've known her from an ample nation
Choose one,
Then close the valves of her attention
Like stone.

SUCCESS IS COUNTED SWEETEST

Success is counted sweetest
By those who ne'er succeed.
To comprehend a nectar
Requires sorest need.

Not one of all the purple host
Who took the flag today
Can tell the definition
So clear of victory

As he defeated, dying,
On whose forbidden ear
The distant strains of triumph
Burst agonized and clear.

SURGEONS MUST BE
VERY CAREFUL

Surgeons must be very careful
When they take the knife.
Underneath their fine incisions
Stirs the culprit, life.

FAITH IS A FINE INVENTION

Faith is a fine invention
When gentlemen can see,
But microscopes are prudent
In an emergency.

HOPE IS THE THING
WITH FEATHERS

Hope is the thing with feathers
That perches in the soul
And sings the tune without the words
And never stops at all.

And sweetest in the gale is heard;
And sore must be the storm
That could abash the little bird
That kept so many warm.

I've heard it in the chillest land
And on the strangest sea,
Yet never in extremity
It asked a crumb of me.

WHAT SOFT CHERUBIC
CREATURES

What soft cherubic creatures
These gentlewomen are.
One would as soon assault a plush
Or violate a star.

Such dimity convictions,
A horror so refined
Of freckled human nature,
Of deity ashamed—

It's such a common glory,
A fisherman's degree.
Redemption, brittle lady,
Be so ashamed of thee.

MUCH MADNESS IS
DIVINIST SENSE

Much madness is divinest sense
To a discerning eye—
Much sense the starkest madness.
'Tis the majority
In this, as all, prevail.
Assent and you are sane:
Demur, you're straightway dangerous
And handled with a chain.

THE HEART ASKS
PLEASURE FIRST

The heart asks pleasure first,
And then excuse from pain,
And then those little anodynes
That deaden suffering,

And then to go to sleep,
And then if it should be
The will of its inquisitor
The privilege to die.

I HAD BEEN HUNGRY ALL
THE YEARS

I had been hungry all the years.
My noon had come to dine.
I trembling drew the table near
And touched the curious wine.

'Twas this on tables I had seen
When turning hungry home
I looked in windows for the wealth
I could not hope for mine.

I did not know the ample bread.
'Twas so unlike the crumb
The birds and I had often shared
In nature's dining room.

The plenty hurt me, 'twas so new.
Myself felt ill and odd,
As berry of a mountain bush
Transplanted to the road.

Nor was I hungry, so I found
That hunger was a way
Of persons outside windows
The entering takes away.

Because I Could Not Stop for Death

Because I could not stop for Death
He kindly stopped for me.
The carriage held but just ourselves
And immortality.

We slowly drove. He knew no haste,
And I had put away
My labor and my leisure too
For his civility.

We passed the school where children strove
At recess in the ring.
We passed the fields of gazing grain;
We passed the setting sun—

Or rather, he passed us.
The dews drew quivering and chill,
For only gossamer my gown,
My tippet only tulle.

We paused before a house that seemed
A swelling of the ground.

The roof was scarcely visible,
The cornice in the ground.

Since then 'tis centuries, and yet
Feels shorter than the day
I first surmised the horses' heads
Were toward eternity.

THE SKY IS LOW, THE CLOUDS ARE MEAN

The sky is low, the clouds are mean.
A traveling flake of snow
Across a barn or through a rut
Debates if it will go.

A narrow wind complains all day
How someone treated him.
Nature, like us, is sometimes caught
Without her diadem.

I NEVER SAW A MOOR

I never saw a moor;
I never saw the sea,
Yet know I how the heather looks
And what a billow be.

I never spoke with God,
Nor visited in heaven.
Yet certain am I of the spot
As if the chart were given.

The Saddest Noise, the Sweetest Noise

The saddest noise, the sweetest noise,
The maddest noise that grows,
The birds, they make it in the spring,
At night's delicious close

Between the March and April line,
That magical frontier
Beyond which summer hesitates,
Almost too heavenly near.

It makes us think of all the dead
That sauntered with us here,
By separation's sorcery
Made cruelly more dear.

It makes us think of what we had,
And what we now deplore.
We almost wish those siren throats
Would go, and sing no more.

An ear can break a human heart
As quickly as a spear;
We wish the ear had not a heart
So dangerously near.

WAS HE HENPECKED?

Phoebe Cary

"I'll tell you what it is my dear,"
  Said Mrs. Dorking, proudly,
"I do not like that chanticleer
  Who crows o'er us so loudly.

"And since I must his laws obey,
  And have him walk before me,
I'd rather like to have my say
  Of who should lord it o'er me."

"*You'd like to vote?*" he answered slow,
  "Why, treasure of my treasures,
What can you, or what should you know
  Of public men, or measures?

"Of course, you have ability,
  Of nothing am I surer;
You're quite as wise, perhaps, as I;
  You're better, too, and purer.

"I'd have you just for mine alone;
  Nay, so do I adore you,
I'd put you queen upon a throne,
  And bow myself before you."

"*You'd put me! you?* now that is what
  I do not want, precisely;
I want myself to choose the spot
  That I can fill most wisely."

"My dear, you're talking like a goose—
  Unhenly, and improper"—
But here again her words broke loose,
  In vain he tried to stop her:

494

"I tell you, though she never spoke
   So you could understand her,
A goose knows when she wears a yoke,
   As quickly as a gander."

"Why, bless my soul! what would you do?
   Write out a diagnosis?
Speak equal rights? join with their crew
   And dine with the Sorosis?

"And shall I live to see it, then—
   My wife a public teacher?
And would you be a crowing hen—
   That dreadful unsexed creature?"

"Why, as to that, I do not know;
   Nor see why you should fear it;
If I can crow, why let me crow,
   If I can't, then you won't hear it!"

"Now, why," he said, "can't such as you
   Accept what we assign them?
You have your rights, 't is very true,
   But then, we should define them!

"We would not peck you cruelly,
   We would not buy and sell you;
And you, *in turn*, should think, and be,
   And do, just what we tell you!

"I do not want you made, my dear,
   The subject of rude men's jest;
I like you in your proper sphere,
   The circle of a hen's nest!

"I'd keep you in the chicken-yard,
   Safe, honored, and respected;
From all that makes us rough and hard,
   Your sex should be protected."

"Pray, did it ever make you sick?
   Have I gone to the dickens?

Because you let me scratch and pick
  Both for myself and the chickens?"

"Oh, that's a different thing, you know,
  Such duties are parental;
But for some work to do, you'd grow
  Quite weak and sentimental."

"Ah! yes, it's well for you to talk
  About a parent's duty!
Who keeps your chickens from the hawk?
  Who stays in nights, my beauty?"

"But, madam, you may go each hour,
  Lord bless your pretty faces!
We'll give you anything, but power
  And honor, trust and places.

"We'd keep it hidden from your sight
  How public scenes are carried;
Why, men are coarse, and swear, and fight"—
  "I know it, dear; I'm married!"

"Why, now you gabble like a fool;
  But what's the use of talking?
'T is yours to serve, and mine to rule,
  I tell you, Mrs. Dorking!

"Oh, yes," she said, "you've all the sense;
  Your sex are very knowing;
Yet some of you are on the fence,
  And only good at crowing."

"Ah! preciousest of precious souls,
  Your words with sorrow fill me;
To see you voting at the polls
  I really think would kill me.

"To mourn my home's lost sanctity;
  To feel you did not love me;
And worse, to see you fly so high,
  And have you roost above me!"

"Now, what you fear in equal rights
   I think you've told precisely;
That's just about the 'place it lights,'"
   Said Mrs. Dorking wisely.

CHAPTER 11
Keeping Capitalism Wholesome

INTRODUCTION

WILLIAM M. GOUGE, 1796–1863
from A Short History of Paper Money
and Banking in the United States (1833)

THOMAS SKIDMORE, 1793–1832
from The Rights of Man to Property! (1829)

ORESTES AUGUSTUS BROWNSON, 1803–1876
from The Laboring Classes (1840)

GEORGE FITZHUGH, 1806–1881
from Sociology for the South (1854)

The country's basic capitalism was as clearly in place by the 1830s as its democracy, and was bein; practiced with equal enthusiasm—and worry. People of all shades of opinion lamented the sediment of moral shoddiness in the system, and many worried, as Robert Coram had, that highly skewed patterns of wealth and poverty might come to mock both democracy and equality of opportunity.

William Gouge, a U.S. Treasury employee, wrote the classic Jacksonian economic tract, which argued that all injustice resulted from government activism, especially the national bank, and that Adam Smith's "natural law" would insure absolute fairness if government didn't intervene. Thomas Skidmore, Jacksonian Orestes Brownson (in his brief radical phase before his conversion to Catholicism), and George Fitzhugh strongly dissented.

Skidmore, a New York City printer, offered the clearest answer: divide wealth equally once, and then, through confiscatory inheritance taxes, distribute the property of the deceased each year equally among those coming of age. This bourgeois egalitarianism, he argued, would strengthen an ethic of work and creativity since all would start with hope, options, and much greater equality of opportunity.

Sharing Gouge's anti-government position and (very gingerly) Skidmore's ideas on inheritance, Brownson came close to asserting Karl Marx's argument of inevitably growing disparities in wealth leading to revolution. Yet he retained some hope that residual democratic decencies and true religion (in contrast to the prevalent "priestcraft") might still check the viciousness.

While Brownson said that wage labor was worse than slavery, Virginian Fitzhugh argued that slavery was the only decent alternative to laissez-faire, where the strong ground up the working poor in their machinery of profits. Fitzhugh insisted that Southern slaves, with cradle to grave security, were much better off than Northern laborers, but avoided advocating white slavery though only whites were, he claimed, intelligent enough to do most work in the factories that the South needed to develop to stave off Northern domination.

CONSIDERATIONS

- What concerns motivate these reformers? Is their concern about gross inequalities in wealth and hence in power reasonable? How effective do you think the solutions they suggest would be?

- Is there a natural economic law that insures justice if government doesn't act? Did and should government take little economic role?

- Isn't some rough economic equality at the start of life necessary if equality of opportunity is to be meaningful, as Skidmore argues? How would your life, and that of your society, be changed if you were about to come into your share of Skidmore's public inheritance?

- Why did not the total impoverishment of the working class happen as these thinkers feared?

- Does free society mean, as Fitzhugh argues, the freedom of the strong or favored to use their advantages to take from the weak? Is capitalism an amoral system?

- Do slavery or democratic socialism offer good answers for those society rewards least? Is there a good answer? Should one care?

from A SHORT HISTORY OF PAPER MONEY AND BANKING IN THE UNITED STATES

William M. Gouge

Our view of the extent to which paper-money banking affects our social condition will be very imperfect if we confine it to the *direct* operations of the system. These are, as it were, but the first links of a long extended chain. Each effect becomes in its turn a cause and the remote consequences are of more importance than the immediate. To prove this, a few plain truths will suffice.

If two men start in life at the same time, and the one gets at the commencement but a small advantage over the other and retains the advantage for twenty or thirty years, their fortunes will, at the end of that period be very unequal.

If a man at the age of twenty-one years is deprived of one hundred dollars which he had honestly earned and honestly saved, the injury done to this man must be estimated by the advantage he would have derived from the use of his little property during the rest of his life. The want of it may prevent his turning his faculties to the best account. The loss may dispirit his future exertion.

If a man is at any period of his life deprived of a property, large or small, accumulated for him by the honest industries and economy of his ancestors, the wrong done to him is of the same character as that which he sustains when he is unjustly deprived of property which was the fruits of his own industry. It is the dictate of nature that parents shall leave their wealth to their children, and the law of the land, in this case, only confirms the dictate of nature. . . .

Where the distribution of wealth is left to natural and just laws, and the natural connection of cause and effect is not violated, the tendency of "money to beget money," or rather of wealth to produce wealth, is not an evil. A man has as strong a natural right to the profits which are yielded by the capital which was formed by his labor as he had to the immediate product of his labor. To deny this would be to deny him a right to the whole product of his labor. The claims of the honest capitalist and of the honest laborer are equally sacred and rest, in fact, on the same foundation. Nor is it the law of nature that the idle and improvident shall suffer temporary inconvenience only. By neglecting to form a capital for themselves, they render their future labor less productive than it otherwise might be; and finally make themselves dependent on others for the means of both subsistence and employment.

But unequal political and commercial institutions *invert* the operation of the natural and just causes of wealth and poverty, take much o the capital of a country from those whose industry produced it and whose economy saved it, and give it to those who neither work nor save. The natural reward of industry then goes to the idle, and the natural punishment of idleness falls on the industrious.

Inasmuch as personal, political, commercial, and accidental causes operate sometimes in conjunction and sometimes in opposition, it is difficult to say, in individual cases, in how great degree wealth or poverty is owing to one cause or to another. Harsh judgments of rich and poor, taking them individually, are to be avoided. But it is notorious that as regards different *classes* in different countries wealth and poverty are the consequences of the positive institutions of those countries. Peculiar political privileges are commonly the ground of the distinction; but peculiar commercial privileges have the same effect and when the foundation of the artificial inequality of fortune is once laid (it matters not whether it be by feudal institutions or money corporations), all the subsequent operations of society tend to increase the difference in the condition of different classes of the community.

One consequence of unequal institutions is increasing the demand for luxuries and diminishing the effective demand for necessaries and comforts. Many being qualified to be producers of necessaries and few to be producers of luxuries, the reward of the n any is reduced and that of the few raised to an enormous height. The inventor of some new means of gratification for the rich is sure to receive his recompense, though thousands of able-bodied men may be starving around him. . . .

Through all the operations of business the effects of an unequal distribution of wealth may be distinctly traced. The rich have the means of rewarding most liberally the professional characters whom they employ and the tradesmen with whom they deal. An aristocracy in one department of society introduces an aristocracy into all. . . .

It is, however, among the hard-working members of society that the ultimate effects of such causes are most observable.

The condition of a multitude of poor women in our large cities has lately attracted the attention of the benevolent. It appears from the statements that have been published, that they can, by working ten or twelve hours every day, earn no more than from seventy-five cents to a dollar a week. Half of this sum goes for house rent and fuel, leaving them from thirty-seven and a half cents to fifty cents a week for food and clothing for themselves and children. Some thousands are said to be in this situation in Philadelphia alone.

Various proposals have been made to better their conditions, some futile, others absolutely pernicious. The laws of supply and demand are too powerful to yield to sermons and essays. The low rate of the wages of these poor women is the effect of general causes; causes which affect, in one way or another, every branch of business. In the great game we have been playing, much of the wealth of the country has passed into a few hands. Many men dying have left nothing to their widows and children; and others, who still live, cannot support their families except by the additional industry of their wives. The work of a seamstress can be done by a woman in her own house in the intervals she can spare from attention to her children. In this way, the number of seamstresses has been increased.

On the other hand, many families who would gladly employ these poor women are compelled by their own straitened circumstances to do this kind of work themselves. In this way the demand for seamstresses is diminished.

Private benevolence may improve the condition of individuals of this class; but the class itself can be benefited by such causes only as will diminish the number of seamstresses or increase the demand for their labor. The cause that will improve the condition of one of the industrious classes of society will improve the conditions of all. When an end shall be put to unfair speculation, then, and not till then, will honest industry have its just reward. . . .

The practices of trade in the United States have debased the standard of commercial honesty. Without clearly distinguishing the causes that have made commerce a game of haphazard, men have come to perceive clearly the nature of the effect. They see wealth passing continually out of the hands of those whose labor produced it or whose economy saved it into the hands of those who neither work nor save.

They do not clearly perceive *how* the transfer takes place, but they are certain of the fact. In the general scramble, they think themselves entitled to some portion of the spoil and, if they cannot obtain it by fair means, they take it by foul.

Hence we find men without scruple incurring debts which they have no prospect of paying.

Hence we find them, when on the very verge of bankruptcy, embarrassing their friends by prevailing on them to indorse notes and sign custom-house bonds.

Instances not unfrequently occur of men who have failed once or twice afterwards accumulating great wealth. How few of these honorably discharge their old debts by paying twenty shillings in the pound.

How many evade the just demands of their creditors by privately transferring their property.

It is impossible in the present condition of society to pass laws which will punish dishonest insolvents and not oppress the honest and unfortunate.

Neither can public opinion distinguish between them. The dishonest share the sympathy which should be given exclusively to their unfortunate neighbors; and the honest are forced to bear a part of the indignation which should fall entirely on the fraudulent.

The standard of commercial honesty can never be raised very high while trade is conducted on present principles. "It is hard," says Dr. Franklin, "for an empty bag to stand upright." The straits to which many men are reduced cause them to be guilty of actions which they would regard with as much horror as their neighbors if they were as prosperous as their neighbors.

We may be very severe in our censure of such men, but what else ought we to expect when the laws and circumstances give to some men so great advantages in the great game in which the fortunes of the whole community are at issue; what else ought we to expect but that those to whom the law gives no such advantage should exert to the utmost such faculties as remain to them in the struggle for riches, and not be very particular whether the means they use are such as the law sanctions or the law condemns.

Let those who are in possession of property which has been acquired according to the strict letter of the law be thankful that they have not been led into such temptations as those on whom the positive institutions of society have had an unfavorable influence.

But banking has a more extensive effect on the moral character of the community, through that distribution of wealth which is the result of its various direct and remote operations. Moralists in all ages have inveighed against luxury. To it they attribute the corruption of morals and the downfall of nations. The word luxury is equivocal. What is regarded as a luxury in one stage of society is in another considered as a comfort, and in a still more advanced stage as a necessary. The desire of enjoyment is the great stimulus to social improvement. If men were content with bare necessaries, no people would in the arts and sciences and in whatever else renders life desirable be in advance of the lowest caste of the Hindoos or the unhappy peasantry of the most unhappy country of Europe.

But whatever moralists have said against luxury is true when applied to that *artificial* inequality of fortune which is produced by *positive* institutions of an unjust character. Its necessary effect is to corrupt one part of the community and debase the other.

The bare prospect of inheriting great wealth damps the energies of a young man. It is well if this is the only evil it produces. "An idle man's brain," says John Bunyan, "is the devil's workshop." Few men can have much leisure and not be injured by it. To get rid of the *ennui* of existence young men of wealth resort to the gambling table, the race ground, and other haunts of dissipation. They cannot have these low means of gratification without debasing those less favored by fortune.

The children of the poor suffer as much in one way as the children of the rich suffer in another. The whole energies of the father and mother are exhausted in providing bread for themselves and their family. They cannot attend properly to the formation of the moral character of their offspring, the most important branch of education. They can ill spare the means to pay for suitable intellectual instruction. Their necessities compel them to put their children to employments unsuited to their age and strength. The foundation is thus laid of diseases which shorten and embitter life.

Instances occur of men by the force of their innate powers overcoming the advantages of excess or defect of wealth; but it is true, as a general maxim, that in early life and in every period of life too much or too little wealth is injurious to the character of the individual, and when it extends through a community, it is injurious to the character of the community.

In the general intercourse of society this artificial inequality of wealth produces baneful effects. In the United States the pride of wealth has more force than in any other country because there is here no other pride to divide the human heart. Some of our good Republicans do, indeed, boast of a descent from the European nobility; but when they produce their coats of arms and their genealogical trees they are laughed at. The question is propounded if their noble ancestors left them any *money*. Genius confers on its possessor a very doubtful advantage. Virtue with us, as in the days of the Roman poet, is viler than seaweed unless it has a splendid retinue. Talent is estimated only as a means of increasing riches. Wealth alone can give permanent distinction, for he who is at the top of the political ladder today may be at the bottom tomorrow.

One mischief this state of things produces is that men are brought to consider wealth as the *only* means of happiness. Hence they sacrifice honor, conscience, health, friends, everything to obtain it.

The other effects of artificial inequality of wealth have been treated of at large by moralists from Solomon and Socrates downwards. To their works and to the modern treatises on crime and pauperism we refer the reader. The last mentioned treatises are for the most part only illustrations of the ultimate effects of positive institutions which operate unequally on different members of the community.

The inferences the intelligent reader must have drawn from what has already been stated preclude the necessity of much detail in this part of our inquiry.

Wealth is, if independently considered, but one among fifty of the causes of happiness; and poverty viewed in the same light is but one among fifty of the causes of misery. The poorest young man having health of body and peace of mind and enjoying the play of the social sympathies in the affections of wife, children, and friends is happier than the richest old man, bowed down with sickness, oppressed with anxiety for the future, or by remorse for the past, having nobody to love, and beloved by nobody. . . .

Some little wealth, at least enough for daily subsistence, is necessary for the enjoyment of life and the pursuit of happiness; and hence it is that the right to property is as important as the right to life and the right to liberty. "You take my life when you do take the means by which I live."

The majority of men are of such temperament that something more than the means of subsistence for the bare twenty-four hours is necessary for their happiness. They must also have a prospect of enjoying the like means of subsistence in future days. But this is a prospect which, with the reflecting part of the poor, is frequently overcast with clouds and gloom. Few journeymen mechanics are able to make adequate provision for sickness and old age. The wages of a laborer will support him and his family while he enjoys health and while employment is steady; but in case of long continued sickness he must look for relief from the hand of public or of private charity. If he casts his eyes on his wife and children, his dying hours are embittered with thoughts of the misery which may be their portion. Corroding care is the inmate of the poor man's breast. It is so heart-withering that it may be made a question if the condition of some slaves in the Southern States is much worse than that of many citizens of the other States. The want of liberty is a great drawback on happiness; but the slave is free from care. He knows that when he grows old or becomes infirm his master is bound to provide for his wants.

There would be less objection to that artificial inequality of wealth which is the result of unjust positive institutions if it increased the happiness of one class of society in the same proportion that it diminishes the happiness of another class. But increase of wealth beyond what is necessary to gratify the rational desires of a man does not increase his happiness. If it gives birth to irrational desires, the gratification of them must produce misery. Even when inordinate wealth does not give birth to irrational desires, it is attended with an increase of care, and this is a foe to happiness.

With some men, the love of wealth seems to be a blind passion. The magpie in hiding silver spoons in its nest appears to act with as much reflection as they do in piling money-bag on money-bag. They have no object in view beyond accumulation. But with most men the desire of great wealth appears subordinate to the love of great power and distinction. This is the end, that the means. They love fine houses, splendid equipage, and large possessions less for any physical gratification they impart than for the distinction they confer and the power they bestow. It is with some as much an object of ambition to be ranked with the richest men as it is with others to be ranked with the greatest warriors, poets, or philosophers.

The love of that kind of distinction which mere wealth confers is not a feeling to be highly commended; but it is hardly to be reprobated when it is constitutional and when it is under the government of proper moral principle. In this case it is a simple stimulus to vigorous industry and watchful economy. With some men the love of ease is the ruling passion, with others the love of pleasure, and with others the love of science. If the love of riches was not with many men stronger than any of the other loves we have mentioned, there might not be enough wealth accumulated to serve the general purposes of society. They may claim the liberty of gratifying their particular passion in a reasonable way; but it is a passion which derives less gratification from the actual possession of a large store, than from the constant increase of a small one. The man whose wealth increases gradually from one hundred dollars to one thousand, thence to five thousand, thence to ten thousand, and thence to fifty thousand, has more satisfaction in the process than he who suddenly becomes possessed of one hundred thousand dollars. As to the distinction which mere wealth confers, it would be obtained in a state of society in which the distribution of wealth was left to natural laws as certainly as in a state in which positive institutions operate to the advantage of the few and to the disadvantage of the many. If the riches of men were made to depend entirely on their industry, economy, enterprise, and prudence, the possession of one hundred thousand dollars would confer as much distinction as the possession of five hundred thousand dollars confers at present. Those worth "a plum," would then rank among the "first men" on change; those who are worth "five plums" can rank no higher now.

But the system has not a merely negative effect on the happiness of the rich. Such is the uncertainty of fortune in the United States that even the most wealthy are not exempt from painful solicitude for the future. Who can be sure that he will be able to navigate his own bark in safety to the end of the voyage when he sees the shore strewed with wrecks? If a man leaves an estate to his children, he knows not how long they will keep possession of it. If he extends his views to his grandchildren, the probability will appear strong that some of them will be reduced to abject poverty. . . .

There is one other evil resulting from the super-extended system of credit which has its origin in banking, and with a few observations on this, we shall close our remarks on this head of the subject. We allude to the *misery* suffered by an honest man who is involved in debts.

We have known cases in which none of the common rules of prudence had been transgressed in incurring the debts, in which the creditors were perfectly convinced of the honesty of the debtor, and neither pressed for payment nor reflected on his disability to comply with his engagements, in which the debtor was sensible that his failure would not subject his creditors to any serious inconvenience; and yet a gloom would over-spread the mind of the debtor, and remain there for years.

• • •

SUMMARY

To place the subject fairly before the reader, we shall bring together the principal propositions that have been supported in this essay and leave the decision to his candid judgment.

We have maintained:

• • •

3. That real money diffuses itself through different countries and through different parts of a country in proportion to the demands of commerce. No prohibitions can prevent its departing from countries where wealth and trade are declining; and no obstacle except spurious money can prevent its flowing into countries where wealth and trade are increasing.

4. That money is the tool of all trades and is, as such, one of the most useful of productive instruments and one of the most valuable of labor saving machines.

• • •

11. That the "flexibility" or "elasticity" of bank medium is not, in excellence, but a defect, and that "expansions" and "contractions" are not made to suit the wants of the community but from a simple regard to the profits and safety of the banks.

12. That the uncertainty of trade produced by these successive "expansions" and "contractions" is but *one* of the evils of the present system. That the banks cause credit dealings to be carried to an extent that is highly pernicious; that they cause credit to be given to men who are not entitled to it, and deprive others of credit to whom it would be useful.

13. That the granting of exclusive privileges to companies or the exempting of companies from liabilities to which individuals are subject is repugnant to the fundamental principles of American govern-

ment; and that the banks, inasmuch as they have exclusive privileges and exemptions and have the entire control of credit and currency, are the most pernicious of money corporations.

• • •

18. That if it was the wish of the Legislature to promote usurious dealings, it could not well devise more efficient means than incorporating paper money banks. That these banks, moreover, give rise to many kinds of stock-jobbing, by which the simple-minded are injured and the crafty benefited.

19. That many legislators have, in voting for banks, supposed that they were promoting the welfare of their constituents; but the prevalence of false views in legislative bodies in respect to money corporations and paper money is to be attributed chiefly to the desire certain members have to make money for themselves, or to afford their political partisans and personal friends opportunities for speculation.

20. That the banking interest has a pernicious influence on the periodical press, on public elections, and the general course of legislation. This interest is so powerful that the establishment of a system of sound currency and sound credit is impracticable, except one or other of the political parties into which the nation is divided makes such an object its primary principle of action.

21. That through the various advantages which the system of incorporated paper-money banking has given to some men over others, the foundation has been laid of an *artificial* inequality of wealth, which kind of inequality is, when once laid, increased by all the subsequent operations of society.

22. That this artificial inequality of wealth adds nothing to the substantial happiness of the rich and detracts much from the happiness of the rest of the community. That its tendency is to corrupt one portion of society and debase another.

23. That the sudden dissolution of the banking system without suitable preparation would put an end to the collection of debts, destroy private credit, break up many productive establishments, throw most of the property of the industrious into the hands of speculators, and deprive laboring people of employment.

24. That the system can be got rid of, without difficulty, by prohibiting, after a certain day, the issue of small notes and proceeding gradually to those of the highest denomination.

•   •   •

31. That, on the abolition of incorporated paper-money banks, private bankers will rise up who will receive money on deposit and allow interest on the same, discount promissory notes, and buy and sell bills of exchange. Operating on sufficient funds and being responsible for their engagements in the whole amount of their estates, these private bankers will not by sudden and great "expansions" and "curtailments" derange the whole train of mercantile operations. In each large city an office of deposit and transfer similar to the Bank of Hamburg will be established, and we shall th is secure all the good of the present banking system and avoid all its evils.

32. That, if the present system of banking and paper money shall continue, the wealth and population of the country will increase from natural causes till they shall be equal for each square mile to the wealth and population of Europe. But, with every year, the state of society in the United States will more nearly approximate to the state of society in Great Britain. Crime and pauperism will increase. A few men will be inordinately rich, some comfortable, and a multitude in poverty. This condition of things will naturally lead to the adoption of that policy which proceeds on the principle that a legal remedy is to be found for each social evil, and nothing left for the operations of nature. This kind of legislation will increase the evils it is intended to cure.

33. That there is reason to *hope* that, on the downfall of moneyed corporations and the substitution of gold and silver for bank medium, sound credit will take the place of unsound, and legitimate enterprise the place of wild speculation. That the moral and intellectual character of the people will be sensibly, though gradually, raised, and the causes laid open of a variety of evils under which society is now suffering. That the sources of legislation will to a certain extent be purified, by taking from members of legislative bodies inducements to pass laws for the special benefit of themselves, their personal friends, and political partisans. That the operation of the natural and just causes of wealth and poverty will no longer be inverted, but that each cause will operate in its natural and just order and produce its natural and just effect: wealth becoming the reward of industry, frugality, skill, prudence, and enterprise; and poverty the punishment of few except the indolent and prodigal.

from THE RIGHTS OF MAN TO PROPERTY!

Thomas Skidmore

There is no man of the least reflection, who has not observed, that the effect, in all ages and countries, of the possession of great and undue wealth, is, to allow those who possess it, to live on the labor of others. And yet there is no truth more readily, cheerfully, and universally acknowledged, than that the *personal* exertions of each individual of the human race, are exclusively and unalienably his own.

It would seem, then, to be no bad specimen of argument, to say, inasmuch as great wealth is an instrument which is uniformly used to extort from others, their property in their personal qualities and efforts—that it ought to be taken away from its possessor, on the same principle, that a sword or a pistol may be wrested from a robber, who shall undertake to accomplish the same effect, in a different, manner.

One thing must be obvious to the plainest understanding; that as long as property is unequal; or rather, as long as it is so enormously unequal, as we see it at present, that those who possess it, *will* live on the labor of others. . . .

It is not possible to maintain a doctrine to the contrary of this position without, at the same time, maintaining an absurdity no longer tolerated in enlightened countries; that a part, and that a very great part, of the human race, are doomed, of right, to the slavery of toil, while others are born, only to enjoy.

•　•　•

[T]he great community of mankind . . . in their general, or collective capacity, are trustees, for the benefit of each individual of the species—and the Creator of the Universe is the being, who has furnished the property, which is the subject-matter of the trust, and ordered it to be distributed to all equally. . . .

We live near to a great epoch, in the history of our own country—the Revolution that separated us from England—we are acquainted with the distinguished men, who performed a prominent part, as well in the separation of the two countries, as in erecting the new government that succeeded. We are able to know their minds, and to judge for ourselves, how far they were adequate to institute government, on principles of original right. . . .

Of all these, no man, more than Mr. Jefferson, deserves to be considered, as possessing in his own mind, not only "the standard of the man," but the standard of the age. If there was any one capable of ascending to first principles, it was he; and if it was not to be expected of him, how was it to be expected of any one else? Yet Mr. Jefferson speaks of the rights of man, in terms, which when they come to be investigated closely, appear to be very defective and equivocal. . . .

Whoever looks over the face of the world, and surveys the population of all countries; our own, as well as any and every other; will see it divided into rich and poor; into the hundred who have every thing, and the million who have nothing. If, then, Mr. Jefferson, had made use of the word *property,* instead of *"the pursuit of happiness,"* I should have agreed with him. Then his language would have been clear and intelligible, and strictly conformable to natural right. For I hold, that man's natural right to *life* or *liberty,* is not more sacred or unalienable, than his right to property. But if property is to descend only to particular individuals from the previous generation, and if the many are born, having neither parents nor any one else, to give them property, equal in amount to that which the sons of the rich receive from their fathers and other testators, how is it established that they are created equal? In the pursuit of happiness, is property of no consequence? Can any one be as happy without property of any kind, as with it? Is even liberty and life to be preserved without it? Do we not every day, see multitudes, in order to acquire property, in the very pursuit of that happiness which Mr. Jefferson classes among the unalienable rights of man, obliged to sacrifice both liberty and health and often ultimately life, into the bargain? If then property be so essential and indispensable in the pursuit of happiness, as it appears to be, how can it be said, that I am created with an equal right to this happiness—with another, when I must purchase property of him, with labor and suffering—and when he is under no necessity to purchase the like of me at the same costly price? If we are created equal—how has he the right to monopolize all, or even an undue share of the property of the preceding generation? If, then, even the rights of liberty and life, are so insecure and precarious, without property—how very essential to *their* preservation is it, that "the pursuit of happiness"—should be so construed, as to afford title to that, without which, the rights of life and liberty are but all empty name?

Let no one attempt to evade the question, by saying, that if the poor have not parents with property which they can give to their children, it is not the fault of this or of any government. It is possible, *under some circumstances*, that this might be true, and yet be altogether foreign to the question. But who, I ask, is it, but government that authorizes and enforces the execution of *wills?* Who is it, that allows a man just as he is about to return into dust, to say what disposition shall be made of that which he now calls his; who shall have it, after he ceases to be; and who shall not? Who is it, that authorizes a man to consider himself the owner of property longer than he lives, even to the remotest generation; and clothes him with power, (if he chooses,) to order that even his own children, and his childrens' children forever, shall have none from *him;* nor from anyone else, unless by servitude it be purchased, from others, who may happen to possess it? . . . It is government, therefore, which has the power of destroying wills altogether, and of making such disposition as it shall judge best, of the effects of deceased persons. If, indeed, it were true, that government had the power, or rather ability, only to make life and liberty equal, and could not make property equal; it would go the full length of proving that government, was an unauthorized institution, alienating the "unalienable rights," with which the Creator has endowed all men, a *very great majority of whom*, have no property of any description; never have had any: and while the present order of things exists, never *will* have any.

The Author of the Declaration of Independence, and those who supported it, "with their lives, their fortunes and their sacred honor," never seemed to have perceived, that, if their system of rights, in its practical effect, went to give to one human being living under it, the privilege of taking so much of the property of the preceding generation (whether it came from a parent is nothing to the question,) as would enable him to live in idleness, on the productions of the labor of others; so should it give the same privilege to all. Otherwise there is no equality in the business; and the declaration, that the Creator had created such an equality, but the legislation of man had destroyed it, becomes at once the *theory* of our government on the one hand, and its *practice* on the other. . . .

Again, let me ask what is the *purpose* of this posthumous dominion over property? Is it to give pleasure to the dead? They cannot feel. And besides if they could, such pleasure might be more than compensated by the pain of the living. Is it to avert any calamity, or procure any blessing during life, which otherwise could not be averted or procured, that he should enjoy this dominion? This is not possible, for no effect of this dominion is to happen until its possessor has ceased to be capable of any sensation of either suffering or joy. Is it to gratify vanity by enabling him to say "Such is the property I leave you?" Generous man! I would reply, who leave behind you, what you cannot carry away with you! As much is your generosity to be admired, as the criminal's on the gallows, who, when he is just about to be executed, declares he is determined to commit murder no more!

•　•　•

The principle which the first of all governments in any country, and, indeed, every succeeding government, should adopt and practice, is this. In dividing that which is the equal and common property of all, the apportionments should be equal; and if it is concluded, as it will be, where men understand how best to pursue their own happiness, that a life-lease of property is better than any other, that will be the term preferred to every other. . . . Society, thus organized, gives notice to all its members, that they are to use their own industry, with a view to their own happiness; and cannot be allowed, on any pretence whatever, whether of kindness or otherwise, to interfere with others in the same pursuit. . . .

Whoever looks at the world as it now is will see it divided into two distinct classes: proprietors, and non-proprietors; those who own the world, and those who own no part of it. If we take a closer view of these two classes, we shall find that a very great proportion even of the proprietors are only nominally so; they possess so little that in strict regard to truth they ought to be classed among the non-proprietors. They may be compared, in fact, to the small prizes in a lottery, which, when they are paid, leave the holder a loser. . . .

But when we see that the system which has prevailed . . . gives to some single descendant of some holder of property under William Penn possessions of the value perhaps of a million dollars, while, it may be, an hundred thousand other inhabitants of Pennsylvania, collectively, have not half that sum; *and all this, merely because of a few beads having been given to some Indians some two hundred years ago;* how is it possible to have had a different result? The system is one that *begins* by making whole nations paupers; and why should it not be expected that they would *continue* so? Indeed it would be a miracle, exceeding everything of the kind that has ever been supposed to have happened, if we had seen from such an organization of things anything but what we now see. . . .

If these remarks be true, there would seem, then, to be no remedy but by commencing anew. And is there any reason why we should not? That which is commenced in error and injustice may surely be set right when we know how to do it. There is *power* enough in the hands of the people of the State of New York or of any other State to rectify any and every thing which requires it, when they shall see wherein the evil exists and wherein lies the remedy. . . . If still there be those who shall say that these unjust and unequal governments ought not to be destroyed, although they may not give to man in society the same equality of property as he would enjoy in a state of nature; then I say that *those are the persons* who, in society, *if anybody,* should be deprived of all their possessions, inasmuch as it is manifestly as proper for them to be destitute of property as it is for any one else. If slavery and degradation are to be the result, they are the proper victims. After an equal division has been once made, there seems nothing wanting but to secure an equal transmission of property to posterity. . . .

Instead, therefore, of this gentleman or any other person in similar circumstances having any right to complain of any dispossession of vast estates thus coming to him by what is called descent, one would naturally think that he ought to congratulate himself that he has enjoyed the sweets they have afforded him so long; and that gratitude to as well as a proper consideration for the rights of each individual around him should make him acquiesce in the decree of this community, if they should think proper so to order, to surrender it up, preparatory to its being divided equally among the whole, himself, of course, being one of the number. . . .

In justification of himself, if he should say, "I was more industrious than others, more temperate, more frugal, more ingenious, more skilful, had greater bodily strength which I did not fail to exercise and therefore, for all these reasons, I ought to be allowed to retain what I have," could we not say it is not true? And admitting it to be true that he was *equally* as industrious, etc., as many thousands of his fellow-citizens, would it not be the most fatal argument that could be urged

against him? For if all these qualities are to be considered as giving
him a title to *his property*, as he calls it, why should it not give a title
also to them to an equal possession with him? And yet they have labored yet have nothing! Such is, at least, the case with the great mass
of mankind. And *all* the rich, we certainly know, cannot pretend to be
proportionally *more* virtuous than they. . . .

This modification will be accomplished by pursuing the following

PLAN

1. Let a new State Convention be assembled. Let it prepare a new
constitution, and let that constitution, after having been adopted by
the people, decree an abolition of all debts, both at home and abroad,
between citizen and citizen, and between citizen and foreigner. Let it
renounce all property belonging to our citizens, without the State. Let
it claim all property within the State, both real and personal, of whatever kind it may be, with the exception of that belonging to resident
aliens, and with the further exception of so much personal property
as may be in the possession of transient owners, not being citizens. Let
it order an equal division of all this property among the citizens, of
and over the age of maturity, in manner yet to be directed. Let it order
all transfers or removals of property, except so much as may belong to
transient owners, to cease until the division is accomplished.

2. Let a census be taken of the people. . . .

3. Let each citizen, association, corporation, and other persons at
the same time when the census is being taken give an inventory of all
personal property, of whatever description it may be, and to whomsoever it may belong, in his, her, or their possession. Let also a similar
inventory of all real property within the State be taken, whoever may
be the owner of it. . . .

4. Let there be next a dividend made of this amount among all such
citizens who shall be of and over the age of eighteen, if this should be
fixed as I am inclined to think it should be as the age of maturity; and
let such dividend be entered in a book for the purpose to the credit of
such persons, male and female.

5. Let public sale be made, as soon after such dividend is made as
may be practicable, to the highest bidder of all the real and personal
property in the State.

•   •   •

8. As it regards personal property which may be secreted or clandestinely put out of the way, order should be given that from the time when any Inventory of any person's property of the kind is made out up to the completion of the General Sale, the owner should be answerable for the forthcoming of so much as may be left in his possession, at the peril of imprisonment for fourteen years as is now the punishment for the crime of grand larceny.

•   •   •

10. There is one exception to the delivering of property to persons who may bid it off. It is to those for whom, from excessive intemperance, insanity, or other incapacitating cause, the law may provide, as it should, proper and suitable trustees or guardians. Under proper regulations, it should be entrusted to *them*.

11. While all this is transacting, persons already arrived at the age of maturity and before they can be put in possession of their own patrimony will die. Of these and others throughout the State, a daily register should be kept from this time forward forever; and so also should be kept another register of the births of those now in minority and of those that shall hereafter be born. The property intended to be given to those who shall thus have died and the property of those who shall have received their patrimony in consequence of the General Division and who shall die before the first day of January ensuing the completion of the General Sales shall be divided equally among all those who shall have arrived at the age of maturity between the time of taking the Census aforesaid and the first day of January just mentioned.

12. An annual dividend forever shall be made of the property left throughout the State by persons dying between the last day of every year and the first day of the next succeeding among those who throughout the State, male and female, shall have arrived at the age of maturity within such period; and it shall be at their option, after the dividend is made, to receive it in cash or to use the credit of it in the future purchase of other property which the State will have constantly on sale in consequence of the decease of other persons in the ensuing year.

•   •   •

16. All native born citizens from the period of their birth to that of their maturity shall receive from the State a sum paid monthly or oth-

er more convenient installments equal to their full and decent maintenance according to age and condition; and the parent or parents, if living and not rendered unsuitable by incapacity or vicious habits to train
up their children, shall be the persons authorized to receive it. Otherwise, guardians must be appointed to take care of such children and
receive their maintenance allowance. They are to be educated also at
the public expense.

17. When the death happens of either of any two married persons,
the survivor retains one half of the sum of their joint property, their
debts being first paid. The other half goes to the State, through the
hands of the Public Administrator; this Office taking charge of the effects of all deceased persons.

18. Punishment by imprisonment for a term of fourteen years
should be visited upon him who during his lifetime gives away his
property to another. Hospitality is, of course, not interdicted but charity is, inasmuch as ample provision will be made by the State for such
persons as shall require it. The good citizen has only to inform the ap-
plicant for charity where his proper wants will be supplied.

19. All persons after receiving their patrimony will be at full liberty to reside within the State, or to take it or its avails to any other part
of the world which may be preferred and there to reside as a citizen or
subject of another state.

20. Property being thus continually and equally divided forever,
and the receivers of such property embarking in all the various pursuits and occupations of life, these pursuits and occupations must be
guaranteed against injury from foreign competition, or otherwise in-
demnity should be made by the State.

I have thus developed the principles of the modification which the
Government of this State should undergo and the means necessary to
accomplish it in order that every citizen may enjoy in a state of society
substantially the rights which belong to him in a state of nature.

• • •

The same eternal and indissoluble rights, exist for all: "all men are
created equal:" and neither governments, nor others, have any right,
so to speak, to *uncreate them.* The black man's right to suffrage, being a
personal right, is as perfect as the white man's; and, so also is his right
of property. But, if the present constitution existed, and the colored citizen were put in possession of his equal portion of the domain of the

State, and all its personal effects, he would not have the same right to appear at the ballot boxes, as the white man. It is necessary that he should have such right; for elsewhere there is no power, but unlawful force, with which he may defend his property. Those who could go to the ballot-boxes, and put in their votes, could, by that very act, take it away from him, without his having a chance to make reprisal or resistance. It would be nonsense on the one hand to say, "this is your property;" and on the other, to tell him; "but you shall not have the same power to defend it, as belongs to another." Nor, can it be pretended, on any account, that what some people call policy, should sanction the with-holding from the black man, the same right of suffrage, which is extended to the white man. . . .

But if the principle is to prevail, that property is given to any human being, in the right which such being holds to it, in virtue of his existence; and that the right of suffrage, being a personal right, co-existent with the being himself, belongs to him also, as a means of its defence and preservation, as well as of his personal liberty; it follows that woman as well as man, is entitled to the same right of suffrage, and ought, on no consideration to be deprived of it. It is not necessary to say one word on the propriety or utility of its exercise; this is a matter to be left, wholly and exclusively to the judgment and pleasure of her or him to whom such right belongs, independent and regardless, even, of the whole community.

from THE LABORING CLASSES

Orestes Augustus Brownson

The middle class is always a firm champion of equality when it concerns humbling a class below it. Manfully have the British commoners struggled against the old feudal aristocracy, and so successfully that they now constitute the dominant power in the state. To their struggles against the throne and the nobility is the English nation indebted for the liberty it so loudly boasts and which, during the last half of the last century, so enraptured the friends of humanity throughout Europe.

But this class has done nothing for the laboring population, the real *proletarii*. It has humbled the aristocracy; it has raised itself to dominion, and it is now conservative . . . .

Their only real enemy is in the employer. In all countries is it the same. The only enemy of the laborer is your employer, whether appearing in the shape of the master mechanic, or in the owner of a factory. A Duke of Wellington is much more likely to vindicate the rights of labor than an Abbot Lawrence, although the latter may be a very kind-hearted man and liberal citizen . . . .

We have little faith in the power of education to elevate a people compelled to labor from twelve to sixteen hours a day and to experience for no mean portion of the time a paucity of even the necessaries of life, let alone its comforts. Give your starving boy a breakfast before you send him to school and your tattered beggar a cloak before you attempt his moral and intellectual elevation. A swarm of naked and starving urchins crowded into a schoolroom will make little proficiency in the "Humanities." Indeed, it seems to us most bitter mockery for the well-dressed and well-fed to send the schoolmaster and priest to the wretched hovels of squalid poverty, a mockery at which devils may laugh but over which angels must weep. Educate the working classes of England; and what then? Will they require less food and less clothing when educated than they do now? Will they be more contented or more happy in their condition? For God's sake beware how you kindle within them the intellectual spark, and make them aware that they too are men, with powers of thought and feeling which ally them by the bonds of brotherhood to their betters. If you will doom them to the external condition of brutes, do in common charity keep their minds and hearts brutish. Render them as insensible as possible, that they may feel the less acutely their degradation and see the less clearly the monstrous injustice which is done them. . . .

What then is the remedy? As it concerns England, we shall leave the English statesman to answer. Be it what it may, it will not be obtained without war and bloodshed. It will be found only at the end of one of the longest and severest struggles the human race has ever been engaged in, only by that most dreaded of all wars, the war of the poor against the rich, a war which, however long it may be delayed, will come, and come with all its horrors. The day of vengeance is sure; for the world after all is under the dominion of a just Providence.

No one can observe the signs of the times with much care without perceiving that a crisis as to the relation of wealth and labor is approaching. It is useless to shut our eyes to the fact, and like the ostrich fancy ourselves secure because we have so concealed our heads that we see not the danger. We or our children will have to meet this crisis. The old war between the King and the Barons is well nigh ended, and so is that between the Barons and the Merchants and Manufacturers, landed capital and commercial capital. The businessman has become the peer of my Lord. And now commences the new struggle between the operative and his employer, between wealth and labor. Every day does this struggle extend further and wax stronger and fiercer; what or when the end will be God only knows.

In this coming contest there is a deeper question at issue than is commonly imagined, a question which is but remotely touched in your controversies about United States banks and sub-treasuries, chartered banking and free banking, free trade and corporations, although these controversies may be paving the way for it to come up. We have discovered no presentiment of it in any king's or queen's speech, nor in any President's message. It is embraced in no popular political creed of the day, whether christened Whig or Tory, *Justemilieu* or Democratic. No popular Senator or deputy or peer seems to have any glimpse of it; but it is working, in the hearts of the million, is struggling to shape itself, and one day it will be uttered, and in thunder tones. Well will it be for him who, on that day, shall be found ready to answer it.

What we would ask is, throughout the Christian world, the actual condition of the laboring classes, viewed simply and exclusively in their capacity of laborers? . . .

All over the world this fact stares us in the face: the workingman is poor and depressed, while a large portion of the non-workingmen, in the sense we now use the term, are wealthy. It may be laid down as a general rule, with but few exceptions, that men are rewarded in an inverse ratio to the amount of actual service they perform. . . . The whole class of simple laborers are poor and in general unable to procure any thing beyond the bare necessaries of life.

In regard to labor two systems obtain: one that of slave labor, the other that of free labor. Of the two, the first is, in our judgment, except so far as the feelings are concerned, decidedly the least oppressive. If the slave has never been a free man, we think, as a general rule, his sufferings are less than those of the free laborer at wages. As to actual freedom one has just about as much as the other. The laborer at wages has all the disadvantages of freedom and none of its blessings, while the slave, if denied the blessings, is freed from the disadvantages. We are no advocates of slavery; we are as heartily opposed to it as any modern abolitionist can be; but we say frankly that, if there must always be a laboring population distinct from proprietors and employers, we regard the slave system as decidedly preferable to the system at wages. It is no pleasant thing to go days without food, to lie idle for weeks, seeking work and finding none, to rise in the morning with a wife and children you love, and know not where to procure them a breakfast, and to see constantly before you no brighter prospect than the almshouse. Yet these are no unfrequent incidents in the lives of our laboring population. Even in seasons of general prosperity, when there was only the ordinary cry of "hard times," we have seen hundreds of people in a not very populous village, in a wealthy portion of our common country, suffering for the want of the necessaries of life, willing to work, and yet finding no work to do. Many and many is the application of a poor man for work, merely for his food, we have seen rejected. These things are little thought of, for the applicants are poor; they fill no conspicuous place in society, and they have no biographers. But their wrongs are chronicled in heaven. It is said there is no want in this country. There may be less than in some other countries. But death by actual starvation in this country is, we apprehend, no uncommon occurrence. The sufferings of a quiet, unassuming but useful class of females in our cities, in general sempstresses, too proud to beg or to apply to the almshouse, are not easily told. They are industrious; they do all that they can find to do, but yet the little there is for them to do, and the miserable pittance they receive for it is hardly sufficient to keep soul and body together. And yet there is a man who employs them to make shirts, trousers, etc., and grows rich on their labors. He is one of our respectable citizens, perhaps is praised in the newspapers for his liberal donations to some charitable institution. He passes among us as a pattern of morality and is honored as a worthy Christian. And why should he not be, since our *Christian* community is made up of such as he, and since our clergy would not dare question his piety lest they should incur the reproach of infidelity and lose their standing and their salaries? Nay, since our clergy are raised up, educated, fashioned, and sustained by such as he? Not a few of our churches rest on Mammon for their foundation. The basement is a trader's shop.

We pass through our manufacturing villages; most of them appear neat and flourishing. The operatives are well dressed and, we are told, well paid. They are said to be healthy, contented, and happy. This is the fair side of the picture; the side exhibited to distinguished visitors. There is a dark side, moral as well as physical. Of the common operatives, few, if any, by their wages, acquire a competence. . . . But the great mass wear out their health, spirits, and morals without becoming one whit better off than when they commenced labor. The bills of mortality in these factory villages are not striking, we admit, for the poor girls when they can toil no longer go home to die. The average life—working life, we mean—of the girls that come to Lowell, for instance, from Maine, New Hampshire, and Vermont, we have been assured, is only about three years. What becomes of them then? Few of them ever marry; fewer still ever return to their native places with reputations unimpaired. "She has worked in a factory," is almost enough to damn to infamy the most worthy and virtuous girl. We know no sadder sight on earth than one of our factory villages presents when the bell, at break of day, or at the hour of breakfast or dinner, calls out its hundreds or thousands of operatives. We stand and look at these hard-working men and women hurrying in all directions and ask ourselves where go the proceeds of their labors? The man who employs them and for whom they are toiling as so many slaves is one of our city nabobs, reveling in luxury; or he is a member of our legislature, enacting laws to put money in his own pocket; or he is a member of Congress, contending for a high tariff to tax the poor for the benefit of the rich; or in these times he is shedding crocodile tears over the deplorable condition of the poor laborer, while he docks his wages twenty-five per cent; building miniature log cabins, shouting Harrison and "hard cider." And this man too would fain pass for a Christian and a republican. He shouts for liberty, stickles for equality, and is horrified at a Southern planter who keeps slaves.

One thing is certain: that, of the amount actually produced by the operative, he retains a less proportion than it costs the master to feed, clothe, and lodge his slave. Wages is a cunning device of the devil for the benefit of tender consciences who would retain all the advantages of the slave system without the expense, trouble, and odium of being slaveholders. . . .

Nevertheless the system of wages will triumph. It is the system which in name sounds honester than slavery and in substance is more profitable to the master. It yields the wages of iniquity, without its opprobrium. It will therefore supplant slavery and be sustained, for a time. . . .

In our own country this condition has existed under its most favorable aspects and has been made as good as it can be. It has reached all the excellence of which it is susceptible. It is now not improving but growing worse. The actual condition of the workingman today, viewed in all its bearings, is not so good as it was fifty years ago. If we have not been altogether misinformed, fifty years ago, health and industrious habits constituted no mean stock in trade, and with them almost any man might aspire to competence and independence. But it is so no longer. The wilderness has receded, and already the new lands are beyond the reach of the mere laborer, and the employer has him at his mercy. . . .

. . . [O]ur business is to emancipate the proletaries as the past has emancipated the slaves. This is our work. There must be no class of our fellow men doomed to toil through life as mere workmen at wages. If wages are tolerated it must be, in the case of the individual operative, only under such conditions that, by the time he is of a proper age to settle in life, he shall have accumulated enough to be an independent laborer on his own capital, on his own farm or in his own shop. Here is our work. How is it to be done? . . .

. . . [T]he evil we speak of is inherent in all our social arrangements, and cannot be cured without a radical change of those arrangements.

... The only way to get rid of its evils is to change the system, not its managers. The evils of slavery do not result from the personal characters of slave masters. They are inseparable from the system, let who will be masters. Make all your rich men good Christians, and you have lessened not the evils of existing inequality in wealth. The mischievous effects of this inequality do not result from the personal characters of either rich or poor, but from itself, and they will continue just so long as there are rich men and poor men in the same community. You must abolish the system or accept its consequences. No man can serve both God and Mammon. If you will serve the devil, you must look to the devil for your wages; we know no other way. . . .

The remedy is first to be sought in the destruction of the priest. . . . What was the mission of Jesus but a solemn summons of every priesthood on earth to judgment and of the human race to freedom? He discomfited the learned doctors and with whips of small cords drove the priests, degenerated into mere money changers, from the temple of God. He instituted himself no priesthood, no form of religious worship. He recognized no priest but a holy life and commanded the construction of no temple but that of the pure heart. He preached no formal religion, enjoined no creed, set apart no day for religious worship. He preached fraternal love, peace on earth, and good will to men. He came to the soul enslaved, "cabined, cribbed, confined," to the poor child of mortality, bound hand and foot, unable to move, and said in the tones of a God, "Be free; be enlarged; be there room for thee to grow, expand, and overflow with the love thou wast made to overflow with." . . .

The priest is universally a tyrant, universally the enslaver of his brethren, and therefore it is Christianity condemns him. . . .

It may be supposed that we Protestants have no priests, but for ourselves we know no fundamental difference between a Catholic priest and a Protestant clergyman, as we know no difference of any magnitude, in relation to the principles on which they are based, between a Protestant church and the Catholic church. Both are based on the principle of authority; both deny in fact, however it may be in manner, the authority of reason and war against freedom of mind; both substitute dead works for true righteousness, a vain show for the reality of piety, and are sustained as the means of reconciling us to God without requiring us to become godlike. Both therefore ought to go by the board. . . .

According to the Christianity of Christ, no man can enter the kingdom of God who does not labor with all zeal and diligence to establish the kingdom of God on the earth—who does not labor to bring down the high and bring up the low; to break the fetters of the bound and set the captive free; to destroy all oppression, establish the reign of justice, which is the reign of equality, between man and man; to introduce new heavens and a new earth, wherein dwelleth righteousness, wherein all shall be as brothers, loving one another, and no one possessing what another lacketh. No man can be a Christian who does not labor to reform society. . . No man can be a Christian who does not refrain from all practices by which the rich grow richer and the poor poorer, and who does not do all in his power to elevate the laboring classes, so that one man shall not be doomed to toil while another enjoys the fruits; so that each man shall be free and independent, sitting under "his own vine and fig tree with none to molest or to make afraid." We grant the power of Christianity in working out the reform we demand; we agree that one of the most efficient means of elevating the workingmen is to Christianize the community. But you must Christianize it. It is the gospel of Jesus you must preach, and not the gospel of the priests. . . . [L]et it be the genuine gospel that you preach, and not that pseudo-gospel which lulls the conscience asleep and permits men to feel that they may be servants of God while they are slaves to the world, the flesh, and the devil, and while they ride roughshod over the hearts of their prostrate brethren. . . .

But what shall government do? Its first doing must be an *un*doing. There has been thus far quite too much government, as well as government of the wrong kind. The first act of government we want is a still further limitation of itself. It must begin by circumscribing within narrower limits its powers. And then it must proceed to repeal all laws which bear against the laboring classes, and then to enact such laws as are necessary to enable them to maintain their equality. We have no faith in those systems of elevating the working classes which propose to elevate them without calling in the aid of government. We must have government and legislation expressly directed to this end. . . .

It is obvious then that, if our object be the elevation of the laboring classes, we must destroy the power of the banks over the Government and place the Government in the hands of the laboring classes themselves or in the hands of those, if such there be, who have an identity of interest with them. But this cannot be done so long as the banks exist.

Such is the subtle influence of credit and such the power of capital that a banking system like ours, if sustained, necessarily and inevitably becomes the real and efficient government of the country. We have been struggling for ten years in this country against the power of the banks, struggling to free merely the Federal Government from their grasp, but with humiliating success. At this moment, the contest is almost doubtful, not indeed in our mind, but in the minds of no small portion of our countrymen. The partisans of the banks count on certain victory. The banks discount freely to build "log cabins," to purchase "hard cider," and to defray the expense of manufacturing enthusiasm for a cause which is at war with the interests of the people. That they will succeed, we do not for one moment believe; but that they could maintain the struggle so long and be as strong as they now are at the end of ten years' constant hostility proves but all too well the power of the banks and their fatal influence on the political action of the community. . . .

Following the destruction of the banks, must come that of all monopolies, of all privilege. There are many of these. We cannot specify them all; we therefore select only one, the greatest of them all, the privilege which some have of being born rich while others are born poor. It will be seen at once that we allude to the hereditary descent of property, an anomaly in our American system, which must be removed o the system itself will be destroyed. . . . [A]s we have abolished hereditary monarchy and hereditary nobility we must complete the work by abolishing hereditary property. A man shall have all he honestly acquires, so long as he himself belongs to the world in which he acquires it. But his power over his property must cease with his life, and his property must then become the property of the State, to be disposed of by some equitable law for the use of the generation which takes his place. . . . We see no means of elevating the laboring classes which can be effectual without this. And is this a measure to be easily carried? Not at all. It will cost infinitely more than it cost to abolish either hereditary monarchy or hereditary nobility. It is a great measure, and a startling. The rich, the business community, will never voluntarily consent to it, and we think we know too much of human nature to believe that it will ever be effected peaceably. It will be effected only by the strong arm of physical force. It will come, if it ever come at all, only at the conclusion of war, the like of which the world as yet has never witnessed, and from which, however inevitable it may seem to the eye of philosophy, the heart of Humanity recoils with horror.

We are not ready for this measure yet. There is much previous work to be done, and we should be the last to bring it before the legislature. The time, however, has come for its free and full discussion.

from SOCIOLOGY FOR THE SOUTH

George Fitzhugh

FREE TRADE

Political economy is the science of free society. Its theory and its history alike establish this position. Its fundamental maxims, *Laissez-faire* and *"Pas trop gouverner,"* are at war with all kinds of slavery, for they in fact assert that individuals and peoples prosper most when governed least. . . . After the abolition of feudalism and Catholicism, an immense amount of unfettered talent, genius, industry and capital, was brought into the field of free competition. The immediate result was, that all those who possessed either of those advantages prospered as they had never prospered before, and rose in social position and intelligence. At the same time, and from the same causes, the aggregate wealth of society, and probably its aggregate intelligence, were rapidly increased. Such was no doubt part of the effects, of unfettering the limbs, the minds and consciences of men. . . .

A philosophy that should guide and direct industry was equally needed with a philosophy of morals. The occasion found and made the man. For writing a one-sided philosophy, no man was better fitted than Adam Smith. He possessed extraordinary powers of abstraction, analysis and generalization. He was absent, secluded and unobservant. He saw only that prosperous and progressive portion of society whom liberty or free competition benefitted, and mistook its effects on them for its effects on the world. He had probably never heard the old English adage, "Every man for himself, and Devil take the hindmost." This saying comprehends the whole philosophy, moral and economical, of the "Wealth of Nations." . . .

Its leading and almost its only doctrine is, that individual well-being and social and national wealth and prosperity will be best promoted by each man's eagerly pursuing his own selfish welfare unfettered and unrestricted by legal regulations, or governmental prohibitions, farther than such regulations may be necessary to prevent positive crime.

. . . His friends and acquaintances were of that class, who, in the war of the wits to which free competition invited, were sure to come off victors. His country, too, England and Scotland, in the arts of trade and in manufacturing skill, was an over-match for the rest of the world. International free trade would benefit his country as much as social free trade would benefit his friends. This was his world, and had it been the only world his philosophy would have been true. But there was another and much larger world, whose misfortunes, under his system, were to make the fortunes of his friends and his country. . . . [T]he unemployed poor, the weak in mind or body, the simple and unsuspicious, the prodigal, the dissipated, the improvident and the vicious. . . . [T]hey were fine subjects out of which the astute and designing, the provident and avaricious, the cunning, the prudent and the industrious might make fortunes in the field of free competition. Another portion of the world which Smith overlooked, were the countries with which England traded. . . Trade is a war of the wits, in which the stronger witted are sure to succeed as the stronger armed in a war with swords. . . . And thus, whether between nations or individuals, the war of free trade is constantly widening the relative abilities of the weak and the strong. It has been justly observed that under this system the rich are continually growing richer and the poor poorer. The remark is true as well between nations as between individuals. Free trade, when the American gives a bottle of whiskey to the Indian for valuable furs, or the Englishman exchanges with the African blue-beads for diamonds, gold and slaves, is a fair specimen of all free trade when unequals meet. Free trade between England and Ireland furnishes the latter an excellent market for her beef and potatoes, in exchange for English manufactures. . . . But far the worst evils of this free trade remain to be told. Irish pursuits depressing education and refinement, England becomes a market for the wealth, the intellect, the talent, energy and enterprise of Ireland. . . . Thus is Ireland robbed of her very life's blood, and thus do our Northern States rob the Southern.

Under the system of free trade a fertile soil, with good rivers and roads as outlets, becomes the greatest evil with which a country can be afflicted. The richness of soil invites to agriculture, and the roads and rivers carry off the crops, to be exchanged for the manufactures of poorer regions, where are situated the centres of trade, of capital and manufactures. In a few centuries or less time the consumption abroad of the crops impoverishes the soil where they are made. No cities or manufactories arise in the country with this fertile soil, because there is no occasion. No pursuits are carried on requiring intelligence or skill; the population is of necessity sparse, ignorant and illiterate; universal absenteeism prevails; the rich go off for pleasure and education, the enterprising poor for employment. . . .

The profits of exclusive agriculture are not more than one-third of those realized from commerce and manufactures. The ordinary and average wages of laborers employed in manufactures and mechanic trades are about double those of agricultural laborers; but, moreover, women and children get good wages in manufacturing countries, whose labor is lost in agricultural ones. But this consideration, great as it is, shrinks to insignificance compared with the intellectual superiority of all other pursuits over agriculture. . . .

THE TWO PHILOSOPHIES

. . . The people in free society feel the evils of universal liberty and free competition, and desire to get rid of those evils. They propose a remedy, which is in fact slavery; but they are wholly unconscious of what they are doing, because never having lived in the midst of slavery, they know not what slavery is. The citizens of the South, who have seen none of the evils of liberty and competition, but just enough of those agencies to operate as healthful stimulants to energy, enterprise and industry, believe free competition to be an unmixed good.

The South, quiet, contented, satisfied, looks upon all socialists and radical reformers as madmen or knaves. It is as ignorant of free society as that society is of slavery. . . . The knowledge of the numerous theories of radical reform proposed in Europe, and the causes that have led to their promulgation, is of vital importance to us. Yet we turn away from them with disgust, as from something unclean and vicious. We occupy high vantage ground for observing, studying and classifying the various phenomena of society; yet we do not profit by the advantages of our position. We should do so, and indignantly hurl back upon our assailants the charge, that there is something wrong and rotten in our system. From their own mouths we can show free society to be a monstrous abortion, and slavery to be the healthy, beautiful and natural being which they are trying, unconsciously, to adopt.

NEGRO SLAVERY

. . . Very wicked men must be put into penitentiaries; lunatics into asylums, and the most wild of them into strait-jackets, just as the most wicked of the sane are manacled with irons; and idiots must have committees to govern and take care of them. Now, it is clear the Athenian democracy would not suit a negro nation, nor will the government of mere law suffice for the individual negro. He is but a grown up child, and must be governed as a child, not as a lunatic or criminal. The master occupies towards him the place of parent or guardian. . . .

The negro is improvident; will not lay up in summer for the wants of winter; will not accumulate in youth for the exigencies of age. He would become an insufferable burden to society. Society has the right to prevent this, and can only do so by subjecting him to domestic slavery. In the last place, the negro race is inferior to the white race, and living in their midst, they would be far outstripped or outwitted in the chase of free competition. Gradual but certain extermination would be their fate. . . . In Africa or the West Indies, he would become idolatrous, savage and cannibal, or be devoured by savages and cannibals. At the North he would freeze or starve.

We would remind those who deprecate and sympathize with negro slavery, that his slavery here relieves him from a far more cruel slavery in Africa, or from idolatry and cannibalism, and every brutal vice and crime that can disgrace humanity; and that it christianizes, protects, supports and civilizes him; that it governs him far better than free laborers at the North are governed. There, wife-murder has become a mere holiday pastime. . . . Our negroes are not only better off as to physical comfort than free laborers, but their moral condition is better.

But abolish negro slavery, and how much of slavery still remains. . . . Children are slaves to their parents, guardians and teachers. Imprisoned culprits are slaves. Lunatics and idiots are slaves also. Three-fourths of free society are slaves, no better treated, when their wants and capacities are estimated, than negro slaves. The masters in free society, or slave society, if they perform properly their duties, have more cares and less liberty than the slaves themselves. . . .

Every negro in the South would be soon liberated, if he would take liberty on the terms that white tenants hold it. The fact that he cannot enjoy liberty on such terms, seems conclusive that he is only fit to be a slave.

But for the assaults of the abolitionists, much would have been done ere this to regulate and improve Southern slavery. Our negro mechanics do not work so hard, have many more privileges and holidays, and are better fed and clothed than field hands, and are yet more valuable to their masters. The slaves of the South are cheated of their rights by the purchase of Northern manufactures which they could produce. Besides, if we would employ our slaves in the coarser processes of the mechanic arts and manufacturers, such as brick making, getting and hewing timber for ships and houses, iron mining and smelting, coal mining, grading railroads and plank roads, in the manufacture of cotton, tobacco, &c., we would find a vent in new employments for their increase, more humane and more profitable than the vent afforded by new states and territories. The nice and finishing processes of manufactures and mechanics should be reserved for the whites, who only are fitted for them, and thus, by diversifying pursuits and cutting off dependence on the North, we might benefit and advance the interest of our whole population. Exclusive agriculture has depressed and impoverished the South. . . . Free trade doctrines, not slavery, have made the South agricultural and dependent, given her a sparse and ignorant population, ruined her cities, and expelled her people. . . .

We need never have white slaves in the South, because we have black ones. Our citizens, like those of Rome and Athens, are a privileged class. We should train and educate them to deserve the privileges and to perform the duties which society confers on them. Instead of, by a low demagoguism, depressing their self-respect by discourses on the equality of man, we had better excite their pride by reminding them that they do not fulfil the menial offices which white men do in other countries. Society does not feel the burden of providing for the few helpless paupers in the South. And we should recollect that here we have but half the people to educate, for half are negroes. . . .

We deem this peculiar question of negro slavery of very little importance. The issue is made throughout the world on the general subject of slavery in the abstract. The argument has commenced. One set of ideas will govern and control after awhile the civilized world. Slavery will every where be abolished, or every where be re-instituted. We think the opponents of practical, existing slavery, are stopped by their own admission; nay, that unconsciously, as socialists, they are the defenders and propagandists of slavery, and have furnished the only sound arguments on which its defence and justification can be rested. We have introduced the subject of negro slavery to afford us a better opportunity to disclaim the purpose of reducing the white man any where to the condition of negro slaves here. It would be very unwise and unscientific to govern white men as you would negroes. . . .

We abhor the doctrine of the "Types of Mankind;" first, because it is at war with scripture, which teaches us that the whole human race is descended from a common parentage; and, secondly, because it encourages and incites brutal masters to treat negroes, not as weak, ignorant and dependent brethren, but as wicked beasts, without the pale of humanity. This Southerner is the negro's friend, his only friend. Let no intermeddling abolitionist, no refined philosophy, dissolve this friendship.

CHAPTER 12
Reforming Society

Introduction

THEODORE DWIGHT WELD, 1803–1895,
ANGELINA GRIMKÉ, 1805–1879,
AND SARAH GRIMKÉ, 1792–1873
Weld-Grimké Letters (1837–1843)

SENECA FALLS DECLARATION OF RIGHTS (1848)

FREDERICK DOUGLASS, 1817–1895
from Fifth of July Speech (1852)

SARAH PAYSON PARTON ("FANNY
FERN"), 1811–1862
from Little Ferns for Fanny's Little Friends (1854)

NATHANIEL HAWTHORNE, 1804–1864
from Earth's Holocaust (1846)

Both democratic and religious ferment spurred broad reform efforts in many directions—better institutions for criminals, the insane, orphans, and the poor; dress, diet and medical changes; and efforts to end war, prostitution, mutilation, and capital punishment. Public education was perhaps the most successful of these efforts; certainly abolition, women's rights, property rights, and temperance were the most controversial.

Several women gained a clearer sense of their own oppression from struggling against that of the slave. The complexity of this tie between abolition and women's rights is clear in the letters between the ablest anti-slavery organizer, Theodore Dwight Weld and Sarah and Angelina Grimké, daughters of a leading South Carolina planter family. In the North, the sisters were among the most prominent abolitionists.

Sarah wrote the earliest American feminist book, unprecedented in its stress on economics as central to women's liberation, and Angelina was so effective an orator that she did much to change Northern attitudes toward women's speaking in public forums. Their letters show the depth of religious and personal feeling (like those of John and Margaret Winthrop two centuries earlier) that motivated abolitionists social efforts. After 1842 Weld and the Grimkés ceased their activism, convinced that the "events" they had helped set in motion were now surely leading to slavery's end, probably through civil war. An 1848 convention in Seneca Falls, New York issued the classic argument for women's rights in form that drew on the nation's earlier Declaration.

Frederick Douglass, who escaped enslavement in Maryland as a young man, supported women's rights but devoted his life to fighting both American slavery and the laws and prejudices that encumbered free black life. A distinguished writer, orator and abolitionist organizer, Douglass was especially famous in the antebellum years for his powerful oratory, well demonstrated in his honest and scathing Fifth of July Speech.

Sarah Payson Parton was perhaps the most popular and best paid writer of the 1850s. Her stories for children show the reform concerns of that decade, to be swamped by growing sectional discord. Nathaniel Hawthorne deemed Parton the best of "the scribbling women," whose success he envied. His allegory on reform efforts was less an attack on the process than an application to it of his basic message to his era: evil resides, and needs to be recognized, in the human heart itself.

CONSIDERATIONS

- What concerns seem to lie behind reformers' efforts in the period? What right or responsibility did they have to tell others in society what to do? How could one define the "common good" on the issues they raised?

- Was the temperance crusade against alcohol different in any basic way from the contemporary opposition to drugs?

- How reasonable was the abolitionist attack on slavery? What should they have said differently, or should they have said nothing?

- What are the differences and who is right, in the Weld-Grimké argument? Were men in the period tyranninizing women? Are they now?

- How different is Douglass's position on slavery from that of the earlier white abolitionists? Is he right/wise to so praise American principles and so scorn American practices?

- What criticisms and what support of reform are found in Parton and Hawthorne? How important are "reform" efforts in society? Do they solve or complicate problems?

WELD-GRIMKÉ LETTERS

Angelina Grimké, Sarah Grimké, and Theodore Weld

ANGELINA AND SARAH GRIMKÉ

Written in New York, about March 1, 1837

*The definite, practical means by which the North
can put an end to Slavery in the South*

Let them see to it that they send no man to Congress who would give his vote to the admission of another slave state into the national union. Let them protest against the injustice and cruelty of delivering the fugitive slave back to his master, as being a direct infringement of the Divine command.—Deut. xxiii. 15, 16. Let them petition their different legislatures to grant a jury trial to the friendless, helpless runaway, and for the repeal of those laws which secure to the slaveholder his legal right to his slave, after he has voluntarily brought him within the verge of their jurisdiction, and for the enactment of such laws as will protect the colored man, woman and child from the fangs of the kidnapper, who is constantly walking about in the northern states, seeking whom he may devour. Let the northern churches refuse to receive slaveholders at their communion tables, or to permit slaveholding ministers to enter their pulpits. . . .

Let northern manufacturers refuse to purchase cotton, for the cultivation of which the laborer has received no wages. Let the grocer refuse to buy the rice and sugar of the South, so long as "the hire of the laborers who had reaped down their fields is kept back by fraud." Let the merchant refuse to receive the articles manufactured of slave grown cotton, and let the consumer refuse to purchase either the rice, sugar or cotton articles, to produce which has cost the slave his unpaid labor, his tears and his blood. Every northerner may, in this way, bear a faithful testimony against slavery at the South, by withdrawing his pecuniary support. . . .

Our fathers and mothers knew that there was a very important *principle* involved in the right claimed by England to lay a tax upon articles exported to the colonies, and they therefore refused to pay that tax. Now we would ask, is there not a very important principle involved in the constant purchase of slave-grown products? Does not every man who purchases them tacitly concede the right of the slave-holder to rob the laborer of his wages? Is not the language of the Psalmist applicable to such, "When thou sawest a thief, then thou consentedst with him?" Do not such purchasers offer to the Southern planter the very strongest inducements to continue his oppression of the poor? It is a maxim in law, that the receiver is as bad as the thief; is not every Northerner, then, who buys or sells the productions of slave labor, involved in the guilt of slavery? Do such obey the apostle's injunction, "Have no fellowship with the unfruitful works of darkness, but rather reprove them?"

Then again we would have Northerners abandon that unholy and unreasonable prejudice which is doing the work of oppression on the free people of color in our midst. Let them learn to measure men, not by their complexions, but by their intellectual and moral worth. Then will they be less ashamed to be found the associates of the worthy colored citizens than the companions of those who rob "the poor because he is poor." Let them in every possible way promote their moral and intellectual elevation, and treat them as though they were men, and American citizens, whenever they meet with people of color in stages or steam boats, taverns, or places of public worship.

WELD TO ANGELINA AND SARAH GRIMKÉ

New York, N. Y. July 22, 37.

Saturday evening

My dear Sister Angelina

. . . [T]he Ex. Com. no more attaches their *sanction* to your public holdings-forth to promiscuous assemblies than it does to your "theeing and thouing" or to your tight crimped caps, seven by nine bonnets, or that impenetrable drab that defieth utterly all amalgamation of colors! If any gainsay your speaking in public and to *men*, they gainsay the *Quakers* and not the *abolitionists*. They fly in the face of a *denominational* tenet, not an *anti slavery* doctrine or *measure*. I mean *distinctively:* I would to God that every anti slavery woman in this land had heart and head and womanhood enough and leisure withal to preach. . . .

If the men wish to come, it is downright *slaveholding* to shut them out. *Slaveholders* undertake to say that *one* class of human beings shall not be profited by public ministrations. I pray you leave slaveholders "alone in their glory". If I should ever be in the vicinity of your meetings I shall act on the principle that he that hath ears to hear hath a right to use them; and if you undertake to stuff them with cotton or to barricade them with brick and mortar, we'll have just as much of a breeze about it as can be made at all consistent with "peace principles".

Why! folks talk about women's preaching as tho' it was next to highway robbery—eyes astare and mouth agape. Pity women were not born with a split stick on their tongues! Ghostly dictums have fairly beaten it into the heads of the whole world save a fraction, that *mind* is *sexed*, and *Human rights* are *sex'd, moral obligation sex'd*. . . .

Now for the scolding. Quarter! quarter! quarter! . . .

Avast there with your railing accusations. Ah, you haven't lived at the South for nothing. "Practice makes perfect". Wonder how long it would take me to get my hand in; quite certain I should be a dull scholar, tho' if I had *you* for teacher, rather think I should come up *fast*—perhaps make a prodigy.

That infinite distinction between the "rights" and the "wrongs" of woman, just exactly the difference between *"pencil marks"* and *pen* strokes. So then nothing but jet black will do for you. Well its a noble labor. I have strong predilections that way myself; think I should carry an *ink* bottle in my pocket if it would [not] put my temperance good name in jeopardy. . . .

So you see I am at my old tricks of fault finding with you. Be patient. In this hollow world where even *most* of those who call themselves *friends* show it only by flattery, you will escape criticism *pretty much;* and even if mine should be unjust you can quickly *neutralize* them. A thousand things crowd upon me, but I have no room. Do take care of your *health* and may God give you his own sweet and ceaseless *communion,* better, better than life. Surely there is no need for me to say again to you and dear Sarah, call on me at all times for whatever I have or can do for you.

Most affectionately your brother in Jesus
T. D. Weld

My dear sister Sarah,

I think it would excite prejudice among the Quakers against the Executive Committee if your address to them were to be published at the A. S. office or kept for sale at the Repository. It would compromise that neutrality which ought to be observed. The anti slavery committee *as such* ought not to have anything to do with *denominational* conflicts. . . .

Most truly your brother in the preciousness of Christ

T. D. Weld

ANGELINA GRIMKÉ TO WELD

Groton [Mass.] 8th Month 12. [1837]

My Dear Brother

No doubt thou hast heard by this time of all the fuss that is now making in this region about our stepping so far out of the bounds of female propriety as to lecture to promiscuous assemblies. My auditors literally sit some times with "mouths agape and eyes astare", so that I cannot help smiling in the midst of "rhetorical flourishes" to witness their perfect amazement at hearing a woman speak in the churches. . . . I am waiting in some anxiety to see what the Executive Committee mean to do in these troublous times, whether to renounce us or not. But seriously speaking, we are placed very unexpectedly in a very trying situation, in the forefront of an entirely new contest—a contest for the *rights* of *woman* as a moral, intelligent and responsible being. Harriet Martineau says "God and man know that the time has not come for women to make their injuries even heard of": but it seems as tho' it had come *now* and that the exigency must be met with the firmness and faith of woman in by gone ages. I cannot help feeling some regret that this sh'ld have come up *before* the Anti Slavery question was settled, so fearful am I that it may injure that blessed cause, and then again I think this must be the Lord's time and therefore the *best* time, for it seems to have been brought about by a concatenation of circumstances over which we had no control. The fact is it involves the interests of every minister in our land and therefore they will stand almost in a solid phalanx against woman's rights and I am afraid the discussion of this question will divide in Jacob and scatter in Israel; it will also touch every man's interests at home, in the tenderest relation of life; it will go down into the very depths of his soul and cause great searchings of heart. . . .

I must confess my womanhood is insulted, my moral feelings outraged when I reflect on these things, and I am sure *I know just* how the free colored people feel towards the whites when they pay them more than common attention; it is *not paid as a* RIGHT, but *given as a* BOUN-

TY on a *little* more than *ordinary* sense. There is not one man in 500 who really understands what kind of attention is alone acceptable to a woman of pure and exalted moral and intellectual worth. Hast thou read Sisters letters in the Spectator? I want thee to read them and let us know what thou thinkest of them . . . As to our being Quakers being an *excuse* for our speaking in public, we do *not* stand on this ground at all; we ask *no* favors for ourselves, but *claim* rights for our *sex*. . . . "[I]n Christ Jesus there is neither male nor female." O! if in our intercourse with each other we realized this great truth, how delightful, ennobling and dignified it would be, . . . I find thou wilt find out *my pride* in whatever form it appear, well keep a watch, for I have a *great deal* of it—so much that I should not like at all to see such "a *distinguished man*" as thyself at one of my lectures; and if *moral suasion* could keep thee out, I assure thee I would NOT let thee come in, unless I was in so *humble* a mood as to be ready for a close criticism on the matter and manner of my talk and gesture, etc. . . . How dost thou think I felt at those great meetings in Lowell? 1500 city people in the blaze of a chandelier. Sister says that before I rose I looked as if I was saying to myself "the time has come and the sacrifice must be offered." Indeed I often feel in our meetings as if I was "as a lamb led to the slaughter," sometimes so sick before I rise that it seems impossible for me to speak 10 minutes; but the Lord is at my right hand. . . .

I am afraid thou art not the only Northern man who thinks I have not lived at the South for nothing, for I do *scold most terribly* when I undertake to tell the brethren *how* the North is implicated in the guilt of slavery; they look at me in utter amazement. I am not at all surprized they are afraid lest such a woman should usurp authority over the men. The fact is, I *was* once a great scold and I am indebted to a *slave* for curing me of it. It was when I was quite a little girl and she shamed me and coaxed me out of the horrible practice by telling me very affectionately how ugly it was and promising to make me a doll and dress it like a soldier if I would give it up. She made the doll, I made the promise and believe [I have] kept it unbroken to this day so far as slaves were concerned. I think this woman did a great deal towards opening my childish heart to sympathize with these poor suffering bleeding ones. I thank the Lord for it: and to this time I remember that doll and her kind advice with feelings which bring tears to my eyes. . . .

What we claim for ourselves, we claim for *every* woman whom God has called and qualified with gifts and graces. Can't *thou* stand *just here* side by side with us?

Thy sister in the bonds of woman and the slave

A. E. Gé.

WELD TO SARAH AND ANGELINA GRIMKÉ

New York, August 15–37

My dear sisters

I had it in my heart to make a suggestion to you in my last letter about your course touching the *"rights of women"*, but it was crowded out by other matters perhaps of less importance. . . .

Now as I have a small sheet (fool that I didn't take a larger) and much to say, I'll make *points*. 1. As to the *rights* and *wrongs* of women, it is an old theme with me. It was the *first* subject I ever *discussed*. In a little debating society when a boy, I took the ground that sex neither *qualified* nor *disqualified* for the discharge of any functions mental, moral or spiritual; that there is no reason why *woman* should not make laws, administer justice, sit in the chair of state, plead at the bar or in the pulpit, if she has the qualifications, just as much as tho she belonged to the other sex. Further, that the proposition of marriage may with just the same propriety be made by the *woman* as the *man,* and that the *existing usage* on that subject, pronouncing it *alone* the province of the *man,* and *indelicacy* and almost, if not quite *immoral* for *woman* to make the first advances, overlooks or rather *perverts* the sacred design of the institution and debases it into the mire of earthliness and gross sensuality, smothering the spirit under the flesh. Now as I have never found man, woman or child who agreed with me in the "ultraism" of womans rights, I take it for granted even *you* will cry out "oh shocking"!! at the *courting* part of the doctrine. Very well, let that pass. What I advocated in boyhood I advocate now, that woman in EVERY *particular* shares equally with man rights and responsibilities. Now I have made this statement of my *creed* on this point to show you that we *fully agree in principle* except that I probably go much farther than you do in a *single* particular. Now notwithstanding this, I do most deeply regret that you have begun a series of articles in the Papers on the rights of woman. Why, my dear sisters, the best possible advocacy which you can make is just what you *are* making day by day. Thousands hear you every week who have all their lives held that woman must not speak in public. Such a practical refutation of the dogma as your speaking furnishes has already converted multitudes. Leading abolitionists, male and female, everywhere are under responsibilities that cover *all* their time, powers and opportunities. How much new good to be explored—facts, principles, processes, relations innumerable yet untraced. How few must do the work! How much to be done! How very short the "*accepted* time" in which to do it. Besides you are *Southerners*, have been slaveholders; your dearest friends are all in the sin and shame and peril. All these things give you great access to northern mind, great sway over it. . . . You can do more at convincing the north than twenty *northern* females, tho' they could speak as well as you. Now this peculiar advantage you *lose* the moment you take *another* subject. . . .

Now can't you leave the *lesser* work to others who can do it *better* than you, and devote, consecrate souls and spirits, to the *greater* work which you can do far better and to far better purpose than any body else. Again, the abolition question is most powerfully preparative and introductory to the *other* question. By pushing the former with all our might we are most effectually advancing the latter. By absorbing the public mind in the greatest of all violations of rights, we are purging its vision to detect other violations. Rights! Rights! Their value, their sacredness, their changeless nature, all these will be made familiar as house hold words. When you get the tide raised to the summit level, you can pour it over all below it. . . .

Let us all *first* wake up the nation to lift millions of slaves of both sexes from the dust, and turn them into MEN and then when we all have our hand in, it will be an easy matter to take millions of females from their knees and set them on their feet, or in other words transform them from *babies* into *women.* One word more. All our opposers . . . will chuckle if only a part of your energies can be directed into *another* chanell, especially if they can be diverted into one which will make you so obnoxious as to cripple your influence on the subject of slavery. I pray our dear Lord to give you wisdom and grace and help and bless you forever

Your brother T. D. Weld

ANGELINA GRIMKÉ TO WELD AND JOHN GREENLEAF WHITTIER

Brookline [Mass.] 8th Mo 20–[1837]

To Theodore D. Weld and J. G. Whittier

Brethren beloved in the Lord.

As your letters came to hand at the same time and both are devoted mainly to the same subject we have concluded to answer them on one sheet and jointly. You seem greatly alarmed at the idea of our advocating the *rights of woman.* . . .

These letters have not been the means of arousing the public attention to the subject of Womans rights, it was the Pastoral Letter which did the mischief. The ministers seemed panic struck at once and commenced a most violent attack. . . .

Now my dear brothers this *invasion of our rights* was just such an attack upon *us,* as that made upon Abolitionists generally when they were told a few years ago that they had no right to discuss the subject of Slavery. Did *you* take no notice of this assertion? Why no! With one heart and one voice you said, *We* will settle *this right before* we go one step further. *The time* to assert a right is *the* time when *that* right is denied. *We must establish this right* for it we do not, it will be impossible for *us* to go *on with the work of Emancipation.* . . . There is an eagerness to understand our views. Now is it wrong to give those views in a series of letters in a paper NOT devoted to Abolition?

And can you not see that women *could* do, and *would* do a hundred times more for the slave if she were not fettered? Why we were gravely told that we are out of our sphere even when we circulate petitions; out of our "appropriate sphere" when we speak to women only; and out of them when we *sing* in the churches. Silence is *our* province, submission *our* duty. If then we "give *no reason* for the hope that is in us," that we have *equal rights* with our brethren, how can we expect to be permitted *much longer to exercise those rights? . . . we* cannot push Abolitionism forward with all our might *until* we take up the stumbling block out of the road. We cannot see with brother Weld in this matter. We acknowledge the excellence of his reasons for urging us to labor in this cause of the Slave, our being Southerners, etc., but then we say how can we expect to be able to hold meetings much longer when people are so diligently taught to *despise us* for thus stepping out of the sphere of woman! . . .

Why, my dear brothers can you not see the deep laid scheme of the clergy against us as lecturers? They know full well that if they can persuade the people it is a *shame* for us to speak in public, and that every time we open our months for the dumb we are breaking a divine command, that even if we spoke with the tongues of *men* or of angels, we should have *no hearers*. They are springing a deep mine beneath our feet, and we shall *very* soon be compelled to retreat for we shall have *no* ground to stand on. If we surrender the right to *speak* to the public this year, we must surrender the right to petition next year and the right to *write* the year after and so on. What *then* can *woman* do for the slave when she is herself under the feet of man and shamed into *silence?* Now we entreat *you* to weigh candidly the *whole subject,* and then we are sure you will see, this is no more than an abandonment of our first love than the effort made by Anti Slavery men to establish the *right* of free discussion. . . .

With regard to brother Welds ultraism on the subject of marriage, he is quite mistaken if he fancies he has got far *ahead of us* in the human rights reform. We do *not* think this doctrine at all shocking: it is *altogether right.* But I am afraid I am *too proud* ever to exercise the right. . . . By the bye it will be very important to establish this right, for the men of Mass. stoutly declare that women who hold such sentiments of *equality* can never expect to be courted. They seem to hold out this as a kind of threat to deter us from asserting our rights, not *knowing wherunto this will grow.* But jesting is inconvenient says the Apostle: to business then.

Anti Slavery men are trying very hard to separate what God hath joined together. I fully believe that so far from keeping different moral reformations entirely distinct that no such attempt can ever be successful. They are bound together in a circle like the sciences; they blend with each other like the colors of the rain bow; they are the parts only of our glorious whole and that whole is Christianity, pure *practical* christianity. The fact is I believe—but dont be alarmed, for it is only I—that . . . [t]he whole Church Government must come down, the clergy stand right in the way of reform, and I do not know but this stumbling block too must be removed *before* Slavery can be abolished, for the system is supported by *them;* . . .

Is Brother Weld frightened at *my ultraism?* Please write to us soon and let us know what you think. . . . May the Lord bless you my dear brothers is the prayer of your sister in Jesus

                                                                    A.E.G

We never mention women's rights in our *lectures* except so far as is necessary to urge them to meet their responsibilities. We speak of their *responsibilities* and leave *them* to *infer* their *rights*.

WELD TO SARAH AND ANGELINA GRIMKÉ

[New York, August 26, 1837]

... [T]he very week that I was converted to Christ in the city of Utica during a powerful revival of religion under brother Finney—and the first time I ever spoke in a religious meeting—I urged females both to pray and speak if they felt deeply enough to do it, and not to be restrained from it by the fact that they were *females*. ...

I had opportunity to feel the pulse of the ministry and church generally, and I did not find one in ten who *believed* it was unscriptural, fully. They grieved and said perhaps, and they didnt know, and they *were opposed to it*, and that it [was] not best; but yet the practice of female praying in promiscuous meetings grew every day and now all over that region nothing is more common in revivals of religion. I found wherever the *practice* commenced *first* it always held its own and gained over crowds; but where it was *first* laid down as a *doctrine* and pushed, it always went hard and generally forestalled the practice and *shut it out*. 2. The feeling of opposition to female praying, speaking, & etc., which *men* generally have is from a stereotyped notion or persuasion that they are not competent for it. It arises from habitually regarding them as *inferior* beings. I know that the majority of men regard woman as *silly*. The proposition that woman can reason and analyze closely is to them an absurdity. They are surprised greatly if a woman speaks or prays to edification, and in this state of mind it is not strange that they stumble at *Paul*. But let intelligent woman begin to pray or speak and men begin to be converted to the true doctrine, and when they get familiar with it they like it and lose all their scruples. True there is a pretty large class of ministers who are fierce about it and will fight, but a still larger class that will come over if they first witness the successful *practice* rather than meet it in the shape of a doctrine to be swallowed. Now if instead of blowing a blast thro' the newspapers, sounding the onset and summoning the ministers and churches to surrender, you had without any introductory flourish just gone right among them and lectured *when* and *where* and *as* you could find opportunity and paid no attention to criticism, but pushed right on without making any ado about "*attacks*" and "*invasions*" and "*opposition*" and have let the barkers bark their bark out, within one year you might have practically brought over 50,000 persons of the very moral elite of New England. You may rely upon it, your *specimens* of female speaking and praying will do fifty times as much to bring over to womans rights the community as your *indoctrinating* under your own name thro' the newspapers those who never saw you.

Another point: you say "anti slavery men are trying very hard to separate what God has joined together"; you then say that "the different moral reformations can only be successfully advanced by combining them together. . . .

Since the world began, Moral Reform has been successfully advanced only in *one* way, and that has been by uplifting a great *self evident central* principle before all eyes . . . then push the *principle*—the *whole* principle, *as* a whole (not split up into fractions) push it in its most obvious import and bearing: *push* it till the community see it, feel it, in so far as the thinking portion are concerned surrender to it. Then when you have drawn them up to the top of the general principle, you can slide them down upon all the derivative principles, *all at once;* but if you attempt to start off on a derivative principle from any other point than the summit level or the main principle you must beat upstream— yes up a *cataract.* . . . Now what is plainer than that the grand primitive principle for which we struggle is HUMAN rights, and that the rights of *woman* is a principle purely *derivative* from the other? . . . See what has been done already by abolition doctrines. I know *personally* hundreds of our leading abolitionists who 3 years ago would have demurred stoutly to the doctrine of womens preaching and divers other particulars of womens rights but have been brought right on the whole subject by their *general principles* of human rights. . . . How? Ans. by lodging in the public mind a principle that involves womans rights and leads to them and gives eyes to see them and prepares hearts to welcome them. . . . I have left unsaid most that I designed. Among other things 20 different reasons why you should let alone womans rights except to exercise them—but must stop.

Adieu! my sisters most dearly beloved. God bless You and speed the right.

Your own brother
Theodore

SARAH AND ANGELINA GRIMKÉ TO WELD

Fitchburg [Mass.] 9/20/37

My dear brother,

Angelina is so wrathy that I think it will be unsafe to trust the pen in her hands to reply to thy two last good long letters. As I feel nothing but gratitude for the kindness which I am sure dictated them, commingled with wonder at the "marvellables" which they contain, I shall endeavor to answer them and as far as possible allay the uneasiness which thou seems to feel at the course we are pursuing. My astonishment is as great at thy misconceptions as thine can be at ours. Truly if I did not know brother Theodore as well as I think I do, I should conclude his mind was beclouded by the fears which seem to have seized some of the brotherhood least we should usurp dominion over our lords and masters. . . .

The mtgs. we have had, generally full, if not crowded, have satisfied our sister that here she was mistaken . . . We have kept steadily on with our A. S. work; we have not held one mtg. less, because we gave a little attention to guard the workmen from the thrusts of the enemies. Thou takes it for granted that our heads are so full of *womans rights, womans rights* that our hearts have grown cold in the cause of the slave, that we have started aside like broken bows. Now we think thou hast verily misjudged us. . . . I know the opposition "arises (in part) from habitually regarding women as inferior beings" but chiefly, I believe, from a desire to keep them in unholy subjection to man, and one way of doing this is to deprive us of the means of becoming their equals, by forbidding us the privileges of education to fit us for the performance of duty. I am greatly mistaken if most men have not a desire that women should be silly. . . . [w]e believe that if women exercised their rights of thinking and acting for themselves, they would labor ten times more efficiently than they now do for the A. S. cause and all other reformations. . . .

Angelina wishes to try her hand at scolding again. Farewell dear brother, may the Lord reward thee ten fold for thy kindness and, keep thee in the hollow of his holy hand—thy sister in Jesus S. M. G.

Sister seems very much afraid that my pen will be transformed into a venomous serpent when it is employed in addressing thee, my Dear Brother, and no wonder, for I like to pay my debts, and as I received $10 worth of scolding I should be guilty of injustice did I not return the favor. Well—*such* a lecture, I never before received. What is the matter with thee? One would really suppose that we had actually abandoned the A. Sl'y cause and were scouring the country preaching *nothing* but *women's rights,* when in fact I can truly say that whenever I lecture I forget *every thing but the SLAVE.* HE is all in all for the time being. And what is the reason that *I* am to be scolded because *Sister* writes letters in the Spectator? . . . And dost thou really think in my answer to C. E. B[eecher]'s absurd views of woman that I had better suppress my own? If so I will do it, as thou makest such a monster out of the molehill. . . .

Suppose in fact that what has frightened thee so was that public lecture I wanted to give in Boston on Womans rights: H. B. S[tanton] must have told thee about it, but our friend[s] there thot I had best not, so I did *not* commit the sin . . .

—thine for the poor stricken slave—A. E. Gé

WELD TO SARAH AND ANGELINA GRIMKÉ

New York, Oct 10. 37

My very Dear Sisters

. . . Verily believing that you felt more about the question of womans rights—your spirit more stirred within you at seeing the *female* in a condition below the male—than at seeing *human beings* crushed by *law,* public sentiment, and the professing Church and ministry, *below* the BRUTES, how could I think otherwise? Why! Angelina in yesterdays letter says she is doubtful whether womans rights are not the *root*—whether they do not *lie deeper* than the rights involved in our great question!! And adds "The slave may be freed and woman be where she is, but woman cannot be freed and the slave remain where he is". . . .

Another subject—Angelina's last letter!! Why dear child! What is the matter with you? Patience! Rally yourself. Recollect your womanhood my sister, and put on charity which is the bond of perfectness, "thinketh no evil" and "hopeth all things". I speak just what I mean and in no spirit of ralliery when I say there are some things in that letter which you ought to be ashamed of and to repent of. . . .

Most affectionately yours with an own brothers love—therefore thus speak—

Theodore D. Weld.

WELD TO ANGELINA GRIMKÉ

New York, Oct 16. 37

My dear Sister Angelina . . .

Further your assertion that the Committee "offered him the alternative of either having his lips padlocked or of ceasing to be their agent" is ALL MOONSHINE. If my fault finding Sister Angelina is determined to swallow camels, pray do *masticate* them *thoroughly*. . . .

Your next charge is "the Ex. Committee have disowned us" . . . and much of the same strange and incomprehensible import!! What a rush of new emotions this last charge raises. It is so utterly *unaccountable*. I *stare* at it, so ludicrous I could laugh aloud, and finally it argues such A STATE OF MIND in you that I could cry like a child. . . .

I *have done* my sister. Doubtless you will call me censorious and harsh if not *ill tempered*. Perhaps you may *resent* what I have said. And yet I am sure that the fearful strength of your *pride* will restrain *exhibitions* of resentment. . . .

If I had time to look over what I have scrawled I have no doubt my conscience would upbraid me with being *miserably unfaithful* to your soul. Long and desperate conflicts with my own tempest wrought spirit have taught me that the souls *grand* conquest is *self* conquest. . . .

Whether or not as the old Greeks said "Know thyself" came down from heaven, it IS the gate at the entrance of the ONLY road that leads there. Oh Angelina! enter in! enter in! . . . May great, great grace rest on thee and Jesus' spirit dwell on thee and abound, my ever dear sister.

Yours for Jesus and the desolate.

T. D. W.

[Endorsed by Angelina Grimké:] Faithfulness.

WELD TO SARAH AND ANGELINA GRIMKÉ

New York, Nov. 6, 37

My ever dear sisters Sarah and Angelina

Perhaps my last letter to Angelina was too unguarded, and in the sentence quoted in her letter the latitude was *certainly* to[o] *wide*. To know that what I said has *pained* her, while it pains me doubly, does yet cause me to *rejoice*. To you both, this is a *contradiction* I doubt not, but let it pass. Ah, my dear sister A., you have sore and long and multiform conflicts yet to wage with the powerful and subtle and endlessly ramified pride of your heart. . . . May the comforter hide you both under the shadow of his wings my own dear sisters.

Your brother Theodore.

ANGELINA GRIMKÉ TO WELD

Brookline [Mass.]—21 inst—[January, 1838]

Very Dear Brother

And now let me tell you how often I have thanked God for such a friend as you have proved to me, one who *will* tell me my faults. I solemnly believe there is, there *can be no* true friendship without it . . . [Y]ou dear brother have, I must acknowledge, dived deeper into the hidden sins of my heart than any one ever did before, and you can therefore do me more good. I know I find it *very hard* to bear, but this only proves the dire necessity which exists that you should probe deep, not suffering your hand to spare or your eye to pity. . . .

And yet, Brother, I think in some things you wronged me in *that letter never to be forgotten,* but never mind, YOU DID NOT HURT ME, even that did me good. I *tho't* too that it was *not* written in the spirit of love, but I will not say *it was not,* for I know I *was* but a poor judge *then.* . . . If we ever meet and *can* talk these things over I think it will do my heart good. Be sure to keep that letter of mine which you said I ought to be ashamed of—all the rest better be destroyed. There will be no use in writing about it—WE CAN NOT UNDERSTAND EACH OTHER, and I have unintentionally said too much perhaps. . . .

You say in view of that War cloud which hangs round the horizon of our country, the conflicts in Congress, etc., you "rejoice and leap for joy, you feel in more than perfect peace" Oh! Brother, how different it is with me my spirit sinks within me and yet I pray God that I may learn to rejoice in his judgements in this Nation as much as I have in his judgements in my own soul. . . .

I remember that all *my* relatives are at the South and I exceedingly fear and quake, and feel ready to go down and die for them or with them. Sometimes the hope gleams across my mind that as we have labored so *publicly* in the cause of the slave, our services will be remembered in the hour of darkness and death and their lives will be spared—at least our Mothers. Are those vain and foolish hopes? You say *she* cannot be a Christian if we have done our duty to her touching slavery. Our witness is in heaven, our record is on high. . . . Farewell.

May our Fathers blessing rest upon and preserve you prays one of his little ones.

WELD TO ANGELINA GRIMKÉ

New York, Feb. 8, '38

Private

A paragraph in your last letter Angelina, went *to my soul*. You feel that I have "wronged" you and think that what I said "was not written in the spirit of love", and express the wish that all the letters you have written me may be destroyed, except one of which you say—"be sure to keep that letter of which you say I ought to be ashamed." You then close the subject by saying "there will be no use in writing about it *we cannot understand each other.*"

Whatever my *aim* may have been, your letter too clearly reveals that my *unkind thrusts* have left an enduring pang, the knowledge of which renders back into my own bosom a double measure, pressed down and running over. And it is well. I deserve it all! . . .

I *would* explain the mystery of the *seeming* unkindness and cruelty of my spirit toward you in reproof, did not higher considerations than *inclination* or self interest forbid me to do it, until I have *first* fulfilled an obligation which I am *now* convinced should have been discharged long ago—a *sacred* duty which I owed to *you*, to my own soul, and to our Father. . . .

I know it will surprise and even amaze you, Angelina, when I say to you as I now do, that for a long time, *you have had my whole heart.*

Not supremely. Grace has restrained me from that extreme. I *do* love the Lord our righteousness *better* than I love *you*. And it is *because* I love him *better* that I love you *as* I do.

Your letter to Wm. Lloyd Garrison formed an era in my feelings and a crisis in my history that drew my spirit toward yours by irrepressible affinities. I read it over and over and over, and in the deep consciousness that I should find in the spirit that dictated that letter the searchless power of *congenial communings*—which I had always been pining for and of which I had never found but one (C. Stuart)—I forgot utterly that you were not of my own sex!

The *Spirit*, the *Spirit*, not a brother nor a Sister spirit but unimbodied spirit with none of the associations or incidents of the physical nature, moved upon me with overcoming power. I felt as tho *commun-*

ion with your spirit was a *law* and a *necessity* of my being. To write you and open a channel of communication with you was my immediate determination—but then it occurred—you were a *woman!* . . . [T]his same state of mind has continued unvarying, except that it has gathered strength with every day until long stilled convictions of duty make it impossible for me longer to refrain myself, and I now tell you the whole. *Less* I cannot say, and *more* I *need* not, than that affection for you, Angelina, has intrenched itself among my deepest susceptibilities and taken the strong holds of my nature. . . .

I cannot close this letter without announcing to you a fact, the knowledge of which may *spare you much pain.* It is this. I have *no expectation* and almost no *hope* that my feelings are in *any degree* RECIPROCATED BY YOU. I have no doubt but you esteem me as a christian brother, respect me as a man of principle and feel as tho I had desired your welfare, and do heartily thank me for having faithfully pointed out your defects, however imperfect the mode of ministration; but that you have in the least degree any other feelings. I have no reason to believe, and as little assurance that the knowledge of my own feelings toward you may give birth to such feelings. . . .

To God and the word of His grace I commit you and in submission to *His will* wait the issue. Theodore D. Weld.

P. S. I have written over the top of this sheet, "Private"—not however because I have the least unwillingness that dear sister Sarah should see it if it is your wish and her desire. I suppose you and she have no *secrets* kept from each other and surely she has been to me as a very dear elder sister in the Lord in all Christian confidence and Christian love, and so far from desiring to conceal from her the feelings of my heart toward you, I feel that to *know* them is her right, from the love she bears you and knit as your heart is to hers.

ANGELINA GRIMKÉ TO WELD

Brookline [Mass.] Febr'y 11th [1838]
Your letter was indeed a great surprise, My Brother, and yet it was no surprise at all. It was a surprise because you have so mastered your feelings as never to betray them; it was no surprise because in the depths of my own heart *there was found a response* which I could not but believe was produced there by an undefinable feeling in yours. Not even the word "private" prepared me for such a disclosure, so full of strength and power. I tho't you had found it your duty to reprove me

again for some darling sin and determined to save my feelings, by hidden admonition, and my heart was lifted in prayer to receive it in the spirit of meekness and love. You say that my letter revealed to you that you had inflicted *"abiding pain;"* Yes! you did, and it was love for you which caused reproof to sink so deep into my heart. I tho't with such views of my character it was impossible you could love me. . . .

And now, Theodore, I will tell you that a letter of yours published in the Liberator two years ago "drew *my* spirit to *yours* by irrepressible affinities". I felt that there was a kindred mind, a congenial soul and I longed to hold communion with you, but never expected the privilege. . . .

I must now say a word to you about my speaking before the Legislative Committee which has the charge of petitions. Yesterday week H. B. S[tanton] was out here, and half in fun and half in earnest proposed my doing so. I treated it as a jest, but after he left, felt to my own great surprize that I *must* do it. I could hardly believe my own feelings, but conviction deepened. [Angelina E. Grimké]

Brother Beloved in the Lord—I bargained beforehand for a part of this sheet but am after all put off with this scrap. Thy letter to my precious sister was not unexpected to me, altho' I sometimes thought circumstances might impose silence. Since our first meeting I have felt as if you were kindred spirits, and that if the Lord inclined your hearts to each other I could bless his holy name.

S. G.

WELD TO ANGELINA AND SARAH GRIMKÉ

New York, Feb. 16, '38

My heart is full! THAT LETTER found me *four* days ago! I tried to answer it *immediately* but could not, and again the next day but could not write a word and again yesterday but in vain. I dared not trust myself to write to you, and even now, were it not that my silence might lead you to infer that I had not received THAT LETTER and thus distress you with the fear that I might still be tortured by suspence, I would even now give it over. My heart aches for *utterance* but oh *not* the utterance of *words!* The truth is Angelina, (for you have a right to know my *weaknesses* and *shall*—the *whole*) I have so long wrestled with myself like a blind giant stifling by violence all the intensities of my nature that when at last they found *vent,* and your voice of love proclaimed a *deliverance* so unlooked for, so full, and free, revealing what I dared [not] *hope* for, and what I had never for a moment dreamed to be possible that *your heart was* and *long had been mine*—it was as the life touch to one *dead* . . .

In Love imperishable *your own* Theodore

My very dear sister Sarah—How shall I sufficiently think you for your precious postscript to our dear A's letter? You amaze me when you say that my letter to our dear A "was not unexpected" to you tho you supposed "that circumstances might for a time impose silence". Verily after all my strife to hide it, did I indeed betray the state of my heart toward her? And have you indeed been long committing us to God as those designed by him for a sacred and enduring union? I marvel and adore!

ANGELINA GRIMKÉ TO WELD

Wednesday evening

[Boston, Mass., Feb. 21, 1838]

O! my Theodore. One of my meetings with the Legislature is over, "Praise the Lord o my soul and *all* that is within me, praise *His* holy name." I wrote you word that Sister was to speak to day and I tomorrow, but she took a violent cold and will not be able to speak at all. She could not even go to the meeting, but Jesus was there. *His* arm was underneath and round about me, He sustained me and brought me through. But I never was so near fainting under the tremendous pressure of feeling. My heart almost died within me. The novelty of the scene, the weight of responsibility, the ceaseless exercise of mind thro' which I had passed for more than a week—all together sank me to the earth. I am well nigh despaired, but our Lord and Master gave me his arm to lean upon and in great weakness, my limbs trembling under me, I stood up and spoke nearly two hours. Now I will tell you just what kind of meeting I had. So far as intellect and power of language was concerned I did *not* excel—it was *not* one of my happiest efforts; but my heart broke over the wrongs of the slave, the deep fountains of sympathy were broken up, and many were melted to tears. It was just such a meeting as I had tried to pray for. . . .

[Yo]ur letters of the 16 and 18th lie before me. What shall I say of them but that they contain an *exact* description of my feelings. Yes "words are mere mockers of the heart, they have *no* room in them, they never can be the circulating medium of the soul". . . .

I[n] great haste I am most truly Thine for ever

[Angelina]

Dear brother, I could not go to the Mtg. yesterday but my heart, my soul, my spirit was there. S. and E. Philbrick say our A. did nobly, and I know she did. I feel it in my inner man. . . . S. M. G.

ANGELINA GRIMKÉ TO WELD

[Brookline, Mass.] 22 of Febr'y [1838]

I gladly embrace this opportunity to send My Dear Theodore some account of my second meeting and of my feelings respecting it. My subjects were the Dangers of Slavery, Safety of Im. Emancipation, Character of Free Colored People and Gradualism. On arriving at the L[egislative] House we found the People coming down stairs, not being able to obtain an entrance and on reaching the hall such thro' the door way and compelled to walk over the seats in order to reach the table which was placed opposite the Speakers desk. After waiting some time, the Chairman announced the Com. ready to hear me. I rose and was greeted by HISSES from a dense crowd at the door. I never felt more perfectly calm in my life, and proceeded. . . .

It is said that the Chairman is an Abolitionist in heart—at any rate he has a heart of flesh, for I never saw any one struggle harder to suppress emotion; the tears were continually rising to his eyes; he was compelled to wipe them away several times. I spoke with far more freedom than I did on Wednesday, and if *I* am any judge of the effect produced, I think it was good. . . .

"What shall I render unto the Lord for all his benefits," for the high and holy Privilege which I have enjoyed this week of pleading the cause of the perishing slave before the rulers of the people? Why Theodore, it seems all like a dream. I can hardly realize *what* I have been doing only three hours ago. . . .

The more I reflect on all you tell me of your love for me, the more I feel amazed. I read your letters over and over in wonder and gratitude and feel as if I can say in regard to the description of your feelings, "as face answereth to face in the waterbrook, so does my heart to *your* heart." . . .

[B]ut remember *Duty* is to be before me and if you cannot come until Thome and Wythe are out of the Press, I can say "Even so rather." I trust the slave will lose *nothing* by our gain in each other. Farewell—I am Thine—Deep calleth unto deep in the ceaseless respondings of my heart to thine.

WELD TO LEWIS TAPPAN

Washington [D. C.] Jan. 23, '43.

Dear brother Tappan,

. . . I write this to beg that my name may not be published as one of the representatives of the A. and F. A. S. S. And for this reason (One which I have no doubt all the committee fully understand) I totally dissent from the *foundation principle* on which that society is based—a *denial* of the equal membership of women—and if my appointment as their representative were made public, I should feel impelled to make equally public the *reasons* forcing me to decline, and to do it *in such a way* as would inevitably bring up anew the questions of womens rights to speak, vote, sit on committees, etc., in connection with the Slave's right to personal ownership with all its attributes and in all its relations.

Now, free to utter and to act out my convictions upon the subject of woman's rights, and doing it at all times and places in my judgement calling for it, as you and all my friends well know, still the agitation of that question in *connection with* abolition societies and their operations I believe always has been, and *must* be, only evil and that continually in its effect on the *slave's deliverance*. I pray therefore that you will not by *publishing* my appointment, make it necessary for me to set that ball in motion again. The question never would have become, as it has, inextricably twisted into the abolition question, but for the persevering attempt to deprive women of what are, in my estimation, their inalienable rights. *You* most conscientiously thought otherwise, and *acted out your conscience*. And you know dear brother how heartily I give to your conscience and all consciences, a *wide birth*, the largest scope, not narrowed in the least by the assurance on my part that its dictates are wrong and their effects disastrous. . . .

As ever most affectionately your brother
Theodore D. Weld

THEODORE D. WELD TO JAMES G. BIRNEY

Washington D. C.

Jan. 22, 1842

My dear brother,

. . . I am glad you have accepted it, though my views of the inexpediency of the Liberty party, receive constant confirmation with increase of reflection, both upon human nature and events.

I am glad, because a very large number of men are working in the *political* harness, who will not draw *steadily* in any other, and because a separate political organization *will exist,* and run its round, and instead of throwing fences across the race course, I say, *give it a clear field;* the clearer the field the shorter the heat. . . . Whoever has not seen, even since so long ago as Jacksons veto of The U. S. Bank, that, from every quarter, the elements of conflict, the last conflict between liberty and slavery, were rushing headlong into the central focus—has been asleep. Nothing short of miracles, constant miracles, and such as the world has never seen can keep at bay the two great antagonist forces, which since the first blow on the currency started from their moorings and drove against each other. They must drive against each other, till *one* of them goes to the bottom. *Events,* the master of men, have for years been silently but without a moments pause, settling the basis of two great parties, the nucleus of one slavery, of the other freedom. This has been the real practical issue for twenty years with the south, but the north has, by incessant shifts of position, (all *false*) succeeded in *staving off* the only true and irrevocable one. Now they begin to see what thoughtful Abolitionists discovered years ago, that where half of a government live by their own work and pay as they go and the other half, by others' work and by the longest possible credit, and where these halves are made by *Climate*—a mighty pecuniary convulsion *must,* if of long continuance, hurl these two systems of labor and living into mortal conflict, and *that must* demolish the basis of all existing parties, and recast them in the mould of necessity upon the all controlling principle, and under the omnipotent affinities of *self preservation.* This *will, must,* make the other *one* party. The great cause now at work producing this, may, in its progress, encounter obstacles, (the third party I think is one) but it cannot be *arrested. The end must come.* . . .

I have been here about four weeks and expect to stay about as much longer. Mr. Adams case, the particulars of which you see in the papers, is doing much for our cause. Gates, Giddings, Andrews and all here favorable to Abo., regard it as having already made more available A. S. capital than all other movements here for 5 years. Mr. A. will probably occupy, a week more in his defense, unless a successful move should be made to lay it on the table. The slaveholding members of Cong. are at their wits end. The pecuniary pressure with no light ahead—the *cotton* prospect—the demonstration of England towards Cuba and warwise—with the other almost innumerable perplexities surrounding them have smitten them with dread if not with panic. . . .

Your concluding remark filled my eyes with tears. Thanks to God that He enables you to cast your cares upon him and to find *sweet peace*. My dear wife, little boys and Sister Sarah are in fine health. . . .

I am as ever your own brother

Theodore D. Weld

SENECA FALLS DECLARATION
OF RIGHTS

(1848)

When, in the course of human events, it becomes necessary for one portion of the family of man to assume among the people of the earth a position different from that which they have hitherto occupied, but one to which the laws of nature and of nature's God entitle them, a decent respect to the opinions of mankind requires that they should declare the causes that impel them to such a course.

We hold these truths to be self-evident: that all men and women are created equal; that they are endowed by their Creator with certain inalienable rights; that among these are life, liberty, and the pursuit of happiness; that to secure these rights governments are instituted, deriving their just powers from the consent of the governed. Whenever any form of government becomes destructive of these ends, it is the right of those who suffer from it to refuse allegiance to it, and to insist upon the institution of a new government, laying its foundation on such principles, and organizing its powers in such Form, as to them shall seem most likely to effect their safety and happiness. Prudence, indeed, will dictate that governments long established should not be changed for light and transient causes; and accordingly all experience hath shown that mankind are more disposed to suffer, while evils are sufferable, than to right themselves by abolishing the forms to which they were accustomed. But when a long train of abuses and usurpations, pursuing invariably the same object evinces a design to reduce them under absolute despotism, it is their duty to throw off such government, and to provide new guards for their future security. Such has been the patient sufferance of the women under this government, and such is now the necessity which constrains them to demand the equal station to which they are entitled.

The history of mankind is a history of repeated injuries and usurpations on the part of man toward woman, having in direct object the establishment of an absolute tyranny over her. To prove this, let facts be submitted to a candid world.

He has never permitted her to exercise her inalienable right to the elective franchise.

He has compelled her to submit to laws in the formation of which she had no voice.

He has withheld from her rights which are given to the most ignorant and degraded men—both natives and foreigners.

Having deprived her of this first right of a citizen, the elective franchise, thereby leaving her without representation in the halls of legislation, he has oppressed her on all sides.

He has made her if married in the eye of the law civilly dead.

He has taken from her all right in property even to the wages she earns.

He has made her morally an irresponsible being as she can commit many crimes with impunity provided they be done in the presence of her husband. In the covenant of marriage she is compelled to promise obedience to her husband, he becoming to all intents and purposes her master—the law giving him power to deprive her of her liberty and to administer chastisement. He has so framed the laws of divorce, as to what shall be the proper causes, and in case of separation, to whom the guardianship of her children shall be given, as to be wholly regardless of the happiness of women—the law, in all cases, going upon a false supposition of the supremacy of man, and giving all power into his hands.

After depriving her of all rights as a married woman, if single, and the owner of property, he has taxed her to support a government which recognizes her only when her property can be made profitable to it.

He has monopolized nearly all the profitable employments, and from those she is permitted to follow, she receives but a scanty remuneration. He closes against her all the avenues to wealth and distinction which he considers most honorable to himself. As a teacher of theology, medicine, or law, she is not known.

He has denied her the facilities for obtaining a thorough education, all colleges being closed against her.

He allows her in Church, as well as State, but a subordinate position, claiming Apostolic authority for her exclusion from the ministry, and, with some exceptions, from any public participation in the affairs of the Church.

He has created a false public sentiment by giving to the world a different code of morals for men and women, by which moral delinquencies which exclude women from society, are not only tolerated, but deemed of little account in man.

He has usurped the prerogative of Jehovah himself, claiming it as his right to assign for her a sphere of action, when that belongs to her conscience and to her God.

He has endeavored, in every way that he could, to destroy her confidence in her own powers, to lessen her self-respect, and to make her willing to lead a dependent and abject life.

NOW in view of this entire disfranchisement of one-half the people of this country, their social and religious degradation—in view of the unjust laws above mentioned, and because women do feel themselves aggrieved, oppressed, and fraudulently deprived of their most sacred rights, we insist that they have immediate admission to all the rights and privileges which belong to them as citizens of the United States.

In entering upon the great work before us, we anticipate no small amount of misconception, misrepresentation, and ridicule; but we shall use every instrumentality within our power to effect our object. We shall employ agents, circulate tracts, petition the State and National legislatures, and endeavor to enlist the pulpit and the press in our behalf. We hope this Convention will be followed by a series of Conventions embracing every part of the country.

from FIFTH OF JULY SPEECH

(1852)

Frederick Douglass

Fellow-citizens, pardon me, allow me to ask, why am I called upon to speak here to-day? What have I, or those I represent, to do with your national independence? Are the great principles of political freedom and of natural justice, embodied in that Declaration of Independence, extended to us? and am I, therefore, called upon to bring our humble offering to the national altar, and to confess the benefits and express devout gratitude for the blessings resulting from your independence to us?

Would to God, both for your sakes and ours, that an affirmative answer could be truthfully returned to these question! . . .

But such is not the state of the case. I say it with a sad sense of the disparity between us. I am not included within the pale of this glorious anniversary! Your high independence only reveals the immeasurable distance between us. The blessings in which you, this day, rejoice, are not enjoyed in common.—The rich inheritance of justice, liberty, prosperity and independence, bequeathed by your fathers, is shared by you, not by me. The sunlight that brought light and healing to you, has brought stripes and death to me. This Fourth July is *yours*, not *mine*. *You* may rejoice, *I* must mourn. To drag a man in fetters into the grand illuminated temple of liberty, and call upon him to join you in joyous anthems, were inhuman mockery and sacrilegious irony. Do you mean, citizens, to mock me, by asking me to speak to-day? . . .

Fellow-citizens, above your national, tumultuous joy, I hear the mournful wail of millions! whose chains, heavy and grievous yesterday, are, to-day, rendered more intolerable by the jubilee shouts that reach them. If I do forget, if I do not faithfully remember those bleeding children of sorrow this day, "may my right hand forget her cunning, and may my tongue cleave to the roof of my mouth!" To forget them, to pass lightly over their wrongs, and to chime in with the popular theme, would be treason most scandalous and shocking, and would make me a reproach before God and the world. My subject, then, fellow-citizens, is American slavery. I shall see this day and its popular characteristics from the slave's point of view. Standing there identified with the American bondman, making his wrongs mine, I do not hesitate to declare, with all my soul, that the character and conduct of this nation never looked blacker to me than on this 4th of July! Whether we turn to the declarations of the past, or to the professions of the present, the conduct of the nation seems equally hideous and revolting. America is false to the past, false to the present, and solemnly binds herself to be false to the future. Standing with God and the crushed and bleeding slave on this occasion, I will, in the name of humanity which is outraged, in the name of liberty which is fettered, in the name of the constitution and the Bible which are disregarded and trampled upon, dare to call in question and to denounce, with all the emphasis I can command, everything that serves to perpetuate slavery—the great sin and shame of America. . . .

At a time like this, scorching irony, not convincing argument, is needed. O! had I the ability, and could reach the nation's ear, I would, to-day, pour out a fiery stream of biting ridicule, blasting reproach, withering sarcasm, and stern rebuke. For it is not light that is needed, but fire; it is not the gentle shower, but thunder. We need the storm, the whirlwind, and the earthquake. The feeling of the nation must be quickened; the conscience of the nation must be roused; the propriety of the nation must be startled; the hypocrisy of the nation must be exposed; and its crimes against God and man must be proclaimed and denounced.

What, to the American slave, is your 4th of July? I answer; a day that reveals to him, more than all other days in the year, the gross injustice and cruelty to which he is the constant victim. To him, your celebration is a sham; your boasted liberty, an unholy license; your national greatness, swelling vanity; your sounds of rejoicing are empty and heartless; your denunciation of tyrants, brass fronted impudence; your shouts of liberty and equality, hollow mockery; your prayers and hymns, your sermons and thanksgivings, with all your religious parade and solemnity, are, to Him, mere bombast, fraud, deception, impiety, and hypocrisy—a thin veil to cover up crimes which would disgrace a nation of savages. There is not a nation on the earth guilty of practices more shocking and bloody than are the people of the United States, at this very hour. . . .

Behold the practical operation of this internal slave-trade, the American slave-trade, sustained by American politics and American religion. Here you will see men and women reared like swine for the market. You know what is a swine-drover? I will show you a man-drover. They inhabit all our Southern States. They perambulate the country, and crowd the highways of the nation, with droves of human stock. You will see one of these human flesh jobbers, armed with pistol, whip, and bowie-knife, driving a company of a hundred men, women, and children, from the Potomac to the slave market at New Orleans. These wretched people are to be sold singly, or in lots, to suit purchasers. They are food for the cotton-field and the deadly sugar-mill. Mark the sad procession, as it moves wearily along, and the inhuman wretch who drives them. . . .

. . . Attend the auction; see men examined like horses; see the forms of women rudely and brutally exposed to the shocking gaze of American slave-buyers. See this drove sold and separated forever; and never forget the deep, sad sobs that arose from that scattered multitude. Tell me, citizens, where, under the sun, you can witness a spectacle more fiendish and shocking. Yet this is but a glance at the American slave-trade, as it exists, at this moment, in the ruling part of the United States. . . .

But a still more inhuman, disgraceful, and scandalous state of things remains to be presented. By an act of the American Congress, not yet two years old, slavery has been nationalized in its most horrible and revolting form. By that act, Mason and Dixon's line has been obliterated; New York has become as Virginia; and the power to hold, hunt, and sell men, women and children, as slaves, remains no longer a mere state institution, but is now an institution of the whole United States. The power is co-extensive with the star-spangled banner, and American Christianity. Where these go, may also go the merciless slave-hunter. Where these are, man is not sacred. He is a bird for the sportsman's gun. By that most foul and fiendish of all human decrees, the liberty and person of every man are put in peril. Your broad republican domain is hunting ground for *men*. *Not* for thieves and robbers, enemies of society, merely, but for men guilty of no crime. Your law-makers have commanded all good citizens to engage in this hellish sport. Your President, your Secretary of State, your *lords, nobles,* and ecclesiastics enforce, as a duty you owe to your free and glorious country, and to your God, that you do this accursed thing. Not fewer than forty Americans have, within the past two years, been hunted down and, without a moment's warning, hurried away in chains, and consigned to slavery and excruciating torture. Some of these have had wives and children, dependent on them for bread; but of this, no account was made. The right of the hunter to his prey stands superior to the right of marriage, and to *all* rights in this republic, the rights of God included! For black men there is neither law nor justice, humanity nor religion. The Fugitive Slave *Law* makes mercy to them a crime; and bribes the judge who tries them. An American judge gets ten dollars for every victim he consigns to slavery, and five, when he fails to do so. The oath of any two villains is sufficient, under this hell-black enactment, to send the most pious and exemplary black man into the remorseless jaws of slavery! His own testimony is nothing. . . .

. . . [T]he church of this country is not only indifferent to the wrongs of the slave, it actually takes sides with the oppressors. It has made itself the bulwark of American slavery, and the shield of American slave-hunters. Many of its most eloquent Divines, who stand as the very lights of the church, have shamelessly given the sanction of religion and the Bible to the whole slave system. They have taught that man may, properly, be a slave; that the relation of master and slave is ordained of God; that to send back an escaped bondman to his master is clearly the duty of all the followers of the Lord Jesus Christ; and this horrible blasphemy is palmed off upon the world for Christianity.

For my part, I would say, welcome infidelity! welcome atheism! welcome anything! in preference to the gospel, *as preached by those Divines!* They convert the very name of religion into an engine of tyranny and barbarous cruelty . . .

Americans! your republican politics, not less than your republican religion, are flagrantly inconsistent. You boast of your love of liberty, your superior civilization, and your pure Christianity, while the whole political power of the nation (as embodied in the two great political parties) is solemnly pledged to support and perpetuate the enslavement of three millions of your countrymen. You hurl your anathemas at the crowned headed tyrants of Russia and Austria and pride yourselves on your Democratic institutions, while you yourselves consent to be the mere *tools* and *body-guards* of the tyrants of Virginia and Carolina. You invite to your shores fugitives of oppression from abroad, honor them with banquets, greet them with ovations, cheer them, toast them, salute them, protect them, and pour out your money to them like water; but the fugitives from your own land you advertise, hunt, arrest, shoot, and kill. You glory in your refinement and your universal education; yet you maintain a system as barbarous and dreadful as ever stained the character of a nation—a system begun in avarice, supported in pride, and perpetuated in cruelty. . . .

Fellow-citizens, I will not enlarge further on your national inconsistencies. The existence of slavery in this country brands your republicanism as a sham, your humanity as a base pretense, and your Christianity as a lie. It destroys your moral power abroad: it corrupts your politicians at home. It saps the foundation of religion; it makes your name a hissing and a bye-word to a mocking earth. It is the antagonistic force in your government, the only thing that seriously disturbs and endangers your *Union*. It fetters your progress; it is the enemy of improvement; the deadly foe of education; it fosters pride; it breeds insolence; it promotes vice; it shelters crime; it is a curse to the earth that supports it; and yet you cling to it as if it were the sheet anchor of all your hopes. Oh! be warned! be warned! a horrible reptile is coiled up in your nation's bosom; the venomous creature is nursing at the tender breast of your youthful republic; *for the love of God, tear away,* and fling from you the hideous monster, and *let the weight of twenty millions crush and destroy it forever!*

But it is answered in reply to all this, that precisely what I have now denounced is, in fact, guaranteed and sanctioned by the Constitution of the United States; that, the right to hold, and to hunt slaves is a part of that Constitution framed by the illustrious Fathers of this Republic. . . .

Fellow-citizens! there is no matter in respect to which the people of the North have allowed themselves to be so ruinously imposed upon as that of the pro-slavery character of the Constitution. In that instrument I hold there is neither warrant, license, nor sanction of the hateful thing; but interpreted, as it ought to be interpreted, the Constitution is a glorious liberty document. Read its preamble, consider its purposes.

Is slavery among them? Is it at the gateway? or is it in the temple? it is neither. While I do not intend to argue this question on the present occasion, let me ask, if it be not somewhat singular that, if the Constitution were intended to be, by its framers and adopters, a slaveholding instrument, why neither slavery, slaveholding, nor slave can anywhere be found in it. . . .

Now, take the Constitution according to its plain reading, and I defy the presentation of a single pro-slavery clause in it. On the other hand, it will be found to contain principles and purposes, entirely hostile to the existence of slavery. . . .

Allow me to say, in conclusion, notwithstanding the dark picture I have this day presented, of the state of the nation, I do not despair of this country. There are forces in operation which must inevitably work the downfall of slavery. "The arm of the Lord is not shortened," and the doom of slavery is certain. I, therefore, leave off where I began, with hope. While drawing encouragement from "the Declaration of Independence," the great principles it contains, and the genius of American Institutions, my spirit is also cheered by the obvious tendencies of the age. . . .

from LITTLE FERNS FOR FANNY'S LITTLE FRIENDS

Sara Payson Parton ("Fanny Fern")

THE LITTLE "MORNING GLORY"

Dear little pet! She was going a journey in the cars with mamma; and her little curly head could not stay on the pillow, for thinking of it. She was awake by the dawn, and had been trying to rouse mamma for an hour. She had told her joy in lisping accents to "Dolly," whose stoical indifference was very provoking, especially when she knew she was going to see "her dear, white-haired old grand-papa," who had never yet looked upon her sweet face, although pen and ink had long since heralded her polite perfections. Yes, little pet must look her prettiest, for grand-papa's eyes are not so dim, that the sight of a pretty face doesn't cheer him like a ray of glad sunlight; so the glossy waves of golden hair are nicely combed, and the bright dress put on, to heighten, by contrast, the dimpled fairness of the neck and shoulders; then, the little white apron, to keep all tidy; then the Cinderella boots, neatly laced. I can see you, little pet! I wish I had you in my arms this minute! . . .

Alas! poor little pet!

Grand-papa's eyes grow weary watching for you, at the little cottage window. Grand-mamma says, "the cakes will be quite spoiled;" and she "knits to her seam needle," and then moves about the sitting-room uneasily; now and then stopping to pat the little Kitty, that is to be pet's play-fellow. And now lame Tim has driven the cows home; and the dew is falling, the stars are creeping out, and the little crickets and frogs have commenced their evening concert, and *still* little pet has n't come! Where *is* the little stray waif?

Listen! Among the "unrecognized dead" by the late RAILROAD ACCIDENT, was a female child, about three years of age; fair complexion and hair; had on a red dress, green sack, white apron, linen gaiters, tipped with patent leather, and white woolen stockings.

Poor little pet! Poor old grand-papa! Go comfort him; tell him it was a *"shocking accident,"* but then *"nobody was to blame;"* and offer him a healing plaster for his great grief, in the shape of "damage" money.

THE CHARITY ORPHANS

"Pleasant sight, is it not?" said my friend, glancing complacently at a long procession of little charity children, who were passing, two and two—two and two—with closely cropped heads, little close-fitting sunbonnets and dark dresses; "pleasant sight, is it not, Fanny?" Yes—no—*no*, said I, courageously, it gives me the heart-ache. Oh, I see as you do, that their clothes are clean and whole, and that they are drilled like a little regiment of soldiers, (heads up,) but I long to see them step out of those prim ranks, and shout and scamper. I long to stuff their little pockets full of anything—everything, that other little pets have. I want to get them round me, and tell them some comical stories to take the care-worn look out of their anxious little faces. I want to see them twist their little heads round when they hear a noise, instead of keeping them straight forward as if they were "on duty." I want to know if anybody tucks them up comfortably when they go to bed, and gives them a good-night kiss. I want to know if they get a beaming smile, and a kind word in the morning. I want to know who soothes them when they are in pain; and if they *dare say so*, when they feel lonely, and have the heart-ache. I want to see the tear roll freely down the cheek, (instead of being wiped slyly away) when they see happy little ones trip gaily past, hand in hand, with a kind father, or mother. I want to know if "Thanksgiving" and "Christmas" and "New Year's" and *"Home"* are anything but empty sounds in their orphan ears.

I know their present state is better than vicious poverty, and so I try to say with my friend, "it is a pleasant sight;" but the words die on my lip; for full well I know it takes something more than food, shelter and clothing, to make a child happy. Its little heart, like a delicate vine, *will* throw out its tendrils for something to *lean on*—something to *cling to*; and so I can only say again, the sight of those charity orphans gives me the heart-ache.

ONLY A PENNY

Now I am going to tell you a story about little Clara. Those of you who live in the city will understand it; but some of my little readers may live in the country, (or at least I hope they do) where a beggar is seldom seen; or if he is, can always get of the good, nice, kind-hearted farmer, a bowl of milk, a fresh bit of bread, and liberty to sleep in the barn on the sweet-scented hay; therefore, it will be hard for you to believe that there is anybody in the wide world with enough to eat, and drink, and wear, who does not care whether a poor fellow creature starves or not; or whether he lives or dies.

But listen to my story.

One bright, sunny morning I was walking in Broadway, (New-York), looking at the ladies who passed, in their gay clothes—as fine as peacocks, and just about as silly—gazing at the pretty shop windows, full of silks, and satins, and ribbons, looking very much as if a rainbow had been shivered there—looking at the rich people's little children, with their silken hose, and plumed hats, and velvet tunics, tiptoeing so carefully along, and looking so frightened lest somebody should soil their nice clothes—when a little, plaintive voice struck upon my ear—

"Please give me a penny, Madam—*only* a penny—to buy a loaf of bread?"

I turned my head: there stood a little girl of six years,—so filthy, dirty—so ragged, that she scarcely looked like a human being. Her skin was coated with dust; her pretty curly locks were one tangled mass; her dress was fluttering in strings around her bare legs and shoeless feet—and the little hand she held out to me for "a penny," so bony that it looked like a skeleton's. She looked so very hungry, I would n't make her talk till I had given her something to eat; so I took her to a baker's, and bought her some bread and cakes; and it would have made you cry (you, who were never hungry in your life,) to see her swallow it so greedily, just like a little animal.

Then I asked her name, and found out 'twas "Clara;" that she had no papa; that while he lived he was very cruel, and used to beat her and her mother; and that now her mother was cruel too, and drank rum; that she sent little Clara out each morning to beg,—or if she couldn't beg, to steal,—but at any rate to bring home something, "unless she wanted a beating."

Poor little Clara!—all alone threading her way through the great, wicked city—knocked and jostled about,—*so* hungry—*so* tired,—*so* frightened! Clara was afraid to steal, (not because God saw her—for she didn't know anything about *Him*,) but for fear of policemen and prisons—so she wandered about, hour after hour, saying pitifully to the careless crowd, "Only a penny—*please* give me a penny to buy a loaf of bread!"

Yes—Clara's mother was very cruel; but God forbid, my little innocent children, that you should ever know how hunger, and thirst, and misery, may sometimes turn even that holy thing—*a mother's love*—to bitterness.

Poor Clara! she had never known a better home than the filthy, dark cellar, where poor people in cities huddle together like hunted cattle. . . . Her little head often pained her. She was foot-weary and heart-sore; and what was worse than all, she had never heard of heaven, "where the weary rest." Wasn't it very pitiful?

Well, little Clara kissed my hand when she had eaten enough—(it was so odd for *Clara* to have *enough*)—and her sunken eyes grew bright, and she said—"Now I shall not be beaten, because I've something left to carry home;" so she told me where she lived, and I bade her good bye, and told her I would come and see her mother to-morrow.

The next day I started again to find little Clara's mother. I was *very* happy going along, because I meant, if I could, to get her away from her cruel mother; to make her clean and neat; to teach her how to read and spell, and show to her that the world was not *all* darkness—not *all* sin, and tears, and sorrow; and to tell her of that kind God who loves *everything* that He has made. So as I told you I was very happy,—the soil looked so bright to me—the sky so fair,—and I could scarcely make my feet go fast enough.

Turning a corner suddenly, I met a man bearing a child's coffin. . . .

Yes—it was she! I was too late—*she* was in the little coffin! No hearse—no mourners—no tolling bell! Borne along—unnoticed—uncared for—through the busy, crowded, noisy, streets. But, dear children, kind Angels looked pitying down, and Clara "hungers no more—nor thirsts any more—neither shall the sun light on her, nor any heat."

A PEEP UNDER GROUND

The Raffertys and the Rourkes

I have made up my mind, that there is nothing lost in New-York. You open your window and toss out a bit of paper or silk, and though it may be no bigger than a sixpence, it is directly snatched up and carried off, by a class of persons the Parisians call, "Chiffoniers" (rag-pickers)! You order a load of coal or wood, to be dropped at your door;—in less than five minutes a whole horde of ragged children are greedily waiting round to pick up the chips, and bits, that are left after the wood or coal is carried in and housed; and often locks of hair are pulled out, and bloody noses ensue, in the strife to get the largest share. You will see these persons round the stores, looking for bits of paper, and silk, and calico, that are swept out by the clerks, upon the pavement; you will see them watching round provision shops, for decayed vegetables, and fruits, and rinds of melons, which they sell to keepers of pigs; you will see them picking up peach stones to sell to confectioners, who crack them and use the kernels; you will see them round old buildings, carrying off, at the risk of cracked heads, pieces of decayed timber, and old nails; you will see them round new buildings, when the workmen are gone to meals, scampering off with boards, shingles, and bits of scaffolding. I thought I had seen all the ingenuity there was to be seen, in picking up odds and ends in New-York, but I had n't then seen Michael Rafferty!

Michael Rafferty, and Terence Rourke, who was a wood sawyer by profession, lived in a cellar together; the little Raffertys, and little Rourkes, with their mammas, filling up all the extra space, except just so much as was necessary to swing the cellar door open. A calico curtain was swung across the cellar for a boundary line, to which the little Rourkes and little Raffertys paid about as much attention, as the whites did to the poor Indians' landmarks.

At the time I became acquainted with the two families, quite a jealousy had sprung up on account of Mr. Rafferty's having made a successful butter speculation. Mrs. Rourke, in consequence, had kept the calico curtain tightly drawn for some weeks, and boxed six of the little Rourkes' ears (twelve in all,) for speaking to the little Raffertys through the rents in the curtain.

All this I learned from Mrs. Rafferty, as I sat on an old barrel in the north-west corner of her cellar. "It was always the way," she said, "if a body got up in the world, there were plenty of envious spalpeens, sure, to spite them for it;" which, I took occasion to remark to Mrs. Rafferty, was as true, as anything I had ever had the pleasure of hearing her say.

Just then the cellar door swung open, and the great butter speculator, Mr. Michael Rafferty, walked in. He nodded his head, and gave an uneasy glance at the curtain, as much as to say, "calicoes have ears." I understood it, and told him we had been very discreet. Upon which he said, "You see, they'll be after staling my thrade, your ladyship, if they know how I manage about the butther."

"Tell me how you do it, Michael," said I; "you know women have a right to be curious."

"Well," said he, speaking in a confidential whisper, "your ladyship knows there are plenty of little grocery shops round in these poor neighborhoods, where they sell onions, and combs, and molasses, and fish, and tape, and gingerbread, and rum. Most of them sell milk, (none of the best, sure, but it does for the likes of us poor folks.) It stands round in the sun in the shop windows, your ladyship, till it gets turned, like, and when they have kept it a day or two, and find they can't sell it," (and here Michael looked sharp at the calico curtain) "I buys it for two cents a quart, and puts it in that churn," (pointing to a dirty looking affair in the corner,) "and my old woman and I make it into butter." And he stepped carefully across the cellar, and pulled *from under the bed*, a keg, which uncovered with a proud flourish, and sticking a bit of wood in it, offered me a taste, "just to thry it."

I could n't have tasted it, if Michael had shot me; but I told him I dare say he understood his trade and hoped he found plenty of customers.

"I sell it as fast as I can make it," said he, putting on the cover and shoving it back under the bed again.

"What do you do with the buttermilk?" said I.

He looked at Mrs. Rafferty, and she pointed to the bright, rainbow ribbon on her cap.

"Sell it?" said I.

"Sure," said Michael, with a grin; "we are making money, your ladyship; we shall be afther moving out of this cellar before long, and away from the likes of them," (pointing in the direction of the curtain); "and, savin' your ladyship's presence," said he, running his fingers through his mop of wiry hair, "Irish people sometimes understhand dhriving a thrade as well as Yankees;" and Michael drew himself up as though General Washington could n't be named on the same day with *him*.

Just then a little snarly headed boy came in with two pennies and a cracked plate, "to buy some butther."

"Didn't I tell your ladyship so?" said Michael. "Holy Mother!" he continued, as he pocketed the pennies, and gave the boy a short allowance of the vile stuff, "how I wish I had known how to make that butther when every bone in me body used to ache sawin' wood, and the likes o' that, to say nothing of the greater respictability of being in the mercantile profession."

from EARTH'S HOLOCAUST

Nathaniel Hawthorne

Once upon a time—but whether in the time past or time to come is a matter of little or no moment—this wide world had become so overburdened with an accumulation of worn-out trumpery that the inhabitants determined to rid themselves of it by a general bonfire. The site fixed upon at the representation of the insurance companies, and as being as central a spot as any other on the globe, was one of the broadest prairies of the West, where no human habitation would be endangered by the flames, and where a vast assemblage of spectators might commodiously admire the show. . . .

"What materials have been used to kindle the flame?" inquired I of a bystander, for I was desirous of knowing the whole process of the affair from beginning to end. . . .

"Oh, some very dry combustibles," replied he, "and extremely suitable to the purpose—no other, in fact, than yesterday's newspapers, last month's magazines, and last year's withered leaves. Here, now, comes some antiquated trash that will take fire like a handful of shavings."

As he spoke some rough-looking men advanced to the verge of the bonfire and threw in, as it appeared, all the rubbish of the herald's office—the blazonry of coat-armor, the crests and devices of illustrious families, pedigrees that extended back like lines of light into the midst of the Dark Ages, together with stars, garters and embroidered collars, each of which, as paltry a bauble as it might appear to the uninstructed eye, had once possessed vast significance, and was still, in truth, reckoned among the most precious of moral or material facts by the worshippers of the gorgeous past. . . .

At sight of these dense volumes of smoke mingled with vivid jets of flame that gushed and eddied forth from this immense pile of earthly distinctions the multitude of plebeian spectators set up a joyous shout and clapped their hands with an emphasis that made the welkin echo.

That was their moment of triumph achieved after long ages over creatures of the same clay and the same spiritual infirmities who had dared to assume the privileges due only to Heaven's better workmanship. . . .

[S]houted a rude figure, spurning the embers with his foot[:] "And henceforth let no man dare to show a piece of musty parchment as his warrant for lording it over his fellows. If he have strength of arm, well and good: it is one species of superiority; if he have wit, wisdom, courage, force of character, let these attributes do for him what they may; but from this day forward no mortal must hope for place and consideration by reckoning up the mouldy bones of his ancestors. That nonsense is done away."

"And in good time," remarked the grave observer by my side—in a low voice, however—"if no worse nonsense comes in its place. But at all events, this species of nonsense has fairly lived out its life." . . .

"Let us get to windward and see what they are doing on the other side of the bonfire."

We accordingly passed around, and were just in time to witness the arrival of a vast procession of Washingtonians—as the votaries of temperance call themselves nowadays—accompanied by thousands of the Irish disciples of Father Mathew with that great apostle at their head. They brought a rich contribution to the bonfire, being nothing less than all the hogsheads and barrels of liquor in the world, which they rolled before them across the prairie. . . .

[H]ere was the whole world's stock of spirituous liquors, which, instead of kindling a frenzied light in the eyes of individual topers, as of yore, soared upward with a bewildering gleam that startled all mankind. It was the aggregate of that fierce fire which would otherwise have scorched the hearts of millions. . . . [T]he multitude gave a shout, as if the broad earth were exulting in its deliverance from the curse of ages.

But the joy was not universal. Many deemed that human life would be gloomier than ever when that brief illumination should sink down. While the reformers were at work I overheard muttered expostulations from several respectable gentlemen with red noses and wearing gouty shoes; and a ragged worthy whose face looked like a hearth where the fire is burnt out now expressed his discontent more openly and boldly.

"What is this world good for," said the last toper, "now that we can never be jolly any more? What is to comfort the poor man in sorrow and perplexity? How is he to keep his heart warm against the cold winds of this cheerless earth? And what do you propose to give him in exchange for that solace that you take away?" . . .

I could not help commiserating the forlorn condition of the last toper, whose boon-companions had dwindled away from his side, leaving the poor fellow without a soul to countenance him in sipping his liquor—nor, indeed, any liquor to sip. Not that this was quite the true state of the case, for I had observed him at a critical moment filch a bottle of fourth-proof brandy that fell beside the bonfire, and hide it in his pocket.

The spirituous and fermented liquors being thus disposed of, the zeal of the reformers next induced them to replenish the fire with all the boxes of tea and bags of coffee in the world. And now came the planters of Virginia, bringing their crops of tobacco. . . .

"Well, they've put my pipe out," said an old gentleman, flinging it into the flames in a pet. "What is this world coming to? Everything rich and racy,—all the spice of life—is to be condemned as useless. Now that they have kindled the bonfire, if these nonsensical reformers would fling themselves into it, all would be well enough."

"Be patient," responded a staunch conservative; "it will come to that in the end. They will first fling us in, and finally themselves."

From the general and systematic measures of reform, I now turned to consider the individual contributions to this memorable bonfire. . . . A widow resolving on a second marriage slyly threw in her dead husband's miniature. A young man jilted by his mistress would willingly have flung his own desperate heart into the flames, but could find no means to wrench it out of his bosom. An American author whose works were neglected by the public threw his pen and paper into the bonfire, and betook himself to some less discouraging occupation. It somewhat startled me to overhear a number of ladies highly respectable in appearance proposing to fling their gowns and petticoats into the flames, and assume the garb, together with the manners, duties, offices and responsibilities, of the opposite sex. . . .

It was now rumored among the spectators that all the weapons and munitions of war were to be thrown into the bonfire. . . .

The blessed tidings were accordingly promulgated, and caused infinite rejoicings among those who had stood aghast at the horror and absurdity of war.

But I saw a grim smile pass over the seared visage of a stately old commander—by his war-worn figure and rich military dress he might have been one of Napoleon's famous marshals—who, with the rest of the world's soldiery, had just flung away the sword that had been familiar to his right hand for half a century.

"Ay, ay!" grumbled he. "Let them proclaim what they please, but in the end we shall find that all this foolery has only made more work for the armories and cannon-founders."

"Why, sir," exclaimed I, in astonishment, "do you imagine that the human race will ever so far return on the steps of its past madness as to weld another sword or cast another cannon?"

"There will be no need," observed, with a sneer, one who neither felt benevolence nor had faith in it. "When Cain wished to slay his brother, he was at no loss for a weapon." . . .

The fire was now to be replenished with materials that had hitherto been considered of even greater importance to the well-being of society than the warlike munitions which we had already seen consumed. A body of reformers had travelled all over the earth in quest of the machinery by which the different nations were accustomed to inflict the punishment of death. . . . Headsmen's axes with the rust of noble and royal blood upon them, and a vast collection of halters that had choked the breath of plebeian victims, were thrown in together. . . . But the loudest roar of applause went up, telling the distant sky of the triumph of the earth's redemption, when the gallows made its appearance. . . .

"That was well done!" exclaimed I.

"Yes, it was well done," replied, but with less enthusiasm than I expected, the thoughtful observer who was still at my side—"well done if the world be good enough for the measure. Death, however, is an idea that cannot easily be dispensed with in any condition between the primal innocence and that other purity and perfection which perchance we are destined to attain after travelling round the full circle. But, at all events, it is well that the experiment should now be tried." . . .

I know not whether it were the excitement of the scene or whether the good people around the bonfire were really growing more enlightened every instant, but they now proceeded to measures in the full length of which I was hardly prepared to keep them company. For instance, some threw their marriage certificates into the flames, and declared themselves candidates for a higher, holier and more comprehensive union than that which had subsisted from the birth of time under the form of the connubial tie. . . . There was then a cry that the period was arrived when the title-deeds of landed property should be given to the flames and the whole soil of the earth revert to the public from whom it had been wrongfully abstracted and most unequally distributed among individuals. . . .

Whether any ultimate action was taken with regard to these propositions is beyond my knowledge, for just then some matters were in progress that concerned my sympathies more nearly.

"See! see! What heaps of books and pamphlets!" cried a fellow who did not seem to be a lover of literature. "Now we shall have a glorious blaze!"

"That's just the thing," said a modern philosopher. "Now we shall get rid of the weight of dead men's thought which has hitherto pressed so heavily on the living intellect that it has been incompetent to any effectual self-exertion.—Well done, my lads! Into the fire with them! Now you're enlightening the world indeed! . . .

From Shakespeare there gushed a flame of such marvellous splendor that men shaded their eyes as against the sun's meridian glory, nor even when the works of his own elucidators were flung upon him did he cease to flash forth a dazzling radiance from beneath the ponderous heap. It is my belief that he is still blazing as fervidly as ever. . . .

I felt particular interest in watching the combustion of American authors, and scrupulously noted by my watch the precise number of moments that changed most of them from shabbily-printed books to indistinguishable ashes. . . .

If it be no lack of modesty to mention my own works, it must here be confessed that I looked for them with fatherly interest, but in vain. Too probably they were changed to vapor by the first action of the heat; at best, I can only hope that in their quiet way they contributed a glimmering spark or two to the splendor of the evening. . . .

"Here comes the fresh fuel that I spoke of," said my companion.

To my astonishment, the persons who now advanced into the vacant space around the mountain-fire bore surplices and other priestly garments, mitres, crosiers, and a confusion of popish and Protestant emblems with which it seemed their purpose to consummate the great Act of Faith. . . .

"All is well," said I, cheerfully. "The wood-paths shall be the aisles of our cathedral; the firmament itself shall be its ceiling. What needs an earthly roof between the Deity and his worshippers? Our faith can well afford to lose all the drapery that even the holiest men have thrown around it, and be only the more sublime in its simplicity."

"True," said my companion. "But will they pause here?"

... [A]s the final sacrifice of human error, what else remained to be thrown upon the members of that awful pile except the Book which, though a celestial revelation to past ages, was but a voice from a lower sphere, as regarded the present race of man? It was done. Upon the blazing heap of falsehood and worn-out truth—things that the earth had never needed or had ceased to need or had grown childishly weary of—fell the ponderous church Bible. ... There, likewise, fell the family Bible which the long-buried patriarch had read to his children—in prosperity or sorrow. ...

"This is terrible!" said I, feeling that my cheek grew pale and seeing a like change in the visages about me.

"Be of good courage yet," answered the man with whom I had spoken so often. He continued to gaze steadily at the spectacle with a singular calmness, as if it concerned him merely as an observer. "Be of good courage, nor yet exult too much; for there is far less both of good and evil in the effect of this bonfire than the world might be willing to believe. ...

" ... Trust me, the world of to-morrow will again enrich itself with the gold and diamonds which have been cast off by the world of to-day. Not a truth is destroyed nor buried so deep among the ashes but it will be raked up at last."

This was a strange assurance, yet I felt inclined to credit it—the more especially as I beheld among the wallowing flames a copy of the Holy Scriptures the pages of which, instead of being blackened into tinder, only assumed a more dazzling whiteness as the finger-marks of human imperfection were purified away. ...

"Listen to the talk of these worthies," said he, pointing to a group in front of the blazing pile. "Possibly they may teach you something useful without intending it."

The persons whom he indicated consisted of that brutal and most earthy figure who had stood forth so furiously in defence of the gallows—the hangman, in short—together with the last thief and the last murderer, all three of whom were clustered about the last toper; the latter was liberally passing the brandy-bottle which he had rescued from the general destruction of wines and spirits. ...

"Poh, poh, my good fellows!" said a dark-complexioned personage who now joined the group. His complexion was indeed fearfully dark, and his eyes glowed with a redder light than that of the bonfire. "Be not so cast down, my dear friends; you shall see good days yet. There is one thing that these wiseacres have forgotten to throw into the fire, and without which all the rest of the conflagration is just nothing at all—yes, though they had burnt the earth itself to a cinder."

"And what may that be?" eagerly demanded the last murderer.

"What but the human heart itself?" said the dark visaged stranger, with a portentous grin. "And unless they hit upon some method of purifying that foul cavern, forth from it will reissue all the shapes of wrong and misery—the same old shapes, or worse ones—which they have taken such a vast deal of trouble to consume to ashes. I have stood by this livelong night and laughed in my sleeve at the whole business. Oh, take my word for it, it will be the old world yet." . . .

CHAPTER 13

Which Minority's Rights?

INTRODUCTION

ABRAHAM LINCOLN, 1809–1865
from The Perpetuation of Our Political Institutions (1838)
and *from* Lincoln-Douglas Debates (1858)

HENRY DAVID THOREAU, 1817–1862
from Civil Disobedience (1849) and
from Slavery in Massachusetts (1856)

JOHN C. CALHOUN
from Disquisition on Government (1850)

SOLOMON NORTHUP, 1808–1869
from Twelve Years a Slave (1853)

By the 1830s few Americans failed to see that popular politics and the party system had made a shambles of Madison's arguments about how democracy would work. Most Americans supported minority rights in general, but few showed much concern about those of groups they judged less worthy than themselves. Such problems, always deep in democratic societies, came to a head as civil war approached. Various minorities pled their oppression and need for protection, but it was impossible to protect the "rights" of some without gutting those of others.

Whig lawyer Abraham Lincoln's first speech (like Beecher's educational argument) was partly a response to the riots of the mid-1830s and stressed the need to respect law to rein in popular passions. This basic position, now related to the rights of the Declartion of Independence, he turned toward sectional issues two decades later in debates with Stephen Douglas that won him the political prominence that led to his presidency. Henry David Thoreau worked out his classic theory of a "majority of one" and of civil disobedience in disgust at the Mexican War, and later seethed at how the Fugitive Slave Law enslaved Massachusetts to the service of slavecatchers. South Carolinian John C. Calhoun powerfully argued his idea for protecting American political civility and minority rights without mentioning slavery or the South, but probably he wished no "concurrent majority" for any group more oppressed than Southern planters.

While Calhoun's probing critique of democratic tendencies shared much with Tocqueville's, his life-long concern was the right to oppress those groups to which Solomon Northup belonged: free blacks and slaves. A New York freeman, Northup was duped, doped, and sold into slavery in Louisiana. Twelve years later his situation became known and he was freed to return to his family. Once home he dictated the most detailed and straight-forward picture of slavery we have.

CONSIDERATIONS

- What rights do and should minorities have in society? Can one trust the majority to do what is right? What is the relation of the rights of unpopular groups to the common good?

- To what degree is respect for law essential in democratic society? Is defiance of law ever justified or useful? Was it in Thoreau's case, or the case of the slaves attempting to escape?

- How good are Thoreau's and Calhoun's "solutions"? Does Thoreau use his idea in the way Ghandi and Martin Luther King applied it later?

- Who were threatened minorites: abolitionists? Massachusetts? Thoreau? the South as Civil War approached? Were the slaves?

- What does Northup's account suggest about the nature of American slavery? of slave character?

- Could the rights of all minorities be protected? Are gays or creationists or militia militants or drug user minorities today deserving of legal protection?

from THE PERPETUATION OF OUR POLITICAL INSTITUTIONS

January 27, 1838

Abraham Lincoln

We find ourselves in the peaceful possession of the fairest portion of the earth, as regards extent of territory, fertility of soil, and salubrity of climate. We find ourselves under the government of a system of political institutions, conducing more essentially to the ends of civil and religious liberty, than any of which the history of former times tells us. We, when mounting the stage of existence, found ourselves the legal inheritors of these fundamental blessings. We toiled not in the acquirement or establishment of them—they are a legacy bequeathed us, by a *once* hardy, brave, and patriotic, but *now* lamented and departed race of ancestors. Theirs was the task (and nobly they performed it) to possess themselves, and through themselves, us, of this goodly land; and to uprear upon its hills and its valleys, a political edifice of liberty and equal rights; 'tis ours only, to transmit these, the former, unprofaned by the foot of an invader; the latter, undecayed by the lapse of time and untorn by usurpation, to the latest generation that fate shall permit the world to know. This task gratitude to our fathers, justice to ourselves, duty to posterity, and love for our species in general, all imperatively require us faithfully to perform.

How then shall we perform it?—At what point shall we expect the approach of danger? By what means shall we fortify against it?—Shall we expect some transatlantic military giant, to step the Ocean, and crush us at a blow? Never!—All the armies of Europe, Asia and Africa combined, with all the treasure of the earth (our own excepted) in their military chest; with a Buonaparte for a commander, could not by force, take a drink from the Ohio, or make a track on the Blue Ridge, in a trial of a thousand years.

At what point then is the approach of danger to be expected? I answer, if it ever reach us, it must spring up amongst us. It cannot come from abroad. If destruction be our lot, we must ourselves be its author and finisher. As a nation of freemen, we must live through all time, or die by suicide.

I hope I am over wary; but if I am not, there is, even now, something of ill-omen, amongst. I mean the increasing disregard for law which pervades the country; the growing disposition to substitute the wild and furious passions, in lieu of the sober judgment of Courts; and the worse than savage mobs, for the executive ministers of justice. This disposition is awfully fearful in any community; and that it now exists in ours, though grating to our feelings to admit, it would be a violation of truth, and an insult to our intelligence, to deny. Accounts of outrages committed by mobs, form the every-day news of the times. They have pervaded the country, from New England to Louisiana;—they are neither peculiar to the eternal snows of the former, nor the burning suns of the latter;—they are not the creature of climate—neither are they confined to the slave-holding, or the non-slave-holding States. Alike, they spring up among the pleasure hunting masters of Southern slaves, and the order loving citizens of the land of steady habits.—Whatever, then, their cause may be, it is common to the whole country.

It would be tedious, as well as useless, to recount the horrors of all of them. Those happening in the State of Mississippi, and at St. Louis, are, perhaps, the most dangerous in example and revolting to humanity. In the Mississippi case, they first commenced by hanging the regular gamblers; a set of men, certainly not following for a livelihood, a very useful, or very honest occupation; but one which, so far from being forbidden by the laws, was actually licensed by an act of the Legislature, passed but a single year before. Next, negroes, suspected of conspiring to raise an insurrection, were caught up and hanged in all parts of the State: then, white men, supposed to be leagued with the negroes; and finally, strangers, from neighboring States, going thither on business, were, in many instances subjected to the same fate. Thus went on this process of hanging, from gamblers to negroes, from negroes to white citizens, and from these to strangers; till dead men were seen literally dangling from the boughs of trees upon every road side; and in numbers almost sufficient, to rival the native Spanish moss of the country, as a drapery of the forest.

Turn, then, to that horror-striking scene at St. Louis. A single victim was only sacrificed there. His story is very short; and is, perhaps, the most highly tragic, of anything of its length, that has ever been witnessed in real life. A mulatto man, by the name of McIntosh, was seized in the street, dragged to the suburbs of the city, chained to a tree, and actually burned to death; and all within a single hour from the time he had been a freeman, attending to his own business, and at peace with the world.

Such are the effects of mob law; and such are the scenes, becoming more and more frequent in this land so lately famed for love of law and order; and the stories of which, have even now grown too familiar, to attract any thing more, than an idle remark.

But you are, perhaps, ready to ask, "What has this to do with the perpetuation of our political institutions?" I answer, it has much to do with it. Its direct consequences are, comparatively speaking, but a small evil; and much of its danger consists, in the proneness of our minds, to regard its direct, as its only consequences. . . . When men take it in their heads to-day, to hang gamblers, or burn murderers, they should recollect, that, in the confusion usually attending such transactions, they will be as likely to hang or burn some one who is neither a gambler nor a murderer as one who is; and that, acting upon the example they set, the mob of to-morrow, may, and probably will, hang or burn some of them by the very same mistake. And not only so; the innocent, those who have ever set their faces against violations of law in every shape, alike with the guilty, fall victims to the ravages of mob law; and thus it goes on, step by step, till all the walls erected for the defence of the persons and property of individuals, are trodden down, and disregarded. But all this even, is not the full extent of the evil.— By such examples, by instances of the perpetrators of such acts going unpunished, the lawless in spirit, are encouraged to become lawless in practice; and having been used to no restraint, but dread of punishment, they thus become, absolutely unrestrained.—Having ever regarded Government as their deadliest bane, they make a jubilee of the suspension of its operations; and pray for nothing so much, as its total annihilation. While, on the other hand, good men, men who love tranquillity, who desire to abide by the laws, and enjoy their benefits, who would gladly spill their blood in the defence of their country; seeing their property destroyed; their families insulted, and their lives endangered; their persons injured; and seeing nothing in prospect that forebodes a change for the better; become tired of, and disgusted with, a Government that offers them no protection; and are not much averse to a change in which they imagine they have nothing to lose. Thus, then, by the operation of this mobocratic spirit, which all must admit, is now abroad in the land, the strongest bulwark of any Government, and particularly of those constituted like ours, may effectually be broken down and destroyed—I mean the *attachment* of the People. Whenever this effect shall be produced among us; whenever the vicious portion of population shall be permitted to gather in bands of hundreds and thousands, and burn churches, ravage and rob provision-stores, throw printing presses into rivers, shoot editors, and hang and burn obnoxious persons at pleasure, and with impunity; depend on it, this Government cannot last. . . .

The question recurs, "how shall we fortify against it?" The answer is simple. Let every American, every lover of liberty, every well wisher to his posterity, swear by the blood of the Revolution, never to violate in the least particular, the laws of the country; and never to tolerate their violation by others. As the patriots of seventy-six did to the support of the Declaration of Independence, so to the support of the Constitution and Laws, let every American pledge his life, his property, and his sacred honor;—let every man remember that to violate the law, is to trample on the blood of his father, and to tear the character of his own, and his children's liberty. Let reverence for the laws be breathed by every American mother, to the lisping babe, that prattles on her lap—let it be taught in schools, in seminaries, and in colleges; let it be written in Primers, spelling books, and in Almanacs;—let it be preached from the pulpit, proclaimed in legislative halls, and enforced in courts of justice. And, in short, let it become the *political religion* of the nation; and let the old and the young, the rich and the poor, the grave and the gay, of all sexes and tongues, and colors and conditions, sacrifice unceasingly upon its altars.

• • •

The experiment is successful; and thousands have won their deathless names in making it so. But the game is caught; and I believe it is true, that with the catching, end the pleasures of the chase. This field of glory is harvested, and the crop is already appropriated. But new reapers will arise, and *they*, too, will seek a field. It is to deny what the history of the world tells us is true, to suppose that men of ambition and talents will not continue to spring up amongst us. And, when they do, they will as naturally seek the gratification of their ruling passion, as others have so done before them. The question then, is, can that gratification be found in supporting and maintaining an edifice that has been erected by others? Most certainly it cannot.... It thirsts and burns for distinction; and, if possible, it will have it, whether at the expense of emancipating slaves, or enslaving freemen. Is it unreasonable then to expect, that some man possessed of the loftiest genius, coupled with ambition sufficient to push it to its utmost stretch, will at some time, spring up among us? And when such a one does, it will require the people to be united with each other, attached to the government and laws, and generally intelligent, to successfully frustrate his designs.

Distinction will be his paramount object, and although he would as willingly, perhaps more so, acquire it by doing good as harm; yet, that opportunity being past, and nothing left to be done in the way of building up, he would set boldly to the task of pulling down. . . .

Passion has helped us; but can do so no more. It will in future be our enemy. Reason, cold, calculating, unimpassioned reason, must furnish all the materials for our future support and defence.—Let those materials be moulded into *general intelligence, sound morality,* and, in particular, *a reverence for the constitution and laws.* . . .

from THE LINCOLN-DOUGLAS DEBATES

Abraham Lincoln

AUGUST 21, 1858

... [A]nything that argues me into his idea of perfect social and political equality with the negro, is but a specious and fantastic arrangement of words, by which a man can prove a horse chestnut to be a chestnut horse. [Laughter.] I will say here, while upon this subject, that I have no purpose directly or indirectly to interfere with the institution of slavery in the States where it exists. I believe I have no lawful right to do so, and I have no inclination to do so. I have no purpose to introduce political and social equality between the white and the black races. There is a physical difference between the two, which in my judgment will probably forever forbid their living together upon the footing of perfect equality, and inasmuch as it becomes a necessity that there must be a difference, I, as well as Judge Douglas, am in favor of the race to which I belong, having the superior position. I have never said anything to the contrary, but I hold that notwithstanding all this, there is no reason in the world why the negro is not entitled to all the natural rights enumerated in the Declaration of Independence, the right to life, liberty and the pursuit of happiness. [Loud cheers.] I hold that he is as much entitled to these as the white man. I agree with Judge Douglas he is not my equal in many respects—certainly not in color, perhaps not in moral or intellectual endowment. But in the right to eat the bread, without leave of anybody else, which his own hand earns, *he is my equal and the equal of Judge Douglas, and the equal of every living man.* [Great applause.]

• • •

But lately, I think—and in this I charge nothing on the Judge's motives—lately, I think, that he, and those acting with him, have placed that institution on a new basis, which looks to the *perpetuity and nationalization of slavery.* [Loud cheers.] And while it is placed upon this new basis, I say, and I have said, that I believe we shall not have peace upon the question until the opponents of slavery arrest the further spread of it, and place it where the public mind shall rest in the belief that it is in the course of ultimate extinction; or, on the other hand, that its advocates will push it forward until it shall become alike lawful in all the States, old as well as new, North as well as South. . . .

A VOICE—Then do you repudiate Popular Sovereignty?

MR. LINCOLN—Well, then, let us talk about Popular Sovereignty! [Laughter.] What is Popular Sovereignty? [Cries of "A humbug," "a humbug."] Is it the right of the people to have Slavery or not have it, as they see fit, in the territories? I will state—and I have an able man to watch me—my understanding is that Popular Sovereignty, as now applied to the question of Slavery, does allow the people of a Territory to have Slavery if they want to, but does not allow them *not* to have it if they *do not* want it. [Applause and laughter.] I do not mean that if this vast concourse of people were in a Territory of the United States, any one of them would be obliged to have a slave if he did not want one; but I do say that, as I understand the Dred Scott decision, if any one man wants slaves, all the rest have no way of keeping that one man from holding them. . . .

SEPTEMBER 18, 1858

. . . I will say then that I am not, nor ever have been in favor of bringing about in any way the social and political equality of the white and black races, [applause]—that I am not nor ever have been in favor of making voters or jurors of negroes, nor of qualifying them to hold office, nor to intermarry with white people; and I will say in addition to this that there is a physical difference between the white and black races which I believe will for ever forbid the two races living together on terms of social and political equality. And inasmuch as they cannot so live, while they do remain together there must be the position of superior and inferior, and I as much as any other man am in favor of having the superior position assigned to the white race. I say upon this occasion I do not perceive that because the white man is to have the superior position the negro should be denied everything. I do not understand that because I do not want a negro woman for a slave I must necessarily want her for a wife. [Cheers and laughter.] My understanding is that I can just let her alone. I am now in my fiftieth year, and I certainly never have had a black woman for either a slave or a wife. So it seems to me quite possible for us to get along without making either slaves or wives of negroes. I will add to this that I have never seen to my knowledge a man, woman or child who was in favor of producing a perfect equality, social and political, between negroes and white men. I recollect of but one distinguished instance that I ever heard of so frequently as to be entirely satisfied of its correctness—and that is the case of Judge Douglas' old friend Col. Richard M. Johnson. [Laughter.] I will also add to the remarks I have made, (for I am not going to enter at large upon this subject,) that I have never had the least apprehension that I or my friends would marry negroes if there was no law to keep them from it, [laughter] but as Judge Douglas and his friends seem to be in great apprehension that they might, if there were no law to keep them from it, [roars of laughter] I give him the most solemn pledge that I will to the very last stand by the law of this State, which forbids the marrying of white people with negroes. [Continued laughter and applause.] I will add one further word, which is this, that I do not understand there is any place where an alteration of the social and political relations of the negro and the white man can be made except in the State Legislature—not in the Congress of the United States—and as I do not really apprehend the approach of any such thing myself, and as Judge Douglas seems to be in constant horror that some such danger is rapidly approaching, I propose as the best means to prevent it that the Judge be kept at home and placed in the State Legislature to fight the measure. [Uproarious laughter and applause.] . . .

OCTOBER 15, 1858

When that Nebraska bill was brought forward four years ago last January, was it not for the "avowed object" of putting an end to the slavery agitation? We were to have no more agitation in Congress; it was all to be banished to the Territories. By the way, I will remark here that, as Judge Douglas is very fond of complimenting Mr. Crittenden in these days, Mr. Crittenden has said there was a falsehood in that whole business, for there was *no slavery agitation at that time to allay.* We were for a little while *quiet* on the troublesome thing and that very allaying plaster of Judge Douglas', stirred it up again. [Applause and laughter.] But was it not understood or intimated with the "confident promise" of putting an end to the slavery agitation. Surely it was. In every speech you heard Judge Douglas make, until he got into this "imbroglio," as they call it, with the Administration about the Lecompton Constitution, every speech on that Nebraska bill was full of his felicitations that we were *just at the end* of the slavery agitation. The last tip of the last joint of the old serpent's tail was just drawing out of view. [Cheers and laughter.] But has it proved so? I have asserted that under that policy that agitation "has not only not ceased, but has constantly augmented." When was there ever a greater agitation in Congress than last winter? When was it as great in the country as today?

There was a collateral object in the introduction of that Nebraska policy which was to clothe the people of the Territories with a superior degree of self-government, beyond what they had ever had before. The first object and the main one of conferring upon the people a higher degree of "self government," is a question of fact to be determined by you in answer to a single question. Have you ever heard or known of a people any where on earth who had as little to do, as, in the first instance of its use, the people of Kansas had with this same right of "self-government"? [Loud applause.] In its main policy, and in its collateral object, *it has been nothing but a living, creeping lie from the time of its introduction, till today.* [Loud cheers.]

I have intimated that . . . [w]e might, by arresting the further spread of it and placing it where the fathers originally placed it, put it where the public mind should rest in the belief that it was in the course of ultimate extinction. Thus the agitation may cease. It may be pushed forward until it shall become alike lawful in all the States, old as well as new, North as well as South. I have said, and I repeat, my wish is that the further spread of it may be arrested, and that it may be placed where the public mind shall rest in the belief that it is in the course of ultimate extinction. [Great applause.] . . .

Again; the institution of slavery is only mentioned in the Constitution of the United States two or three times, and in neither of these cases does the word "slavery" or "negro race" occur; but covert language is used each time, and for a purpose full of significance. . . .

In all three of these places, being the only allusions to slavery in the instrument, covert language is used. Language is used not suggesting that slavery existed or that the black race were among us. And I understand the contemporaneous history of those times to be that covert language was used with a purpose, and that purpose was that in our Constitution, which it was hoped and is still hoped will endure forever—when it should be read by intelligent and patriotic men, after the institution of slavery had passed from among us—there should be nothing on the face of the great charter of liberty suggesting that such a thing as negro slavery had ever existed among us. [Enthusiastic applause.] This is part of the evidence that the fathers of the Government expected and intended the institution of slavery to come to an end. . . .

The exact truth is, that they found the institution existing among us, and they left it as they found it. But in making the government they left this institution with many clear marks of disapprobation upon it. They found slavery among them and they left it among them because of the difficulty—the absolute impossibility of its immediate removal. And when Judge Douglas asks me why we cannot let it remain part slave and part free as the fathers of the government made, he asks a question based upon an assumption which is itself a falsehood; and I turn upon him and ask him the question, when the policy that the fathers of the government had adopted in relation to this element among us was the best policy in the world—the only wise policy—the only policy that we can ever safely continue upon—that will ever give us peace unless this dangerous element masters us all and becomes a national institution—*I turn upon him and ask him why he could not let it alone?* [Great and prolonged cheering.] . . .

You may say and Judge Douglas has intimated the same thing, that all this difficulty in regard to the institution of slavery is the mere agitation of office seekers and ambitious Northern politicians. He thinks we want to get "his place," I suppose. [Cheers and laughter.] I agree that there are office seekers amongst us. The Bible says somewhere that we are desperately selfish. I think we would have discovered that fact without the Bible. I do not claim that I am any less so than the average of men, but I do claim that I am not more selfish than Judge Douglas. [Roars of laughter and applause.]

But is it true that all the difficulty and agitation we have in regard to this institution of slavery springs from office seeking—from the mere ambition of politicians? Is that the truth? How many times have we had danger from this question? Go back to the day of the Missouri Compromise. Go back to the Nullification question, at the bottom of which lay this same slavery question. Go back to the time of the Annexation of Texas. Go back to the troubles that led to the Compromise of 1850. You will find that every time, with the single exception of the Nullification question, they sprung from an endeavor to spread this institution. . . . Is this the work of politicians? Is that irresistible power which for fifty years has shaken the government and agitated the people to be stilled and subdued by pretending that it is an exceedingly simple thing, and we ought not to talk about it? [Great cheers and laughter.] If you will get everybody else to stop talking about it, I assure I will quit before they have half done so. [Renewed laughter.] But where is the philosophy or statesmanship which assumes that you can quiet that disturbing element in our society which has disturbed us for more than half a century, which has been the only serious danger that has threatened our institutions—I say, where is the philosophy or the statesmanship based on the assumption that we are to quit talking about it [applause], and that the public mind is all at once to cease being agitated by it? Yet this is the policy here in the North that Douglas is advocating—that we are to care nothing about it! I ask you if it is not a false philosophy? Is it not a false statesmanship that undertakes to build up a system of policy upon the basis of caring nothing about *the very thing that every body does care the most about?* ["Yes, yes," and applause]—a thing which all experience has shown we care a very great deal about? [Laughter and applause.] . . .

How many Democrats are there about here ["a thousand"]—who have left slave States and come into the free State of Illinois to get rid of the institution of slavery. [Another voice—"a thousand and one."] I reckon there are a thousand and one. [Laughter.] I will ask you, if the policy you are now advocating had prevailed when this country was in a Territorial condition, where would you have gone to get rid of it? [Applause.] Where would you have found your free State or Territory to go to? And when hereafter, for any cause, the people in this place shall desire to find new homes, if they wish to be rid of the institution, where will they find the place to go to? [Loud cheers.]

Now irrespective of the moral aspect of this question as to whether there is a right or wrong in enslaving a negro, I am still in favor of our new Territories being in such a condition that white men may find a home—may find some spot where they can better their condition—where they can settle upon new soil and better their condition in life. [Great and continued cheering.] I am in favor of this not merely, (I must say it here as I have elsewhere,) for our own people who are born amongst us, but as an outlet for *free white people everywhere,* the world over—in which Hans and Baptiste and Patrick, and all other men from all the world, may find new homes and better their conditions in life. [Loud and long continued applause.]

... The real issue in this controversy—the one pressing upon every mind—is the sentiment on the part of one class that looks upon the institution of slavery *as a wrong,* and of another class that *does not* look upon it as a wrong. The sentiment that contemplates the institution of slavery in this country as a wrong is the sentiment of the Republican party. It is the sentiment around which all their actions—all their arguments circle—from which all their propositions radiate. They look upon it as being a moral, social and political wrong; and while they contemplate it as such, they nevertheless have due regard for its actual existence among us, and the difficulties of getting rid of it in any satisfactory way and to all the constitutional obligations thrown about it. Yet having a due regard for these, they desire a policy in regard to it that looks to its not creating any more danger. They insist that it should as far as may be, *be treated* as a wrong, and one of the methods of treating it as a wrong is to *make provision that it shall grow no larger.* [Loud applause.] They also desire a policy that looks to a peaceful end of slavery at sometime, as being wrong. ...

Try it by some of Judge Douglas' arguments. He says he "don't care whether it is voted up or voted down" in the Territories. I do not care myself in dealing with that expression, whether it is intended to be expressive of his individual sentiments on the subject, or only of the national policy he desires to have established. It is alike valuable for my purpose. Any man can say that who does not see anything wrong in slavery, but no man can logically say it who does see a wrong in it; because no man can logically say he don't care whether a wrong is voted up or voted down. He may say he don't care whether an indifferent thing is voted up or down, but he must logically have a choice between a right thing and a wrong thing. He contends that whatever community wants slaves has a right to have them. So they have if it is not a wrong. But if it is a wrong, he cannot say people have a right to do wrong. He says that upon the score of equality, slaves should be allowed to go in a new Territory, like other property. This is strictly logical if there is no difference between it and other property. If it and other property are equal, his argument is entirely logical. But if you insist that one is wrong and the other right, there is no use to institute a comparison between right and wrong. You may turn over everything in the Democratic policy from beginning to end, whether in the shape it takes on the statute book, in the shape it takes in the Dred Scott decision, in the shape it takes in conversation or the shape it takes in short maxim-like arguments—it everywhere carefully excludes the idea that there is anything wrong in it.

That is the real issue. That is the issue that will continue in this country when these poor tongues of Judge Douglas and myself shall be silent. It is the eternal struggle between these two principles—right and wrong—throughout the world. They are the two principles that have stood face to face from the beginning of time; and will ever continue to struggle. The one is the common right of humanity and the other the divine right of kings. It is the same principle in whatever shape it develops itself. It is the same spirit that says, "You work and toil and earn bread, and I'll eat it." [Loud applause.] No matter in what shape it comes, whether from the mouth of a king who seeks to bestride the people of his own nation and live by the fruit of their labor, or from one race of men as an apology for enslaving another race, it is the same tyrannical principle. I was glad to express my gratitude at Quincy, and I re-express it here to Judge Douglas—*that he looks to no end of the institution of slavery.* That will help the people to see where the struggle really is. It will hereafter place with us all men who really do wish the wrong may have an end. And whenever we can get rid of the fog which obscures the real question—when we can get Judge Douglas and his friends to avow a policy looking to its perpetuation—we can get out from among them that class of men and bring them to the side of those who treat it as a wrong. Then there will soon be an end of it, and that end will be its "ultimate extinction." Whenever the issue can be distinctly made, and all extraneous matter thrown out so that men can fairly see the real difference between the parties, this controversy will soon be settled, and it will be done peaceably too. There will be no war, no violence. . . .

. . . [H]e sustains the Dred Scot decision, that the people of the Territories can still somehow exclude slavery. The first thing I ask attention to is the fact that Judge Douglas constantly said, before the decision, that whether they could or not, *was a question for the Supreme Court.* [Cheers.] But after the Court has made the decision he virtually says it is *not* a question for the Supreme Court, but for the people. [Renewed applause.] And how is it he tells us they can exclude it? He says it needs "police regulations," and that admits of "unfriendly legislation." . . . Can he withhold the legislation which his neighbor needs for the enjoyment of a right which is fixed in his favor in the Constitution of the United States which he has sworn to support? Can he withhold it without violating his oath? And more especially, can he pass unfriendly legislation to violate his oath? Why this is a monstrous sort of talk about the Constitution of the United States! [Great applause.] *There has never been as outlandish or lawless a doctrine from the mouth of any respectable man on earth.* [Tremendous cheers.]

from CIVIL DISOBEDIENCE

Henry David Thoreau

I heartily accept the motto,—"That government is best which governs least;" and I should like to see it acted up to more rapidly and systematically. Carried out, it finally amounts to this, which also I believe,—"That government is best which governs not at all;" and when men are prepared for it, that will be the kind of government which they will have. . . . The standing army is only an arm of the standing government. The government itself, which is only the mode which the people have chosen to execute their will, is equally liable to be abused and perverted before the people can act through it. Witness the present Mexican war, the work of comparatively a few individuals using the standing government as their tool. . . .

This American government . . . is a sort of wooden gun to the people themselves. But it is not the less necessary for this; for the people must have some complicated machinery or other, and hear its din, to satisfy that idea of government which they have. . . . Yet this government never of itself furthered any enterprise, but by the alacrity with which it got out of its way. *It* does not keep the country free. *It* does not settle the West. *It* does not educate. The character inherent in the American people has done all that has been accomplished; and it would have done somewhat more, if the government had not sometimes got in its way. . . .

. . . [A] government in which the majority rule in all cases cannot be based on justice, even as far as men understand it. Can there not be a government in which majorities do not virtually decide right and wrong, but conscience? . . . It is not desirable to cultivate a respect for the law, so much as for the right. The only obligation which I have a right to assume is to do at any time what I think right. . . .

The mass of men serve the state . . . not as men mainly, but as machines, with their bodies. They are the standing army, and the militia, jailors, constables, posse comitatus, etc. In most cases there is no free exercise whatever of the judgment or of the moral sense; but they put themselves on a level with wood and earth and stones; and wooden men can perhaps be manufactured that will serve the purpose as well. . . . A very few, as heroes, patriots, martyrs, reformers in the great sense, and *men*, serve the state with their consciences also, and so necessarily resist it for the most part; and they are commonly treated as enemies by it. . . .

All machines have their friction; and possibly this does enough good to counterbalance the evil. At any rate, it is a great evil to make a stir about it. But when the friction comes to have its machine, and oppression and robbery are organized, I say, let us not have such a machine any longer. In other words, when a sixth of the population of a nation which has undertaken to be the refuge of liberty are slaves, and a whole country is unjustly overrun and conquered by a foreign army, and subjected to military law, I think that it is not too soon for honest men to rebel and revolutionize. What makes this duty the more urgent is the fact that the country so overrun is not our own, but ours is the invading army. . . .

Practically speaking, the opponents to a reform in Massachusetts are not a hundred thousand politicians at the South, but a hundred thousand merchants and farmers here, who are more interested in commerce and agriculture than they are in humanity, and are not prepared to do justice to the slave and to Mexico, *cost what it may*. I quarrel not with far-off foes, but with those who, near at home, coöperate with, and do the bidding of, those far away, and without whom the latter would be harmless. . . .

All voting is a sort of gaming, like checkers or backgammon, with a slight moral tinge to it, a playing with right and wrong, with moral questions; and betting naturally accompanies it. The character of the voters is not staked. I cast my vote, perchance, as I think right; but I am not vitally concerned that that right should prevail. I am willing to leave it to the majority. . . .

O for a man who is a *man*, and, as my neighbor says, has a bone in his back which you cannot pass your hand through! Our statistics are at fault: the population has been returned too large. How many *men* are there to a square thousand miles in this country? Hardly one. Does not America offer any inducement for men to settle here? The American has dwindled into an Odd Fellow,—one who may be known by the development of his organ of gregariousness, and a manifest lack of intellect and cheerful self-reliance; whose first and chief concern, on coming into the world, is to see that the Almshouses are in good repair. . . .

It is not a man's duty, as a matter of course, to devote himself to the eradication of any, even the most enormous wrong; he may still properly have other concerns to engage him; but it is his duty, at least, to wash his hands of it, and, if he gives it no thought longer, not to give it practically his support. If I devote myself to other pursuits and contemplations, I must first see, at least, that I do not pursue them sitting upon another man's shoulders. I must get off him first, that he may pursue his contemplations too. . . .

Action from principle, the perception and the performance of right, changes things and relations; it is essentially revolutionary . . .

Unjust laws exist: shall we be content to obey them, or shall we endeavor to amend them, and obey them until we have succeeded, or shall we transgress them at once? Men generally, under such a government as this, think that they ought to wait until they have persuaded the majority to alter them. They think that, if they should resist, the remedy would be worse than the evil. But it is the fault of the government itself that the remedy *is* worse than the evil. *It* makes it worse. Why is it not more apt to anticipate and provide for reform? Why does it not cherish its wise minority? Why does it cry and resist before it is hurt? Why does it not encourage its citizens to be on the alert to point out its faults, and *do* better than it would have them? Why does it always crucify Christ, and excommunicate Copernicus and Luther, and pronounce Washington and Franklin rebels? . . .

I do not hesitate to say, that those who call themselves Abolitionists should at once effectually withdraw their support, both in person and property, from the government of Massachusetts and not wait till they constitute a majority of one, before they suffer the right to prevail through them. I think that it is enough if they have God on their side, without waiting for that other one. Moreover, any man more right than his neighbors constitutes a majority of one already. . . .

[I]f one thousand, if one hundred, if ten men whom I could name— if ten *honest* men only,—ay, if *one* HONEST man, in this State of Massachusetts, *ceasing to hold slaves*, were actually to withdraw from this copartnership, and be locked up in the county jail therefor, it would be the abolition of slavery in America. For it matters not how small the beginning may seem to be: what is once well done is done forever. But we love better to talk about it. . . .

Under a government which imprisons any unjustly, the true place for a just man is also a prison. The proper place to-day, the only place which Massachusetts has provided for her freer and less desponding spirits, is in her prisons, to be put out and locked out of the State by her own act, as they have already put themselves out by their principles. It is there that the fugitive slave, and the Mexican prisoner on parole, and the Indian come to plead the wrongs of his race should find them; on that separate, but more free and honorable ground, where the State places those who are not *with* her, but *against* her,—the only house in a slave State in which a free man can abide with honor. . . . Cast your whole vote, not a strip of paper merely, but your whole influence. A minority is powerless while it conforms to the majority; it is not even a minority then; but it is irresistible when it clogs by its whole weight. If the alternative is to keep all just men in prison, or give up war and slavery, the State will not hesitate which to choose. . . .

[T]he rich man—not to make any invidious comparison—is always sold to the institution which makes him rich. Absolutely speaking, the more money, the less virtue; for money comes between a man and his objects, and obtains them for him; and it was certainly no great virtue to obtain it. It puts to rest many questions which he would otherwise be taxed to answer. . . .

I can afford to refuse allegiance to Massachusetts, and her right to my property and life. It costs me less in every sense to incur the penalty of disobedience to the State than it would to obey. . . .

I have paid no poll-tax for six years. I was put into a jail once on this account, for one night. . . . I did not for a moment feel confined, and the walls seemed a great waste of stone and mortar . . . I could not but smile to see how industriously they locked the door on my meditations, which followed them out again without let or hindrance, and *they* were really all that was dangerous. As they could not reach me, they had resolved to punish my body; just as boys, if they cannot come at some person against whom they have a spite, will abuse his dog. I saw that the State was half-witted, that it was timid as a lone woman with her silver spoons, and that it did not know its friends from its foes, and I lost all my remaining respect for it, and pitied it. . . .

The night in prison was novel and interesting enough. . . . The rooms were white-washed once a month; and this one, at least, was the whitest, most simply furnished, and probably the neatest apartment in the town. . . .

When I came out of prison,—for some one interfered, and paid that tax,—I did not perceive that great changes had taken place on the common. . . .

I was put into jail as I was going to the shoemaker's to get a shoe which was mended. When I was let out the next morning, I proceeded to finish my errand, and, having put on my mended shoe, joined a huckleberry party, who were impatient to put themselves under my conduct; and in half an hour,—for the horse was soon tackled,—was in the midst of a huckleberry field, on one of our highest hills, two miles off, and then the State was nowhere to be seen. . . .

[T]he government does not concern me much, and I shall bestow the fewest possible thoughts on it. It is not many moments that I live under a government, even in this world. If a man is thought-free, fancy-free, imagination-free, that which *is not* never for a long time appearing *to be* to him, unwise rulers or reformers cannot fatally interrupt him. . . .

I please myself with imagining a State at last which can afford to be just to all men, and to treat the individual with respect as a neighbor; which even would not think it inconsistent with its own repose if a few were to live aloof from it, not meddling with it, nor embraced by it, who fulfilled all the duties of neighbors and fellow-men. A State which bore this kind of fruit, and suffered it to drop off as fast as it ripened, would prepare the way for a still more perfect and glorious State, which also I have imagined, but not yet anywhere seen.

from SLAVERY IN MASSACHUSETTS

Henry David Thoreau

I lately attended a meeting of the citizens of Concord, expecting, as one among many, to speak on the subject of slavery in Massachusetts; but I was surprised and disappointed to find that what had called my townsmen together was the destiny of Nebraska, and not of Massachusetts, and that what I had to say would be entirely out of order. I had thought that the house was on fire, and not the prairie; but though several of the citizens of Massachusetts are now in prison for attempting to rescue a slave from her own clutches, not one of the speakers at that meeting expressed regret for it, not one even referred to it. It was only the disposition of some wild lands a thousand miles off, which appeared to concern them. The inhabitants of Concord are not prepared to stand by one of their own bridges, but talk only of taking up a position on the highlands beyond the Yellowstone river. . . . There is not one slave in Nebraska; there are perhaps a million slaves in Massachusetts. . . .

Again it happens that the Boston Court House is full of armed men, holding prisoner and trying a MAN, to find out if he is not really a SLAVE. Does any one think that Justice or God awaits Mr. Loring's decision? For him to sit there deciding still, when this question is already decided from eternity to eternity, and the unlettered slave himself, and the multitude around, have long since heard and assented to the decision, is simply to make himself ridiculous. . . .

The whole military force of the State is at the service of a Mr. Suttle, a slaveholder from Virginia, to enable him to catch a man whom he calls his property; but not a soldier is offered to save a citizen of Massachusetts from being kidnapped! Is this what all these soldiers, all this *training* has been for these seventy-nine years past? Have they been trained merely to rob Mexico, and carry back fugitive slaves to their masters? . . .

Massachusetts sat waiting Mr. Loring's decision, as if it could in any way affect her own criminality. Her crime, the most conspicuous and fatal crime of all, was permitting him to be the umpire in such a case. It was really the trial of Massachusetts. Every moment that she hesitated to set this man free—every moment that she now hesitates to atone for her crime, she is convicted. The Commissioner on her case is God; not Edward G. God, but simple God.

I wish my countrymen to consider, that whatever the human law may be, neither an individual nor a nation can ever commit the least act of injustice against the obscurest individual, without having to pay the penalty for it. A government which deliberately enacts injustice, and persists in it, will at length ever become the laughing-stock of the world.

Much has been said about American slavery, but I think that we do not even yet realize what slavery is. If I were seriously to propose to Congress to make mankind into sausages, I have no doubt that most of the members would smile at my proposition, and if any believed me to be in earnest, they would think that I proposed something much worse than Congress had ever done. But if any of them will tell me that to make a man into a sausage would be much worse,—would be any worse, than to make him into a slave,—than it was to enact the Fugitive Slave Law, I will accuse him of foolishness, of intellectual incapacity, of making a distinction without a difference. The one is just as sensible a proposition as the other. . . .

[I]f the majority vote the devil to be God, the minority will live and behave accordingly, and obey the successful candidate, trusting that some time or other, by some Speaker's casting vote, perhaps, they may reinstate God. This is the highest principle I can get out of or invent for my neighbors. These men act as if they believed that they could safely slide down hill a little way—or a good way—and would surely come to a place, by and by, where they could begin to slide up again. . . .

[W]hat I had lost was a country. I had never respected the Government near to which I had lived, but I had foolishly thought that I might manage to live here, minding my private affairs, and forget it. For my part, my old and worthiest pursuits have lost I cannot say how much of their attraction, and I feel that my investment in life here is worth many per cent. less since Massachusetts last deliberately sent back an innocent man, Anthony Burns, to slavery. I dwelt before, perhaps, in the illusion that my life passed somewhere only *between* heaven and hell, but now I cannot persuade myself that I do not dwell *wholly within* hell. . . .

Slavery and servility . . . are merely a decaying and a death, offensive to all healthy nostrils. We do not complain that they *live,* but that they do not *get buried.* Let the living bury them; even they are good for manure.

from A DISQUISITION ON GOVERNMENT

John C. Calhoun

That constitution of our nature which makes us feel more intensely what affects us directly than what affects us indirectly through others, necessarily leads to conflict between individuals. Each, in consequence, has a greater regard for his own safety or happiness, than for the safety or happiness of others; and, where these come in opposition, is ready to sacrifice the interests of others to his own. And hence, the tendency to a universal state of conflict, between individual and individual; accompanied by the connected passions of suspicion, jealousy, anger and revenge,—followed by insolence, fraud and cruelty;—and, if not prevented by some controlling power, ending in a state of universal discord and confusion, destructive of the social state and the ends for which it is ordained. This controlling power, wherever vested, or by whomsoever exercised, is GOVERNMENT.

It follows, then, that man is so constituted, that government is necessary to the existence of society, and society to his existence, and the perfection of his faculties. It follows, also, that government has its origin in this twofold constitution of his nature; the sympathetic or social feelings constituting the remote,—and the individual or direct, the proximate cause. . . . [S]ociety is the greater. It is the first in the order of things, and in the dignity of its object; that of society being primary, —to preserve and perfect our race; and that of government secondary and subordinate, to preserve and perfect society. Both are, however, necessary to the existence and well-being of our race, and equally of Divine ordination. . . .

To the Infinite Being, the Creator of all, belongs exclusively the care and superintendence of the whole. He, in his infinite wisdom and goodness, has allotted to every class of animated beings its condition and appropriate functions; and has endowed each with feelings, instincts, capacities, and faculties, best adapted to its allotted condition. . . .

But government, although intended to protect and preserve society, has itself a strong tendency to disorder and abuse of its powers, as all experience and almost every page of history testify. . . .

How can those who are invested with the powers of government be prevented from employing them, as the means of aggrandizing themselves, instead of using them to protect and preserve society? . . .

There is but one way in which this can possibly be done; and that is, by such an organism as will furnish the ruled with the means of resisting successfully this tendency on the part of the rulers to oppression and abuse. Power can only be resisted by power. . . .

. . . [N]othing is more difficult than to equalize the action of the government, in reference to the various and diversified interests of the community; and nothing more easy than to pervert its powers into instruments to aggrandize and enrich one or more interests by oppressing and impoverishing the others. . . .

. . . [T]he community will be divided into two great parties,—a major and minor,—between which there will be incessant struggles on the one side to retain, and on the other to obtain the majority,—and, thereby, the control of the government and the advantages it confers. . . .

. . . [T]he very uncertainty of the tenure, combined with the violent party warfare which must ever precede a change of parties under such governments, would rather tend to increase than diminish the tendency to oppression.

As, then, the right of suffrage, without some other provision, cannot counteract this tendency of government, the next question for consideration is—What is that other provision? . . .

There is . . . but one mode in which this can be effected; and that is, by taking the sense of each interest or portion of the community, which may be unequally and injuriously affected by the action of the government, separately, through its own majority, or in some other way by which its voice may be fairly expressed; and to require the consent of each interest, either to put or to keep the government in action. This, too, can be accomplished only in one way,—and that is, by such an organism of the government, and, if necessary for the purpose, of the community also,—as will, by dividing and distributing the powers of government, give to each division or interest, through its appropriate organ, either a concurrent voice in making and executing the laws, or a veto on their execution. . . .

. . . [T]he effect of organism is neither to supersede nor diminish the importance of the right of suffrage; but to aid and perfect it. The object of the latter is, to collect the sense of the community. The more fully and perfectly it accomplishes this, the more fully and perfectly it fulfils its end. But the most it can do, of itself, is to collect the sense of the greater number; that is, of the stronger interests, or combination of interests; and to assume this to be the sense of the community. It is only when aided by a proper organism, that it can collect the sense of the entire community,—of each and all its interests; of each, through its appropriate organ, and of the whole, through all of them united. This would truly be the sense of the entire community; for whatever diversity each interest might have within itself,—as all would have the same interest in reference to the action of the government, the individuals composing each would be fully and truly represented by its own majority or appropriate organ, regarded in reference to the other interests. In brief, every individual of every interest might trust, with confidence, its majority or appropriate organ, against that of every other interest.

It results, from what has been said, that there are two different modes in which the sense of the community may be taken; one, simply by the right of suffrage, unaided; the other, by the right through a proper organism. . . . The former of these I shall call the numerical, or absolute majority; and the latter, the concurrent, or constitutional majority. . . .

A written constitution certainly has many and considerable advantages; but it is a great mistake to suppose, that the mere insertion of provisions to restrict and limit the powers of the government, without investing those for whose protection they are inserted with the means of enforcing their observance, will be sufficient to prevent the major and dominant party from abusing its powers. . . .

. . . [O]f what possible avail could the strict construction of the minor party be, against the liberal interpretation of the major, when the one would have all the powers of the government to carry its construction into effect,—and the other be deprived of all means of enforcing its construction? In a contest so unequal, the result would not be doubtful. The party in favor of the restrictions would be overpowered. At first, they might command some respect, and do something to stay the march of encroachment; but they would, in the progress of the contest, be regarded as mere abstractionists; and, indeed, deservedly, if

they should indulge the folly of supposing that the party in possession of the ballot-box and the physical force of the country, could be
successfully resisted by an appeal to reason, truth, justice, or the obligations imposed by the constitution. . . .

. . . [T]he government of the concurrent majority, where the organism is perfect, excludes the possibility of oppression, by giving to each
interest, or portion, or order,—where there are established classes,—
the means of protecting itself, by its negative, against all measures
calculated to advance the peculiar interests of others at its expense. Its
effect, then, is, to cause the different interests, portions, or orders,—as
the case may be,—to desist from attempting to adopt any measure
calculated to promote the prosperity of one, or more, by sacrificing that
of others; and thus to force them to unite in such measures only as
would promote the prosperity of all, as the only means to prevent the
suspension of the action of the government,--and, thereby, to avoid
anarchy, the greatest of all evils. It is by means of such authorized and
effectual resistance, that oppression is prevented, and the necessity of
resorting to force superseded, in governments of the concurrent majority;—and, hence, compromise, instead of force, becomes their conservative principle. . . .

. . . [T]he object to be won or lost appeals to the strongest passions
of the human heart,—avarice, ambition, and rivalry. It is not then wonderful, that a form of government, which periodically stakes all its
honors and emoluments, as prizes to be contended for, should divide
the community into two great hostile parties; or that party attachments,
in the progress of the strife, should become so strong among the members of each respectively, as to absorb almost every feeling of our nature, both social and individual; or that their mutual antipathies should
be carried to such an excess as to destroy, almost entirely, all sympathy
between them, and to substitute in its place the strongest aversion. . . .

That which corrupts and debases the community, politically, must also
corrupt and debase it morally. The same cause, which, in governments of
the numerical majority, gives to party attachments and antipathies such
force, as to place party triumph and ascendency above the safety and
prosperity of the community, will just as certainly give them sufficient force
to overpower all regard for truth, justice, sincerity, and moral obligations
of every description. It is, accordingly, found that in the violent strifes between parties for the high and glittering prize of governmental honors

and emoluments,—falsehood, injustice, fraud, artifice, slander, and breach of faith, are freely resorted to, as legitimate weapons;—followed by all their corrupting and debasing influences.

In the government of the concurrent majority, on the contrary, the same cause which prevents such strife, as the means of obtaining power, and which makes it the interest of each portion to conciliate and promote the interests of the others . . . —truth, justice, integrity, fidelity, and all others, by which respect and confidence are inspired, would be the most certain and effectual means of acquiring it. . . .

Liberty, indeed, though among the greatest of blessings, is not so great as that of protection; inasmuch, as the end of the former is the progress and improvement of the race,—while that of the latter is its preservation and perpetuation. And hence, when the two come into conflict, liberty must, and ever ought, to yield to protection; as the existence of the race is of greater moment than its improvement.

It follows, from what has been stated, that it is a great and dangerous error to suppose that all people are equally entitled to liberty. It is a reward to be earned, not a blessing to be gratuitously lavished on all alike;—a reward reserved for the intelligent, the patriotic, the virtuous and deserving;—and not a boon to be bestowed on a people too ignorant, degraded and vicious, to be capable either of appreciating or of enjoying it. . . .

Such are the many and striking advantages of the concurrent over the numerical majority. Against the former but two objections can be made. The one is, that it is difficult of construction, . . . and the other, that it would be impracticable to obtain the concurrence of conflicting interests, where they were numerous and diversified; or, if not, that the process for this purpose, would be too tardy to meet, with sufficient promptness, the many and dangerous emergencies, to which all communities are exposed. . . .

When something must be done,—and when it can be done only by the united consent of all,—the necessity of the case will force to a compromise;—be the cause of that necessity what it may. On all questions of acting, necessity, where it exists, is the overruling motive; and where, in such cases, compromise among the parties is an indispensable condition to acting, it exerts an overruling influence in predisposing them to acquiesce in some one opinion or course of action. Experience furnishes many examples in confirmation of this important truth. Among these, the trial by jury is the most familiar.

from TWELVE YEARS A SLAVE

Solomon Northup

Having been born a freeman, and for more than thirty years enjoyed the blessings of liberty in a free State—and having at the end of that time been kidnapped and sold into Slavery, where I remained, until happily rescued in the month of January, 1853, after a bondage of twelve years. . . .

Though born a slave, and laboring under the disadvantages of which my unfortunate race is subjected, my father was a man respected for his industry and integrity, as many now living, who well remember him, are ready to testify. His whole life was passed in the peaceful pursuits of agriculture, never seeking employment in those more menial positions, which seem to be especially allotted to the children of Africa. Besides giving us an education surpassing that ordinarily bestowed upon children of our condition, he acquired, by his diligence and economy, a sufficient property qualification to entitle him to the right of suffrage. He . . . comprehended the system of Slavery, and dwelt with sorrow on the degradation of his race. He endeavored to imbue our minds with sentiments of morality, and to teach us to place our trust and confidence in Him who regards the humblest as well as the highest of his creatures. How often since that time has the recollection of his paternal counsels occurred to me, while lying in a slave hut in the distant and sickly regions of Louisiana, smarting with the undeserved wounds which an inhuman master had inflicted, and longing only for the grave which had covered him, to shield me also from the lash of the oppressor. . . .

Up to this period I had been principally engaged with my father in the labors of the farm. The leisure hours allowed me were generally either employed over my books, or playing on the violin—an amusement which was the ruling passion of my youth. It has also been the source of consolation since, affording pleasure to the simple beings with whom my lot was cast, and beguiling my own thoughts. . . .

On Christmas day, 1829, I was married to Anne Hampton, a colored girl then living in the vicinity of our residence. . . .

From the time of my marriage to this day the love I have borne my wife has been sincere and unabated; and only those who have felt the glowing tenderness a father cherishes for his offspring, can appreciate my affection for the beloved children which have since been born to us. . . .

. . . [W]e were the parents of three children—Elizabeth, Margaret, and Alonzo. Elizabeth, the eldest, was in her tenth year; Margaret was two years younger, and little Alonzo had just passed his fifth birth-day. They filled our house with gladness. Their young voices were music in our ears. Many an airy castle did their mother and myself build for the little innocents. . . .

[Northup was hired to play music, taken to Washington, D.C., drugged, and sold as a slave first in D.C. and then in New Orleans.]

Strange as it may seem, within plain sight of this same house, looking down from its commanding height upon it, was the Capitol. The voices of patriotic representatives boasting of freedom and equality, and the rattling of the poor slave's chains, almost commingled. A slave pen within the very shadow of the Capitol! . . .

"Well, my boy, how do you feel now?" said Burch, as he entered through the open door. I replied that I was sick, and inquired the cause of my imprisonment. He answered that I was his slave—that he had bought me, and that he was about to send me to New-Orleans. I asserted, aloud and boldly, that I was a free man—a resident of Saratoga, where I had a wife and children, who were also free, and that my name was Northup. . . . He denied that I was free, and with an emphatic oath, declared that I came from Georgia. . . . With blasphemous oaths, he called me a black liar, a runaway from Georgia, and every other profane and vulgar epithet that the most indecent fancy could conceive. . . .

Burch ordered the paddle and cat-o'-ninetails to be brought in. . . .

As soon as these formidable whips appeared, I was seized by both of them, and roughly divested of my clothing. . . . Blow after blow was inflicted upon my naked body. When his unrelenting arm grew tired, he stopped and asked if I still insisted I was a free man. I did insist upon it, and then the blows were renewed, faster and more energetically, if possible, than before. When again tired, he would repeat the same question, and receiving the same answer, continued his cruel labor. . . .

At length . . . Burch desisted, saying, with an admonitory shake of his fist in my face, and hissing the words through his firm-set teeth, that if ever I dared to utter again that I was entitled to my freedom, that I had been kidnapped, or any thing whatever of the kind, the castigation I had just received was nothing in comparison with what would follow. He swore that he would either conquer, or kill me. . . .

Next day many customers called to examine Freeman's "new lot." The latter gentleman was very loquacious, dwelling at much length upon our several good points and qualities. He would make us hold up our heads, walk briskly back and forth, while customers would feel of our hands and arms and bodies, turn us about, ask us what we could do, make us open our months and show our teeth, precisely as a jockey examines a horse which he is about to barter for or purchase. Sometimes a man or woman was taken back to the small house in the yard, stripped, and inspected more minutely. Scars upon a slave's back were considered evidence of a rebellious or unruly spirit, and hurt his sale. . . .

The same man also purchased Randall. The little fellow was made to jump, and run across the floor, and perform many other feats, exhibiting his activity and condition. All the time the trade was going on, Eliza was crying aloud, and wringing her hands. She besought the man not to buy him, unless he also bought herself and Emily. She promised, in that case, to be the most faithful slave that ever lived. The man answered that he could not afford it, and then Eliza burst into a paroxysm of grief, weeping plaintively. Freeman turned round to her, savagely, with his whip in his uplifted hand, ordering her to stop her noise, or he would flog her. He would not have such work—such snivelling; and unless she ceased that minute, he would take her to the yard and give her a hundred lashes. Yes, he would take the nonsense out of her pretty quick—if he didn't, might he be d—d. Eliza shrunk before him, and tried to wipe away her tears, but it was all in vain. She wanted to be with her children, she said, the little time she had to live. All the frowns and threats of Freeman could not wholly silence the afflicted mother. She kept on begging and beseeching them, most piteously, not to separate the three. Over and over again she told them how she loved her boy. . . . The bargain was agreed upon, and Randall must go alone. Then Eliza ran to him; embraced him passionately; kissed him again and again; told him to remember her—all the while her tears falling in the boy's face like rain.

Freeman damned her, calling her a blubbering, bawling wench, and ordered her to go to her place, and behave herself, and be somebody. He swore he wouldn't stand such stuff but a little longer. He would soon give her something to cry about, if she was not mighty careful, and *that* she might depend upon.

The planter from Baton Rouge, with his new purchases, was ready to depart.

"Don't cry, mama. I will be a good boy. Don't cry," said Randall, looking back, as they passed out of the door.

What has become of the lad, God knows. It was a mournful scene indeed. I would have cried myself if I had dared. . . .

After some further inspection, and conversation touching prices, he finally offered Freeman one thousand dollars for me, nine hundred for Harry, and seven hundred for Eliza. . . .

As soon as Eliza heard it, she was in an agony again. By this time she had become haggard and hollow-eyed with sickness and with sorrow. It would be a relief if I could consistently pass over in silence the scene that now ensued. It recalls memories more mournful and affecting than any language can portray. . . . [N]ever have I seen such an exhibition of intense, unmeasured, and unbounded grief as when Eliza was parted from her child. She broke from her place in the line of women, and rushing down where Emily was standing, caught her in her arms. The child, sensible of some impending danger, instinctively fastened her hands around her mother's neck and nestled her little head upon her bosom. Freeman sternly ordered her to be quiet, but she did not heed him. He caught her by the arm and pulled her rudely, but she only clung closer to the child. Then, with a volley of great oaths, he struck her such a heartless blow, that she staggered backward, and was like to fall. . . . "Mercy, mercy, master!" she cried, falling on her knees. "Please, master, buy Emily. I can never work any if she is taken from me; I will die.". . .

Finally, after much more supplication, the purchaser of Eliza stepped forward, evidently affected, and said to Freeman he would buy Emily, and asked him what her price was.

"What is her *price*! *Buy* her?" was the responsive interrogatory of Theophilus Freeman. And instantly answering his own inquiry, he added, "I won't sell her. She's not for sale."

The man remarked he was not in need of one so young—that it would be of no profit to him, but since the mother was so fond of her, rather than see them separated, he would pay a reasonable price. But to this humane proposal Freeman was entirely deaf. He would not sell her then on any account whatever. There were heaps and piles of money to be made of her, he said, when she was a few years older. There were men enough in New-Orleans who would give five thousand dollars for such an extra, handsome, fancy piece as Emily would be. . . .

Freeman, out of patience, tore Emily from her mother by main force, the two clinging to each other with all their might.

"Don't leave me, mama—don't leave me," screamed the child, as its mother was pushed harshly forward. "Don't leave me—come back, mama," she still cried, stretching forth her little arms imploringly. But she cried in vain. . . .

Eliza never after saw or heard of Emily or Randall. Day nor night, however, were they ever absent from her memory. In the cotton field, in the cabin, always and everywhere, she was talking of them—often *to* them, as if they were actually present. Only when absorbed in that illusion, or asleep, did she ever have a moment's comfort afterwards. . . .

In the autumn, I left the mills, and was employed at the opening. One day the mistress was urging Ford to procure a loom, in order that Sally might commence weaving cloth for the winter garments of the slaves. He could not imagine where one was to be found, when I suggested that the easiest way to get one would be to make it, informing him at the same time, that I was a sort of "Jack at all trades," and would attempt it, with his permission. It was granted very readily, and I was allowed to go to a neighboring planter's to inspect one before commencing the undertaking. At length it was finished and pronounced by Sally to be perfect. . . . I was continued in the employment of making looms, which were taken down to the plantation on the bayou.

At this time one John M. Tibeats, a carpenter, came to the opening to do some work on master's house. I was directed to quit the looms and assist him. . . .

John M. Tibeats was the opposite of Ford in all respects. He was a small, crabbed, quick-tempered, spiteful man. He had no fixed residence that I ever heard of, but passed from one plantation to another, wherever he could find employment. He was without standing in the community, not esteemed by white men, nor even respected by slaves. He was ignorant, withal, and of a revengeful disposition.

. . . During my residence with Master Ford I had seen only the bright side of slavery. His was no heavy hand crushing us to the earth. *He* pointed upwards, and with benign and cheering words addressed us as his fellow-mortals, accountable, like himself, to the Maker of us all. I think of him with affection, and had my family been with me, could have borne his gentle servitude, without murmuring, all my days. . . .

William Ford unfortunately became embarrassed in his pecuniary affairs. . . . He was also indebted to John M. Tibeats to a considerable amount in consideration of his services in building the mills. . . . It was therefore necessary, in order to meet these demands, to dispose of eighteen slaves, myself among the number. Seventeen of them, including Sam and Harry, were purchased by Peter Compton, a planter also residing on Red River.

I was sold to Tibeats, in consequence, undoubtedly, of my slight skill as a carpenter. This was in the winter of 1842. . . .

I bade farewell to my good friends at the opening, and departed with my new master Tibeats. We went down to the plantation on Bayou Boeuf, distant twenty-seven miles from the Pine Woods, to complete the unfinished contract. . . .

On my arrival at Bayou Boeuf, I had the pleasure of meeting Eliza, whom I had not seen for several months. She had not pleased Mrs. Ford, being more occupied in brooding over her sorrows than in attending to her business, and had, in consequence, been sent down to work in the fields on the plantation. She had grown feeble and emaciated, and was still mourning for her children. She asked me if I had forgotten them, and a great many times inquired if I still remembered how handsome little Emily was—how much Randall loved her—and wondered if they were living still, and where the darlings could then be. She had sunk beneath the weight of an excessive grief. Her drooping form and hollow cheeks too plainly indicated that she had well nigh reached the end of her weary road.

Ford's overseer on this plantation, and who was the exclusive charge of it, was a Mr. Chapin, a kindly disposed man, and a native of Pennsylvania. In common with others, he held Tibeats in light estimation, which fact, in connection with the four hundred dollar mortgage, was fortunate for me.

I was now compelled to labor very hard. From earliest dawn until late at night, I was not allowed to be a moment idle. Notwithstanding which, Tibeats was never satisfied. He was continually cursing and complaining. He never spoke to me a kind word. I was his faithful slave, and earned him large wages every day, and yet I went to my cabin nightly, loaded with abuse and stinging epithets.

We had completed the corn mill, the kitchen, and so forth, and were at work upon the weaving-house, when I was guilty of an act, in that State punishable with death. . . .

As the day began to open, Tibeats came out of the house to where I was, hard at work. He seemed to be that morning even more morose and disagreeable than usual. He was my master, entitled by law to my flesh and blood, and to exercise over me such tyrannical control as his mean nature prompted; but there was no law that could prevent my looking upon him with intense contempt. I despised both his disposition and his intellect. I had just come round to the keg for a further supply of nails, as he reached the weaving-house.

"I thought I told you to commence putting on weatherboards this morning," he remarked.

"Yes, master, and I am about it," I replied.

"Where?" he demanded.

"On the other side," was my answer.

He walked round to the other side, examined my work for a while, muttering to himself in a fault-finding tone.

"Didn't I tell you last night to get a keg of nails of Chapin?" he broke forth again.

"Yes, master, and so I did; and the overseer said he would get another size for you, if you wanted them when he came back from the field."

Tibeats walked to the keg, looked a moment at the contents, then kicked it violently. Coming towards me in a great passion, he exclaimed,

"G—d d—n you! I thought you *knowed* something."

I made answer: "I tried to do as you told me, master. I didn't mean anything wrong. Overseer said—" But he interrupted me with such a flood of curses that I was unable to finish the sentence. At length he ran towards the house, and going to the piazza, took down one of the overseer's whips. The whip had a short wooden stock, braided over with leather, and was loaded at the butt. The lash was three feet long, or thereabouts, and made of raw-hide strands.

At first I was somewhat frightened, and my impulse was to run. . . . I felt, moreover, that I had been faithful—that I was guilty of no wrong whatever, and deserved commendation rather than punishment. My fear changed to anger, and before he reached me I had made up my mind fully not to be whipped, let the result be life or death.

Winding the lash around his hand, and taking hold of the small end of the stock, he walked up to me, and with a malignant look, ordered me to strip.

"Master Tibeats," said I, looking him boldly in the face, "I will *not*." I was about to say something further in justification, but with concentrated vengeance, he sprang upon me, seizing me by the throat with one hand, raising the whip with the other, in the act of striking. Before the blow descended, however, I had caught him by the collar of the coat, and drawn him closely to me. Reaching down, I seized him by the ankle, and pushing him back with the other hand, he fell over on the ground. Putting one arm around his leg, and holding it to my breast, so that his head and shoulders only touched the ground, I placed my foot upon his neck. He was completely in my power. My blood was up. It seemed to course through my veins like fire. In the frenzy of my madness I snatched the whip from his hand. He struggled with all his power; swore that I should not live to see another day; and that he would tear out my heart. But his struggles and his threats were alike in vain. I cannot tell how many times I struck him. Blow after blow fell fast and heavy upon his wriggling form. At length he screamed— cried murder—and at last the blasphemous tyrant called on God for mercy. But he who had never shown mercy did not receive it. The stiff stock of the whip wrapped round his cringing body until my right arm ached.

Until this time I had been too busy to look about me. Desisting for a moment, I saw Mrs. Chapin looking from the window, and Rachel standing in the kitchen door. Their attitudes expressed the utmost excitement and alarm. His screams had been heard in the field. Chapin was coming as fast as he could ride. I struck him a blow or two more, then pushed him from me with such a well-directed kick that he went rolling over on the ground.

Rising to his feet, and brushing the dirt from his hair, he stood looking at me, pale with rage. We gazed at each other in silence. Not a word was uttered until Chapin galloped up to us.

"What is the matter?" he cried out.

"Master Tibeats wants to whip me for using the nails you gave me," I replied.

"What is the matter with the nails?" he inquired, turning to Tibeats.

Tibeats answered to the effect that they were too large, paying little heed, however, to Chapin's question, but still keeping his snakish eyes fastened maliciously on me.

"I am overseer here," Chapin began. "I told Platt to take them and use them, and if they were not of the proper size I would get others on returning from the field. It is not his fault. Besides, I shall furnish such nails as I please. I hope you will understand *that*, Mr. Tibeats."

Tibeats made no reply, but, grinding his teeth and shaking his fist, swore he would have satisfaction, and that it was not half over yet. Thereupon he walked away. . . .

As I stood there, feelings of unutterable agony overwhelmed me. I was conscious that I had subjected myself to unimaginable punishment. The reaction that followed my extreme ebullition of anger produced the most painful sensations of regret. An unfriended, helpless slave—what could I *do*, what could I *say*, to justify, in the remotest manner, the heinous act I had committed, of resenting a *white* man's contumely and abuse. . . . [L]ooking up, I beheld Tibeats, accompanied by two horsemen, coming down the bayou. They rode into the yard, jumped from their horses, and approached me with large whips, one of them also carrying a coil of rope.

"Cross your hand," commanded Tibeats, with the addition of such a shuddering expression of blasphemy as is not decorous to repeat.

"You need not bind me, Master Tibeats, I am ready to go with you anywhere," said I.

One of his companions then stepped forward, swearing if I made the least resistance he would break my head—he would tear me limb from limb—he would cut my black throat—and giving wide scope to other similar expressions. Perceiving any importunity altogether vain, I crossed my hands, submitting humbly to whatever disposition they might please to make of me. Thereupon Tibeats tied my wrists, drawing the rope around them with his utmost strength. Then he bound my ankles in the same manner. . . . With a remaining piece of rope Tibeats made an awkward noose, and placed it about my neck.

"Now, then," inquired one of Tibeats' companions, "where shall we hang the nigger?"

One proposed such a limb, extending from the body of a peach tree, near the spot where we were standing. His comrade objected to it, alleging it would break, and proposed another. Finally they fixed upon the latter.

During this conversation, and all the time they were binding me, I uttered not a word. . . . Surely my time had come. I should never behold the light of another day—never behold the faces of my children—the sweet anticipation I had cherished with such fondness. I should that hour struggle through the fearful agonies of death! None would mourn for me—none revenge me. Soon my form would be mouldering in that distant soil, or, perhaps, be cast to the slimy reptiles that filled the stagnant waters of the bayou! Tears flowed down my cheeks, but they only afforded a subject of insulting comment for my executioners.

At length, as they were dragging me towards the tree, Chapin, who had momentarily disappeared from the piazza, came out of the house and walked towards us. He had a pistol in each hand, and as near as I can now recall to mind, spoke in a firm, determined manner, as follows:

"Gentlemen, I have a few words to say. You had better listen to them. Whoever moves that slave another foot from where he stands is a dead man. In the first place, he does not deserve this treatment. It is a shame to murder him in this manner. I never knew a more faithful boy than Platt. You, Tibeats, are in the fault yourself. You are pretty much of a scoundrel, and I know it, and you richly deserved the flogging you have received. In the next place, I have been overseer of this plantation seven years, and, in the absence of William Ford, am master here. My duty is to protect his interests, and that duty I shall perform. You are not responsible—you are a worthless fellow. Ford holds a mortgage on Platt of four hundred dollars. If you hang him, he loses his debt. Until that is canceled you have no right to take his life. You have no right to take it any way. There is a law for the slave as well as for the white man. You are no better than a murderer.

"As for you," addressing Cook and Ramsay, a couple of overseers from neighboring plantations, "as for you—begone! If you have any regard for your own safety, I say, begone."

Cook and Ramsay, without a further word, mounted their horses and rode away. Tibeats, in a few minutes, evidently in fear, and overawed by the decided tone of Chapin, sneaked off like a coward, as he was, and mounting his horse, followed his companions. . . .

I remembered the words of Chapin, his precautions, his advice to beware, lest in some unsuspecting moment he might injure me. They were always in my mind, so that I lived in a most uneasy state of apprehension and fear. One eye was on my work, the other on my master. I determined to give him no cause of offence, to work still more diligently, if possible, than I had done, to bear whatever abuse he might heap upon me, save bodily injury, humbly and patiently, hoping thereby to soften in some degree his manner towards me, until the blessed time might come when I should be delivered from his clutches.

The third morning after my return, Chapin left the plantation for Cheneyville, to be absent until night. Tibeats, on that morning, was attacked with one of those periodical fits of spleen and ill-humor to which he was frequently subject, rendering him still more disagreeable and venomous than usual. . . .

"You are not planing that down enough," said he.

"It is just even with the line," I replied.

"You're a d—d liar," he exclaimed passionately.

"Oh, well, master," I said, mildly, "I will plane it down more if you say so," at the same time proceeding to do as I supposed he desired. Before one shaving had been removed, however, he cried out, saying I had now planed it too deep—it was too small—I had spoiled the sweep entirely. Then followed curses and imprecations. I had endeavored to do exactly as he directed, but nothing would satisfy the unreasonable man. . . . His anger grew more and more violent, until, finally, with an oath, such a bitter, frightful oath as only Tibeats could utter, he seized a hatchet from the work-bench and darted towards me, swearing he would cut my head open.

It was a moment of life or death. The sharp, bright blade of the hatchet glittered in the sun. In another instant it would be buried in my brain, and yet in that instant—so quick will a man's thoughts come to him in such a fearful strait—I reasoned with myself. If I stood still, my doom was certain; if I fled, ten chances to one the hatchet, flying from his hand with a too-deadly and unerring aim, would strike me in the back. There was but one course to take. Springing towards him with all my power, and meeting him full halfway, before he could bring down the blow, with one hand I caught his uplifted arm, with the other seized him by the throat. We stood looking each other in the eyes. In his I could see murder. I felt as if I had a serpent by the neck, watching the slightest relaxation of my grip, to coil itself round my body, crushing and stinging it to death. I thought to scream aloud, trusting that some ear might catch the sound—but Chapin was away; the hands were in the field; there was no living soul in sight or hearing.

The good genius, which thus far through life has saved me from the hands of violence, at that moment suggested a lucky thought. With a vigorous and sudden kick, that brought him on one knee, with a groan, I released my hold upon his throat, snatched the hatchet, and cast it beyond reach.

Frantic with rage, maddened beyond control, he seized a white oak stick, five feet long, perhaps, and as large in circumference as his hand could grasp, which was lying on the ground. Again he rushed towards me, and again I met him, seized him about the waist, and being the stronger of the two, bore him to the earth. While in that position, I obtained possession of the stick, and rising, cast it from me, also.

He likewise arose and ran for the broad-axe, on the work bench. Fortunately, there was a heavy plank lying upon its broad blade, in such a manner that he could not extricate it, before I had sprung upon his back. . . .

There have been hours in my unhappy life, many of them, when the contemplation of death as the end of earthly sorrow—of the grave as a resting place for the tired and worn out body—has been pleasant to dwell upon. But such contemplations vanish in the hour of peril. . . .

. . . [O]nce more I seized him by the throat, and this time, with a vice-like grip that soon relaxed his hold. He became pliant and un-strung. His face, that had been white with passion, was now black from suffocation. Those small serpent eyes that spat such venom, were now full of horror—two great white orbs starting from their sockets!

There was a "lurking devil" in my heart that prompted me to kill the human blood-hound on the spot—to retain the grip on his accursed throat till the breath of life was gone! I dared not murder him, and I dared not let him live. If I killed him, my life must pay the forfeit—if he lived, my life only would satisfy his vengeance. A voice within whispered me to fly. . . .

. . . [Northup hides in a swamp until white friends arrange his sale.]

Edwin Epps, of whom much will be said during the remainder of this history, is a large, portly, heavy-bodied man with light hair, high cheek bones, and a Roman nose of extraordinary dimensions. He has blue eyes, a fair complexion, and is, as I should say, full six feet high. He has the sharp, inquisitive expression of a jockey. His manners are repulsive and coarse, and his language gives speedy and unequivocal evidence that he has never enjoyed the advantages of an education. . . .

At the time I came into his possession, Edwin Epps was fond of the bottle, his "sprees" sometimes extending over the space of two whole weeks. Latterly, however, he had reformed his habits, and when I left, was as strict a specimen of temperance as could be found on Bayou Boeuf. When "in his cups," Master Epps was a roystering, blustering, noisy fellow, whose chief delight was in dancing with his "niggers," or lashing them about the yard with his long whip, just for the pleasure of hearing them screech and scream, as the great welts were planted on their backs. When sober, he was silent, reserved and cunning, not beating us indiscriminately, as in his drunken moments, but sending the end of his rawhide to some tender spot of a lagging slave, with a sly dexterity peculiar to himself.

He had been a driver and overseer in his younger years, but at this time was in possession of a plantation on Bayou Huff Power. . . . His principal business was raising cotton, and in as much as some may read this book who have never seen a cotton field, a description of the manner of its culture may not be out of place. . . .

In the latter part of August begins the cotton picking season. At this time each slave is presented with a sack. A strap is fastened to it, which goes over the neck, holding the mouth of the sack breast high, while the bottom reaches nearly to the ground. Each one is also presented with a large basket that will hold about two barrels. This is to put the cotton in when the sack is filled. The baskets are carried to the field and placed at the beginning of the rows.

When a new hand, one unaccustomed to the business, is sent for the first time into the field, he is whipped up smartly, and made for that day to pick as fast as he can possibly. At night it is weighed, so that his capability in cotton picking is known. He must bring in the same weight each night following. If it falls short, it is considered evidence that he has been laggard, and a greater or less number of lashes is the penalty.

An ordinary day's work is considered two hundred pounds. A slave who is accustomed to picking, is punished, if he or she brings in a less quantity than that. There is a great difference among them as regards this kind of labor. Some of them seem to have a natural knack, or quickness, which enables them to pick with great celerity, and with both hands, while others, with whatever practice or industry, are utterly unable to come up to the ordinary standard. Such hands are taken from the cotton field and employed in other business. Patsey, of whom I shall have more to say, was known as the most remarkable cotton picker on Bayou Boeuf. She picked with both hands and with such surprising rapidity, that five hundred pounds a day was not unusual for her.

Each one is tasked, therefore, according to his picking abilities, none, however, to come short of two hundred weight. I, being unskillful always in that business, would have satisfied my master by bringing in the latter quantity, while on the other hand, Patsey would surely have been beaten if she failed to produce twice as much. . . .

The hands are required to be in the cotton fields as soon as it is light in the morning, and with the exception of ten or fifteen minutes, which is given them at noon to swallow their allowance of cold bacon, they are not permitted to be a moment idle until it is too dark to see, and when the moon is full, they often times labor till the middle of the night. They do not dare to stop even at dinner time, nor return to the quarters, however late it be, until the order to halt is given by the driver.

The day's work over in the field, the baskets are "toted," or in other words, carried to the gin-house, where the cotton is weighed. No matter how fatigued and weary he may be—no matter how much he longs for sleep and rest—a slave never approaches the gin-house with his basket of cotton but with fear. If it falls short in weight—if he has not performed the full task appointed him, he knows that he must suffer. And if he has exceeded it by ten or twenty pounds, in all probability his master will measure the next day's task accordingly. So, whether he has too little or too much, his approach to the gin-house is always with fear and trembling. Most frequently they have too little, and therefore it is they are not anxious to leave the field. After weighing, follow the whippings; and then the baskets are carried to the cotton house, and their contents stored away like hay, all hands being sent in to tramp it down. If the cotton is not dry, instead of taking it to the gin-house at once, it is laid upon platforms, two feet high, and some three times as wide, covered with boards or plank, with narrow walks running between them.

This done, the labor of the day is not yet ended, by any means. Each one must then attend to his respective chores. One feeds the mules, another the swine—another cuts the wood, and so forth; besides, the packing is all done by candle light. Finally, at a late hour, they reach the quarters, sleepy and overcome with the long day's toil. Then a fire must be kindled in the cabin, the corn ground in the small hand-mill, and supper, and dinner for the next day in the field, prepared. All that is allowed them is corn and bacon, which is given out at the corncrib and smoke-house every Sunday morning. Each one receives, as his weekly allowance, three and a half pounds of bacon, and corn enough to make a peck of meal. That is all—no tea, coffee, sugar, and with the exception of a very scanty sprinkling now and then, no salt. . . . Master Epps' hogs were fed on *shelled* corn—it was thrown out to his "niggers" in the ear. The former, he thought, would fatten faster by shelling, and soaking it in the water—the latter, perhaps, if treated in the same manner, might grow too fat to labor. Master Epps was a shrewd calculator, and knew how to manage his own animals, drunk or sober. . . .

The majority of slaves have no knife, much less a fork. They cut their bacon with the axe at the woodpile. The corn meal is mixed with a little water, placed in the fire, and baked. When it is "done brown," the ashes are scraped off, and being placed upon a chip, which answers for a table, the tenant of the slave hut is ready to sit down upon the ground to supper. By this time it is usually midnight. The same fear of punishment with which they approach the gin-house, possesses them again on lying down to get a snatch of rest. It is the fear of oversleeping in the morning. Such an offence would certainly be attended with not less than twenty lashes. . . .

The softest couches in the world are not to be found in the log mansion of the slave. The one whereon I reclined year after year, was a plank twelve inches wide and ten feet long. My pillow was a stick of wood. The bedding was a coarse blanket, and not a rag or shred beside. Moss might be used, were it not that it directly breeds a swarm of fleas.

The cabin is constructed of logs, without floor or window. The latter is altogether unnecessary, the crevices between the logs admitting sufficient light. In stormy weather the rain drives through them, rendering it comfortless and extremely disagreeable. The rude door hangs on great wooden hinges. In one end is constructed an awkward fire-place.

An hour before day light the horn is blown. Then the slaves arouse, prepare their breakfast, fill a gourd with water, in another deposit their dinner of cold bacon and corn cake, and hurry to the field again. It is an offence invariably followed by a flogging, to be found at the quarters after daybreak. Then the fears and labors of another day begin;

and until its close there is no such thing as rest. He fears he will be caught lagging through the day; he fears to approach the gin-house with his basket-load of cotton at night; he fears, when he lies down, that he will oversleep himself in the morning. Such is a true, faithful, unexaggerated picture and description of the slave's daily life, during the time of cottonpicking, on the shores of Bayou Boeuf. . . .

On my arrival at Master Epps', in obedience to his order, the first business upon which I entered was the making of an axe-helve. The handles in use there are simply a round, straight stick. I made a crooked one, shaped like those to which I had been accustomed at the North. When finished, and presented to Epps, he looked at it with astonishment, unable to determine exactly what it was. He had never before seen such a handle, and when I explained its conveniences, he was forcibly struck with the novelty of the idea. He kept it in the house a long time, and when his friends called, was wont to exhibit it as a curiosity.

It was now the season of hoeing. I was first sent into the corn-field, and afterwards set to scraping cotton. In this employment I remained until hoeing time was nearly passed, when I began to experience the symptoms of approaching illness. I was attacked with chills, which were succeeded by a burning fever. I became weak and emaciated, and frequently so dizzy it caused me to reel and stagger like a drunken man. Nevertheless, I was compelled to keep up my row. When in health I found little difficulty in keeping pace with my fellow-laborers, but now it seemed to be an utter impossibility. Often I fell behind, when the driver's lash was sure to greet my back, infusing into my sick and drooping body a little temporary energy. I continued to decline until at length the whip became entirely ineffectual. The sharpest sting of the rawhide could not arouse me. Finally, in September, when the busy season of cotton picking was at hand, I was unable to leave my cabin. Up to this time I had received no medicine, nor any attention from my master or mistress. The old cook visited me occasionally, preparing me corncoffee, and sometimes boiling a bit of bacon, when I had grown too feeble to accomplish it myself.

When it was said that I would die, Master Epps, unwilling to bear the loss, which the death of an animal worth a thousand dollars would bring upon him, concluded to incur the expense of sending to Holmesville for Dr. Wines. He announced to Epps that it was the effect of the climate, and there was a probability of his losing me. He directed me to eat no meat. . . . One morning, long before I was in a proper condition to labor, Epps appeared at the cabin door, and, presenting me a sack, ordered me to the cotton field. At this time I had had no experience whatever in cotton picking. It was an awkward business indeed. While others used both hands, snatching the cotton and depositing it in the mouth of the sack, with a precision and dexterity that was incomprehensible to me, I had to seize the boll with one hand, and deliberately draw out the white, gushing blossom with the other.

. . . After a most laborious day I arrived in the gin-house with my load. When the scale determined its weight to be only ninety-five pounds, not half the quantity required of the poorest picker, Epps threatened the severest flogging, but in consideration of my being a "raw hand," concluded to pardon me on that occasion. The following day, and many days succeeding, I returned at night with no better success—I was evidently not designed for that kind of labor. I had not the gift—the dexterous fingers and quick motion of Patsey, who could fly along one side of a row of cotton, stripping it of its undefiled and fleecy whiteness miraculously fast. Practice and whipping were alike unavailing, and Epps, satisfied of it at last, swore I was a disgrace—that I was not fit to associate with a cotton-picking "nigger"—that I could not pick enough in a day to pay the trouble of weighing it, and that I should go into the cotton field no more. I was now employed in cutting and hauling wood, drawing cotton from the field to the ginhouse, and performed whatever other service was required. Suffice to say, I was never permitted to be idle.

It was rarely that a day passed by without one or more whippings. This occurred at the time the cotton was weighed. The delinquent, whose weight had fallen short was taken out, stripped, made to lie upon the ground, face downwards, when he received a punishment proportioned to his offence. It is the literal, unvarnished truth, that the crack of the lash, and the shrieking of the slaves, can be heard from dark till bed time, on Epps' plantation, any day almost during the entire period of the cotton-picking season. . . .

During the two years Epps remained on the plantation at Bayou Huff Power, he was in the habit, as often as once in a fortnight at least, of coming home intoxicated from Holmesville. The shooting-matches almost invariably concluded with a debauch. At such times he was boisterous and half-crazy. Often he would break the dishes, chairs, and whatever furniture he could lay his hands on. When satisfied with his amusement in the house, he would seize the whip and walk forth into the yard. Then it behooved the slaves to be watchful and exceeding wary. The first one who came within reach felt the smart of his lash. Sometimes for hours he would keep them running in all directions, dodging around the corners of the cabins. . . .

All of us would be assembled in the large room of the great house, whenever Epps came home in one of his dancing moods. No matter how worn out and tired we were, there must be a general dance. When properly stationed on the floor, I would strike up a tune.

"Dance you d—d niggers, dance," Epps would shout.

Then there must be no halting or delay, no slow or languid movements; all must be brisk, and lively, and alert. "Up and down, heel and toe, and away we go," was the order of the hour. Epps' portly form mingled with those of his dusky slaves, moving rapidly through all the mazes of the dance.

Usually his whip was in his hand, ready to fall about the ears of the presumptuous thrall, who dared to rest a moment. . . .

Ten years I toiled for that man without reward. Ten years of my incessant labor has contributed to increase the bulk of his possessions. . . .

A rough, rude energy, united with an uncultivated mind and an avaricious spirit, are his prominent characteristics. He is known as a "nigger breaker," distinguished for his faculty of subduing the spirit of the slave. . . . When the evidence, clear and indisputable, was laid before him that I was a free man, and as much entitled to my liberty as he—when, on the day I left, he was informed that I had a wife and children, as dear to me a his own babes to him, he only raved and swore, denouncing the law that tore me from him. . . .

Old Abram was a kind-hearted being—a sort of patriarch among us, fond of entertaining his younger brethren with grave and serious discourse. He was deeply versed in such philosophy as is taught in the cabin of the slave; but the great absorbing hobby of Uncle Abram was General Jackson, whom his younger master in Tennessee had followed to the wars. He loved to wander back, in imagination, to the place where he was born, and to recount the scenes of his youth during those stirring times when the nation was in arms. He had been athletic, and more keen and powerful than the generality of his race, but now his eye had become dim, and his natural force abated. Very often, indeed, while discussing the best method of baking the hoe-cake, or expatiating at large upon the glory of Jackson, he would forget where he left his hat, or his hoe, or his basket; and then would the old man be laughed at, if Epps was absent, and whipped if he was present. So was he perplexed continually, and sighed to think that he was growing aged and going to decay. Philosophy and Jackson and forgetfulness had played the mischief with him, and it was evident that all of them combined were fast bringing down the gray hairs of Uncle Abram to the grave. . . .

Patsey was slim and straight. She stood erect as the human form is capable of standing. There was an air of loftiness in her movement, that neither labor, nor weariness, nor punishment could destroy. Truly, Patsey was a splendid animal, and were it not that bondage had enshrouded her intellect in utter and everlasting darkness, would have been chief among ten thousand of her people. She could leap the highest fences, and a fleet hound it was indeed, that could outstrip her in a race. No horse could fling her from his back. She was a skillful teamster. She turned as true a furrow as the best, and at splitting rails there were none that could excel her. When the order to halt was heard at night, she would have her mules at the crib, unharnessed, fed and curried, before uncle Abram had found his hat. Not, however, for all or any of these, was she chiefly famous. Such lightning-like motion was in her fingers as no other fingers ever possessed, and therefore it was, that in cotton picking time, Patsey was queen of the field.

She had a genial and pleasant temper, and was faithful and obedient. Naturally, she was a joyous creature, a laughing, light-hearted girl, rejoicing in the mere sense of existence. Yet Patsey wept oftener, and suffered more, than any of her companions. She had been literally excoriated. Her back bore the scars of a thousand stripes; not because she was backward in her work, nor because she was of an unmindful and rebellious spirit, but because it had fallen her lot to be the slave of a licentious master and a jealous mistress. She shrank before the lustful eye of the one, and was in danger even of her life at the hands of the other, and between the two, she was indeed accursed. . . .

Uncle Abram, also, was frequently treated with great brutality, although he was one of the kindest and most faithful creatures in the world. He was my cabin-mate for years. There was a benevolent expression in the old man's face, pleasant to behold. He regarded us with a kind of parental feeling, always counseling us with remarkable gravity and deliberation.

Returning from Marshall's plantation one afternoon whither I had been sent on some errand of the mistress, I found him lying on the cabin floor, his clothes saturated with blood. He informed me that he had been stabbed! While spreading cotton on the scaffold, Epps came home intoxicated from Holmesville. He found fault with every thing, giving many orders so directly contrary that it was impossible to execute any of them. Uncle Abram, whose faculties were growing dull, became confused, and committed some blunder of no particular consequence. Epps was so enraged thereat, that, with drunken recklessness, he flew upon the old man, and stabbed him in the back. It was a long, ugly wound. . . .

It was no uncommon thing with him to prostrate Aunt Phebe with a chair or stick of wood; but the most cruel whipping that ever I was doomed to witness—one I can never recall with any other emotion than that of horror—was inflicted on the unfortunate Patsey. . . .

. . . [H]e ordered four stakes to be driven into the ground, pointing with the toe of his boot to the places where he wanted them. When the stakes were driven down, he ordered her to be stripped of every article of dress. Ropes were then brought, and the naked girl was laid upon her face, her wrists and feet each tied firmly to a stake. Stepping to the piazza, he took down a heavy whip, and placing it in my hands, commanded me to lash her. Unpleasant as it was, I was compelled to obey him. Nowhere that day, on the face of the whole earth, I venture to say, was there such a demoniac exhibition witnessed as then ensued.

Mistress Epps stood on the piazza among her children, gazing on the scene with an air of heartless satisfaction. The slaves were huddled together at a little distance, their countenances indicating the sorrow of their hearts. Poor Patsey prayed piteously for mercy, but her prayers were vain. . . .

I absolutely refused to raise the whip. He then seized it himself, and applied it with ten-fold greater force than I had. The painful cries and shrieks of the tortured Patsey, mingling with the loud and angry curses of Epps, loaded the air. She was terribly lacerated—I may say, without, exaggeration, literally flayed. The lash was wet with blood. . . .

A blessed thing it would have been for her—days and weeks and months of misery it would have saved her—had she never lifted her head in life again. Indeed, from that time forward she was not what she had been. The burden of a deep melancholy weighed heavily on her spirits. She no longer moved with that buoyant and elastic step—

there was not that mirthful sparkle in her eyes that formerly distinguished her. . . .

She had been reared no better than her master's beast—looked upon merely as a valuable and handsome animal—and consequently possessed but a limited amount of knowledge. And yet a faint light cast its rays over her intellect, so that it was not wholly dark. She had a dim perception of God and of eternity, and a still more dim perception of a Saviour who had died even for such as her. She entertained but confused notions of a future life. . . . Her idea of the joy of heaven was simply *rest* . . . .

CHAPTER 14

The Decision of War

INTRODUCTION

DEBATE ON JOHN P. HALE'S BILL TO OUTLAW
RIOTING, APRIL 20, 1848

GEORGE TEMPLETON STRONG, 1820–1875
from The Diary of George Templeton Strong, 1836–1856

MARY BOYKIN CHESNUT, 1823–1886
from The Diary of Mary Boykin Chesnut, 1861–1865

THOMAS WENTWORTH HIGGINSON, (1823–1911)
Army Life in a Black Regiment (1867)

ABRAHAM LINCOLN
Letter to Horace Greeley, Address Delivered at the
Dedication of the Cemetery at Gettysburg, and
Second Inaugural Address (1862–1865)

The dynamics of accelerating sectional anger are clear in the U.S. Senate's most spontaneous debate on slavery. In 1848 over 50 Washington, DC, slaves tried to escape to freedom on a boat down the Potomac, but ill winds and tides allowed their recapture. A proslavery mob was preparing to attack the city's jail and its antislavery newspaper, when the nation's only antislavery senator, John Hale of New Hampshire, introduced an innocuous anti-riot bill. Hale knew it would be a red flag to Southerners, and they charged. By the end of the debate, Northern attention, much to moderates' distress, was turned from abolitionist "slave theft" to the extremism of Calhoun, Jefferson Davis and "Hangman" Foote.

Wall Street lawyer George Templeton Strong and Southern planter Mary Boykin Chesnut were the best diarists and among the best prose stylists of the era. Strong's vigorous observations of events reveal his sharp views on many issues, including his growing anger at the South despite small sympathy with the slave. Chesnut wrote her diary during the Civil War, and spent much of the rest of her impoverished life editing it. It well documents the charm and the tragedy of the antebellum South, and also the need planters felt, once the war began, to deny that slavery had anything to do with their profits or their battle.

A Unitarian minister and rioter in aid of fugitive slaves, Thomas Wentworth Higginson jumped at the chance to lead a Union regiment of ex-slaves, because he rightly saw this was the best way for blacks to earn their freedom and the respect of much of the North. Sharply observant of the character and culture of his troops, he was the first American to record the depth and beauty of slave spirituals. His taste proved better here than when he later took on briefly the hard business of mentoring Emily Dickinson's muse.

The reasons for fighting the Civil War have been endlessly debated, but no one has gone far beyond Abraham Lincoln's statements about its changing motivations and meaning.

CONSIDERATIONS

- Was slavery compatible with American principles? Was there a way to end it short of Civil War? What are the implications about this of the riot debate?

- Why was Lincoln elected and why did the South secede? What clues or explanations for these things do you find in the diaries?

- Does Chesnut or Higginson better understand black character and culture? Did African American soldiers earn their race's freedom?

- Is individual freedom real if governments can order young men into situations where hundreds of thousands of them will lose their lives? In war should individuals be willing to sacrifice everything for the common good?

- Could anything have been done to avoid civil war or to make more just and less harsh its results for Southern whites and blacks?

Debate on John P. Hale's Bill to Outlaw Rioting

April 20, 1848

Mr. Hale. I wish to make a single remark, in order to call the attention of the Senate to the necessity of adopting the legislation proposed by this bill. The bill itself is nearly an abstract of a similar law now in force in the adjoining State of Maryland, and also in many other States of the Union. The necessity for the passage of the bill will be apparent to the Senate from facts which are probably notorious to every member of the body. Within the present week large and riotous assemblages of people have taken place in this District, and have not only threatened to carry into execution schemes utterly subversive to all law, with respect to the rights of property, but have actually carried these threats into execution, after having been addressed, upheld, and countenanced by men of station in society, whose character might have led us to suppose that they would have taken a different course, and given wiser counsels to those whom they addressed. It seems to me, then, that we have approached a time when the decision is to be made in this Capitol, whether mob-law or constitutional law is to reign paramount. The bill which I now propose to introduce simply makes any city, town, or incorporated place within the District liable for all injuries done to property by riotous or tumultuous assemblages. Whether any further legislation on the part of Congress will be necesary, time will determine. But I may be permitted to say, that at the present moment we present a singular spectacle to the people of this country and to the world. The notes of congratulation which this Senate sent across the Atlantic to the people of France on their deliverance from thraldom, have hardly ceased, when the supremacy of mob-law and the destruction of the freedom of the press are threatened in this capital of the Union. Without further remark, I move that this bill be referred to the Committee on the judiciary.

Mr. Bagby. I rise for the purpose of giving notice that whenever that bill shall be reported by the committee—if it ever should be—I shall propose to amend it by a section providing a sufficient penalty for the crime of kidnapping in this District. I was struck by a remark made by the Senator from New Hampshire. He adverts to the rejoicing of the people of this country at the events now in progress in Europe, and thence infers that the slaves of this country are to be permitted to cut the throats of their masters. I shall certainly, sir, attend to this subject.

MR. HALE. To avoid misapprehension, I purposely abstained from saying a word in regard to anything that might even be supposed to lie beyond the case which it is the object of this bill to meet. I did not make the most distant allusion to slavery. I refrained from it purposely, because I wanted to present to the consideration of the Senate the simple question of the integrity of the law and the rights of property unembarrassed by considerations of the character alluded to by the honorable Senator from Alabama. . . .

MR. CALHOUN. I suppose no Senator can mistake the object of this bill, and the occurrence which has led to its introduction. Now, Sir, I am amazed that even the Senator from New Hampshire should have so little regard for the laws and the Constitution of the country, as to introduce such a bill as this, without including in it the enactment of the severest penalties against the atrocious act which has occasioned this excitement. Sir, gentlemen, it would seem, have at last come to believe that the southern people and southern members have lost all sensibility or feeling upon this subject. I know to what this leads. I have known for a dozen years to what all this is tending. When this subject was first agitated, I said to my friends, there is but one question that can destroy this Union and our institutions, and that is this very slave question, for I choose to speak of it directly. I said further, that the only way by which such a result could be prevented was by prompt and efficient action; that if the thing were permitted to go on, and the Constitution to be trampled on; that if it were allowed to proceed to a certain point, it would be beyond the power of any man, or any combination of men, to prevent the result. We are approaching that crisis, and evidence of it is presented by the fact that such a bill upon such an occurrence should be brought in to repress the just indignation of our people from wreaking their vengeance upon the atrocious perpetrators of these crimes, or those who contribute to them, without a denunciation of the cause that excited that indignation. I cannot but trust that I do not stand alone in these views.

I have for so many years raised my voice upon this subject that I have been considered almost the exclusive defender of this great institution of the South, upon which not only its prosperity but its very existence depends. . . . If you do not regard the stipulations of the Constitution in our favor, why should we regard those in your favor? If your vessels cannot come into our ports without the danger of such piratical acts; if you have caused this state of things by violating the provisions of the Constitution and the act of Congress for delivering up fugitive slaves, by passing laws to prevent it, and thus make it impossible to recover them when they are carried off by such acts, or seduced from us, we have the right, and are bound by the high obligation of safety to ourselves, to retaliate, by preventing any of your seagoing vessels from entering our ports. That would apply an effectual remedy, and make up the issue at once on this, the gravest and most vital of all questions to us and the whole Union. . . .

MR. DAVIS, of Mississippi. . . . Is this District to be made the field of abolition struggles? Is this Chamber to be the hot-bed in which plants of sedition are to be nursed? Why is it that in this body, once looked to as the conservative branch of the Government—once looked to as so dignified that it stood above the power of faction—that we find the subject of this contest so insulting to the South—so irritating always when it is agitated—introduced on such an occasion? Is this debatable ground? No! It is ground upon which the people of this Union may shed blood, and that is the final result. If it be pressed any further, and if this Senate is to be made the theatre of that contest, let it come—the sooner the better. We who represent the southern States are not here to be insulted on account of institutions which we inherit. And if civil discord is to be thrown from this Chamber upon the land—if the fire is to be kindled here with which to burn the temple of our Union—if this is to be made the centre from which civil war is to radiate, here let the conflict begin. I am ready, for one, to meet it with any incendiary, who, dead to every feeling of patriotism, attempts to introduce it. . . .

MR. FOOTE. I undertake to say that there is not a man who has given his countenance to this transaction in any shape, who is not capable of committing grand larceny; or, if he happened to be a hero, as such men are not, of perpetrating highway robbery on any of the roads of this Union. He is not a gentleman. He would not be countenanced by any respectable person anywhere. He is amenable to the law. I go further—and I dare say my sentiments will meet the approbation of many even who do not live in slave States—and I maintain, that when the arm of the law is too short to reach such a criminal, he may be justly punished by a sovereignty not known to the law. Such proceedings have taken place, and there are circumstances which not only instigate, but justify such acts. I am informed, upon evidence on which I rely, that this very movement out of which the bill originates, has been instigated and sanctioned by persons in high station. It is even rumored, and it is believed by many—I am sorry for the honor of this body to say so—that a Senator of the United States is concerned in the movement. Certain it is, that a member of another body, meeting in a certain Hall not far distant, was yesterday morning engaged in certain reprehensible contrivances, and that but for his abject flight from the place of his infamous intrigues, he would have been justly punished, not by the mob, but by high-spirited citizens convened for the purpose of vindicating their rights, thus unjustly assailed.

Why is it that this question is continually agitated in the Senate of the United States—that it is kept here as the subject of perpetual discussion? Is it simply that gentlemen wish to be popular at home? I suppose so. Is it because of their peculiar sympathies for that portion of the population which constitutes slavery as recognized in the South? What is the motive? Is the object to attain popularity? Is it to gain high station? Is it to keep up a local excitement in some portions of the North, with the view of obtaining political elevation as the reward of such factious conduct? But I care not for the motives of such acts. I undertake to say that in no country where the principles of honesty are respected, would such a movement as that now attempted be promoted, or even countenanced for a moment. . . . The Senator from New Hampshire is evidently attempting to get up a sort of civil war in the country, and is evidently filled with the spirit of insurrection and incendiarism. He may bring about a result which will end in the spilling of human blood. I say to him, however, let him come forward boldly, and take the proper responsibility. Let him say, "Now I am ready to do battle in behalf of the liberties of my friends, the blacks—the slaves of the District of Columbia." Let him buckle on his armor; let him unsheath his sword, and at once commence the contest, and I have no doubt be will have a fair opportunity of shedding his blood in this holy cause on the sacred soil of the District of Columbia. If he is really in earnest, he is bound, as a conscientious man, to pursue his course, which cannot be persevered in, without all those awful scenes of bloodshed and desolation long anticipated by good men in every part of this Republic. . . .

All must see that the course of the Senator from New Hampshire is calculated to embroil the Confederacy —to put in peril our free institutions—to jeopard that Union which our forefathers established, and which every pure patriot throughout the country desires shall be perpetuated. Can any man be a patriot who pursues such a course? Is he an enlightened friend of freedom, or even a judicious friend of those with whom he affects to sympathize, who adopts such a course? Who does not know that such men are practically the worst enemies of the slaves? I do not beseech the gentleman to stop; but if he perseveres, he will awaken indignation everywhere: and it cannot be, that enlightened men, who conscientiously belong to the faction of the North, of which he is understood to be the head, can sanction or approve everything that he may do, under the influence of excitement, in this body. I will close by saying, that if he really wishes glory, and to be regarded as the great liberator of the blacks; if he wishes to be particularly distinguished in this cause of emancipation, as it is called, let him, instead of remaining here in the Senate of the United States, or, instead of secreting himself in some dark corner of New Hampshire, where he may possibly escape the just indignation of good men throughout this Republic—let him visit the good State of Mississippi, in which I have the honor to reside, and no doubt he will be received with such hosannas and shouts of joy as have rarely marked the reception of any individual in this day and generation. I invite him there, and will tell him beforehand, in all honesty, that he could not go ten miles into the interior, before he would grace one of the tallest trees of the forest, with a rope around his neck, with the approbation of every virtuous and patriotic citizen; and that, if necessary, I should myself assist in the operation.

Mr. Hale. I beg the indulgence of the Senate for a few moments. Though I did not exactly anticipate this discussion, yet I do not regret it. Before I proceed further, as the honorable Senator from Mississippi has said that it has been asserted, and he thinks on good authority, that a Senator of the United States connived at this kidnapping of slaves, I ask him if he refers to me?

Mr. Foote. I did.

Mr. Hale. I take occasion, then, to say, that the statement that I have given the slightest countenance to the procedure is entirely without the least foundation in truth. I have had nothing to do with the occurrence, directly or indirectly, and I demand of the honorable Senator to state the ground upon which he has made his allegation.

MR. FOOTE. It has been stated to me, and I certainly believed it; and believing it, I denounced it. I did not make the charge directly. My remarks were hypothetical. I am glad to hear the Senator say that he has had no connection with the movement; but whether he had or not, some of his brethren in the great cause in which he was engaged no doubt had much to do with it.

MR. HALE. The sneer of the gentleman does not affect me. I recognize every member of the human family as a brother; and if it was done by human beings, it was done by my brethren. Once for all, I utterly deny, either by counsel, by silence, or by speech, or in any way or manner, having any knowledge, cognizance, or suspicion of what was done, or might be done, until I heard of this occurrence as other Senators have heard of it. . . .

MR. FOOTE. I ask the Senator—and beg to remind him that twenty millions of people are listening to his answer—in the circumstances of the case, evidently known to him, does he suppose that this occurrence could have taken place without extensive countenance and aid from men of standing in this District, whether members of Congress or others?

MR. HALE. I have no doubt that those persons could not have got away without some aid. It is enough that I have disclaimed all knowledge of it. I thought that when the honorable Senator was speaking, more than twenty millions of people were listening. He invites me to visit the State of Mississippi, and kindly informs me that he would be one of those who would act the assassin, and put an end to my career. He would aid in bringing me to public execution—no, death by a mob. Well, in return for his hospitable invitation, I can only express the desire that he would penetrate into some of the dark corners of New Hampshire, and if he do, I am much mistaken if he would not find that the people in that benighted region would be very happy to listen to his arguments, and engage in an intellectual conflict with him, in which the truth might be elicited. . . .

I think, if I did not misunderstand the honorable Senator from South Carolina, that he is surprised at the temerity of the Senator from New Hampshire in introducing this bill. Let me ask, what is this bill? What is this incendiary bill that has elicited such a torrent of invective? Has it been manufactured by some "fanatical abolitionist?" Why, it is copied, almost word for word, from a law on the statute-book which has been in operation for years, in the neighboring State of Maryland. It has no allusion, directly or indirectly, to the subject of slavery. Yet I am accused of throwing it in as a firebrand, and in order to make war upon the institutions of the South! How? In God's name, is it come to this, that the American Senate, and in the year of grace one thousand eight hundred and forty-eight, the rights of property cannot be named but the advocates of slavery are in arms, and exclaim that war is made upon their institutions; because it is attempted to cast the protection of the law around the property of an American citizen, who appeals to an American Senate! It has long been held by you that your peculiar institution is incompatible with the right of speech; but if it be also incompatible with the safeguards of the Constitution being thrown around property of American citizens, let the country know it! If that is to be the principle of your action, let it be proclaimed throughout the length and breadth of the land, that there is an institution so omnipotent—so almighty—that even the sacred rights of life and property must bow down before it!

Do not let it be said that I have introduced this subject. I have simply asked that the plainest provisions of the common law—the clearest dictates of justice—shall be extended and exercised for the protection of the property of citizens of this District; and yet, the honorable Senator from South Carolina is shocked at my temerity!

MR. BUTLER. Allow me to ask one question with perfect good temper. The Senator is discussing the subject with some feeling; but I ask him whether he would vote for a bill, properly drawn, inflicting punishment on persons inveigling slaves from the District of Columbia?

MR. HALE. Certainly not, and why? Because I do not believe that slavery should exist here.

MR. CALHOUN, (in his seat.) He wishes to arm the robbers, and disarm the people of the District.

MR. HALE. The honorable Senator is alarmed at my temerity—

MR. CALHOUN, (in his seat.) I did not use the word, but did not think it worth while to correct the Senator.

MR. HALE. The Senator did not use that term?

MR. CALHOUN. No. I said brazen, or something like that.

MR. HALE. The meaning was the same. It was brazen then, that I should introduce a bill for the protection of property in this District—a bill perfectly harmless, but which he has construed into an attack upon the institutions of the South. I ask the Senator and the country wherein consists the temerity? I suppose it consists in the section of the country from which it comes. He says that we seem to think that the South has lost all feeling. Ah! there is the temerity. The bill comes from the wrong side of a certain parallel! Why, did the honorable Senator from South Carolina imagine that we of the North, with our faces bowed down to the earth, and with our backs to the sun, had received the lash so long that we dared not look up? Did he suppose that we dared not ask that the protection of the law should be thrown around property in the District to which we come to legislate? . . .

And here let me tell the Senator from Alabama, that he will have my full cooperation in any measure to prevent kidnapping. I shall expect him to redeem his pledge. Again: I am shocked to hear the honorable Senator from South Carolina denounce this bill as a measure calculated to repress those citizens from the expression of their just indignation.

MR. CALHOUN. If the Senator will allow me, I will explain. I said no such thing. But I will take this occasion to say, that I would just as soon argue with a maniac from bedlam, as with the Senator from New Hampshire, on this subject.

SEVERAL SENATORS. "Order, order."

MR. CALHOUN. I do not intend to correct his statements. A man who says that the people of this District have no right in their slaves, and that it is no robbery to take their property from them, is not entitled to be regarded as in possession of his reason.

MR. HALE. It is an extremely novel mode of terminating a controversy by charitably throwing the mantle of maniacal irresponsibility over one's antagonist! . . .

MR. FOOTE. The Senator seems to suppose that I wanted to decoy him to the State of Mississippi. I have attempted no such thing. I have thought of no such thing. I have openly challenged him to present himself there or anywhere uttering such language and breathing such an incendiary spirit as he has manifested in this body, and I have said that just punishment would be inflicted upon him for his enormous criminality. I have said further, that, if necessary, I would aid in the infliction of the punishment. My opinion is, that enlightened men would sanction that punishment. But, says the Senator, that would be assassination! I think not. I am sure that the Senator is an enemy to the Constitution of his country—an enemy of one of the institutions of his country which is solemnly guaranteed by the organic law of the land—and in so far he is a lawless person. I am sure, if he would go to the State of Mississippi, or any other slave State of this Confederacy, and utter such language, he would justly be regarded as an incendiary in heart and in fact, and as such, guilty of the attempt to involve the South in bloodshed, violence, and desolation; and if the arm of the law happened to be too short, or the spirit of the law to be slumberous, I have declared that the duty of the people whose rights were thus put in danger would be to inflict summary punishment upon the offender. But, says the Senator, victims have been made, and there are other victims ready. I am sure that he could not persuade me that he would ever be a victim. I have never deplored the death of such victims, and I never shall deplore it. Such officious intermeddling deserved its fate. I believe no good man who is not a maniac, as the Senator from New Hampshire is apprehended to be, can have any sympathy for those who lawlessly interfere with the rights of others. He, however, will never be a victim! He is one of those gusty declaimers—a windy speaker—a—

MR. CRITTENDEN. If the gentlemen will allow me, I rise to a question of order. Gentlemen have evidently become excited, and I hear on all sides language that is not becoming. I call the gentleman to order for his personal reference to the Senator from New Hampshire.

MR. FOOTE. I only said, in reply to the remarks of the Senator from New Hampshire—

MR. CRITTENDEN. I did not hear what the Senator from New Hampshire said, but the allusion of the gentleman from Mississippi I consider to be contrary to the rules of the Senate.

MR. FOOTE. I am aware of that. But such a scene has never occurred in the Senate—such a deadly assailment of the rights of the country.

MR. JOHNSON, of Maryland. Has the Chair decided?

MR. FOOTE. Let my words be taken down.

THE PRESIDING OFFICER. In the opinion of the Chair, the gentleman from Mississippi is not in order.

MR. FOOTE. I pass it over. But the Senator from New Hampshire has said, that if I would visit that State, I would be treated to an argument. Why, I would not argue with him. What right have they of New Hampshire to argue upon this point? It is not a matter in which they stand in the least connected. . . .

His sentiments will find no response or approval in any enlightened vicinage in New England, and therefore he has no right to say that those who are faithful to the principles of the Constitution, and fail to re-echo the fierce, fanatical, and factious declarations of the Senator, are "cravens" in heart, and deficient in any of the noble sentiments which characterize high-spirited republicans. . . .

The declarations of the Senator from New Hampshire just amount to this: that if he met me on the highway and addressing me gravely or humorously—for he is quite a humorous personage—should say, I design to take that horse which is now in your possession; and then announce that he wished to enter into an argument with me as to whether I should prefer that the animal should be stolen from the stable or taken from me on the road; how could I meet such a proposition? Why, I should say to him, either you are a maniac, or, if sane, you are a knave . . . .

How are we to understand the Senator? He will not acknowledge that his object is to encourage such conduct, and he shuns the responsibility. When we charge upon him that he himself has breathed, in the course of his harangue this morning, the same spirit which has characterized this act, he says most mildly and quietly, "by no means—I have only attempted to introduce a bill corresponding substantially with the law on the statute books of most of the States of this Confederacy." And the Senator supposes that all of us are perfectly demented, or do not know the nature of the case, the circumstances, or the motives which have actuated the Senator. . . .

I trust that the indignation of the country will be so aroused, that even in the quarter of the country from which he comes, the Senator from New Hampshire, although his sensibilities are not very approachable, will be made to feel ashamed of his conduct. . . .

Mr. Magnum. Why should we pursue this discussion? Is it believed that we are to be reasoned out of our rights? Are we to be reasoned out of our convictions? No, Sir. Then why discuss the subject? Why not stand upon our rights; upon our constitutional compromises? Why not stand thus perfectly passionless, but prepared to defend them when they shall be assailed? But are they to be assailed? Sir, nothing has occurred during this session that has afforded me more satisfaction than to hear from some of the ablest and most distinguished men in this Union, the declaration that whilst they are opposed to an extension of the area of slavery, they are not disposed to trample upon the compromises of the Constitution. This is our strength. It is to be found in the patriotism of those who love the institutions of our country better than party. I believe the great body of the people are prepared to stand upon the compromises of the Constitution. It is upon this ground that I stand content and passionless, and if I know myself I shall ever continue to do so.

Sir, no good can result from this discussion. . . .

MR. FOOTE. Will the honorable Senator allow me to ask him whether, in the case of a conspiracy to excite insurrection among the slaves, it would not, in his opinion, justify mob proceedings?

MR. MAGNUM. Oh! my dear sir, in former years we had a compendious mode of disposing of such cases. We have now a mode equally certain, though not so compendious. Upon a matter of that nature we take a strong ground. But I am not to be driven hastily into legislation that is proposed by gentlemen who entertain extreme opinions on either side.

MR. CALHOUN. I disagree with my worthy friend, the Senator from North Carolina, in several particulars. I do not look upon a state of excitement as a dangerous state. On the contrary, I look upon it as having often a most wholesome tendency. The state to be apprehended as dangerous in any community is this, that when there is a great and growing evil in existence, the community should be in a cold and apathetic state. Nations are much more apt to perish in consequence of such a state than through the existence of heat and excitement. . . .

I differ also from my honorable friend from North Carolina in this respect: he seems to think that the proper mode of meeting this great question of difference between the two sections of the Union is to let it go on silently, not to notice it at all, to have no excitement about it. I differ from him altogether. . . . The very inaction of the South is construed into one of two things—indifference or timidity. And it is this construction which has produced this bold and rapid movement towards the ultimate consummation of all this. And why have we stood and done nothing? I will tell you why. Because the press of this Union, for some reason or other, does not choose to notice this thing. One section does not know what the other section is doing. . . . I do not stand here as a southern man. I stand here as a member of one of the branches of the Legislature of this Union—loving the whole, and desiring to save the whole. How are you to do it? . . . Sir, I hold equality among the confederated States to be the highest point, and any portion of the confederated States who shall permit themselves to sink to a point of inferiority—not defending what really belongs to them, as members, sign their own death warrant, and in signing that, sign the doom of the whole.

MR. DOUGLAS. On the occurrence I desire to say a word. In the first place, I must congratulate the Senator from New Hampshire on the great triumph which he has achieved. He stands very prominently before the American people, and is, I believe, the only man who has a national nomination for the Presidency. I firmly believe that on this floor, to-day, by the aid of the Senator from Mississippi, he has more than doubled his vote at the Presidential election, and every man in this Chamber from a free State knows it! . . . If they had gone into a caucus with the Senator from New Hampshire, and after a night's study and deliberation, had devised the best means to manufacture abolitionism and abolition votes in the North, they would have fallen upon precisely the same kind of procedure which they have adopted to-day. It is the speeches of southern men, representing slave States, going to an extreme, breathing a fanaticism as wild and as reckless as that of the Senator from New Hampshire, which creates abolitionism in the North. The extremes meet. It is no other than southern Senators acting in concert, and yet without design, that produces abolition.

MR. CALHOUN. Does the gentleman pretend to say, that myself, and southern gentlemen who act with me upon this occasion, are fanatics? Have we done anything more than defend our rights, encroached upon at the North? Am I to understand the Senator that we make abolition votes by defending our rights? If so, I thank him for the information, and do not care how many such votes we make.

MR. DOUGLAS. Well, I will say to the Senator from South Carolina, and every other Senator from the South, that far be it from me to entertain the thought, that they design to create abolitionists in the North, or elsewhere. Far be it from me to impute any such design. Yet I assert that such is the only inevitable effect of their conduct.

MR. CALHOUN, (in his seat.) We are only defending ourselves.

MR. DOUGLAS. No, they are not defending themselves. . . . My friend from Mississippi, [MR. FOOTE] in his zeal and excitement this morning, made a remark, in the invitation which he extended to the Senator from New Hampshire to visit Mississippi, which is worth ten thousand votes to the Senator, and I am confident that that Senator would not allow my friend to retract that remark for ten thousand votes.

MR. FOOTE. Will you allow me?

MR. DOUGLAS. Certainly.

MR. FOOTE. If the effect of that remark will be to give to that Senator all the abolition votes, he is fairly entitled to them. Had the Senator from Illinois lived where I have resided—had he seen insurrection exhibiting its fiery front in the midst of the men, women, and children of the community—had he had reason to believe that the machinery of insurrection was at such a time in readiness for purposes of the most deadly character, involving life, and that dearer than life, to every southern man—had he witnessed such scenes, and believed that movements like that of this morning were calculated to engender feelings out of which were to arise fire, blood, and desolation, the destruction finally of the South, he would regard himself as a traitor to the best sentiments of the human heart, if he did not speak out the language of manly denunciation. I can use no other language. I cannot but repeat my conviction, that any man who dares to utter such sentiments as those of the Senator from New Hampshire, and attempts to act them out anywhere in the sunny South, will meet death upon the scaffold, and deserves it.

MR. DOUGLAS. I must again congratulate the Senator from New Hampshire on the accession of five thousand votes! Sir, I do not blame the Senator from Mississippi for being indignant at any man from any portion of this Union, who would produce an incendiary excitement—who would kindle the flame of civil war—who would incite a negro insurrection, hazarding the life of any man in the southern States. The Senator has, I am aware, reason to feel deeply on this subject. . . .

MR. DAVIS, of Mississippi. I do not wish to be considered as participating in the feeling to which the Senator alludes. I have no fear of insurrection; no more dread of our slaves than I have of our cattle. Our slaves are happy and contented. They bear the kindest relation that labor can sustain to capital. It is a paternal institution. They are rendered miserable only by the unwarrantable interference of those who know nothing about that with which they meddle. I rest this case on no fear of insurrection; and I wish it to be distinctly understood, that we are able to take care of ourselves, and to punish all incendiaries. It was the insult offered to the institutions which we have inherited, that provoked my indignation. . . .

MR. DOUGLAS. All that I intended to say was, that the effect of this excitement—of all these harsh expressions—will be the creation of abolitionists at the North.

MR. FOOTE. The more the better!

MR. DOUGLAS. The gentleman may think so; but some of us at the North do not concur with him in that opinion. Of course the Senator from New Hampshire will agree with him, because he can fan the flame of excitement so as to advance his political prospects. And I can also well understand how some gentlemen at the South may quite complacently regard all this excitement, if they can persuade their constituents to believe that the institution of slavery rests upon their shoulders—that they are the men who meet the Goliath of the North in this great contest about abolition. It gives them strength at home. But we of the North, who have no sympathy with abolitionists, desire no such excitement.

MR. CALHOUN. I must really object to the remarks of the Senator. We are merely defending our rights. Suppose that we defend them in strong language; have we not a right to do so? Surely the Senator cannot mean to impute to us the motives of low ambition. He cannot realize our position. For myself, (and I presume I may speak for those who act with me,) we place this question upon high and exalted grounds. Long as he may have lived in the neighborhood of slaveholding States, he cannot have realized anything on the subject. I must object entirely to his course, and say that it is at least as offensive as that of the Senator from New Hampshire. . . .

MR. FOOTE. . . . I would say with all possible courtesy to the Senator from Illinois, for whom I entertain the highest respect, and whose general feelings of justice for us in the South we all understand and appreciate, he will permit me to say to him, in a spirit of perfect courtesy, that there are various ways of becoming popular. Our constituents will have confidence in us, if they see we are ready here to maintain their interests inviolate. And it may be, also, that the Senator from New Hampshire will strengthen himself in proportion as his conduct is denounced. But I beg the Senator from Illinois to recollect, that there is another mode of obtaining that popularity, which is expressed in the adage—"*in medio tutissimus ibis,*" and that there is such a thing as winning golden opinions from all sorts of people; and it may be that a man of mature power—young and aspiring as he may be to high places—may conceive that, by keeping clear of all union with the two leading factions, he will more or less strengthen himself with the great body of the American people, and thus attain the high point of elevation to which his ambition leads. But if the Senator from Illinois thinks that a middle course in regard to this question is best calculated to serve his purpose, he is mistaken.

MR. DOUGLAS. The Senator has hit it precisely when he says that sometimes the course advised in the familiar adage which he has quoted, is, indeed, the course of duty and of wisdom. I do believe that upon this question that is the only course which can "win golden opinions" from reflecting men throughout the country.

MR. FOOTE, (in his seat.) "Golden opinions from all sorts of people."

MR. DOUGLAS. In the North it is not expected that we should take the position that slavery is a positive good—a positive blessing. If we did assume such a position, it would be a very pertinent inquiry, Why do you not adopt this institution? We have moulded our institutions at the North as we have thought proper; and now we say to you of the South, if slavery be a blessing, it is your blessing; if it be a curse, it is your curse; enjoy it—on you rest all the responsibility! . . . But my object was to inform the people of the South how it is that gentlemen professing the sentiments of the Senator from New Hampshire, get here; how it is that they will see others coming here with similar sentiments, unless they reflect more calmly and coolly, and take a different course; and how this imprudent and violent course is calculated to crush us who oppose abolitionism. If any unpleasant feeling has been excited by these remarks of mine, I regret it. I know that it is not always pleasant to tell the truth plainly and boldly, when it comes home to an individual. But what I have said is the truth, and we all know it and feel it. . . .

MR. BUTLER. From the course which this discussion has taken, is clearly indicated the approaching storm which will ere long burst upon this country. I am persuaded that the part of the country which I represent is destined to be in a minority—a doomed minority. . . .

from THE DIARY OF
GEORGE TEMPLETON STRONG

OCTOBER 7, 1836

By the way, speaking of *ultraism*, who, in the name of wonder,
would have suspected Henry J. Anderson, the upright, steady, stiff,
immutable, cool, cautious, rational, judgmatical, reasoning, accurate,
mathematical, matter-of-fact, sober, anti-enthusiastic, clear-headed,
moneymaking, real-estate-buying, demonstrating Prof. Harry—that
incarnation of a right angle—*who* would ever have suspected him of
being a furiously enthusiastic Democrat? No—not a Democrat, the
expression's certainly too tame, but a *"Pas eauto-*crat" (the word's
coined for the occasion), an "every man himself-ocrat"—a man who
believes in the utter perfectibility of the human race, and regards all
law as an encumbrance, a shackle on that freedom which is the birth-
right of all mankind? Yet such he is—on the very best authority. Trevett has heard him argue on it; he grows perfectly rabid the moment
he gets into the subject, e.g., "The fire laws are nuisances—every man
has a right to have his house burnt down, and himself in it, if he likes";
"The laws prohibiting omnibusses from Wall Street are atrocious—
shameful—*infernal—*" (on this topic he was particularly indignant, and
in Trevett's hearing) "a shameful infringement on our liberties." Agrarianism, too, he supports. In religion no one knows his sentiments—
they are not far from Deism—though he always speaks with respect
of the Bible, and lives a moral life. Who would have thought it of Harry
Anderson! . . .

APRIL 27, 1837

Matters very bad out of doors. Confidence annihilated, the whole
community, big and little, traveling to ruin in a body. Strong fears entertained for the banks, and if they go, God only knows what the consequences will be. Ruin here, and on the other side of the Atlantic, and
not only private ruin but political convulsion and revolution, I think. . . .

MAY 2, 1837

Workmen thrown out of employ by the hundred daily. Business at a stand; the coal mines in Pennsylvania stopped and no fuel in prospect for next winter—delightful prospects, these.

MAY 3, 1837

Went up to the office at six. Fresh failures, Talbot Olyphant & Co., among them. So they go—smash, crash. Where in the name of wonder is there to be an end of it? Near two hundred and fifty failures thus far! . . .

Locofoco meeting in the Park this morning—and such a meeting! It looked like a convention of loafers from all quarters of the world.

MAY 4, 1837

Terrible news in Wall Street. [John] Fleming, late president of the Mechanics Bank, found dead in his bed this morning. Some say prussic acid; others (and the coroner's jury) say "mental excitement" and apoplexy.

Anyhow there's a run on the bank—street crowded—more feeling of alarm and despondency in Wall Street than has appeared yet. . . .

MAY 10, 1837

Extensive news in this morning's paper. The banks (except three) have concluded to stop specie payment!!! Glory to the Old General! Glory to little Matty, second fiddler to the great Magician! Glory—ay, and double patent glory—to the experiment, the specie currency, and all the glorious humbugs who have inflicted them on us.

Commerce and speculation here have been spreading of late like a card house, story after story and ramification after ramification till the building towered up to the sky and people rolled up their eyes in amazement, but at last one corner gave way and every card that dropped brought down a dozen with it, and *sic transit gloria mundi!*

NOVEMBER 5, 1838

Two things I'm sorry to see in this election: one, the introduction of abolitionism into politics, which may play the devil with our institutions and which is at any rate a new force brought into the system, with an influence now almost inappreciable, but which may grow greater and greater till it brings the whole system into a state of discord and dissension, from which heaven preserve it! The other is the increasing tendency of the Whig party to absorb all the wealth and respectability, and of the Democratic (so called) to take in all the loaferism of the nation, a tendency which may bring us finally to be divided into two great factions, the rich and the poor; and then for another French Revolution, so far as American steadiness and good sense can imitate French folly and bloodthirstiness. . . .

FEBRUARY 3, 1840

. . . [A] good, steady, old-fashioned conflagration, in which the dramatic interest was well sustained throughout, and fire and water were "head and head" till the grand finale when the walls tumbled down in various directions with a great crash, and then fire triumphed, which as the hero of the piece it was very proper and perfectly regular that it should do. On the whole, this was a very fair fire. I'm getting quite a connoisseur.

It's very amusing to notice the view the loaferage (i.e., the majority of the lookers-on at fires) take of the subject. They consider it a sort of grand exhibition (admission gratis) which they have a perfect right to look at from any point they like and to choose the best seats to see the performance; the interests of the owners never seem to enter their heads, and any attempt to keep them back, or to keep a passage open, or any other effort to save property by which their freedom of locality or locomotion is impaired, they consider an unwarrantable interference, of course. . . .

But the state of things is really too bad. Here, in the two first days of last week $2,500,000 of property were destroyed by fire. Now comes another, the loss of which can't be under $80,000, and as to the little fires that have taken place during the interval, I don't take count of them. One committee, appointed by the merchants on Saturday, at their meeting, to devise means for stopping this extraordinary inflammability, don't seem yet to have done much. From all I've seen of fires of late, I'm fully convinced that our fire department is utterly and shamefully incompetent. The engines are not powerful enough to throw water to any considerable height, the hose are so full of rips and holes that a third of the water must be lost, the hydrants never seem to have any water in them, a large part of the firemen do nothing but bustle about in their caps, swear at everybody and try to look tremendous, the engines are never worked for five minutes in succession, and everything in short is as badly conducted as possible. It's a wonder to me at every large fire that half the city don't burn up; some night it will, and then they'll get to work to reform in earnest.

MAY 8, 1840

. . . [T]he procession and fuss tonight surpassed in spirit and numbers anything of the sort that I ever saw here—except during the excitement of election. The procession seemed interminable. I thought as the Irishman did that somebody must have cut off the other end of it. Banners, log cabins on wheels, barrels supposed to be full of hard cider, and all sorts of glories adorned its march. Getting into Niblo's wasn't to be thought of; not more than a third of the procession accomplished it. The Locos, of course, disgraced themselves as usual, by a fierce attack on one banner in particular—representing Matty shinning away from the White House with O. K. under it, i.e., "Off to Kinderhook." Brick bats were thrown and heads broken and an attack was made on the Garden (subsequently), but the siege was raised by a few sticks and stones dropped on the heads of the assailants from above. Altogether it was a grand affair—Harrison forever!

OCTOBER 11, 1840

I took a walk up to Eighth Street and down again. It's a pity we've no street but Broadway that's fit to walk in of an evening. The street is always crowded, and whores and blackguards make up about two-thirds of the throng. That's one of the advantages of uptown; the streets there are well paved, well lighted, and decently populated.

MARCH 28, 1841

Went to church. Heard [the Reverend John Murray] Forbes this morning. Matty Van Buren was there, in the pew of his brother president, Duer of Columbia College, and by a curious coincidence the subject of the sermon was the spiritual blessings that flow from retiracy and seclusion for a season from the busy world and the cares of active life. If I wasn't nearsighted I've no doubt I should have observed Matty wince considerably.

APRIL 5, 1841

Mournful news this morning. General Harrison died on Saturday night, a few hours less than one month from his inauguration. The news was most unexpected to me, for I didn't suppose him very seriously ill, and he was said on Saturday to be recovering. I confess I never was so sincerely sorry for the death of any one whom I knew of merely as a *public* character. Though not possessed of any great talent, I believe he was a good, honest, benevolent, right-minded man—qualities far more rare among our political people.

SEPTEMBER 23, 1842

Left for the Yankee Metropolis Saturday afternoon in the *Cleopatra*. Beautiful evening, and I smoked cigars on deck during the greater part of it. They burn anthracite coal on board that boat—it's dangerous but cheap, and that's the main point. I didn't like it a bit, for we went off at near twenty miles an hour (we were abreast of the *Oldfield* at eight o'clock), and with two great flickering, waving streams of pale yellow fire pouring out of flues it looked downright awful.

JUNE 22, 1843

Entered into conversation with a man who told me he'd never been on board a steamboat before—rather an intelligent person, too, from Delaware county. Hitherto "father had gone down to York, but father was gittin' old." Such greenness in an enlightened American I'd never dreamed possible and I involuntarily felt my pockets, in doubt whether he wasn't a wolf in sheep's clothing, bent on abstracting my valuables. Had a curiosity to ascertain the sensations of the subject on first experiencing this novel kind of locomotion. He said it made him kind o' dizzy. Considering our nomadic habits as a people, I regard this person as a curiosity deserving the attention of the scientific world.

NOVEMBER 18, 1843

Took tea in Murray Street and went with Templeton to the *First Philharmonic*.

Great crowd: all the aristocracy and "gig respectability" and wealth and beauty and fashion of the city there on the spot an hour beforehand. For myself, being superior to such vanities I selected the little side gallery where I could look down in a calm and philosophical manner on the splendors below, and especially upon George Anthon making very strong love apparently to one of the —s! and upon Schermerhorn making himself generally ornamental, and Fanning Tucker trying to devise outlets for his legs and barking his knees on the bench next in front of him, and Mr. Wilmerding dozing off regu-larly at the soft passages and waking up with a jump at the loud ones, and so forth.

Beethoven's Symphony in A was the *opus magnum* of the evening. . . . I hold this the finest symphony I've heard yet. . . .

MAY 27, 1844

The sole shadow of a chance of nomination that John Tyler ever possessed is gone. Don't much care; "country's risin', Clay and Frelinghuysen, quite surprizin', give the Loco pisen," and so on. It don't matter much which Loco is selected to be made a martyr of. . . .

Whether the jacobinical spirit and the antipathy to law and order and the overthrow of everything worth preserving, which is the unconscious principle of the one party, and the temper and final result of its unchecked development, be worse than commercial, speculating, bankswindling, money-worshipping *primum mobile* of the other is a question.

Certainly since the downfall of Federalism there has been no conservative party in the country which has ventured to avow any higher aim than the cultivation of tariffs and credit systems, trade and manufactures.

Its unchecked development would make us a commercial aristocracy which is mean enough everywhere, but here 'twould be a fluctuating mushroom aristocracy and the meanest the world has seen yet.

NOVEMBER 8, 1844

. . . [T]he illustrious Pork is President-Elect.

And the Whig Party is defunct, past all aid from warm blankets, galvanic batteries, and the Humane Society; it's quite dead and the sooner it's buried the better. What form of life will be generated from its decomposition remains to be seen.

Two causes have mainly brought all this to pass: Native Americanism, and the great difference between the candidates in conspicuousness and vulnerability. Everybody could talk about Clay's long career as a prominent politician and find something in it to use against him fairly or falsely, while his opponent was impregnable from the fact that he'd never done or said anything of importance to anybody. . . .

Henceforth I think political wire-pullers will be careful how they nominate prominent and well-known men for the Presidency; they'll find it safer to pick up the first man they may find in the street. . . .

MARCH 31, 1845

Somebody was recommending . . . to get out a Greek Testament with English notes mainly for the benefit of Harper's friends of the Methodist clerical corps, who, being generally men of rather limited education, would find it much more convenient than the Latin notes and commentaries that belong to most standard editions. "Don't," said Harper; "they're nice people, they are—but they all think the New Testament was written in English, and it would only unsettle their minds and throw them into horrid perplexities to be undeceived; they do very well as they are—let 'em alone."

DECEMBER 23, 1845

Well, last night I spent . . . at Mrs. Mary Jones's great ball. Very splendid affair—"the ball of the season," I heard divers bipeds more or less asinine observe in regard to it. Two houses open—standing supper table—"dazzling array of beauty and fashions." Polka for the first time brought under my inspection. It's a kind of insane Tartar jig performed to a disagreeable music of an uncivilized character. Everybody was there and I loafed about in a most independent manner and found it less of a bore than I had expected. Mrs. Jones, the hostess, is fat but comely; indeed, there's enough of her to supply a small settlement with wives. . . .

MAY 11, 1849

Row last night at the Opera House, whereof I was a spectator. Mob fired upon, some twelve or fifteen killed and four times as many wounded, a real battle, for the b'hoys fought well and charged up to the line of infantry after they had been fired upon. Prospect of a repetition of the performances tonight on a larger scale, for the blackguards swear they'll have vengeance. The houses of the gentlemen who signed the invitation to Macready to perform last night threatened.

JUNE 15, 1849

There's that prodigious Twenty-first Street house staring me in the face, and saying from every one of its drawing rooms and boudoirs: "We shall have to be furnished next fall." . . .

It's a terrible daily source of anxiety and depression. . . . Ruskin is right—no man's happiness was ever promoted by the splendors of rosewood and brocatelle and ormolu and tapestry carpets; they never give pleasure to their possessor or to those who come and see them. . . . It is a slavery to which we submit in the meekest silence, though it darkens life with needless cares and shuts us out from other and real enjoyments that might be purchased with the wasted cost of this pernicious trumpery. . . .

JULY 31, 1849

A terrible business will be the tottle of the bills growing out of that charming specimen of domestic architecture. The primal curse that condemned man to earn his bread by the sweat of his brow was heavy, but far heavier is the curse that man has laid upon himself by the artificial habits and conventional necessities and social fictions of the system of luxury and extravagance and ostentation to which he has bound himself in these latter days. Toil and labor may be happiness; they are so to a healthy mind; but there never is aught but wretchedness in the bitter, corrosive cares and sickening anxieties of debt, of position too expensive for the real abilities of its occupant.

JULY 11, 1850

The President died at half-past ten Tuesday evening. A very unhappy event, not only because he was a good and upright man, such as is uncommon in high office, but because everybody North and South had a vague sort of implicit confidence in him, which would have enabled him to guide us through our present complications much better than his "accidental" successor, of whom nobody knows much, and in whom no party puts any very special trust or faith.

SEPTEMBER 2, 1850

Jenny Lind has arrived, and was received with such a spontaneous outbreak of rushing, and crowding, and hurrahing, and serenading as this city has never seen before. The streets round the Irving House blocked up with a mob night and day; horses hardly permitted to carry her through the streets, so vehemently did the mob thirst for the honor of drawing her carriage, and so on. Really it's very strange—Miss Jenny is a young lady of very great musical taste, and possessed of a larynx so delicately organized that she can go up to A *in alto* with brilliancy and precision, and sing with more effect than any other living performer. Furthermore, she is a good, amiable, benevolent woman, fully equal, I dare say, to the average of our New York girls; and having in her vocal apparatus a fortune of millions, she devotes a liberal share of it to works of charity. But if the greatest man that has lived for the last ten centuries were here in her place, the uproar and excitement could not be much greater and would probably be much less. . . .

JANUARY 8, 1851

Henry Long, the interesting black representative of the Rights of Man, adjudged this morning to be lawfully held to service and delivered up to the Philistines of Virginia, notwithstanding the rhetoric of John Jay. . . .

JANUARY 16, 1851

Bad accident in this street between Fifth and Sixth Avenues yesterday. The houses Tom Emmet and Ferris Pell (or rather his widow) were putting up and on which the Bank has a rather large loan, tumbled down spontaneously, killing or mangling and mutilating some two dozen people. Cause, the criminal economy of the contractor. Saw some of the *mortar*, a greasy, pulverulent earth or clay, apparently far less tenacious than an average specimen of Broadway mud. The contractor, who certified to the sufficiency of his work three hours before the crash, has discreetly run away.

MAY 27, 1851

Tremendous row at Hoboken yesterday; a battle of the peoples, like Leipzig. German loaferism warring with the Aaron Burrs of New York, the gutterborn soaplocks and shortboys of the wharves and their Irish allies. Some lives lost, and strong possibility that the fight may be renewed here.

Mr. Ruggles's affairs worse and worse and worse and worse, and as he falls he will propagate ruin and spread desolation and devastation around him. I wish some new nineteenth century saint would arise and preach a curse upon all credit systems, a crusade against negotiable paper, and proclaim all the woes of the Apocalyptic Babylon against that complex work of devilish ingenuity whereby ruin, bankruptcy, and dishonor are made so fearfully familiar to this enlightened age; the system that makes the utmost fruit of steady industry vulgar and cheap when compared with the glittering results that form exceptions only to its legitimate and usual result, but yet occur often enough to lure the multitude and make us a nation of gamblers, easily classified as a minority of millionaires sprinkled through a majority of bankrupt beggars.

God deliver me from *debt!* Yet the insolvent debtor, I suppose, cares but little for the incubus, as a general rule, after he has become resigned to the conviction that it can't be thrown off, and that he must live under it as he best may. That is the worst of our wretched "financial" system. It degrades, debases, demoralizes its victims. They look men in the face whom they have ruined by breaking their promises, and have nothing to say but that it was a "business transaction." It dissolves out all the sterling integrity there may be in the great mass of people, and leaves the dross and dirt behind. . . .

JULY 7, 1851

Talk of the ennobling pursuits of literature, historic research, art, music, the elevating influence of investigations into natural science, the noble object of reviving a fit and reverent style of church architecture, and the other subjects which the better class of cultivated men select as their business or their relaxation—they are all good. But . . . it strikes me that most "liberal pursuits," no matter how purifying to the tastes and invigorating to the intellect, are something like a wretched waste of time and perversion of talent and an insane misapplication of energy and industry, while men and women and children in multiplying thousands lie rotting alive, body and soul at once, in those awful catacombs of disease and crime, and even the question how to save them is yet unsolved.

We have our Five Points, our emigrant quarters, our swarms of seamstresses to whom their utmost toil in monotonous daily drudgery gives only bare subsistence, a life barren of hope and of enjoyment; our hordes of dock thieves, and of children who live in the streets and by them. No one can walk the length of Broadway without meeting some hideous troop of ragged girls, from twelve years old down, brutalized already almost beyond redemption by premature vice, clad in the filthy refuse of the rag-picker's collections, obscene of speech, the stamp of childhood gone from their faces, hurrying along with harsh laughter and foulness on their lips that some of them have learned by rote, yet too young to understand it; with thief written in their cunning eyes and whore on their depraved faces, though so unnatural, foul, and repulsive in every look and gesture, that that last profession seems utterly beyond their aspirations. On a rainy day such crews may be seen by dozens. They haunt every other crossing and skulk away together, when the sun comes out and the mud is dry again. And such a group I think the most revolting object that the social diseases of a great city can produce. A gang of blackguard boys is lovely by the side of it.

Meantime, philanthropists are scolding about the fugitive slave law, or shedding tears over the wretched niggers of the Carolinas who have to work and to eat their victuals on principles inconsistent with the rights of man, or agitating because the unhanged scoundrels in the City Prison occupy cells imperfectly ventilated. "Scholars" are laboriously writing dissertations for the Historical Society on the First Settlement of the Township of Squankum. . . . And what am I doing, I wonder? I'm neither scholar nor philanthropist nor clergyman, nor in any capacity a guide or ruler of the people, to be sure—there is that shadow of an apology for my sitting still. But if Heaven will permit and enable me, I'll do something in the matter before I die—to have helped one dirty vagabond child out of such a pestilential sink would be a thing one would not regret when one came to march out of this world—and if one looks at FACTS, would be rather more of an achievement than the writing another *Iliad*. . . .

July 29, 1852

Heard that the *Henry Clay* had been burnt. . . .

The loss of life seems to have been fearful, and the transaction a case of wholesale murder. Reckless racing leading to mischief, and then panic and frenzy among the passengers, imbecility in the officers, and murderous absence even of *boats* to save a dozen or two.

July 30

Went up by railroad last night. The funeral took place this morning, attended by nearly every one on the Point; a melancholy business it was. I shall never forget poor Bailey's figure, and look of apathy—almost of stupor; and the three little boys clinging round him and crying, unnoticed; the still sunlight on the cemetery, the burial service, the multitude of sad faces, the two coffins with which we all felt that all the life and hope and heart of one man were sinking into the earth to wither into dust. And all this and so much beside, *that the Henry Clay might beat the Armenia.*

It is time that this drowning and burning to death of babies and young girls and old men to gratify the vanity of steamboat captains were stopped. I would thank God for the privilege of pulling the cap over the eyes of the captain and owners of this boat, and feel as I completed my hangman's office that I had not lived utterly in vain. . . .

The scene at the wreck yesterday morning was hideous: near thirty bodies exposed along the shore—many children among them.

And some enterprising undertakers from Yonkers and New York had sent up their stock of coffins on speculation.

"Looking for deceased friend, sir?" "Buying a coffin, sir?" "Only five dollars, sir, and warranted."

Public feeling is very strong now. But it will die out within the week. These scoundrels will never be punished, not even indicted. *Damn them!* No, I retract that, for God knows we all stand in need of something less than the rigor of justice. But a thousand years or so of fire and brimstone after hanging in this world, would be a moderate award of retribution. . . .

FEBRUARY 16, 1853

Visit from Edward A. Strong this morning, discussing the drunkenness, whoremongering, insubordination, and total worthlessness of poor Bob [Strong], and with much feeling and distress. Poor Bob!—and poor young America generally, from Jem Pendleton and the "Pup-Club" down. Was there ever among the boys of any city so much gross dissipation redeemed by so little culture and so little manliness and audacity even of the watchman-fighting sort? It has grown to be very bad, the tone of morals and manners has, even among the better class of young men about town.

MARCH 11, 1853

Stocks down. Wonder whether I'd better invest some loose savings in another Erie bond at present prices, or wait for a farther depression? Alas, alas, alas, for all the dreams of former times, the dreams to which this journal bears witness! Is it the doom of all men in this nineteenth century to be weighed down with the incumbrance of a desire to make money and save money, all their days? I suppose if my career is prosperous, it will be spent in the thoughtful, diligent accumulation of dollars, till I suddenly wake up to the sense that the career is ended and the dollars dross. So are we gradually carried into the social currents that belong to our time, whether it be the tenth century, or this cold-blooded, interest-calculating age of our own. . . .

MAY 7, 1853

Another murderous *noyade* on the New Haven Railroad yesterday. More than fifty lives lost; a car full of people pitched over an open draw into the Norwalk River, as a trap with its rats is soused into a wash-tub, by the brute stolidity of the engineer, who didn't see the appointed signal that told him to pull up. Or quite as truly by the guilty negligence of the directors who reappointed this man after he'd been dismissed two years ago for causing an accident by some piece of gross recklessness. What is to be done? . . . I should have thought the surviving passengers and the good people of Norwalk far from clearly unjustifiable in this case had they administered Lynch Law to the criminal on the spot. . . .

JULY 6, 1854

Wall Street all agog with the fraud on the New Haven Railroad Company by its President Robert Schuyler, whose failure was announced last week. A swindle of near two millions, by no nameless money-making speculator, but by one of our "first" people in descent and social position and supposed wealth. . . .

MAY 28, 1856

Never was the country in such a crazy state as just now. Civil war impending over Kansas. . . . I believe civilization at the South is retrograde and that the Carolinas are decaying into barbarism. Brooks comes on Sumner at his desk unawares, stuns him with a cudgel, and belabors the prostrate orator till the cudgel breaks and splinters, and Southern editors and Congressmen talk about the "chivalry," "gallantry," and manliness of the act, and they're getting up a testimonial for Brooks in Charleston.

MAY 29, 1856

No new vagaries from the wild men of the South since yesterday. The South is to the North nearly what the savage Gaelic race of the Highlands was to London *tempore* William and Mary, *vide* Macaulay's third volume; except that they've assumed to rule their civilized neighbors instead of being oppressed by them, and that the simple, barbaric virtues of their low social development have been thereby deteriorated.

A few fine specimens have given them a prestige the class don't deserve. We at the North are a busy money-making democracy, comparatively law-abiding and peace-loving, with the faults (among others) appropriate to traders and workers. A rich Southern aristocrat who happens to be of fine nature, with the self-reliance and high tone that life among an aristocracy favors, and culture and polish from books and travel, strikes us (not as Brooks struck Sumner but) as something different from ourselves, more ornamental and in some respects better. He has the polish of a highly civilized society, with the qualities that belong to a ruler of serfs. Thus a notion has got footing here that "Southern gentlemen" are a high-bred chivalric aristocracy, something like Louis XIV's noblesse, with grave faults, to be sure, but on the whole, very gallant and generous, regulating themselves by "codes of honor" (that are *wrong*, of course, but very grand); not rich, but surrounded by all the elements of real refinement. Whereas I believe they are, in fact, a race of lazy, ignorant, coarse, sensual, swaggering, sordid, beggarly barbarians, bullying white men and breeding little niggers for sale.

MAY 30, 1856

On my way up at eight, I stopped at the Tabernacle, where the citizens of New York were summoned to meet and declare their sentiments about Sumner and the South. A vast crowd, earnest, unanimous, and made up of people who don't often attend political gatherings. Significant that John A. Stevens called the meeting to order and old Griswold presided; men not given to fits of enthusiasm or generous sympathy, unlike to be prominent in anything wherein the general voice of the community does not sustain them. Evarts read the resolutions, which seemed discreetly framed and not intemperate. The meeting was prepared to swallow much stronger language. The roar of the great assemblage when Sumner's name occurred, and its spontaneous outburst of groaning and hissing at the sound of "Preston S. Brooks" impressed me. They seemed expressions of deep and strong feeling. I guess the North is roused at last.

from THE DIARY OF
MARY BOYKIN CHESNUT

FEBRUARY 15TH, 1861

I came to Charleston on November 7th and then went to Florida to see my mother. On the train, just before we reached Fernandina, a woman called out: "That settles the hash!" Tanny touched me on the shoulder and said: "Lincoln's elected." "How do you know?" "The man over there has a telegram." Someone cried: "Now that the black radical Republicans have the power I suppose they will Brown us all."

I have always kept a journal, with notes and dates and a line of poetry or prose, but from today forward I will write more. I now wish I had a chronicle of the two delightful and eventful years that have just passed. Those delights have fled, and one's breath is taken away to think what events have since crowded in. . . .

It is hard for me to believe these people are in earnest. They are not putting the young, active, efficient, in place anywhere. Whenever there is an election, they hunt up some old fossil who was ages ago laid on the shelf. There never was such a resurrection of the dead and forgotten. This does not look like business. My first doubts came when I saw who were elected to any office and that efficiency was never thought of but political maneuvering still ruled. My father was a South Carolina nullifier, Governor of the state at the time of the nullification row, and then United States Senator; so I was of necessity a rebel born. My husband's family being equally pledged to the Union Party rather exasperated my zeal. Yet I felt a nervous dread and horror of this break with so great a power as the United States, but I was ready and willing. South Carolina had been rampant for years. She was the torment of herself and everybody else. Nobody could live in this state unless he were a fire-eater. Come what would, I wanted them to fight and stop talking. South Carolinians had exasperated and heated themselves into a fever that only bloodletting could ever cure. It was the inevitable remedy. So I was a seceder. . . .

I wonder if it be a sin to think slavery a curse to any land. Men and women are punished when their masters and mistresses are brutes, not when they do wrong. Under slavery, we live surrounded by prostitutes, yet an abandoned woman is sent out of any decent house. Who thinks any worse of a Negro or mulatto woman for being a thing we can't name? God forgive us, but ours is a monstrous system, a wrong and an iniquity! Like the patriarchs of old, our men live all in one house with their wives and their concubines; and the mulattoes one sees in every family partly resemble the white children. Any lady is ready to tell you who is the father of all the mulatto children in everybody's household but her own. Those, she seems to think, drop from the clouds. My disgust sometimes is boiling over. Thank God for my country women, but alas for the men! They are probably no worse than men everywhere, but the lower their mistresses, the more degraded they must be.

I think this journal will be disadvantageous for me, for I spend my time now like a spider spinning my own entrails, instead of reading as my habit was in all spare moments.

APRIL 13TH

. . . Fort Sumter has been on fire. He has not yet silenced any of our guns or so the aids—still with swords and red sashes by way of uniform—tell us. But the sound of those guns makes regular meals impossible. None of us go to table, but tea trays pervade the corridors going everywhere. Some of the anxious hearts lie on their beds and moan in solitary misery. Mrs. Wigfall and I solace ourselves with tea in my room. These women have all a satisfying faith. "God is on our side," they cry. When we are shut in, we, Mrs. Wigfall and I, ask: "Why?" Answer: "Of course, He hates the Yankees! You'll think that well of Him."

Not by one word or look can we detect any change in the demeanor of these Negro servants. Lawrence sits at our door, as sleepy and as respectful and as profoundly indifferent. So are they all. They carry it too far. You could not tell that they even hear the awful noise that is going on in the bay, though it is dinning in their ears night and day. And people talk before them as if they were chairs and tables, and they make no sign. Are they stolidly stupid, or wiser than we are, silent and biding their time.

APRIL 16TH

. . . So Maria Whitaker came, all in tears. She brushes hair delightfully, and as she stood at my back I could see her face in the glass. "Maria, are you crying because all this war talk scares you?" said I. "No ma'am." "What is the matter with you?" . . .

And then came the story of her troubles. "Now Miss Mary, you see me married to Jeems Whitaker yourself. I was a good and faithful wife to him, and we were comfortable every way, good house, everything. He had no cause of complaint. But he has left me." "For Heaven's sake! Why?" "Because I had twins. He says they are not his, because nobody named Whitaker ever had twins."

Maria is proud in her way, and the behavior of this bad husband has nearly mortified her to death. She has had three children in two years. No wonder the man was frightened! But then Maria does not depend on him for anything. . . .

Bad books are not allowed house room except in the library and under lock and key, the key in the Master's pocket; but bad women, if they are not white and serve in a menial capacity, may swarm the house unmolested. The ostrich game is thought a Christian act. These women are no more regarded as a dangerous contingent than canary birds would be.

If you show by a chance remark that you see that some particular creature more shameless than the rest has no end of children and no beginning of a husband, you are frowned down. You are talking on improper subjects. There are certain subjects pure-minded ladies never touch upon, even in their thoughts.

JULY 4TH

Russell abuses us in his letters from New Orleans. People here care a great deal for what Russell says because he "represents the Times," and the London Times reflects the sentiment of the English people. How we do cling to the idea of an alliance with England or France. Without France, even Washington could not have done it. Somebody said today: "Is not the South as much our country, and as able to declare its independence, as the colonies? We were not even Colonies from New England." "Might makes right" was the answer. . . .

Dr. Gibbes says he was at a country house near Manassas when a Federal soldier who had lost his way came in exhausted. He asked for brandy, which the lady of the house gave him. Upon second thought he declined it; she brought it to him so promptly, he said, he thought it might be poisoned. Certainly, his mind was! She, naturally, was enraged. "Sir, I am a Virginia woman. Do you think I could be as base as that? Here Tom! Bill! Disarm this man! He is our prisoner." The Negroes came running, and the man surrendered without more ado. Another Federal was drinking at the well. A Negro girl said: "You go in and see Missus." The man went in, and she followed crying triumphantly: "Look here, Missus, I got a prisoner too!" The Negroes were not ripe for John Brown, you see. This lady sent in her two prisoners, and Beauregard complimented her on her pluck and patriotism and presence of mind.

These Negroes were rewarded by their owners. Now if slavery is as disagreeable as we think it, why don't they all march over the border where they would be received with open arms. It amazes me. I am always studying these creatures. They are to me inscrutable in their ways, and past finding out.

Dr. Gibbes says the faces of the dead on the battlefield have grown as black as charcoal, and they shine in the sun. Now this horrible vision of the dead on the battlefield haunts me.

AUGUST 27TH

. . .Today I saw a letter from a girl crossed in love. Her parents object to the social position of her fiancé; in point of fact, they forbid the banns. She writes: "I am misserable." Her sister she calls a "mean retch." For such a speller, a man of any social status would do. They ought not to expect so much for her. If she wrote her "pah" a note I am sure that "stern parient" would give in.

I am miserable too today, but with one "s." The North is consolidated. They move as one man, with no states but with the army organized by the central power. . . .

Negro women are married, and after marriage behave as well as other people. Marrying is the amusement of their life. They take life easily. So do their class everywhere. Bad men are hated here as elsewhere.

I hate slavery. You say there are no more fallen women on a plantation than in London, in proportion to numbers; but what do you say to this? A magnate who runs a hideous black harem with its consequences under the same roof with his lovely white wife, and his beautiful and accomplished daughters? He holds his head as high and poses as the model of all human virtues to these poor women whom God and the laws have given him. From the height of his awful majesty, he scolds and thunders at them, as if he never did wrong in his life. Fancy such a man finding his daughter reading "Don Juan." "You with that immoral book!" And he orders her out of his sight. You see, Mrs. Stowe did not hit the sorest spot. She makes Legree a bachelor.

Someone said: "Oh, I know half a Legree, a man said to be as cruel as Legree. But the other half of him did not correspond. He was a man of polished manners, and the best husband and father and churchmember in the world." "Can that be so?" "Yes, I know it. And I knew the dissolute half of Legree. He was high and mighty, but the kindest creature to his slaves; and the unfortunate results of his bad ways were not sold. They had not to jump over ice blocks. They were kept in full view, and were provided for, handsomely, in his will. His wife and daughters, in their purity and innocence, are supposed never to dream of what is as plain before their eyes as the sunlight. And they play their parts of unsuspecting angels to the letter. They profess to adore their father as the model of all earthly goodness."

"Well, yes. If he is rich, he is the fountain from whence all bessings flow."

September 6th

. . . In Missouri, Ben McCulloch caught a Dutch parson in the act of making some men take the oath of allegiance to the Union. He ordered him "to take his Bible again in his hand and unswear them as quick as possible!" It is encouraging when one hears of a piece of fun, however broad. If one can afford to laugh, things are mending. . . .

September 18th

. . . We had actually a reception, six men and a boy. Two of the interesting creatures came to ask for overseers' places, and sat for hours. One of the men was Jackson Revel, a sandhill neighbour from his youth upwards. The young ladies of this house taught him to read, and his son is named for my husband. Oh, the leisure these people have! Some of these stupid, slow, heavy-headed louts sat from twelve o'clock till five; and Mr. Chesnut would never have forgiven me if I had shown impatience. The boy came to beg, while his mother and sisters sat at the gate. Mr. Chesnut was in imminent danger of going mad, but they sat steadfast. All remained to dinner, boy included, even though he knew his family waited all day at the gate.

SEPTEMBER 19TH

. . . A painful piece of news came to us yesterday. Our cousin, Mrs. Witherspoon of Society Hill, was found dead in her bed. She was quite well the night before. Killed, people say, by family troubles; by contentions, wrangling, ill blood among those nearest and dearest to her. She was a proud and high-strung woman, of a warm and tender heart, truth and uprightness itself. Few persons have ever been more loved and looked up to. A very handsome old lady, of fine presence, dignified and commanding. "Killed by family troubles!" So they said when Mr. John N. Williams died, so Uncle John said yesterday of his brother Burwell. "Death deserts the army," said that quaint old soul, "and takes fancy shots of the most eccentric kind nearer home."

The high and disinterested conduct our enemies seem to expect of us is involuntary and unconscious praise. They pay us the compliment to look for from us— and execrate us for the want of it— a degree of virtue they were never able to practice themselves. They say our crowning misdemeanour is to hold in slavery still those Africans they brought over here from Africa, or sold to us when they found to own them did not pay. They gradually slid them off down here, giving themselves years to get rid of them in a remunerative way. We want to spread them too, west and south, or northwest, where the climate would free them or kill them; would improve them out of the world as the Yankees do Indians. If they had been forced to keep them in New England, I dare say they would have shared the Indians' fate; for they are wise in their generation, these Yankee children of light. Those pernicious Africans!

SEPTEMBER 21ST

Last night when the mail came in, I was seated near the lamp. Mr. Chesnut, lying on a sofa at a little distance, called out to me: "Look at my letters and tell me whom they are from?" I began to read one of them aloud. It was from Mary Witherspoon, and I broke down; horror and amazement was too much for me. Poor cousin Betsey Witherspoon was murdered! She did not die peacefully in her bed, as we supposed, but was murdered by her own people, her Negroes. I remember when Dr. Keith was murdered by his Negroes, Mr. Miles met me and told me the dreadful story. "Very awkward indeed, this sort of thing. There goes Keith in the House always declaiming about the 'Benificent Institution'—How now?" Horrible beyond words! Her household Negroes were so insolent, so pampered, and insubordinate. She lived alone. She knew, she said, that none of her children would have the patience she had with these people who had been indulged and spoiled by her until they were like spoiled children, simply intolerable. . . .

SEPTEMBER 24TH

The men who went to Society Hill (the Witherspoon home) have come home again with nothing very definite. William and Cousin Betsey's old maid, Rhody, are in jail; strong suspicion but as yet no proof of their guilt. The neighborhood is in a ferment. Evans and Wallace say these Negroes ought to be burnt. Lynching proposed! But it is all idle talk. They will be tried as the law directs, and not otherwise. John Witherspoon will not allow anything wrong or violent to be done. He has a detective there from Charleston.

Hitherto I have never thought of being afraid of Negroes. I had never injured any of them; why should they want to hurt me? Two thirds of my religion consists in trying to be good to Negroes, because they are so in our power, and it would be so easy to be the other thing. Somehow today I feel that the ground is cut away from under my feet. Why should they treat me any better than they have done Cousin Betsey Witherspoon?

Kate and I sat up late and talked it all over. Mrs. Witherspoon was a saint on this earth, and this is her reward. Kate's maid Betsey came in—a strong-built, mulatto woman—dragging in a mattress. "Missis, I have brought my bed to sleep in your room while Mars' David is at Society Hill. You ought not to stay in a room by yourself these times." She went off for more bed gear. "For the life of me," said Kate gravely, "I cannot make up my mind. Does she mean to take care of me, or to murder me?" I do not think Betsey heard, but when she came back she said: "Missis, as I have a soul to be saved, I will keep you safe. I will guard you." We know Betsey well, but has she soul enough to swear by? She is a great stout, jolly, irresponsible, unreliable, pleasant-tempered, bad-behaved woman, with ever so many good points. Among others, she is so clever she can do anything, and she never loses her temper; but she has no moral sense whatever.

That night, Kate came into my room. She could not sleep. The thought of those black hands strangling and smothering Mrs. Witherspoon's grey head under the counterpane haunted her; we sat up and talked the long night through. . . .

Went over just now to have a talk with that optimist, my mother-in-law. Blessed are the pure in mind, for they shall see God. Her mind certainly is free from evil thoughts. Someone says, the most unhappy person is the one who has bad thoughts. She ought to be happy. She thinks no evil. And yet, she is the cleverest woman I know. She began to ask me something of Charlotte Temple (I call her this to keep back her true name). "Has she ever had any more children?" "She has one more." "Is she married?" "No." "Is she a bad girl, really?" "Yes." "Oh! Don't say that. Poor thing! Maybe after all she is not really bad, only to be pitied!" I gave it up. I felt like a fool. Here was one thing I had made sure of as a fixed fact. In this world, an unmarried girl with two children was, necessarily, not a good woman. If that can be waved aside, I give up, in utter confusion of mind. Ever since she came here sixty or seventy years ago, as a bride from Philadelphia, Mrs. Chesnut has been trying to make it up to the Negroes for being slaves. . . .

Mrs. Chesnut has a greediness of books such as I never saw in anyone else. Reading is the real occupation and solace of her life. In the soft luxurious life she leads, she denies herself nothing that she wants. In her well-regulated character she could not want anything that she ought not to have. Economy is one of her cherished virtues, and strange to say she never buys a book, or has been known to take a magazine or periodical; she has them all. They gravitate toward her, they flow into her room. Everybody is proud to send, or lend, any book they have compassed by any means, fair or foul. Other members of the family who care nothing whatever for them buy the books and she reads them.

She spends hours every day cutting out baby clothes for the Negro babies. This department is under her supervision. She puts little bundles of things to be made in everybody's work basket and calls it her sewing society. She is always ready with an ample wardrobe for every newcomer. Then the mothers bring their children for her to prescribe and look after whenever they are ailing. She is not at all nervous. She takes a baby and lances its gums quite coolly and scientifically. She dresses all hurts, bandages all wounds. These people are simply devoted to her, proving they can be grateful enough when you give them anything to be grateful for. . . .

One begins to understand the power which the ability to vote gives the meanest citizen. We went to one of Uncle Hamilton's splendid dinners, plate, glass, china and everything that was nice to eat. In the piazza, when the gentlemen were smoking after dinner, in the midst of them sat Squire MacDonald, the well-digger. . . . Said Louisa—"Look, the mud from the well is sticking through his toes! See how solemnly polite and attentive Mr. Chesnut is to him!" "Oh that's his way. The raggeder and more squalid the creature, the more polite and the softer Mr. Chesnut grows."

OCTOBER 7TH

. . . An appalling list of foreigners in the Yankee army, just as I feared; a rush of all Europe to them, as soon as they raised the cry that this war is for the extirpation of slavery. If our people had read less of Mr. Calhoun's works, and only read the signs of the times a little more; if they had known more of what was going on around them in the world.

And now comes back on us that bloody story that haunts me night and day, Mrs. Witherspoon's murder. The man William, who was the master spirit of the gang, once ran away and was brought back from somewhere west; and then his master and himself had a reconciliation and the master henceforth made a pet of him. The night preceding the murder, John Witherspoon went over to his mother's to tell her of some of William's and Rhody's misdeeds. While their mistress was away from home, they had given a ball fifteen miles away from Society Hill. To that place they had taken their mistress's china, silver, house linen, etc. After his conversation with his mother, as he rode out of the gate, he shook his whip at William and said: "Tomorrow I mean to come here and give every one of you a thrashing." That night Mrs. Witherspoon was talking it all over with her grandson, a half-grown boy who lived with her and slept indeed in a room opening into hers. "I do not intend John to punish these Negroes. It is too late to begin discipline now. I have indulged them past bearing. They all say I ought to have tried to control them, that it is all my fault." Mrs. Edwards, who was a sister of Mrs. Witherspoon, sometime ago was found dead in her bed. It is thought this suggested their plan of action to the Negroes. What more likely than she should die as her sister had done! When John went off, William said: "Listen to me and there will be no punishment here tomorrow." They made their plan, and then all of them went to sleep, William remaining awake to stir up the others at the proper hour.

What first attracted the attention of the family to the truth about her death was the appearance of black and blue spots about the face and neck of the body of their mother. Then someone, in moving the candle from the table at her bedside, found blood upon their fingers. Looking at the candlestick, they saw the print of a bloody hand which had held it. There was an empty bed in the entry, temporarily there for some purpose, and as they were preparing to lay her out, someone took up the counterpane from this bed to throw over her. On the under side of it, again, bloody fingers. Now they were fairly aroused. Rhody was helping Mary Witherspoon, a little apart from the rest. Mary cried: "I wish they would not say such horrid things. Poor soul, she died in peace with all the world. It is bad enough to find her dead, but nobody ever touched a hair of her head. To think any mortal could murder her. Never! I will not believe it!" To Mary's amazement, Rhody drew near her and, looking strangely in her eyes, she said: "Miss Mary, you stick to dat! You stick to dat!" Mary thrilled all over with suspicion and dread.

There was a trunk in Mrs. Witherspoon's closet where she kept money and a complete outfit ready for travelling at any moment; among other things, some new and very fine night gowns. One of her daughters noticed that her mother must have opened that trunk, for she was wearing one of those night gowns. They then looked into the closet and found the trunk unlocked and all the gold gone. The daughters knew the number of gold pieces she always kept under lock and key in that trunk. Now they began to scent mischief and foul play in earnest, and they sent for the detective.

The detective dropped in from the skies quite unexpectedly. He saw that one of the young understrappers of the gang looked frightened and uncomfortable. This one he fastened upon, and got up quite an intimacy with him; and finally, he told this boy that he knew all about it, that William had confessed privately to him to save himself and hang the others. But he said he had taken a fancy to this boy, and if he would confess everything, he would take him as State's evidence instead of William. The young man fell in the trap laid for him and told every particular from beginning to end. Then they were all put in jail, the youth who had confessed among them, as he did not wish them to know of his treachery to them.

This was his story. After John went away that night, Rhody and William made a great fuss. They were furious at Mars' John threatening them after all these years. William said: "Mars' John more than apt to do what he say he will do, but you all follow what I say and he'll have something else to think of beside stealing and breaking glass and china. If ole Marster was alive now, what would he say to talk of whipping us!" Rhody always kept the key to the house to let herself in every morning, so they arranged to go in at twelve, and then William watched and the others slept the sleep of the righteous. Before that, however, they had a "real fine supper and a heap of laughing at the way dey'd all look tomorrow." They smothered her with a counterpane from a bed in the entry. They had no trouble the first time, because they found her asleep and "done it all 'fore she waked." But after Rhody took her keys and went into the trunk and got a clean night gown—for they had spoiled the one she had on—and fixed everything, candle, medicine and all, she came to! Then she begged them hard for life. She asked them what she had ever done that they should want to kill her? She promised them before God never to tell on them. Nobody should ever know! But Rhody stopped her mouth with the counterpane, and William held her head and hands down, and the other two sat on her legs. Rhody had a thrifty mind and wished to save the sheets and night gown, so she did not destroy them. They were found behind her mantelpiece. There the money was also, all in a hole made among the bricks behind the wooden mantelpiece. A grandson of Rhody's slept in her house. Him she locked up in his room. She did not want him to know anything of this fearful night.

That innocent old lady and her grey hair moved them not a jot. Fancy how we feel. I am sure I will never sleep again without this nightmare of horror haunting me.

Mrs. Chesnut, who is their good angel, is and has always been afraid of Negroes. In her youth, the San Domingo stories were indelibly printed on her mind. She shows her dread now by treating every one as if they were a black Prince Albert or Queen Victoria. We were beginning to forget Mrs. Cunningham, the only other woman we ever heard of who was murdered by her Negroes. Poor cousin Betsey was goodness itself. After years of freedom and indulgence and tender kindness, it was an awful mistake to threaten them like children. It was only threats. Everybody knew she would never do anything. Mr. Cunningham had been an old bachelor, and the Negroes had it their own way till he married. Then they hated her. They took her from her room, just over one in which her son-in-law and her daughter slept. They smothered her, dressed her, and carried her out—all without the slightest noise—and hung her by the neck to an apple tree, as if she had committed suicide. If they want to kill us, they can do it when they please, they are noiseless as panthers. They were discovered because, dressing her in the dark, her tippet was put on hindpart before, and she was supposed to have walked out and hung herself in a pair of brand new shoes whose soles obviously had never touched the ground.

We ought to be grateful that anyone of us is alive, but nobody is afraid of their own Negroes.

OCTOBER 13TH

Mulberry. We went in the afternoon to the Negro church on the plantation. Manning Brown, a Methodist minister, preached to a very large black congregation. Though glossy black, they were well dressed and were very stylishly gotten up. They were stout, comfortable looking Christians.... Manning Brown preached Hell fire so hot, I felt singed, if not parboiled. . . .

Jim Nelson, the driver, the stateliest darky I ever saw, tall and straight as a pine tree, with a fine face, and not so very black but a full-blooded African, was asked to lead in prayer. He became wildly excited, on his knees, facing us with his eyes shut. He clapped his hands at the end of every sentence, and his voice rose to the pitch of a shrill shriek, yet was strangely clear and musical, occasionally in a plaintive minor key that went to your heart. Sometimes it rang out like a trumpet. I wept bitterly. It was all sound, however, and emotional pathos. There was literally nothing in what he said. The words had no meaning at all. It was the devotional passion of voice and manner which was so magnetic. The Negroes sobbed and shouted and swayed backward and forward, some with aprons to their eyes, most of them clapping their hands and responding in shrill tones: "Yes, God!" "Jesus!" "Savior!" "Bless de Lord, amen," etc. It was a little too exciting for me. I would very much have liked to shout, too. . . .

Now all this leaves not a trace behind. Jim Nelson is a good man, honest and true; but those who stole before, steal on, in spite of sobs and shouts on Sunday. Those who drink, continue to drink when they can get it. Except that for any open, detected sin they are turned out of church. A Methodist parson is no mealy-mouth creature.

OCTOBER 18TH

Mrs. Witherspoon's death has clearly driven us all wild. Mrs. Chesnut, although she talks admirably well and is a wonderfully clever woman, bored me by incessantly dwelling upon the transcendant virtues of her colored household, in full hearing of the innumerable Negro women who literally swarm over this house. She takes her meals in her own rooms, but today came in while we were at dinner. "I warn you, don't touch that soup! It is bitter. There is something wrong about it!" The family answered her pleasantly, but continued calmly to eat their soup. The men who waited at table looked on without change of face. . . .

NOVEMBER 11TH

Yesterday Mr. John DeSaussure came, absolutely a lunatic, his preposterous and ill-timed gayety all gone. He was in a state of abject fright because the Negroes show such exultation at the enemy's making good their entrance at Port Royal. I cannot see any change in them, myself; their faces are as unreadable as the Sphinx. Certainly they are unchanged in their good conduct. That is, they are placid, docile, kind and obedient—and as lazy and dirty as ever. . . .

NOVEMBER 12TH

. . . Minnie F. says they are hanging Negroes in Louisiana and Mississippi like birds in the trees, for an attempted insurrection; but out there they say the same thing of South Carolina, and we know it is as quiet as the grave here, and as peaceful. We have no reason to suppose a Negro knows there is a war. I do not speak of the war to them; on that subject, they do not believe a word you say. A genuine slave owner, born and bred, will not be afraid of Negroes. Here we are mild as the moonbeams, and as serene; nothing but Negroes around us, white men all gone to the army. Mrs. Reynolds and Mrs. Withers, two of the very kindest and most considerate of slave owners, aver that the joy of their Negroes at the fall of Port Royal is loud and open; but there is no change of any kind whatever with ours. . . .

Mrs. Reynolds's conversation with her jet-black butler, Ammon. "Missis, at Beaufort they are burning the cotton and killing the Negroes. They do not mean the Yankees to have cotton or Negroes." She tried to make him understand, in vain: "Would I kill you, or let anybody

else kill you? You know nobody kills Negroes here. Why will you believe they do it there?" "We know you won't own up to anything
against your side. You never tell us anything that you can help." Ammon has been that nuisance, a pampered menial, for twenty years. . . .

NOVEMBER 28TH.

"Ye who listen with credulity to the whispers of fancy"—pause, and
look on this picture and that.

On one side Mrs. Stowe, Greeley, Thoreau, Emerson, Sumner. They
live in nice New England homes, clean, sweet-smelling, shut up in libraries, writing books which ease their hearts of their bitterness against
us. What self-denial they do practice is to tell John Brown to come down
here and cut our throats in Christ's name. Now consider what I have
seen of my mother's life, my grandmother's, my mother-in-law's.
These people were educated at Northern schools, they read the same
books as their Northern contemporaries, the same daily papers, the
same Bible. They have the same ideas of right and wrong, are
high-bred, lovely, good, pious, doing their duty as they conceive it.
They live in Negro villages. They do not preach and teach hate as a
gospel, and the sacred duty of murder and insurrection; but they strive
to ameliorate the condition of these Africans in every particular. They
set them the example of a perfect life, a life of utter self-abnegation.
Think of these holy New Englanders forced to have a Negro village
walk through their houses whenever they see fit, dirty, slatternly, idle,
ill-smelling by nature. These women I love have less chance to live their
own lives in peace than if they were African missionaries. They have
a swarm of blacks about them like children under their care, not as Mrs.
Stowe's fancy painted them, and they hate slavery worse than Mrs.
Stowe does. Book-making which leads you to a round of visits among
crowned heads is an easier way to be a saint than martyrdom down
here, doing unpleasant duty among the Negroes with no reward but
the threat of John Brown hanging like a drawn sword over your head
in this world, and threats of what is to come to you from blacker devils in the next.

The Mrs. Stowes have the plaudits of crowned heads; we take our
chances, doing our duty as best we may among the woolly heads. My
husband supported his plantation by his law practice. Now it is running him in debt. Our people have never earned their own bread. . . .

This old man's goes to support a horde of idle dirty Africans, while he is abused as a cruel slave owner. I say we are no better than our judges in the North, and no worse. We are human beings of the nineteenth century and slavery has to go, of course. All that has been gained by it goes to the North and to Negroes. The slave owners, when they are good men and women, are the martyrs. I hate slavery. I even hate the harsh authority I see parents think it their duty to exercise toward their children.

NOVEMBER 30TH

. . . Mr. John Raven Matthews has burned his cotton, his gin houses and his Negro houses. The Moscow idea is rampant. How old Mr. Chesnut sneers whenever he hears of "another such fool as that." He is deaf and blind and ninety years old, but he hears everything, and his comments are racy indeed. The papers are read to him in a shrieking voice every night. He dozes until you stop, then he wakes and sternly demands: "What's the matter? Who told you to stop?" Sometimes he breaks out in talk of his own. "I was always a Union man. The world's against us. But for the strong power of the United States, repressing insurrections and keeping the hands of outsiders off, we would not keep slavery a day. The world will not tolerate a small slave power."

DECEMBER 6TH

. . . Mr. Team was here today. He is a stalwart creature, a handsome old man, perhaps the finest black eyes I ever saw. He has been an overseer all his life. Most people detest overseers, but Mr. Team is an exception. He has the good will and respect of all the world; of our small world, I mean. How those magnificent eyes blazed today. He is disgusted at the way Mr. Chesnut has been left out in the cold. He said today: "In all my life I have only met one or two womenfolk who were not abolitionists in their hearts, and hot ones too. Mrs. Chesnut is the worst. They have known that of her here for years." We told him Uncle Tom's story, as invented or imagined by Mrs. Stowe. He said he had not seen many of that sort. If there were any, "money couldn't buy 'em." We said: "Daddy Abram was as good." "I never knew a Negro to be murdered or burnt. But, if the Marsters are bad or drunken, look out. Slavery is a thing too unjust, too unfair to last. Let us take the bull by the horns, set 'em free, let 'em help us fight, to pay for their freedom."

Old Mr. Chesnut did not hear, and I noticed no voice was raised to enable him to hear. He is a Prince of Slaveholders, and so he will die. His forefathers paid their money for them, and they are his by that right divine—he thinks. Our votes are not counted. We are women, alas!

Team said: "Slavery does not make good masters." Then he told a tale of a woman so lazy she tied her child to her back and jumped in the river. She said she did not mean to work, nor should her child after her! He had had us crying over his stories, but now we laughed, so that we might not cry.

The Southern landscape is always sad. Now the freshet is up on every side, and the river comes to our doors. The lower limbs of the trees dip mournfully in the water. Many sheep and cattle have been driven up. This house is a Noah's Ark, and their lowing and bleating adds to the general despairing effect. We are surrounded by water on three sides. This is not at all like the Sandy Hill house, with all its God-forsaken make-shift wretchedness. Here everything is fresh, bright, cool, sweet-scented; and a mocking bird is singing and a woodpecker at work—or a yellow hammer, for I cannot see the small bird which is making such a noise. I hear loud laughing among the Negroes, and every sound comes up of a jolly contented life. There is neither silence nor solitude. All the same, it is mournful; a 'dismal swamp' feeling hangs around us still.

Another Russell letter says the Yankees are satisfied they will get what cotton they want; the almighty dollar always wins its way. That was written before Port Royal. Russell thinks he knows the fervid beating of this strong Southern heart, and that we will destroy everything before their approaching footsteps. He finds our courage a fact past controversy, and says that if our money was as palpable a fact, as visible to the naked eye as our soldierly qualities, no mortal could doubt the issue of this conflict.

DECEMBER 8TH

. . . The circuit rider is here. (I mean the colored church.) He looks into everything, and if commandments are not kept, he turns out church members. They dislike to be up before the church and excommunicated more than aught else in the world, so it is a wholesome discipline. . . . Mr. Shuford begins each sentence in a low chanting voice, distinct enough; then he works himself up, shuts his eyes, clenches his fists, and the end of the sentence might be addressed to a congregation over the river, so loud and shrill is the shriek. It is like nothing I have ever heard, except calling the ferry man. And oh, the bridal party, all as black as the ace of spades. The bride and her bridesmaids in white swiss muslin, the gayest of sashes, and bonnets too wonderful to be described. . . .

Maria was hard on Mr. Shuford as she combed my hair at night. She likes Manning Brown. "He is ole Marster's nephew, a gentleman born, and he preaches to black and to white just the same. There ain't but one gospel for all. He tells us 'bout keeping the Sabbath holy, honoring our fathers and mothers, and loving our neighbors as ourselves. Mr. Shuford he goes for low life things, hurting people's feelings. 'Don't you tell lies! Don't you steal!' Worse things, real indecent. Before God, we are white as he is, and in the pulpit he no need to make us feel we are servants."

I took up the cudgels for Mr. Shuford. Years ago I went to see some sick Negroes, and I left the carriage at the overseer's house and with my basket went down the line on foot. I passed what I knew to be an unoccupied house and heard coming from it queer sounds, so I softly drew near. It was Mr. Shuford teaching the little Negroes. They were answering all together, and seemed to know their catechism wonderfully well. I sat there listening more than an hour. I know how hard it is to teach them, for I have tried it, and I soon let my Sunday School all drift into singing hymns. I determined to wait until they developed more brains, but Mr. Shuford's patience was sublime. How he wrestled in prayer for those imps of darkness, and he thought only God saw or heard him. . . .

Mr. Shuford unconsciously took a shot at us. "Go to, you rich men. Weep, howl, for your miseries have come upon ye." Hitherto I have felt so poor, and have fancied my life so devoid of pleasure that I was inclined to grumble at providence. Today under Mr. Shuford's ministrations I began to tremble, to shiver. Maybe, after all, we were the rich who were threatened with howling.

I went whimpering to Mr. Chesnut. He said coolly: "Let the galled jade wince!" He said the saddle was on the other horse; that his Negroes owed him about fifty thousand dollars now for food and clothes. "Why the lazy rascals steal all of my hogs, and I have to buy meat for them, and they will not make cotton. Well, if they don't choose to make cotton, and spin it and weave it, they may go naked for me. There are plenty of sheep. Let them shear the sheep and spin that too." . . .

One joke at Mr. Chesnut's expense always made him very angry. At an agricultural dinner, Mr. Taylor told the story. "Chesnut offered his crop to his overseer for his wages. The overseer answered: 'La, Colonel, you don't catch me that way!'"

He is like his mother in feeling, but he likes to be thought like his father, whose bark is worse than his bite. How men can go blustering around, making everybody uncomfortable, simply to show that they are masters and we are only women and children at their mercy! My husband's father is kind, and amiable when not crossed, given to hospitality on a grand scale, jovial, genial, friendly, courtly in his politeness. But he is as absolute a tyrant as the Czar of Russia, the Khan of Tartary, or the Sultan of Turkey.

•   •   •

Team was here. Mr. Chesnut lent his Gold Branch plantation to the Trapiers and Jenkins. "Jenkins," said Team, "is a parson. Two of his Niggers run away a'ready. They are from the ocean wave. They call our river—the big Wateree—a spring branch. They swim like ducks across the river. They laughs at ferries and bridges and toll gates. Did you all ever have a runaway?"

"Never," said Mr. Chesnut. "It's pretty hard work to keep me from running away from them! Have these Negroes gone back to the fleet at Beaufort?"

"Straight as the crow flies."

MARCH 13TH [1862]

. . . Read "Uncle Tom's Cabin" again. These Negro women have a chance here that women have nowhere else. They can redeem themselves—the "impropers" can. They can marry decently, and nothing is remembered against these colored ladies. It is not a nice topic, but Mrs. Stowe revels in it. How delightfully Pharisaic a feeling it must be to rise superior, and fancy we are so degraded as to defend and like to live with such degraded creatures around us—such men as Legree and his women.

The best way to take Negroes to your heart is to get as far away from them as possible. As far as I can see, Southern women do all that missionaries could do to prevent and alleviate evils. The social evil has not been suppressed in old England or in New England, in London or in Boston. People in those places expect more virtue from a plantation

African than they can insure in practice among themselves, with all their own high moral surroundings—light, education, training, and support. Lady Mary Montagu says, "Only men and women at last." "Male and female created he them," says the Bible. There are cruel, graceful, beautiful mothers of angelic Evas North as well as South, I dare say. The Northern men and women who came here were always hardest, for they expected an African to work and behave as a white man. We do not. . . .

People can't love things dirty, ugly, and repulsive, simply because they ought to do so, but they can be good to them at a distance; that's easy. . . .

MARCH 14TH

. . . Mr. Venable interrupted the fun, which was fast and furious, with the very best of bad news! Newbern shelled and burned, cotton, turpentine—everything. There were 5000 North Carolinians in the fray, 12,000 Yankees. Now there stands Goldsboro. One more step and we are cut in two. The railroad is our backbone, like the Blue Ridge and the Alleghenies, with which it runs parallel. So many discomforts, no wonder we are down-hearted.

MARCH 17TH

Back to the Congaree House to await my husband, who has made a rapid visit to the Wateree region. As we drove up Mr. Chesnut said: "Did you see the stare of respectful admiration E. R. bestowed upon you, so curiously prolonged? I could hardly keep my countenance." "Yes, my dear, I feel the honor of it, though my individual self goes for nothing in it. I am the wife of the man who has the appointing power just now, with so many commissions to be filled. I am nearly forty, and they do my understanding the credit to suppose I can be made to believe they admire my mature charms. They think they fool me into thinking that they believe me charming. There is hardly any farce in the world more laughable."

Last night a house was set on fire; last week two houses. "The red cock crows in the barn!" Our troubles thicken, indeed, when treachery comes from that dark quarter. . . .

Mary P. was giving Wade Manning's story of his Aunt Camilla's Bed of justice. The lady is of the stoutest, with a fiery red face and straggling grey hair. Her room opens on a stairway up and down which all the world goes, and is obliged to go, for it is the only staircase in the house. With her door wide open, she sat in bed with a bundle of switches; and every Monday morning, everybody in the yard was there to give an account of their deeds or misdeeds for the past week. They were mustered in a row and waited. She solemnly rehearsed their misdemeanors. Some were adroit enough to avert their fate. Those whom she condemned stepped up to the bedside and received their punishment, screaming, howling and yelling to the utmost of their ability to soften her heart. She belabored them with her night cap flying, and her gown in horrid disarray from the exercise of her arm. Wade found her dreadful to think of as he fled from the sight and sound. Peace once restored and everybody once more at the daily avocations, they were as jolly as larks, with perspiration streaming. Wade moaned: "It shocks and makes me miserable, but they don't seem to mind a switching, Cousin Mary, not ten seconds after it is over! And this is the place my father sends me to be educated!"

MAY 6TH

. . . The Hampton Estate has fifteen hundred Negroes on Lake Washington, in Mississippi; but neither Wade nor Preston, that splendid boy, would lay a lance in rest, or couch it—which is the right phrase? —for the sake of slavery. They hate slavery as we do. Someone asked: "Then what are they fighting for?" "For Southern rights, whatever that is! And they do not want to be understrappers forever for those nasty Yankees."

They talk well enough about it, but I forget what they say. John Chesnut says: "No use to give a reason. A fellow could not stay away you know, not very well." Johnny is not sound on the goose, either; but then it takes four Negroes to wait on him satisfactorily.

MAY 14TH

. . . Hanging all the state officials was proposed. "Save the country that way, and spare the rank and file." "I won't mind," said Mrs. Pickens, radiantly young and beautiful. "Let them hang the Governor, if it can save the state." Whereupon a horse-laugh. This was one of the jokes repeated as having occurred down at the State House. Mrs. Pickens calls the Governor's other wives gone before her, Number One and Number Two. The men say she is as clever as she is handsome. "She put it this way: 'Let them hang an old husband, if that would save the country!'" added Mr. Preston, who is verbally correct always, when he repeats.

The best and the bravest went first. Now the lag-lasts do not want to be conscripted. As officers, they would gladly face the music, but the few that are left are old, or middle-aged, and nothing remains for them but the ranks. They hoped to reap where others had sowed, to win where they did not work. Without a murmur they sent their sons, but they grumbled when asked for money, though they gave it. Kill a man's wife (or son) and he may brook it, but keep your hands out of his breeches pocket. Their own sacred skins they respect, but there was not a regular shrinking until sacred property was touched.

NOVEMBER 18TH

. . . On the first of last January, all his servants left him but four. To these faithful few he gave free papers at once, that they might lose naught by loyalty should the Confederates come into authority once more. He paid high wages and things worked smoothly for some weeks. One day his wife saw some Yankee officers' cards on a table, and said to her maid: "I did not know any of these people had called." "Oh, Missis!" the maid replied, "They come to see me, and I have been waiting to tell you. It is too hard! I cannot do it! I cannot dance with those nice gentlemen at night at our Union Balls and then come here and be your servant the next day. I can't!" "So," said Mr. Gordon, "freedom must be followed by fraternity and equality." One by one, the faithful few slipped away, and the family were left to their own devices. Why not? . . .

And now comes a stange story. Today I had a letter from my sister, who wrote to inquire for her old playmate, friend, and even lover, Boykin McCaa. "I had almost forgotten Boykin's existence, but he came here last night. He stood by my bedside and spoke to me kindly and affectionately. I said, holding out my hand: 'Boykin, you are very pale?' He answered, 'I have come to tell you good-bye.' Then he seized both of my hands, and his were as cold and hard as ice. I screamed again and again, my whole household came rushing in, and the Negroes came from the yard. All had been wakened by my piercing shrieks. This dream haunts me."

"Stop," said Mr. Chesnut, and he read from that day's Examiner: "Captain Burwell Boykin McCaa was found dead upon the battlefield.

He died leading a cavalry charge, at the head of his company. He was shot through the head." Coincidences are queer, sometimes.

MARCH 8TH, [1864]

. . . Shopping, I paid thirty dollars for a pair of gloves, fifty dollars for a pair of slippers, twenty-four dollars for six spools of thread, and thirty-two dollars for five miserable, shabby, little pocket handkerchiefs.

[MARCH 9TH]

. . . They had been in Vicksburg during the siege, and during the bombardment they sought refuge in a cave. The roar of the cannon ceasing, they came out for a breath of fresh air; and at the moment they emerged a bomb burst among them, struck the son already wounded, and smashed off the arm of a beautiful little grandchild not three years old. This poor little girl with her touchingly lovely face and her arm gone is here now.

MARCH 12TH

. . . General Grant is charmed with Sherman's successful movements, and says he has destroyed millions upon millions of our property in Mississippi. I hope that may not be true, hope Sherman may fail as Kilpatrick did. If we had Stonewall or Albert Sidney Johnson where Joe Johnston and Polk are, I would not give a fig for Sherman's chances. The Yankees say that at last they have scared up a man who succeeds, and they expect him to remedy all that is gone, so they have made their brutal Grant a lieutenant general.

MARCH 18TH

. . . Buck cried: "Don't waste your delicacy! Sally is going to marry a man who has lost an arm, so he is also a maimed soldier, you see; and she is proud of it. The cause glorifies such wounds." Annie said meekly: "I fear it will be my fate to marry one who has lost his head!" "Tudy has her eye on one who lost an eye! What a glorious assortment of noble martyrs and heroes!" The bitterness of this kind of talk is appalling.

General Lee had tears in his eyes when he spoke of his daughter-in-law, now dead; that lovely little Charlotte Wickham, Mrs. Roony Lee. Roony Lee says "Beast" Butler was very kind to him while he was a prisoner; and the "Beast" has sent him back his war horse. The Lees are men enough to speak the truth of friend or enemy, not fearing consequences.

MARCH 31ST

. . . I met Preston Hampton. Conny was with me. She showed her regard for him by taking his overcoat and leaving him in a drenching rain. What boyish nonsense he talked! He said he was in love with Miss Dabney now, that his love was so hot within him that he was waterproof and the rain sizzed and smoked off and did not so much as dampen his ardour or his clothes.

NOVEMBER 28TH

. . . Halcott Green tries to raise our spirits. "Take my word for it, good news, wonderful news is coming." It had better hurry up. Time is short now. We have lost nearly all of our men, and we have no money, and it looks as if we had taught the Yankees to fight. Here we stand, despair in our hearts ("Oh, Cassandra, don't!" shouts Isabella) and our houses are burnt—or about to be—over our heads.

The Yankees have just got things shipshape; a splendid army, perfectly disciplined, and new levies coming in day and night to them. Their gentry do not go into the ranks. They pile up shoddy fortunes cheating their government; they dwell in their comfortable cities, tranquil, in no personal fear. The war is to them only a pleasurable excitement.

Someone said: "If we had only freed the Negroes at first, and put them in the Army, that would have trumped their trick." I remember when Mr. Chesnut spoke to his Negroes about it, his head men were keen to go in the Army, to be free and get a bounty after the War. Now they say coolly that they don't want freedom if they have to fight for it. That means they are pretty sure of having it anyway.

DECEMBER 1ST

Through the deep waters we wade! . . . Our troops down there are raw militia, old men and boys who were never under fire before. "The cradle and the grave" is robbed by us, they say. Sherman goes to Savannah and not to Augusta.

The girls went with the Martins to the State House. The Senate was deliberating how much cotton they would allow a man to plant next year, while the House put off until noon tomorrow a bill to raise men for home defense. While the enemy is thundering at their gates, they can still fool themselves with words.

FEBRUARY 16TH [1865]

. . . Here in Lincolnton I am broken-hearted, an exile. Such a place. Bare floors. For a featherbed, a pine table and two chairs, I pay $30.00 a day. Such sheets! But I have some of my own. At the door, before I was well out of the hack, the woman of the house packed Lawrence out, neck and heels. She would not have him at any price. She said his clothes were too fine for a Nigger. "His airs indeed!" Poor Lawrence was so humble and silent. He said at last: "Miss Mary, send me back to Mars' James!" I began to look for a pencil to write a note to my husband, and in the flurry could not find it. "Here is one," said Lawrence, producing a gold pencil case. "Go away," she shouted. "I wants no Niggers here with pencils and airs." . . .

The Fants are refugees here. They are Viginians, and have been in exile since Second Manassas. They tried to go back to their own house and found one chimney standing.

The day I left home, I had packed a box of flour, sugar, rice, coffee, etc.; but my husband would not let me bring it. He said I was coming to a land of plenty, to unexplored North Carolina, where the foot of Yankee marauders was unknown. Now I have written to send me that box and many other things by Lawrence or I will starve.

The Middletons have come, and Mrs. Ben Rutledge. They describe the hubbub in Columbia, everybody flying in every direction like a flock of swallows. She heard the enemy's guns booming in the distance.

APRIL 22ND

. . . Colonel Cadwallader Jones came with a dispatch, sealed and secret. It was for General Chesnut. I opened it. Lincoln, Old Abe Lincoln, killed, murdered! Seward wounded! Why? By whom? It is simply maddening. I sent off messenger after messenger for General Chesnut. I have not the faintest idea where he is, but I know this foul murder will bring down worse miseries on us.

Mary Darby says: "But they murdered him themselves! There are no Confederates in Washington." "But if they see fit to accuse us of instigating it?"

Met Mr. Heyward. He said the army is deserting. Joe Johnston said: "That is the peoples' vote against a continuance of the war. And the death of Lincoln, I call that a warning to tyrants. He will not be the last president put to death in the Capital, though he is the first."

MAY 3RD

. . . Floride Cantey heard an old Negro say to his master: "When you'all had de power you was good to me, and I'll protect you now. No niggers nor Yankees shall touch you. If you want anything, call for Sambo. I mean, call for Mr. Samuel—that's my name now."

MAY 10TH

. . . E. M. Boykin is awfully sanguine. His main idea is joy that he has no Negroes to support, and can hire only those that he really wants.

MAY 16TH

We are scattered, stunned, the remnant of heart left alive in us filled with brotherly hate. We sit and wait until the drunken tailor who rules the United States of America issues a proclamation and defines our anomalous position.

Such a hue and cry, everybody blamed by somebody else. Only the dead heroes left stiff and stark on the battle field escape.

MAY 18TH

Colonel Chesnut, ninety-three, blind and deaf, is apparently as strong as ever and certainly as resolute of will. African Scipio walks always at his side. He is six feet two, a black Hercules and as gentle as a dove in all his dealings with the blind old master, who boldly strides forward, striking with his stick to feel where he is going. The Yankees left Scipio unmolested. He told them he was absolutely essential to his master; and they said: "If you want to stay so bad, he must have been good to you." Scipio was silent. He says: "It made them mad if you praised your Master."

Partly patriarch, partly *grand seigneur*, this old man is of a species that we will see no more; the last of the lordly planters who ruled this Southern world. His manners are unequalled still, but underneath this smooth exterior lies the grip of a tyrant whose will has never been crossed.

Sometimes this old man will stop himself, just as he is going off in a fury because they try to prevent his attempting some impossible feat. He will stop, and say gently: "I hope that I never say or do anything unseemly—sometimes I think I am subject to mental aberrations."

At every footfall he calls out: "Who goes there?" If a lady's name is given, he uncovers and stands hat in hand until she passes. He has still the Old World art of bowing low and gracefully. He came of a race that would brook no interference with their own sweet will by man, woman, or devil; but then such manners would clear any man's character if it needed it.

ARMY LIFE IN A BLACK REGIMENT

Thomas Wentworth Higginson

Had an invitation reached me to take command of a regiment of Kalmuck Tartars, it could hardly have been more unexpected. I had always looked for the arming of the blacks, and had always felt a wish to be associated with them; had read the scanty accounts of General Hunter's abortive regiment, and had heard rumors of General Saxton's renewed efforts. But the prevalent tone of public sentiment was still opposed to any such attempts; the government kept very shy of the experiment, and it did not seem possible that the time had come when it could be fairly tried. . . .

Fortunately it took but a few days in South Carolina to make it clear that all was right, and the return steamer took back a resignation of a Massachusetts commission. Thenceforth my lot was cast altogether with the black troops, except when regiments or detachments of white soldiers were also under my command, during the two years following.

These details would not be worth mentioning except as they show this fact: that I did not seek the command of colored troops, but it sought me. And this fact again is only important to my story for this reason, that under these circumstances I naturally viewed the new recruits rather as subjects for discipline than for philanthropy. . . . Fortunately, I felt perfect confidence that they could be so trained,—having happily known, by experience, the qualities of their race, and knowing also that they had home and household and freedom to fight for, besides that abstraction of "the Union." Trouble might perhaps be expected from white officials, though this turned out far less than might have been feared; but there was no trouble to come from the men, I thought, and none ever came. On the other hand, it was a vast experiment of indirect philanthropy, and one on which the result of the war and the destiny of the negro race might rest; and this was enough to tax all one's powers. I had been an abolitionist too long, and had known and loved John Brown too well, not to feel a thrill of joy at last on finding myself in the position where he only wished to be.

In view of all this, it was clear that good discipline must come first; after that, of course, the men must be helped and elevated in all ways as much as possible. . . .

The first need, therefore, was of an unbroken interval of training. During this period, which fortunately lasted nearly two months, I rarely left the camp, and got occasional leisure moments for a fragmentary journal, to send home, recording the many odd or novel aspects of the new experience. Camp-life was a wonderfully strange sensation to almost all volunteer officers, and mine lay among eight hundred men suddenly transformed from slaves into soldiers, and representing a race affectionate, enthusiastic, grotesque, and dramatic beyond all others. Being such, they naturally gave material for description. There is nothing like a diary for freshness,—at least so I think,—and I shall keep to the diary through the days of camp-life . . .

I am under pretty heavy bonds to tell the truth, and only the truth; for those who look back to the newspaper correspondence of that period will see that this particular regiment lived for months in a glare of publicity, such as tests any regiment severely, and certainly prevents all subsequent romancing in its historian. As the scene of the only effort on the Atlantic coast to arm the negro, our camp attracted a continuous stream of visitors, military and civil. . . . It was no pleasant thing to live under such constant surveillance; but it guaranteed the honesty of any success, while fearfully multiplying the penalties had there been a failure. A single mutiny,—such as has happened in the infancy of a hundred regiments,—a single miniature Bull Run, a stampede of desertions, and it would have been all over with us; the party of distrust would have got the upper hand, and there might not have been, during the whole contest, another effort to arm the negro.

I may now proceed, without farther preparation, to the Diary. . . .

Three miles farther brought us to the pretty town of Beaufort, with its stately houses amid Southern foliage. Reporting to General Saxton, I had the luck to encounter a company of my destined command, marched in to be mustered into the United States service. They were unarmed, and all looked as thoroughly black as the most faithful philanthropist could desire; there did not seem to be so much as a mulatto among them. Their coloring suited me, all but the legs, which were clad in a lively scarlet, as intolerable to my eyes as if I had been a turkey. I saw them mustered; General Saxton talked to them a little, in his direct, manly way; they gave close attention, though their faces looked impenetrable. Then I conversed with some of them. The first to whom I spoke had been wounded in a small expedition after lumber, from which a party had just returned, and in which they had been under fire and had done very well. I said, pointing to his lame arm,—

"Did you think that was more than you bargained for, my man?"

His answer came promptly and stoutly,—

"I been a-tinking, Mas'r, *dat's jess what I went for.*"

I thought this did well enough for my very first interchange of dialogue with my recruits. . . .

It needs but a few days to allow the absurdity of distrusting the military availability of these people. They have quite as much average comprehension as whites of the need of the thing, as much courage (I doubt not), as much previous knowledge of the gun, and, above all, a readiness of ear and of imitation, which, for purposes of drill, counterbalances any defect of mental training. To learn the drill, one does not want a set of college professors; one wants a squad of eager, active, pliant school-boys; and the more childlike these pupils are the better. There is no trouble about the drill; they will surpass whites in that. As to camp-life, they have little to sacrifice; they are better fed, housed, and clothed than ever in their lives before, and they appear to have few inconvenient vices. They are simple, docile, and affectionate almost to the point of absurdity. The same men who stood fire in open field with perfect coolness, on the late expedition, have come to me blubbering in the most irresistibly ludicrous manner on being transferred from one company in the regiment to another. . . .

. . . [T]hese companies can be driven with a looser rein than my former one, for they restrain themselves; but the moment they are dismissed from drill every tongue is relaxed and every ivory tooth visible. This morning, I wandered about where the different companies were target-shooting, and their glee was contagious. Such exulting shouts of "Ki! ole man," when some steady old turkey-shooter brought his gun down for an instant's aim, and then unerringly hit the mark and then, when some unwary youth fired his piece into the ground at half-cock, such infinite guffawing and delight, such rolling over and over on the grass, such dances of ecstasy, as made the "Ethiopian minstrelsy" of the stage appear a feeble imitation.

Evening.—Better still was a scene on which I stumbled to-night. Strolling in the cool moonlight, I was attracted by a brilliant light beneath the trees, and cautiously approached it. A circle of thirty or forty soldiers sat around a roaring fire, while one old uncle, Cato by name, was narrating an interminable tale, to the insatiable delight of his audience. I came up into the dusky background, perceived only by a few, and he still continued. It was a narrative, dramatized to the last degree, of his adventures in escaping from his master to the Union vessels; and even I, who have heard the stories of Harriet Tubman, and such wonderful slave-comedians, never witnessed such a piece of acting. When I came upon the scene he had just come unexpectedly upon a plantation-house, and, putting a bold face upon it, had walked up to the door.

"Den I go up to de white man, berry humble, and say, would he please gib ole man a mouthful for eat?

"He say he must hab de valeration ob half a dollar.

"Den I look berry sorry, and turn for go away.

"Den he say I might gib him dat hatchet I had.

"Den I say" (this in a tragic vein) "dat I must hab dat hatchet for defend myself *from de dogs!*"

[Immense applause, and one appreciating auditor says, chuckling, "Dat was your *arms,* ole man," which brings down the house again]

"Den he say de Yankee pickets was near by, and I must be very keerful.

"Den I say, 'Good Lord, Mas'r, am dey?' "

Words cannot express the complete dissimulation with which these accents of terror were uttered,—this being precisely the piece of information he wished to obtain. . . .

Yet to-morrow strangers will remark on the hopeless, impenetrable stupidity in the daylight faces of many of these very men, the solid mask under which Nature has concealed all this wealth of mother-wit. . . . This is their university; every young Sambo before me, as he turned over the sweet potatoes and peanuts which were roasting in the ashes, listened with reverence to the wiles of the ancient Ulysses, and meditated the same. It is Nature's compensation; oppression simply crushes the upper faculties of the head, and crowds everything into the perceptive organs. Cato, thou reasonest well! When I get into any serious scrape, in an enemy's country, may I be lucky enough to have you at my elbow, to pull me out of it! . . .

. . . [S]ince I took command I have heard of no man intoxicated, and there has been but one small quarrel. I suppose that scarcely a white regiment in the army shows so little swearing. Take the "Progressive

Friends" and put them in red trousers, and I verily believe they would fill a guard-house sooner than these men. If camp regulations are violated, it seems to be usually through heedlessness. They love passionately three things besides their spiritual incantations; namely, sugar, home, and tobacco. . . .

I have seen none of that disposition to connive at the offences of members of one's own company which is so troublesome among white soldiers. Nor are they lazy, either about work or drill; in all respects they seem better material for soldiers than I had dared to hope.

There is one company in particular, all Florida men, which I certainly think the finest-looking company I ever saw, white or black; they range admirably in size, have remarkable erectness and ease of carriage, and really march splendidly. Not a visitor but notices them . . .

One of their favorite songs is full of plaintive cadences; it is not, I think, a Methodist tune, and I wonder where they obtained a chant of such beauty.

> I can't stay behind, my Lord, I can't stay behind!
> O, my father is gone, my father is gone,
> My father is gone into heaven, my Lord!
>> I can't stay behind!
> Dere's room enough, room enough,
> Room enough in do heaven for de sojer:
>> Can't stay behind!"

It always excites them to have us looking on, yet they sing these songs at all times and seasons. . . .

The most eloquent, perhaps, was Corporal Prince Lambkin, just arrived from Fernandina, who evidently had a previous reputation among them. His historical references were very interesting. He reminded them that he had predicted this war ever since Fremont's time, to which some of the crowd assented; he gave a very intelligent account of that Presidential campaign, and then described most impressively the secret anxiety of the slaves in Florida to know all about President Lincoln's election, and told how they all refused to work on the fourth of March, expecting their freedom to date from that day. He finally brought out one of the few really impressive appeals for the American flag that I have ever heard. "Our mas'rs dey hab lib under de flag, dey got dere wealth under it, and ebryting beautiful for dere chilen.

Under it dey hab grind us up, and put us in dere pocket for money. But de fus' minute dey tink dat ole flag mean freedom for we colored people, dey pull it right down, and run up de rag ob dere own." [Immense applause]. "But we'll neber desert de ole flag, boys, neber; we hab lib under it for *eighteen hundred sixty-two years,* and we'll die for it now." With which overpowering discharge of chronology-at-long-range, this most effective of stump-speeches closed. . . .

They seem peculiarly fitted for offensive operations, and especially for partisan warfare; they have so much dash and such abundant resources, combined with such an Indian-like knowledge of the country and its ways. These traits have been often illustrated in expeditions sent after deserters. For instance, I despatched one of my best lieutenants and my best sergeant with a squad of men to search a certain plantation, where there were two separate negro villages. They went by night, and the force was divided. The lieutenant took one set of huts, the sergeant the other. Before the lieutenant had reached his first house, every man in the village was in the woods, innocent and guilty alike. But the sergeant's mode of operation was thus described by a corporal from a white regiment who happened to be in one of the negro houses. He said that not a sound was heard until suddenly a red leg appeared in the open doorway, and a voice outside said, "Rally." Going to the door, he observed a similar pair of red legs before every hut, and not a person was allowed to go out, until the quarters had been thoroughly searched, and the three deserters found. This was managed by Sergeant Prince Rivers . . . There is not a white officer in this regiment who has more administrative ability, or more absolute authority over the men; they do not love him, but his mere presence has controlling power over them. He writes well enough to prepare for me a daily report of his duties in the camp; if his education reached a higher point, I see no reason why he should not command the Army of the Potomac. . . .

If Sergeant Rivers was a natural king among my dusky soldiers, Corporal Robert Sutton was the natural prime-minister. If not in all respects the ablest, he was the wisest man in our ranks. As large, as powerful, and as black as our good-looking Color-Sergeant, but more heavily built and with less personal beauty, he had a more massive brain and a far more meditative and systematic intellect. Not yet grounded even in the spelling-book, his modes of thought were nevertheless strong, lucid, and accurate; and he yearned and pined for intellectual companionship beyond all ignorant men whom I have ever met. I believe that he would have talked all day and all night, for days together, to any officer who could instruct him, until his companion, at least, fell asleep exhausted. His comprehension of the whole problem of Slavery was more thorough and far-reaching than that of any Abolitionist, so far as its social and military aspects went; in that direction I could teach him nothing and he taught me much. . . .

He was a Florida man, and had been chiefly employed in lumbering and piloting on the St. Mary's River, which divides Florida from Georgia. Down this stream he had escaped in a "dug-out," and after thus finding the way, had returned (as had not a few of my men in other cases) to bring away wife and child. " I would n't have leff my child, Cunnel," he said, with an emphasis that sounded the depths of his strong nature. And up this same river he was always imploring to be allowed to guide an expedition. . . .

. . . [I]t was the first stand-up fight in which my men had been engaged, though they had been under fire, in an irregular way, in their small early expeditions. To me personally the event was of the greatest value: it had given us all an opportunity to test each other, and our abstract surmises were changed into positive knowledge. Hereafter it was of small importance what nonsense might be talked or written about colored troops; so long as mine did not flinch, it made no difference to me. . . .

We knew neither the numbers of the enemy, nor their plans, nor their present condition: whether they had surprised us or whether we had surprised them was all a mystery. Corporal Sutton was urgent to go on and complete the enterprise. All my impulses said the same thing; but then I had the most explicit injunctions from General Saxton to risk as little as possible in this first enterprise, because of the fatal effect on public sentiment of even an honorable defeat. We had now an honorable victory, so far as it went; the officers and men around me were in good spirits, but the rest of the column might be nervous; and it seemed so important to make the first fight an entire success, that I thought it wiser to let well alone . . .

Attending to the wounded, therefore, and making as we best could stretchers for those who were to be carried, including the remains of the man killed at the first discharge (Private William Parsons of Company G), and others who seemed at the point of death, we marched through the woods to the landing,—expecting at every moment to be involved in another fight. This not occurring, I was more than ever satisfied that we had won a victory; for it was obvious that a mounted force would not allow a detachment of infantry to march two miles through open woods by night without renewing the fight, unless they themselves had suffered a good deal. . . .

In the morning, my invaluable surgeon, Dr. Rogers, sent me his report of killed and wounded; and I have been since permitted to make the following extracts from his notes: "One man killed instantly by ball through the heart, and seven wounded, one of whom will die. Braver men never lived. One man with two bulletholes through the large muscles of the shoulders and neck brought off from the scene of action, two miles distant, two muskets ; and not a murmur has escaped his lips. Another, Robert Sutton, with three wounds,—one of which, being on the skull, may cost him his life,—would not report himself till compelled to do so by his officers. While dressing his wounds, he quietly talked of what they had done, and of what they yet could do. To-day I have had the Colonel *order* him to obey me. He is perfectly quiet and cool, but takes this whole affair with the religious bearing of a man who realizes that freedom is sweeter than life. Yet another soldier did not report himself at all, but remained all night on guard, and possibly I should not have known of his having had a buck-shot in his shoulder, if some duty requiring a sound shoulder had not been required of him to-day. This last, it may be added, had persuaded a comrade to dig out the buckshot, for fear of being ordered on the sick-list. And one of those who were carried to the vessel—a man wounded through the lungs—asked only if I were safe, the contrary having been reported. An officer may be pardoned some enthusiasm for such men as these. . . .

NEGRO SPIRITUALS

The war brought to some of us, besides its direct experiences, many a strange fulfilment of dreams of other days. For instance, the present writer had been a faithful student of the Scottish ballads, and had always envied Sir Walter the delight of tracing them out amid their own heather, and of writing them down piecemeal from the lips of aged crones. It was a strange enjoyment, therefore, to be suddenly brought into the midst of a kindred world of unwritten songs, as simple and indigenous as the Border Minstrelsy, more uniformly plaintive, almost always more quaint, and often as essentially poetic. . . .

The music I could only retain by ear, and though the more common strains were repeated often enough to fix their impression, there were others that occurred only once or twice.

The words will be here given, as nearly as possible, in the original dialect; and if the spelling seems sometimes inconsistent, or the misspelling insufficient, it is because I could get no nearer. . . .

The favorite song in camp was the following,—sung with no accompaniment but the measured clapping of hands and the clatter of many feet. It was sung perhaps twice as often as any other. This was partly due to the fact that it properly consisted of a chorus alone, with which the verses of other songs might be combined at random.

I. Hold Your Light.

"Hold your light, Brudder Robert,—
Hold your light,
Hold your light on Canaan's shore.

"What make ole Satan for follow me so?
Satan ain't got notin' for do wid me.
Hold your light,
Hold your light,
Hold your light on Canaan's shore."

This would be sung for half an hour at a time, perhaps each person present being named in turn. It seemed the simplest primitive type of "spiritual." The next in popularity was almost as elementary, and, like this, named successively each one of the circle. It was, however, much more resounding and convivial in its music.

II. Bound to Go.

"Jordan River, I'm bound to go,
Bound to go, bound to go,—
Jordan River, I'm bound to go,
And bid 'em fare ye well.

"My Brudder Robert, I'm bound to go,
Bound to go," &c.

. . . It was a very ringing song, though not so grandly jubilant as the next, which was really impressive as the singers pealed it out, when marching or rowing or embarking.

V. My Army Cross Over.

"My army cross over,
    My army cross over,
O, Pharaoh's army drownded!
    My army cross over.

"We'll cross de mighty river,
    My army cross over;
We'll cross de river Jordan,
    My army cross over;
We'll cross de danger water,
    My army cross over;
We'll cross de mighty Myo,
    My army cross over. (*Thrice.*)
O, Pharaoh's army drownded!
    My army cross over."

I could get no explanation of the "mighty Myo," except that one of the old men thought it meant the river of death. Perhaps it is an African word. In the Cameroon dialect, "Mawa" signifies "to die." . . .

In the next, the conflict is at its height, and the lurid imagery of the Apocalypse is brought to bear. This book, with the books of Moses, constituted their Bible; all that lay between, even the narratives of the life of Jesus, they hardly cared to read or to hear.

XII. Down in the Valley.

"We'll run and never tire,
We'll run and never tire,
We'll run and never tire,
    Jesus set poor sinners free.
Way down in de valley,
    Who will rise and go with me?
You've heern talk of Jesus,
    Who set poor sinners free.

"De lightnin' and de flashin'

> De lightnin' and de flashin',
> De lightnin' and de flashin',
>> Jesus set poor sinners free.
> I can't stand the fire. (*Thrice.*)
>> Jesus set poor sinners free,
> De green trees a-flamin'. (*Thrice.*)
>> Jesus set poor sinners free,
>> Way down in de valley,
>> Who will rise and go with me?
>> You've heern talk of Jesus
>> Who set poor sinners free."

"De valley and "de lonesome valley" were familiar words in their religious experience. To descend into that region implied the same process with the "anxious-seat" of the camp-meeting. . . .

XVIII. I Know Moon Rise.

> "I know moon-rise, I know star-rise,
>> Lay dis body down.
> I walk in de moonlight, I walk in de starlight,
>> To lay dis body down.
> I'll walk in de graveyard, I'll walk through de graveyard,
>> To lay dis body down.
> I'll lie in de grave and stretch out my arms;
>> Lay dis body down.
> I go to de judgment in de evenin' of de day,
>> When I lay dis body down;
> And my soul and your soul will meet in de day
>> When I lay dis body down."

"I'll lie in de grave and stretch out my arms." Never, it seems to me, since man first lived and suffered, was his infinite longing for peace uttered more plaintively than in that line.

The next is one of the wildest and most striking of the whole series: there is a mystical effect and a passionate striving throughout the whole. The Scriptural struggle between Jacob and the angel, which is only dimly expressed in the words, seems all uttered in the music. I think it impressed my imagination more powerfully than any other of these songs.

XIX. Wrestling Jacob.

"O wrestlin' Jacob, Jacob, day's a-breakin';
    I will not let thee go!
O wrestlin' Jacob, Jacob, day's a-breakin';
    He will not let me go!
O, I hold my brudder wid a tremblin' hand;
    I would not let him go!
I hold my sister wid a tremblin' hand;
    I would not let her go!

O, Jacob do hang from a tremblin' limb,
    He would not let him go!
O, Jacob do hang from a tremblin' limb,
    De Lord will bless my soul.
O wrestlin' Jacob, Jacob," &c.

. . . Some of the songs had played an historic part during the war. For singing the next, for instance, the negroes had been put in jail in Georgetown, S. C., at the outbreak of the Rebellion. "We'll soon be free" was too dangerous an assertion; and though the chant was an old one, it was no doubt sung with redoubled emphasis during the new events. "De Lord will call us home," was evidently thought to be a symbolical verse; for, as a little drummer-boy explained to me, showing all his white teeth as he sat in the moonlight by the door of my tent, "Dey tink *de Lord* mean for say de *Yankees.*"

XXXIV. We'll Soon Be Free.

"We'll soon be free,
We'll soon be free,
We'll soon be free,
    When de Lord will call us home.
My brudder, how long,
My brudder, how long,
My brudder, how long,
    'Fore we done sufferin' here?
It won't be long (*Thrice.*)
    'Fore de Lord will call us home.
We'll walk de miry road (*Thrice.*)
    Where pleasure never dies.

We'll walk de golden street (*Thrice.*)
    Where pleasure never dies.
My brudder, how long (*Thrice.*)
    'Fore we done sufferin' here?

    We'll soon be free (*Thrice.*)
    When Jesus sets me free,
We'll fight for liberty (*Thrice.*)
    When de Lord will call us home."

The suspicion in this case was unfounded, but they had another song to which the Rebellion had actually given rise. This was composed by nobody knew whom,—though it was the most recent, doubtless, of all these "spirituals,"—and had been sung in secret to avoid detection. It is certainly plaintive enough. The peck of corn and pint of salt were slavery's rations.

XXXV. Many Thousand Go.

"No more peck o' corn for me,
    No more, no more,—
No more peck o' corn for me,
    Many tousand go.

"No more driver's lash for me, (*Twice.*)
    No more, &c.

"No more pint o' salt for me, (*Twice.*)
    No more, &c.

"No more hundred lash for me, (*Twice.*)
    No more, &c.

"No more mistress' call for me,
    No more, no more,—

"No more mistress' call for me,
    Many tousand go."

Even of this last composition, however, we have only the approximate date and know nothing of the mode of composition. Allan Ramsay says of the Scotch songs, that, no matter who made them, they were soon attributed to the minister of the parish whence they sprang. And I always wondered, about these, whether they had always a conscious and definite origin in some leading mind, or whether they grew by gradual secretion, in an almost unconscious way. On this point I could get no information, though I asked many questions, until at last, one day when I was being rowed across from Beaufort to Ladies' Island, I found myself, with delight, on the actual trail of a song. One of the oarsmen, a brisk young fellow, not a soldier, on being asked for his theory of the matter, dropped out a coy confession. "Some good sper-ituals," he said, "are start jess out o' curiosity. I been a-raise a sing, myself, once."

My dream was fulfilled, and I had traced out, not the poem alone, but the poet. I implored him to proceed.

"Once we boys," he said, "went for tote some rice and de nigger-driver he keep a-callin' on us; and I say, 'O, de ole nigger-driver!' Den anudder said, 'Fust ting my mammy tole me was, notin' so bad as nig-ger-driver.' Den I made a sing, just puttin' a word, and den anudder word."

Then he began singing, and the men, after listening a moment, joined in the chorus, as if it were an old acquaintance, though they evidently had never heard it before. I saw how easily a new "sing" took root among them.

XXVI. The Driver.

> "O, de ole nigger-driver!
>> O, gwine away!
> Fust ting my mammy tell me,
>> O, gwine away!
> Tell me 'bout de nigger-driver,
>> O, gwine away!
> Nigger-driver second devil,
>> O, gwine away!
> Best ting for do he driver,
>> O, gwine away!
> Knock he down and spoil he labor,
>> O, gwine away!"

• • •

At any rate, this ungenerous discouragement had this good effect, that it touched their pride; they would deserve justice, even if they did not obtain it. This pride was afterwards severely tested during the disgraceful period when the party of repudiation in Congress temporarily deprived them of their promised pay. In my regiment the men never mutinied, nor even threatened mutiny; they seemed to make it a matter of honor to do their part, even if the Government proved a defaulter; but one third of them, including the best men in the regiment, quietly refused to take a dollar's pay, at the reduced price. "We'se gib our sogerin' to de Guv'ment, Cunnel," they said, "but we won't 'spise ourselves so much for take de seben dollar." They even made a contemptuous ballad, of which I once caught a snatch.

> "Ten dollar a month!
> Tree ob dat for clothin'!
> Go to Washington
> Fight for Linkum's darter!"

This "Lincoln's daughter " stood for the Goddess of Liberty, it would seem. They would be true to her, but they would not take the half-pay. This was contrary to my advice, and to that of their other officers; but I now think it was wise. Nothing less than this would have called the attention of the American people to this outrageous fraud.

The same slow forecast had often marked their action in other ways. One of our ablest sergeants, Henry McIntyre, who had earned two dollars and a half per day as a master-carpenter in Florida, and paid one dollar and a half to his master, told me that he had deliberately refrained from learning to read, because that knowledge exposed the slaves to so much more watching and suspicion. This man and a few others had built on contract the greater part of the town of Micanopy in Florida, and was a thriving man when his accustomed discretion failed for once, and he lost all. He named his child William Lincoln, and it brought upon him such suspicion that he had to make his escape.

I cannot conceive what people at the North mean by speaking of the negroes as a bestial or brutal race. Except in some insensibility to animal pain, I never knew of an act in my regiment which I should call brutal. In reading Kay's "Condition of the English Peasantry" I was constantly struck with the unlikeness of my men to those therein described. This could not proceed from my prejudices as an abolitionist, for they would have led me the other way, and indeed I had once written a little essay to show the brutalizing influences of slavery. I learned to think that we abolitionists had underrated the suffering produced by slavery among the negroes, but had overrated the demoralization.

Or rather, we did not know how the religious temperament of the negroes had checked the demoralization. Yet again, it must be admitted that this temperament, born of sorrow and oppression, is far more marked in the slave than in the native African. . . .

It used to seem to me that never, since Cromwell's time, had there been soldiers in whom the religious element held such a place. "A religious army," "a gospel army," were their frequent phrases. In their prayer-meetings there was always a mingling, often quaint enough, of the warlike and the pious. "If each one of us was a praying man," said Corporal Thomas Long in a sermon, "it appears to me that we could fight as well with prayers as with bullets,—for the Lord has said that if you have faith even as a grain of mustard-seed cut into four parts, you can say to the sycamore-tree, Arise, and it will come up." And though Corporal Long may have got a little perplexed in his botany, his faith proved itself by works, for he volunteered and went many miles on a solitary scouting expedition into the enemy's country in Florida, and got back safe, after I had given him up for lost.

I am bound to say that this strongly devotional turn was not always accompanied by the practical virtues; but neither was it strikingly divorced from them. A few men, I remember, who belonged to the ancient order of hypocrites, but not many. . . .

Another man of somewhat similar quality went among us by the name of Henry Ward Beecher, from a remarkable resemblance in face and figure to that sturdy divine. I always felt a sort of admiration for this worthy, because of the thoroughness with which he outwitted me, and the sublime impudence in which he culminated. He got a series of passes from me, every week or two, to go and see his wife on a neighboring plantation, and finally, when this resource seemed exhausted, he came boldly for one more pass, that he might go and be married.

We used to quote him a good deal, also, as a sample of a certain Shakespearian boldness or personification in which the men sometimes indulged. . . .

Simon was one of the shrewdest old fellows in the regiment, and he said to me once, as he was jogging out of Beaufort behind me, on the Shell Road, "I'se goin' to leave de Souf, Cunnel, when de war is over. I'se made up my mind dat dese yer Secesh will neber be cibilized in my time." . . .

We who served with the black troops have this peculiar satisfaction, that, whatever dignity or sacredness the memories of the war may have to others, they have more to us. . . . We had touched the pivot of the war. Whether this vast and dusky mass should prove the weakness of the nation or its strength, must depend in great measure, we knew, upon our efforts. Till the blacks were armed, there was no guaranty of their freedom. It was their demeanor under arms that shamed the nation into recognizing them as men.

from LETTER TO HORACE GREELEY

Abraham Lincoln

Executive Mansion
Washington, August 22, 1862.

Hon. Horace Greeley:
Dear Sir.

I have just read yours of the 19th. addressed to myself through the New-York Tribune. . . . If there be perceptable in it an impatient and dictatorial tone, I waive it in deference to an old friend, whose heart I have always supposed to be right.

As to the policy I "seem to be pursuing" as you say, I have not meant to leave any one in doubt.

I would save the Union. I would save it the shortest way under the Constitution. The sooner the national authority can be restored; the nearer the Union will be "the Union as it was." If there be those who would not save the Union, unless they could at the same time *save* slavery, I do not agree with them. If there be those who would not save the Union unless they could at the same time *destroy* slavery, I do not agree with them. My paramount object in this struggle *is* to save the Union, and is *not* either to save or to destroy slavery. If I could save the Union without freeing *any* slave I would do it, and if I could save it by freeing *all* the slaves, I would do it; and if I could save it by freeing some and leaving others alone I would also do that. What I do about slavery, and the colored race, I do because I believe it helps to save the Union; and what I forbear, I forbear because I do *not* believe it would help to save the Union. I shall do *less* whenever I shall believe what I am doing hurts the cause, and I shall do *more* whenever I shall believe doing more will help the cause. I shall try to correct errors when shown to be error; and I shall adopt new views so fast as they shall appear to be true views.

I have here stated my purpose according to my view of *official* duty; and I intend no modification of my oft-expressed *personal* wish that all men everywhere could be free.

Yours,

A. Lincoln.

ADDRESS DELIVERED AT THE
DEDICATION OF
THE CEMETERY AT GETTYSBURG

November 19, 1863

Abraham Lincoln

Four score and seven years ago our fathers brought forth on this continent, a new nation, conceived in Liberty, and dedicated to the proposition that all men are created equal.

Now we are engaged in a great civil war, testing whether that nation, or any nation so conceived and so dedicated, can long endure. We are met on a great battle-field of that war. We have come to dedicate a portion of that field, as a final resting place for those who here gave their lives that that nation might live. It is altogether fitting and proper that we should do this.

But in a larger sense, we can not dedicate—we can not consecrate—we cannot hallow—this ground. The brave men, living and dead, who struggled here, have consecrated it, far above our poor power to add or detract. The world will little note, nor long remember what we say here, but it can never forget what they did here. It is for us the living, rather, to be dedicated here to the unfinished work which they who fought here have thus far so nobly advanced. It is rather for us to be here dedicated to the great task remaining before us—that from these honored dead we take increased devotion to that cause for which they gave the last full measure of devotion—that we here highly resolve that these dead shall not have died in vain—that this nation, under God, shall have a new birth of freedom—and that government of the people, by the people, for the people, shall not perish from the earth.

SECOND INAUGURAL ADDRESS
March 4, 1865

Abraham Lincoln

At this second appearing to take the oath of the presidential office, there is less occasion for an extended address than there was at the first. Then a statement, somewhat in detail, of a course to be pursued, seemed fitting and proper. Now, at the expiration of four years, during which public declarations have been constantly called forth on every point and phase of the great contest which still absorbs the attention, and engrosses the energies of the nation, little that is new could be presented. The progress of our arms, upon which all else chiefly depends, is as well known to the public as to myself; and it is, I trust, reasonably satisfactory and encouraging to all. With high hope for the future, no prediction in regard to it is ventured.

On the occasion, corresponding to this four years ago, all thoughts were anxiously directed to an impending civil war. All dreaded it— all sought to avert it. While the inaugeral address was being delivered from this place, devoted altogether to *saving* the Union without war, insurgent agents were in the city seeking to *destroy* it without war— seeking to dissole the Union, and divide effects, by negotiation. Both parties deprecated war; but one of them would *make* war rather than let the nation survive; and the other would *accept* war rather than let it perish. And the war came.

One eighth of the whole population were colored slaves, not distributed generally over the Union, but localized in the Southern part of it. These slaves constituted a peculiar and powerful interest. All knew that this interest was, somehow, the cause of the war. To strengthen, perpetuate, and extend this interest was the object for which the insurgents would rend the Union, even by war; while the government claimed no right to do more than to restrict the territorial enlargement of it. Neither party expected for the war, the magnitude, or the duration, which it has already attained. Neither anticipated that the *cause* of the conflict might cease with, or even before, the conflict itself should cease. Each looked for an easier triumph, and a result less fundamen-

712

tal and astounding. Both read the same Bible, and pray to the same God; and each invokes His aid against the other. It may seem strange that any men should dare to ask a just God's assistance in wringing their bread from the sweat of other men's faces; but let us judge not that we be not judged. The prayers of both could not be answered; that of neither has been answered fully. The Almighty has his own purposes. "Woe unto the world because of offences! for it must needs be that offences come; but woe to that man by whom the offence cometh!" If we shall suppose that American Slavery is one of those offences which, in the providence of God, must needs come, but which, having continued through His appointed time, He now wills to remove, and that He gives to both North and South, this terrible war, as the woe due to those by whom the offence came, shall we discern therein any departure from those divine attributes which the believers in a Living God always ascribe to Him? Fondly do we hope—fervently do we pray—that this mighty scourge of war may speedily pass away. Yet, if God wills that it continue, until all the wealth piled by the bond-man's two hundred and fifty years of unrequited toil shall be sunk, and until every drop of blood drawn with the lash, shall be paid by another drawn with the sword, as was said three thousand years ago, so still it must be said "the judgments of the Lord, are true and righteous altogether"

With malice toward none; with charity for all; with firmness in the right, as God gives us to see the right, let us strive on to finish the work we are in; to bind up the nation's wounds; to care for him who shall have borne the battle, and for his widow, and his orphan—to do all which may achieve and cherish a just and lasting peace, among ourselves, and with all nations.